P9-BBN-318

English Skills
with Readings

JOHN LANGAN
Atlantic Community College

SHARON WINSTANLEY
Seneca College

McGraw-Hill Ryerson

Toronto Montréal New York Burr Ridge Bangkok Bogotá Caracas
Lisbon London Madrid Mexico City Milan
New Delhi Seoul Singapore Sydney Taipei

McGraw-Hill
Ryerson Limited
*A Subsidiary of The **McGraw·Hill** Companies*

ENGLISH SKILLS WITH READINGS
Second Canadian Edition

ISBN: 0-07-560970-3

4 5 6 7 8 9 0   GTC   0 9 8 7 6 5 4 3

Printed and bound in Canada

Editorial Director and Publisher: Evelyn Veitch
Senior Sponsoring Editor: Veronica Visentin
Developmental Editor: Marianne Minaker
Senior Supervising Editor: Margaret Henderson
Production Editor: Nancy Carroll
Marketing Manager: Ralph Courtney
Senior Production Co-ordinator: Nicla Dattolico
Cover & Inside Design: Liz Harasymczuk
Cover Images: Copyright © Digital Stock
Typesetter: Bookman Typesetting Company
Typeface: Minion
Printer: Transcontinental Printing Inc.

Canadian Cataloguing in Publication Data

Langan, John, 1942–
   English skills with readings

2nd Canadian ed.
Includes index.
ISBN 0-07-560970-3

1. English language — Rhetoric.   I. Winstanley, Sharon.   II. Title.

PE1408.L28 2000   808'.0427   C99-931964-7

Explaining a Process • Examining Cause and Effect • comparing or contrasting • Definin
• Dividing and Classifying • Describing a Scene or Person • Narrating an Event • Argu
sition • Explaining a Process • Examining Cause and Effect • comparing or contrastin
ning a Term • Dividing and Classifying • Describing a Scene or Person • Narrating an Ev
guing a Position • Explaining a Process • Examining Cause and Effect • comparing

Contents

Readings Listed by Rhetorical Mode

Note: Some selections are listed more than once because they illustrate more than one rhetorical* mode of development.

* The word "rhetorical" refers to a particular structuring method or format chosen by a writer for its effectiveness in communicating the selection's message to an audience. Many of these selections, and most writers, make use of more than one rhetorical mode or format in any one piece of writing; for example, an essay may be *narrative* in basic style, but may also *contrast* two different ideas.

Process

Cause–Effect

Comparison–Contrast

Definition

Division and Classification

Argumentation

*aining a Process · Examining Cause and Effect · comparing or contrasting · Defining
· Dividing and Classifying · Describing a Scene or Person · Narrating an Event · Argu
sition · Explaining a Process · Examining Cause and Effect · comparing or contrastin
ning a Term · Dividing and Classifying · Describing a Scene or Person · Narrating an Ev
guing a Position · Explaining a Process · Examining Cause and Effect · comparin

Preface

English Skills with Readings, Second Canadian Edition, will help students understand, learn, and apply the basic rules of effective writing and communication. The
text will also help them master essential reading and response-writing skills. This
new Canadian edition is even more clear and explicit in its arrangement of information, goals, and procedural steps within each chapter, but, like its predecessor, it
is based on the following assumptions about the processes of reading and writing:

- First, *English Skills with Readings,* Second Canadian Edition, assumes that
  four principles in particular are keys to and goals for effective writing: unity,
  support, coherence, and sound sentence skills. These four principles are
  highlighted on the inside cover and reinforced throughout the book. Part
  One focuses in depth on the first three principles, and touches on aspects of
  the fourth; Part Four treats sentence skills fully. Part Two demonstrates the
  application of the four principles to different methods of paragraph development; Part Three demonstrates their application to the traditional five-
  paragraph essay. Part Five prompts students to see how professional writers
  use these principles, and again demonstrates their application in both
  paragraph- and essay-writing assignments.
- This book also reflects the belief that, in addition to the four principles,
  there are other important factors in writing effectively. First among these
  factors is the student's recognition that writing is a process whose initial and
  revising stages require serious attention. Hence, the second chapter both discusses and demonstrates the theories and practices of prewriting, purposeful
  rewriting, revising, and editing. As well as demonstrating the process of
  writing, the chapter also asks students to examine their attitude about writing, to write on what they know or can learn about, and to consider keeping
  a writing journal. Finally, students are strongly advised to follow a consistent
  outlining pattern as part of the writing process.
- *English Skills with Readings,* Second Canadian Edition, assumes that writing
  from personal experience is a good way for "underprepared" students or

unwilling writers to begin writing. After mastering the skill of presenting a point and providing support from personal experience, such students are ready to move on to developing an idea by extrapolating from their own reasoning or by providing information from secondary sources. Students are asked to write on experience-based and more objective topics in Parts Two and Three, with some emphasis on, and preference given to, the third-person point of view and less personalised treatment of subjects. The reading selections in Part Five generate a variety of first- and third- person assignments.

■   The book also assumes that beginning writers at a college level are more likely to learn composing skills through contact with lively, engaging, and realistic models than through meeting material remote from common experiences of everyday life. When one sample writer explains the annoyances of college Net servers, or another warmly recalls how her grandmother's cooking led her to enter training to become a chef, or yet another discusses why TV wrestling is so popular, students are more apt to remember and follow the writing principles that may be involved. After reading vigorous student samples originating from a mainly Canadian context, and after reading some of the stimulating professional selections in Part Five, students will understand better the power that good writing can exert. They will then be more likely to aim for similar honesty, realism, and detail in their own work.

■   Another premise basic to *English Skills with Readings*, Second Canadian Edition, is that mastery of the paragraph should precede extension of basic compositional principles and skills into the longer essay. Thus Part One illustrates the basic principles of composition using paragraph models, and the assignments in Part Two aim at developing the ability to support ideas within a variety of paragraph forms. The essential principles of writing a deductively structured paragraph are then applied to the traditional five-paragraph essays in Part Three. Finally, in Part Five, each reading selection is followed by two paragraph assignments and one essay assignment.

■   Another assumption of this book is that, since no two people will use an English text in exactly the same way, the material should be organized in a highly accessible way. Because each of the five parts of the book deals with a distinct area of the book's subject, instructors can turn quickly and easily to the skills or knowledge they wish to present. Some ideas for sequencing are offered in the boxes titled "What to Do Next" appearing in the first chapters of the book. Additionally, a detailed syllabus is provided in the Instructor's Manual.

■   Finally, especially central to this text is the assumption that reading and writing are inextricably connected skills, so that practising one helps the other. Part Five enables students to work on becoming better readers as well as better writers. The introduction to Part Five offers a series of tips on effective reading, and ten questions after each selection provide practice in key reading comprehension skills. Discussion questions that follow each selection will deepen students' understanding of content and sensitize them to basic matters of structure, style, and tone. Last, three writing assignments for each selection offer guidelines to help students think about and begin these assignments.

Helpful learning aids accompany the book. The *Instructor's Manual and Test Bank (Canadian edition)* includes the Instructor's Guide along with twenty-eight supplementary activities and tests. Also available is *AllWrite! (Canadian edition)*—a high-interest, interactive grammar tutorial program on CD-ROM. Please contact your local McGraw-Hill Ryerson representative for details concerning policies, prices, and availability as some restrictions may apply.

THE READINGS

- The fifteen selections have been chosen for their content and timeliness as much as for rhetorical mode. They are organized thematically into three groups: "Goals and Values," "Education and Self-Improvement," and "Human Groups and Society." Some readings reflect current Canadian and international concerns: "Are We Raising Morally Illiterate Kids?," "Decoys and Denial," and "'The Boy Code' of Our Culture Breeds Bullies." Some offer information students may find helpful during their college years: "Why Should We Hire You?," "Power Learning," and "How to Write a Test." Still other selections discuss basic human experiences and ethical questions: "Adolescent Confusion," "Letter," and "Truth or Consequences." Finally, some selections provoke thought with a light touch: "Wolverine," "Have You Seen My Missing Math Gene?," and "The Importance of Cooking Dinner." Twelve of the fifteen selections are Canadian, and speak to the context and concerns of students in Canadian society today. All the selections should capture the interest of a wide range of students in the varied program areas offered by Canadian community colleges. (A list on pages xi-xii presents the readings by rhetorical mode.)
- Each reading begins with a preview that supplies background information as needed and stimulates interest in the subject of the selection.
- The ten reading comprehension questions that follow each selection give students practice in five key skills: summarizing (by choosing an alternative title), determining the main idea, recognizing key supporting details, making inferences, and understanding vocabulary in context. These are among the most crucial comprehension skills. A special chart at the back of the book enables students to track their progress as they practise these skills.
- Discussion questions following the reading comprehension questions deal with matters of content as well as aspects of structure, style, and tone. Through the questions on structure, in particular, students will see that professional authors practise some of the same basic composing techniques (such as the use of transitions and emphatic order to achieve coherence) that they have been asked to practise in their own writing.

CHANGES TO THE SECOND CANADIAN EDITION

The authors of the Canadian and U.S. editions have watched with pleasure and gratitude as the audience for *English Skills with Readings* expands each year. Instructors continue to say that the four bases really do help students learn to write effectively, and continue to comment that students find the model passages, activities, assignments, and readings especially interesting and worthwhile.

English Skills with Readings, Second Canadian Edition reflects both significant changes made to the fourth U.S. edition of the text, and major changes made to suit and speak to the specific Canadian community college audiences for this book.

Here is an overview of what is new to the second Canadian edition:

- Beginning with Chapter 2, "Important Factors in Writing," each chapter in Part One opens with Learning Outcomes for the student. These focus and personalize the text for the student, enabling him or her to engage closely with chapter content and activities, and to measure progress and outcomes with each chapter's skills and knowledge. Each chapter in Part One through Part Three ends with a Review of the Learning Outcomes, prompting the student to assess content understanding and evaluate progress and achievement in specific ways. Instructors may find it useful to use the Outcomes and Reviews as monitoring or evaluating methods in class and individually, especially for the chapters on methods of paragraph development and essay writing.
- In "Important Factors in Writing," the section on the student's attitude towards writing has been expanded with a new activity. Students will be better able to recognize and deal with the fact that a realistic and positive attitude is an important component of learning to write well.
- Material on outlining in Part One has been enlarged by the addition of an outline diagram—meant for use by students—as well as two new activities. Outlining is stressed as an essential stage in the writing process and consistently reintroduced at appropriate points in the text.
- The text now emphasizes careful internal construction of the paragraph with the introduction of, and continued attention to, both "topics" and "subtopics" and their support within any unit of writing. Exercises based on discovering topics and subtopics within sample pieces of writing have been included in Part One to reinforce the need for careful and logical construction of any piece of writing. A series of new class-tested activities will help students better understand the nature of specific details and how to generate and use such details. Learning to write concretely is a key step in becoming an effective writer. A new exercise has been added on topic sentences as well.
- The second Canadian edition reinforces in greater depth the concept of writing as iterative process, and strongly reinforces this concept throughout the text, beginning in Part One, with the process broken down into stages. Throughout Parts One, Two, and Three, students follow the progress of other student writers as they work through various writing tasks. New material on specific aspects of revising, editing, and proofreading has been added to Parts One through Three.
- In Part One a section on word processing and its usefulness at various stages of the writing process is now included as one of the key factors in writing.
- Each chapter in Part Two that covers a pattern of rhetorical development opens with specific Learning Outcomes related to writing a paragraph based on that pattern. As well, each chapter in this section of the book opens with

a description of the origin and potential uses and applications for each pattern of development. Within each of these chapters, a "How-To" box appears for each pattern, to reinforce and clarify the step-by-step procedure offered in the first of the writing assignments. Thus, these chapters offer a pedagogical continuum, beginning with Learning Outcomes, continuing with samples and questions, then reinforcing the Outcomes with the "How-To" instructions, the assignments, and concluding with the Review of the Learning Outcomes based on completion of an assignment that ends each chapter.

■ *English Skills with Readings,* Second Canadian Edition places more emphasis on issues involving voice in students' writing, emphasizing the importance of writing effectively in the third-person point of view for the purposes of career communications needs.

■ Throughout the text, most of the sample paragraphs have been replaced with samples grounded in a Canadian context. The samples have been updated to reflect as far as possible the interests and experiences of the diverse demographic of Canadian community college students in a wide range of programs.

■ A number of changes have been made in the sentence-skills material in Part Four. Diagnostic and Achievement tests have been added, along with five additional editing tests. Materials, in general, have been updated, and related to the Canadian college context. The chapters on run-ons and subject-verb agreement have been expanded.

■ A new chapter, "ESL Pointers," has been added to offer specific assistance to students writing in English as a second or third language. Explanations of some grammatical points covered may also prove useful to first-language speakers.

■ Many small changes appear throughout the second Canadian edition. Transitions are given more focus within chapters on rhetorical patterns in Part Two, with boxed inserts suggesting transitional words and phrases appropriate to various rhetorical modes. Narration and Description are placed first among patterns of development, as essential modes to be treated prior to expository patterns.

■ Finally, four new Canadian selections are now part of the fifteen selections in Part Five: "Letter," by Judith MacKenzie, "Are We Raising Morally Illiterate Kids?," by Caroline Medwell, "Wolverine," by Paul Jay, and "'The Boy Code' of Our Culture Breeds Bullies," by Michele Landsberg. The new selections offer a range of contemporary themes that should engage students and make for rewarding writing assignments.

ACKNOWLEDGMENTS

Reviewers who have provided helpful ideas and feedback include Bev Allix, Humber College; Arlene Davies-Fuhr, Grant MacEwan Community College; Mary Dunn, Sir Sandford Fleming; Peter Fahlman, Algonquin College; Barb Graham, St. Clair College; Peter Miller, Seneca College; Kay Oxford, George Brown College; Edeet Ravel, John Abbott College; and Pat Rogin, Durham College.

Again I am grateful for the support, good humour, and encouragement of the editors at McGraw-Hill Ryerson Canada: Developmental Editor Marianne Minaker and Senior Supervising Editor Margaret Henderson. Their help and kindness have been invaluable to me in the completion of this project. My thanks must also go to the many students at Seneca College who have shared their valued thoughts, feelings, and insights with me.

SHARON WINSTANLEY
JOHN LANGAN

Basic Principles of
Effective Writing

PREVIEW

Part One begins by introducing you to the book and to paragraph form. As you work through the brief activities in "Getting Started," you will gain a quick understanding of the book's purpose, how it is organized, and how it will help you develop your writing skills. After presenting a series of important general factors that will help you create good papers, Part One then describes four basic steps that can make you an effective writer. The four steps are:

1   Make a point.
2   Support the point with specific evidence.
3   Organize and connect the specific evidence.
4   Write clear, error-free sentences.

Explanations, examples, and activities are provided to help you master the first three steps. (You will be referred to Part Four of the book for a detailed treatment of the fourth step.) After seeing how these steps can help you write a competent paper, you will learn how they lead to four standards, or "bases," of effective writing: unity, support, coherence, and sentence skills. You will then practise evaluating a number of papers in terms of these four bases.

CHAPTER 1

Getting Started

LEARNING OUTCOMES

After working through this chapter and completing its assignments,

- **you will know the basic principles of effective writing;**
- **you will apply those principles as you write a simple paragraph; and**
- **you will grasp the overall organization of this book.**

English Skills with Readings grows out of the experiences of both its authors and the students they have been privileged to know. This text continues to grow and develop out of everything its authors have learned, and are still learning, as they continue to work at the process of writing.

Students sometimes assume that the writer of an English text could never share the difficulties they experience with writing tasks. The author, they assume, is part of a cold, hostile camp of "enemies," a group of people armed with red pens who were born knowing how to punctuate perfectly, spell flawlessly, and most intimidating of all, write three effortless drafts of an "A" essay without breaking a sweat.

No wonder students feel anxiety as they try to express their ideas. No wonder many students, including those writing in English as their second or third language, feel defeated before their fingers pick up a pen or touch a keyboard.

Anxiety is the real enemy of communicating. Anxiety's usual companions are unpleasant memories of past experiences and uncertainty about how to approach writing tasks: together, this threesome are enough to make anyone apprehensive about writing.

The aim of this text is to release students from "communication anxiety," with a realistic, experience-based, step-by-step approach to writing tasks.

The first important point to understand is that virtually no one is a "born writer." Writing is one large part of the lifelong process of communication. Like speaking, drawing, or communicating with actions, the patterns and rules for writing arose gradually from the success or failure of those who tried to write in various ways. Patterns and rules grew from seeing "what worked." Like anything whose end-result seems magical or mysterious, writing is actually only a matter of practice, perseverance, and gradually increasing skill. Becoming an effective writer involves no mysteries and no impossible tasks.

English Skills with Readings explains in a clear and direct way the basic principles and skills to help you learn to write effectively. It provides a number of practice materials so that you can work on these skills enough to make them habits. Each chapter begins with specific learning outcomes showing clearly what you can achieve and learn as you work through the chapter's tasks. This chapter introduces the most basic principles of effective writing. You will also discover how the rest of the book is organized and how it can help you become an effective writer.

I AN INTRODUCTION TO THE BASIC PRINCIPLE OF EFFECTIVE WRITING

Point and Support: An Important Difference between Writing and Talking

Every act of communication has a point. Humans are rarely aimless creatures; even when we wave to a friend in the hall, we have a reason to do so. Speech is even more purposeful: in everyday conversation, we make all kinds of points. We may say, "I love my job"; "Sherifa's a really generous person"; or "That exam was unfair." The points may concern personal matters or larger issues: "A lot of doctors are arrogant"; or "Rises in tuition fees make students suffer."

Points raised in conversation often lack support for two reasons. First, conversations are brief, unless we intend to argue or pursue a point more thoroughly. Second, the people with whom we speak do not always challenge us to support our statements. They may know why we feel as we do, or they may already agree with us, or they simply may not want to put us on the spot. Thus, they do not always ask "Why?" But the people who *read* what we write may not know us, agree with us, or feel in any way obliged to us.

Points made in print need support. First, we rarely write as briefly as we speak. Second, a reading audience may have many viewpoints. Third, and perhaps most significant, print allows readers to consider our views at their leisure and form their own responses.

Therefore, communicating effectively means making a point understood by the audience. To communicate effectively with readers, an effective writer provides solid evidence for any point he or she makes. An important difference between writing and talking is that *in writing, any idea advanced must be supported with specific reasons or details.*

Readers are generally reasonable people. They will not take our views on faith, but they *are* willing to consider what we say *as long as we support it*. Therefore, we must remember to support any statements that we make with specific evidence.

Point and Support in a Paragraph

A *paragraph* is a short unit of writing of 150 words or more. It usually consists of an opening point called a *topic sentence* followed by a *series of specifics,* in the form of sentences, that support the point. Much of the writing featured in this book will be paragraphs.

A Sample Paragraph: Following is a paragraph on why the writer finds her college's Internet server annoying:

Net Eats Student's Time!

Using my college's Net server can be a terrible waste of time. Yesterday evening was typical of how irritating "collegenet" can be. First of all, the server itself was down for two hours. This happened on the evening when I wanted to check the college library site for an article my marketing professor mentioned. I was determined to find the article, so I kept checking the site, and I was too restless to concentrate on my accounting assignment. Once the server started up again at 10:30 p.m., I found the article, printed it, and then decided to check my e-mail. The second stage in my growing irritation began with the twenty-three pointless messages I found. A lot of mail that the college sends out means nothing to me, like postings about parking charges at other campuses, and announcements from student groups I've never heard of, so scrolling through these e-mails just to delete and trash them is a time-waster. The final stage in my annoyance was still waiting for me. Unlike the college notices, these were mysterious posts that took forever to download. As I sat there at midnight, yawning and drumming my fingers on the desk, the mystery mails finally revealed themselves as chain letters with huge headers on them. The headers were the names and e-mail addresses of dozens of students— everyone the sender knew. Students who send these chain letters, complete with the usual threats about "breaking the chain," obviously have more time on their hands than I do.

Notice what the details in this paragraph do. They provide you, the reader, with a basis for understanding why the writer feels as she does. Through specific evidence, the writer has explained and communicated her point successfully. The evidence that supports the point in a paragraph often consists of a series of reasons or subtopics introduced by signal words (*First of all, second,* and the like) and followed by examples and details that support the reasons or expand on the subtopics. That is true of the sample paragraph above: three reasons are provided, followed by examples and details that back up those reasons.

Activity 1

Complete the following outline of the sample paragraph. Summarize in a few words the details that develop each reason, rather than writing the details out in full.

Point: _____

_____

Reason 1: _____

Details that develop reason 1: _____

_____

_____

Reason 2: _____

Details that develop reason 2: _____

_____

_____

Reason 3: _____

Details that develop reason 3: _____

_____

_____

Activity 2

Complete the statements below.

1. An important difference between writing and talking is that in writing we absolutely must _____ any statement we make.

2. A _____ is a collection of specifics that support a point.

Writing a Paragraph: An excellent way to get a feel for the paragraph is to write one. Your instructor may ask you to do that now. The only guidelines you need to follow are the ones described here and on the previous pages. There is an advantage to writing a paragraph right away, at a point where you have had almost no instruction. This first paragraph will give a quick sense of your needs as a writer and will provide a benchmark or baseline—a standard of comparison that you and your instructor can use to measure your writing progress during the semester.

II WRITING YOUR FIRST PARAGRAPH

Activity

Write a paragraph on the best or worst job you have ever had. Provide three reasons why your job was the best or the worst, and give plenty of details to develop each of your three reasons. Note that the sample paragraph, "Net Eats Student's Time," has the same format your paragraph should have. The author:

1 states a point in her first sentence,
2 gives three reasons to support the point,
3 introduces each reason clearly with signal words (*First of all, Second,* and *Finally*), and then
4 provides details that develop each of the three reasons. Write your paragraph on a separate sheet of paper.

III AN INTRODUCTION TO THIS BOOK

How the Book Is Organized

English Skills with Readings is divided into five parts. Read the Table of Contents, then skim through Parts One and Two. Brief questions about Parts One through Four appear below, not to test you but simply to introduce you to the central ideas in the text and the organization of the book. Your instructor may ask you to write the answers in class or just to note the answers in your head.

1. What are the eight "Important Factors in Writing" listed as subheadings in Chapter 2 of Part One of this text?
   - Which of these factors seems most important to you? Why?
   - Which of these factors had you not considered before?

2. According to Chapters 3 and 4 of Part One, what are the first, second, third, and fourth steps in writing?
   - How many of these steps have you used as parts of previous writing experience?
   - How many stages do you feel there would be in writing an effective paper, using these steps?
   - What would those stages be, according to your experience?

3. The final chapter of Part One, "Four Bases for Evaluating Writing," introduces you to four guidelines and goals for all your writing. List the four bases, and write or discuss briefly what each term means to you at this time. (You will also find these bases or standards summarized on the inside front cover of this text.)

4. Part Two is concerned with the different ways of developing your ideas within a paragraph or essay's structure.
   - How many methods of development are listed in the Table of Contents?
   - How many of these patterns have you already encountered?

5. Part Three deals with essay writing.
   - Based on your previous experience, how is an essay similar to a paragraph, and in what ways is it different?

6. Part Four is the largest section of the text; why do you think this is the case?
   - Which specific aspects of sentence skills do you wish to work on this semester?

How to Use the Book

Here is a suggested sequence for using this book if you are working on your own.

1. After completing this introduction, read the remaining four chapters in Part One and work through as many of the activities as you need to master the ideas in these chapters. Your instructor may give you answer sheets so that you can check your answers. At that point, you will have covered all the basic theory needed to write effective papers.

2   Turn to Part Four and do the introductory projects. These projects will help you identify the sentence skills you need to review. Study those skills one or two at a time while you continue to work on other parts of the book.

3   What you do next depends on course requirements, individual needs, or both. You will want to practise at least several different kinds of paragraph development in Part Two. If your time is limited, be sure to include "Providing Examples," "Explaining a Process," "Comparing or Contrasting," and "Arguing a Position." After that, you could logically go on to write one or more of the several-paragraph essays described in Part Three.

4   Read at least one of the fifteen selections in Part Five every week, always being sure to work through the two sets of questions that follow each reading.

5   Follow the instructions in the "Suggestions on What to Do Next" boxes that appear at the end of Chapters 3 to 5 in Part One.

AS YOU BEGIN. . .

English Skills with Readings will help you learn, practise, and apply the writing skills you need to communicate clearly and effectively. But the starting point must be your determination to do the work needed to become an independent writer. If you decide—*and only you can decide*—that you want to learn to write effectively, this book will help you reach that goal.

laining a Process · *Examining Cause and Effect* · *Comparing or Contrasting* · *Defini*
n · *Dividing and Classifying* · *Describing a Scene or Person* · *Narrating an Event* · *Argu*
sition · *Explaining a Process* · *Examining Cause and Effect* · *Comparing or Contrasti*
ning a Term · *Dividing and Classifying* · *Describing a Scene or Person* · *Narrating an E*
guing a Position · *Explaining a Process* · *Examining Cause and Effect* · *Comparing*

C H A P T E R   2

Important Factors in Writing

LEARNING OUTCOMES

After reading this chapter and working through its activities,

- you will have a more realistic and confident attitude about writing;
- you will begin to understand writing for a specific purpose and audience;
- you will learn to discover an appropriate subject;
- you will understand the value of keeping a journal;
- you will learn the importance of working through the four stages of the writing process:
  - discover your topic and message by prewriting
  - structure and order your ideas by outlining
  - write your first draft
  - revise for content quality, edit and proofread for errors; and
- you will discover how using a word processor can help at every stage of the writing process.

The preceding chapter introduced you to the paragraph form, and the chapters that follow in Part One will explain the basic steps in writing a paragraph and basic standards for evaluating a paragraph. The purpose of this chapter is to advance you along the road to effective writing by introducing you to *writing as a process with a purpose*. This chapter describes a number of important general factors that will help you create good papers. These factors cover the creation of a paper from beginning to end. They are:

1 having the right attitude about writing,
2 writing for a specific purpose and audience,
3 knowing or discovering your subject,
4 keeping a journal,

5 prewriting,

6 outlining,

7 using a word processor, and

8 revising, editing, and proofreading.

I YOUR ATTITUDE ABOUT WRITING

Negative experiences in the past and personal uncertainties colour everyone's feelings about writing. To begin building a positive, realistic attitude towards writing, consider honestly your own responses to the following questions and answers concerning common attitudes about writing.

■ *How do you feel as you prepare for a writing task?* Most people feel *vulnerable.* Everyone feels that their writing will expose them, their feelings, and their ideas to their readers. Will their work be unfairly criticized, now that any shortcomings are on paper for all to see? One of this chapter's recommendations is to keep a journal. Keeping a private, personal journal may help you to overcome "writer's block" connected with an audience's response to your writing. Journals allow you to write to *yourself* in daily entries, and are therefore a good way to lessen fears of imagined or real audiences.

■ *Are you worried about your instructor's evaluation of your first paper?* Every student is. As you will learn from this text, knowing your audience is basic to any writing task. You are giving your first submission to an audience you do not yet know: your professor. Most students fear that their professor will see them as unintelligent or hopeless at writing upon seeing that first writing sample. Actually, college English instructors enjoy reading students' ideas and helping students who want to learn the skill or knowledge they teach. If you do not understand what is required, ask for information. Then write your thoughts down as clearly and honestly as possible. Do not expect perfection. Learning to write well is a lifelong process. Your instructor and this text are there to work *with you* on this process.

■ *Do you feel that you have "nothing to say," when confronted with a writing task?* Relax. For one thing, ideas will not come to you when you are tense. There are many subjects on which many people feel they have "nothing to say." Everyone has unique experiences; everyone has opinions. After some thought, or after "downtime" in which you do some activity, perhaps unrelated to writing, you will probably find you have any number of ideas. The mind-freeing activities called "prewriting" in this chapter are designed to help you to overcome exactly this sort of feeling; the more you use these activities, the more you will find that you *do* have "something to say." Each time you begin the writing process by discovering your own good ideas, your confidence will increase.

■ ***Do you believe that writing well is a natural gift?*** Such an attitude excludes the thousands of students and working people who write competently and effectively every day. A person who says that writing well is an innate gift usually means that he or she does not have this gift. Chances are, this same person may have written a letter that touched someone, or may have succeeded in correcting a billing error by writing to some company. In other words, he or she can write effectively. But, based on negative past experiences, and self-defeating anxiety, people in a classroom situation sometimes decide that writing is a gift given only to others. Suddenly their mistaken view tells them everyone else finds writing easy, or at least tolerable. Psychologists call this "playing old tapes," or allowing the past to rule the present. As a result of this attitude, once inside a classroom, people do not do their best when they write, or they may hardly try at all. The truth is that that everyone who can learn, can learn to write well. All that anyone needs is enough confidence to begin, and enough perseverance to keep working.

Adopt a realistic attitude about writing. Realize two things: you communicate effectively every day, and you can progress step by step in clearly set-out stages to become an effective and confident writer. Base your attitude towards writing on four crucial ideas:

1 ***Writing is hard work for almost everyone.*** It is difficult, and sometimes lonely, to do the intense, active thinking that clear writing demands. Everyone feels some fear as he or she sits down before a blank sheet of paper or screen, only to find that sometimes, not much that he or she writes may be worth keeping. It is always a challenge to transfer thoughts and feelings from one's mind onto a page. And often, an apparently simple writing subject turns out to be complicated. But people are complicated beings: discovering and then translating thoughts into writing takes energy, time, and effort.

2 ***Writing is not a straightforward process.*** Writing is not an automatic process: no one gets something for nothing. Good writing almost never emerges from hasty first drafts; the mind approaches different tasks in different ways. Writing is a process of many different tasks: discovering, patterning, refining, and composing. Perhaps the writer may return to any of those stages several times before he or she is satisfied. Competent writing results from learning how to manage the various stages of the process and from having the perseverance to work through those stages with care.

3 ***Writing is a skill.*** Writing is a skill like driving, drawing, or cooking, and like any skill, it can be learned. Any learning or acquisition of a skill begins with a desire and a decision: *if* you decide that you want to write well, and *if* you then decide to work at it, you will write well. This book will give you the extensive practice needed to develop your writing skills.

4 ***Writing is rewarding.*** Writing effectively brings lifelong rewards. On a personal level, writing effectively brings the satisfaction of knowing you have expressed thoughts and feelings in such a way that readers understand, and perhaps act on, what you have written. On a professional or career level, effective communication skills are the first requirement of all employers, and the great-

est asset in any field. Since technology has made communications the basis for the global economy, writing well is a necessity in the twenty-first century.

Activity

To perform a final check on reasons for attitudes towards writing, read the following four statements. Note the statements with which you agree, and try to be as honest as possible.

Now read the following statements and comments. The comments will help you see how your attitude may affect your efforts to become a better writer.

Comments

- Statement 1: *"A good writer should be able to sit down and write a paper straight through without stopping."*
  Statement 1 is not true. Writing is a process. It is done not in one easy step but in a series of steps, and seldom at one sitting. If you cannot do a paper all at once, that simply means you are like most of the other people on the planet. It is harmful to carry around the false idea that writing should be an easy matter.

- Statement 2: *"I'll never be good at writing because I make too many mistakes in spelling, grammar, and punctuation."*
  The first concern in good writing should be content: what you have to say. Your ideas and feelings are what matter most. You should not worry about spelling, grammar, or punctuation while working on content.

  Unfortunately, some people are so self-conscious about making mistakes that they do not focus on what they want to say. They need to realize that a paper is best done in stages, and that applying the rules can and should wait until a later stage in the writing process. Through review and practice, you will eventually learn how to follow the rules with confidence.

- Statement 3: *"Because I dislike writing, I always start a paper at the last possible minute."*
  This is all too common. You feel you are going to do poorly, and then behave in a way that ensures you will receive a low mark! You defeat yourself by not allowing enough time to make a fair effort.

  Again, what you need to realize is that writing is a process. Because it is done in steps, you do not have to get it right all at once. If you allow yourself enough time, you will find a way to make a paper come together.

- Statement 4: *"English was not really my favourite subject, and I don't expect that to change."*
  How you may have performed in the *past* does not control how you can perform in the *present*. Even if English was not your favourite subject in high school, you can make English one of your best subjects in college. If you believe writing can be learned and then work hard at it, you *will* become a better writer.

In conclusion, your attitude is crucial. If you realize you can become a better writer, chances are you will improve. Your success or failure depends on your attitude as you begin.

II WRITING FOR A SPECIFIC PURPOSE AND AUDIENCE

The three most common purposes of writing are *to inform*, *to persuade*, and *to entertain*. Most of the writing you will do in this book will involve some form of persuasion. You will advance a point or topic sentence and then support it in a variety of ways. To some extent, you will also write papers to inform: to provide readers with information about a particular subject.

Your audience will be primarily your instructor, and sometimes other students as well. Your instructor is really a symbol of the larger audience you should see yourself as writing for: an educated, adult audience that expects you to present your ideas in a clear, direct, and organized way. If you can learn to write to persuade or inform such a general audience, you will have accomplished a great deal.

It will also be helpful for you to write some papers for a more specific audience. By so doing, you will develop an ability to choose words and adopt a tone that is just right for a given purpose and a given group of people. For example, Part Two of this book includes assignments asking you to write with very specific purposes in mind, and for very specific audiences.

III KNOWING OR DISCOVERING YOUR SUBJECT

KNOWING YOUR SUBJECT

Whenever possible, try to write on a subject that interests you. You will then find it easier to put more time and energy into your work. More important, try to write on a subject that you already know something about. If you do not have direct experience with the subject, you should at least have indirect experience—knowledge gained through thinking, prewriting (to be explained on pages 17–23), reading, or talking about the subject.

If you are asked to write on a topic about which you have no experience or knowledge, do enough research to gain the information you need. Without direct or indirect experience, or the information you gain through research, you will be unable to provide the specific evidence needed to develop the point you are trying to make. Your writing will be starved for specifics.

To find the information you need, visit your college or local library or use an Internet search engine to find websites on your topic. At the library, look up your topic in the "Subject" index of the computerized or card index. Note the titles of books or of articles in journals or magazines that seem most related to your topic.

(See page 355 in this text for information on how to cite the titles of works.) Be prepared to spend some time scanning material relevant to your assignment. Remember to write down the author, title of the publication, and page number of any material you want to quote or paraphrase in your own words. If you use the Internet for your research, use your topic and synonyms for it as search keywords. Be ready to spend some time reading and perhaps printing information from sites most related to your topic. Bookmark these sites on your computer's server, or write down the titles of the sites and their URLs. For further information on how to insert direct quotations into your assignment or how to list the works you use in your paper, ask your professor or go to this website: *www.mla.org.*

DISCOVERING YOUR SUBJECT AND YOUR FOCUS

At times you will not know your subject when you begin to write. Instead, you will discover it in the actual process of writing. For example, when a student named Silvio sat down to write a paper about a memorable job (see page 38), he thought for a while that his topic was going to be an especially depressing moment on that job. As he began to accumulate details, however, he realized that his topic was really the job itself and all the drawbacks it entailed. Silvio only *thought* he knew the focus of his paper when he began to write. In fact, *he discovered his subject in the course of writing.*

Another student, Lisa, explained that at first her topic was how she relaxed with her children. But as she accumulated details, she realized after a page of writing that the words *relax* and *children* simply did not go together. Her details were really examples of how she *enjoyed* her children, not how she *relaxed* with them. She sensed that the real focus of her writing should be what she did by herself to relax, and then she suddenly thought that the best time of her week was Thursdays after school. "A light clicked on in my head," she explained. "I knew I had my paper." Then it was a matter of detailing exactly what she did to relax on Thursday evenings. Her paper, "How I Relax," is on page 79.

Sometimes you must write a bit in order to find out just what you want to write. Writing can help you think about and explore your topic and decide just what direction your paper will finally take. The techniques presented in "Prewriting"—the section starting on page 17—will suggest specific ways to discover and develop a subject.

ALLOWING YOUR IDEAS TO EMERGE

One related feature of the writing process bears mention. Do not feel that you must proceed in a linear fashion when you write. The writing process is not a railroad track going straight from your central point to supporting detail 1 to supporting detail 2 to supporting detail 3 to your concluding paragraph. Instead, as you draft the paper, proceed in whatever way seems most comfortable. You may want to start by writing the closing section or by developing your third supporting detail.

Do whatever is easiest. As you get material down on the page, it will make what you have left to do a bit easier. Sometimes as you work on one section, it may happen that a new focal point for your paper will emerge. If your writing tells you that it wants to be something else, then revise or start over as needed to take advantage of that discovery. Your goal is to wind up with a paper that solidly makes and supports a point. Be ready and open to change direction and to make whatever adjustments are needed to reach your goal.

Activity 1

Answer the following questions.

1. What are three ways of gaining information to write a paper?
2. How does having enough information about a subject make the writing process easier?
3. You are freewriting to discover material for a paper on using technology at college, and find that most of the points you have written down concern your enjoyment of computer graphics software. What has happened? What should you do?

Activity 2

Write for five minutes about the house, residence, or apartment where you live. Simply write down whatever details come to you. Don't worry about being neat; just pile up as many details as you can.

Afterward, go through the material. Try to find a potential focus within all those details. Do the details suggest a simple point that you could make about the place where you live? If so, you've seen a small example of how writing about a topic can be an excellent way of discovering a point about that topic.

IV KEEPING A JOURNAL

Because writing is a skill, it makes sense that the more you practise writing, the better you will write. One excellent way to get practice in writing is to keep a daily or almost-daily journal.

At some point during the day—perhaps in free time after your last class, or before dinner, or before going to bed, spend fifteen minutes or so writing in your journal. You do not have to prepare what to write or be in the mood or worry about making mistakes; just write down whatever words come to you. As a minimum, you should complete at least one page in each writing session.

You may want to use a notebook that you can easily carry with you for on-the-spot writing. Or you may decide to write on loose-leaf paper that can be transferred later to a journal folder or binder on your desk. No matter how you proceed, be sure to date all your entries.

The content of your journal could be some of the specific happenings, thoughts, and feelings of the day. Your starting point may be a comment by an instructor, a classmate, or a family member; a gesture or action that has amused, angered, confused, or depressed you; something you have read or seen on television—anything, really, that has caught your attention and that you decide to explore in writing. Some journal entries may focus on a single subject; others may wander from one topic to another. *You* are your main audience.

Your instructor may ask you to make journal entries a set number of times a week, for a set number of weeks. He or she may ask you to turn in your journal every so often for review and feedback. If you are keeping the journal on your own, try to make entries three to five times a week, every week of the semester.

Your journal can serve as a sourcebook of ideas for possible papers. More important, keeping a journal will help you become confident about the habit of thinking on paper, and it can help you make writing a familiar part and a pleasing record of your life.

Following is an excerpt from one student's journal. (Sentence-skills and spelling mistakes have been corrected to improve readability.) As you read, look for a general point and supporting material that could be the basis for an interesting paper.

October 6, 1999

Today I felt like quitting my job. A man came to the Customer Service counter to return a food processor. Working in Customer Service still makes me nervous. I'm not used to taking responsibility for store policy, and I'm afraid I'll make the wrong decision a lot of the time. It was easier being a cashier because I didn't have to deal with Mr. Priddy, the manager, so much. I don't always know if I should accept returned merchandise or not and there are so many forms to fill out. Mr. Priddy's temper scares me, and today he was close enough to hear everything that went on. Anyway, this customer bought a food processor for his wife, and supposedly the first time she used it, the motor cut out and wouldn't restart. On top of that, he didn't have his Zellers receipt or the guarantee that came with the processor. He hadn't even washed the thing before he brought it back. What really upset me was how aggressive he was, and he just kept repeating himself in a louder and louder voice. I wanted to take the processor back, give him a refund, and make him go away. But Mr. P was in the next aisle. He heard the whole conversation and he knew I was stuck for an answer. I could see his face out of the corner of my eye. He was itching for an opportunity to interrupt me and take over. Finally, just as he started to edge closer to my counter, while the customer was yelling about Zellers' customer satisfaction policy, the customer's wife appeared. She should have had *my* job; she was so polite. She calmly explained that all she really wanted was to have the processor sent back to be checked out. She even apologized for not having the guarantee and magically produced her husband's credit card receipt out of the bottom of her purse . . .

■ If the writer of this journal is looking for an idea for an essay, she can probably find several in this single entry. For example, she might write a narrative supporting the point that "In my new job I have to deal with some irritating customers." See if you can find another idea in this entry that might be the basis for an interesting paragraph. Write your point in the space below.

_____

■ Take fifteen minutes to prepare a journal entry right now on this day in your life. On a separate sheet of paper, just start writing about anything that you have seen, said, heard, thought, or felt, and let your thoughts take you where they may.

V THE FOUR STAGES OF THE WRITING PROCESS
STAGE ONE: PREWRITING

If you are like many people, you sometimes have trouble getting started writing.

A mental block may develop when you sit down before a blank sheet of paper. You may not be able to think of a topic or an interesting slant on a topic. Or you may have trouble coming up with interesting and relevant details to support your topic. Even after starting a paper, you may hit snags: moments when you wonder "Where do I go next?"

The following pages describe four techniques that will help you think about and develop a topic and get words down on paper:

■ questioning,
■ freewriting,
■ making a list, and
■ diagramming.

These techniques, which are often called *prewriting techniques,* are a central part of the writing process.

TECHNIQUE 1: QUESTIONING

In *questioning,* you generate ideas and details by asking as many questions as you can think of about your subject. Such questions include *What? When? Why? How? Where?* and *Who?*

Following is an example of how one student, Scott, used questioning to generate material for a paper. Scott felt that he could write about a painful moment he had experienced, but he was having trouble getting started. So he asked himself a series of questions about the experience. As a result, he accumulated a series of details that provided the basis for the paper he finally wrote.

Here are the questions Scott asked and the answers he wrote:

Questions	Answers
<u>Where</u> did the experience happen?	In my younger brother's residence room at the University of Alberta

Questions	Answers
<u>When</u> did it happen?	A week before his first-year spring break
<u>Who</u> was involved?	My brother Josh, his roommate, and I
<u>What</u> happened?	I found out my brother was failing every course but one, and wasn't even planning to tell our parents. His marks in December weren't good, and his bulletin board was covered with tests with big red "Fs" on them. He'd even changed the address for his spring transcripts by claiming his main residence was his roommate's mother's house.
<u>Why</u> was the experience so painful?	My brother always did better than I did in school, and my parents were paying for his tuition and residence fees. They really wanted him to succeed at university. I worked for five years before I started putting myself through college for the last two years. The trip from Winnipeg cost me a lot of money, and I was really looking forward to it.
<u>How</u> did my brother react?	He tried to lie to me at first, pretending that nothing was was wrong when I asked how his marks were. Then he got tense and defensive, saying he wasn't sure what he was doing yet anyway and that he needed time off to travel.
<u>How</u> did I react?	I was in a rage. I couldn't believe how dishonest he was and how he could let down our parents this way. I wanted to get out of there and call home, then I thought better of it. I was jealous of all the advantages he was ready to waste. Then I decided to wait and see if he would admit what he was doing to the family.

After discovering all these details from his questioning, Scott's next step was to prepare an outline. He then worked his way through several drafts of the paper, focusing on revealing his own responses to his disappointment with his brother. The effective paragraph that eventually resulted from Scott's prewriting techniques appears in the chapter on Narration on page 130.

Activity

To get a sense of questioning, use a sheet of paper to ask yourself a series of questions about a restaurant you particularly enjoy. See how many details you can accumulate about that place in ten minutes.

TECHNIQUE 2: FREEWRITING

When you do not know what to write about a subject or when you are blocked in writing, freewriting sometimes helps. In *freewriting*, you write on your topic for ten minutes. You do not worry about spelling or punctuating correctly, about erasing mistakes, or about finding exact words. You just write without stopping. If you get stuck for words, you write "I am looking for something to say" or repeat words until something comes. There is no need to feel inhibited, since mistakes do not count and you do not have to hand in your paper.

Freewriting will limber up your writing muscles and make you familiar with the act of writing. It is a way to break through mental blocks about writing and overcome the fear of making errors. As you do not have to worry about making mistakes, you can concentrate on discovering what you want to say about a subject. Your initial ideas and impressions will often become clearer after you have gotten them down on paper. Through continued practice in freewriting, you will develop the habit of thinking as you write. And you will learn a technique that is a helpful way to get started on almost any paper.

Here is the freewriting that one student did to accumulate details for a paper on why his town is changing for the worse.

> Two years ago, the town where I grew up on the shore of Lake Erie started to dry up and disappear. The biggest employer, the car-parts factory, had just closed down for its third strike in five years, and the labour problems were getting worse and worse. More workers were being laid off as more and more parts were being made in Mexico or in the East. Last night's paper said the U.S. parent company is going to close the factory for good. There isn't anywhere near here for all those hundreds of people to work. Will all those families still be able to live here? One of the two big chain stores just outside of town closed in the last year, and the other one became part of an American chain. Walmart took over the Woolco store, but they brought in their own management and people from some of their other stores, so a third of the Woolco employees didn't end up working at the new store. The saddest sight of all is Queen Street, the town's old main street. Everybody used to walk along Queen Street; it always looked like it would never change and it was the real heart of town. A year ago, a big new mall was built just outside of London, only a half hour's drive away. People drive there to do all their shopping, and

even to do their banking, or go to the movies. Half the stores on Queen Street are closed and empty today, and two of the bank branches have shut down. No one has any reason to "go downtown" any more. Right now, it feels like my home town is on the way to becoming a ghost town.

The writer's next step was to use the freewriting as the basis for an outline for a paper about the causes of the changes in his home town. An effective paper that eventually resulted from the author's freewriting, an outline, and a good deal of rewriting appears on page 165.

Activity

To get a sense of freewriting, use a sheet of paper to freewrite about your everyday worries. See how many ideas and details you can accumulate in ten minutes.

TECHNIQUE 3: MAKING A LIST

Another way to get started is to make a list of as many different items as you can think of concerning your topic. Do not worry about repeating yourself, about sorting out major details from minor ones, or about spelling or punctuating correctly. Simply make a list of everything about your subject that occurs to you. Your aim is to generate details and to accumulate as much raw material for writing as possible.

Following is a list prepared by one student, Paulina, who was gathering details for a paper on abuse of public parks. Her first stage in doing the paper was simply to make a list of thoughts and details that occurred to her about the topic. Here is her list:

    Messy picnickers (most common)
    Noisy radios
    Graffiti on buildings and fences
    Frisbee games that disturb others
    Dumping car ashtrays
    Stealing park property
    Nude sunbathing
    Destroying flowers
    Damaging fountains and statues
    Litter

Notice that Paulina puts in parentheses a note to herself that messy picnickers are the most common type of park abusers. Very often as you make a list, ideas about how to develop a paper will occur to you. Jot them down.

Activity

To get a sense of making a list, use a sheet of paper to list specific problems you will face this semester. See how many ideas and details you can accumulate in ten minutes.

TECHNIQUE 4: DIAGRAMMING

Diagramming, also known as *mapping* or *clustering*, is another prewriting activity that can help you generate ideas and details about a topic. In diagramming, you use lines, boxes, arrows, and circles to show relationships among the ideas and details that come to you.

Diagramming is helpful to people who like to think visually. Whether you use a diagram, and just how you proceed with it, is up to you.

Here is the diagram that one student, Devon, prepared for a paper on differences between his job as he imagined it and as it turned out to be. The diagram, with its clear picture of relationships, was especially helpful for the comparison-contrast paper that Devon was doing. His final essay appears on pages 180–181.

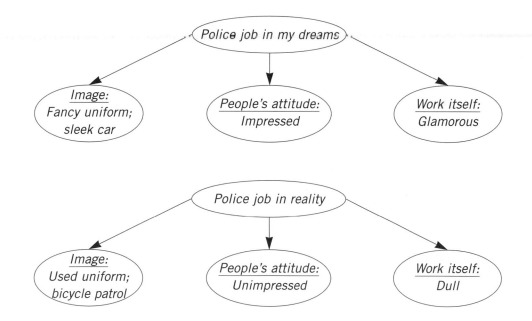

Activity

To get a sense of diagramming, use a sheet of paper to make a diagram of differences between two instructors or two jobs. See how many ideas and details you can accumulate in ten minutes.

USING ALL FOUR TECHNIQUES

Prewriting techniques are designed to open up your mind, to allow you to discover ideas and the connections between those ideas. No rules govern your use of prewriting techniques; go with what works for you. You may use several techniques almost simultaneously when writing a paper. You may, for example, ask questions while making a list; you may diagram and perhaps sort through a list as you write it; you may ask yourself questions and then freewrite answers to them. And keep in mind that if you try one technique and are not satisfied, you can simply go on to another one. All the techniques are at your disposal. Choose ones that work best for you.

Activity 1

Answer the following questions.

1. Which prewriting technique have you used previously?
2. Which prewriting technique do you think might work best for you? Why?
3. Why do people prewrite at all, rather than trying immediately to write a first draft?

Activity 2

Following are examples of how the four prewriting techniques could be used to develop the topic "Inconsiderate Drivers." Identify each technique by writing *Q* (for *questioning*), *F* (for *freewriting*), *D* (for the *diagram*), or *L* (for the *list*) in the answer space.

_____

High beams on

Weave in and out at high speeds

Treat street like a garbage can

Open car door onto street without looking

Stop on street looking for an address

Don't use turn signals

High speeds in low-speed zones

Don't take turns merging

Use horn when they don't need to

Don't give walkers the right of way

_____

What is one example of an inconsiderate driver?	A person who suddenly turns without using a signal to let the drivers behind know in advance.
When does this happen?	At city intersections or on smaller country roads.
Why is this dangerous?	You have to be alert to slow down yourself to avoid rear-ending the car in front.
What is another example of inconsideration on the road?	Drivers who come toward you at night with their high beams on.

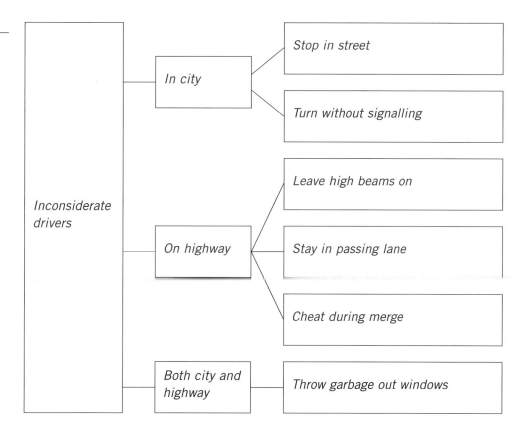

I was driving home last night after class and had three people try to blind me by coming at me with their high beams on. I had to zap them all with my high beams. Rude drivers make me crazy. The worst are the ones that use the road as a garbage can. People who throw bags and cups and hamburger wrappings and other stuff out the car windows should be tossed into a dumpster. If word got around that this was the punishment maybe they would wise up. Other people do dumb things as well. I hate the person who will just stop in the middle of the street and try to figure out directions or look for a house address. Why don't they pull over to the side of the street? That hardly seems like too much to ask. Instead, they stop all traffic while doing their own thing. Then there are the people who keep what they want to do a secret. They're not going to tell you they plan to make a right- or left-hand turn. Instead, you've got to figure it out yourself when they suddenly slow down in front of you.

STAGE TWO: OUTLINING

As mentioned on the first page of this chapter, outlining or mapping your paper is an essential second step in the writing process. At times, you may first have to do a fair amount of writing to discover your topic and focus on the point you wish to make about that topic, but a time will come when outlining, or re-outlining is needed to untangle and clarify your prewriting.

- A formal outline helps you to sort out and state your topic and each of your supporting points, or subtopics and the details that clarify or explain each. The best way to structure your ideas and decide on their value before drafting a paragraph is to create an ordered outline.
- Outlining is a different kind of mental activity from prewriting. It is an an ordering and selecting activity, and an organizational skill that will develop your ability to think clearly and logically. An outline lets you work on and see the bare bones of a paper, without the distraction of a clutter of words and sentences. Outlining provides a quick check on whether your paper is *unified*. It suggests at the start whether your paper will be adequately *supported*. And it shows you how to plan a paper that is *well organized*.

CREATING AN OUTLINE FOR AN EFFECTIVE PARAGRAPH

As you outline, remember that the process may not proceed in exactly the order set out below. You may find it easier to note your main supporting points or subtopics before you are able to write a suitable topic sentence. Or, you may find that one of your details supporting a subtopic is actually a subtopic itself. Discovering the structure within your prewriting is one of the values of making an outline.

Following these instructions is an outline diagram to use with each of your paragraph writing assignments. Make photocopies of it, or set up its pattern of points and numbering as a disk document called "paragraph outline." Simply cut and paste the blank outline onto a new document page each time you need to create an outline.

1 Begin by making a trial statement of your point, which is your topic and your attitude towards that point. Write this as your topic sentence: it should be general enough to cover all your subtopics (supporting points). Moreover, each of your subtopics or supporting points should accurately reflect the attitude you express, or *the focus* of your approach to your topic.

2 Examine your prewriting. Look for possible subtopics, or main supporting points for your topic. Note these in a few words in each of the spaces provided on your paragraph outline sheet.

3 Consider an appropriate *order* for your supporting points. Do you wish to state your supporting points as they occurred *in time,* or do you wish to put them in order of *increasing importance*?

4 For each supporting point or subtopic, list in point form details from your prewriting or any new details that occur to you. To ensure balance in your paragraph, it is desirable to have approximately the same number of details to support each suptopic.

The exercises following this section will help you to discern the difference between more general subtopics, or supporting points, and the specific details that clarify, explain, or make vivid those subtopics.

PARAGRAPH OUTLINING FORM

To write an effective paragraph, first prepare an outline. Photocopy this outline pattern, or set it up as a blank document to save to your computer disk.

Topic sentence: _____

_____

_____

Subtopic or Supporting Point (1): _____

_____

Details:

_____

_____

_____

_____

Subtopic or Supporting Point (2): _____

_____

Details:

_____

_____

_____

_____

Subtopic or Supporting Point (3): _____

_____

Details:

_____

_____

_____

_____

The following series of exercises will help develop the outlining skills that are so important to writing an effective paper.

Activity 1

One key to effective outlining is the ability to distinguish between general ideas and specific ideas. Read each group of specific ideas below. Then circle the letter of the general idea that tells what the specific ideas have in common. Note that the general idea should not be too broad or too narrow. Begin by trying the example item, and then read the explanation that follows.

Example   *Specific ideas:* egg salad; tuna salad; bacon, lettuce, and tomato; peanut butter and jelly
The general idea is:
a. foods.
b. sandwich fillings.
c. salads used as sandwich fillings.

Explanation: It is true that the specific ideas are all food, but they have in common something even more specific—they are all sandwich fillings. Therefore, answer *a* is too broad; the correct answer is *b*. Answer *c* is too narrow because it doesn't cover all of the specific ideas: two of the sandwich fillings are not salads.

1. *Specific ideas:* Easter, Thanksgiving, Valentine's Day, New Year's Day
   The general idea is:
   a. days.
   b. holidays.
   c. religious holidays.

2. *Specific ideas:* hide and seek, tag, jacks, hopscotch
   The general idea is:
   a. games.
   b. toys.
   c. children's games.

3. *Specific ideas:* runny nose, coughing, sneezing, sore throat
   The general idea is:
   a. cold symptoms.
   b. symptoms.
   c. throat problems.

4. *Specific ideas:* yes, no, maybe, okay
   The general idea is:
   a. negative answers.
   b. positive answers.
   c. answers.

5. *Specific ideas:* OPEN, STOP, FIRE EXIT, YIELD
   The general idea is:
   a. words.

    b. words on signs.

    c. words on traffic signs.

6. *Specific ideas:* leaking toilet, no hot water, broken window, roaches
   The general idea is:
   a. problems.
   b. kitchen problems.
   c. apartment problems.

7. *Specific ideas:* tornado, earthquake, sunrise, spring
   The general idea is:
   a. natural disasters.
   b. natural events.
   c. events.

8. *Specific ideas:* big and small, short and tall, fat and lean, kind and mean
   The general idea is:
   a. words.
   b. sizes.
   c. opposites.

Activity 2

In the following items, specific items are given but general ideas are unstated. Fill in each blank with a general heading that accurately encompasses the list provided.

Example   General idea: <u>*Breakfast choices*</u>

                Specific ideas: doughnuts
                                        bacon and eggs
                                        cereal
                                        pancakes

1. *General idea:* _____
   Specific ideas: vanilla fudge
                       chocolate
                       strawberry
                       butter almond

2. *General idea:* _____
   Specific ideas: birthday
                       anniversary
                       get well
                       graduation

3. *General idea:* _____
   Specific ideas: robbery
                       assault
                       murder
                       kidnapping

4. *General idea:* _____
    Specific ideas: salesperson
                     hair stylist
                     welder
                     insurance agent

5. *General idea:* _____
    Specific ideas: Bufferin
                     Tylenol
                     Anacin
                     Advil

6. *General idea:* _____
    Specific ideas: washing dishes
                     preparing meals
                     taking out garbage
                     dusting

7. *General idea:* _____
    Specific ideas: writing
                     listening
                     speaking
                     reading

8. *General idea:* _____
    Specific ideas: order the invitations
                     get the bride's gown
                     rent the tuxedos
                     hire a photographer

Activity 3

Major and minor ideas, or subtopics and details, are mixed together in the two paragraphs outlined below. Place subtopics in spaces labelled *a, b,* and *c.* Place appropriate detail or minor idea under each subtopic in numbered spaces.

1. *Topic sentence:* People can be classified by how they treat their cars.
    Seldom wax or vacuum car
    Keep every mechanical item in top shape
    Protective owners
    Deliberately ignore needed maintenance
    Indifferent owners
    Wash and polish car every week
    Accelerate too quickly and brake too hard
    Abusive owners
    Inspect and service car only when required by provincial law

    a. _____

        (1) _____

        (2) _____

b. _____

   (1) _____

   (2) _____

c. _____

   (1) _____

   (2) _____

2. *Topic sentence:* Living with an elderly parent has many benefits.
Advantages for elderly person
Live-in babysitter
Learn about the past
Advantages for adult children
Serve useful role in family
Help with household tasks
Advantages for grandchildren
Stay active and interested in young people
More attention from adults

a. _____

   (1) _____

   (2) _____

b. _____

   (1) _____

   (2) _____

c. _____

   (1) _____

   (2) _____

Activity 4

Again, major and minor ideas (subtopics and details) are mixed together. In addition, in each outline one of the three major ideas or subtopics is missing and must be added. Put the subtopics and details in logical order by filling in the outlines that follow (summarizing as needed) and adding a third major idea or subtopic.

1. *Topic sentence:* Extending the school day would have several advantages.
Help children academically
Parents know children are safe at the school
More time to spend on basics
Less pressure to cover subjects quickly
More time for extras like art, music, and sports
Help working parents
More convenient to pick up children at 4 or 5 p.m.
Teachers' salaries would be raised

a. _____

    (1) _____

    (2) _____

b. _____

    (1) _____

    (2) _____

c. _____

    (1) _____

    (2) _____

2. *Topic sentence:* By following hints about food, exercise, and smoking, you
    can increase your chances of dying young.
    Don't ever walk if you can ride instead.
    Choose foods such as bacon and lunch meats that are laced with nitrates and
        other preservatives.
    Be very selective about what you eat.
    Develop the habit of smoking.
    If you begin to cough or feel short of breath, keep smoking.
    If a friend invites you to play an outdoor sport, open a beer instead and head
        for your reclining chair.
    Resist the urge to exercise.
    Choose foods from one of four essential groups: fat, starch, sugar, and grease.
    Smoke on a regular basis.

a. _____

    (1) _____

    (2) _____

b. _____

    (1) _____

    (2) _____

c. _____

    (1) _____

    (2) _____

Activity 5

Read the following two student paragraphs. Then outline each one in the space
provided. Write out the topic sentence in each case and summarize in a few words
the subtopic (primary details). Then note secondary supporting details that fit
under each subtopic.

1.   **Commuter Complaints**

    Three hours a day in the car, caused by delays resulting from weather, road repairs, and other drivers, make commuting a very annoying part of life. At a steady one hundred kilometres per hour, a one-way trip across the top of Toronto *should* take less than an hour. But Toronto is a city with two seasons, winter and construction, so the trip takes a lot longer. Winter means icy surfaces, salt trucks, and ploughs with their blue lights winking as they slow traffic to a crawl. Snowstorms bring traffic to a complete halt, leaving drivers sitting in the early morning or evening darkness listening to repeated road reports. Summer brings construction-season slowdowns. Out come the road crews to repave the same sections of the 401 they repaved last year, causing lane closings and bumper-to-bumper traffic. In nice weather, drivers glare at crews having lunch in the closed lanes as they sit starving, or sweating because they can not catch a breeze while doing ten kilometres an hour. The terrible habits of some drivers make endless commutes even more annoying. "Speed demons" think that tailgating, suddenly speeding up, and then crazily changing lanes over and over will get them to their destination more quickly. These drivers show up half an hour later, their cars off to the side, smashed into the back of the car in front. They have already slowed traffic by frightening other drivers with their moves, then entertained them with the eventual accidents that make everyone slow down to take a look. Cell-phone-addicted drivers who concentrate more on conversations than on driving may be even more dangerous. No one can dial, talk, and drive all at the same time; cell-phone drivers never seem to look in their rear-view mirrors, so they change speeds for no apparent reason, and then weave slowly out of their lanes without signalling. Other drivers slow down to avoid them, and everyone suffers together. In fact, after considering all these annoyances, there might be one consolation for commuters. They are never suffering alone.

Topic sentence: _____

_____

Subtopic a. _____

   (1) _____

   (2) _____

Subtopic b. _____

   (1) _____

   (2) _____

Subtopic c. _____

   (1) _____

   (2) _____

2.

Cooking is My Life

I love to cook for many reasons; in fact, cooking will truly be my life when I graduate from the culinary arts program at Niagara College. My love of cooking begins in my childhood, so my first reason must be early memories of wonderful smells and funny kitchen conversations with my grandmother. Today I still prefer the fragrance of her white cornbread baking to the scent of any perfume. Some day I hope to attract customers to a restaurant of my own with the aromas of the Portugese soups and stews she made for the family. I also associate cooking with laughter, because my grandmother had the interesting habit of talking to food. If a piece of meat she was trimming would not do what she wanted it to, she would say, "Come on, Senhor Lambleg, you must obey me." The meat, the fish, and the vegetables always understood her and obeyed, even the potatoes she hated peeling and occasionally cursed. Talk and laughter were always part of family dinners, so they are the second reason I love to cook. Dinners lasted at least an hour. They held us together as a family because meals were often the only time I saw my older sisters and brothers and my father. Even though I liked sharing in the conversations, what I loved best about those dinners was the respect and love my grandmother received for everything she put on the table. Each dish was always tasted, smelled, and praised when it arrived on the table. Finally, perhaps the most important reason I love to cook is that from a very early age, I always received my share of praise for cooking. When my grandmother kneaded bread dough, she would hand me a piece, put me on a stool at the counter beside her, and let me pound the dough any way I pleased. Even if I made a mess, she would always bake my little "loaf" beside her big ones, and give everyone some of my bread at dinner so they could say how good it was. For all these reasons, I can say that I look forward to a lifetime of cooking ... and talking to the food as I cook.

Topic sentence: _____

_____

Subtopic a. _____

    (1) _____

    (2) _____

Subtopic b. _____

    (1) _____

    (2) _____

Subtopic c. _____

    (1) _____

    (2) _____

STAGE THREE: WRITING FIRST DRAFTS

Writing an effective paper is never done all at once. First, prewrite until you feel confident about your topic, subtopics, and supporting details. Then work with your prewriting until you are satisfied that you can create a complete and logical paragraph outline. Now, you are ready for the third stage of the writing process: creating a first draft.

All your work on the first two stages will now pay off. Instead of staring at that blank screen or empty sheet of paper, you have ideas and details ready to turn into sentences. If possible, allow some time between outlining and writing a draft. A day, or even a few hours, will let you approach your material with a fresh mind, and sometimes a new perspective on what you want to say. Following are tips on creating a first draft:

- Never try to make a first draft a *final* draft. You will defeat the purpose of working on writing as a process. A first draft is only one part—*the third stage after prewriting and outlining*—In creating your effective paragraph; It represents your first try at putting your ideas and structure into sentence and paragraph form. Second, you will cramp and inhibit yourself by trying to make each sentence "perfect." Saying exactly what you mean in the way you want to say it takes time. In your first draft, concentrate on getting the points and details on your outline down as sentences. Trying to write a finished piece of work in one draft forces your mind to do too many things at once: creating, choosing the right words, spelling correctly, and all the other tasks you perform as you write. Do one thing at a time. *Concentrate on your content.*
- Write on every other line, or, after keying in your draft, highlight it and change it from single-spacing to double-spacing. Doing so enables you to make changes, to add and subtract ideas, words, and phrases in your revision drafts.
- Do not worry about spelling errors or sentence problems. Correcting these belongs to the final stage of the writing process: *editing and proofreading.* Focus on getting your ideas down in sentences. Any other concern will only distract you.
- Do not worry if you leave out an idea or detail in your outline or add some new point or detail. The writing process is never straightforward. Do not sacrifice a potentially good idea or vivid example for the sake of sticking rigidly to your outline. You can always revise your outline, and you will be revising your draft.

Your instructor may want you to include your first draft with the draft you submit, so be sure to save it. Alternatively, you may participate in peer evaluations of your first draft with your classmates. In such evaluations, focus is always on *content*: how clear is your point, and how well is it supported?

STAGE FOUR: REVISING, EDITING, AND PROOFREADING

Revising is the first part of the fourth stage of the writing process. Revising means literally "re-seeing" material; *it focuses on content* and how accurately or fully that content is expressed. Working with your first draft, *you shape, add to, and perhaps subtract from your raw material* as you take your paper through two or more drafts.

Your goal in revising is to* make clear the single point *of your paper. Achieving this goal involves working on two activities: development of evidence and organization of evidence.

1   *Develop fully* the specific evidence needed to support your point.

-   Be sure that your paper's main point is fully developed. Ask yourself, *"What's missing?"* Remember that your audience does not see your point through your eyes. For another person to "see" your point through your words, he or she needs you to be as specific and complete as possible. Either leave some time between drafts so that you read your work with a "fresh eye," or have someone else read your paper.
-   Look for *balance* in the distribution of your supporting details for each of your subtopics. If you have two examples as details to support one subtopic, but four examples detailing both your other subtopics, then your paragraph will not seem *balanced,* and one supporting point or subtopic may seem weak. You must add more support to one of your subtopics and delete your weakest items from your other subtopics.
-   Look carefully for *repetition,* for ideas or details that do not add to your point, or that merely say the same thing in different words. Delete such repetitions and work at supplying examples and details that are different, distinct, and aimed at making your point clear.

2   *Organize* and *connect* the specific evidence. Look at the way you explained or backed up your point.

-   Are your supporting points set out in the order in which they happened? If you have used *time order,* be sure all your material follows this order.
-   Is one of your points more important than the others? If you want to *emphasize* this point, place it last so that your other subtopics and details lead up to it.
-   To ensure that your reader sees the *connections and relationships* between your supporting points, be sure to use *transition words and phrases.* If the *sequence* of your subtopics is important, use words like "first," "next," "second," and so on. If there is a growing *order of importance* to your supporting points, use words like "more" and "most" when you introduce these increasingly important points. If one idea simply follows another *in time,* use phrases like "then," "next," or "after that," and if one idea is *caused by* another, use words like "because" or "therefore."

Editing and proofreading are the final stages in this fourth step of the writing process.

-   You *edit* the next-to-final draft; that is, you check it carefully for sentence skills —grammar, mechanics, punctuation, and usage. Run the spell checker on your final draft or note and look up any words you are likely to have misspelled. More information on editing follows in Chapter 4 of Part One of this text, and page references for all sentence-skills issues appear on the inside front cover.

▪ You *proofread* the final copy of the paper for any mistakes in keying or hand-writing.

Editing and proofreading are important steps that some people avoid, often because they have worked so hard (or so little) on the previous stages.

Ideally, you should have enough time to set your paper aside for a while, so that you can check it later from a fresh point of view. Remember that locating and correcting sentence-skills mistakes can turn an average paper into a better one and a good paper into an excellent one. A later section of this book will give you practice in editing and proofreading in a series of editing tests (pages 427–439).

USING A WORD PROCESSOR

Computers have changed nearly everything in the last half of the twentieth century. Computers and current word-processing software can modify the way you handle writing tasks. Sitting at the keyboard, you can quickly add or delete anything, from a word to an entire section. You can "cut" material and "paste" it elsewhere in seconds. Word processing also makes it easy to set margins, space lines, and number pages. It can also help you check your spelling and grammar. You can store each of your drafts on disk, and at any point during your work, one or more copies of your text can be printed out whenever you like.

In most cases, you will have been using word processing softwares and various computer programs during earlier stages of your education, and at work. If not, word processing is easy to learn. Even if you have never touched a computer keyboard, you can enrol in an introductory computer applications course at your college. You will be entering and formatting your first document within an hour. You do not even need to own your own computer; all you need is a box of disks. Nearly every college has at least one computer centre, with rows of computers and staff members to provide assistance.

SOME TIPS ON WORD PROCESSING

▪ Allow enough time if you are using your school's computer centre. You may have to wait for a computer or printer to be free. You may also need several sessions at the computer and printer to complete your paper.

▪ Every word-processing program allows you to "save" your writing by hitting one or more keys. Save your work frequently as you work on a draft. Work that is not saved is lost when the file you are working on is closed, when the computer is turned off—or if there is a power or system failure.

▪ Keep your work on two disks—the disk you routinely work on and a backup disk. At the end of each session at the computer, copy your work onto the backup disk. Then if your working disk becomes damaged or gets lost, you will have the backup copy.

▪ Print your work at the end of every session. Then not only will you have your most recent draft to work on away from the computer; you will also have a copy in case something should happen to your disks.

▪ Work in single-spacing so you can see as much of your writing on the screen at one time as possible. Just before you print your work, change to double-spacing.

■ Before making major changes in a paper, create a copy of your file. For example, if your file is titled "Worst Job," create a file called "Worst Job 2." Then make all your changes in that file. If the changes do not work out, you can always go back to the original file.

WAYS TO USE A COMPUTER IN EACH STAGE OF THE WRITING PROCESS

Following are some ways to make word processing a part of your writing. If you are still becoming familiar with working on the computer, you will find your own best way to proceed.

Prewriting

You may or may not wish to use a computer for prewriting. Working in longhand allows you to work at convenient times and places when and where a computer may not be available. On the other hand, if you keyboard fast, ideas appear on the screen when you are word processing almost as quickly as they occur to you. A passing thought that could prove productive is not likely to get lost. Because of its speed, word processing is especially well suited for freewriting.

After any initial freewriting, questioning, and listing on a computer, you may wish to print a copy of your prewriting material. You can then see everything at once and work from the printed copy as you develop an outline of your paper.

If you have prepared a list of items, you may be able to turn that list into an outline right on the screen. Delete the ideas you feel should not be in your paper (saving them at the end of the file in case you change your mind), and add any new ideas that occur to you. Then use the cut and paste functions to shuffle the supporting ideas around until you find the best order for your paper.

Word processing also makes it easy for you to experiment with the wording of the point of your paper. You can try a number of versions in a short time, deleting any version with which you are not happy.

Writing Your First Draft

Like many writers, you may wish to write your first draft by hand and then key it into the computer for revision. However, if you feel comfortable composing directly on the screen, you can benefit from the computer's special features. A draft on the screen, or a hard copy of it, is easier to revise than a handwritten one. Also, if you have written an anecdote in your freewriting that you plan to use, simply copy the story from your freewriting file and insert it where it fits in your paper. You can refine it then or later. If you discover that a sentence or more is out of place, simply cut it from where it is, and paste it wherever you wish.

Revising

During revision, the virtues of word processing really shine. All substituting, adding, deleting, and rearranging can be done easily within an existing file. All changes instantly take their proper places within the paper, rather than being scribbled above the line or squeezed into the margins. While concentrating on each change you want to make, you never have to start from scratch or work on a messy draft. You can, for instance, easily go through your paper to check that all your supporting evidence is relevant and to add new support where needed. Anything you decide to eliminate can be deleted in a keystroke. Anything you add can be inserted precisely where you choose. All you have to do is delete or cut and paste. Then you can easily sweep through the paper, focusing on other changes such as improving word choice, increasing sentence variety, eliminating wordiness, and so on.

You may find it convenient to print a copy of your file at various points throughout the revision. You can then revise in longhand: adding, crossing out, and indicating changes, and later quickly make those changes in the document.

EDITING AND PROOFREADING

Editing and proofreading are also easier with word processing. Instead of crossing out or whiting out mistakes, or rewriting an entire paper if you have found numerous errors, you can make all necessary changes within the most recent draft. If you find proofreading on the screen hard on your eyes, print out a double-spaced copy. Mark any corrections on that copy, and then transfer them to the final draft.

If the word-processing package you are using includes spelling and grammar checkers, by all means use them. The spell checker tells you when a word is not in its dictionary. Keep in mind, however, that the spell-checker cannot tell you how to spell a name correctly or when you have mistakenly used, for example, *their* instead of *there*. To a spell-checker, *Thank ewe four the complement* is as correct as *Thank you for the compliment*. Also, use the grammar checker with caution. Any errors it does not uncover are still your responsibility. Grammar checkers may also substitute phrases that change the meaning of what you want to say. Use a grammar checker *in conjunction with* Part Four of this text, not as a substitute for learning to correct your sentences.

A word-processed paper, with its clean look and handsome formatting, looks so good that you may feel it is in better shape than it really is. Do not be fooled by your paper's appearance. Take sufficient time to review your grammar and punctuation carefully.

Even after you hand in your paper, save the computer file. Your instructor may ask you to do some revising; the file will save you from having to type the paper from scratch.

PRACTICE IN SEEING THE ENTIRE WRITING PROCESS

This section will show you the stages, mentioned on page 17 in writing an effective paper. You will see what one student, Silvio, does in preparing a paper about his worst job.

There is no single sequence that all people follow in writing a composition. However, the different stages in composing that Silvio goes through in writing his paper should give you some idea of what to expect. Silvio does not just sit down and proceed neatly from start to middle to finish. Writing seldom works like that.

STAGE 1: PREWRITING

Silvio's assignment is to write a paper on the best or worst job he ever had. His first step is to do some freewriting on his topic, as shown below:

"I have had good and bad jobs, that's for sure. The job I remember most is the worst job I ever had. I worked in an apple plant. Putting in long hours and being totally wiped out at the end of my shift. I lifted cartons and cartons and cartons of apple juice, bottles of apple juice or large cans of apple juice. There is no other job that compares to this job, it was a lot worse than it seems. The boss treated us like slaves and so did the company. I put in a lot of time each day. Starting early in the evening all the way through the night to when the sun was rising in the morning. Other people would be going to work and I would be going home from work, all this for not a heck of a lot of money.

At this point Silvio moves on to another prewriting technique—making up a list of initial details about the job. Here is the list he prepares:

Apple factory job—worst one I ever had

Boss was a madman
Working conditions were poor
Went to work at 5 p.m., got back at 7 a.m.
Lifted cartons of apple juice for ten hours
Slept, ate, and worked—no social life
Gas money to and from work
Loaded onto wooden skids in a truck
Short breaks and breakneck pace
No real companions at work
Cold outside
Floors of trucks ice-cold metal
Had to clean apple vats

STAGE 2: MORE PREWRITING AND CREATING AN OUTLINE

Freewriting and list making helped Silvio to accumulate material for his paragraph. He *thought* he was ready to begin lining up his details about why he hated his job. Then, two problems occurred to him. Did he want to focus on his boss? What was the best order for the items listed to support the point he wanted to make? He decided to omit details about his boss, but thought he needed more reasons why the job was so bad. Before he became too frustrated by trying to order the items in his existing list, or figure out subtopics, he decided to "step backwards." He tried another type of prewriting: *he asked himself why he had hated his job so much.* Silvio found he had many details about how hard the work itself was. Then he remembered he had also really hated the job because of the conditions in the factory and the low pay he received.

I hated my job in the apple factory. *Why?*
1. the work was hard
    − there was a lot of physical lifting to do
    − the production line was always moving, and I had to be always moving
    − I loaded cartons of apple juice onto wooden skids in tractor trailers
    − there were two parts to the job--ten hours on the line, and two hours spent cleaning
2. the working conditions were bad
3. the pay was poor

Knowing he needed to add details about the working conditions and the pay, Silvio asked himself *why specifically* those two aspects of the job were so bad. In doing so, he generated the details he needed.

Why were working conditions bad?
Outside weather cold
Usually zero degrees
Floor of tractor trailer was cold steel
Breaks were limited—10 minutes every 2½ hours
½ hour for lunch

Why was pay poor?
$6.35 an hour
(minimum wage at the time)
Quarter more for working the second shift
Only money was in overtime—when you got time-and-a-half
No double time
I would work twenty hours Friday into Saturday to get as much overtime as possible

Looking at the two steps he had worked through, Silvio now knew he had some organization for his points, and he could create a reasonable outline. He started to fill in the copy of the "Outline" document he had saved on his disk. As he did so, he found new details to add.

Note: *To keep Silvio's work as readable as possible, his spelling and sentence-skills mistakes have been corrected. Ordinarily, a number of such mistakes might be present, and editing a paper for them would be a later part of the writing process.*

Topic Sentence:
Working in an apple plant was the worst job I ever had.

Supporting Point # 1
The work was physically hard.
Supporting Details
- stacking cartons onto a rolling track
- cartons held 12 litres—they were heavy to lift
- ?

Supporting Point # 2
The pay was bad.
Supporting Details
- $6.35 an hour, minimum wage
- a quarter an hour extra for late shift
- worked a lot of hours plus overtime to make up a decent cheque

Supporting Point # 3
Working conditions were poor.
Supporting Details
- short breaks
- cold temperature on the loading dock
- lonely, nothing to talk about with other guys

STAGE 3: WRITING A FULL DRAFT

Silvio now moves on to a first full draft:

> Working in an apple plant was the worst job I ever had. The work was physically hard. For ~~a long time~~ ten hours a night, I stacked cartons that rolled down a metal track in a tractor trailer. ~~Each carton was very heavy Each carton was heavy with cans or bottles of apple juice~~ Each carton contained twelve one litre cans or bottles of apple juice, and they were heavy. ~~At the same time, I had to keep a mental count of all the cartons I had loaded.~~ The pay for the job was a bad feature. I was getting the minimum wage at that time plus a quarter extra for night shift. I had to work a lot to get a decent take-home pay. Working conditions were poor at the apple plant. We were limited to ~~short breaks~~ two ten-minute breaks. The truck-loading dock where I was most of the time had zero-degree temperatures. It was a lonely job to have, since I had little in common with the other truck loaders. Then at the end of the shift I had to work by myself cleaning the apple vats.

Comments and Activity on Stage 3

Notice that Silvio, after writing his first draft, is still trying to make his details more specific. He strikes out the vague phrase "a long time" and replaces it with an exact detail: "ten hours a night." He works on his sentences as well, once he is able to see his first draft printed out, rewriting one sentence three times until he is satisfied with it.

- Which sentence does Silvio rewrite? Why?

He also notices one sentence that does not support his main point and eliminates it.

- Which sentence does Silvio eliminate? Why, exactly?

STAGE 4A: REVISING

Silvio puts his work aside for a day and begins to revise his paper the next morning. Revising is as important a stage in the writing process as prewriting and doing the first draft. *Revising* means that you rewrite a paper, building on what has been done to make it stronger and better. One writer has said about revision, "It's like cleaning house—getting rid of all the junk and putting things in the right order." **A typical revision means writing at least one or two more drafts.**

Shown below is part of Silvio's revision. After doing his early work in longhand, Silvio has now moved his paper onto a word processor and printed out the first draft. He has double-spaced the lines, allowing room for his revisions, which he adds in longhand. (If you are not using a word processor, you will want to write a draft on every other line of a page so that there is room to revise. Also, write on only one side of a page, so that you can see your entire paper at one time.)

First of all,
Working in an apple plant was the worst job I ever had. The work was
took
physically hard. For ten hours a night, I ~~stacked~~ cartons that rolled down a
and stacked them onto wooden skids
metal track in a tractor trailer. Each carton contained twelve one-litre cans or
The second bad feature of the job was
bottles of apple juice, and they were heavy. The pay ~~for the job was a bad~~
$6.35 an hour,
~~feature~~. I was getting the minimum wage at that time plus a quarter extra for
over sixty hours a week   *The worst feature of*
night shift. I had to work ~~a lot~~ to get a decent take-home pay. ~~Also poor at~~ the
job was
apple plant ~~were~~ the working conditions. We were limited to two ten-minute

breaks . . . .

STAGE 4B: EDITING AND PROOFREADING

On completing the revision, Silvio enters all of his changes into his processed document and prints the almost-final draft of his paper. He is now ready to do careful editing and proofreading.

Editing and proofreading, the final stage in the writing process, means checking a paper carefully for spelling, grammar, punctuation, and other errors. You are ready for this stage when you are satisfied with your content: your choice of supporting points and details; the order in which they are presented; and the way they and your topic sentence are worded.

Using the hints in the box below, Silvio reads through his paper carefully, looking for keying errors, omitted words, and any other errors he may have missed so far. He refers to a grammar handbook to be sure about his grammar, punctuation, and usage. He uses both his dictionary and the spell checker on his word processor for final checks on his spelling. At this stage such close and attentive work is often hard to do—students have spent so much time on their papers, or so little, that they want to avoid any more work. But if it is done carefully, this important final stage will ensure that a paper looks as good as possible.

Hints for Editing and Proofreading

- One helpful trick at this stage is to read your paper out loud. You will probably hear awkward wordings and become aware of spots where the punctuation needs to be improved. Make the changes needed for your sentences to read smoothly and clearly.
- Another helpful technique is to use a sheet of paper to cover your paragraph so that you can expose and check carefully just one line at a time.
- A third strategy is to read your paper backward, from the last sentence to the first. Doing so helps keep you from getting caught up in the flow of the paper and missing small mistakes—which is easy to do, since you're so familiar with what you meant to say.

After editing and proofreading, Silvio writes the final draft of his paper.

My Job in an Apple Plant

Working in an apple plant was the worst job I ever had. First of all, the work was physically hard. For ten hours a night, I took cartons that rolled down a metal track and stacked them onto wooden skids in a tractor trailer. Each carton contained twelve one-litre cans or bottles of apple juice, and they were heavy. The second bad feature of the job was the pay. I was getting the minimum wage at that time, $6.35 an hour, plus extra for working the night shift. I had to work over sixty hours a week to get a decent take-home pay. The worst feature of the apple plant job was the working conditions. We were limited to two ten-minute breaks and an unpaid half hour for lunch. Most of my time was spent outside on the truck-loading dock in near-zero-degree temperatures. And I was very lonely on the job, since I had no interests in common with the other truck loaders. I felt this isolation especially when the production line shut down for the night, and I worked by myself for two hours cleaning the apple vats. The vats were an ugly place to be on a cold morning, and the job was a bitter one.

Activity 1

Listed in the box below are five of six stages one student worked through in the process of composing a paragraph titled "My Favourite Places":

> 1. Prewriting (list)
> 2. Prewriting (freewriting and questioning)
> 3. First draft
> 4. Second draft
> 5. Final draft

The five stages appear in scrambled order below and on the next page. Write the number *1* In the blank space in front of the first stage of development and number the remaining stages in sequence.

_____

There are some places that always make me feel happy. For example, video rental stores. ~~The posters out front and on the walls~~ The posters for new movies outside the front door ~~make me excited and eager to see what's new~~ draw me inside and make me eager to see movies I've heard about. I also feel happy whenever I walk into the animation lab at college. ~~On days when I have computer animation classes, I just feel happy. Even at eight o'clock in the morning, I feel quite cheerful.~~ Any day when I have an animation class or lab time is a happy day, because I love the whole process of creating pictures and stories. ~~Not many people feel as happy as I do in a room full of computers.~~ I feel happiest of all in the bedroom of my new apartment … a big room on the third floor, with a huge bay window … built-in shelves for my books and treasures … shiny wood floors … my stereo and VCR … an old dresser I spent months refinishing …

_____

Favourite Places
the park at the end of my block
movie houses and video stores
feel happy in the animation lab
with a small group of my best friends—at a show, or just hanging out together
music stores
flea markets in the country
with my dogs at my parents' house
the bus on the way home from college

My Favourite Places

I have three favourite places that make me feel happy for different reasons. Video stores, for example, always brighten me up. The bright coloured posters in the windows excite me, making me curious and eager to see new movies I've heard about. Inside the stores, the shelves full of thousands of movies seem like an endless buffet of entertainment. I feel I will never really be bored or unhappy as long as there are so many movies to take me away from my worries. My spirits also lift every time I enter the computer animation lab at college. Whenever I walk through the door, I'm in an environment where

I really enjoy myself, and where every skill I learn adds to my happiness. I love the whole process of making images on the screen, and then making those images act out stories. But I most enjoy creating bizarre new creatures out of bits and pieces of images that were never together before. The place where I am happiest of all is the bedroom of my new apartment; it's a world all its own. Every time I climb the stairs to the top floor, I peek in just to see my kingdom. Part of my pleasure comes from the sheer size; my room is big, airy, and always full of light from its bay window. I can sit on the built-in window seat and look out over the treetops at the street, or I can look into my room and enjoy the shiny wood floors, my old iron-frame bed, and the shelves full of my books, stereo equipment, and personal treasures. Maybe the fact that room is a reflection of me is what makes me happy there. I feel like I have three "secret weapons" for when I'm down: the video store, the animation lab, and my room.

_____

There are some places that always make me happy. For example, I always feel excited and happy in video stores. When I stand outside looking at the poster, I feel excited and eager to see the new movies, and then I see all the shelves full of movies. The computer animation lab at college is another favourite place of mine. I love to sit at the computer and create images and stories. And to design whole new creatures on screen. I love learning anything new in animation. The place where I'm happiest is my big new third-floor bedroom. There is a bay window with a window seat where I can sit, and shiny wood floors. I love to sit and look at the shelves full of my belongings and all the things that reflect me. Video stores, the animation lab, and my bedroom are three of my favourite places to be.

_____

Some places just make me happy. For example, I always enjoy going into video stores and seeing the posters and all the movies. Sitting on the shelves waiting for me. Also I cheer up every time I walk into the animation lab for a class or free time. My bedroom and the park at the end of my street are the best, though. I feel like myself in those places.

Why am I so happy in the animation lab?	What makes my bedroom my favourite place?
Learn new things all the time	Big, bay window and seat, shiny floors
Making new creatures	Shelves with all my favourite things
Telling stories with pictures on screen	Light, trees outside, looking outside
I'm good at what I do there	Things I've worked on—the dresser, the bed

Activity 2

The author of "My Favourite Places" in Activity 1 made a number of revising and editing changes between the second draft and the final draft. Compare the two drafts and identify five of the changes in the spaces provided below.

1. _____
2. _____
3. _____
4. _____
5. _____

REVIEWING THE LEARNING OUTCOMES FOR CHAPTER 2

To assure yourself that you have met the Learning Outcomes for this chapter, answer the following questions:

1 What are the three main purposes for writing? Which will you encounter most often in college? Why?

2 Describe your main reading audience. What is your audience looking for in any paper you write?

3 Why is the writing process not necessarily straightforward?

4 What is the goal of all prewriting techniques? Why are there several different techniques?

5 What is revising? Why and how is revising different from editing? What is proofreading?

Explaining a Process · Examining Cause and Effect · Comparing or Contrasting · Defini
Term · Dividing and Classifying · Describing a Scene or Person · Narrating an Event · Arg
a Position · Explaining a Process · Examining Cause and Effect · comparing or contrasti
Defining a Term · Dividing and Classifying · Describing a Scene or Person · Narrating an E
Arguing a Position · Explaining a Process · Examining Cause and Effect · Comparir

CHAPTER 3

The First and Second Steps in Writing

LEARNING OUTCOMES

After reading this chapter and working through its activities and writing assignments,

- you will have practised beginning a paper by making a point;
- you will know how to decide on and provide specific details and adequate evidence to support that point; and
- you will have achieved a level of competence in writing an effective paragraph.

The four basic elements in writing an effective paragraph are

1 Make a point.
2 Support the point with subtopics and supporting details.
3 Organize and connect the supporting material.
4 Write clear, error-free sentences.

This chapter will present steps 1 and 2, and Chapter 4 (page 78) will present steps 3 and 4. Then Chapter 5 starting on page 98, will present the four steps that lead to achieving the four bases of effective writing. When you make a point and stick to it, your paper will be *unified*. When you provide specific evidence, your paper will be *supported*. When you organize the specific evidence, your paper will be *coherent*. And when you write clear, error-free sentences, your paper will reflect effective *sentence skills*.

STEP 1: MAKE A POINT

Your first step in writing is to think about your subject, decide what point you want to make about that subject, and to write that point in a single sentence. The point is commonly known as a *topic sentence*. As a guide to yourself and to the reader, put that point in the first sentence of your paragraph. Everything else in the paragraph should then develop and support in specific ways the single point given in the first sentence.

Activity

Your goal is to develop your awareness of two things: a clear, single point and focused, specific support for that point.

Read the two paragraphs below, written by students on the topic "Cheating in Everyday Life." Which paragraph starts with a clear, single point and goes on to support that point? Which paragraph fails to start with a clear point and rambles on in many directions, introducing a number of ideas but developing none of them?

Paragraph A

Cheating

Cheating has always been a part of life, and it will be so in the future. An obvious situation is that students have many ways of cheating in school. This habit can continue after school is over and become part of their daily lives. There are steps that can be taken to prevent cheating, but many teachers do not seem to care. Maybe they are so burned out by their jobs that they do not want to bother. The honest student is often the one hurt by the cheating of others. Cheating at work also occurs. This cheating may be more dangerous, because employers watch out for it more. Businesses have had to close down because cheating by employees took away a good deal of their profits. A news story recently concerned a server who was fired for taking a steak home from the restaurant where he worked, but his taking the steak may have been justified. Cheating in the sense of being unfaithful to a loved one is a different story because emotions are involved. People will probably never stop cheating unless there is a heavy penalty to be paid.

Paragraph B

Everyday Cheating

Cheating is common in everyday life. For one thing, cheating at school is common. Many students will borrow a friend's homework and copy it in their own handwriting. Other students take essays from Internet sites and claim them as their own. People also cheat on the job. They use the postage meter at work for personal mail, spend hours of company time sending personal e-mails, or take home office supplies such as tape, paper, or pens. Some people who are not closely supervised or who are out on the road may cheat an employer by taking dozens of breaks or using work time for personal chores. Finally, many people cheat when they deal with large businesses. For instance, few customers will report an incorrect bill in their favour. Visitors in a hotel may take home towels, and restaurant patrons may take home silverware. A customer in a store may change price tags because "This is how much the shirt cost last month." For many people, daily cheating is an acceptable way to behave.

Complete the following statement: Paragraph _____ is effective because it makes a clear, single point in the first sentence and goes on in the remaining sentences to support that single point.

Paragraph B starts with a *single idea,* that people cheat in everyday life, and then supports that idea with several different examples. But paragraph A does not begin by making a definite point. Instead, we get two broad, obvious statements: that cheating "has always been a part of life" and "will be so in the future." Because the author has not focused on a clear, single point, what happens in this paragraph is inevitable.

The line of thought in paragraph A swerves about in various directions. In the second sentence, we read that "students have many ways of cheating in school," and we think for a moment that this will be the author's point: he or she will give us supporting details about different ways students cheat in school. But the next sentence makes another point: that after school is over, students may continue to cheat as "part of their daily lives." We therefore expect the author to give us details backing up the idea that students who cheat continue to cheat after they leave or finish school. However, the next sentence makes two additional points: "There are steps that can be taken to prevent cheating, but many teachers do not seem to care." These are two more ideas that could be, but are not, the focus of the paragraph. By now we are not really surprised at what happens in the following sentences. Several more points are made: "The honest student is often the one hurt by the cheating of others," cheating at work "may be more dangerous," an employee who stole a steak "may have been justified," and cheating by being unfaithful is different "because emotions are involved." *No single idea is developed; the result is confusion.*

In summary, while paragraph B is unified, paragraph A shows a complete lack of unity.

STEP 2: SUPPORT THE POINT WITH SPECIFIC EVIDENCE

The first essential element in writing effectively is to *start with a clearly stated point.* The second basic step is to *support that point with specific evidence.* Following are the two examples of supported points that you have already read, on page 5 and on page 47.

Example I

Point 1

Using the college's Net server can be a waste of time.

Subtopics or Supporting Points for Point 1

1. The server can go down for hours.
2. The college sends out a lot of e-mail I do not need.
3. Students clog up e-mail with chain letters.

Example II

Point 2

Cheating is common in everyday life.

Subtopics (or Supporting Points) and Details for Point 2

1. At school
    a. Copying homework
    b. Cheating on essays
2. At work
    a. Using postage meter and company Net time
    b. Stealing office supplies
    c. Taking breaks and doing errands on company time
3. With large businesses
    a. Not reporting error on bill
    b. Stealing towels and silverware
    c. Switching price tags

The supporting points and details are needed so that we can see and understand for ourselves that each writer's point is sound. By providing us with particulars about her experiences with the college Internet server, the first writer shows why she believes it can be a waste of time. We can see that she has made a sound point. Likewise, the author of "Everyday Cheating" has supplied specific supporting examples of how cheating is common in everyday life. That paragraph, too, has provided the evidence (in the form of subtopics and details to support each) that is needed for us to understand and agree with the writer's point.

Activity

Your goal for this activity is to develop a sense of the varied and specific details that let a reader "see" the writer's point.

Both of the paragraphs that follow resulted from an assignment to "Write a paper that details your reasons for being in college." Both writers make the point that they have various reasons for attending college. Which paragraph then goes on to provide plenty of specific evidence to back up its point? Which paragraph is vague and repetitive and lacks the concrete details needed to show us exactly why the author decided to attend college?

Hint: Imagine that you've been asked to make a short film based on each paragraph. Which one suggests specific pictures, locations, words, and scenes you could shoot?

Paragraph A

Reasons for Going to College

I decided to attend college for various reasons. One reason is self-respect. For a long time now, I have felt little self-respect. I spent a lot of time doing nothing, just hanging around or getting into trouble, and eventually I began to feel bad about it. Going to college is a way to start feeling better about myself. By accomplishing things, I will improve my self-image. Another reason for going to college is that things happened in my life that made me think about a change. For one thing, I lost the part-time job I had. When I lost the job, I realized I would have to do something in life, so I thought about school. I was in a rut and needed to get out of it but did not know how. But when something happens that is out of your control, then you have to make some kind of decision. The most important reason for college, though, is to fulfill my dream. I know I need an education, and I want to take the courses I need to reach the position that I think I can handle. Only by gaining confidence and experience, can I get what I want. Going to college will help me fulfill this goal. These are the main reasons why I am attending college.

Paragraph B

Why I'm in School

There are several reaons I'm in school. First of all my father's attitude made me want to succeed in school. One night last year, after I had come in at 3 a.m., my father said, "Sean, you're losing all respect for yourself. When I look at my son, all I see is a young man who doesn't care about himself." I was angry, but I knew my father was right in a way. I had spent the last two years working at odd jobs delivering pizza and repairing bikes, then spending all night at raves with my friends. That night, though, I decided I would prove my father wrong. I would go to college and be a success. Another reason I'm in college is my girlfriend's encouragement. Marie has already been in school for a year, and she is doing well in her computer technology courses. Marie helped me fill out my application and register for courses. She even lent me a hundred dollars for textbooks. On her day off, she lets me use her car so I don't have to take the bus. The main reason I am in college is to fulfill a personal goal: I want to finish something, for the first time in my life. For example, I quit high school at the end of grade eleven. Then I enrolled in a provincial job-training program, but I dropped out after six months. I tried to get my grade twelve certificate, but I started missing classes and eventually gave up. Now I am registered as a mature student in a special program where I will make up my missing high school credits at night as part of first-semester work. I am determined to accomplish this goal and to then go on and work for a diploma in broadcast technology.

Complete the following statement: Paragraph _____ provides clear, vividly detailed reasons why the writer decided to attend college.

Paragraph B is the one that solidly backs up its point. The writer gives us specific reasons why he is in school. On the basis of such evidence, we can clearly understand his opening point. The writer of paragraph A offers only vague, general reasons for being in school. We do not get specific examples of how the writer was "getting into trouble," what events occurred that forced the decision, or even what kind of job he or she wants to qualify for. We sense that the feeling expressed is sincere; but without particular examples we cannot really see why the writer decided to attend college.

THE IMPORTANCE OF SPECIFIC DETAILS

The point that opens a paper is a general statement. The evidence that supports a point is generally made up of subtopics and their specific details, reasons, examples, and facts.

Specific details have two key functions:

- Details and specific ideas *excite the reader's interest.* They make writing a pleasure to read, for we all enjoy learning particulars about other people— what they do and think and feel.
- Details *support and explain a writer's point*; they give the evidence needed for us to see and understand a general idea.

For example, the writer of "Net Eats Student's Time!" provides details that make vividly clear why she feels using the college's Net server wastes her time. She specifies a precise occasion when she had to wait while the server was down (and how long she had to wait—two hours), and describes how restless and distracted she was while waiting for service to resume. She mentions checking the e-mail function on the server and finding many messages from the college to scroll through, then goes on to specify exactly why these posts were a waste of time (they were irrelevant to her and she had to read them to discover this and then delete them). She then tells us two specific details of her final reason for frustration with spending time on the Net: (1) she finds a number of messages so heavily coded that they take a long time to load, and (2) the messages turn out to be student "chain-letters" with massive addresses on them.

The writer of "Why I'm in School" provides equally vivid details. He gives clear reasons for being in school (his father's attitude, his girlfriend's encouragement, and his wish to fulfill a personal goal) and backs up each reason with specific details. His details give us many sharp pictures. For instance, we hear the exact words his father spoke: "Sean, you're losing all respect for yourself." He tells us exactly how he was spending his time ("delivering pizza and repairing bikes, then spending all night at raves with my friends"). He describes how his girlfriend helped him (filling out the college application, lending money and her car). Finally, instead of stating generally that "you have to make some kind of decision," as the writer of "Reasons for Going to College" does, he specifies that he has a strong desire to finish college because he dropped out of schools and programs in the past: high school, a job-training program, and another try at high school.

In both "Net Eats Student's Time!" and "Why I'm in School," the vivid, exact details capture our interest and enable us to share in the writer's experience. We see people's actions and hear their words; the details provide pictures that make each of us feel "I am there." The particulars also allow us to understand each writer's point clearly. We are *shown* exactly why the first writer finds the Net a time-waster and exactly why the second writer is attending college.

Activity

In this activity, you will continue to sharpen your sense of what makes good specific support. Each of the five points below is followed by two attempts at support (*a* and *b*). Write S (for *specific*) in the space next to the one that succeeds in providing specific support for the point. Write X in the space next to the one that lacks supporting details.

1. My two-year-old son was in a stubborn mood today.
_____   a. When I asked him to do something, he gave me nothing but trouble. He seemed determined to make things difficult for me, for he had his mind made up.
_____   b. When I asked him to stop playing in the yard and come indoors, he looked me square in the eye and shouted "No!" and then spelled it out, "N … O!"

2. The prices in the amusement park were outrageously high.
_____   a. The food seemed to cost twice as much as it would in a supermarket and was sometimes of poor quality. The rides also cost a lot, and so I had to tell the children that they were limited to a certain number of them.
_____   b. The cost of the log flume, a ride that lasts roughly 3 minutes, was $5.75 a person. Then I had to pay $2 for a 250 ml soft drink and $3.75 for a hot dog.

3. My brother-in-law is accident-prone.
_____   a. Once he tried to open a tube of Krazy Glue with his teeth. When the cap came loose, glue squirted out and sealed his lips shut. They had to be pried open in a hospital emergency room.
_____   b. Even when he does seemingly simple jobs, he seems to get into trouble. This can lead to hilarious, but sometimes dangerous, results. Things never seem to go right for him, and he often needs the help of others to get out of one predicament or another.

4. The so-called "bargains" at the yard sale were junk.
_____   a. The tables at the yard sale were filled with useless stuff no one could possibly want. They were the kinds of things that should be thrown away, not sold.
_____   b. The "bargains" at the yard sale included two headless dolls, blankets filled with holes, scorched pot holders, and a plastic Christmas tree with several branches missing.

5. The key to success in college is organization.
   a. Knowing what you're doing, when you have to do it, and so on is a big help for a student. A system is crucial in achieving an ordered approach to study. Otherwise, things become very disorganized, and it is not long before your grades begin to drop.
   b. Organized students never forget paper or exam dates, which are marked on a calendar above their desks. And instead of having to cram for exams, they study their clear, neat classroom and textbook notes on a daily basis.

Comments: The specific support for point 1 is answer *b*. The writer does not just tell us that the little boy was stubborn but provides an example that shows us. In particular, the detail of the son's spelling out "N … O!" makes his stubbornness vividly real for the reader. For point 2, answer *b* gives specific prices ($5.75 for a ride, $2 for a soft drink, and $3.75 for a hot dog) to support the idea that the amusement park was expensive. For point 3, answer *a* vividly backs up the idea that the brother-in-law is accident-prone by detailing an accident with Krazy Glue. Point 4 is supported by answer *b*, which lists specific examples of useless items that were offered for sale—from headless dolls to a broken plastic Christmas tree. We cannot help agreeing with the writer's point that the items were not bargains but junk. Point 5 is backed up by answer *b*, which identifies two specific strategies of organized students: they mark important dates on calendars above their desks, and they take careful notes and study them on a daily basis.

In each of the five cases, the specific evidence enables us to *see for ourselves* that the writer's point is valid.

THE IMPORTANCE OF ADEQUATE DETAILS

One of the most common and most serious problems in students' writing is inadequate development. You must provide *enough* specific details to support fully the point you are making. You could not, for example, submit a paragraph about how your brother-in-law is accident-prone and provide only a single short example. You would have to add several other examples or provide an extended example of your brother-in-law's accident-proneness. Without such additional support, your paragraph would be underdeveloped.

At times, students try to disguise an undersupported point by using repetition and wordy generalities. You saw this, for example, in paragraph A ("Reasons for Going to College") on page 50. Be prepared to do the plain hard work needed to ensure that each of your paragraphs has full and solid support.

Activity

Your goal in this activity is to develop a sense of when support is sufficient to make a point clear. The following paragraphs were written on the same topic, and each has a clear opening point. Which one is adequately developed? Which one has few particulars and uses mostly vague, general, wordy sentences to conceal the fact that it is starved for specific details?

Paragraph A

New Uses for Public Parks

Canadians are finding new ways to use city parks. Instead of visiting large parks for playgrounds or for walks among the trees, people may go to the park to exercise in groups. People of every age do Tai Chi stretches every morning, while others band together for organized walks each evening. Each park has its joggers, runners, and cyclists, while others bring their weights to do workouts in the park's fresh air and quiet. Canadian city parks also host concerts, art shows, and plays. Suburban and waterfront parks offer children's festivals every summer; musicians return to parks for annual folk and world music events, and Shakespeare comes to a stage in Toronto's High Park every July. Perhaps the most interesting "new" use of parks is really an old one: public rental gardens. Large parks rent "allotment gardens" where apartment dwellers plant and cultivate gardens each year. These park-gardeners fence off their spaces, plant flowers, fruits, and vegetables, and faithfully tend their plots every day. Allotment gardens began in the Depression when families on tight budgets tried to supplement their diets, and recently a group of U. of T. students started growing fruit and vegetables for the university's food bank, to help feed hungry people in today's economy. Some gardeners are from cultures used to growing their own produce, and still others simply enjoy the contact with nature and the seasons. Parks are made for people, and today, people are finding new ways to use and enjoy the peace, space, and land that parks offer.

Paragraph B

Uses for Public Parks

People use parks for many hobbies and activities. Exercising in the open air is healthy, and many people choose to take advantage of this in a variety of ways. Different types of people can be seen every day getting different forms of exercise in various parks. In fact, every season is suitable for some form of exercise in the park. But working at fitness in the fresh air is not the only reason people go to parks. Parks offer entertainment of every kind these days, which benefits the cultural life of the cities where the parks are located and draws many visitors. Many of these people might not otherwise visit a public park. Today, parks are full of children and their parents, people working at fitness, people admiring the trees and flowers, and people walking their pets. It is certainly obvious that parks have many attractions for people in today's cities.

Complete the following statement: Paragraph _____ provides an adequate number of specific details to support its point.

Paragraph A offers a series of detailed examples of new ways in which people are using public parks. Paragraph B, on the other hand, is underdeveloped. Paragraph B mentions only "different types of people…getting different forms of exercise," while paragraph A refers specifically to people who "do their Tai Chi stretches, joggers, runners, and cyclists, weightlifters, and groups of walkers." Paragraph B talks generally of "entertainment of every kind" in parks, while paragraph A specifies "concerts, art shows, and plays," as well as children's festivals, music events, and Shakespeare in High Park's outdoor theatre. Moreover, there is no parallel in paragraph B for paragraph A's point and details about allotment gardens and the people who cultivate them. In summary, paragraph B lacks the full, specifically detailed support needed to develop its opening point convincingly.

Review Activity

To check your understanding of the chapter so far, see if you can answer the following questions.

1. It has been observed: "To write well, the first thing that you must do is decide what nail you want to drive home." What is meant by *nail*?

   _____

2. How do you *drive home the nail* in a paper?

   _____

3. What are the two reasons for using specific details in your writing?

   a. _____
   b. _____

PRACTICE IN MAKING AND SUPPORTING A POINT

You now know the two most important steps in competent writing: (1) making a point and (2) supporting that point with specific and adequate evidence. The purpose of this section is to expand and strengthen your understanding of these two basic steps.

You will first work through a series of activities on *making* a point:

1 Identifying Common Errors in Topic Sentences
2 Understanding the Two Parts of a Topic Sentence
3 Selecting a Topic Sentence
4 Writing a Topic Sentence I
5 Writing a Topic Sentence II

You will then sharpen your understanding of specific details by working through a series of activities on *supporting* a point:

6 Recognizing Specific Details I
7 Recognizing Specific Details II
8 Making Words and Phrases Specific

1 IDENTIFYING COMMON ERRORS IN TOPIC SENTENCES

When writing the main point in a topic sentence, people sometimes make mistakes that undermine their chances of producing an effective paper. One mistake is to substitute an *announcement of the topic* for a true topic sentence. Other mistakes include *writing statements that are too broad or too narrow.* Following are examples of all three errors, along with contrasting examples of effective topic sentences.

Announcement

My Ford Escort is the concern of this paragraph.

The statement above is a simple announcement of a subject, rather than a topic sentence in which an idea is expressed about the subject.

Statement That Is Too Broad

Many people have problems with their cars.

The statement above is too broad to be supported adequately with specific details in a single paragraph.

Statement That Is Too Narrow

My car is a Ford Escort.

The statement above is too narrow to be expanded into a paragraph. Such a narrow statement is sometimes called a *dead-end statement* because there is no place to go with it. It is a simple fact that does not need or call for any support.

Effective Topic Sentence

I hate my Ford Escort.

The statement above expresses an opinion that could be supported in a paragraph. The writer could offer a series of specific supporting reasons, examples, and details to make it clear why he or she hates the car.

Here are additional examples:

Announcements

The subject of this paper will be my apartment.
I want to talk about increases in the divorce rate.

Statements That Are Too Broad

The places where people live have definite effects on their lives.
Many people have trouble getting along with others.

Statements That Are Too Narrow

I have no hot water in my apartment at night.
Almost one of every two marriages ends in divorce.

Effective Topic Sentences

My apartment is a terrible place to live.
The divorce rate is increasing for several reasons.

Activity 1

For each pair of sentences below, write *A* beside the sentence that only *announces* a topic. Write *OK* beside the sentence that *advances an idea* about the topic.

1. _____ a. This paper will deal with flunking math.

    _Ok_ b. I flunked math last semester for several reasons.

2. _____ a. I am going to write about my job as a gas station attendant.

    _Ok_ b. Working as a gas station attendant was the most demanding job I ever had.

3. _____ a. Telemarketing is the subject of this paragraph.

    _Ok_ b. People should know what to do when they receive a tele-marketing phone call.

4. _Ok_ a. In several ways, my college library is very easy to use.

    _____ b. This paragraph will deal with the college library.

5. _____ a. My paper will discuss the topic of procrastinating.

    _Ok_ b. The following steps will help you stop procrastinating.

Activity 2

For each pair of sentences below, write *TN* beside the statement that is *too narrow* to be developed into a paragraph. (Such a narrow statement is also known as a *dead-end sentence*.) Write *OK* beside the statement in each pair that calls for support or development of some kind.

1. _TN_ a. I do push-ups and sit-ups each morning.

    _Ok_ b. Exercising every morning has had positive effects on my health.

2. _TN_ a. Farid works nine hours a day and then goes to school three hours a night.

_OK_   b. Farid is an ambitious man.

3. _TN_   a. I started college after being away from school for seven years.

_OK_   b. Several of my fears about returning to school have proved to be groundless.

4. _OK_   a. Parts of the NFB film _Get a Job_ are interesting to college students.

_TN_   b. Our class watched the NFB film _Get a Job_ yesterday.

5. _OK_   a. My brother was depressed yesterday for several reasons.

_TN_   b. Yesterday my brother had to pay fifty-two dollars for a motor tune-up.

Activity 3

For each pair of sentences below, write _TB_ beside the statement that is _too broad_ to be supported adequately in a short paper. Write _OK_ beside the statement that makes a limited point.

1. _OK_   a. Professional hockey is a dangerous sport.

_TB_   b. Professional sports are violent.

2. _TB_   a. Married life is the best way of living.

_OK_   b. Teenage marriages often end in divorce for several reasons.

3. _OK_   a. Aspirin has several beneficial side effects.

_TB_   b. Drugs have different effects on different people.

4. _TB_   a. I've always done fairly well in school.

_OK_   b. I got an A in math last semester for several reasons.

5. _TB_   a. Computers are changing our society.

_OK_   b. Using computers to teach children is having excellent results.

2 UNDERSTANDING THE TWO PARTS OF A TOPIC SENTENCE

As stated earlier, the point that opens and controls the content of a paragraph is often called a _topic sentence_. When you look closely at a point, or topic sentence, you can see that it is made up of two parts:

1 The _limited topic_
2 The writer's _attitude_ about the limited topic

The writer's attitude or point of view or idea is usually expressed in one or more _keywords_. All the details in a paragraph should support the idea expressed in the keywords. In each of the topic sentences below, a single line appears under the <u>topic</u> and a double line under the <u>idea or attitude about the topic</u> (expressed in a <u>key-word</u> or <u>keywords</u>):

My <u>girlfriend</u> is very <u>assertive</u>.

<u>Highway accidents</u> are often caused by <u>absent-mindedness</u>.

The <u>kitchen</u> is the <u>most widely used</u> room in my house.

<u>Voting</u> should be <u>required by law</u> in Canada.

My <u>pickup</u> truck is the most <u>reliable</u> vehicle I have ever owned.

In the first sentence, the topic is *girlfriend*, and the keyword that expresses the writer's idea about his topic is that his girlfriend is *assertive*. In the second sentence, the topic is *highway accidents*, and the keyword that determines the focus of the paragraph is that such accidents are often caused by *absent-mindedness*. Notice each topic and keyword or keywords in the other three sentences as well.

Activity

For each point below, draw a single line under the topic and a double line under the idea about the topic.

1. Billboards should be abolished.

2. My boss is an ambitious woman.

3. Politicians are often self-serving.

4. The apartment needed repairs.

5. Television commercials are often misleading.

6. My parents have rigid racial attitudes.

7. The middle child is often a neglected member of the family.

8. The language in many movies today is offensive.

9. Doctors are often insensitive.

10. Homeowners today are more energy-conscious than ever before.

3   SELECTING A TOPIC SENTENCE

Remember that a paragraph is made up of a topic sentence and a group of related sentences that develop and support the topic sentence. It is also helpful to remember that the topic sentence is a *general* statement. The other sentences provide specific support for the general statement. Supporting sentences include *subtopics*, or subsections, or categories of the topic presented. Each subtopic requires *specific details* or examples to make it clear.

Activity

Each group of sentences below could be written as a short paragraph. Circle the letter of the topic sentence in each case. To find the topic sentence, ask yourself, "Which is a general statement supported by the specific details in the other three statements?"

Begin by trying the example item below. First circle the letter of the sentence you think expresses the main idea. Then read the explanation.

Example
    a. If you stop carrying matches or a lighter, you can cut down on impulse smoking.
    b. If you sit in no-smoking areas, you will smoke less.
    c. You can behave in ways that will help you smoke less.
    d. By keeping a record of when and where you smoke, you can identify the most tempting situations and then avoid them.

Explanation: Sentence *a* explains one way to smoke less. Sentences *b* and *d* also provide specific ways to smoke less. In sentence *c*, however, no one specific way is explained. The words *ways that will help you smoke less* refer only generally to such methods. Therefore, sentence *c* is the topic sentence; it expresses the author's main idea. The other sentences support that idea by providing examples.

1. a. "I couldn't study because I forgot to bring my book home."
     b. "I couldn't take the final because my grandmother died."
     c. Students give instructors some common excuses.
     d. "I couldn't come to class because I had a migraine headache."

2. a. Its brakes are badly worn.
     b. My old car is ready for the junk pile.
     c. Its floor has rusted through, and water splashes on my feet when the highway is wet.
     d. My mechanic says its engine is too old to be repaired, and the car isn't worth the cost of a new engine.

3. a. Tobacco is one of the most addictive of all drugs.
     b. Selling cigarettes ought to be against the law.
     c. Nonsmokers are put in danger by breathing the smoke from other people's cigarettes.
     d. Cigarette smoking kills many more people than all illegal drugs combined.

4. a. Contract workers are valuable commodities for employment agencies and for employers with specific needs.
     b. Contract workers are self-employed, for tax purposes, so they can write off many expenses such as gas used during the drive to work and back.
     c. Contract workers earn slightly less than permanent employees, but may have the same net income because of fewer company deductions.
     d. Contract workers have distinct advantages in the 1990s workplace.

5. a. The last time I ate there, I discovered two new flavours I now love: lemon grass and coriander.
     b. Although it is only a small local restaurant, it has received great reviews.
     c. The new Thai restaurant near my house is a favourite of mine and of people from all over Vancouver.
     d. The seafood is really fresh, and all the dishes are cooked to order.

4 WRITING A TOPIC SENTENCE: I

Activity

The following activity will give you practice in writing an accurate topic sentence—one that is neither too broad nor too narrow for the supporting material in a paragraph. Sometimes you will construct your topic sentence after you have decided what details you want to discuss. An added value of this activity is that it shows you how to write a topic sentence that will exactly match the subtopics or details you have developed.

1. *Topic sentence:* There are several causes of forest fires.

   a. Some are caused by careless people tossing matches out of car windows.
   b. A few are started when lightning strikes a tree.
   c. Some result from campers who fail to douse cooking fires.
   d. The majority of forest fires are deliberately set by arsonists.

2. *Topic sentence:* We loved last night's dinner at the Bistro for several reasons.

   a. The bistro owner greeted us with a smile and seated us at a window table as soon as we arrived.
   b. Our appetizers and main courses were delicious.
   c. Our server brought us extra bread and more water.
   d. The desserts were homemade and garnished with whipped cream.

3. *Topic sentence:* I have several problems with my net server.

   a. My Net server goes dead at certain times of the day.
   b. When I am online, I experience slow loading times.
   c. The line to server does not always connect quickly.
   d. Sometimes, the server connection will cut out in mid-session.

4. *Topic sentence:* The "monster" movie was terrible for several reasons.

   a. The crowd scenes were crudely spliced from another film.
   b. Mountains and other background scenery were just painted cardboard cutouts.
   c. The "sync" was off, so that the audience heard voices even when the actors' lips were not moving.
   d. The so-called monster was just a spider that had been filmed through a magnifying lens.

5 WRITING A TOPIC SENTENCE: II

Often you will start with a general topic or a general idea of what you want to write about. You may, for example, want to write a paragraph about some aspect of school life. To come up with a point about school life, begin by limiting your topic. One way to do this is to make a list of all the limited topics, or subtopics, you can think of that fit under the general topic.

Activity

On the following pages are four general topics and a series of limited topics, or subtopics, that fit under them. Make a point out of *one* of the limited topics in each group.

Hint: To create a topic sentence, ask yourself, "What point do I want to make about _____ (*my limited topic*)?"

Example   Recreation
- Movies
- Dancing
- TV shows
- Reading
- Sports parks

Your point: *Sports parks today have some truly exciting games.* _____

1. Your college
   - Instructor
   - Cafeteria
   - Specific class
   - Particular room or building
   - Particular policy (attendance, grading, etc.)
   - Classmate

Your point: _____

2. Job
   - Pay
   - Boss
   - Working conditions
   - Duties
   - Co-workers
   - Customers or clients

Your point: _____

3. Money
   - Budgets
   - Credit cards
   - Dealing with a bank

- School expenses
- Ways to get it
- Ways to save it

Your point: _____

4. Cars
   - First car
   - Driver's licence test
   - Road conditions
   - Accident
   - Speed limit
   - Safety problems

Your point: _____

6 RECOGNIZING SPECIFIC DETAILS: I

Specific details are examples, reasons, particulars, and facts. Such details are needed to support and explain a topic sentence effectively. Each subtopic sentence needs specific details to clarify and explain it, as well. Specific details provide the evidence needed for readers to understand, as well as to feel and experience, a writer's point. Specific details allow readers to *see* your point clearly.

Here is a topic sentence followed by two sets of supporting sentences. Which set provides sharp, specific details?

Topic Sentence

Some poor people must struggle to make meals for themselves.

Set A

They gather up whatever free food they can find in fast-food restaurants and take it home to use however they can. Unless they have access to foodbanks, they base their diet on anything they can buy that is cheap and filling.

Set B

Some add hot water to the free packets of ketchup they get at McDonald's to make tomato soup. Others buy cheap canned dog food and fry it like hamburger.

Set B provides specific details: instead of a general statement about "free food they find in fast-food restaurants and take … home to use however they can," we get a vivid detail we can see and picture clearly: "free packets of ketchup they get at McDonald's to make tomato soup." Instead of a general statement about how the poor will "base their diet on anything they can buy that is cheap and filling," we get exact and vivid details: "Others buy cans of cheap dog food and fry it like hamburger."

Specific details are often like the information we might find in a movie script. They provide us with such clear pictures that we could make a film of them if we wanted to. You would know just how to film the information given in set B. You would show a poor person breaking open a packet of ketchup from McDonald's and mixing it with water to make a kind of tomato soup. You would show someone opening a can of dog food and frying its contents like hamburger.

In contrast, the writer of set A fails to provide the specific information needed. If you were asked to make a film based on set A, you would have to figure out for yourself just what particulars you were going to show.

When you are working to provide specific supporting information in a paper, it might help to ask yourself, "Could someone easily film this information?" If the answer is "yes," you probably have good details. Your specific details help you to *show*, not *tell*.

Activity

Your aim in this activity is to strengthen your "eye" for specific details. Each topic sentence below is followed by two sets of supporting details (*a* and *b*). Write S (for *specific*) in the space next to the set that provides specific support for the point. Write G (for *general*) next to the set that offers only vague, general support.

1. *Topic sentence:* My roommate is messy.

    _G_ a. He doesn't seem to mind that he can't find any clean clothes or dishes. He never puts anything back in its proper place; he just drops it wherever he happens to be. His side of the room looks as if a hurricane has gone through.

    _S_ b. His coffee cup is covered inside with a thick layer of green mold. I can't tell you what colour his easy chair is; it has disappeared under a pile of dirty laundry. When he turns over in bed, I can hear the crunch of cracker crumbs beneath his body.

2. *Topic sentence:* Antonetta is very assertive.

    _____ a. Her assertiveness is apparent in both her personal and her professional life. She is never shy about extending social invitations. And while some people are turned off by her assertiveness, others are impressed by it and enjoy doing business with her.

    _____ b. When she meets a man she likes, she is quick to say, "Let's go out for coffee sometime." In her job as a furniture salesperson, she will call potential customers to let them know when new stock is coming in.

3. *Topic sentence:* Our new kitten causes us lots of trouble.

    _____ a. He has shredded the curtains in my bedroom with his claws. He nearly drowned when he crawled into the washing machine. And my hands look like raw hamburger from his playful bites and scratches.

_____ b. He seems to destroy everything he touches. He's always getting into places where he doesn't belong. Sometimes he plays too roughly, and that can be painful.

7 RECOGNIZING SPECIFIC DETAILS: II

Activity

At several points in the following paragraphs you are given a choice of two sets of supporting details. Write *S* (for *specific*) in the space next to the set that provides specific support for that point. Write *G* (for *general*) next to the set that offers only vague, general support.

Paragraph 1

My daughter's boyfriend is a good-for-nothing young man. After knowing him for just three months, everyone in our family is opposed to the relationship. For one thing, Russell is lazy.

_____ a. He is always finding an excuse to avoid putting in an honest day's work. He never pitches in and helps with chores around our house, even when he's asked directly to do so. And his attitude about his job isn't any better. To hear him tell it, he deserves special treatment in the workplace. He thinks he's gone out of his way if he just shows up on time.

_____ b. After starting a new job last week, he announced this Monday that he wasn't going to work because it was his *birthday*—as if he were somebody special. And when my husband asked Russell to help put storm windows on the house next Saturday, Russell answered that he uses his weekends to catch up on sleep.

Another quality of Russell's which no one likes is that he is cheap.

_____ c. When my daughter's birthday came around, Russell said he would take her out to Baldoni's, a fancy Italian restaurant. Then he changed his mind. Instead of spending a lot of money on a meal, he said, he wanted to buy her a really nice pair of earrings. So my daughter cooked dinner for him at her apartment. But there was no present, not even a little one. He claims he's waiting for a jewellery sale at Birks. I don't think my daughter will ever see that "really nice" gift.

_____ d. He makes big promises about all the nice things he's going to do for my daughter, but he never comes through. His words are cheap, and so is he. He's all talk and no action. My daughter isn't greedy, but it hurts her when Russell says he's going to take her someplace nice or give her something special and then nothing happens.

Worst of all, Russell is mean.

_____ e. Russell seems to get special pleasure from hurting people when he feels they have a weak point. I have heard him make remarks that to him were funny but were really very insensitive. It is hard to understand someone who needs to be ugly to other people just for the sake of being powerful. Sometimes I want to let him know how I feel.

_____ f. When my husband was out of work, Russell said to him, "Well, you've got it made now, living off your wife." After my husband glared at him, he said, "Why're you getting sore? I'm just kidding." Sometimes he snaps at my daughter, saying things like "Don't make me wait—there are plenty of other babes who would like to take your place." At such times I want to throw him out the door.

Everyone in the family is waiting anxiously for the day when my daughter will see Russell the way the rest of us see him.

Paragraph 2

Many adult children move back in with their parents for some period of time. Although living with Mom and Dad again has some advantages, there are certain problems that are likely to arise. One common problem is that children may expect their parents to do all the household chores.

_____ a. They never think that they should take on their share of work around the house. Not only do they not help with their parents' chores, they don't even take responsibility for the extra work that their presence creates. Like babies, they go through the house making a mess that they expect their parents to clean up. It's as if they think their parents are their servants.

_____ b. They expect meals to appear on the table as if by magic. After they've eaten, they go off to work or play, never thinking about who's going to do the dishes. They drop their dirty laundry beside the washing machine, assuming that Mom will attend to it and return clean, folded clothes to their bedroom door. And speaking of their bedroom: every day they await the arrival of Mom's Maid Service to make the bed, pick up the floor, and dust the furniture.

Another problem that frequently arises is that parents forget their children are no longer adolescents.

_____ c. Parents like this want to know everything about their adult children's lives. They don't think their kids, even though they are adults, should have any privacy. Whenever they see their children doing anything, they want to know all the details. It's as though their children are still teenagers who are expected to report all their activities. Naturally, adult children get irritated when they are treated as if they were teenagers.

_____ d. They may insist upon knowing far more about their children's comings and goings than the children want to share. For example, if such parents see their adult son heading out the door, they demand to know: Where is he going? Who will he be with? What will he be doing? What time will he be back? In addition, they may not let their adult child have any privacy. If their daughter and a date are sitting in the living room, for instance, they may join them there and start asking the young man questions about his family and his job, as if they were interviewing him for the position of son-in-law.

Finally, there may be financial problems when an adult child returns to live at home.

_____ e. Having an extra adult in the household creates extra expenses. But many adult children don't offer to help deal with those extra costs. Adult children often eat at home, causing the grocery bill to climb. They may stay in a formerly unused room, which now needs to be heated and lit. They produce extra laundry to be washed. They use the telephone, adding to the long-distance bill. For all these reasons, adult children should expect to pay a reasonable amount to their parents for room and board.

_____ f. It's expensive to have another adult living in the household. Adult children would be paying a lot of bills on their own if they weren't staying with their parents. It's only fair that they share the expenses at their parents' house. They should consider all the ways that their living at home is increasing their parents' expenses. Then they should insist upon covering their share of the costs.

8 MAKING WORDS AND PHRASES SPECIFIC

To be an effective writer, you must use specific, rather than general, words. Specific words create pictures in the reader's mind. They help capture the reader's interest and make your meaning clear.

Activity

This activity will give you practice in replacing vague, indefinite words with sharp, specific words. Add three or more specific words to replace the general word or words underlined in each sentence. Make changes in the wording of a sentence as necessary.

Example   My bathroom cabinet contains <u>many drugs</u>.

My bathroom cabinet contains aspirin, antibiotics, herbel sedative,

and cough medicine.

1. At the shopping centre, we visited <u>several stores</u>.

    _____

    _____

2.   Sunday is my day to take care of <u>chores</u>.

_____

_____

3.   Hoi Yee enjoys <u>various activities</u> in her spare time.

_____

_____

4.   I spent most of my afternoon doing <u>homework</u>.

_____

_____

5.   We returned home from vacation to discover that <u>several pests</u> had invaded the house.

_____

_____

9   MAKING SENTENCES SPECIFIC

Again, you will practise replacing vague, indefinite writing with lively, image-filled writing that captures your reader's interest and makes your meaning clear. Compare the following sentences:

General	*Specific*
The boy came down the street.	Voytek ran down Woodlawn Avenue.
A bird appeared on the grass.	A blue jay swooped down onto the frost-covered lawn.
She stopped the car.	Wanda slammed on the brakes of her Escort.

The specific sentences create clear pictures in your reader's mind. The details *show* readers exactly what has happened.

Here are four ways to make your words and sentences specific:

1   Use exact names.

She loves her *motorbike*.
Kellie loves her *Honda*.

2   Use lively verbs.

The garbage truck *went* down Front Street.
The garbage truck *rumbled* down Front Street.

3   Use descriptive words (modifiers) before nouns.

A girl peeked out the window.
A *chubby, six-year-old* girl peeked out the *dirty kitchen* window.

4 Use words that relate to the five senses: sight, hearing, taste, smell, and touch.

That woman is a karate expert.
That *tiny, silver-haired* woman is a karate expert. (*Sight*)

When the dryer stopped, a signal sounded.
When the *whooshing* dryer stopped, a *loud buzzer* sounded. (*Hearing*)

Natasha offered me an orange slice.
Natasha offered me a *sweet, juicy* orange slice. (*Taste*)

The real estate agent opened the door of the closet.
The real estate agent opened the door of the *cedar-scented* closet. (*Smell*)

I pulled the blanket around me to fight off the wind.
I pulled the *scratchy* blanket around me to fight off the *chilling* wind. (*Touch*)

Activity

Using the methods described above, add specific details to any eight of the ten sentences that follow. Use a separate sheet of paper.

Examples   The person got out of the car.

The elderly man painfully lifed himself out of the white station wagon.

The fans enjoyed the victory.

Many of the fifty-thousand fans stood, waved Leafs sweaters, and

cheered wildly when Tretiak scored the winning goal.

1. The lunch was not very good.
2. The animal ran away.
3. An accident occurred.
4. The instructor came into the room.
5. The machine did not work.
6. The crowd grew restless.
7. I relaxed.
8. The room was inviting.
9. The child threw the object.
10. The driver was angry.

10 PROVIDING SPECIFIC EVIDENCE

Activity

Provide three details that logically support each of the following points made in the following topic sentences. Your details can be drawn from your own experience, or they can be invented. In each case, the details should show in a specific way what the point expresses in only a general way. State your details briefly in phrases rather than in complete sentences.

Example   The student had several ways of passing time during the dull lecture.

Shielded his eyes with his hand and dozed for a while.

Read the sports magazine he had brought to class.

Made an elaborate drawing on a page of his notebook.

1. I could tell I was coming down with the flu.

   _____

   _____

   _____

2. Canadians should vacation in their own country.

   _____

   _____

   _____

3. I had car problems recently.

   _____

   _____

   _____

4. When your money gets tight, there are several ways to economize.

   _____

   _____

   _____

5. Some people are excellent drivers.

   _____

   _____

   _____

11 IDENTIFYING ADEQUATE SUPPORTING EVIDENCE

Activity

Two of the following paragraphs provide clear supporting points (subtopics) and sufficient details to support their topic sentences convincingly. Write *AD,* for *adequate development,* beside those paragraphs. There are also three paragraphs that, for the most part, use vague, general, or wordy sentences as a substitute for clear subtopics and concrete details. Write *U,* for *underdeveloped,* beside those paragraphs.

1.

My Husband's Stubbornness

My husband's worst problem is his stubbornness. He simply will not let any kind of weakness show. If he isn't feeling well, he refuses to admit it. He will keep on doing whatever he is doing and will wait until the symptoms get almost unbearable before he will even hint that anything is the matter with him. Then things are so far along that he has to spend more time recovering than he would if he had a different attitude. He also hates to be wrong. If he is wrong, he will be the last to admit it. This happened once when we went shopping, and he spent an endless amount of time going from one place to the next. He insisted that one of them had a fantastic sale on things he wanted. We never found a sale, but the fact that this situation happened will not change his attitude. Finally, he never listens to anyone else's suggestions on a car trip. He always knows he's on the right road, and the results have led to a lot of time wasted getting back in the right direction. Every time one of these incidents happens, it only means that it is going to happen again in the future.

2.

Street Hockey: Tradition or Torture?

Street hockey has always been popular with boys and girls in Red Deer Alberta, so we feel we have a tradition to keep up, but it is becoming an increasingly dangerous pastime. Games are constantly interrupted by cars and trucks. This fall, one of the new girl players, who was captain of her school's field hockey team, believed she had to prove herself to us. Unaware of the amount of traffic on seemingly quiet streets, she ploughed forward, head down, eyes focused on the ball, and nearly wound up as the hood ornament on a minivan. Late-night drinking drivers make street hockey even more hazardous. Bottles thrown out the windows shatter on the pavement, and large chunks of glass get picked up by hockey sticks as we chase the ball. Two players ended up in Emergency, one with a dangerous cut over his eye, the other with six stitches in his forearm, both injuries caused by flying glass. The most dangerous incident, though, had nothing to do with traffic; it was a combination of ordinary carelessness and modern lawn care. A wild shot sent the ball onto someone's newly treated front yard. Our forward sprinted to retrieve the ball, tripped over the "dangerous chemical" sign, and fell face-forward into damp grass, freshly soaked in weed killer. He turned out to be violently allergic to the ingredients, and went into something like an asthma attack. We had to call 911 for paramedics with inhalers and oxygen. So, a traditional teenage prairie sport has lost some of its appeal these days and, in fact, has become more of a hazard than a tradition for its players.

3.

Attitudes about Food

Attitudes that we form as children about food are not easily changed. In some families, food is love. Not all families are like this, but some children grow up with this attitude. Some families think of food as something precious and not to be wasted. The attitudes children pick up about food are hard to change in adulthood. Some families celebrate with food. If a child learns an attitude, it is hard to break this later. Someone once said: "As the twig is bent, so grows the tree." Children are very impressionable, and they can't really think for themselves when they are small. Children learn from the parent figures in their lives, and later from their peers. Some families have healthy attitudes about food. It is important for adults to teach their children these healthy attitudes. Otherwise, the children may have weight problems when they are adults.

_____   4.

Qualities in a Friend

There are several qualities I look for in a friend. A friend should give support and security. A friend should also be fun to be around. Friends can have faults, like anyone else, and sometimes it is hard to overlook them.. But a friend can't be dropped because he or she has faults. A friend should stick by a friend, even in bad times. There is a saying that "a friend in need is a friend indeed." I believe this means that there are good friends and fair-weather friends. The second type is not a true friend. He or she is the kind of person who runs when there's trouble. Friends don't always last a lifetime. Someone believed to be a best friend may lose contact if a person moves to a different area or goes around with a different group of people. A friend should be generous and understanding. A friend does not have to be exactly like you. Sometimes friends are opposites, but they still like each other and get along. Since I am a very quiet person, I can't say that I have many friends. But these are the qualities I believe a friend should have.

_____   5.

Schoolyard Cardsharks

There is something odd about the evenings-only men's club and casino in the nearby school playground. As dusk gathers over Halifax, under the arc lights provided for the children's protection, a group of gentlemen with peculiar habits gather to socialize. The members of this society have a uniform: ballcaps worn back-to-front, XXLL-size T-shirts, and huge unlaced athletic shoes. Sheltering behind the wooden "climbing castle," they arrange their chosen furniture, worn folding chairs stolen from the neighbourhood's front porches. Next, raised ritual handgrips are exchanged, and the fraternal greetings are heard: "How the h--- are ya?" "So where were ya last night?" As a rough circle is formed by the players' chairs, packs of Export As emerge from pockets and sleeves, and the sacramental beverages of Molson Ex and Gatorade are readied for the tense action to follow. Finally, the stakes are agreed upon, and the equipment is carefully placed on a pilfered card table: two dog-eared decks of playing cards. Is their game five-card stud, or blackjack, deuces wild? No, it's euchre…the same game their grandparents play in their retirement homes. Youth and age meet in odd ways, in odd locations.

12 ADDING DETAILS TO COMPLETE A PARAGRAPH

Activity

Each of the following paragraphs needs specific details to back up its supporting points. In the spaces provided, add a sentence or two of realistic details for each supporting point. The more specific you are, the more convincing your details are likely to be.

1.

An Inspiring Instructor

After only a class or two, it was clear that the new Computer Graphics instructor was very good at her job. First of all, she made personal contact with every student in the class. _____

_____

_____

_____

In addition, she gave out extremely clear course requirements. _____

_____

_____

_____

Finally, she encouraged all the students to ask questions. _____

_____

_____

_____

2.

Helping a Parent in College

    There are several ways a family can help a parent who is attending college. First, family members can take over some of the household chores that the parent usually does. _____

_____

_____

_____

Also, family members can make sure that the student has some quiet study time. _____

_____

_____

_____

Last, families can take an interest in the student's problems and accomplishments. _____

_____

_____

_____

---

13 WRITING A SIMPLE PARAGRAPH

You know now that an effective paragraph does two essential things: (1) it makes a point, and (2) it provides specific details to support that point. You have considered a number of paragraphs that are effective because they follow these two basic steps or are ineffective because they fail to follow them.

    You are ready, then, to write a simple paragraph of your own. Choose one of the three assignments below, and follow carefully the guidelines provided.

■ Assignment 1

Turn back to the activity on page 70 and select the point for which you have the best supporting details. Develop that point into a paragraph by following these steps:

a If necessary, rewrite the point so that the first sentence is more specific or suits your purpose more exactly. For example, you might want to rewrite the second point so that it includes a specific place: "Taking a vacation in and around Vancouver has many attractive possibilities."

b Use one or two methods of prewriting to generate details about your topic. When you are satisfied with what you have accumulated, see if the details can be grouped under more general or subtopic headings. You are looking for three supporting points for your topic. For example, a student writing about vacationing near Vancouver might find that he or she had details that fit under three headings: city attractions like Stanley Park, Whistler and ski resorts, and Victoria and the coastal islands. You may find it useful to reread Silvio's experience with the writing process on pages 38–42.

c   Using your disk copy or a photocopy of the paragraph outline form on page 25, provide several details to develop fully each of your three supporting points or subtopics. Make sure that all the information in your outline truly supports your point.

d   Write your first draft based on your outline. Conclude your paragraph with a sentence that refers to your opening point. This last sentence "rounds off" the paragraph and lets the reader know that your discussion is complete. For example, the first paragraph about cheating on page 47 begins with "Cheating is common in everyday life." It closes with a statement that refers to, and echoes, the opening point: "For many people, daily cheating is an acceptable way to behave."

e   Revise your first draft. Does each sentence truly support your topic? Is the order in which you stated your ideas reasonable? Check to make sure that you use transition words like *First of all, Second* or *Next*, and *Finally, Most,* or *Last* to introduce your three supporting details.

f   Supply a title based on the point. For instance, point 4 on page 70 might have the title "Ways to Economize."

g   If you have not been prewriting or drafting on a word processor, key in your draft now and run the spell checker over your paper, correcting any spelling errors before you print your final copy. If you are writing in class, use a dictionary to check the spelling in your final draft.

Use the following list to check your paragraph for each of the above items:

YES   NO

_____   Do you begin with a point?

_____   Do you provide relevant, specific details that support the point?

_____   Do you use the words *First of all, Second,* and *Finally* to introduce your three supporting details?

_____   Do you have a closing sentence that refers back to your opening point?

_____   Do you have a title based on the point?

_____   Are your sentences clear and free from obvious errors?

Assignment 2

In this chapter you have read two paragraphs (page 50) on reasons for being in college. For this assignment, write a paragraph describing your own reasons for being in college. You might want to look first at the following list of common reasons students give for going to school. Use the ones that apply to you (making them as specific as possible) or supply your own. Select three of your most important reasons for being in school as subtopics or supporting points and generate specific supporting details for each reason.

Before starting, reread paragraph B on page 50. *You must provide comparable specific details of your own.* Make your paragraph truly personal; do not fall back on vague generalities like those in paragraph A on page 50. Use the checklist for Assignment 1 as a guideline as you work on the paragraph.

APPLY IN
MY CASE

Reasons Students Go to College

_____   • To acquire employment-related skills

_____   • To prepare for a specific career

_____   • To please their families

_____   • To educate and enrich themselves

_____   • To be with friends

_____   • To take advantage of an opportunity they didn't have before

_____   • To see if college has anything to offer them

_____   • To do more with their lives than they've done so far

_____   • To take advantage of provincial or federal assistance programs or other special funding

_____   • To earn the status that they feel comes with a college diploma

_____   • To get a new start in life

Assignment 3

Write a paragraph about stress in your life. Choose three of the following stressful areas and provide specific examples and details to develop each area.

Stress at school
Stress at work
Stress at home
Stress with a friend or friends

Use the checklist for Assignment 1 as a guideline while working on the paragraph.

REVIEWING THE LEARNING OUTCOMES FOR CHAPTER 3

1 What is the first sentence in an effective paper called?

_____

_____

2   How does this first sentence affect all other sentences in a paragraph unit?

_____

_____

_____

3   List three reasons why specific supporting evidence is necessary in any piece of effective writing:

a _____

b _____

c _____

4   What is the difference between a supporting point or subtopic and a supporting detail?

_____

_____

_____

5   In what way specifically do you feel your writing skills have improved after working through the writing tasks in the last two chapters?

_____

_____

_____

Suggestions on What to Do Next

1   Work through the next chapter in Part One: "The Third and Fourth Steps in Writing" (page 78).

2   Read "Providing Examples" (page 147) in Part Two and do the first writing assignment.

3   Take the "Sentence-Skills Diagnostic Test" or do the introductory projects in Part Four and begin working on the sentence skills you need to review.

CHAPTER 4

The Third and Fourth Steps in Writing

LEARNING OUTCOMES

By working through activities and writing assignments in this chapter,

- you will write papers whose ideas are clearly connected by using a clear method of organization for your supporting material;
- you will make your point more effectively by stating your supporting material in an order appropriate to your content;
- you will connect your specific evidence with transitional methods and words so that your readers move easily and logically through your papers; and
- you will refine your editing skills and write clearer sentences containing fewer errors by referring to the rules in Part Four of this book.

The third and fourth steps in effective writing are

3 Organize and connect the specific evidence.
4 Write clear, error-free sentences.

You know from the previous chapter that steps 1 and 2 in writing an effective paragraph are stating a point and supporting it with specific evidence. Step 3 is organizing and connecting the specific evidence. Most of this chapter will deal with the chief ways to organize and connect this supporting information in a paper. The chapter will then look briefly at the sentence skills that make up step 4 in writing a successful paper.

STEP 3: ORGANIZE AND CONNECT THE SPECIFIC EVIDENCE

At the same time that you are generating the specific details needed to support a point, you should be thinking about ways to organize and connect those details.

All the details in your paper must **cohere**, or **stick together**; when they do, your reader is able to move smoothly and clearly from one bit of supporting information to the next. This chapter will discuss the following ways to organize and connect supporting details: (1) common methods of organization, (2) transitions, and (3) other connecting words.

COMMON METHODS OF ORGANIZATION: TIME ORDER AND EMPHATIC ORDER

Time order and emphatic order are common methods used to organize the supporting material in a paper. You will learn more specialized methods of development in Part Two of the book.

Time order simply means that details are listed as they occur in time. *First* this is done; *next* this; *then* this; *after* that, this; and so on. Here is a paragraph that organizes its details through time order:

How I Relax

After my last class on Thursday nights, my concentration is strained to the limit, and I have a ritual I follow to relax. The first part of my ritual is a necessity. I have to pick up my son and daughter from the sitter, listen to the events of their day, and put them to bed. Next come the personal treats I *choose.* I start with some "aromatherapy," running hot water into the tub along with lots of patchouli-scented bubble bath. As the bubbles rise, I light two fat, perfumed candles and then get into the tub. I shut out the bathroom lights, enjoy the candlelight, and get into the tub to soothe my tired muscles. The bubbles are tingly on my skin as I lie back and put my feet on the water spigots, with everything but my head under the water. After about ten minutes of soaking, I wash myself with scented soap, get out and dry myself off, and put on my flannelette "bunnyjamas." Then I go to the kitchen and unwrap one of my Thursday take-out treats. My usual choice is a huge chickpea roti oozing curry sauce, which I reheat in the microwave and eat with a vanilla ice-cream float. I carry these into the living room and turn on the television. To get comfortable, I sit on the couch with a pillow behind me and my legs under me. The final treat is watching—surprise—Hong Kong action movies! Somehow, watching Chow Yun-Fatt and Jackie Chan going through their moves just leaves me totally relaxed after a long, hard day of being a part-time mother and full-time student.

Fill in the missing words: "How I Relax" uses the following words to help show time order: _____, _____, _____, _____, and _____.

Emphatic order is sometimes described as "*save-the-best-till-last*" order. It means that the most interesting or important detail is placed in the last part of a paper.

(In cases where all the details seem equal in importance, the writer should impose a personal order that seems logical or appropriate to the details in question.) The last position in a paper is the most emphatic position because the reader is most likely to remember the last thing read. *Finally, last of all,* and *most important* are typical words showing emphasis. The following paragraph organizes its details through emphatic order.

Why Wrestling Rules

According to my classmates in Media Studies, there are several reasons why wrestling is so popular now. First of all, wrestling is promoted everywhere to catch any possible audience. On the corner store racks, magazines feature StoneCold and Goldberg on the covers, and at the checkout counters boxes of WWF trading cards wait for collectors. Cable stations show wrestling every day, and when The Undertaken, Edge, and The Rock, come to Skydome, every seat is sold. Entertainment programs and news broadcasts cover the latest antics of wrestlers, and toy stores carry action figures for wrestling-crazed children. Next, TV wrestling has attracted a vast and measurable audience from an unexpected source. Who are these new fans of men and women in tights? Former soap opera viewers are the fastest growing new audiences for wrestling, according to ratings surveys. Why would soap fans switch to wrestling? Well, my classmates say wrestling has four things in common with soaps: heroes and villains, strong female characters, continuing stories, and lots of grudges and revenge. Somehow it is hard to picture Erica Kane going into the ring against Chyna, but wrestling and soap opera must grab people's emotions. Maybe both are larger than life and give people something to fantasize about. But the biggest reason of all for wrestling's popularity is the universal desire to watch action, if not violence. Although other professional sports and even video games offer action, wrestling is theatrical, showy, and full of special effects like pyros and theme music. Wrestlers are actors, living cartoons who bounce around and come back in the next episode. Perhaps wrestlers without their costumes and makeup would just be better-trained versions of the people on *Springer*; so it must be promotion, the drama, the action; in fact, the whole package that keeps its audiences growing.

Fill in the missing words: The paragraph lists a total of _____ different reasons wrestling is growing in popularity. The writer of the paragraph feels that the most important reason is _____. He or she signals this reason by using the emphasis words _____.

Some paragraphs use a *combination of time order and emphatic order*. For example, "Net Eats Student's Time!" on page 5 includes time order: it moves from the time the writer tried to access the server to the end of the evening. In addition, the writer uses emphatic order, ending with her greatest source of irritation, signaled by the words *the final stage in my annoyance.*

TRANSITIONS

Transitions are *signal words and phrases* that help readers *follow the direction of the writer's thought.* They show the relationship between ideas, connecting one thought with the next. They can be compared to road signs that guide travellers.

To see the value of transitions, look at the following pairs of examples. Put a check beside the example in each pair that is easier and clearer to read and understand.

1. _____ a. Our building manager recently repainted our apartment. He replaced our faulty air conditioner.

   _____ b. Our building manager recently repainted our apartment. Also, he replaced our faulty air conditioner.

2. _____ a. I carefully inserted a disk into the computer. I turned on the power button.

   _____ b. I carefully inserted a disk into the computer. Then I turned on the power button.

3. _____ a. Moviegoers usually dislike film monsters. Filmgoers loved Chucky and could not wait for him to return and take a bride.

   _____ b. Moviegoers usually dislike film monsters. However, filmgoers loved Chucky and could not wait for him to return and take a bride.

You should have checked the second example in each pair. The transitional words in those sentences—*Also, Then,* and *However*—make the relationship between the sentences clear. Like all effective transitions, they help connect the writer's thoughts.

In the following box are common transitional words and phrases, grouped according to the kind of signal they give readers. Note that certain words provide more than one kind of signal. In the paragraphs you write, you will often use addition signals: words like *first of all, also, another,* and *finally* will help you move from one supporting reason or detail to the next.

Transitions

Addition signals: first of all, for one thing, second, the third reason, also, next, another, and, in addition, moreover, furthermore, finally, last of all

Time signals: first, then, next, after, as, before, while, meanwhile, now, during, finally

Space signals: next to, across, on the opposite side, to the left, to the right, in front, in back, above, below, behind, nearby

Change-of-direction signals: but, however, yet, in contrast, otherwise, still, on the contrary, on the other hand

Illustration signals: for example, for instance, specifically, as an illustration, once, such as

Conclusion signals: therefore, consequently, thus, then, as a result, in summary, to conclude, last of all, finally

Activity

1. Underline the three *addition* signals in the following paragraph:

I am opposed to provincial lotteries for a number of reasons. First of all, by supporting lotteries, provinces are supporting gambling. I don't see anything morally wrong with gambling, but it is a known cause of suffering for many people who do it to excess. Provinces should be concerned with improving people's lives, not causing more misery. Another objection I have to the province lotteries is the kind of advertising they do on television. The commercials promote the lotteries as an easy way to get rich. In fact, the odds against getting rich are astronomical. Last, the lotteries take advantage of the people who can least afford them. Studies have shown that people with lower incomes are more likely to buy lottery tickets than people with higher incomes. This is the harshest reality of the lotteries: provinces are encouraging people of limited means not to save their money but to throw it away on a provincial pipe dream.

2. Underline the four *time* signals in the following paragraph:

A few things make it easy for a Canadian to know that he or she is home when crossing the border. First is always seeing the word "Douane" underneath the word "Customs." Of course, unless someone is entering Quebec, it is unlikely that the traveller will actually hear any French, but there is something comforting and familiar about two languages on all the signs. Then, after getting back on the highway, another signal tips off the Canadian that he or she is home: no more trying to figure out how far 276 miles might be. Road signs are in international kilometres again. Next, the driver lifts a weary eye to the roadside scenery, noticing something different about the view: not the trees, the gas stations, or the malls, but the fact that there aren't any advertising billboards! And finally, desperate for a few minutes rest and a snack, the returning Canadian stops at a doughnut shop named for a hockey player and is again able to order the one thing never seen south of the border: a butter tart.

3. Underline the three *space* signals in the following paragraph:

Standing in the burned-out shell of my living room was a shocking experience. Above my head were charred beams, all that remained of our ceiling. In front of me, where our television and stereo had once stood, were twisted pieces of metal and chunks of blackened glass. Strangely, some items seemed little damaged by the fire. For example, I could see the TV tuner knob and a dusty CD under the rubble. I walked through the gritty ashes until I came to what was left of our couch. Behind the couch had been a wall of family photographs. Now, the wall and the pictures were gone. I found only a waterlogged scrap of my wedding picture.

4.   Underline the four *change-of-direction* signals in the following paragraph:

In some ways, train travel is superior to air travel. People always marvel at the speed with which airplanes can zip from one end of the country to another. Trains, on the other hand, definitely take longer. But sometimes longer can be better. Travelling across Canada by train allows people to experience the trip more completely. They get to see the cities and towns, mountains and prairies that too often pass by unnoticed when they fly. Another advantage of train travel is comfort. Travelling by plane means wedging into a narrow seat with knees bent and bumping the back of the seat in front and being handed a "snack" consisting of a bag of ten roasted peanuts. In contrast, the seats on most trains are spacious and comfortable, permitting even the longest-legged traveller to stretch out and watch the scenery just outside the window. And when train travellers grow hungry, they can get up and stroll to the dining car, where they can order anything from a simple snack to a complete meal. There's no question that train travel is definitely slow and old-fashioned compared with air travel. However, in many ways it is much more civilized.

5.   Underline the three *illustration* signals in the following selection:

At the start of the twenty-first century, the most desirable status symbols are the smallest ones, and they are all powered by microchips. The home computer everyone secretly craves, for instance, is <u>not</u> the powerful-looking model with external drives, modems, and speaker boxes hanging off its side. No, the status computer is probably one of those cute little candy-coloured items that sings old Rolling Stones songs and floats around in a circle. Or it might be a nearly invisible model, with a tiny console that fits in a drawer and an elegant flat screen mounted on a collapsible arm. And, of course, the laptop, so small that it slides into a backpack, is still a hot item. But there is an even trendier example of tiny technology, something for the person who really wants to look organized: the Palm Pilot. With the arrival of the millennium, the big leatherbound daybook has gone out of style. Instead, the busy person lists all of his or her appointments, phone numbers, and vital information on a little piece of equipment that looks like a grown-up GameBoy. And when this busy individual wants to make a call, he or she uses the tiniest piece of status technology of all: specifically, one of the itty bitty new cell phones. These wee marvels are the size of a deck of cards, fit into a pocket or purse, and let their owners "reach out and touch someone" or even access their e-mail. Status symbols are shrinking all the time; who knows if one day, they will be built right into their owners?

6.   Underline the *conclusion* signal in the following paragraph:

A hundred years ago, miners used to bring caged canaries down into the mines with them to act as warning signals. If the bird died, the miner knew that the oxygen was running out. The smaller animal would be affected much more quickly than the miners. In the same way, animals are acting as warning signals to us today. Baby birds die before they can hatch because pesticides in the environment cause the adults to lay eggs with paper-thin shells. Fish die because the Great Lakes are contaminated with acid rain or poisonous mercury. The dangers in our environment will eventually affect all life on earth, including humans. Therefore, we must pay attention to these early warning signals. If we don't, we will be as foolish as a miner who ignored a dead canary—and we will die.

OTHER CONNECTING WORDS

In addition to transitions, there are three other kinds of connecting words that help tie together the specific evidence in a paper: repeated words, pronouns, and synonyms. Each will be discussed in turn.

Repeated Words

Many of us have been taught by English instructors, and correctly so, not to repeat ourselves in our writing. On the other hand, repeating keywords can help tie a flow of thought together. In the paragraph that follows, the word *retirement* is repeated to remind readers of the key idea on which the discussion is centred. Underline the word the five times it appears.

Oddly enough, retirement can pose more problems for the spouse than for the retired person. For a person who has been accustomed to a demanding job, retirement can mean frustration and a feeling of uselessness. This feeling will put pressure on the spouse to provide challenges at home equal to those of the workplace. Often, these tasks will disrupt the spouse's well-established routine. Another problem arising from retirement is filling up all those empty hours. The spouse may find himself or herself in the role of social director or tour guide, expected to come up with a new form of amusement every day. Without sufficient challenges or leisure activities, a person can become irritable and take out the resulting boredom and frustration of retirement on the marriage partner. It is no wonder that many of these partners wish their spouses would come out of retirement and do something—anything—just to get out of the house.

Pronouns

Pronouns (*he, she, it, you, they, this, that,* and others) are another way to connect ideas as you develop a paper. Using pronouns to take the place of other words or ideas can help you avoid needless repetition. Be careful, though, to use pronouns with care in order *to avoid unclear or inconsistent pronoun reference* described on pages 300–306 of this book. Underline the eight pronouns in the passage below, noting at the same time the words to which the pronouns refer.

A professor of nutrition at a major university recently advised his students that they could do better on examinations by eating lots of sweets. He told them that the sugar in cakes and candy would stimulate their brains to work more efficiently, and that if the sugar was eaten for only a month or two, it would not do them any harm.

Synonyms

Using synonyms (words that are alike in meaning) can also help move the reader clearly from one thought to the next. In addition, the use of synonyms increases variety and reader interest by avoiding needless repetition of the same words. Underline the three phrases used as synonyms for *ATMs* in the following passage:

ATMs make it too tempting for the average Canadian to overspend. Because bank machines run *twenty four/seven*, we can take out another forty dollars any time of day or night instead of waiting for the bank to open and perhaps reconsidering how much we really need that extra money. Automated cash windows are temptingly placed nearly everywhere just for our spending convenience. "Instant tellers" sit in convenience stores, gas stations, and all over malls, waiting to catch us when we are weakest. ATMs look so bright, friendly, and appealing that somehow we feel less guilty about withdrawing money from them than we might after filling out a withdrawal slip, waiting in line, and facing a teller. Perhaps it is just easier to face a screen that reads "Insufficient funds," than it is to hear a live bank teller say, "I'm sorry, but your account is overdrawn."

Activity

To sharpen your sense of how *coherence*, or a sense of connection is maintained throughout a paper, read the selection below and then answer the questions about it that follow.

The Worst Experience of My Week

[1]The registration process at McKenzie College was a nightmare. [2]The night before registration for my course officially began, I went to bed anxious about the whole thing, and nothing that happened the next day eased any of my tension. [3]First, even though I had paid my registration fee early last spring, the staff in the registration office had no record of my payment. [4]For some bizarre reason, they wouldn't accept the receipt I had. [5]Consequently, I had to stand in a special numbered line for two hours, waiting for someone to give me a paper that stated that I had, in fact, paid my registration fee. [6]The need for this new receipt seemed ridiculous to me, since, all along, I had proof that I had paid. [7]Next, I was told that I had to see my program co-ordinator in the International Business Faculty and that this faculty was in Section C, Phase 2, of the Champlain Building. [8]I had no idea what or where the Champlain Building was. [9]Finally, I found the ugly cinder-block structure. Then I began looking for Section C and Phase 2. [10]When I found these, everyone there was a member of the Communications Department. [11]No one seemed to know where International Business had gone. [12]Finally, one instructor said she thought

International Business was in Section A. [13]"And where is Section A?" I asked. [14]"I don't know," the teacher answered. "I'm new here." [15]She saw the bewildered look on my face and said sympathetically, "You're not the only one who's confused." [16]I nodded and walked numbly away. [17]I felt as if I were fated to spend the rest of the semester trying to complete the registration process, and I wondered if I would ever become an official college student.

Questions

1. How many times is the key idea *registration* repeated? _____;

2. Write here the pronoun that is used for *staff in the registration office* (sentence 4): _____; *Section C, Phase 2* (sentence 10): _____; *instructor* (sentence 15): _____.

3. Write here the words that are used as a synonym for *receipt* (sentence 5):

    _____;

    the words that are used as a synonym for *Champlain* (sentence 9):

    _____;

    the word that is used as a synonym for *instructor* (sentence 14):

    _____.

STEP 4: WRITE CLEAR, ERROR-FREE SENTENCES

The fourth step in writing an effective paper is to follow the agreed-upon rules, or conventions, of written English. These conventions, or, as they are called in this book, sentence skills, must be followed if your sentences are to be clear and error-free. Here are some of the most important of these skills.

1 Write complete sentences rather than fragments.
2 Do not write run-on sentences.
3 Use verb forms and tenses correctly and consistently.
4 Make sure that subjects and verbs agree.
5 Use pronoun forms and types correctly.
6 Use adjectives and adverbs correctly.
7 Eliminate faulty modifiers and faulty parallelism.
8 Use correct paper format.
9 Use capital letters where needed.
10 Use numbers and abbreviations correctly.
11 Use the following punctuation marks correctly: apostrophe, quotation marks, comma, colon, semi-colon, dash, hyphen, and parentheses.
12 Always use the spell checker when processing assignments, and use the dictionary as necessary to eliminate spelling errors.

13 Use words accurately by developing your vocabulary and distinguishing between commonly confused words.

14 Choose words effectively to avoid slang, clichés, and wordiness.

15 Vary your sentences.

16 Edit and proofread to eliminate careless errors.

The sentence skills are explained in detail, and activities are provided, in Part Four, where they can be referred to easily as needed. A diagnostic test on pages 440–445 will help you identify skills you may need to review. Your instructor will also identify such skills in marking your papers and may use the correction symbols shown on the inside back cover. Note that the correction symbols, and also the checklist of sentence skills on the inside front cover, include page references, so that you can turn quickly to those skills that give you problems.

■ Review Activity

To check your progress with the Learning Outcomes for this chapter, complete the following statements.

1. The four steps in writing a paper are:

   a. _____

   b. _____

   c. _____

   d. _____

2. *Time order* means _____

   _____

3. *Emphatic order* means _____

   _____

4. What are the *transitions?* What is their function? _____

   _____

5. In addition to transitions, three other kinds of connecting words that help

   link sentences and ideas are repeated words, _____, and

   _____.

PRACTICE IN ORGANIZING AND CONNECTING SPECIFIC EVIDENCE

You now know the third step in effective writing: *organizing the specific evidence used to support the main point of a paper.* You also know that the fourth step—writing clear, error-free sentences—will be treated in detail in Part Four of the book. As you work through the activities in this section, you will expand and strengthen your understanding of the third step in writing. You will achieve mastery of this chapter's Learning Outcomes connected to gaining and increasing your competence in organizing and linking ideas.

To do so, work through the following series of activities:

1 Organizing with Time Order
2 Organizing with Emphatic Order
3 Organizing with a Combination of Time Order and Emphatic Order
4 Identifying Transitions
5 Providing Transitions
6 Identifying Transitions and Other Connecting Words

1 ORGANIZING THROUGH TIME ORDER

Activity

Use time order to organize the scrambled list of sentences below.

First choose the point that all the other sentences support, and number it #1. Then, choose one of three methods for completing the exercise:

1 Simply read all the items through, and number each supporting sentence as it occurs in time sequence in the spaces provided.
2 Key in each supporting item and use the "cut and paste" functions on your computer to move the sentences around until they are in the correct time sequence. Number your sentence choices, and then print your document.
3 Write the sentences on a sheet of paper, leaving a space between each, and then cut out each item. Move the strips of paper containing the sentences around until they are in time sequence; then number the sentences. Transfer the numbers for the correctly-ordered sentences to the spaces below.

_____ The table is right near the garbage pail.

_____ So you reluctantly select a gluelike tuna-fish sandwich, a crushed-in apple pie, and watery, lukewarm coffee.

_____ You sit at the edge of the table, away from the garbage pail, and gulp down your meal.

_____ Trying to eat in the cafeteria is an unpleasant experience.

_____ Suddenly you spot a free table in the corner.

_____ With a last swallow of the lukewarm coffee, you get up and leave the cafeteria as rapidly as possible.

_____ Flies are flitting into and out of the pail.

_____ By the time it is your turn, the few things that are almost good are gone.

_____ There does not seem to be a free table anywhere.

_____   Unfortunately, there is a line in the cafeteria.

_____   The submarine sandwiches, coconut-cream pie, and iced tea have all disappeared.

_____   You hold your tray and look for a place to sit down.

_____   You have a class in a few minutes, and so you run in to grab something to eat quickly.

2 ORGANIZING THROUGH EMPHATIC ORDER

Activity

Use emphatic order (order of importance) to arrange the following scrambled list of sentences. Write the number 1 beside the point that all the other sentences support. Then, using one of the three methods suggested in the preceding activity, number each supporting sentence, starting with what seems to be the least important detail and ending with the most important detail.

_____   The people in my area of Swift Current are all around my age and seem to be genuinely friendly and interested in me.

_____   The place where I live has several important advantages.

_____   The schools in this neighbourhood have a good reputation, so I feel that my daughter is getting a good education.

_____   The best thing of all about this area, though, is the school system.

_____   Therefore, I don't have to put up with public transportation or worry about how much it's going to cost to park each day.

_____   The school also has an extended daycare program, so I know my daughter is in good hands until I come home from work.

_____   First of all, I like the people who live in the other apartments near mine.

_____   Another positive aspect of this area is that it's close to where I work.

_____   That's more than I can say for the last place I lived, where people never seemed to say hello.

_____   The office where I'm a receptionist is only a six-block walk from my house.

_____   In addition, I save a lot of wear and tear on my car.

3 ORGANIZING THROUGH A COMBINATION OF TIME ORDER AND EMPHATIC ORDER

Activity

Use a _combination_ of time and emphatic order to arrange the scrambled list of sentences below. Write the number 1 beside the point that all the other sentences support. Then, using one of the three methods suggested in the two preceding activities, number each supporting sentence. Paying close attention to transitional words and phrases will help you organize and connect the supporting sentences.

_____ I did not see the snake, but visited my friend in the Gravenhurst hospital where he suffered for days because of the snakebite venom.

_____ We were taking our time, dawdling along sideroads when we decided to eat lunch in the woods by the roadside.

_____ As I walked back to the car, I saw a long dark shape on the path in front of me.

_____ After my two experiences, I suspect that my fear of snakes will be with me for life.

_____ The first experience occurred when my best friend received a bite from a Massassauga rattler.

_____ I looked down at my feet, but it was shady and dark in the woods and my legs were shaking.

_____ I had two experiences when I was eighteen that are the cause of my *herpetophobia,* or terrible and uncontrollable fear of snakes.

_____ We stopped the car at the side of the road, took out our lunches, and then I decided to walk into the woods a little farther.

_____ When I got back in the car, I felt sick to my stomach, light-headed, and faint.

_____ I saw the huge bandage on his calf and the discoloured, puffy swelling when the bandage was removed.

_____ Then it curved its horrible slinky body off sideways out of my way and slithered into the dark bushes nearby.

_____ I sat in the car for an hour afterward, shaking and sweating, trying to reassure myself that snakes could not open car doors.

_____ But my more direct experience with snakes happened one day when when another friend and I were driving south to Barrie to buy concert tickets.

_____ Nearly touching the toe of my running shoe was a long, fat, grey snake, with a huge diamond-shaped head, looking straight at me.

_____ Most of all, I saw the ugly red scabs on his leg where the snake's fangs had ripped the flesh of his calf.

_____ I imagined the evil, muscular-looking snake lunging at me, opening its mouth wide, and attaching itself to my ankle.

_____ At the same time I cried out "Arghh!", ran towards the car, and never looked back.

_____ For a long, horrible second, the snake raised its head and eyed me coldly, as if it were thinking about how I would taste.

4 IDENTIFYING TRANSITIONS

The following three activities will increase your awareness of, and your competence in using, various transitional methods. In meeting this Learning Outcome, you will achieve two necessities for effective writing: (1) you will connect your supporting ideas and details in ways that reflect your intention as a writer, and (2) you will make your point, and the sequence of your supporting material easier to follow for your readers.

Activity

Locate the major transitions used in the following two selections. Then write the transitions in the spaces provided. Mostly, you will find addition words such as *another* and *also*. You will also find several change-of-direction words such as *but* and *however*.

1.

Watching Hockey on TV

Watching a hockey game on television may seem like the easiest thing in the world. However, like the game of hockey itself, watching a game correctly is far more complicated than it appears. First is the matter of the company. The ideal number of people depends on the size of your living-room floor. Also, at least one of your guests should be rooting for the opposite team. There's nothing like a little rivalry, the potential for a fight, to increase the enjoyment of hockey. Next, consider the refreshments. Make sure you have plenty of everyone's favourite drinks, along with the essential chips, dips, and pretzels. You may even want something more substantial on hand, like wings or pizza. If you do, make everyone wait until the moment the puck is dropped before eating. Waiting will make everything taste much better. Finally, there are the last items to have on hand, or in this case, on upper body: team jerseys. The purpose of these garments is not to keep people warm, but to reinforce loyalties during the game—and to use as weapons after. If your team happens to be getting trounced, you may just decide to wrap up your friends in the Oilers jerseys in your blue-and-white Leafs sweaters.

a. _____

b. _____

c. _____

d. _____

e. _____

2.

Avoidance Tactics

Getting down to studying for an exam or writing a paper is hard, and so it is tempting for students to use one of the following five avoidance tactics in order to put the work aside. For one thing, students may say to themselves, "I can't do it." They adopt a defeatist attitude at the start and give up without a struggle. They could get help with their work by using such college services as tutoring programs and access and learning resources. However, they refuse even to try. A second avoidance technique is to say, "I'm too busy." Students may take on an extra job, become heavily involved in social activities, or allow family problems to become so time-consuming that they cannot concentrate on their studies. Yet if college really matters to a student, he or she will make sure that there is enough time to do the required work. Another avoidance technique is expressed by the phrase "I'm too tired." Typically, sleepiness occurs when it is time to study or go to class and then vanishes when the school pressure is off. This sleepiness is a sign of work avoidance. A fourth excuse is to say, "I'll do it later." Putting things off until the last minute is practically a guarantee of poor grades on tests and papers. When everything else seems more urgent than studying—watching TV, calling a friend, or even cleaning the oven—a student may simply be escaping academic work. Last, some students avoid work by saying to themselves, "I'm here and that's what counts." Such students live under the dangerous delusion that, since they possess a student card, a parking sticker, and textbooks, the course work will somehow take care of itself. But once a student has a student card, he or she has only just begun. Doing the necessary studying, writing, and reading will bring real results: good grades, genuine learning, and a sense of accomplishment.

a. _____

b. _____

c. _____

d. _____

e. _____

f. _____

g. _____

h. _____

5 PROVIDING TRANSITIONS

Activity

In the spaces provided, add logical transitions to tie together the sentences and ideas in the following paragraphs. Use the words in the boxes that precede each paragraph.

1.

however	a second	last of all
for one thing	also	on the other hand

Why School May Frighten a Young Child

Topic senten ce.
1st subtopic

(Schools may be frightening to young children for a number of reasons.) ___For one thing___, the regimented environment may be a new and disturbing experience. At home children may have been able to do what they wanted when they wanted to do it. In school,

2nd ___However other hand___, they are given a set time for talking, working,

playing, eating, and even going to the toilet. ___A second___ source of anxiety may be the public method of discipline that some teachers use. Whereas at home children are scolded in private, in school they may be held up to embarrassment and ridicule in front of their peers. "Fatima," the teacher may say, "why are you the only one in the class who didn't do your homework?" Or, "David, why are you the only one who can't work quietly at

3 your seat?" Children may ___also___ be frightened by the loss of personal attention. Their little discomforts or mishaps, such as tripping on the stairs, may bring instant sympathy from a parent; in school, there is often no one to notice, or the teacher is frequently too busy to care and just

4 says, "Go do your work. You'll be all right." ___Last of all___, a child may be scared by the competitive environment of the school. At home, one hopes, such competition for attention is minimal. In school,

___On the other hand___, children may vie for the teacher's approving glance or tone of voice, or for stars on a paper, or for favoured seats in the front row. (For these and other reasons, it is not surprising that children may have difficulty adjusting to school.) *Conclusion senten ce.*

2.

as a result	once	finally
second	when	first of all
	but	

Joining a Multicultural Club

Canadians are pround of the "diversity" of our population, but I learned first-hand about diversity when I joined a multicultural club. ___First of all___, the club has helped me become friends with a diverse group of people. At any time in my apartment, I can have someone from Pakistan chatting about music to someone from Portugal, or someone from Russia talking about politics to someone from Uganda.

___Once___ I watched an Israeli student give falafels to three students from China. They had never eaten such things, but they liked them.

A ___second___ benefit of the club is that it's helped me realize

how similar people are. ___when___ the

whole club first assembled, we wound up having a conversation about dating and sex that included the perspectives of fifteen countries and six continents! It was clear we all shared the feeling that sex was fascinating. The talk lasted for hours, with many different persons describing the wildest or funniest experience they had had with the opposite sex. Only a few students, particularly those from Canada and Japan, seemed bashful.

_____*Finally*_____, the club has reminded me about the dangers of stereotyping. Before I joined the club, most of my experience with Chinese-Canadians was limited to some shy, fellow high-school students.

_____*As a result*_____, I believed that most Chinese people worked in the computer or food service industries. _____*But*_____ in the club, I met Chinese people who were soccer players, English majors, and graphic designers. I've also seen Jewish and Muslim students, people who I thought would never get along, drop their preconceived notions and become friends. Even more than my classes, the club has been an eye-opener for me.

6 IDENTIFYING TRANSITIONS AND OTHER CONNECTING WORDS

Activity

This activity will give you practice in identifying *transitions, repeated words, synonyms, and pronouns* that are used to help tie ideas together.

Section A: Transitions In the space provided, write the transitional words.

1. I decided to pick up a drop-add form from the registrar's office. However, I changed my mind when I saw the long line of students waiting there.

   _____

2. In England, drivers use the left-hand side of the road. Consequently, steering wheels are on the right side.

   _____

3. Crawling babies will often investigate new objects by putting them in their mouths. Therefore, parents should be alert for any pins, tacks, or other dangerous items on floors and carpets.

   _____

4. One technique that advertisers use is to have a celebrity endorse a product. The consumer then associates the star qualities of the celebrity with the product.

   _____

Section B: Repeated Words   In the space provided, write the repeated words.

5. We absorb radiation from many sources in our environment. Our colour television sets and microwave ovens, among other things, give off low-level radiation.

   _____

6. Many researchers believe that people have weight set-points that their bodies try to maintain. This may explain why many dieters return to their original weight.

   _____

7. At the end of the Our Lady Peace concert, thousands of fans held up disposable lighters in the darkened area. The sea of lighters signalled that the fans wanted an encore.

   _____

8. Establishing credit is important for a woman. A good credit history is often necessary when she is applying for a consumer loan or mortgage.

   _____

Section C: Synonyms   In the space provided, write the synonym for the underlined word.

9. I checked my <u>car's</u> tires, oil, water, and belts before the trip. But the ungrateful machine blew a gasket about fifty kilometres from home.

   _____

10. Women's <u>clothes</u>, in general, use less material than men's clothes. Yet women's garments usually cost more than men's.

   _____

11. Temperance movements in various countries sought to ban <u>alcohol</u>. Drinking liquor, movement leaders said, led to violence, poverty, prostitution, and insanity.

   _____

12. For me, <u>apathy</u> quickly sets in when the weather becomes hot and sticky. This listlessness disappears when the humidity decreases.

   _____

Section D: Pronouns In the space provided, write the word referred to by the underlined pronoun.

13. At the turn of the century, bananas were still an oddity in North America. Some people even attempted to eat <u>them</u> with the skins on.

    _____

14. Canning vegetables is easy and economical. <u>It</u> can also be very dangerous.

    _____

15. There are a number of signs that appear when students are under stress. For example, <u>they</u> start to have trouble studying, eating, and even sleeping.

    _____

REVIEWING THE LEARNING OUTCOMES FOR CHAPTER 4

1 The two requirements for a paper that is _____ are (1) a clear method of _____ and (2) use of _____ and other _____ _____ to connect the supporting ideas.

2 Two of the most common methods of organizing material for a paper are _____ order, which places ideas or events in the sequence in which they _____, and _____ order, which saves the _____ idea or supporting point until _____.

3 List three common *addition-signal transitions:*

    _____, _____, _____.

    List three common *space-signal transitions:*

    _____, _____, _____.

    List three common *conclusion-signal transitions:*

    _____, _____, _____.

4 Three other methods of indicating transition or connection between ideas are

    a _____

    b _____

    c _____

5 The main purposes for providing transitional words and phrases are

    a _____

    b _____

Suggestions on What to Do Next

1   Work through the final chapter in Part One: "Four Bases for Evaluating Writing."

2   Read "Explaining a Process" (page 156) in Part Two and do the first writing assignment.

3   Read "Vocabulary Development" in Part Four.

4   Continue your review of sentence skills in Part Four. If you plan to make a general review of all the skills, here is an appropriate sequence to follow:

   (1) Paper Format
   (2) Capital Letters
   (3) Subjects and Verbs
   (4) Fragments
   (5) Run-Ons
   (6) Standard English Verbs
   (7) Irregular Verbs
   (8) Subject-Verb Agreement
   (9) Apostrophe
   (10) Comma
   (11) Quotation Marks
   (12) Sentence Variety

CHAPTER 5

Four Bases for Evaluating Writing

LEARNING OUTCOMES

By completing the activities and exercises in this chapter,

- you will apply your understanding of the four bases of effective writing in working through practical exercises which require you to judge and revise aspects of student papers, and
- You will learn the goals and practise the skills needed for *revising and editing* as essential parts of the writing process:
  - you will evaluate papers for focused support of a single point, or unity;
  - you will decide what constitutes adequate, and specific support that communicates a point clearly to readers;
  - you will see the importance of clearly organizing ideas and carefully choosing and placing transitional devices for creating coherence (effective sequencing and connecting of supporting material); and
  - you will learn to recognize how effective sentence skills carry your paper's message.

As you complete these activities based on the four standards of effective writing, you will prepare to succeed in the writing, revising, and editing stages of writing tasks in the following chapters of this text. You will increase your knowledge of how to proceed and your confidence in your ability to create effective papers.

In the preceding two chapters, you learned four essential steps in writing an effective paper. The box below shows how these steps lead to four bases, or standards, you can use in evaluating a paper.

Four Steps ⟶	*Four Bases* ⟶	*Four Goals Defined*
1 If you make a point and stick to that point,	your writing will have *unity.*	**Unity:** a single main idea pursued and supported by the points and details of your writing
2 If you back up the point with specific evidence,	your writing will have *support.*	**Support:** for each supporting point, specific and definite details
3 If you organize and connect the specific evidence,	your writing will have *coherence.*	**Coherence:** supporting points and details organized and connected clearly
4 If you write clear, error-free sentences,	your writing will reflect effective *sentence skills.*	**Effective Sentence Skills:** sentence structure, grammar, spelling, and punctuation free of errors

BASE 1: UNITY

Activity

The following two paragraphs were written by students on the topic "Why Students Drop Out of College." Read them and decide which one makes its point more clearly and effectively, and why.

Paragraph A

Why Students Drop Out

Students drop out of college for many reasons. First of all, some students are bored in school. These students may enter college expecting nonstop fun or a series of undemanding courses. When they find out that college is often routine, they quickly lose interest. They do not want to take dull required courses or spend their nights studying, and so they drop out. Students also drop out of college because the work is harder than they thought it would be. These students may have gotten decent marks in high school simply by showing up for class. In college, however, they may have to prepare for two-hour exams, write lengthy reports, or make detailed presentations to a class. The hard work comes as a shock, and students give up. Perhaps the most common reason students drop out is that they are having personal or emotional problems. Younger students, especially, may be attending college at an age when they are also feeling confused, lonely, or depressed. These students may have problems with roommates, family, boyfriends, or girlfriends. They become too unhappy to deal with both hard academic work and emotional troubles. For many types of students, dropping out seems to be the only solution they can imagine.

Paragraph B

Student Dropouts

There are three main reasons students drop out of college. Some students, for one thing, are not really sure they want to be in school and lack the desire to do the work. When exams come up, or when a course requires a difficult project or demanding essay, these students will not do the required studying or research. Eventually, they may drop out because their grades are so poor they are about to fail anyway. Such students sometimes come back to school later with a completely different attitude about school. Other students drop out for financial reasons. The pressures of paying tuition, buying textbooks, and possibly having to support themselves can be overwhelming. These students can often be helped by the school or the province because financial aid is available, and some schools offer work-study programs. Finally, students drop out because they have personal problems. They cannot concentrate on their courses because they are unhappy at home, they are lonely, or they are having trouble with boyfriends or girlfriends. Instructors should suggest that such troubled students see counsellors or join support groups. If instructors would take a more personal interest in their students, more students would make it through troubled times.

Fill in the blanks: Paragraph _____ makes its point more clearly and effectively because _____

_____

_____

UNDERSTANDING AND EVALUATING UNITY

Paragraph A is more effective because it is *unified.* All the details in paragraph A are *on target;* they support and develop the single point expressed in the first sentence—that there are many reasons students drop out of college. On the other hand, paragraph B contains some details irrelevant to the opening point—that there are three main reasons students drop out. These details should be omitted in the interest of paragraph unity. Go back to paragraph B and cross out the sections that are off target—the sections that do not support the opening idea.

You should have crossed out the following sections: "Such students sometimes … attitude about school"; "These students can often … work-study programs"; and "Instructors should suggest … through troubled times."

The difference between these two paragraphs leads us to the first base, or standard, of effective writing: *unity.* **To achieve unity is to have all the details in your paper related to the single point expressed in the topic sentence, the first sentence.** Each time you think of something to put in, ask yourself whether it relates to your main point. If it does not, leave it out. For example, if you were writing about a certain job as the worst job you ever had and then spent a couple of sentences talking about the interesting people that you met there, you would be missing the first and most essential base of good writing.

CHECKING FOR UNITY

To check a paper for unity, ask yourself these questions:

1 Is there a clear opening statement of the point of the paper?

2 Is all the material on target in support of the opening point?

BASE 2: SUPPORT

Activity

The following student paragraphs were written on the topic "A Quality of Some Person or Animal You Know." Both are unified, but one communicates more clearly and effectively. Which one, and why?

Paragraph A

Laziness Defined

Cats may be the laziest creatures on earth, but they are also the smartest. Every day is divided up according to their pleasures and needs. They always find time to eat, without ever having to cook or prepare a meal. Enough complaining will make sure that their dishes are filled on time. Cats know they need exercise, too, so they take care of that by climbing the furniture and suddenly running up and down the stairs, usually at night. If they need someone to play with, they know enough not to strain themselves. Their radar can usually locate an owner who is busy at the computer or snoozing in front of the television, all ready for an eager furry playmate to nudge him or her into cooperating. Cats know their greatest need is for many hours of deep soothing sleep. Any time is the right time to sleep, and any place where humans are busy or where a fuzzy patch of cat fur will be appreciated is the right spot. Meeting all three needs keeps a cat healthy and occupied, and shows humans just how smart a lazy creature can be.

Paragraph B

My Generous Grandfather

My grandfather is the most generous person I know. He has given up a life of his own in order to give his grandchildren everything they want. Not only has he given up many years of his life to raise his children properly, but he is now sacrificing many more years to his grandchildren. His generosity is also evident in his relationship with his neighbours, his friends, and the members of his church. He has been responsible for many good deeds and has always been there to help all the people around him in times of trouble. Everyone knows that he will gladly lend a helping hand. He is so generous that I almost have to feel sorry for him. If one day he suddenly became selfish, it would be earthshaking. That's my grandfather.

Fill in the blanks: Paragraph _____ makes its point more clearly and effectively because _____

_____

_____

UNDERSTANDING SUPPORT

Paragraph A is more effective, for it offers **specific examples that show** us the laziness of cats in action. We see for ourselves why the writer describes cats as extremely lazy, but clever. Paragraph B, on the other hand, gives us no specific evidence. The writer of paragraph B **tells us repeatedly** that the grandfather is generous **but never shows us** examples of that generosity. Just how, for instance, did the grandfather sacrifice his life for his children and grandchildren? Did he hold two jobs so that his son could go to college, or so that his daughter could have her own car? Does he give up time with his wife and friends to travel every day to his daughter's house to babysit, go to the store, and help with the dishes? Does he wear threadbare suits and coats and eat Kraft Dinner and other inexpensive meals (with no desserts) so that he can give money to his children and toys to his grandchildren? We want to see and judge for ourselves whether the writer is making a valid point about the grandfather, but without specific details we cannot do so. In fact, we have almost no picture of him at all. The best writing **shows**; it does not **tell.**

Consideration of these two paragraphs leads us to the second base of effective writing: *support.* After realizing the importance of specific supporting details, one student writer revised a paper she had done on a restaurant job as the worst job she ever had. In the revised paper, instead of talking about "unsanitary conditions in the kitchen," she referred to such specifics as "green mold on the bacon" and "ants in the potato salad." All your papers should include many vivid details!

CHECKING FOR SUPPORT

To check a paper for support, ask yourself these questions:

1 Are there *specific supporting points* to support the opening point?
2 Is there *enough specific evidence*?
3 Are *specific details* included?

BASE 3: COHERENCE

Activity

The following two paragraphs were written on the topic "The Best or Worst Job You Ever Had." Both are unified and both are supported. However, one communicates more clearly and effectively. Which one, and why?

Paragraph A

Pantry Helper

My worst job was as a pantry helper in one of Vancouver's well-known restaurants. I had an assistant from three to six in the afternoon who did little but stand around and eat the whole time she was there. She kept an ear open for the sound of the back door opening, which was a sure sign the boss was coming in. The boss would testily say to me, "You've got a lot of things to do here, Lina. Try to get a move on." I would come in at two o'clock to relieve the woman on the morning shift. If her day was busy, that meant I would have to prepare salads, prepare soup stocks, and so on. Orders for appetizers and cold plates would come in and have to be prepared. The worst thing about the job was that the heat in the kitchen, combined with my nerves, would give me an upset stomach by seven o'clock almost every night. I might be going to the storeroom to get some supplies, and one of the servers would tell me she wanted an order of fried calamari. I would put the fryer basket on and head for the supply room, and a waitress would holler out that her customer was in a hurry. Flies would come in through the torn screen in the kitchen window and sting me. I was getting paid only $6.50 an hour. At five o'clock, when the dinner rush began, I would be dead tired. Roaches scurried in all directions whenever I moved a box or picked up a head of lettuce to cut.

Paragraph B

My Worst Job

The worst job I ever had was as a server at the Westside Inn. First of all, many of the people I waited on were rude. When a baked potato was hard inside or a salad was limp or their steak wasn't just the way they wanted it, they blamed me, rather than the kitchen. Or they would ask me to pick up their cutlery from the floor, or bring them different wineglasses, or even take their children to the bathroom. Also, I had to contend not only with the customers but with the kitchen staff as well. The cooks and bussers were often undependable and surly. If I didn't treat them just right, I would wind up having to apologize to customers because their meals came late or their water glasses weren't filled. Another reason I didn't like the job was that I was always moving. Because of the constant line at the door, as soon as one group left, another would take its place. I usually had only a twenty-minute lunch break and a ten-minute break in almost nine hours of work. I think I could have put up with the job if I had been able to pause and rest more often. The last and most important reason I hated the job was my boss. She played favourites, giving some of the servers the best-tipping repeat customers and preferences on holidays. She would hover around during my break to make sure I didn't take a second more than the allotted time. And even when I helped out by working through a break, she never had an appreciative word but would just tell me not to be late for work the next day.

Fill in the blanks: Paragraph _____ makes its point more clearly and effectively because _____

_____

_____

UNDERSTANDING COHERENCE

Paragraph B is more effective *because the material is organized clearly* and logically. Using emphatic order, the writer gives us a list of four reasons why the job was so bad: rude customers, unreliable kitchen staff, constant motion, and—most of all—an unfair boss. Further, the writer includes transitional words that act as signposts, making movement from one idea to the next easy to follow. The major transitions are *First of all, Also, Another reason,* and *The last and most important reason.*

While paragraph A is unified and supported, the writer does not have any clear and consistent way of organizing the material. Partly, emphatic order is used, but this is not made clear by transitions or by saving the most important reason for last. Partly, a time order is used, but it moves inconsistently from two to seven to five o'clock.

These two paragraphs lead us to the third base of effective writing: *coherence.* The supporting ideas and sentences in a composition must be organized so that they cohere or "stick together." As has already been mentioned, key techniques for tying material together are:

- a clear method of organization (such as time order or emphatic order),
- transitions, and
- other transitional phrases and connecting words.

CHECKING FOR COHERENCE

To check a paper for coherence, ask yourself these questions:

1   Does the paper have a clear method of organization?
2   Are transitions and other connecting words used to tie the material together?

BASE 4: SENTENCE SKILLS

Activity

Two versions of a paragraph are given below. Both are *unified, supported,* and *organized,* but one version communicates more clearly and effectively. Which one, and why?

Paragraph A

Falling Asleep Anywhere

[1]There are times when people are so tired that they fall asleep almost anywhere. [2]For example, there is a lot of sleeping on the bus or subway on the way home from work in the evenings. [3]A man will be reading the newspaper, and seconds later it appears as if he is trying to eat it. [4]Or he will fall asleep on the shoulder of the stranger sitting next to him. [5]Another place where unplanned naps go on is the lecture hall. [6]In some classes, a student will start snoring so loudly that the professor has to ask another student to shake the sleeper awake. [7]A more embarrassing situation occurs when a student leans on one elbow and starts drifting off to sleep. [8]The weight of the head pushes the elbow off the desk, and this momentum carries the rest of the body along. [9]The student wakes up on the floor with no memory of getting there. [10]The worst time to fall asleep is when driving a car. [11]Police reports are full of accidents that occur when people lose consciousness and go off the road. [12]If the drivers are lucky, they are not seriously hurt. [13]One woman's car, for instance, went into the river. [14]She woke up in a metre of water and thought it was raining. [15]When people are really tired, nothing will stop them from falling asleep—no matter where they are.

Paragraph B

Falling Asleep Anywhere

[1]There are times when people are so tired that they fall asleep almost anywhere. [2]For example, on the bus or subway on the way home from work. [3]A man will be reading the newspaper, seconds later it appears as if he is trying to eat it. [4]Or he will fall asleep on the shoulder of the stranger sitting next to him. [5]Another place where unplanned naps go on are in the lecture hall. [6]In some classes, a student will start snoring so loudly that the professor has to ask another student to shake the sleeper awake. [7]A more embarrassing situation occurs when a student leans on one elbow and starting to drift off to sleep. [8]The weight of the head push the elbow off the desk, and this momentum carries the rest of the body along. [9]The student wakes up on the floor with no memory of getting there. [10]The worst time to fall asleep is when driving a car. [11]Police reports are full of accidents that occur when people conk out and go off the road. [12]If the drivers are lucky they are not seriously hurt. [13]One womans car, for instance went into the river. [14]She woke up in a metre of water. [15]And thought it was raining. [16]When people are really tired, nothing will stop them from falling asleep—no matter where they are.

Fill in the blanks: Paragraph _____ makes its point more clearly and effectively because _____

_____

_____

UNDERSTANDING SENTENCE SKILLS

Paragraph A is more effective because it incorporates *sentence skills,* the fourth base of competent writing. See if you can identify the ten sentence-skills mistakes in paragraph B. Do this, first of all, by going back and underlining the ten spots in paragraph B that differ in wording or punctuation from paragraph A. Then try to identify the ten sentence-skills mistakes by circling what you think is the correct answer in each of the ten statements below.

Note: Comparing paragraph B with the correct version may help you guess correct answers even if you are not familiar with the names of certain skills.

Sentences have been designated "word groups," because some of the paragraph's "sentences" do not fulfill the grammatical requires for a sentence. Answers are on page 108.

1. In word group 2, there is a
   a. missing comma
   b. missing apostrophe
   c. fragment
   d. dangling modifier
2. In word group 3, there is a
   a. run-on
   b. fragment
   c. mistake in subject-verb agreement
   d. mistake involving an irregular verb
3. In word group 5, there is a
   a. fragment
   b. spelling error
   c. run-on
   d. mistake in subject-verb agreement
4. In word group 7, there is a
   a. misplaced modifier
   b. dangling modifier
   c. mistake in parallelism
   d. run-on
5. In word group 8, there is a
   a. nonstandard English verb
   b. run-on
   c. comma mistake
   d. missing capital letter
6. In word group 11, there is a
   a. mistake involving an irregular verb
   b. fragment
   c. slang phrase
   d. mistake in subject-verb agreement
7. In word group 12, there is a
   a. missing apostrophe
   b. missing comma
   c. mistake involving an irregular verb
   d. fragment
8. In word group 13, there is a
   a. mistake in parallelism
   b. mistake involving an irregular verb
   c. missing apostrophe
   d. missing capital letter
9. In word group 13, there is a
   a. missing comma around an interrupter
   b. dangling modifier
   c. run-on
   d. cliché
10. In word group 15, there is a
    a. missing quotation mark
    b. mistake involving an irregular verb
    c. fragment
    d. mistake in pronoun point of view

Part Four of this book explains these and other sentence skills. You should review all the skills carefully. Doing so will ensure that you know the most important rules of grammar, punctuation, and usage—rules needed to write clear, error-free sentences.

CHECKING FOR SENTENCE SKILLS

Sentence skills are summarized in the following chart and on the inside front cover of the book.

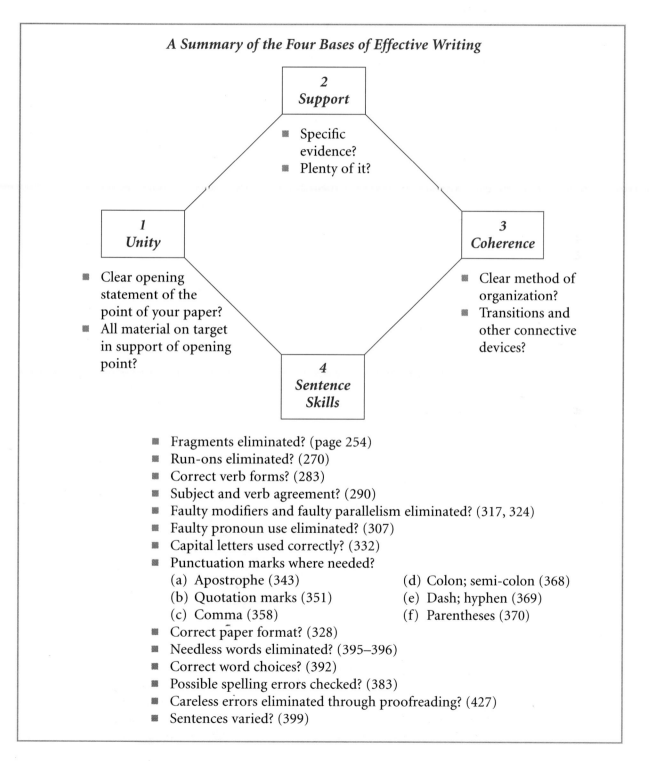

A Summary of the Four Bases of Effective Writing

2
Support

- Specific evidence?
- Plenty of it?

1
Unity

- Clear opening statement of the point of your paper?
- All material on target in support of opening point?

3
Coherence

- Clear method of organization?
- Transitions and other connective devices?

4
Sentence Skills

- Fragments eliminated? (page 254)
- Run-ons eliminated? (270)
- Correct verb forms? (283)
- Subject and verb agreement? (290)
- Faulty modifiers and faulty parallelism eliminated? (317, 324)
- Faulty pronoun use eliminated? (307)
- Capital letters used correctly? (332)
- Punctuation marks where needed?
  - (a) Apostrophe (343)
  - (b) Quotation marks (351)
  - (c) Comma (358)
  - (d) Colon; semi-colon (368)
  - (e) Dash; hyphen (369)
  - (f) Parentheses (370)
- Correct paper format? (328)
- Needless words eliminated? (395–396)
- Correct word choices? (392)
- Possible spelling errors checked? (383)
- Careless errors eliminated through proofreading? (427)
- Sentences varied? (399)

You should have chosen the following answers for the questions on page 106:

1. c	3. d	5. a	7. b	9. a
2. a	4. c	6. c	8. c	10. c

PRACTICE IN USING THE FOUR BASES

You are now familiar with four bases, standards, and goals of effective writing: unity, support, coherence, and sentence skills. In this closing section, you will expand and strengthen your understanding of the four bases as you work through the following activities:

1 Evaluating Outlines for Unity
2 Evaluating Paragraphs for Unity
3 Evaluating Paragraphs for Support
4 Evaluating Paragraphs for Coherence
5 Revising Paragraphs for Coherence
6 Evaluating Paragraphs for All Four Bases: Unity, Support, Coherence, and Sentence Skills

1 EVALUATING OUTLINES FOR UNITY

The best time to check a paper for unity is when it is in outline form. An outline, as explained on pages 23–25, is one of the best techniques for getting started with a paper.

Look at the rough beginning of an outline that one student prepared and then corrected for unity:

I had a depressing weekend.

1. Hay fever bothered me

2. Had to pay seventy-seven-dollar car bill

3. ~~Felt bad~~

4. Boyfriend and I had a fight

5. ~~Did poorly in my math test today as a result~~

6. My mother yelled at me unfairly

Four reasons support the opening statement that the writer was depressed over the weekend. The writer crossed out "Felt bad" because it was not a reason for her depression. Saying that she felt bad is only another way of saying that she was depressed. She also crossed out the item about the day's math test because the point she is supporting is that she was depressed over the weekend.

Activity

In each outline, cross out items that do not support the opening point. These items must be omitted in order to achieve paragraph unity.

1. The cost of raising a child keeps increasing.
   a. Education taxes get higher every year.
   b. A pair of children's running shoes now costs over $100.
   c. Overpopulation is a worldwide problem.
   d. Providing nutritious food is more costly because of inflated prices.
   e. Children should work at age sixteen.

2. My father's compulsive gambling hurt our family life.
   a. We were always short of money for bills.
   b. Luckily, my father didn't drink.
   c. My father ignored his children to spend time at the racetrack.
   d. Gamblers' Anonymous can help compulsive gamblers.
   e. My mother and father argued constantly.

3. There are several ways to get better mileage in your car.
   a. Check air pressure in tires regularly.
   b. Drive at no more than ninety kilometres per hour.
   c. Orange and yellow cars are the most visible.
   d. Avoid jackrabbit starts at stop signs and traffic lights.
   e. Always have duplicate ignition and trunk keys.

2 EVALUATING PARAGRAPHS FOR UNITY

Activity

Each of the following four paragraphs contains *sentences that are off target*—sentences that do not support the opening point—and so the paragraphs are *not unified*. In the interest of paragraph unity, such sentences must be omitted.

Cross out the irrelevant sentences and write the numbers of those sentences in the spaces provided. The number of spaces will tell you the number of irrelevant sentences in each paragraph.

1.
A Kindergarten Failure

[1]In kindergarten I experienced the fear of failure that haunts many schoolchildren. [2]My moment of panic occurred on my last day in kindergarten at Laurier Public School in Dauphin, Manitoba. [3]My family lived in Manitoba for three years before we moved to Toronto, where my father was a Human Resources manager for The Co-operators Insurance Company. [4]Our teacher began reading a list of names of all those students who were to line up at the door in order to visit the grade one classroom. [5]Our teacher was a pleasant-faced woman who had resumed her career after raising her own children. [6]She called every name but mine, and I was left sitting alone in the class while everyone left, the teacher included. [7]I sat there in absolute horror. [8]I imagined

that I was the first kid in human history who had flunked things like crayons, sandbox, and sliding board. [9]Without getting the teacher's permission, I got up and walked to the bathroom and threw up into a sink. [10]Only when I ran home in tears to my mother did I get an explanation of what had happened. [11]Since I was to go to a separate school in the fall, I had not been taken with the other children to meet the grade one teacher at the public school. [12]My moment of terror and shame had been only a misunderstanding.

The numbers of the irrelevant sentences: _____   _____

2.
How to Prevent Cheating

[1]Instructors should take steps to prevent students from cheating on exams. [2]To begin with, instructors should stop reusing old tests. [3]A test that has been used even once is soon known via the student grapevine. [4]Students will check with their friends to find out, for example, what was on Dr. Thompson's marketing final last term. [5]They may even manage to find a copy of the test itself, "accidentally" not turned in by a former student of Dr. Thompson's. [6]Instructors should also take some commonsense precautions at test time. [7]They should make students separate themselves, by at least one seat, during an exam, and they should watch the class closely. [8]The best place for the instructor to sit is in the rear of the room, so that a student is never sure if the instructor is looking at him or her. [9]Last of all, instructors must make it clear to students that there will be stiff penalties for cheating. [10]One of the problems with our educational systems is a lack of discipline. [11]Instructors never used to give in to students' demands or put up with bad behaviour, as they do today. [12]Anyone caught cheating should immediately receive a zero for the exam. [13]A person even suspected of cheating should be forced to take an alternative exam in the instructor's office. [14]Because cheating is unfair to honest students, it should not be tolerated.

The numbers of the irrelevant sentences: _____   _____

3.
Other Uses for Cars

[1]Many people who own a car manage to turn the vehicle into a garbage can, a clothes closet, or a storage room. [2]People who use their cars as garbage cans are easily recognized. [3]Empty snack bags, hamburger wrappers, pizza cartons, pop cans, and doughnut boxes litter the floor. [4]On the seats are old CDs, blackened fruit skins, crumpled receipts, crushed candy boxes, and used tissues. [5]At least the garbage stays in the car, instead of adding to the litter on our highways. [6]Other people use a car as a clothes closet. [7]The car contains several pairs of shoes, pants, or shorts, along with a suit or dress that's been hanging on the car's clothes hanger for over a year. [8]Sweaty, smelly gym clothes will also find a place in the car, a fact passengers quickly discover. [9]The world would be better off if people showed more consideration of others. [10]Finally, some people use a car as a spare garage or basement. [11]In the back

seats or trunks of these cars are bags of fertilizer, beach chairs, old textbooks, chainsaws, or window screens that have been there for months. [12]The trunk may also contain an extra spare tire, a dented hub cap, a four-litre container of window washer fluid, and old stereo equipment. [13]If apartments offered more storage space, probably fewer people would resort to using their cars for such storage purposes. [14]All in all, people get a lot more use out of their cars than simply the kilometres they travel on the road.

The numbers of the irrelevant sentences: _____ _____ _____

4.   **Why Adults Visit Amusement Parks**

[1]Adults visit amusement parks for several reasons. [2]For one thing, an amusement park is a place where it is acceptable to "pig out" on junk food. [3]At the park, everyone is drinking pop and eating chips, ice cream, or hot dogs. [4]No one seems to be on a diet, so buying huge amounts of junk food is a guilt-free experience. [5]Parks should provide stands where healthier food, such as salads or cold chicken, would be sold. [6]Another reason people visit amusement parks is to prove themselves. [7]They want to visit the park that has the newest, scariest ride in order to say that they went on the Parachute Drop, the seven-storey Elevator, the Water Chute, or the Death Slide. [8]Going on a scary ride is a way to feel courageous and adventurous without taking much of a risk. [9]Some rides, however, can be dangerous. [10]Rides that are not properly inspected or maintained have killed people all over the country. [11]A final reason people visit amusement parks is to escape from everyday pressures. [12]When people are poised at the top of a gigantic roller coaster, they are not thinking of bills, work, or personal problems. [13]A scary ride empties the mind of all worries—except making it to the bottom alive. [14]Adults at an amusement park may claim they have come for their children, but they are there for themselves as well.

The numbers of the irrelevant sentences: _____ _____ _____

3 EVALUATING PARAGRAPHS FOR SUPPORT

Activity

The five paragraphs that follow lack sufficient supporting details. In each paragraph, identify the spot or spots where more specific details are needed.

1.   **Chicken: Our Best Friend**

[1]Chicken is the best-selling meat today for a number of good reasons. [2]First of all, its reasonable cost puts it within everyone's reach. [3]Chicken is popular, too, because it can be prepared in so many different ways. [4]It can, for example, be cooked by itself, in spaghetti sauce, or with noodles and gravy. [5]It can be baked, boiled, broiled, or fried. [6]Chicken is also convenient. [7]Last and

most important, chicken has a high nutritional value. [8]Two hundred and fifty grams of chicken contain twenty-eight grams of protein, which is almost half the recommended daily dietary allowance.

Fill in the blanks: The first spot where supporting details are needed occurs after sentence number _____. The second spot occurs after sentence number _____.

2.

A Car Accident

[1]I was on my way home from work when my terrible car accident took place. [2]As I drove my car around the curve of the expressway exit, I saw a number of cars ahead of me, backed up because of a red light at the main road. [3]I slowly came to a stop behind a dozen or more cars. [4]In my rear-view mirror, I then noticed a car coming up behind me that did not slow down or stop. [5]I had a horrible, helpless feeling as I realized the car would hit me. [6]I knew there was nothing I could do to signal the driver in time, nor was there any way I could get away from the car. [7]Minutes after the collision, I picked up my glasses which were on the seat beside me. [8]My lip was bleeding, and I got out a tissue to wipe it. [9]The police arrived quickly, along with an ambulance for the driver of the car that hit me. [10]My car was so damaged that it had to be towed away. [11]Today, eight years after the accident, I still relive the details of the experience whenever a car gets too close behind me.

Fill in the blank: The point where details are clearly needed occurs after sentence number _____.

3.

Tips on Bringing Up Children

[1]In some ways, children should be treated as mature people. [2]For one thing, adults should not use baby talk with children. [3]Using real words with children helps them develop language skills more quickly. [4]Baby talk makes children feel patronized, frustrated, and confused, for they want to understand and communicate with adults by learning their speech. [5]So animals should be called cows and dogs, not "moo-moos" and "bow-wows." [6]Second, parents should be consistent when disciplining children. [7]For example, if a parent tells a child, "You cannot have dessert unless you put away your toys," it is important that the parent follow through on the warning. [8]By being consistent, parents will teach children responsibility and give them a stable centre around which to grow. [9]Finally, and most important, children should be allowed and encouraged to make simple decisions. [10]Parents will thus be helping their children prepare for the complex decisions that they will have to deal with in later life.

Fill in the blank: The spot where supporting details are needed occurs after sentence number _____.

4.

Culture Conflict

[1]I am in a constant tug-of-war with my parents over conflicts between their Vietnamese culture and Canadian society. [2]To begin with, my parents do not like me to have so many friends from Canada. [3]They think that I should spend all my time with other Vietnamese people and speak English only when necessary. [4]I get into an argument whenever I want to go to a fast-food restaurant or a movie at night with my friends from school. [5]The conflict with my parents is even worse when it comes to plans for a career. [6]My parents want me to get a degree in science and then go on to medical school. [7]On the other hand, I think I want to become a teacher. [8]So far I have been taking science courses, but soon I will have to apply for Carleton's education program. [9]The other night my father made his attitude about what I should do very clear. [10]The most difficult aspect of our cultural differences is the way our family is structured. [11]My father is the centre of our family, and he expects that I will always listen to him. [12]Although I am twenty-one years old, I still have a nightly curfew at an hour which I consider insulting. [13]Also, I am expected to help my mother perform certain household chores that I've really come to hate. [14]My father expects me to live at home until I am married to a Vietnamese man. [15]When that happens, he assumes I will obey my husband just as I obey him. [16]I do not want to be a bad daughter, but I want to live like my Canadian female friends.

Fill in the blanks: The first spot where a supporting detail or details are needed occurs after sentence number _____. The second spot occurs after sentence number _____. The third spot occurs after sentence number _____.

4   EVALUATING PARAGRAPHS FOR COHERENCE

Activity

Answer the questions about coherence that follow each of the two paragraphs below.

1.

Living Just Enough for the City

[1]There are so many good reasons to live in the city that it is hard to know why suburbs even exist. [2]Most important, there is no reason ever to sit inside, become a TV-bound vegetable, trapped in a maze of courts, crescents, and curving streets going nowhere. [3]Any day or evening, the city and its attractions are only a walk or subway ride away. [4]There is no need to rely on a car and add to the general pollution by driving to a movie, a concert, a museum, or an interesting stretch of stores or clubs. [5]Anything new listed in the paper, or discussed in class, is easily accessible to the city dweller and never involves a carefully planned or lengthy expedition "downtown." [6]Walking the streets is one secret pleasure of city folks; they can walk everywhere. [7]And city streets

are fascinating and full of life. [8]These streets may not be as well manicured or as spacious as suburban residential areas, but they are "people-sized," and meant for walking and looking. [9]Each store window has its stories to tell, and every old house is unique. [10]There are no vast empty parking lots or stretches of closed business strip malls; every block is cluttered with people, dogs, storefronts, and sidewalk displays. [11]Every metre of city streets grabs the attention; the walker's eye is never starved for something interesting. [12]Walking only a block or so to shop every day at small stores where the owners say hello makes shopping a pleasure, not a chore. [13]The fruits and vegetables are fresh and not sealed under plastic so cleverly that the bruises don't show. [14]And the friendly human contact makes the city person's shopping a social activity as much as a consumer activity. [15]Somehow, living in the city makes it easier to be alert, alive, and human.

a. The paragraph should use emphatic order. Write *1* before the reason that seems slightly less important than the other two, *2* before the second-most-important reason, and *3* before the most important reason.

_____ Closeness to attractions

_____ Ability to shop near home

_____ The pleasures of walking

b. Before which of the three reasons could the transitional words *First of all* be added? _____

c. Before which of the three reasons could the transition *In addition* be added? _____

d. What words show emphasis in sentence 2? _____

e. How many times are the keywords *city, city folks,* and *city dwellers* repeated in the paragraph? _____

2.   **Apartment Hunting**

[1]Apartment hunting is a several-step process. [2]Visit and carefully inspect the most promising apartments. [3]Check each place for signs of unwanted guests such as roaches or mice. [4]Make sure that light switches and appliances work and that there are enough electrical outlets. [5]Turn faucets and flush the toilet to be sure that the plumbing works smoothly. [6]Talk to the building manager for a bit to get a sense of him or her as a person. [7]If a problem develops after you move in, you want to know that a capable person will be there to handle the matter. [8]Find out what stores and services that match your interests are available in the neighbourhood. [9]Your local newspaper and real estate offices can provide you with a list of apartments for rent. [10]Family and friends may be able to give you leads. [11]And your college may have a housing office that keeps a list of apartments for rent. [12]Decide just what you need. [13]If you can afford no more than six hundred dollars a month, you need to

find a place that will cost no more than that. ¹⁴If you want a location that's close to work or school, you must take that factor into account. ¹⁵If you plan to cook, you want a place with a workable kitchen. ¹⁶By taking these steps, you should be ready to select the apartment that is best for you.

a. The paragraph should use time order. Write *1* before the step that should come first, *2* before the intermediate step, and *3* before the final step.

_____ Visit and carefully inspect the most promising apartments.

_____ Decide just what you need.

_____ Find out what's available that matches your interests.

b. Before which of the three steps could the transitional words *The first step is to* be added? _____

c. Before which step could the transitional words *After you have decided what you are looking for, the next step is to* be added? _____

d. Before which step could the transitional words *The final step* be added?

_____

e. To whom does the pronoun *him or her* in sentence 6 refer? _____

f. What is a synonym for *building manager* in sentence 7? _____

g. What is a synonym for *apartment* in sentence 13? _____

5 REVISING PARAGRAPHS FOR COHERENCE

The two paragraphs in this section begin with a clear point, but in each case the supporting material that follows the point is not coherent. Read each paragraph and the comments that follow it on how to organize and connect the supporting material. Then do the activity for the paragraph.

Paragraph 1

A Difficult Period

Since I arrived on the West Coast in midsummer, I have had the most difficult period of my life. I had to look for an apartment. I found only one place that I could afford, but the owner said I could not move in until it was painted. When I first arrived in Vancouver, my thoughts were to stay with my father and stepmother. I had to set out looking for a job so that I could afford my own place, for I soon realized that my stepmother was not at all happy having me live with them. A three-week search led to a job shampooing rugs for a house-cleaning company. I painted the apartment myself, and at least that problem was solved. I was in a hurry to get settled because I was starting school at Simon Fraser in September. A transportation problem developed because my stepmother insisted that I return my father's bike, which I was using at first to get to school. I had to rely on a bus that often arrived late, with the result that I missed some classes and was late for others. I had already had a problem with registration in early September. My counsellor had made a mistake with my classes, and I had to register all over again. This meant that I was one week late for class. Now I'm riding to school with a classmate and no longer have to depend on the bus. My life is starting to order itself, but I must admit that at first I thought it was hopeless to stay here.

Comments The writer of this paragraph has provided a good deal of specific evidence to support the opening point. The evidence, however, needs to be organized. Before starting the paragraph, the writer should have decided to arrange the details by using time order. He or she could then have listed in an outline the exact sequence of events that made for such a difficult period.

Activity 1

Here is a list of the various events described by the writer of paragraph 1. Number the events in the correct time sequence by writing *1* in front of the first event that occurred, *2* in front of the second event, and so on.

Since I arrived on the West Coast in midsummer, I have had the most difficult period of my life.

_____ I had to search for an apartment I could afford.

_____ I had to find a job so that I could afford my own place.

_____ My stepmother objected to my living with her and my father.

_____ I had to paint the apartment before I could move in.

_____ I had to find an alternative to unreliable bus transportation.

_____ I had to reregister for my courses because of a counsellor's mistake.

Your instructor may now have you rewrite the paragraph on a separate sheet of paper. If so, be sure to use time signals such as *first, next, then, during, when, after,* and *now* to help guide your reader from one event to the next.

Paragraph 2

Sometimes Dreams Pay Off

When I was in elementary school, there was one boy my friends and I called "David the Dreamer," and we thought there were lots of good reasons for that nickname. Most of the time in class, David looked half asleep. In fact, he had long floppy bangs and rather droopy eyelids that seemed to cover his light blue eyes, and we usually knew he was drifting away at his desk, because teachers would startle him from his snoozy posture each time they called his name during classes. Every year, we heard some teacher ask, "David, are you awake, or does none of this interest you?" Instead of looking sheepish or guilty, David always smiled, dreamily. He never showed any concern, he just went back to whatever he was thinking about as he slumped with his head on his elbows. We knew from talking to him in the schoolyard that he loved comic books. He had a huge collection, and knew every character, every plot, and all the artists who drew the characters. Those comics characters seemed more real to him than we were, so we decided that *they* were what he was dreaming about in class. At recess, he loved to make up stories of his own about the characters, and to give them whole new adventures; some of his plots were better than the originals. When he was spinning his "X-Men" stories, he did not look sleepy at all, and his blue eyes were wide open and fixed on his listeners. Even in gym class, he leaned sleepily against a tree or the gym wall, unfazed by the loud insults of the gym teacher, who called him "Mr. Relaxation" and never chose him for a single team, probably out of frustration that he could not seem to upset the dreamer. David had his own world that he was happy enough to share, but he just never worried much about anyone else's world; he was too busy dreaming. A year ago, I was reading the "Arts" section of the newspaper, and I realized how busy David had been during all that dreaming. There was a picture of David, floppy bangs, sleepy blue eyes and all, winning an award at the Toronto Film Festival for "Best Independent Film of 1998." Apparently, he made the winning team, after all.

Comments on Paragraph 2: The writer of this paragraph provides a number of specifics that support the opening point. However, the supporting material has not been organized clearly. Before writing this paragraph, the author should have (1) decided to arrange the supporting evidence by using emphatic order and (2) listed in an outline the reasons why David's dreaminess was so intriguing and all-consuming, and the supporting details for each reason. The writer could also have determined which reason to use in the emphatic final position of the paper.

Activity 2

Create a clear outline for paragraph 2 by filling in the scheme below. The outline is partially completed.

When I was in elementary school, there was one boy my friends and I called "David the Dreamer," and we thought...

REASON/SUBTOPIC 1. *David's appearance* _____

DETAILS a. _____

b. _____

REASON/SUBTOPIC 2. _____

DETAILS a. _____

b. *Dozing at desk* _____

c. _____

d. _____

REASON/SUBTOPIC   3.   *His fascination with comic books* _____

DETAILS   a. _____

                      b. _____

                      c. _____

Your instructor may have you rewrite the paragraph on a separate sheet of paper. If so, be sure to introduce each of the four reasons with transitions such as *First, Second, Another reason*, and *Finally*. You may also want to use repeated words, pronouns, and synonyms to help tie your sentences together.

6 EVALUATING PARAGRAPHS FOR ALL FOUR BASES: UNITY, SUPPORT, COHERENCE, AND SENTENCE SKILLS

Activity

In this activity, you will evaluate paragraphs in terms of all four bases: *unity, support, coherence*, and *sentence skills*. Evaluative comments follow each paragraph below. Circle the letter of the statement that best applies in each case.

1.
Drunk Drivers

    People caught driving while drunk, even first offenders, should be jailed. Drunk driving, first of all, is more dangerous than carrying a loaded gun. In addition, a jail term would show drivers that society will no longer tolerate such careless and dangerous behaviour. Finally, severe penalties might encourage solutions to the problem of drinking and driving. People who go out for a good time and intend to have several drinks should follow media advice and always designate one person, who would stay completely sober, as the driver.

    a. The paragraph is not unified.
    b. The paragraph is not adequately supported.
    c. The paragraph is not well organized.
    d. The paragraph does not show a command of sentence skills.
    e. The paragraph is well written in terms of the four bases.

2.
A Frustrating Moment

    A frustrating moment happened to me several days ago. When I was shopping. I had picked up a tube of toothpaste and a jar of skin cream. After the cashier rang up the purchases, which came to $4.15. I handed her $10. Then got back my change, which was only $0.85. I told the cashier that she had made a mistake. Giving me change for $5 instead of $10. But she insist that I had only gave her $5, I became very upset and insist that she return the rest of my change. She refused to do so instead she asked me to step aside so she could wait on the next customer. I stood very rigid, trying not to lose my temper. I simply said to her, I'm not going to leave here without my change for $10. Giving in at this point a bell was rung and the manager was summoned. After the situation was explain to him, he ask the cashier to ring off her register to check for the change. After doing so, the cashier was $5 over her sale receipts. Only then did the manager return my change and apologize for the cashier mistake.

a. The paragraph is not unified.
b. The paragraph is not adequately supported.
c. The paragraph is not well organized.
d. The paragraph does not show a command of sentence skills.
e. The paragraph is well written in terms of the four bases.

3.

Asking Men Out

There are several reasons I have trouble asking guys to go out with me. I have asked some of the fellows in my classes and have been turned down. This is one reason that I can't talk to them. At one time I was very shy and quiet, and people sometimes didn't even know I was present. I can talk to boys and men now as friends, but as soon as I want to ask them out, I usually start to become quiet, and a little bit of shyness comes out. When I get up I the nerve finally, the guy sometimes turns me down, and I swear that I will never ask another one out again. I feel sure I will get a refusal, and I have no self-confidence. Also, my friends mock me, though they aren't any better than I am. It can become discouraging when girlfriends are not there for you. Sometimes I just stand there and wait to hear what line the fellow will use. The one they use a lot is "I like you as a friend, Terri, but it's better that things stay that way." Sometimes I want to have the line on tape, so they won't have to waste their breath on me. All my past experiences with boys and men have been just as bad. One guy used me to make his old girlfriend jealous. Then when he succeeded, he started going out with her again. I had a bad experience when I asked a man I knew to the end-of-semester dance. I spent a lot of money on the evening. Two days later, he told me that he was going steady with another girl. I feel that when I meet someone male, I have to be sure I can trust him. I don't want him to turn on me.

a. The paragraph is not unified.
b. The paragraph is not adequately supported.
c. The paragraph is not well organized.
d. The paragraph does not show a command of sentence skills.
e. The paragraph is well written in terms of the four bases.

4.

A Change in My Writing

A technique in my present English class has corrected a writing problem that I've always had. In past English courses, I had major problems with commas in the wrong places, bad spelling, capitalizing the wrong words, sentence fragments, and run-on sentences. I never had any big problems with unity, support, or coherence, but the sentence skills were another matter. They were like little bugs that always appeared to infest my writing. My present instructor asked me to rewrite papers, just concentrating on sentence skills. I thought that the instructor was crazy because I didn't feel that rewriting would do any good. I soon became certain that my instructor was out of his mind, for he made me rewrite my first paper four times. It was very frustrating, for I became tired of doing the same paper over and over. I wanted to curse at my instructor when I'd show him each new draft and he'd find skills mistakes and say "Rewrite." Finally, my papers began to improve and the sentence skills began to fall into place. I was able to see them and correct them before turning in a paper, whereas I couldn't before. Why or how this happened I don't know, but I think that rewriting helped a lot. It took me most of the semester, but I stuck it out and the work paid off.

a. The paragraph is not unified.
b. The paragraph is not adequately supported.
c. The paragraph is not well organized.
d. The paragraph does not show a command of sentence skills.
e. The paragraph is well written in terms of the four bases.

REVIEWING THE LEARNING OUTCOMES FOR CHAPTER 5

1 What is involved in revising a paper to meet the standard of *unity?*

2 What are the functions of *specific details?*

3 What activities are involved in creating a paper that is *coherent?* How do these two writing and revising activities lead to this standard or goal?

4 At which stage is evaluating and correcting a paper's *sentence skills* appropriate and why?

5 Why are *evaluating activities* needed at so many stages of the writing process?

Suggestions on What to Do Next

1 Read "Providing Examples" (page 147) or "Narrating an Event" (page 129) in Part Two and do the writing assignments. Then go on to the other types of paragraph development in Part Two.

2 When you have mastered the different types of paragraph development, you may want to work through "Writing the Essay" in Part Three and do one or more of the writing assignments.

3 Continue your review of sentence skills in Part Four.

Paragraph
Development

PREVIEW

Part Two introduces you to paragraph development and gives you practice in the following common types of paragraph development:

Narrating an Event
Describing a Scene or Person
Providing Examples
Explaining a Process
Examining Cause and Effect
Comparing or Contrasting
Defining a Term
Dividing and Classifying
Arguing a Position

After a brief explanation of each type of paragraph development, student paragraphs illustrating each type are presented, followed by questions about those paragraphs. The questions relate to the standards of effective writing described in Part One. You are then asked to write your own paragraph. In each case, writing assignments progress from personal-experience topics to more formal and objective topics, with the last assignment in each section requiring some simple research. At times, points or topic sentences for development are suggested, so that you can concentrate on (1) making sure your evidence is on target in support of your opening idea, (2) providing plenty of specific supporting details to back up your point, and (3) organizing your supporting material clearly. The last chapter in Part Two provides some additional assignments.

Introduction to Paragraph Development

aining a process • Examining Cause and Effect • Comparing or Contrasting • Defining
• Dividing and classifying • Describing a scene or person • Narrating an Event • Argu
ition • Explaining a process • Examining Cause and Effect • comparing or contrastin
ung a Term Dividing and classifying • Describing a scene or person • Narrating an Ev
uing a position • Explaining a process • Examining Cause and Effect • comparing

LEARNING OUTCOMES

After reading this chapter,

- **you will know how to work through the progression of each chapter of Part Two; and**
- **you will be prepared to use two tools for revision of your writing: peer review and a personal checklist.**

NINE PATTERNS OF PARAGRAPH DEVELOPMENT

Traditionally, writing has been divided into the following patterns of development:

- Narration
- Description
- Exposition

Examples	Comparison or contrast
Process	Definition
Cause and effect	Division and classification

- Argumentation or persuasion

Individual chapters within Part Two are devoted to each of the methods for developing and patterning ideas listed above.

- **Narration** and **description** are basic modes of expression and are present, to some degree, in all methods of development.

  Narration is the shaping or storytelling voice of writing. Much writing relies on narrative to support other methods of development, but when narration is dominant, the reader mainly follows the "narrative line" or writer's voice through a series of events.

Description is the sharp pencil or paintbrush of writing. All writing contains various sorts of description to lend specificity, vividness, and clarity. Describing in words is the attempt to translate the mind's images of people, places, and things into word-pictures, and when description predominates in a piece of writing, it is these word-pictures that make the writer's point.

- **Exposition** includes a group of methods of development which *explain*. In any method of *exposition,* the writer provides information about and seeks to clarify a particular subject. *Exposition* or explaining may be achieved by (1) giving examples, (2) detailing the process of doing or making something, (3) analyzing causes or effects, (4) comparing or contrasting, (5) defining a term or concept, and (6) dividing something into parts or grouping it into categories. Each of the six patterns of exposition is presented in a separate chapter.
- **Argumentation** is an attempt to prove a point or defend an opinion. *Argumentation* is writing with a single goal; it generally makes use of a variety of methods of exposition and specific techniques to reach its goal most effectively. Since writing tasks in this text are aimed at making a clear point, most paragraph and essay writing will contain some elements of argumentation or persuasion.

You will have a chance, then, to learn how nine different patterns can help organize material in your papers. Each of the nine patterns has its own internal logic and provides its own special strategies for imposing order on ideas.

As you practise each pattern, you should keep the following two points in mind:

- In each paragraph that you write, one pattern will predominate, but very often one or more additional patterns may also be involved. For instance, "Net Eats Student's Time!"—a paragraph you have already read (page 5)—presents a series of causes leading to an effect: that the writer feels using the college's Net server wastes her time. But the writer also presents examples to explain each of the causes (the server's two-hour downtime left her too anxious to concentrate, college e-mail was irrelevant and time-consuming to read, student chain letters clogged the mail and slowed down service.) There is also an element of narration, as the writer presents examples that occur from the beginning to the end of an evening meant for homework.
- More important, a paragraph you write in almost any pattern will probably involve some form of argumentation. You will advance a point and then go on to support your point. To convince the reader that your thesis is valid, you may use a series of examples, or narration, or description, or some other pattern of organization. Among the paragraphs you will read in Part Two, one writer supports the point that a certain pet shop is depressing by providing a number of descriptive details. Another writer labels a certain experience in his life a "moment of losing faith" and then uses a narrative to demonstrate the truth of his statement. A third writer advances the opinion that good horror movies can be easily distinguished from bad horror movies and then supplies comparative information about both to support her claim. Much of your writing, in short, will have the purpose of persuading your reader that the idea you have advanced is valid.

WRITER, PURPOSE, AND AUDIENCE

As was noted in "Important Factors in Writing" in Part One, the purpose of most writing is to inform, persuade, or entertain; in this book, most of your writing will involve some form of persuasion or information. The audience for your writing is primarily your instructors and sometimes other students, who are really a symbol for any general audience of educated adults. Sometimes, however, you must write for more specific audiences; therefore, it is important to develop the skills of choosing appropriate words, and adopting an appropriate tone of writing voice, for a particular purpose and particular readers.

This part of the book, then, includes assignments at or near the ends of chapters that ask you to write with a very specific purpose in mind and for a very specific audience. You will be asked, for example, to imagine yourself as a TV critic addressing parents at a school, as someone advising your MPP about possible effects of privatising healthcare in Canada, as an aide at a daycare centre preparing instructions for children, as an apartment tenant complaining to a building owner about neighbours, or as a client of a video introduction service introducing himself or herself to potential acquaintances. Through these and other assignments, you will learn how to adjust your style and tone of voice to a given writing situation.

TOOLS FOR PARAGRAPH DEVELOPMENT

USING PART TWO: THE PROGRESSION IN EACH CHAPTER

Each type of development method is explained; then student papers illustrating that type are presented, followed by questions about the papers. The questions relate to *unity, support,* and *coherence*—principles of effective writing explained earlier in the book. You are then asked to write your own paragraph. In most cases, the first assignment is fairly structured and provides a good deal of guidance for the writing process. The other assignments offer a wide choice of writing topics. The fourth assignment requires writing with a specific purpose and for a specific audience, and the fifth assignment relates to one of the reading selections in Part Five.

USING PEER REVIEW

In addition to having your instructor as an audience for your writing, you will benefit by having another student in your class as an audience. On the day a paper is due, or on a day when you are writing papers in class, your instructor may ask you to pair up with another student. That student will read your paper, and you will read his or her paper.

Ideally, try to read the other paper aloud while your partner listens. If that is not practical, read the assignment in a whisper while he or she looks on. As you read, both you and your partner should look and listen for spots where the paper does not flow smoothly and clearly. Check or circle the trouble spots where your reading hesitates.

Your partner should then read your paper, marking possible trouble spots while doing so. Then each of you should do three things: (1) identify yourself, (2) make an X-Ray outline, and (3) make comments.

1 Identification

On a separate sheet of paper, write at the top the title and author of the paper you have read. Underneath that, put your name as the reader of the paper.

2 X-Ray Outline

"X-ray" the paper for its inner logic by making up an outline. The outline need be no more than twenty words or so, but it should show clearly the logical foundation on which the paper is built. It should identify and summarize the overall point of the paper and the three areas of support for the main point.

Your outline can look as follows.

Point: _____

Support:

(1) _____

(2) _____

(3) _____

For example, here is an outline of the paper on a new puppy in the house on page 165:

Point: A new puppy can have drastic effects on a house.

Support:

(1) Keeps family awake at night

(2) Destroys possessions

(3) Causes arguments

3 Comments

Under the outline, write the heading "Comments." Here is what you should comment on:

- First, make note of something you really liked about the paper, such as good use of transitions or an especially realistic or vivid specific detail.
- Look at the spots where your reading of the paper hesitated: Are words missing or misspelled? Is there a lack of parallel structure? (See pages 324–327.) Are there mistakes with punctuation? Is the meaning of a sentence confused? Try to figure out what the problems are and suggest ways of fixing them.
- Are there spots in the paper where you see problems with *unity, support,* or *organization?* If so, offer comments. For example, you might say, "More

details are needed in the first supporting paragraph," or "Some of the details in the last supporting paragraph don't really back up your point."

After you have completed your evaluation of the paper, give it to your partner. Ideally you will make revisions to your paper in light of this feedback. Remember to weigh your peer marker's comments against your own views. Whether or not you have time to rewrite, be sure to hand in the peer evaluation form with your paper.

USING A PERSONAL CHECKLIST

After you have completed your next-to-final draft of a paper, there are three ways you should check it yourself. You should *always* do the first two checks, which take only a couple of minutes. Ideally, you should take the time to do the detailed final check as well.

1 Read the paper *out loud.* If it does not sound right—that is, if it does not read smoothly and clearly—then make the changes needed to ensure that it does.

2 Make sure you can answer clearly and concisely two basic questions: "What is the point of my paragraph or essay? What are the three distinct bits of support for my point?"

3 Last, evaluate your paper in terms of the detailed checklist given on the next page. The checklist is also reproduced on the inside front cover of this book.

REVIEWING THE LEARNING OUTCOMES FOR PARAGRAPH DEVELOPMENT

1 What are the main functions of narration and description?

2 What is the main function of exposition, and what are the major forms of exposition?

3 Why is argumentation nearly always an element of most papers?

4 What considerations must be taken into account in writing for a specific purpose and audience, and why?

5 What must you do to prepare for peer review of your paper?

Checklist of the Four Bases in Effective Writing

Use the questions below as a guide in both writing and evaluating a paper. Numbers in parentheses refer to the pages that explain each skill.

Base 1: Unity

☐ Clear opening statement of the point of your paper? (46–48; 55–58)
☐ All material on target in support of opening point? (99–100; 108–111)

Base 2: Support

☐ Specific evidence? (48–53; 67–70; 101–102)
☐ Plenty of it? (53–55; 70–74; 111–113)

Base 3: Coherence

☐ Clear method of organization? (78–80; 87–90; 103–104; 115–118)
☐ Transitions and other connective devices? (81–86; 91–96)

Base 4: Sentence Skills

☐ Fragments eliminated? (254)
☐ Run-ons eliminated? (270)
☐ Correct verb forms? (283)
☐ Subject and verb agreement? (290)
☐ Faulty pronouns eliminated? (307)
☐ Faulty modifiers and faulty parallelism eliminated? (320, 324)
☐ Capital letters used correctly? (332)
☐ Punctuation marks where needed?
  a Apostrophe (343)
  b Quotation marks (351)
  c Comma (358)
  d Colon; semi-colon (368)
  e Dash; hyphen (369)
  f Parentheses (370)
☐ Correct paper format? (328)
☐ Possible spelling errors checked? (383)
☐ Correct word choices? (392)
☐ Needless words eliminated? (395)
☐ Sentences varied? (399)
☐ Careless errors removed through editing and proofreading? (427)

CHAPTER 7

Narrating an Event

LEARNING OUTCOMES

By working through the activities and writing tasks in this chapter you will create a narrative paper that

- displays the point of internal or external conflict within an experience: i.e., the focus of your narrative;
- shows careful selection of details related to your point;
- organizes and sequences your supporting material in time order to create an accurate and coherent narrative paper;
- is revised to include vivid and important details to "show" readers your point and recreate your events as accurately as possible; and
- concludes by returning to its point, rather than ending with its last event.

Narrative paragraphs and essays work towards the same purpose as the forms of exposition: such papers seek *to explain*. A narrative-based paper uses a storyline to explain and deepen the meaning of its point. Unlike a made-up story or fictional narrative where the meaning may reveal itself slowly as the story unrolls, a narrative paper announces its meaning in its topic sentence. Expository narrative, then, (1) makes a statement *clear* by relating a detailed storyline about something that has happened, and (2) presents its details *in the order in which they happened*.

Here is a typical narrative illustrating the point "I was embarrassed yesterday."

"I was hurrying across campus to get to a class. It had rained heavily all morning, so I was hopscotching my way around puddles in the pathway. I called to two friends ahead to wait for me, and right before I caught up to them, I came to a large puddle that covered the entire path. I had to make a quick choice of either stepping into the puddle or trying to jump over it. I jumped, wanting to seem cool, since my friends were watching, but didn't clear the puddle. Water splashed everywhere, drenching my shoe, sock, and pants cuff, and spraying the pants of my friends as well. I felt the more embarrassed because I had tried to look so casual."

This narrative or linked sequence of details is a vivid and real explanation of the writer's embarassment: we see and understand just why he felt as he did.

Narrative's uses in college and career writing are numerous. Childcare and social services workers write narrative-based case studies and reports; course- and career-writing in business and technology requires reports of situations and procedures written as accurate recountings of events. Law enforcement officers must record every situation with which they are involved.

In this section, you will be asked to write narratives that illustrate a specific point. The paragraphs below both present narrative experiences that support a particular point. Read them, and then answer the questions that follow.

PARAGRAPHS TO CONSIDER

A Loss of Faith

[1]My younger brother Josh was always the "star" of the family, so six months ago our parents rewarded his good marks by paying for university tuition and residence fees. [2]A week before his spring break this past March, I used my own break from college to fly out to see him at the University of Alberta. [3]When I knocked on the door of his room, he looked surprised, but not in a pleasant way. [4]He introduced me to his roommate, who looked uncomfortable and quickly left. [5]I asked Josh how classes were going, and because Josh's jumpiness was making me nervous, I started to look around the room; the first thing I noticed was the big bulletin board above the desk. [6]As I focused my eyes on the board, dozens of papers tacked up there caught my eye. [7]Most of the papers were tests and lab reports, each one marked with either a big red "F" or an "0", but the largest paper up there was an official document from the university—an official notice of change of address for Josh McKenna. [8]"What's going on?" I said. [9]I stood there stunned and then felt my anger start to grow. [10]"Who lives at 488 West 3rd Street in Calgary?" I asked. [11]Josh just shrugged and said, "What's it to you? Are you supposed to report back on me?" [12]I don't really remember all that he told me, except that he tried to lie at first, to pretend his marks were all right before he admitted the truth: he was failing nearly every course and had stopped going to classes—he had even arranged to send his next transcripts to his roommate's mother's house, the Calgary address. [13]I felt a sharp pain in the pit of my stomach, and I wanted to be anywhere but in that residence room. [14]I wanted to hit him, or tear down the papers and run out to call our parents, but I did nothing. [15]Clumsily I pulled on my jacket. [16]My stomach felt sick, and I worried that my rage would take control of my body. [17]I opened the room door, and suddenly more than anything I wanted to slam the door on my brother and his lies. [18]Instead, I managed to close the door quietly. [19]I walked away understanding what was meant by a loss of faith.

A Childhood Disappointment

[1]The time I almost won a car when I was ten years old was probably the most disappointing moment of my childhood. [2]One hot summer afternoon I was wandering around a local Bay store, waiting for my mother to finish shopping. [3]Near the toy department, I was attracted to a crowd of people gathered around a bright blue car that was on display in the main aisle. [4]A sign indicated that the car was the first prize in a sweepstakes celebrating the store's tenth anniversary. [5]The sign also said that a person did not have to buy anything to fill out an entry form. [6]White entry cards and shiny yellow pencils were scattered on a card table nearby, and the table was just low enough for me to write on, so I filled out a card. [7]Then, feeling very much like an adult, I slipped my card into the slot of a heavy blue wooden box that rested on another table nearby. [8]I then proceeded to the toy department, completely forgetting about the car. [9]However, about a month later, just as I was walking into the house from my first day back at school, the telephone rang. [10]When my mother answered it, a man asked to speak to a Mark Wellesley. [11]My mother said, "There's a Mark Castaldo here, but not a Mark Wellesley." [12]He asked, "Is this 862-9715 at 29 Castaldo Street?" [13]My mother said, "That's the right number, but this is 29 Wellesley Street." [14]She then asked him, "What is this all about?" and he explained to her about the sweepstakes contest. [15]My mother then called me to ask if I had ever filled out an application for a sweepstakes drawing. [16]I said that I had, and she told me to get on the phone. [17]The man by this time had realized that I had filled in my first name and street name on the line where my full name was to be. [18]He told me I could not qualify for the prize because I had filled out the application incorrectly. [19]For the rest of the day, I cried whenever I thought of how close I had come to winning the car. [20]I am probably fated for the rest of my life to think of the "almost" prize whenever I fill out any kind of contest form.

▓ Questions

About Unity

1. Which paragraph lacks a topic sentence?

   _____

   Write a topic sentence for the paragraph:

   _____

   _____

   _____

2. Which sentence in "A Childhood Disappointment" should be omitted in the interest of paragraph unity? (*Write the sentence number here.*) _____

About Support

3. What is for you the best (most real and vivid) detail or image in the paragraph "A Loss of Faith?"

    _____

    _____

    What is the best detail or image in "A Childhood Disappointment?"

    _____

    _____

    What is the most effective detail in "A Loss of Faith?"

    _____

    _____

4. Which paragraph or paragraphs provide details in the form of the actual words used by the participants?

    _____

    _____

About Coherence

5. Do the two paragraphs use time order or emphatic order to organize details?

    _____

6. List the transition words used in one of the two paragraphs:

    a. _____

    b. _____

    c. _____

    d. _____

NOTES ABOUT NARRATIVE WRITING

All narratives relate a time-ordered series of events, but not all narrative writing is personal or deeply emotional.

Personal Narratives

- This chapter includes personal narrative paragraphs which show *why* people feel the way they do, or *how* they learned some lesson in life. Narratives often point to a moral or teach a lesson.
- Personal narratives are often effective because of their intimate connection between reader and writer. The use of "I," or first-person point of view, offers this immediacy when the writer's purpose is to to share his or her experience.

Other Forms of Narrative

- Many narratives, including some personal stories, may be less personal in focus or tone. Writing a narrative in the third-person point of view places the reader's focus on the events or experience itself, rather than on the writer. There is no "I" to distract the reader. Such narratives allow readers more "distance" between themselves and the subject-matter; their tone is cooler, less intimate.

- More objective third-person narratives may also relate the "story" of a marketing campaign, the stages in a technical process, or the events occurring as part of an accident. Such narratives must naturally be more "impersonal," but their general purpose is the same as that of all narrative: the vivid and accurate recreation of some experience or events.

Writers must decide whether their purpose is to focus on the events they narrate or on their connection to these events. The writer's decision dictates both the point of view used and the ultimate tone of the narrative.

WRITING A NARRATIVE PARAGRAPH

How to Write a Narrative Paragraph

1 Think of an event or experience that seems meaningful to you. Such an experience will probably have caused you to change, learn something, or grow in some way.

2 Prewrite to pile up details of your experience. Do not be concerned if you do not immediately find an easy-to-state single point.

3 After your initial prewriting, look for a *conflict*, some moment when your actions or expectations met with something unexpected, causing you to change direction. This is probably your "moment of enlightenment," your focus for your paragraph. Try to state what you learned at this moment, or to name your dominant emotion: this will become the topic, the point of your paper.

4 Write out your point as a topic sentence and create an outline for your narrative. *Organize* your details in time sequence as they occurred. *Select* details from your prewriting that (1) cover only a limited amount of time, and (2) truly support your point.

5 Draft and revise your paragraph with one aim: to *recreate* emotions, actions, and speech as vividly as possible. "Show" readers your experience, and achieve accuracy in your writing by doing so.

Writing Assignment 1

Write a paragraph about an experience in which a certain emotion was predominant. The emotion might be fear, pride, satisfaction, embarrassment, or any of the following:

Frustration	Sympathy	Shyness
Love	Bitterness	Disappointment
Sadness	Violence	Happiness
Terror	Surprise	Jealousy
Shock	Nostalgia	Anger
Relief	Loss	Hate
Envy	Silliness	Nervousness

The experience should be *limited in time*. Note that the two paragraphs presented in this chapter detail experiences that occurred within relatively short time periods. One writer describes the anger he felt at his brother's dishonesty during a brief visit; another describes the disappointing loss of a prize.

A good way to recreate an event is to *include some dialogue*, as the writers of the two paragraphs in this chapter have done. Repeating what you have said or what you have heard someone else say helps make the situation come alive. First, though, be sure to check the section on quotation marks on pages 351–357.

How to Proceed

a Begin by prewriting. Think of an experience or event in your life in which you felt a certain emotion strongly. Then spend ten minutes freewriting about the experience. Do not worry at this point about such matters as spelling or grammar or putting things in the right order; instead, just try to get down all the details you can think of that seem related to the experience.

b This preliminary writing will help you decide whether your topic is promising enough to develop further. If it is not, choose another emotion. If it is, do three things:

  - First, write your topic sentence, underlining the emotion you will focus on. For example, "My first day in kindergarten was one of the *scariest* days of my life."
  - Second, make up a list of all the details involved in the experience. Then arrange these details in time order.
  - Third, write an outline or detailed plan for your paragraph.

c Using the list and outline as guides, prepare a rough draft of your paper. Use time signals such as *first, then, next, after, while, during,* and *finally* to help connect details as you move from the beginning to the middle to the end of your narrative.

d As you work on the drafts of your paper, refer to the checklist on the inside front cover to make sure that you can answer *Yes* to the questions about unity, support, and coherence. Also use the checklist to edit the next-to-final draft of your paper for sentence-skills mistakes, including spelling.

■ Writing Assignment 2

Write a paragraph that shows, through some experience you have had, the truth *or* falsity of a popular belief. You might write about any one of the following statements or some other popular saying.

Haste makes waste.
Don't count your chickens before they're hatched.
A bird in the hand is worth two in the bush.
It isn't what you know, it's who you know.
Borrowing can get you into trouble.
What you don't know won't hurt you.
Keeping a promise is easier said than done.
You never really know people until you see them in an emergency.
If you don't help yourself, nobody will.
An ounce of prevention is worth a pound of cure.
Hope for the best but expect the worst.
Never give advice to a friend.
You get what you pay for.
A stitch in time saves nine.
A fool and money are soon parted.
There is an exception to every rule.
Nice people finish last.

Begin your narrative paragraph with a topic sentence that expresses your attitude, your agreement or disagreement, with a popular saying. For example, "My sister learned recently that 'Keeping a promise is easier said than done.'" Or "'Never give advice to a friend' is not always good advice, as I learned after helping a friend reunite with her boyfriend."

Refer to the suggestions about "How to Proceed" on page 134 when doing your paper. Remember that the purpose of your story is to *support* your topic sentence. Feel free to select carefully from your experience and even add to it so that the details truly support the point of your story.

■ Writing Assignment 3

Write an account of a memorable personal experience. Make sure that your story has a point, expressed in the first sentence of the paragraph. If necessary, tailor your narrative to fit your purpose. Use *time order* to organize your details (*first* this happened; *then* this; *after* that, this; *next*, this; and so on). Concentrate on providing as many specific details as possible so that the reader can really "see" and share your experience. Try to make it as vivid for the reader as it was for you when you first experienced it.

You might want to use one of the topics below, or a topic of your own choosing. Regardless, remember that every sentence of your story must illustrate or support a point stated in the first sentence of your paragraph.

The first time you felt grown-up
A major decision
A moment you knew you were happy
Your best or worst date
A foolish risk
An argument you will never forget
An incident that changed your life
A time when you did or did not do the right thing

Your best or worst holiday or birthday
A time you learned a lesson or taught one to someone else
A triumph in sports or some other event

You may want to refer to the suggestions on "How to Proceed" in Writing Assignment 1.

■ Writing Assignment 4

Imagine that a younger brother or sister, or a young friend, has to make a difficult decision of some kind. Perhaps he or she must decide how to go about preparing for a job interview, whether or not to get help with a difficult class, or what to do about a co-worker who is taking money from the cash register. Write a third-person point-of-view narrative based on your own experience (or that of someone you know) that will teach a younger person something about the decision he or she must make. In your paragraph, include a comment or two about the lesson your story teaches. You may narrate an experience about any problem young people face, including any of those already mentioned or those listed below. (See "My Ghost Town" on page 165, for an example of a third-person narrative.)

Should he or she save a little from a weekly paycheque?
Should he or she live at home or move to an apartment with some friends?
How should he or she deal with a group of friends who are involved with drugs, stealing, or both?

■ Writing Assignment 5

Writing about a Reading Selection: Read Maya Angelou's article "Adolescent Confusion" on pages 538–541. Most teenagers are, at times, as impulsive and unthinking as Angelou was. Write a narrative about a time during your teenage years when you did something impulsively, with little regard for the possible consequences—something that you later regretted. You may have committed this act because you, like Angelou, wanted to know about something or because you were pressured into it by others.

REVIEWING THE LEARNING OUTCOMES FOR NARRATIVE WRITING

When you complete any of the writing assignments in this chapter, review your paper to decide how well you have met the learning outcomes for narrative writing. Decide how well your paper fulfills each of these outcomes:

1   Does your paper open with a clear statement of its point about the emotion, experience, or lesson that is its subject?
2   Does each detail of your storyline contribute specifically to clarifying your point or lesson?
3   Are your details arranged in time order, with transitional words and phrases to show the relationships between events?
4   Are your details specific and vividly described: do they recreate your experience?
5   Do you conclude with a return to your point, rather than with the last event in your story?

ataining a Process • Examining Cause and Effect • Comparing or Contrasting • Defining
• Dividing and Classifying • Describing a Scene or Person • Narrating an Event • Argu
sition • Explaining a Process • Examining Cause and Effect • Comparing or Contrastin
ting a Term • Dividing and Classifying • Describing a Scene or Person • Narrating an Ev
juing a Position • Explaining a Process • Examining Cause and Effect • Comparing

CHAPTER 8

Describing a Scene or Person

LEARNING OUTCOMES

By working through the activities and writing tasks in this chapter, you will create a descriptive paper that

- opens with a dominant impression of its subject in its topic sentence;
- offers a rich, focused, careful selection of sense-oriented details to confirm and strengthen aspects of your dominant impression;
- guides your readers with a clear point of view and a consistent method of tracking observations about your subject; and
- concludes with a thought that fixes your dominant impression in the reader's mind.

Descriptive writing gives readers pictures in words. Describing is a basic communication activity that serves all forms of writing. Narration succeeds because of the power of its descriptive details; readers' thoughts and emotions are touched directly by description that provokes reactions or persuades; and locations, technical processes, or situations are explained and recreated in words by accurate description.

Descriptive "word-pictures" may have many purposes, but to be effective, they must be as vivid and real as possible. You perceive the subject you describe through your senses, so you must, in turn, record your subject in specific details to appeal to your readers' senses: sight, hearing, taste, smell, and touch. More than any other type of writing, a descriptive paragraph needs sharp, colourful details.

Here is a description in which only the sense of sight is used:

"A rug covers the living-room floor."

In contrast, here is a description rich in sense impressions:

"A thick, forest green, plush broadloom rug stretches wall to wall across the living-room floor. The deep and densely woven fibres of the carpet hush your steps as you walk through them in your bare feet, and as your feet relax into the cushiony pile, the soft wool pushes back at you with a spongy resilience."

How many senses do the writer's details speak to?

- Sight: *thick, forest green, plush broadloom rug; stretches wall to wall; walk through them in your bare feet; cushiony pile*
- Hearing: *hush*
- Touch: *bare feet, deep and densely woven fibres, pushes back, spongy resilience*

Sharp, vivid images provided by the sensory details create a clear picture of the rug: we are able to share in the writer's experience.

Descriptive writing skills and techniques are essential to any college assignment where an event, procedure, human behaviour pattern, or strategy must be carefully tracked and recreated. Advertising and sales rely on description; training manuals require careful description of objects, gestures, and processes; in fact, every form of career writing demands the accuracy, precision, and careful detail selection of effective descriptive writing.

In this section, you will be asked to describe a person, place, or thing for your readers by using words rich in sensory details. To help you prepare for the assignment, first read the next two paragraphs, and then answer the questions that follow.

PARAGRAPHS TO CONSIDER

An Athlete's Room

[1]As I entered the bright, cheerful space, with its beige walls and practical, flat-pile carpet, I noticed a closet to my right with the door open. [2]On the shelf above the bunched-together clothes were a red baseball cap, a fielder's glove, and a battered brown gym bag. [3]Turning from the closet, I noticed a single bed with its wooden headboard against the far wall. [4]The bedspread was a brown, orange, and beige print of basketball, football, and baseball scenes. [5]A lamp shaped like a baseball and a copy of <u>Sports Illustrated</u> were on the top of a nightstand to the left of the bed. [6]A sports schedule and several yellowing newspaper clippings were tacked to the cork bulletin board on the wall above the nightstand. [7]A desk with a bookcase top stood against the left wall. [8]I walked toward it to examine it more closely. [9]As I ran my fingers over the items on the dusty shelves, I noticed some tarnished medals and faded ribbons for track accomplishments. [10]These lay next to a heavy gold trophy that read, "MVP: Windsor Varsity Basketball." [11]I accidentally tipped an autograph-covered, slightly deflated basketball off one shelf, and the ball bounced with dull thuds across the width of the room. [12]Next to the desk was a window with brightly printed curtains that matched the bedspread. [13]Between the window and the left corner stood a dresser with one drawer half open, revealing a tangle of odd sweat socks and a few stretched-out T-shirts

emblazoned with team insignias. ¹⁴As I turned to leave the room, I carefully picked my way around scattered pairs of worn-out athletic shoes.

A Depressing Place

¹The pet shop in the mall is a depressing place. ²A display window attracts passersby who stare at the prisoners penned inside. ³In the right-hand side of the window, two puppies press their forepaws against the glass and attempt to lick the human hands that press from the outside. ⁴A cardboard barrier separates the dogs from several black-and-white kittens piled together in the opposite end of the window. ⁵Inside the shop, rows of wire cages line one wall from top to bottom. ⁶At first, it is hard to tell whether a bird, hamster, gerbil, cat, or dog is locked inside each cage. ⁷Only an occasional movement or clawing, shuffling sound tells visitors that living creatures are inside. ⁸Running down the centre of the store is a line of large wooden perches that look like coat racks. ⁹When customers pass by, the parrots and mynahs chained to these perches flutter their clipped wings in a useless attempt to escape. ¹⁰At the end of this centre aisle is a large plastic tub of dirty, stagnant-looking water containing a few motionless turtles. ¹¹The shelves against the left-hand wall are packed with all kinds of pet-related items. ¹²The smell inside the entire shop is an unpleasant mixture of strong chemical deodorizers, urine-soaked newspapers, and musty sawdust. ¹³Because so many animals are crammed together, the normally pleasant, slightly milky smell of the puppies and kittens is sour and strong. ¹⁴The droppings inside the uncleaned birdcages give off a dry, stinging odour. ¹⁵Visitors hurry out of the shop, anxious to feel fresh air and sunlight. ¹⁶The animals remain there.

▪ Questions

About Unity

1. Which paragraph lacks a topic sentence?

_____

2. Which sentence in the paragraph in "A Depressing Place" should be omitted in the interest of paragraph unity? (*Write the sentence number here.*)

_____

About Support

3. Label as *sight, touch, hearing,* or *smell* all the sensory details in the following sentences taken from the three paragraphs. The first one is done for you as an example.

       touch   *sight*   *sight*

a. I accidentally tipped an autograph-covered, slightly deflated basketball off

      sight   *hearing*   *sight*

one shelf, and the ball bounced with dull thuds across the width of the room.

  b. Because so many animals are crammed together, the normally pleasant, slightly milky smell of the puppies and kittens is sour and strong.

  c. As I ran my fingers over the items on the dusty shelves, I noticed some tarnished medals and faded ribbons for track accomplishments.

4. After which sentence in "A Depressing Place" are specific details needed?

  ———

About Coherence

5. Spatial signals (*above, next to, to the right,* and so on) are often used to help organize details in descriptive paragraphs. List four space signals that appear in "An Athlete's Room":

  _____

  _____

  _____

  _____

NOTES ABOUT DESCRIPTIVE WRITING

All effective description records its subject by using a consistent and clear method of tracking or viewing that subject and by using the most accurate and vivid details appropriate for its purpose. While subjectively focused description relies on the writer's impressions of a subject, objective description seeks to present an impersonal and accurate "word picture" recorded by a camera-like "invisible writer."

Subjective Descriptions

- This chapter shows primarily personally-based subjective descriptions. As part of their dominant impression and as a guiding principle for their selection of details, such descriptions convey the attitude, personal viewpoint, and connection to the subject of the writer. The writer's response to his or her subject guides every aspect of a subjective description.
- The focus of a personal or subjective description may be subtly shifted by the writer's use of third-person point of view. An example of this difference in focus is the paragraph "A Depressing Place;" it focuses on the pet shop itself, not on the writer's feelings as he or she walks through it. Many details included could be considered objective details; anyone entering the pet shop would observe the sights, sounds, and smells. This choice of third-person focus often makes the paragraph more persuasive.

Objective Descriptions

- Some college and career writing requires more objectivity, or less personal involvement in description. Objective descriptions are always written in the third-person point of view; the writer's aim is to record his or her subject with the impersonal accuracy of a camera.
- The focus of objective description is totally on its subject, and on offering the reader an obvious and clear "path" to follow as he or she reads the description. The dominant impression in objective description is simply an overview of the object or situation to be described; it does not include any indication of the writer's presence.

A writer approaching a writing task that requires effective description must first decide whether the purpose of that writing is to provide a personal response to the subject, or to record that subject as accurately and impersonally as possible.

WRITING A DESCRIPTIVE PARAGRAPH

How to Write a Descriptive Paragraph

1   Use all of your senses as you remember or observe your subject. In your prewriting, accumulate as many kinds of details as you can come up with. Try questioning yourself: "What do I feel when I touch this?" "What do I see when I look at it from this angle?"

2   When you have recorded as many details as possible, decide on the best way to "track" your progress as you describe your subject. If you describe a place, how will you take your reader along with you? If you describe a person or an object, where will you begin, and what path will you follow as you show your subject to your reader?

3   Decide on your main impression of, or feeling about your subject, and write this down as a trial topic sentence.

4   Begin your formal outline with this topic sentence, and order your details in the outline according to the way your reader will view your subject along with you.

5   As you begin to draft your paragraph, revise and select only those details that contribute to your dominant impression. Try to use the most precise and accurate descriptive words possible for your details.

6   Conclude with a sentence that reminds the reader of your opening dominant impression.

Writing Assignment 1

Write a paragraph describing a special kind of room. Use as your topic sentence "I could tell by looking at the room that a _____ lived there." There are many kinds of people who could be the focus for such a paragraph. You can select any one of the following, or think of some other type of person.

Photographer	Music lover	Carpenter
Cook	TV addict	Baby
Student	Camper	Cat or dog lover
Musician	Grandparent	World traveller
Hunter	Hockey player	Little boy or girl
Slob	Actor	Alcoholic
Outdoors person	Prostitute	Rollberblader or Skateboarder

How to Proceed

a **Prewrite to accumulate details on your topic.** Begin by prewriting. After choosing a topic, spend a few minutes making sure it will work. Prepare a list of all the details you can think of that support the topic. Next, list the five senses, and group as many details as possible under each sense heading. For example, the writer of "An Athlete's Room" made this list:

Sports trophy
Autographed basketball
Sports Illustrated
Baseball lamp
Sports schedule
Medals and ribbons
Sports print on bedspread, curtains
Sweat socks, T-shirts
Baseball cap
Baseball glove
Gym bag
Sports clippings

If you don't have enough details, then choose another type of person, and check your new choice with a list of details before committing yourself to the topic.

b As you work on the paragraph, you should keep in mind all four bases of effective writing.

Base 1: Unity. **Develop your dominant impression and work to support it.** Everything in the paragraph should support your point. For example, if you are writing about an athlete's room, all the details should serve to show that the person who lives in the room is an athlete. Other details should be omitted. Then, after your paragraph is finished, imagine omitting the keyword in your topic sentence. Your details alone should make it clear to the reader what word should fit in that empty space.

Base 2: Support. **Sharpen your focus.** Description depends on the use of *specific* rather than *general* descriptive words. For example:

General	Specific
Old sports trophies	Tarnished medals and faded ribbons for track accomplishments
Ugly turtle tub	Large plastic tub of dirty, stagnant-looking water containing a few motionless turtles
Unpleasant smell	Unpleasant mixture of strong chemical deodorizers, urine-soaked newpapers, and musty sawdust

Remember that you want your readers to *see,* or experience the room vividly as they read. Your words should be as detailed as a clear photograph and should give your readers a clear idea of the room. Use as many senses as possible in describing the room. Chiefly you will use sight, but to an extent you may be able to use touch, hearing, and smell as well.

Base 3: Coherence. **Track your subject carefully.** Organize your descriptive paragraph by using spatial order. Spatial order means that you move from right to left or from larger items to smaller ones, just as a visitor's eye might move around a room. For instance, the writer of "An Athlete's Room" presents an orderly description in which the eye moves from right to left around the room. Here are transition words that will help you connect your sentences as you describe the room:

to the left	across from	on the opposite side
to the right	above	nearby
next to	below	

Such transitions will help prevent you—and your reader—from getting lost as the description proceeds.

Base 4: Sentence skills. In the later drafts of your paper, edit carefully for sentence-skills mistakes. Refer to the checklist of such skills on the inside front cover of the book.

■ Writing Assignment 2

Write a paragraph about a particular place that you can observe carefully or that you already know well. It might be one of the following or some other place:

Student lounge area	Hair salon
Car showroom	Doctor's or dentist's office
Gymnasium	Classroom
Fast-food restaurant	Bank
Inside of a car	Dressing room
Ladies' or men's washroom	Attic
Movie theatre	Street market
Auto repair garage	Place where you work
Music store	Porch

How to Proceed

a **Consider the dominant impression you want to create.** Remember that, like all paragraphs, a descriptive paper must have an opening point. This point, or topic sentence, should state a dominant impression about the place you are describing. State the place you want to describe and the dominant impression you want to make in a single short sentence. The sentence can be refined later. For now, you just want to find and express a workable topic, an overview to guide your readers. You might write, for example, a sentence like one of the following:

The student lounge was hectic.
The music store was noisy.
The car's interior was very clean.
The dressing room in the department store was stifling.
The dentist's office was soothing.
The movie theatre was freezing.
The gymnasium was tense.
The attic was gloomy.
The restaurant was classy.
The office where I work was strangely quiet.

b **Accumulate supporting details.** Now make a list of all the details you can think of that support the general impression. For example, the writer of "A Depressing Place" made the following list:

A Depressing Place
Puppies behind glass
Unpleasant smell
Chained birds
Rows of cages
Dirty tub of turtles
Stuffy atmosphere
Kittens in window
Sounds of caged animals
Droppings and urine on newspapers

c **Make your details specific and appealing to the senses.** Use as many senses as possible in describing a scene. Chiefly, you will use sight, but to some extent you may be able to use touch, hearing, smell, and perhaps even taste as well. Remember that it is through the richness of your sense impressions that the reader will gain a picture of the scene.

d **Chose a method of organization to "track" your subject.** Organize your paper by using any one or a combination of the following methods.

In terms of physical order: That is, move from left to right, or far to near, or in some other consistent order. (Or, move your subject around, if it is small.)

In terms of size: That is, begin with large features or objects and work down to smaller ones.

In terms of a special order: Use a special order appropriate to the subject.

For instance, the writer of "A Depressing Place" organizes the paper in terms of physical order (from one side of the pet shop to the centre to the other side).

e As you are working on the drafts of your paper, refer to the checklist on the inside front cover. Make sure you can answer *Yes* to the questions about unity, support, coherence, and sentence skills.

Writing Assignment 3

Write a paragraph describing a person. Decide on a dominant impression you have of the person, and use only those details that will add to that impression. Here are some examples of people you might want to write about.

TV or movie personality	Co-worker
Instructor	Clergymember
Employer	Police officer
Child	Store owner or manager
Older person	Bartender
Close friend	Joker
Enemy	Neighbour

Before you begin, you may want to look carefully at the paragraphs earlier in this chapter and at "How to Proceed" in Writing Assignment 2.

Here are some possible topic sentences. Your instructor may let you develop one of these or may require you to write your own.

Brendan gives the impression of being permanently nervous.
The old man was as faded and brittle as a dying leaf.
The child was a cherubic little figure.
Our high school principal resembled a cartoon drawing.
The young woman seemed to belong to another era.
Our neighbour is a fussy person.
The rock singer seemed to be plugged in to some special kind of energy source.
The drug addict looked as lifeless as a corpse.
My friend Mike is a slow, deliberate person.
The owner of that grocery store seems burdened with troubles.

Writing Assignment 4

Option 1: You have just subscribed to a video introduction service. Clients of this service are required to make a three-minute presentation, which will be recorded on videotape. In this presentation, clients describe the kind of person they would like to meet as a friend, or possibly date. Write a one-paragraph description for your video presentation. Begin by brainstorming for a few minutes on what your "ideal first meeting" would be like. Then arrange the details you come up with into some or all of the following categories:

- *Character and personality* (Are his or her attitudes important to you? Do you prefer someone who is quiet or someone who is outgoing?)

- *Interests* (Should your companion have some of the same interests as you? If so, which ones?)
- *Personal habits* (Do you care, for instance, if the person you will meet is a nonsmoker?)
- *Physical qualities* (How might your ideal new friend look and dress?)

Option 2: Alternatively, write a similar presentation in which you describe *yourself*. Your aim is to present yourself as honestly as possible, so that interested clients of the introduction service will get a good sense of what you are like.

Writing Assignment 5

Writing About a Reading Selection: Read the selection "'The Boy Code' of Our Culture Breeds Bullies" on pages 510–511. Landsberg lists examples of men bullied in their youth and their responses to such treatment. Everyone, in fact, male or female, has either been a bully or been bullied at some time, and many people have been on both the giving and receiving end of bullying.

Write a descriptive paragraph about one such experience of your own, and of its long-term and short-term effects on you. As you prepare to write, think of the main, or dominant impression with which your experience left you. Write this out as a trial thesis statement and list the events and your emotions under this statement. As you revise the drafts of your paragraph, be sure that all your subtopics and details reinforce this dominant impression. As well, be sure to use vivid descriptive words and precise details to make your emotions and the situation you describe come to life for your readers.

REVIEWING THE LEARNING OUTCOMES FOR DESCRIPTIVE WRITING

When you complete any of the writing assignments in this chapter, review your paper to decide how well your paper responds to the following questions.

1 Does your paper open with a well-focused statement of your dominant impression of your subject? Is this dominant impression supported by each idea and supporting detail in your paragraph?

2 Are all your details specific and vivid? Are your descriptive words as precise as they can be? Do your details appeal to several different senses?

3 Can your reader follow your descriptive path as you move through or around your subject? Have you provided transitional words and phrases to help the reader and to reinforce your tracking of your subject?

4 Does your concluding sentence return to and reinforce your dominant impression?

ailing a Process • Examining cause and Effect • comparing or contrasting • Definin
• Dividing and classifying • Describing a scene or Person • Narrating an Event • Argu
sition • Explaining a Process • Examining cause and Effect • comparing or contrastin
ing a Term • Dividing and classifying • Describing a scene or Person • Narrating an Ev
quing a Position • Explaining a Process • Examining cause and Effect • comparing

CHAPTER 9

Providing Examples

LEARNING OUTCOMES

By completing the activities and writing tasks in this chapter, you will write a paragraph that explains its point with examples, a paper that effectively

- **opens with a topic sentence or controlling idea that makes a specific and clear point about a subject;**
- **offers three subtopics (supporting ideas) that are primary examples to support your point;**
- **supplies secondary or supporting details (which may themselves be examples) for each subtopic or supporting-idea example; and**
- **ends with a conclusion that returns to your main point and sums up what your examples have clarified or explained.**

Examples in exposition provide readers with clarifications or explanations of the writer's ideas. If narration offers sharing of experience, and description sharing of impressions, exposition with examples offers a chance to share knowledge or understanding of a subject. Each time an idea is supported with apt, specifc, and sharply written examples, the reader's ability to grasp that idea is increased; examples help readers to see fully what the writer means.

Our daily conversations are full of *examples*—that is, details, particulars, specific instances—to *explain or make clear* statements that we make:

Statement	*Example*
The IGA was crowded today.	There were at least four carts lined up at each of the checkout counters, and it took me forty-five minutes to get through a line.

Examples sometimes provide *reasons why* we make a particular point, and may help to prove to readers the truth of that statement.

Statement	*Example*
The corduroy shirt I bought is badly made.	The first time I washed it, the colour began to fade, one button cracked and another fell off, and the sleeves shrank almost five centimetres.

Examples offer *specifics*, or hooks, for readers to grasp and remember.

The cat can be very annoying.	She howls for fifteen minutes at a time, and uses her claws to climb the curtains, only to get stuck at the top and howl some more.

In each case, the examples help us *see for ourselves* the truth of the statement that has been made. In paragraphs, too, explanatory examples help the audience fully understand and perhaps be persuaded by a point. Lively, specific examples also add interest to a paper. Consider the sentences you have just read; they are *examples* used to support the point that examples are essential to effective writing. Instructors and textbooks teach by constantly using examples.

All forms of expository and persuasive writing required during college and careers make use of examples; explaining by example is a basic and essential skill that is practised throughout life.

In this chapter, you will be asked to provide a series of examples to support a topic sentence. First read the next two paragraphs; they both use examples to develop their points. Then answer the questions that follow.

PARAGRAPHS TO CONSIDER

The Cruelty of Children

[1]Children can be very cruel. [2]For one thing, they start very early to use words that wound. [3]Three-year-olds in nursery school, for example, call each other "dum-dum" or "weirdo," and slightly older children use nicknames like "fatty" or "four-eyes" to tease their schoolmates. [4]Children who are just a bit older learn facts about other kids from their parents, and use those facts to make someone break down and cry. [5]Children also attack each other physically. [6]For instance, whenever a group of elementary-school children come home from school, there is a lot of pushing, tripping, punching, and pinching. [7]An argument may end in shoving and hair-pulling. [8]But far worse than harsh words or physical violence is the emotional hurt that children can cause their classmates by their cruelty. [9]By junior high school days, for example, young teenagers start to shut out the people they do not like. [10]They ignore the kids whose looks, clothes, interests, or finances differ from their own. [11]Popular kids form groups, and the unpopular ones are left to face social isolation, loneliness, and depression. [12]Many adults think that childhood is an ideal time, but terribly cruel things can happen at this stage in life.

An Egotistical Neighbour

¹I have an egotistical neighbor named Alice. ²If I tell Alice how beautiful I think her dress is, she will take the time to tell me the name of the store where she bought it, the type of material that was used in making it, and the price. ³Alice is also egotistical when it comes to her children. ⁴Because they are hers, she thinks they are the best children on the block. ⁵I am wasting my time trying to tell her I have seen her kids be mean to other children on the street or scratch parked cars. ⁶I do not think parents should praise their children too much. ⁷Kids learn how to be good at home and simply awful when they are not at home. ⁸Finally, Alice is quick to describe the furnishings of her home for someone who is meeting her for the first time. ⁹She tells how much she paid for the panelling in her dining room. ¹⁰She mentions that she has two televisions and that they were bought at an expensive furniture store. ¹¹She lets the person know that the stereo and DVD player in her living room cost more than a thousand dollars, and that she has such a large collection of CDs that she would not be able to play them all in one week. ¹²Poor Alice is so self-centred that she never realizes how boring she can be.

▨ Questions

About Unity

1. Which two sentences in "An Egotistical Neighbour" are irrelevant to the point that Alice is egotistical? *(Write the sentence numbers here.)* _____ _____

About Support

2. In "The Cruelty of Children," how many examples are given of children's cruelty?

   _____ one   _____ two   _____ three   _____ four

3. After which sentence in "The Cruelty of Children" are specific details needed?

   _____

About Coherence

4. What are the three main transition words used in "The Cruelty of Children"?

   a. _____

   b. _____

   c. _____

5. What are the two main transition words in "An Egotistical Neighbour"?

   a. _____

   b. _____

6. Which paragraph clearly uses emphatic order to organize its details, saving for last what the writer regards as the most important example?

_____

_____

WRITING AN EXAMPLES PARAGRAPH

How to Write a Paragraph that Explains with Examples

1 Begin by prewriting to accumulate details about your subject. Questioning, listmaking, and diagramming are good methods for generating examples. Visualising a place, person, situation helps you discover your ideas.

2 Write a few trial topic sentences until you decide on which one best states a clear point of view or controlling attitude about your subject. Examples papers sometimes begin by specifying how many subtopic examples the paper will provide: for example, "Three situations that occurred last week show how stubborn my friend Javier can be."

3 Begin your paragraph outline with your best topic sentence, and select three subtopic examples to explain, clarify, or prove your topic's point. Write these as subtopic sentences (subtopic + attitude). Next, note in point form under each subtopic any details or secondary examples that further illustrate your subtopics. (See Writing Assignment 1 for an illustration of outlining.)

4 As you draft and revise, ask yourself if your major or primary examples and details or secondary examples truly support your point. Eliminate nonsupporting material and add any clarifying details that may occur to you.

5 In your concluding sentence, sum up the way in which your examples have demonstrated your point.

■ Writing Assignment 1

The assignment here is to complete an unfinished paragraph (in the box), which has as its topic sentence, "My husband Sean is a selfish person." Provide the supporting details needed to fill out the subtopic examples of Sean's selfishness. The first subtopic example out of four has been done for you.

How to Proceed: For this assignment, you will provide secondary examples, examples that support the subtopic examples provided on the outline on the following page. To do so, jot down on a separate piece of paper a couple of answers for each of the following questions. Note that this paragraph outline will show two types of examples: primary or subtopic examples (refusal to move, Sean's constant choice of vacations, selfish spending habits, and ignoring childcare) and secondary supporting examples for each subtopic.

a What specific vacations did the family go on because Sean wanted to go? Give places, length of stay, time of year. What vacations has the family never gone on (for example, to visit the wife's relatives), even though the wife wanted to?

b What specific items has Sean bought for himself (rather than for the whole family's use) with leftover budget money?

c What chores and duties involved in the everyday caring for the children has Sean never done?

Note about working in groups: Your instructor may ask you to work with one or two other students in generating the details needed to develop the three examples in the paragraph. Each group may then be asked to read their details aloud, with the class deciding which details are the most effective for each example.

Here and in general in your writing, try to generate *more* supporting material than you need. You are then in a position to choose the *most convincing details* for your paper. Now take your best details, reshape them as needed, and use them to complete the paragraph about Sean.

A Selfish Person

My husband Sean is a selfish person. For one thing, he refuses to move out of the city, even though it is a bad place to raise the children. *We inherited some money when my parents died, and it might be enough for a down payment on a small house in a nearby town. But Sean says he would miss his buddies in the neighbourhood.*

Also, when we go on vacation, we always go where Sean wants to go. ____

____

Another example of Sean's selfishness is that he always spends any budget money that is left over. ____

____

____

____

Finally, Sean leaves all the work of caring for the children to me. ____

____

____

____

____

■ Writing Assignment 2

Write a paragraph providing examples that clarify and explain one quality of a person you know well. The person might be a member of your family, a friend, a roommate, a boss or supervisor, a neighbour, an instructor, or someone else. Following are some descriptive words that can be applied to people. They are only suggestions; you can write about any other specific quality.

Honest	Hardworking	Jealous
Bad-tempered	Supportive	Materialistic
Ambitious	Suspicious	Sarcastic
Bigoted	Open-minded	Self-centred
Considerate	Lazy	Spineless
Argumentative	Independent	Good-humoured
Softhearted	Stubborn	Cooperative
Energetic	Flirtatious	Disciplined
Patient	Irresponsible	Sentimental
Reliable	Stingy	Defensive
Generous	Trustworthy	Dishonest
Persistent	Aggressive	Insensitive
Shy	Courageous	Unpretentious
Sloppy	Compulsive	Neat

How to Proceed

a **Use any method of prewriting.** Begin by prewriting. Make a list of examples that will support and clearly explain the point of your topic sentence. For example, if you decide to write about your brother's irresponsibility, jot down several examples of times when he showed this quality. Part of your list might look like this:

Lost rent money
Forgot to return borrowed textbooks
Didn't show up for big family dinner
Left dog alone in the apartment for two days
Left my bike out in the rain
Missed conference with instructor

Another way to get started is to ask yourself questions about your topic and write down the answers. Again, if you were writing about your brother's irresponsibility, you might ask yourself questions such as these:

How has he been irresponsible?
What are examples of times he's shown this quality?
What happened on these occasions?
Who was involved?
What were the results of his actions?

The answers to these questions should serve as an excellent source of details for the paragraph.

b **Make an outline showing subtopics and support.** Your outline should be made up of the strongest examples from the prewriting material you have generated. Note that as you make this outline, you should group related details together, creating subtopics or subheadings. For example, the items in the list about the irresponsible brother might be categorized into subtopics as follows:

<u>At apartment</u>
Lost rent money
Left dog alone in apartment

<u>At home</u>
Missed family dinner
Left bike in rain

<u>At school</u>
Didn't return textbooks
Missed conference

c **Write a topic sentence containing your subject and overall attitudes towards it.** Next, write out your topic sentence. This first sentence should tell the name of the person you are writing about, your relationship to the person, and the specific quality you are focusing on. For example, you might write, "Linda is a flirtatious girl I know at school," or "Stubbornness is Uncle Carl's outstanding characteristic."

Do not make the mistake of beginning with more than one quality ("I have a cousin named Jamal who is softhearted and generous") or with a general quality ("My boss is a good person"). Focus on *one specific quality.*

d **Develop and select specific and typical examples.** Develop your examples with specific details. Remember that you don't want to *tell* us about the person; rather, you want to *show* the person to us by detailing words, actions, or both. You might want to go back and reread the examples provided in "An Egotistical Neighbour."

e **Revise for adequate and clearly related details.** As you are writing drafts of your paragraph, ask yourself repeatedly: "Do my examples truly show that my subject has a certain quality?" Your aims in this assignment are twofold: (1) to provide *truly specific* closely related details of the quality in question and (2) to provide *enough* specific details so that you solidly support your point.

f **Write a concluding sentence that sums up your examples and reinforces your point.**

g When you are satisfied that you have provided effective examples, edit your paragraph carefully for the sentence-skills mistakes listed on the inside front cover. In addition, make sure you can answer *Yes* to the questions on unity, support, and coherence.

■ Writing Assignment 3

Write a paragraph that uses examples to develop one of the following statements or a related statement of your own.

1. _____ is a distracting place to try to study.

2. The daily life of a student is filled with conflicts.

3. Abundant evidence exists that Canada has become a health-conscious nation.

4. Despite computerized techniques, animated films are still time-consuming to make!

5. One of my instructors, _____, has some good (*or* unusual) teaching techniques.

6. Wasted electricity is all around us.

7. Life in Canada (or your city or town) is faster-paced than ever before.

8. Violence on television is widespread.

9. Women (*or* men) today are wearing some ridiculous fashions.

10. Some students here at _____ do not care about learning (*or* are overly concerned about grades).

Be sure to choose specific and related examples that truly support your point. They should be relevant facts, statistics, personal experiences, or incidents you have heard or read about. Organize your paragraph by grouping several examples that support your point. Save the most vivid, most convincing, or most important example for last.

■ Writing Assignment 4

Imagine that you are a television critic and are still living near the high school you attended. The principal is planning a special parents' evening and would like you to make a speech on the topic "Television and the Responsible Parent." You accept the invitation and decide to organize your talk around this thesis: "There are three television programs that represent worthwhile viewing for families." Write a one-paragraph summary of your talk.

To make an outline of your speech, think of three programs you would recommend for viewing by all members of a family. Write down the titles of the programs, as your subtopics and then list under each title the specific features that made you choose that show.

■ Writing Assignment 5

Writing about a Reading Selection: Everyone has or has had a hero or heroine at some time in his or her life. Some people know their heroes intimately; some people never meet their heroes; in fact, some people's heroes are fictional, historical, or movie characters.

Read Paul Jay's article "Wolverine" on page 535. Who is, or has been a hero to *you* at some time in your life, and why? Write a paragraph using examples to explain specifically why some real person or character has been a hero to you. This person need never have done anything the world might call "heroic." What is important is *your connection to this person as a hero in your life.*

In your prewriting, you may want to ask yourself questions like the following:

- *When* did I need _____'s example as a hero to help me?
- *Why* did I identify with _____ as my hero?
- *What* did _____ do that makes (or made) me connect to him or her as my particular hero?

REVIEWING THE LEARNING OUTCOMES FOR PROVIDING EXAMPLES

After completing any of the writing assignments in this chapter, review your work, using the following questions, to see how well it meets the learning outcomes for this chapter.

1   Do you open with a topic sentence that makes a specific and clear point about your subject?

2   Is your main point supported by three subtopics or supporting ideas that are your primary examples?

3   For each subtopic or primary example, are there specific and adequate details or secondary examples to explain or clarify your subtopics and add to your main point?

4   Do you conclude with a statement that returns to your main point and sums up the meaning of your paper?

Explaining a Process · Examining Cause and Effect · Comparing or Contrasting · Definin
Term · Dividing and classifying · Describing a Scene or Person · Narrating an Event · Arg
a Position · Explaining a Process · Examining Cause and Effect · Comparing or Contrast
Defining a Term · Dividing and classifying · Describing a Scene or Person · Narrating an t
Arguing a Position · Explaining a Process · Examining Cause and Effect · Compari

C H A P T E R   1 0

Explaining a Process

LEARNING OUTCOMES

The goal of any process writing is for its readers to be able to successfully complete the procedure set out by the paper. By working through this chapter's activities and following carefully the instructions for writing assignments, you will write a process paper that

- is appropriate to the knowledge level and ability of its readers;
- opens with a clear statement of the value and purpose of the process to be followed and of its approximate degree of difficulty;
- tells readers exactly what they will need (equipment, time, space, tools, and so on) to complete the process successfully;
- offers complete, carefully ordered steps and explanations for each stage of the process;
- mentions both possible problems or potential difficulties that may occur; and
- concludes with a reassurance of the value of the process for the reader.

Process writing explains how to do something, or describes how something occurred. The most common and useful form of process writing is *instructive*; its purpose is to explain *how to* do something and *why* following its instructions will achieve the desired result. Process writing always sets out its goal or end-product and offers a time-sequenced series of steps for reaching that goal.

Everyone performs activities that are processes, or series of steps carried out in a definite order. Many of these processes are familiar and automatic: tying shoelaces, using a vending machine, and starting a car. Similarly, everyone routinely follows written instructions every day: working through textbook exercises, or even following the commands in any word-processing program. These activities are so familiar that we are seldom aware of the sequence of steps involved. In other cases, when we are asked for directions to a particular place, or when we try to read and follow the directions for some new piece of technology, we are painfully conscious of the whole series of steps involved in the process. Process writing requires us to become aware of the steps in a procedure and of the stages into which we group these steps for ease of following them.

Process writing skills and techniques are used constantly in college and career writing requirements. Students in business, human services, and technology programs must frequently write both instructions and step-by-step descriptions of procedures and changes in situations.

In this section, you will be asked to write a process paragraph—one that explains clearly how to do or make something. To prepare for this assignment, you should first read the student process papers and respond to the questions that follow.

Note: In process writing, where you are often giving instruction, the pronoun *you* can appropriately be used. Two of the model paragraphs here use *you*. Indeed much of this book, which gives instruction on how to write effectively, uses *you* as direct address.

PARAGRAPHS TO CONSIDER

Sneaking into the House at Night

¹The first step I take is bringing my key along with me. ²Obviously, I don't want to have to knock on the door at 1:30 in the morning and rouse my parents out of bed. ³Second, I make it a point to stay out past midnight. ⁴If I come in before then, my father is still up. ⁵I find it hard to face his disapproving look after a night out. ⁶All I need in my life right now is for him to make me feel guilty. ⁷Trying to make it as a college student is as much as I'm ready to handle. ⁸Next, I am careful to be very quiet upon entering the house. ⁹This involves lifting the front door up slightly as I open it, so that it does not creak. ¹⁰It also means treating the floor and steps to the second floor like a minefield, stepping carefully over the spots that squeak. ¹¹Finally, I stop briefly in the bathroom without turning on the light and then tiptoe to my room, put my clothes in a pile on a chair, and slip quietly into bed. ¹²With my careful method of sneaking into the house at night, I have avoided some major hassles with my parents.

How Shareen Broke the "D" Barrier

¹Shareen decided she wanted to excel when she returned to college at twenty-nine, but she just was not sure how. ²Her first semester transcripts were a long list of Bs, with a glaring D in English. ³First, she knew the biggest problem she had to tackle: the D, and the writing problems it represented. ⁴The fact that she couldn't seem to write clearly was dragging down her marks on written assignments in business courses as well. ⁵So after avoiding the campus' tutorial centre for three months, she decided her second move would be to gather up her red-ink-scarred essays and register for weekly sessions with a tutor. ⁶At the same time, Shareen realized she had to face another

potential problem: time. ⁷As a next step, she would either have to cut back on hours at her part-time job or keep her daughter in daycare for several more hours a day. ⁸Shareen decided the best decision was to stop working Wednesday evenings. ⁹A stroke of luck followed her decision: her Aunt Bharati offered to loan Shareen her computer and printer, so she could work at home instead of waiting to use the college computers. ¹⁰Now she could work more conveniently, without paying for extra daycare; she was motivated to follow her tutor's advice and not try to write every essay in a single draft. ¹¹The computer allowed Shareen to take the final step towards improving her writing. ¹²She started to spend twice as long revising a paper as she had writing her first draft. ¹³Because Shareen no longer felt the need to try to write a "perfect" first draft, she actually started to enjoy writing, seeing it as a puzzle to solve. ¹⁴The final step was pure lucky coincidence, because Shareen was a born problem-solver. ¹⁵The result of her decision, her follow-up, and her revising efforts began to arrive when three English papers came back to her with Bs and encouraging comments on them, instead of Ds. ¹⁶And the final most satisfying moment arrived the last week of classes, when Shareen received an A on both a business report and an English research paper. ¹⁷She had broken both the B and the D barriers, and was on the way to excelling at college.

Note: This paragraph *describes* a process or a transitional series of stages. The writer is analyzing a situation or result and tracing the steps by which his or her subject arrived at that result. *Descriptive process writing* does not show "how to;" it analyzes a result and describes each stage that led to it. Students in technological and science-based programs will find descriptive process writing skills extremely useful.

▮ Questions

About Unity

1. Which paragraph lacks a topic sentence?

    _____

2. Which two sentences in "Sneaking into the House at Night" should be eliminated in the interest of paragraph unity? (*Write the sentence numbers here.*)

    _____ _____

About Support

3. After which sentence in "How Shareen Broke the 'D' Barrier" are supporting details needed? _____

4. Summarize the four steps in the process of breaking the D barrier.

    a. _____

    b. _____

c. _____

d. _____

About Coherence

5. Do these paragraphs use time order or emphatic order?

    _____

6. List the four main transition words in "Sneaking into the House at Night."

    a. _____   c. _____

    b. _____   d. _____

WRITING A PROCESS PARAGRAPH

How to Write a Process Paragraph

1 Decide how much your readers are likely to know about the process you will describe. Ask yourself what information they would need to understand and follow your instructions successfully.

2 Prewrite until you have listed details, pieces of equipment, possible problems, and steps: any ideas about your process that occur to you.

3 Note considerations such as time involved, equipment, ingredients, or other items at the top of another page. Under these notes, begin to number and order the steps in your process in point form phrases.

4 Group the steps in your process into approximately three general stages, using time order.

5 Transfer your stages and steps to an outline sheet. The stages in your process paper are your three subtopics or supporting ideas. Leaving space for additional details or examples that may be needed, add the necessary number of steps involved in each stage.

6 Write a topic sentence that gives the purpose, value, and relative level of difficulty of your process; then draft your pararaph from your outline.

7 Revise your paper to ensure
   - that you have mentioned any possible warnings needed or problems that might occur, and have not omitted any details and
   - that you have used transitional words and phrases to assist understanding of your process.

8 Conclude by refocusing on the value or importance of having performed the actions described.

■ Writing Assignment 1

Choose one of the topics below to write about in a process paper.

> How to change a car or bike tire
> How to bathe a dog or cat
> How to get rid of house or garden pests such as mice, cockroaches, or wasps
> How to fall asleep (if you need to and can't)

How to play a simple game like checkers, tic-tac-toe, or an easy card game
How to load a van
How to choose the rigt college for you
How to live on a limited budget
How to shorten a skirt or pants
How to plant a garden
How to use a search engine on the Internet
How to fix a leaky faucet, a clogged drain, or the like
How to enjoy a Canadian winter
How to make your house look lived-in when you are away
How to study for an important exam
How to paint a ceiling
How to conduct a yard or garage sale
How to wash dishes efficiently, clean a bathroom, do laundry, or the like

How to Proceed

a **Prewrite to generate as many "steps" or details for your topic as possible.**
Begin by prewriting. Freewrite for ten minutes on the topic you have chosen.
Do not worry about spelling, grammar, organization, or other matters of cor-
rect form. Just write whatever comes into your head regarding the topic.

Write for more than ten minutes if added details about the topic occur to
you. This freewriting will give you a base of raw material that you can draw on
in the next phase of your work on the paragraph. After freewriting, you should
have a sense of whether there is enough material available for you to write a
process paragraph about the topic. If so, continue as explained below. If not,
choose another topic and freewrite about *it* for ten minutes.

b **List all the steps you can think of that may be part of the process.** Don't
worry, at this point, about how each step fits or whether certain steps overlap.
Here, for example, is the list prepared by the author of "Sneaking into the
House at Night":

Quiet on stairs
Come in after Dad's asleep
House is freezing at night
Bring key
Know which steps to avoid
Lift up front door
Late dances on Saturday night
Don't turn on bathroom light
Avoid squeaky spots on floor
Get into bed quietly

c **Number your items in time order and revise for completeness.** Strike out
items that do not fit in the list; add others that come to mind. Thus:

~~Quiet on stairs~~
2   Come in after Dad's asleep

~~House is freezing at night~~
1 Bring key
5 Know which steps to avoid
3 Lift up front door
~~Late dances on Saturday night~~
6 Don't turn on bathroom light
4 Avoid squeaky spots on floor
8 Get into bed quietly
7 *Undress quietly*

d **Write a clear, direct topic sentence about the process you are going to describe.** In your topic sentence, you can (1) say that it is *important* for your audience to know about the process ("Knowing how to study effectively for a major exam can mean the difference between passing and failing a course"), or (2) state your *opinion of the value* of the process ("My technique for building a campfire is almost foolproof"), or (3) state the *results* of the process.

e **Use your list as a guide to write the outline and first rough draft of your paper.** As you write, try to think of additional details that will support your opening sentence. Group the details of your process into three or more stages, or subtopics. Make sure each stage omits no needed details. Do not expect to finish your paper in one draft. You should, in fact, be ready to write a series of lists and drafts as you work toward the goals of unity, support, and coherence.

f **Be sure that the point of view in your paragraph is consistent.** For example, if you begin to write "How *I* got rid of mice" (first person), do not switch suddenly to "*You* must buy the right traps" (second person). Write your paragraph either from the first-person point of view (*I-we*) *or* from the second-person point of view (*you*). As noted at the beginning of this chapter, do not hesitate to use the second-person (*you*) point of view. A process paragraph in which you give instructions is one of the few situations in formal writing where the second-person *you* is acceptable.

g **Be sure to use some transitions** such as *first, next, also, then, after, now, during,* and *finally* so that your paper moves smoothly and clearly from one step in the process to the next.

h While working on your paper, refer to the checklist on the inside front cover to make sure you can answer *Yes* to the questions about unity, support, and coherence. Also, refer to the checklist when you edit the next-to-final draft of your paper for sentence-skills mistakes, including spelling.

Transitions for Process Papers

first	next, then	finally
as you begin	while this is happening	to finish
first of all	during this step	at last
to start out	the second (third, fourth) step	as a last step
the first step	after you have	to complete

Writing Assignment 2

Write a paragraph about one of the following processes. For this assignment, you will be working with more general topics than those in Writing Assignment 1. You will find, in many cases, that you must invent your own steps in a particular process. You will also have to make decisions about how many steps to include, the order in which to present them, and about the number of stages or subtopics in your process.

How to break a bad habit such as smoking, overeating, or excess drinking
How to improve a course you have taken
How to make someone you know happy
How to go about meeting people
How to discipline a child
How to improve the place where you work
How to show appreciation to others
How to make someone forgive you
How to make yourself depressed
How to get over a broken relationship
How to enjoy a day off

Writing Assignment 3

Everyone is an expert at something. Write a *descriptive* process paragraph that explains some skill that you can perform very well. The skill might be, for example, "refereeing a game," "fishing for perch," "playing goalie," "putting up a tent," "making an ice cream soda," "becoming a long-distance runner," or "fine-tuning a car engine." Write from the point of view that "This is how _____ should be done." Be sure that your paragraph *describes* and *explains* how your process occurs. A *descriptive* process paper does *not* give instructions.

Writing Assignment 4

Option 1: You have a part-time job helping out in a daycare centre. The director, who is pleased with your work and wants to give you more responsibility, has assigned you to be in charge of a group activity (for example, an exercise session, an alphabet lesson, or a valentine-making project). But before you actually begin the activity, the director wants to see a summary of how you would go about it. What advance preparation would be needed, what supplies or equipment would be needed, and what exactly would you be doing throughout the time of the project? Write a paragraph explaining the steps you would follow in conducting the activity.

Option 2: Alternatively, write an explanation that you might give to a friend at college who is *not in your program*. Examples might include explaining how a particular piece of software is used, or how to do some special activity in a lab, how to make a demo tape, or an other specialized activity unique to your program. Explain each step of the task in a way that a friend would understand.

■ Writing Assignment 5

Writing about a Reading Selection:
Read the selection titled "Power Learning" on pages 487–493. Then write a process paragraph or essay on how you could go about improving your study skills. Your topic sentence or thesis might be, "To become a better student, I will take the following steps to strengthen my time control, my classroom notetaking, and my textbook study."

To get started, read through "Power Learning" again and jot down a list of all the suggestions that will be helpful for you. Then pull out the five or six that seem most important. Next, put the steps into a sequence: put hints on time control first, hints on notetaking second, and hints on textbook study third. Then prepare a rough draft of your paper in which you present each step and explain briefly why it is valuable for you. Use transitions and synonyms such as *One step, Another way, A third study aid, Next, A fifth means,* and *Last* as you develop your ideas.

REVIEWING THE LEARNING OUTCOMES FOR PROCESS WRITING

After completing any of the writing assignments in this chapter, answer the following questions to decide how well your paper meets the learning outcomes for process writing:

1 Overall, have you supplied enough information or background material to make your process understandable to your readers? Have you explained any technical or specialized points you have included?

2 Do you open with a topic sentence that states the value of your process and its approximate level of difficulty?

3 Have you mentioned any necessary equipment or supplies? Have you indicated the amount of time needed for your process and each of its stages?

4 Are your steps grouped into logical stages?

5 Is each step completely and carefully described with enough details or examples to make it clear and easy to follow? Have you mentioned any possible problems that may occur while following your instructions?

6 Do you conclude with a reassurance of the value of the process to the reader?

Explaining a Process • Examining Cause and Effect • Comparing or Contrasting • Defini
Term • Dividing and Classifying • Describing a Scene or Person • Narrating an Event • Arg
a Position • Explaining a Process • Examining Cause and Effect • comparing or contrast
Defining a Term • Dividing and Classifying • Describing a Scene or Person • Narrating an E
Arguing a Position • Explaining a Process • Examining Cause and Effect • Compari

CHAPTER 11

Examining Cause
and Effect

LEARNING OUTCOMES

By carefully working through this chapter's activities and successfully
completing one or more of its writing assignments, you will write a cause/effect
paper that

- opens with a topic sentence that states your point of view on your subject
  and indicates whether you will examine causes *or* effects;
- shows a selection of causes and/or effects focused on proving the point of
  the paper;
- uses true and logical causes and/or effects to support its point;
- presents its supporting point causes and/or effects in order of importance;
- supports its subtopic causes and/or effects with sufficient and specific
  details; and
- concludes with a reassurance that its point is effectively supported.

Cause and effect writing examines the *reasons why* things happen (cause), and the
results of those things happening (effects). Writing a paper that discusses causes
and/or effects demands clear thinking and observation. The challenging type of
thinking needed to discover and decide on causes and effects is called *analysis*.
To analyze is to break a subject down into its component parts. An event or situation may have many causes and many effects, and not all these may even be true
causes or effects; they may simply have happened before or after the event or situation. So to write about causes or effects, a writer must first break down the subject into component causes or effects to examine the truth of them. As a form of
exposition, cause/effect writing seeks to explain causal or resultant relationships
between events.

   Every day we ask questions about why things happen: this is a normal response
to our environment. We ask why someone seems unhappy or why our car stopped
working, and we look for answers. We realize that many actions do not occur with-

out causes, and we also realize that a given action can have a series of effects—good or bad. By examining the causes or effects of an action, we seek to understand and explain things that happen in our lives.

Much career and college writing and speaking focuses on cause and effect. Why does a product not sell? Why is a specific piece of software inefficient? Why does a particular biochemical process yield these results? The skills and techniques in analyzing and communicating cause and effect are in constant use in any number of communications formats.

In this section, you will be asked to do some detective work to examine the causes or the effects of something. First read the two paragraphs that follow and answer the questions about them. Both paragraphs support their opening points by explaining a series of causes or a series of effects.

PARAGRAPHS TO CONSIDER

New Puppy in the House

[1]Buying a new puppy can have drastic effects on a quiet household. [2]For one thing, the puppy keeps the entire family awake for at least two solid weeks. [3]Every night when the puppy is placed in its box, it begins to howl, yip, and whine. [4]Even after the lights go out and the house quiets down, the puppy continues to moan. [5]Since it is impossible to sleep while listening to a heartbroken, trembling "Woo-woooo," the family soon begins to suffer the effects of loss of sleep. [6]Soon people become hostile, short-tempered, depressed, and irritable. [7]A second effect is that the puppy tortures the family by destroying its material possessions. [8]Every day something different is damaged. [9]Family members find chewed belts and shoes, gnawed table legs, and leaking sofa cushions. [10]In addition, the puppy usually ruins the wall-to-wall carpeting and makes the house smell like a public washroom at a big-city bus station. [11]Worst of all, though, the puppy causes family disagreements. [12]Parents argue with children about who is supposed to feed and walk the dog. [13]Children argue among themselves about whose turn it is to play with the puppy. [14]Everyone argues about whose idea it was to get the puppy in the first place. [15]These continual arguments, along with the effects of sleeplessness and the loss of valued possessions, seriously disrupt a household. [16]Only when the puppy gets a bit older will the house become peaceful again.

My Ghost Town

[1]My home town near Lake Erie is drying up and disappearing. [2]First, there are an increasing number of problems for employees of the company that used to be the biggest employer in town. [3]The huge car-parts factory supported hundreds of families, but there have been three strikes in five years, and the workers' complaints never seem to be addressed. [4]Also, more workers are being laid off because more and more parts are made in Mexico or the East. [5]Then this week the U.S. parent company admits the plant is unprofitable and it will close the factory completely. [6]Another reason the town looks unhappy

and deserted is that one of our largest stores closed down and relocated last year. [7]The other chain store was sold to Wal-Mart, an American company. [8]The Wal-Mart store brought in management and employees from other locations, so one third of the Woolco people were out of a job, and are either still looking for a new job, getting ready to move away, or both. [9]There are very few new jobs available, and there are no new companies opening near here. [10]But the most visibly depressing cause of all for my town's empty streets is a half-hour's drive away: a big new mall built last year. [11]People drive there for entertainment as they do their shopping and banking. [12]No one wants to use the little family-owned businesses on the main street anymore. [13]So, more Queen Street stores sit empty every week and the two banks are closing their branches, which means fewer jobs for even fewer people. [14]All these changes leave my town looking and feeling as lonely and sad as a frontier ghost town.

■ Questions

About Unity

1. Which sentences in "New Puppy in the House" repeat an idea already stated and so should be omitted? (*Write the sentence numbers here.*) _____

2. Which sentence in "My Ghost Town" does not directly support the paragraph's point?

_____

About Support

3. How many causes are given to support the opening idea in "My Ghost Town"?

_____ one   _____ two   _____ three   _____ four

4. How many effects of bringing a new puppy into the home are given in "New Puppy in the House"?

_____ one   _____ two   _____ three   _____ four

About Coherence

5. What are the five major transition words used in "My Ghost Town"?

a. _____   c. _____   e. _____

b. _____   d. _____

6. What words signal the most important effect in "New Puppy in the House"?

_____

Activity 1

Complete the following outline of "My Ghost Town." The effect is that the the author's town has become empty and lifeless; the causes are what make up the paragraph. Summarize each in a few words. The first cause and details are given for you as an example.

Point

There are a number of reasons why my town turned into a "ghost town."

1. *Reason:* _Workers for the town's biggest employer have lost jobs and are unhappy._

   Details: _Three strikes in five years_

2. *Reason:* _____

   Details: _____

3. *Reason:* _____

   Details: _____

4. *Reason:* _____

   Details: _____

5. *Reason:* _____

   Details: _____

6. *Reason:* _____

   Details: _____

Activity 2

This exercise will help you tell the difference between *reasons* that back up a point and the supporting *details* that go with each of the reasons or subtopics. The scrambled list below contains both reasons (subtopics) and supporting details. Complete the outline following the list by writing the reasons in the lettered blanks (a, b, c, d) and the appropriate supporting details in the numbered blanks (1, 2, 3). Arrange the reasons in what you feel is their order of importance. Also, summarize the reasons and details in a few words rather than writing them out completely.

Point

There are a number of reasons why college students find first semesters difficult.

There are so many kinds of expensive supplies to buy, like drafting materials and zip disks.

Reading, doing assignments, and attending labs take up many hours.

Assignments are often more difficult than previous school tasks.

Most students work several hours a week at part-time jobs.

Travelling to and from college is costly, whether the student pays for a car, gas, and parking, or whether the student must buy monthly public transit passes.

College classes and course work are demanding and unfamiliar to many students.

Classes usually take up at least twenty hours a week

Students find time management to be a problem.

It is hard for a student who lives away from home to pay for tuition, rent, and food.

Lectures are often an intimidating experience for students used to informal classes.

Attending college is frequently financially draining.

Managing assignments for four or more courses, attending required lab hours, and attempting extracurricular interests can be a major worry.

Textbooks for several courses may cost hundreds of dollars.

Almost all the course material is totally new to students and may be quite difficult to grasp.

Students often find there is no time left for families, friends, or children.

Outline

a. _____

    (1) _____

    (2) _____

    (3) _____

    (4) _____

b. _____

    (1) _____

    (2) _____

    (3) _____

    (4) _____

c. _____

    (1) _____

    (2) _____

    (3) _____

    (4) _____

A Note About Causes, Effects, and Logic

Two types of problems occur in cause and effect writing. The first is an error in logic caused by confusing time order with causality, and the second is caused by assuming there is only a single cause or effect in any situation.

- Sometimes facts or events appear to be causes or effects when they merely *precede* or *follow* something *in time.* For instance, if a dog crosses the road just before your car stalls, the dog is not the cause of the situation. The dog's crossing the road simply occurs before your car stalls, but the two events have no causal relationship.

- There are also often multiple or underlying causes and effects. If a writer stated that catching frequent colds is caused by being in constant contact with people with colds, he or she could be ignoring other less apparent causes, such as low resistance due to fatigue or persistent conditions like asthma.

WRITING A CAUSE-EFFECT PARAGRAPH

How to Write a Cause/Effect Paragraph

1 Look at your topic. Does it require a paper on causes or on effects, or may you choose one or the other? After deciding on either a causes or an effects paragraph, begin to prewrite.

2 Use listing or questioning to create either causes or effects for your topic. Examine your lists or notes to be sure that your points are true and logical causes or effects; are there other or deeper causes or effects that you may have missed in your prewriting?

3 Number and try to group points or details that are related or similar. Check to be sure that similar points are not merely repetitions of each other. If you have several points that are related, group them under a common subheading as a possible subtopic cause or effect. (See Writing Assignment 1 below for an example of this.)

4 Use your outline to list your major or subtopic causes or effects and the details that support each. Write a topic sentence that both states your point of view on your subject and indicates whether your paper is about causes or effects.

5 As you work on drafts based on your outline, use an order that is most effective for your supporting points and details: is one cause or effect more important than the others? Is the order in time in which your causes or effects occur important to your point?

6 Be sure to use transitional words and phrases appropriate to cause/ effect writing to help readers to follow your thoughts.

7 Conclude by reinforcing your main point with a reference to the evidence you have presented.

■ Writing Assignment 1

Listed below are topic sentences and brief outlines for three cause *or* effect paragraphs. Choose one of them to develop into a paragraph.

Option 1

Topic sentence: There are several reasons why some high school graduates are unable to read or write adequately for college requirements.

(a) Failure of parents (*cause*)

(b) Failure of schools (*cause*)

(c) Failure of students themselves (*cause*)

Option 2

Topic sentence: Attending college has changed my personality in positive ways.
(a) More confident (*effect*)
(b) More knowledgeable (*effect*)
(c) More assertive (*effect*)

Option 3

Topic sentence: Living with roommates (*or* family) makes attending college difficult.
(a) Late night hours (*cause*)
(b) More temptations to cut class (*cause*)
(c) More distractions from studying (*cause*)

How to Proceed

a **Begin by prewriting.** On a separate sheet of paper, make a list of details (in this case of *causes*, or of *effects*) that might go under each of the supporting points. Provide *more* details than you can actually use. Here, for example, are some of the details generated by the writer of "New Puppy in the House" while working on the paragraph:

Whines and moans	Loss of sleep
Arguments about walking dog	Visits to vet
Arguments about feeding dog	Short tempers
Purchase collar, leash, food	Accidents on carpet
Chewed belts and shoes	Chewed cushions and tables
Arguments about playing with dog	

b **Edit, order, and select details. Look for possible subtopics.** Decide which details you will use to develop the paragraph. Also, number the details in the order in which you will present them. Here is how the writer of "New Puppy in the House" made decisions about the details that were the *effects* of having a puppy.

2   Whines and moans
6   Arguments about walking dog
6   Arguments about feeding dog
       ~~Purchase collar, leash, food~~
4   Chewed belts and shoes
6   Arguments about playing with dog
1   Loss of sleep
       ~~Visits to vet~~
3   Short tempers
5   Accidents on carpet
4   Chewed cushions and tables

Notice that the writer has found possible subtopics and put the same number in front of certain details that go together. For example, there is a "4" in front of "Chewed belts and shoes" and also in front of "Chewed cushions and tables."

c **Organize your subtopics and details into an outline.** Group details that are related (as indicated by numbers), and arrange them in outline form under subtopic headings.

1. Lack of sleep
   a) puppy whines alone in its box—cause
   b) short tempers—effect

2. Damage to house and belongings
   a) clothes, shoes, table legs, cushions—chewing
   b) carpet smells—dog isn't trained

3. Causes arguments
   a) parents & children—who should walk the puppy?
   b) who gets to play with the puppy?
   c) whose idea was the puppy?

Topic sentence? Having a puppy in the house is disruptive...

d As you are working on your outline and paper, keep checking your material to make sure it is unified, supported, and coherent. Use transitions to guide your readers.

e Finally, edit the next-to-final draft of your paper for sentence-skills mistakes, including spelling.

Transitions for Cause/Effect Papers

Transitions for Causes	*Transitions for Effects*
is a result of; results from	so, so that, so then
the reason for	is a consequence of, consequently
since	therefore, thus, then
because (of)	for this reason
is caused by	as a result

Writing Assignment 2

Below are ten topic sentences for a cause or effect paragraph. In outline form on a separate sheet of paper, provide brief supporting points for five of the ten statements.

List the Causes

1. There are several reasons so many accidents occur on _____ (*name a local road, highway, or intersection*).

2. _____ is (*or* is not) a good instructor (*or* employer), for several reasons.

3. _____ is a sport that cannot be appreciated on television.

4. _____ is the most difficult course I have ever taken.

5. For several reasons, many students live at home while going to school.

List the Effects

6. Watching too much American TV can have a bad effect on Canadians.

7. When I heard the news that _____, I was affected in various ways.

8. Conflicts between parents can have harmful effects on a child.

9. Breaking my bad habit of _____ has changed my life (*or* would change my life).

10. My fear of _____ has affected my everyday life.

Decide which of your outlines would be most promising to develop into a paragraph. Make sure that your causes or effects are logical ones that truly support the point in the topic sentence. Then follow the directions on "How to Proceed" in Writing Assignment 1.

▨ Writing Assignment 3

Most of us criticize others readily, but we find it more difficult to give compliments. For this assignment, write a one-paragraph letter praising someone. The letter may be to a person you know (parent, relative, friend); to a public figure (actor, politician, musician, sports star, and so on); or to a company or organization (for example, the people who manufactured a product you own, a newspaper, a TV network, or a government agency).

To start, make a list of **reasons why** you admire the person or organization. Here are examples of reasons for praising an automobile manufacturer:

My car's dependability
Prompt action on a complaint
Well-thought-out design
Friendly dealer service

Follow the suggestions on "How to Proceed" in Writing Assignment 1.

▨ Writing Assignment 4

Option 1: Assume that Canada's federal government has asked the provinces to change their health care policies, making them more like U.S. policies. There would no longer be government-funded insurance to cover medical procedures, operations, hospitalization, or doctor's appointments. What would be some of the effects of such a change? Spend some time thinking about specific results, good or bad, that could occur.

Now, taking into account both any opinions you may have read on the possibility and your own personal views, write a letter to your local MPP detailing your thoughts about the results of such a change.

Option 2: Your roommate has been complaining that it is impossible to succeed in Mr. X's class because the class is too stressful. You volunteer to attend the class and see for yourself. Afterward, you decide to write a letter to the instructor, calling attention to the stressful conditions in the class and suggesting concrete ways that he or she could deal with these conditions. Write this letter, dealing with the causes and effects of stress in the class.

Writing Assignment 5

Writing about a Reading Selection: Read the selection titled "Truth or Consequences" by Laura J. Turner on pages 482–483. Each of us lies sometimes. The reasons for our lies may be major or minor and may have consequences for ourselves or for others which may be significant or insignificant. Think of a lie that you told consciously; think about the reasons you told the lie, and about the effects that lie had on you or on others. Write a causes paragraph which begins by relating the lie that you told, and your feelings about why you did so. Your topic sentence might be something like "I always regretted lying to my mother about my boyfriend's habits, and there are three reasons why I told her that story." As you develop each cause for your decision, use "cause" and order-of-importance transitions to introduce and emphasize the order of your reasons. Conclude with your most important point.

As an alternative, you could write about the consequences, or effects, of the lie that you told. Once again, be sure to include effects and supporting details in the order of importance.

REVIEWING THE LEARNING OUTCOMES FOR CAUSE/EFFECT WRITING

After completing any of the writing assignments in this chapter, review your paper to decide how well your paper responds to the following questions:

1 Does your paper open with a topic sentence that states your point of view on your subject and indicates whether your paper deals with causes or effects?
2 Is each cause or effect in your paper truly a cause or effect? Does each clearly support the point you make?
3 Are your causes or effects presented in an effective order with appropriate transitions to guide your reader and reinforce your point?
4 Are your supporting points or subtopics adequately supported by adequate and specific details?
5 Do you conclude with a reinforcement of your point that sums up your paragraph?

*Explaining a Process • Examining Cause and Effect • comparing or contrasting • Defini
erm • Dividing and classifying • Describing a Scene or Person • Narrating an Event • Arg
a Position • Explaining a Process • Examining Cause and Effect • comparing or contrasti
efining a Term • Dividing and classifying • Describing a Scene or Person • Narrating an E
Arguing a Position • Explaining a Process • Examining Cause and Effect • comparin*

CHAPTER 12

Comparing or Contrasting

LEARNING OUTCOMES

By working through this chapter's activities, practising the skills involved in both types of comparison/contrast patterns of development, and completing one or more of its writing assignments, you will write a comparison or contrast paper that

- compares or contrasts limited aspects of two subjects that have a logical reason to be considered together;
- begins with a limited, clear topic sentence stating (1) both its subjects, (2) its intention either to compare or to contrast, and (3) your point in comparing or contrasting these subjects;
- uses either the one-side-at-a-time or the point-by-point method to state and develop its comparison or contrast;
- carefully compares or contrasts each subject within one of these structures according to several major points or bases for comparing or contrasting; and
- concludes with a summing up of the results of comparing or contrasting your two subjects and a confirmation of your point of view or judgment on these results.

Papers that *compare* two things show *similarities;* papers that *contrast* two things show *differences.* Comparison papers may *inform* readers by showing them similarities between familiar concepts and unknown or seemingly dissimilar concepts. Contrast papers may *persuade* readers by allowing them to examine the differences between two points, then align their views with one side or the other. Both types of paper involve *analysis,* or thinking that breaks down concepts into their component ideas. Both types of papers begin with a judgment (or viewpoint) on the part of the writer and lead to a judgment on the part of the reader.

Comparing and contrasting are two thought processes we constantly perform in everyday life. We compare or contrast two brand-name products: for example, Fila versus Reeboks shoes; two television shows, two instructors, two friends, or two possible courses of action in a situation. We compare or contrast to understand each of the two things more clearly and to make judgments about them. Comparison/contrast writing structures simply imitate and extend our thinking habits.

Comparing and contrasting occur constantly in college and career writing. Why is digital reproduction superior to photographic processing? Why does one employee perform better than another? How does one accounting software package compare to another? How does one advertising campaign's use of media coverage differ from another? Responding to any such question requires competence in the techniques of comparing or contrasting to structure your thinking and achieve the response you desire from readers.

In this section, you will be asked to write a paper of comparison or contrast. First, however, you must learn the two common methods of developing a comparison or contrast paragraph. Read the two paragraphs that follow and try to explain the difference in the two methods of development.

PARAGRAPHS TO CONSIDER

Last Dance

[1]My graduation dance was nothing like what I had expected it to be. [2]From the start of grade twelve, I had pictured getting dressed in a blue gown that my aunt would make and that would cost five hundred dollars in any store. [3]No one else would have a gown as attractive as mine. [4]I imagined my boyfriend coming to the door with a lovely blue corsage, and I pictured myself happily inhaling its perfume all evening long. [5]I saw us setting off for the evening in his brother's Mazda Miata. [6]We would make a flourish as we swept in and out of a series of parties before the dance. [7]Our evening would be capped by a delicious steak dinner and by dancing closely together into the early morning hours. [8]The formal was held on May 17, 1996, at the Riding Club on the Pembina Highway. [9]However, because of sickness in her family, my aunt had no time to finish my gown and I had to buy an ugly pink one at the last minute for eighty dollars. [10]My corsage of yellow carnations looked terrible on my pink gown, and I do not remember its having any scent. [11]My boyfriend's brother was out of town, and I stepped outside to the stripped-down Chevy that he used at races on weekends. [12]We went to one party where I drank a glass of wine that made me sleepy and upset my stomach. [13]After we arrived at the dance, I nibbled on a roll and some celery sticks. [14]Worst of all, we left early without dancing because my boyfriend and I had had a fight several days before, and at the time, we did not really want to be with each other.

Day versus Evening Students

[1]As a part-time college student who has taken both day and evening courses, I have observed notable differences between day and evening

students. [2]First of all, the students in my daytime classes are all about the same age, with similar clothing styles and similar interests. [3]Most are in their late teens to early twenties, and whether male or female, they pretty much dress alike. [4]Their uniform consists of jeans, T-shirts, running shoes, baseball caps and maybe a gold earring or two. [5]They use the same popular slang, talk about the same movies and TV shows, and know the same musical artists. [6]But students in my evening courses are much more diverse. [7]Some are in their late teens, but most range from young married people in their twenties and thirties to people my grandparents' age. [8]Generally, their clothing is more formal than the day students'. [9]They are dressed for the workplace, not for a typical college classroom. [10]Many of the women wear suits, while the men often wear dress shirts or sweaters. [11]As well, they are more comfortable talking about their mortgages or work schedules or child care than about what was on TV last night. [12]Second, for day students, college is generally their only major responsibility. [13]They have plenty of time to study and get assignments done. [14]However, evening students lead much more complicated lives than most day students. [15]They may come to campus after putting in a nine-to-five day at work. [16]Most have children to raise or grandchildren to babysit. [17]When they miss a class or hand in an assignment late, it's usually because of a real problem, such as a sick child or an important deadline at work. [18]Finally, day and evening students definitely have different attitudes toward school. [19]Day students often seem more interested in the view out the window or the attractive classmate in the next row than in what the instructor is saying. [20]They doze, draw cartoons, whisper, and write notes instead of paying attention. [21]Evening students sit up straight, listen hard, and ask the instructor lots of questions. [22]They obviously are there to learn, and they don't want their time wasted. [23]In short, day students and night students are as different as … day and night.

Complete this comment: The difference in the methods of contrast in the two paragraphs is _____

_____

_____

_____

_____

Compare your answer with the following explanation of the two methods of development used in comparison or contrast paragraphs.

METHODS OF DEVELOPMENT

There are two common methods, or formats, of development in a comparison or contrast paper. Details can be presented *one side at a time* or *point by point.* Each format is illustrated below.

One Side at a Time

Look at the outline of "Last Dance":

Topic sentence: My senior prom was nothing like what I had expected it to be.

    a.   Expectations (<u>first half of paper</u>)
       (1) Gown (expensive, blue)
       (2) Corsage (lovely, fragrant blue)
       (3) Car (Mazda Miata)
       (4) Partying (much)
       (5) Dinner (steak)
       (6) Dancing (all night)
    b.   Reality (<u>second half of paper</u>)
       (1) Gown (cheap, pink)
       (2) Corsage (wrong colour, no scent)
       (3) Car (stripped-down Chevy)
       (4) Partying (little)
       (5) Dinner (roll and celery sticks)
       (6) Dancing (didn't because of quarrel)

The first half of the paragraph fully explains *one side* of the contrast; the second half of the paragraph deals entirely with *the other side*. In using the one-side-at-a-time method, be sure to follow the same order of points of contrast (or comparison) for each side.

Point by Point

Now look at the outline of "Day versus Evening Students":

Topic sentence: There are notable differences between day and evening students.

    a.   Age and related tastes in clothing and interests
       (1) Youthful nature of day students
       (2) Older nature of evening students
    b.   Amount of responsibility
       (1) Lighter responsibilities of day students
       (2) Heavier responsibilities of evening students
    c.   Attitude toward school
       (1) Casual attitude of day students
       (2) Serious attitude of evening students

The outline shows how the two kinds of students are contrasted point by point under three subtopics, or bases of comparison. First, the writer compares the ages, clothing styles, and interests of the young daytime students and the older evening students. Next, the writer compares the limited amount of responsibility of the daytime students with the heavier responsibilities of the evening students. Finally, the writer compares the casual attitudes toward school of the daytime students to the serious attitudes of the evening students.

    When you begin a comparison or contrast paper, you should decide right away whether you are going to use the one-side-at-a-time format or the point-by-point format. Your subject matter will often help you determine which format is preferable. Following are some of the advantages and disadvantages of each format:

One-Side-at-a-Time format (also called "block" format) is most effective when you wish to explore each idea in great depth. When you present one side of your subject in an uninterrupted way, you are able to examine any complexities at length or build a detailed or dramatic argument or description. *But,* presenting one side at a time requires you, in the second part of your paper, to carefully remind readers of each point of comparison or contrast as you present the other side of your subject.

Point-by-Point format works best with brief, specific points of comparison or contrast for two subjects or two aspects of the same subject. The reader sees both sides one after the other; he or she is constantly reminded of the comparing or contrasting activity and is less likely to forget points being examined. Point-by-point format is also best for a subject with numerous bases of comparison or contrast for this reason.

An outline is an essential step in helping you decide which format will be more workable for your topic.

Activity 1

Complete the partial outlines provided for the two paragraphs that follow.

1.   **How My Parents' Divorce Changed Me**

In the three years since my parents' divorce, I have changed from a spoiled brat to a reasonably normal college student. Before the divorce, I expected my mother to wait on me. She did my laundry, cooked and cleaned up after meals, and even straightened up my room. My only response was to complain if the meat was too well done or if the sweater I wanted to wear was not clean. In addition, I expected money for anything I wanted. Whether it was an expensive ski trip or a new school jacket, I expected Mom to hand over the money. If she refused, I would get it from Dad. However, he left when I was fifteen, and things changed. When Mom got a full-time job to support us, I was the one with the free time to do housework. I did the laundry, started the dinner, and cleaned, not only my own room, but the whole house. Fortunately, Mom was tolerant. She did not even complain when my first laundry project left us with streaky blue underwear. Also, I no longer asked her for money since I knew there was none to spare. Instead, I got a part-time job on weekends to earn my own spending money. Today I have my own car that I am paying for, and I am putting myself through college. Things have been hard sometimes, but I am glad not to be that spoiled kid any more.

Topic sentence: In the three years since my parents' divorce, I have changed from a spoiled brat to a reasonably normal college student.

a. Before the divorce

(1) _____

(2) _____

b. After the divorce

    (1) _____

    (2) _____

Complete the following statement: Paragraph 1 uses a _____ method of development.

2.
Good and Bad Horror Movies

A good horror movie is easily distinguished from a bad one. A good horror movie, first of all, has both male and female victims. Both sexes suffer terrible fates at the hands of monsters and maniacs. Therefore, everyone in the audience has a chance to identify with the victim. Bad horror movies, on the other hand, tend to concentrate on women, especially half-dressed or seemingly sluttish ones. These movies are obviously prejudiced against half the human race. Second, a good horror movie inspires compassion for its characters. For example, the audience will feel sympathy for the victims of Freddy or Dracula, and also for Freddy or Dracula, who are themselves shown to be sad victims of fate. In contrast, a bad horror movie encourages feelings of aggression and violence in viewers. For instance, in the *Halloween* or *Scream* films, the murder scenes use the murderer's point of view. The effect is that the audience stalks the victims along with the killer and feels the same thrill he does. Finally, every good horror movie has a sense of humour. In *Dracula*, the Count says meaningfully at dinner, "I don't drink wine," as he stares at Jonathan Harker's juicy neck. Humour provides relief from the horror and makes the characters more human. A bad horror movie, though, is humourless and boring. One murder is piled on top of another, and the characters are just cardboard figures. Bad horror movies may provide cheap thrills, but the good ones touch our emotions and live forever.

Topic sentence: A good horror movie is easily distinguished from a bad one.

a. Kinds of victims

    (1) _____

    (2) _____

b. Effect on audience

    (1) _____

    (2) _____

c. Tone

    (1) _____

    (2) _____

Complete the following statement: Paragraph 2 uses a _____ method of development.

Activity 2

Write the number *1* beside the point that all the other scrambled sentences in the list below support. Then number the rest of the sentences in a logical order. To do this, you will have to decide whether the sentences should be arranged according to *one-side-at-a-time* order or *point-by-point* order.

A Change in Attitude

_____   Eventually I could not find a dress or pair of slacks in my wardrobe that I could wear while still continuing to breathe.

_____   In the evening when I got hungry, I made myself tomato, lettuce, and onion salad with vinegar dressing.

_____   I have kicked my chocolate habit, saved my wardrobe, and enabled myself to breathe again.

_____   I also could seldom resist driving over to the nearby Sugar Shack in the evening to get a large chocolate shake.

_____   For dessert at lunch I had an orange or some other fruit.

_____   I gobbled chocolate bars during breaks at work, had chocolate cake for dessert at lunch, and ate chocolate-covered butter creams in the evening.

_____   At this point I began using willpower to control my urge for chocolate.

_____   As a result, the eight kilos that I didn't want dropped off steadily and eventually disappeared.

_____   When the kilos began to multiply steadily, I tried to console myself.

_____   I have been able to lose weight by changing my attitude about chocolate.

_____   I said, "Well, that's only one kilo; I can lose that next week."

_____   Also, I made myself go and step on the bathroom scale whenever I got the urge to drive over to the Sugar Shack.

_____   There was a time when I made chocolate a big part of my daily diet.

_____   Instead of eating chocolate bars on my break, I munched celery and carrots.

Complete the following statement: The sentences can be organized using _____ order.

ADDITIONAL PARAGRAPHS TO CONSIDER

Read these additional paragraphs of comparison or contrast, and then answer the questions that follow.

My Broken Dream

[1]When I became a police officer in Hamilton, the job was not as I had dreamed it would be. [2]I began to dream about being a police officer at about age

ten. ³I could picture myself wearing a handsome blue uniform and having an impressive-looking badge. ⁴I could also picture myself driving a powerful patrol car through town and seeing everyone stare at me with envy. ⁵But most of all, I dreamed of working on a SWAT team using all the equipment that "TV cops" use. ⁶I just knew everyone would be proud of me. ⁷I could almost hear the guys on the block saying, ⁸"Boy, Devon made it big. Did you hear he's a cop?" ⁹I dreamed of leading an exciting life, solving big crimes, and meeting lots of people. ¹⁰I just knew that if I became a cop everyone in town would look up to me. ¹¹However, when I actually did become a police officer, I soon found out that the reality was different. ¹²My first disappointment came when I was sworn in and handed a well-used, baggy uniform. ¹³My disappointment continued when I was given a badge that looked like something pulled out of a cereal box. ¹⁴I was assigned bicycle patrol duty and given a used bike. ¹⁵I got to wear navy Bermuda shorts and knee socks while dodging traffic. ¹⁶Disappointment seemed to continue. ¹⁷I soon found out that I was not the envy of all my friends. ¹⁸When I cycled through town, they acted as if they had not seen me. ¹⁹I was told I was crazy doing this kind of job by people I thought would look up to me. ²⁰My job was not as exciting as I had dreamed it would be either. ²¹Instead of solving robberies and murders every day, I found that I spent a great deal of time comforting a local resident because a neighbourhood dog had watered his favourite bush.

Two Views on Toys

¹There is a vast difference between children and adults where presents are concerned. ²First, there is the matter of taste. ³Adults pride themselves on taste, while children ignore the matter of taste in favour of things that are fun. ⁴Adults, especially grandparents, pick out educational and tasteful toys that go unused, while children love the trendy playthings advertised on television. ⁵Then, of course, there is the matter of money. ⁶The new games on the market today are a case in point. ⁷Have you ever tried to lure a child away from some expensive game in order to get him or her to play with an old-fashioned game or toy? ⁸Finally, there is a difference between an adult's and a child's idea of what is educational. ⁹Adults, filled with memories of their own childhoods, tend to be fond of the written word. ¹⁰Today's children, on the other hand, concentrate on anything electronic. ¹¹These things mean much more to them than to adults. ¹²Next holiday season, examine the toys that adults choose for children. ¹³Then look at the toys the children prefer. ¹⁴You will see the difference.

▨ Questions

About Unity

1. Which sentence in "My Broken Dream" does not directly add to the support for its topic? (Write the sentence number.)

_____

2. Which paragraph has a topic sentence that is too broad?

_____

About Support

3. Which paragraph contains virtually no specific details?

   _____

4. Which paragraph do you feel offers the most effective details?

   _____

About Coherence

5. What method of development (one side at a time or point by point) is used in "My Broken Dream"?

   _____

6. What transitional words are used in "Two Views on Toys"?

   _____

WRITING A COMPARISON OR CONTRAST PARAGRAPH

How to Write a Comparison or Contrast Paragraph

1 An effective comparison/contrast paper examines two subjects that have some relationship to each other, and examines the same specific aspects of each subject. Do your two subjects share a common quality or category so you can find points or bases on which to compare or contrast them? Second, can you focus your two-part topic enough to create a *limited* comparison or contrast paper that addresses specific points about both your subjects?

2 When prewriting for a comparison/contrast paper, always divide your document or sheet of paper into two columns: one for each side of your comparison or contrast. List or freewrite for one side (or for one of your subjects) in one column, and for your other side in the other column.

3 Decide whether your paper will compare or contrast either both sides of your subject or both of your subjects. Prewrite, using the two-column method, to accumulate enough details for both sides of your paper. Then revise your prewriting to be sure one side's points of comparison or contrast have "matching" points for the other side. Eliminate any details or points which cannot apply to both sides.

4 Decide which method of development best suits your subject: one side at a time, or point by point. Set up your outline to reflect the format you choose. (See the outlines for the two paragraphs on page 177 for examples of both.) Begin your outline by stating your reason for making a comparison or contrast, and state this point, as well as whether you will compare or contrast your two sides, in a trial topic sentence. In the body of your outline, create subtopics or groupings for your major points of comparison or contrast. Under each subtopic or supporting point (base for comparison or contrast), list details for each side.

---

5 As you create drafts based on your outline, be sure to use transitional words and phrases (see page 185) appropriate to comparing or contrasting to assist your readers and to clarify the point your paper will make.

6 Be sure to write a conclusion that reaffirms the point of your comparison or contrast, based on the information your paper has presented.

▨ Writing Assignment 1

Below are topic sentences and subtopics or supporting points for three *contrast* paragraphs. Choose one of the three to develop into a point-by-point paragraph.

Option 1

Topic sentence. I abused my body when I was twenty, but I treat myself much differently at the age of thirty.

a. At twenty, I was a heavy smoker. . . .
   Now, instead of smoking, I . . .

b. At twenty, I had a highly irregular diet. . . .
   Today, on the other hand, I eat . . .

c. Finally, at twenty, I never exercised. . . .
   Today, I work out regularly. . . .

Option 2

Topic sentence: College graduates find the job search easier than university graduates do.

a. Graduates at many college programs are trained for specific areas of the workforce…
   In contrast, university graduates…

b. Many college graduates have internship experience and valuable contacts from those co-op positions. . .
   University graduates, on the other hand, often have no workplace experience…

c. By the end of a two-year college program, studets are trained for realistic workplace situations and in specific skills…
   Whereas university students have studied more theoretical and less work-oriented subjects…

Option 3

Topic sentence: My marketing instructor teaches a class quite differently from my accounting instructor.

a. For one thing, Ms. X demands many hours of homework each week. …
   In contrast, Mr. Y does not believe in much work outside class. …

b. In addtion, Ms. X gives difficult tests—with no study aids. …
    Mr. Y's tests, on the other hand, are easy. …

c. Finally, Ms. X keeps every class strictly on the subject of the day. …
    But Mr. Y will wander off onto any topic that snags his interest. …

How to Proceed

a Begin by dividing your page into two columns (one for each side of your topic), and prewriting. To develop supporting details for each side of your topic, freewrite for five minutes.

b Use focused questioning to add to your freewriting material. Using another sheet of paper divided into two columns (in the example following, the two columns are labelled "Then" and "Now"), ask yourself questions focused on each side of your topic. If you are writing about how you treat your body differently at thirty than you did at twenty, you might ask yourself:

Then—at twenty	Now—at thirty
Smoking & Habits	Smoking & Habits
– How many cigarettes did I smoke at twenty?	– What have I substituted for smoking?
Eating Habits	Eating Habits
– What kinds of foods did I eat?	– How regularly did I eat?
– What kinds of foods do I eat?	– What eating patterns do I have now?
Exercise	Exercise
– Why didn't I exercise at twenty?	– Why do I exercise now? What are the benefits?
	– How often do I exercise?

Write down whatever answers occur to you for these and other questions. As with the freewriting, do not worry at this stage about writing correctly. Instead, concentrate on getting down all the information you can think of that supports each point.

c Revise and edit your material. Now go through all the material you have accumulated. Perhaps some of the details you have written down may help you think of even better details that would fit. If so, write them down.

d Make sure all your details support and clarify the point of your topic sentence. Any point of comparison or contrast in a paper should strongly lead to, or reinforce, a point made in the topic sentence.

e Create a formal outline for your paper. Be sure that every point of contrast for one side is balanced by a point and details for the other side of your topic.

f Use contrast and linking transitions. As you work on the drafts of your paper, use words such as *in contrast, but, on the other hand,* and *however* to tie together your material.

g Be sure to edit the next-to-final draft of your paper for sentence-skills mistakes, including spelling.

> ### Transitions for Comparison or Contrast Papers
>
> | *Comparison Transitions* | *Contrast Transitions* |
> |---|---|
> | just as, just like | on the other hand |
> | like, likewise | in contrast to, contrasting |
> | similarly, in a similar way, similar to | as opposed to, in opposition to |
> | also, too, again | although, even though |
> | moreover, further, furthermore | whereas, while |
> | | but, still, nonetheless, nevertheless, yet |

■ Writing Assignment 2

Write a comparison or contrast paragraph on one of the twenty topics below.

Two holidays	Two jobs
Two instructors	Two characters in the same
Two children	movie or TV show
Two kinds of eaters	Two commercials
Two drivers	Two methods of studying
Two co-workers	Two cartoon strips or comic book series
Two members of a team	Two cars
(*or* two teams)	Two friends
Two singers or groups	Two crises
Two animals	Two employees
Two parties	Two magazines

How to Proceed

a **Make two decisions.** (1) What will your topic be? and (2) will you write a comparison paper or a contrast paper? Many times, students choose to do essays centred on the differences between two things. For example, you might write about how a math instructor you have in college differs from a math teacher you had in high school. You might discuss important differences between two co-workers or between two of your friends. You might contrast a factory job you had packing vegetables with a white-collar job you had as a salesperson in a clothing store.

b **Prewrite on your topic, using two columns for points on each side.** As you list points for each side of your comparison or contrast, begin to think of the *point* your paper will make about comparing or contrasting your two sides. It is vital that any effective comparison/contrast paper makes a point about its two subjects (or the two sides of its single subject). As you prewrite and outline, think about the *result* of comparing or contrasting your sides: what conclusion do you reach as you prewrite; what do you want to say by comparing or contrasting? This is most likely your point.

c   Write a trial topic sentence and a two-column outline. After choosing a tentative topic, write a topic sentence that states three things: (1) the two subjects you will compare or contrast; (2) your intention either to compare or to contrast; and (3) the point you will make about your subject by doing so. Then see what kind of support you can generate for that topic. For instance, if you plan to contrast two cars, see if you can think of and jot down three distinct ways they differ. In other words, prepare an outline. An outline is a necessary technique to use when preparing any paragraph; it is almost indispensable when you are planning a comparison or contrast paragraph. For a model, look back at the outlines given on page 177.

Keep in mind that this planning stage is probably the *single most important phase* of work you will do on your paper. Without clear planning, you are not likely to write an effective paragraph.

d   Decide on your bases (or subtopics) for comparing or contrasting. Look for items in the two columns of your outline that can be grouped under one heading, or base for comparing or contrasting. Be sure that for each point of comparison or contrast for one side, you have a "matching point" for the other side.

e   Decide on a method of development appropriate to your subject. After you have decided on a topic and the main lines of support, you must decide whether to use a one-side-at-a-time or a point-by-point method of development. The advantages and uses of both methods are explained on pages 176–178 of this chapter.

f   Freewrite, if necessary, to accumulate more details. Freewrite for ten minutes on the topic you have chosen to ensure that you have an equal number of details for each side. Do not worry about punctuation, spelling, or other matters relating to correct form. Just get as many details as you can onto the page. You want a base of raw material that you can add to and select from as you now work on the first draft of your paper. After you do a first draft, try to put it aside for a day or at least several hours. You will then be ready to return with a fresh perspective on the material and build upon what you have already done.

g   Use transitions to show comparison, contrast, or *linked ideas*. Linking and emphasis transactions are *first, in addition, also, moreover,* and *most important*; they make your paper logical and coherent.

h   As you continue working on your paper, refer to the checklist on the inside front cover. Make sure that you can answer *Yes* to the questions about unity, support, and coherence.

i   Finally, use the checklist on the inside front cover to edit the next-to-final draft of your paper for sentence-skills mistakes, including spelling.

■ Writing Assignment 3

Write a contrast paragraph on one of the fifteen topics below.

Neighbourhood stores versus a shopping mall
Driving on an expressway versus driving on sideroads
Shift versus *Wired* (or any other two popular magazines)
Working parents versus stay-at-home parents

Last year's fashions versus this year's
Used car versus new car
CDs versus tapes
Hip Hop versus R&B, "machine," or another music style.
News in a newspaper versus news on television
Yesterday's toys versus today's
One Canadian TV series versus a similar U.S. network series.
"Winning" locker room after a game versus "losing" locker room
Ad on television versus ad (for the same product) in a magazine
Your values versus those of your parents and their generation.

Follow the directions on "How to Proceed" given in Writing Assignment 2.

Writing Assignment 4

You have volunteered to contribute a monthly column to the students' section of your college's website. On your link-page, you are asked to post helpful advice and information about various issues of interest to your peers. This month's column is dedicated to first-semester students.

Write an open letter comparing or contrasting *specific aspects* of two sides of one of the following subjects:

- life as a first-semester college student versus life as _____
  (a working person, a high school student, or other option)
- issues faced by the "mature student" versus those faced by the "just out of high school student."

Writing Assignment 5

Writing About a Reading Selection: Read the selection "Are We Raising Morally Illiterate Kids?" on pages 514–518. Then consider a situation in your life when you were confronted by the need to make a choice between two courses of action. One option open to you was likely "wrong" by most ethical standards, and the other option was probably the "right" moral choice. Which course of action did you choose, and why? Write a paragraph that examines your situation and decision by comparing or contrasting the appeals, rewards, or problems of each possible course of action.

To get started, write a brief description of your decision and its circumstances at the top of a sheet of paper. Under that description, make two lists: one containing the appealing aspects and problems of making the "wrong" choice, and one containing the appeals, difficulties, and rewards of making the "right" choice. You may want to further subdivide the lists into headings such as "short-term" and "long-term," or "personal" and "affecting others," depending on your situation and decision.

Next, decide whether you will use a side-by-side or point-by-point method of development. Whichever method you use, counter each point for the "wrong" side with a comparable point for the "right" side. If you use the side-by-side method, be sure to use transitions to remind readers of your first "side's" points as you cover the points for the other "side" of your moral issue.

REVIEWING THE LEARNING OUTCOMES FOR
COMPARISON/CONTRAST WRITING

After completing one of the writing assignments in this chapter, review your paper
to see how well your work responds to the following questions:

1   Does your paper compare or contrast two sides of an idea or two subjects that
    have a logical reason to be considered together? Does a worthwhile point emerge
    from the activity of comparing or contrasting the two parts of your topic?

2   Do you open with a topic sentence that states (1) both parts of your subject,
    (2) your intention either to compare or contrast, and (3) the point your paper
    makes by comparing or contrasting your two subjects?

3   Have you carefully and consistently used the method most appropriate to your
    subject matter? If you have many specific details on each side, have you used
    the point-by-point format? If you wished to pursue each side in some depth,
    have you used the one-side-at-a-time format?

4   Within either format, are your points of comparison or contrast, and your sup-
    porting details for each, relatively equal and balanced for both sides or both
    subjects?

5   Do you conclude with a summing up of the points you have made in your
    paper and an indication of how these points reaffirm and strengthen your
    main point?

Defining a Term

ining a Process · Examining Cause and Effect · Comparing or Contrasting · Defining
· Dividing and Classifying · Describing a Scene or Person · Narrating an Event · Argu
ition · Explaining a Process · Examining Cause and Effect · Comparing or Contrastin
ing a Term · Dividing and Classifying · Describing a Scene or Person · Narrating an Ev
uing a Position · Explaining a Process · Examining Cause and Effect · Comparing

LEARNING OUTCOMES

By working through this chapter's activities and completing one or more of its writing assignments, you will write a definition paper that

- sets its subject in an appropriately limited category or classification of similar subjects, and then sets its subject apart from other members of that category with adequate explanations of how the subject differs from them;
- begins with a topic sentence placing the subject in its category, differentiating the subject as somehow unique, and indicating the relative degree of formality or objectivity involved in the definition to follow;
- offers at least three supporting points (or one extended point) to clarify and limit the meaning of its subject; such points may be examples, brief anecdotes, or comparisons or contrasts with other closely related concepts;
- offers meanings appropriate to both the subject and to the needs of the reader for either an objective or a personal and subjective definition; and
- concludes with a summary of the meaning of the term and its significance, based on what has been stated in the paper.

Defining is essential to clear communication. Unless people agree on what a speaker or writer means by a given term, misunderstandings occur, and communication may fail. Definition papers explain the meaning of some term or concept and are forms of extended definitions: extended beyond the limited definitions found in dictionaries. Although a paragraph defining some concrete or abstract term may initially use elements of a dictionary definition, such a paper's purpose is to state fully the writer's sense of that term's meaning. The writer's task, in defining, is to do three things: (1) to *classify* the subject appropriately in terms of other items of its type, (2) to *make specific* his or her explanation of the subject's meaning by limiting that meaning, and (3) to offer meanings *relevant to the needs of the readers* of the paper.

Every day we offer informal definitions to explain what we mean by a particular term. We may say, "Mario is an anxious person." Then, without pausing, we try to be more exact about what we mean by "anxious." We expand on our definition by giving *examples:* "He's always worrying about the future. Yesterday he was talking about how many bills he'll have this year." Or, we offer a *story* to show Mario's anxiety in a specific circumstance. Or perhaps we may *compare or contrast* Mario's anxiety with what we feel in similar situations. We even describe the stages in the *process* by which Mario became so anxious. Our aim is to *set limits* around exactly what we mean by "anxious" *in the context of our conversation*, as opposed to what a dictionary may mean by "anxious," or what a psychologist may mean by the term. Even in ordinary conversations, we use the same assortment of methods for defining that we use in writing definition papers.

The word "definition," as derived from its Latin origin, refers to putting "fines," or limits around a subject—this boundary-setting activity always exists within specific contexts that colour and shape definitions. Throughout your life, in both personal and professional situations, you will work with and create definitions for many purposes—as language and situations change, so does the way words are used. Misunderstandings may be remedied quickly in conversation, but there is little tolerance for risking misunderstanding or not knowing a term in career contexts. The growth of technology has obviously increased the need for definitions of new words and of existing words with new meanings; business constantly creates its own terminologies, and human and social services careers rely on precise definitions for terms in reports and studies.

In this section, you will be asked to write a paragraph in which you define a term. The two student papers below are examples of definition paragraphs. Read them, and then answer the questions that follow.

PARAGRAPHS TO CONSIDER

Luck

¹Luck is putting $1.75 into a vending machine and getting the money back with your snacks. ²It is an instructor's decision to give a retest on a test where you first scored thirty. ³Luck refers to moments of good fortune that happen in everyday life. ⁴It is not going to the dentist for two years and then going and finding out that you do not have any cavities. ⁵It is calling up a plumber to fix a leak on a day when the plumber has no other work to do. ⁶Luck is finding a used car for sale at a good price at exactly the time when your car rolls its last mile. ⁷It is driving into a traffic bottleneck and choosing the lane that winds up moving most rapidly. ⁸Luck is being late for work on a day when your boss arrives later than you do. ⁹It is having a new check-out aisle at the supermarket open up just as your cart arrives. ¹⁰The best kind of luck is winning a new TV set with a raffle ticket for which you paid only a quarter.

Disillusionment

¹Disillusionment is the feeling of having one of our most cherished beliefs stolen from us. ²I learned about disillusionment firsthand the day Mr. Khalid,

our grade eight teacher, handed out the marks on our class biology projects. [3]I had worked hard to assemble what I thought was the best insect collection any school had ever seen. [4]For weeks, I had set up homemade traps around our house, in the woods, and in vacant lots. [5]At night, I would stretch a white sheet between two trees, shine a lantern on it, and collect the night-flying insects that gathered there. [6]With my own money, I had bought killing jars, insect pins, gummed labels, and display boxes. [7]I carefully arranged related insects together, with labels listing each scientific name and the place and date of capture. [8]Slowly and painfully, I processed and printed the report that accompanied my project at the Moosejaw school science fair. [9]In contrast, my friend Michael did almost nothing for his project. [10]He had his father, a doctor, build an impressive maze complete with live rats and a sign that read, "You are the trainer." [11]A person could lift a little plastic door, send a rat running through the maze, and then hit a button to release a pellet of rat food as a reward. [12]This exhibit turned out to be the most popular one at the fair. [13]I felt sure that our teacher would know that Michael could not have built it, and I was certain that my hard work would be recognized and rewarded. [14]Then the grades were finally handed out, and I was crushed. [15]Michael had an A+, but my grade was a B. [16]I suddenly realized that honesty and hard work don't always pay off in the end. [17]The idea that life is not fair, hit me with such force that I felt sick. [18]I will never forget that moment.

■ Questions

About Unity

1. Which paragraph places its topic sentence within the paragraph rather than, more appropriately, at the beginning?

   _____

2. Which sentence in "Disillusionment" is somewhat repetitious, and might be revised for paragraph unity? (*Write the sentence number here.*) _____

About Support

3. Which paragraph develops its definition through a series of short examples?

   _____

   _____

4. Which paragraph develops its definition through a single extended example?

   _____

About Coherence

5. Which paragraph uses emphatic order, saving its best detail for last?

   _____

6. Which paragraph uses time order to organize its details?

_____

WRITING A DEFINITION PARAGRAPH

How to Write a Definition Paragraph

1 Looking at the subject for your paragraph, first ask yourself this question: is your subject a *concrete* thing, or an *abstract* concept? Concrete objects, like dogs or computers, have precise basic (denotative) definitions, to which personal experience-based shadings (connotative descriptions) may be added. Abstract ideas like honour or ambition are defined almost completely according to personal interpretations and understandings of their meaning. Some terms occupy a "middle space" between the concrete and the abstract, like "an ideal employee."

2 Next, consider the degree of objectivity most suitable to defining your subject. Is your paper a personal definition of some abstract subject or quality best explained by your own experience with that quality, or is your paper an extended definition of some concrete subject where more objective, even scientific or factual details are required? Although the methods for writing a definition are the same for both types of subjects, the tones, points of view, types of details, and needs of readers differ.

3 Prewrite to accumulate as many details of any sort about your subject. As you prepare to create an outline for your paper, consider the methods that will best define your subject: examples, comparing or contrasting with other subjects of its type, brief anecdotes, or a description of how your subject works. Decide on a method of development for your definition and create an outline based on that method.

4 Write a topic sentence that places your subject in a logical category and includes at least one specific detail that distinguishes your subject. Include an indication of the nature and tone of your definition: subjective and personal, or objective and factual.

5 Be sure that the body of your definition truly clarifies the meaning of your subject and does not merely repeat itself or offer unclear synonyms as alternative definitions. Make sure that your examples or distinguishing details are vivid and logically connected. The details or support for your definition may also state what your subject is by setting out what it is not.

6 Conclude with a summation of your understanding of your term, and its significance.

▧ Writing Assignment 1

Following are a topic sentence and three supporting points for a paragraph that defines the term *TV addict.* Using a separate sheet of paper, plan and write the secondary supporting details and closing sentence needed to complete the paragraph. Refer to the suggestions on "How to Proceed" that follow.

Topic sentence: Television addicts are people who will watch all the programs they can, for as long as they can, rather than do anything else.

a. TV addicts, first of all, will watch anything on the tube, no matter how bad it is. …

b. In addition, addicts watch TV more hours than normal people do. …

c. Finally, addicts feel that TV is more important than any other activities or events that might be going on. …

How to Proceed

a   **Begin by prewriting.** Prepare examples that expand on each of the three qualities of a TV addict. For each quality, you should have at least two or three sentences that provide either an extended example or shorter examples of this quality in action.

b   **Generate supporting details.** Ask yourself the following questions:

What are some examples of terrible shows that I (or people I know) watch just because the television is turned on?

What are some examples of how frequently I (or people I know) watch TV?

What are some other activities or events that I (or people I know) give up in order to watch TV?

Look for possible comparisons or contrasts within your examples. Comparisons and contrasts are useful ways to limit and clarify subjects being defined. For example, how much TV does an addict watch, compared to someone else?

Write down quickly whatever answers occur to you. Do not worry about writing correct sentences; just concentrate on getting down all the details about television addicts that you can think of.

c   **Work on a first draft based on your prewriting.** As you draw from and add to your material, and work on your draft, focus on the main thrust of your definition. What general impression of a TV addict emerges from your prewriting? Make sure that your defining paragraph's details all relate to this main point so that your final draft is unified, supported, and coherent.

d   Finally, edit the next-to-final draft of your paper for sentence-skills mistakes, including spelling.

■ Writing Assignment 2

Our conversations are full of labels for people. These labels are a convenient kind of verbal shorthand, but how often do people know exactly what we mean by our terms? Write a paragraph that states your definition of what is meant by one of these labels. Each term refers to a certain kind of person.

Bigmouth	Clown	Good example
Charmer	Jellyfish	Hypocrite
Loser	Leader	Perfectionist
Lazybones	Nerd	Pack rat
Net Freak	Good neighbour	Hard worker
Con artist	Optimist	Tree hugger
Fair-weather friend	Pessimist	Team player

How to Proceed

a **Classify your term to limit your definition.** To write a topic sentence for your definition paragraph, your first step should be to *place the term in a class or category.* Then *describe what you feel are the special features that distinguish your term from all the other members of its class.*

In the sample topic sentences below, underline the class, or category, that the term belongs to and double-underline the distinguishing details of that class, or category. One is done for you as an example.

A klutz is a <u>person</u> who <u>stumbles through life.</u>

A worrywart is a person who sees danger everywhere.

The class clown is a student who gets attention in the wrong way.

A clothes horse is a person who needs new clothes to be happy.

b **Develop your definition.** Use one of the following methods:

Examples. Give several examples that support your topic sentence.
Extended example. Use one longer example to support your topic sentence.
Contrast. Support your topic sentence by showing what your term is *not.* For instance, you may want to define a "fair-weather friend" by contrasting his or her actions with those of a true friend.

c **Write an outline.** Once you have created a topic sentence and decided how to develop your paragraph, write an outline. This step is especially important if you are using a contrast method of development.

d Be sure your writing touches the four bases—unity, support, coherence, and sentence skills.

■ Writing Assignment 3

Write a paragraph that defines one of the abstract terms below.

Persistence	Responsibility	Fear
Rebellion	Insecurity	Arrogance
Sense of humour	Assertiveness	Conscience
Escape	Jealousy	Class
Danger	Nostalgia	Innocence
Curiosity	Gentleness	Freedom
Common sense	Depression	Violence
Family	Obsession	Shyness
Practicality	Self-control	

Defining an abstract term or concept requires you to select certain specific examples or circumstances that make your view of that term's meaning clear to your reader. Definition papers make use of many methods of paragraph development.

Following are several approaches to writing such a paper:

■ Begin with an objective definition of your concept, then compare or contrast that meaning with your own specific experiences with or knowledge of that concept.

- Consider explaining what your concept or term means by using *negation*; explain what something is by stating clearly what it is *not,* or need not be.
- Sometimes using an anecdote, or brief story, can vividly show an abstract quality in action.
- Dividing your abstract quality into different aspects or categories, with examples for each, often makes a broad concept clearer to readers.

As a guide in writing your paper, use the suggestions on "How to Proceed" in Writing Assignment 2. Remember always begin by placing your term in a class, or category, and then describe what you feel are the distinguishing features of that term. Three examples follow.

Laziness is a quality that doesn't deserve its bad reputation.
Jealousy is the emotion that hurts most.
Persistence is the quality of not giving up even during rough times.

Writing Assignment 4

Option 1: At the place where you work, one employee has just quit, creating a new job opening. Since you have been working there for a while, your boss has asked you to write a job description of the position. That description, which is really a detailed definition of the job, will be sent to employment services. These services will be responsible for interviewing candidates. Choose any position you know about, and write a job description for it. First, give the purpose of the job, and then list its duties and responsibilities. Finally, give the qualifications for the position.

Option 2: Alternatively, imagine that a new worker has been hired, and your boss has asked you to explain "team spirit" to him or her. The purpose of your explanation will be to give the newcomer an idea of the teamwork that is expected in this workplace. Write a paragraph that defines in detail what your boss means by *team spirit.* Use examples or one extended example to illustrate your general statements.

Writing Assignment 5

Writing about a Reading: Read the selection titled "What Good Families Are Doing Right" on pages 464–472. Then write a definition paragraph on the hallmarks of a *bad* family. Your topic sentence might be, "A bad family is one that

is _____, _____, and _____."

To get started, you should first reread the features of a good family explained in the selection. Doing so will help you think about what qualities are found in a bad family. Prepare a list of as many bad qualities as you can think of. Then go through the list and decide upon the qualities that seem most characteristic of a bad family.

Next, spend some time thinking of and jotting down *examples* of each of these qualities. You will note that the selection provides examples of the hallmarks of a good family; your goal will be to provide examples of the hallmarks of a bad family. Your examples can be drawn from your own experience or observation, or they can be hypothetical examples—examples that you invent but that you feel are realistic. Perhaps your examples will be composites of several bad families or of behaviours that may occur at different times in any family.

Finally, decide on the order in which to present these qualities, keeping in mind that you will want to end with the most telling quality. And remember that you will want to use transition words and synonyms such as The *first hallmark, another quality, a third feature,* and so on.

You should now be ready to write the first draft of your paper.

REVIEWING THE LEARNING OUTCOMES FOR DEFINITION WRITING

After completing any of the writing assignments in this chapter, review your paper to see how well your work responds to the following questions:

1 Does your paper open with a topic sentence that both places your subject to be defined in an appropriate category and sets it off from other members of that category?

2 Does your topic sentence indicate your paper's tone and the degree of objectivity or subjectivity with which you will define your subject?

3 Do you offer at least three supporting points and details for your definition of your subject? Are your points and details specific, and does each directly support your topic sentence's point about your subject?

4 Have you used a method of development for your supporting material that is appropriate to the subject you define, i.e., examples, comparison or contrast, negation, or anecdote?

5 Does your paper conclude with a summary of your meanings, a reminder of your topic sentence's point, and a suggestion of the significance of your definition?

 aining a Process · Examining Cause and Effect · comparing or contrasting · Definin
· Dividing and classifying · Describing a Scene or Person · Narrating an Event · Argu
sition · Explaining a Process · Examining Cause and Effect · comparing or contrastin
uing a Term · Dividing and classifying · Describing a Scene or Person · Narrating an Ev
guing a Position · Explaining a Process · Examining Cause and Effect · Comparing

CHAPTER 14

Dividing and Classifying

LEARNING OUTCOMES

By working through this chapter's activities and completing at least one of its writing assignments, you will write a classification and division paper that

- divides its subject according to a consistent classifying principle logically related to your purpose in analysing that subject;
- arranges its categories or subject-divisions in a sequence that best supports the point and purpose of the paper;
- begins with a topic sentence that states the paper's subject, the divisions of its subject, and your point in making those divisions;
- offers a balanced number of specific and adequate details for each supporting point or subject-division; and
- concludes with a return to your subject as a whole, and offers a closing thought based on your paper's examination of your subject-divisions.

Dividing a subject into classes or categories occurs constantly in everyday life. People break groups of things or ideas into subgroups, based on some purpose or need, hoping to manage situations or understand ideas more easily. The process of dividing and classifying seeks to create order out of apparent confusion and often leads to decision making. Division and classification papers are expository forms that imitate a natural human tendency to open up a subject and examine its parts according to some logical pattern.

If you were doing the laundry, you would probably separate the clothing into piles. If your purpose was to decide when to use bleach, you would sort all the whites into one pile and all the colours into another. If your purpose was to see how many types of washing cycles were needed, you might put all cottons in one pile, polyesters in another, silks in a third, and so on. Or you might divide and classify the laundry not according to colour or fabric type, but on the basis of use. You might put bath towels in one pile, bed sheets in another, personal garments in a third, and so on. Such ordinary processes of sorting according to various principles demonstrate how we organize and order our environment in order to make decisions.

Division and classification activities are ongoing parts of your college and career communications tasks at every level. Writing a paragraph, essay, or report outline to display the arrangement of ideas explaining a subject; sorting a mass of consumers into demographic groups to examine and report on buying patterns; dividing components of a software program into categories to analyze their effectiveness: all involve the same set of structuring and analyzing skills.

In this section, you will be asked to write a paragraph in which you divide or classify a subject according to a single principle. To prepare for this assignment, first read the division and classification paragraphs below and then work through the questions and the activity that follow.

PARAGRAPHS TO CONSIDER

Studying for a Test

[1]The time a student spends studying for a test can be divided into three distinct phases. [2]Phase 1, often called the "no problem" phase, runs from the day the test is announced to approximately forty-eight hours before the dreaded exam is passed out. [3]During phase 1, the student is carefree, smiling, and kind to helpless animals and small children. [4]When asked by classmates if he or she has studied for the test yet, the reply will be an assured "No problem." [5]During phase 1, no actual studying takes place. [6]Phase 2 is entered two days before the test. [7]For example, if the test is scheduled for 9 a.m. Friday, phase 2 begins at 9 a.m. Wednesday. [8]During phase 2, again, no actual studying takes place. [9]Phase 3, the final phase, is entered twelve hours before "zero hour." [10]This is the acute phase, characterized by sweaty palms, nervous twitches, and confused mental patterns. [11]For a test at nine o'clock on Friday morning, a student begins exhibiting these symptoms at approximately nine o'clock on Thursday night. [12]Phase 3 is also termed the "shock" phase, since the student is shocked to discover the imminent nature of the exam and the amount of material to be studied. [13]During this phase, the student will probably be unable to sleep and will mumble meaningless phrases like "$a^2 + c^2$." [14]This phase will not end until the exam is over. [15]If the cram session has worked, the student will fall gratefully asleep. [16]On waking up, he or she will be ready to go through the whole cycle again with the next test.

The Dangers of Tools

[1]Tools can be divided into three categories according to how badly people can injure themselves with them. [2]The first group of tools causes dark-purple bruises to appear on the user's feet, fingers, or arms. [3]Hammers are famous for this, as millions of cartoons and comic strips have shown. [4]Mallets and crowbars, too, can go a bit off target and thud onto a bit of exposed flesh. [5]But first-class bruises can also be caused by clamps, pliers, vise grips, and wrenches. [6]In a split second, any one of these tools can lash out and badly

squeeze a stray finger. [7]Later, the victim will see blue-black blood forming under the fingernail. [8]The second type of tool usually attacks by cutting or tearing. [9]Saws seem to enjoy cutting through human flesh as well as wood. [10]Keeping a hand too close to the saw, or using a pair of knees as a sawhorse, will help the saw satisfy its urge. [11]Planes, chisels, and screwdrivers also cut into skin. [12]And the utility knife—the kind with a razor blade projecting from a metal handle—probably cuts more people than it does linoleum. [13]The most dangerous tools, however, are the mutilators, the ones that send people directly to the emergency room. [14]People were definitely not made to handle monster tools like chain saws, table saws, power drills, and power hammers. [15]Newspapers are filled with stories of shocking accidents people have had with power tools. [16]In summary, if people are not careful, tools can definitely be hazardous to their health.

■ Questions

About Unity

1. Which sentence in "The Dangers of Tools" does not support the paragraph's point? _____

About Support

2. Which of the three phases in "Studying for a Test" lacks specific details?

    _____

3. Which sentence in "The Dangers of Tools" seems to be out of order? _____

About Coherence

4. Which paragraph uses time order to organize its details?

    _____

5. Which paragraph uses emphatic order to organize its details?

    _____

6. What words in the emphatic-order paragraph signal the most important detail?

    _____

Activity

Classification *always* divides items in a group according to some criterion, or *principle of classification*. This principle is used both for *dividing* a group into its members and for maintaining *unity* of the classifications. This activity will sharpen your sense of the classifying process. In each of the following ten groups, cross out the one item that has not been classified on the same basis as the other three. Also, indicate in the space provided the single *principle of classification* used for the three items. Note the examples.

Examples   Water   Household pests
               a. Cold   ~~a. Mice~~
               ~~b. Lake~~   b. Ants
               c. Hot   c. Roaches
               d. Lukewarm   d. Flies
               Unifying principle: Unifying principle:
               Temperature   *insects*

1. Eyes
   a. Blue
   b. Nearsighted
   c. Brown
   d. Hazel
   Unifying principle:

   _____

2. Mattresses
   a. Double
   b. Twin
   c. Queen
   d. Firm
   Unifying principle:

   _____

3. Zoo animals
   a. Flamingo
   b. Peacock
   c. Polar bear
   d. Ostrich
   Unifying principle

   _____

4. Vacation
   a. Summer
   b. Holiday
   c. Seashore
   d. Weekend
   Unifying principle:

   _____

5. College classes
   a. Enjoy
   b. Dislike
   c. Tolerate
   d. Morning
   Unifying principle:

   _____

6. Wallets
   a. Leather
   b. Plastic
   c. Stolen
   d. Fabric
   Unifying principle:

   _____

7. Newspaper
   a. Wrapping garbage
   b. Editorials
   c. Making paper planes
   d. Covering floor while painting
   Unifying principle

   _____

8. Music
   a. Metal
   b. Country
   c. Melodic
   d. Punk
   Unifying principle:

   _____

9. Exercise
   a. Running
   b. Swimming
   c. Gymnastics
   d. Fatigue
   Unifying principle:

   _____

10. Leftovers
    a. Cold chicken
    b. Feed to dog
    c. Reheat
    d. Use in a stew
    Unifying principle:

    _____

WRITING A DIVISION AND CLASSIFICATION PARAGRAPH

How to Write a Division and Classification Paragraph

1   As you begin your prewriting, think about your reason or purpose for dividing up your subject. Consider your audience: who are your readers, and what would they want to know about your subject? What do you know about your subject, and how will that help you to divide and classify your subject into interesting and appropriate categories? Write down your purpose and subject in a trial sentence at the top of your prewriting page.

2   Divide your subject into at least three groups, and set up your prewriting as three columns, one for each of your groups. Be sure that your groups all follow a single principle for classification. List, freewrite, or question until you have a fairly equal number of details for each of your categories.

3   Read over and revise your prewriting to discover the clear *point* that emerges from your divisions and details: what are you saying about your subject? Edit any details that do not directly support your point as well as your purpose for dividing and classifying your subject. State your point about your subject, your purpose for dividing it as you do, and your divisions or categories in a topic sentence. Proceed to create a detailed outline, showing each division and its supporting details.

4   As you write your drafts based on your outline, be sure that each point and support (each division/category and details) relates clearly to your subject as a whole and the point you make about your subject.

5   Conclude by refocusing your reader on your subject as a whole and on the significance of what your dividing and classifying has shown about your subject.

■ ## Writing Assignment 1

Below are four possible division and classification writing assignments, along with possible divisions or subtopics. Choose *one* of them to develop into a paragraph.

Option 1	*Option 3*
Supermarket shoppers	Methods of housekeeping
a. Slow, careful	a. Never clean
b. Average	b. Clean regularly
c. Rushed, hurried	c. Clean constantly

Option 2	*Option 4*
Eaters	Attitudes toward money
a. Super-conservative	a. Tightfisted
b. Typical	b. Sometimes splurge
c. Adventurous	c. Spendthrift

How to Proceed

a **Prewrite.** Try dividing your page into three columns (one for each division) and listing words and phrases in each column as ideas occur to you. To develop some ideas for the paragraph, freewrite for five or ten minutes on your topic.

b **Generate more details by questioning yourself.** Add to the material you have written by asking yourself questions. If you are writing about supermarket shoppers, for example, you might ask:

How do the three kinds of shoppers pick out the items they want?
How many aisles will each type of shopper visit?
Which shoppers bring lists, calculators, coupons, and so on?
How much time does it take each type of shopper to finish shopping?

Continuing to use a "three column" method for your divisions, write down whatever answers occur to you for these and other questions. As with freewriting, do not worry at this stage about writing correctly. Instead, concentrate on getting down all the information you can think of that supports each of the three points, or that fits each of your classifications.

c **Revise your material and decide on an appropriate order.** Now go through all the material you have accumulated. Perhaps some of the details you have written down may help you think of even better details that would fit. If so, write them down. Then make decisions about the exact information you will use to support each point. Number the details within each classification *1, 2, 3,* and so on, in the order you will present them. To ensure a balanced paragraph, try to have roughly the same number of supporting details for each of your three classifications.

d As you work on the drafts of your paragraph, make sure that it touches three of the four bases: unity, support, and coherence.

e Finally, make sure your paper touches the fourth base: sentence skills. Edit the next-to-final draft for sentence-skills mistakes, including spelling.

■ Writing Assignment 2

Write a division and classification paragraph on one of the following subjects:

Instructors	Drivers
Sports fans	Mothers or fathers
Eating places	Women's or men's magazines
Attitudes toward life	Presents
Commercials	Neighbours
Employers	Rock, pop, or country singers
Jobs	Amusement parks or rides
Bars	Guests or company
Family get-togethers	Ways to get an A (or F) in a course
Shoes	Car accessories

How to Proceed

a **Choose a single logical principle for dividing your subject.** The first step in writing a division and classification paragraph is to divide your tentative topic into three reasonably complete parts. *Always use a single principle of division when you form your three parts.* For example, if your topic was "Automobile Drivers" and you divided them into slow, moderate, and fast drivers, your single basis for division would be "rate of speed." It would be illogical, then, to have as a fourth type "teenage drivers" (the basis of such a division would be "age") or "female drivers" (the basis of such a division would be "sex"). You could probably classify automobile drivers on the basis of age or sex or another division, for almost any subject can be analyzed in more than one way. What is important, however, is that *in any single paper you choose only one basis for division and stick to it.* Be consistent.

In "Studying for a Test," the writer divides the process of studying into three time phases: from the time the test is announced to forty-eight hours before the test; the day and a half before the test; the final twelve hours before the test. In "The Dangers of Tools," the single basis for dividing tools into three categories is the kind of injury each type inflicts: bruises, cuts, and major injuries.

b Decide on your purpose for making such a decision. Remember that your topic sentence and your paragraph must *make a point.* It is not enough simply to *announce* "there are three categories of shoes." *What point* do you wish to make by dividing up your topic? Do you wish to *explain* more about your topic, to *describe* each classification in greater detail? As part of your prewriting, aim at discovering your point.

c Freewrite to accumulate details about your subtopics or divisions. Divide your page into three columns, each headed by the name of one of your divisions. List details for each division under your headings for ten minutes.

d Outline your paragraph. To ensure a clear three-part division in your own paragraph, fill in the outline below before starting your paper and make sure you can answer *Yes* to the questions that follow. You should expect to do a fair amount of thinking before coming up with a logical plan for your paper.

Topic (subject, point, and divisions): _____

Three-part division of the topic and purpose: _____

(1) _____

(2) _____

(3) _____

Is there a single basis of division for the three parts? _____

Is the division reasonably complete? _____

e Refer to the checklist of the four bases on the inside front cover while writing the drafts of your paper. Make sure you can answer *Yes* to the questions about unity, support, coherence, and sentence skills. Also, use the checklist when you edit the next-to-final draft of your paper for sentence-skills mistakes, including spelling.

■ **Writing Assignment 3**

There are many ways you could classify the students around you. Pick out one of your courses and write a division and classification paragraph on the students in that class. You might want to categorize the students according to one of the principles of division below:

Attitude toward class	Attendance
Participation in the class	Level of confidence
Method of taking notes in class	Performance during oral reports,
Method of taking a test in class	speeches, presentations, lab
Punctuality	sessions

Of course, you may use any other principle of division that seems appropriate. Follow the steps listed in "How to Proceed" for Writing Assignment 2.

■ **Writing Assignment 4**

Along with students from other colleges and universities in your area, you have been invited to be part of a group panel speaking to graduating students at local high schools. You are to give your audience an overview of student life at your college, or at your campus of your college.

Write a script for a brief presentation that discusses aspects of "Life at _____ College." Divide the college experience into three categories you feel would be of use and interest to your audience. Be sure to (1) indicate your purpose in having chosen each aspect of college life you include in your presentation, and (2) include enough specifics about each aspect to help and inform students who have not yet had any experience of postsecondary education.

■ **Writing Assignment 5**

Writing About a Reading Selection: Read the selection "Letter" on pages 460–461, and consider what the author has to say about generosity and its rewards. Using the concept of charity (or generosity) as your topic, and based on your own experience, write a paragraph that divides charity into different types or forms according to the classifying principle of the rewards involved.

To get started, think carefully about two things: the forms of generosity or charity you have offered to others, and those you have received from others. Start your prewriting with whichever form of charity you find easiest to write about. Write only and specifically about your own experience; do not generalize. Focus on one specific situation and the rewards that arose from it, and look for headings under which to classify those rewards: possibilities might be "personal rewards," "material rewards," "unexpected rewards," and so on. As appears in the reading selection, look for an overall "lesson" or summarising statement about your experience and its meaning with which to conclude your paragraph.

REVIEWING THE LEARNING OUTCOMES FOR
CLASSIFICATION AND DIVISION WRITING

After completing any of the writing assignments in this chapter, review your paper
to see how well your work responds to the following questions:

1 Do the divisions in your paper's subject follow a consistent principle? Is this
dividing principle logically related to your purpose in examining your subject?
Does it lead to new and interesting information about your subject?

2 Does your paper open with a topic sentence that states your purpose for dividing and classifying your subject, your point about doing so, and your categories
or divisions?

3 Do your divisions and supporting details appear in an order that makes your
point most strongly?

4 Do you have a balanced number of supporting details for each subject-
division, and is each detail closely related to your point about your subject?

5 Does your conclusion remind readers of your opening point about your subject and reinforce whatever has been shown in examining your divisions of
your subject?

CHAPTER 15

Arguing a Position

LEARNING OUTCOMES

By completing this chapter's activities and at least one of its writing assignments, you will write an argumentation paper that

■ opens with a clear and definite statement of the point to be argued;

■ shows in its opening section, based on some knowledge of its audience, possible counterarguments and responses to them;

■ uses a method of development most appropriately suited to stating logical and well-reasoned points and details to support the point to be argued;

■ in its supporting points and details, shows logic and knowledge of the specifics of its subject;

■ argues its point and support cleanly, without slanting its point with emotional appeals or insulting its audience; and

■ concludes by reaffirming its point, as justified by the evidence presented in the paper.

A paper whose main purpose is to argue a point, or to persuade, is aimed at influencing the thought and action of the reader. Since responding to persuasion or to an argument usually involves some degree of emotion, many people assume that a paper arguing a position will use non-rational techniques to sway its readers. The opposite is actually true for an effective piece of argumentation. Logic, reason, and knowing the interests of the audience are the most potent tactics for effectively arguing a point.

Every day, based on feelings, we make general statements of opinion. In the ordinary course of things, we do not expect to be challenged, so we do not exercise our ability to defend a point very often. Occasionally, though, someone will greet one of our statements with the question, "Why do you say that?" or "What are your reasons for saying that?" Our questioner then listens carefully as we work to muster our reasons, waiting to see if we really do have solid evidence to support our point of view. Such a questioner may make us feel nervous, but we may also feel grateful to him or her for helping us think through our opinions.

The ability to advance sound and compelling arguments is an important skill in everyday life. We may use persuasion to get an extension on a term paper, or convince an employer that we are the right person for a job. Understanding persuasion based on clear, logical reasoning can also help develop critical awareness of arguments advanced by advertisers, artists, editors, and politicians. Argumentation skills are essential to college and career communications needs. Oral and written presentations are generally persuasive in nature, and proposals and reports often require competent use of the skills and techniques of argumentation and persuasion.

In this section, you will be asked to argue a position and defend it with a series of solid reasons. You are in a general way doing the same thing—making a point and then supporting it   with all the paragraphs in the book. The difference here is that, in a more direct and formal manner, you will advance a point about which you feel strongly and seek to persuade others to agree with you.

PARAGRAPHS TO CONSIDER

"Teensploitation" Insults Teenagers

[1]Some people my age never question all the "teensploitation" movies and TV shows these days, but I believe they are insulting to the audiences they are made for. [2]One reason is that the creators of these movies and programs present unrealistic main characters, teenagers who are all good-looking, well off, and basically idle, self-centred consumers. [3]Teen watchers are separated into "the ones who idolize the characters" and "the ones who feel inadequate because they're not Buffy or Dawson." [4]Being either of those types of watchers can cause any sensitive young person to feel dissatisfied and unhappy with himself or herself after a while. [5]Another problem is that these movies and shows suggest that high school is the most important stage in life, an unreal stage that never ends. [6]Many Canadian teenagers cope with very real financial pressures and demanding family and home situations every day; to them, endless worries about a dance or riding around in a friends' HumVee seem as unrealistic as Buffy's vampires. [7]These shows and movies are candy-coloured dreams that leave many young people feeling lied-to and miserable when they consider their own lives by comparison. [8]Perhaps the main reason "teensploitation" entertainment is so insulting is that it assumes that teenagers are empty-headed, and waiting to be told what is good or bad. [9]Also teens are assumed to be assumed to be so dull and gullible that they only want sequels or copies of the last ten successful teen movies or TV shows. [10]Creators of these repetitive "copycat" products insult their teen audiences by boring them to death. [11]Teens and college-age audiences are not so stupid that new or interesting ideas must be sugar-coated with new titles, flashy settings,

and renamed characters played by Ryan Philippe or Sarah Michelle Gellar. [12]In fact, teens often end up watching the shows and movies they do simply because there don't seem to be any other choices available. [13]And teenagers and young people are no different from other consumers: they buy what is advertised—every teen mag and every entertainment TV show and magazine promotes "teensploitation" stars, shows, and movies. [14]No one can resist forever, especially teens who already feel pressure to conform to the tastes of their peers and the media. [15]For all these reasons, creators of entertainment for young people should stop insulting and maybe damaging their target audiences.

Living Alone

[1]Living alone is quite an experience. [2]People who live alone, for one thing, have to learn to do all kinds of tasks by themselves. [3]They must learn—even if they have had no experience—to reset circuit breakers, put up curtains and shades, temporarily dam an overflowing toilet, cook a meal, and defrost a refrigerator. [4]When there are no fathers, husbands, mothers, or wives to depend on, a person can't fall back on the excuse, "I don't know how to do that." [5]Those who live alone also need the strength to deal with people. [6]Alone, singles must face noisy neighbours, unresponsive property managers, and dishonest repair people. [7]Because there are no buffers between themselves and the outside world, people living alone have to handle every visitor—friendly or unfriendly—alone. [8]Finally, singles need a large dose of courage to cope with occasional panic and unavoidable loneliness. [9]That weird thump in the night is even more terrifying when there is no one in the next bed or the next room. [10]Frightening weather or unexpected bad news is doubly bad when the worry can't be shared. [11]Even when life is going well, little moments of sudden loneliness can send shivers through the heart. [12]Struggling through such bad times taps into reserves of courage that people may not have known they possessed. [13]Facing everyday tasks, confronting all types of people, and handling panic and loneliness can shape singles into brave, resourceful, and more independent people.

▓ Questions

About Unity

1. The topic sentence in "Living Alone" is too broad. Circle the topic sentence below that states accurately what the paragraph is about.

    a. Living alone takes courage.

    b. Living alone can create feelings of loneliness.

    c. Living alone should be avoided.

2. Which sentence in "Teensploitation Insults Teens" should be eliminated in the interest of paragraph unity? (*Write the sentence number here.*) _____

About Support

3. How many reasons are given to support the topic sentence in each paragraph?

    a. In "Teensploitation Insults Teens"

    _____ one   _____ two   _____ three   _____ four

    b. In "Living Alone"

    _____ one   _____ two   _____ three   _____ four

4. After which sentence in "Teensploitation Insults Teens" are more specific details needed? _____

About Coherence

5. Why is emphatic order the most logical choice for both paragraphs?

    _____

6. What are the three main transition words in "Living Alone"?

    a. _____   c. _____   e. _____

Activity

Complete the outline below of a paragraph about "A Terrible Vacation." Summarize in a few words the primary and secondary supporting material that fits under the topic sentence. Two items have been done for you as examples.

Topic sentence: Despite much advertising to the contrary, taking a cruise is a terrible way to spend a vacation.

a. _____

    (1) _____

    (2) _____

b. _____

    (1) _____

    (2) *Little room for jogging* _____

c. _____

    (1) _____

    (2) *Dull conversations with other passengers* _____

    (3) _____

WRITING AN ARGUMENT PARAGRAPH

How to Write an Argument Paragraph

1 If your topic is one with which you are not very familiar, or one where you will need more facts to support your viewpoint, take some time to look up some information on your topic at the library or on the Net. Try to read both supporting and opposing views of your topic so that you can anticipate likely counterarguments and your own responses. Be sure you are firm in your point of view on your subject.

2 Prewrite, using as many methods as needed to accumulate as many facts to support your viewpoint on your topic. Add any points you may have found during research.

3 Begin your outline by looking for the main points to support your viewpoint. Rank your main points (subtopics) in order of increasing importance, or emphatic order. Under each point, note any examples, details, facts or statistics, or anecdotes to support that point. Compose a trial topic sentence that states your topic and your viewpoint; many such topic sentences use the words "should," "must," or "ought."

4 Look over your outline and think about your audience. How much does your reader know about your subject? If you feel that your reader will be more ready to accept your views if you supply some information, do so. What will be your reader's attitude towards your topic? Think of any possible objections your reader might have, and counter these with appropriate facts as part of the first section of your paper.

5 Be prepared to work on your drafts until you are satisfied that your audience will see your viewpoint as clearly as you do. Make sure all the facts and details that support your argument follow logically from each other.

6 Conclude with a statement that both reinforces your viewpoint and is justified by the facts you have presented.

▪ Writing Assignment 1

On a separate piece of paper, make up brief outlines for any four of the eight statements that follow. Note the example. Make sure that you have three separate and distinct reasons for each statement.

Example   Large cities should outlaw passenger cars.
   a.   Cut down on smog and pollution
   b.   Cut down on noise
   c.   Create more room for pedestrians

1.   Condoms should (*or* should not) be made available in schools.

2.   _____ (*name a specific hockey team*) should win the Stanley Cup.

3. The computer is one of the best (*or* worst) inventions of this century.

4. _____ are the best (*or* worst) pets.

5. All cigarette and alcohol advertising should be banned.

6. Canadian immigration laws should be changed.

7. _____ is one public figure today who can be considered a hero.

8. This college needs a better _____ (cafeteria *or* library *or* student centre *or* marks policy *or* attendance policy).

How to Proceed

a **Choose an outline to work on.** Decide, perhaps through discussion with your instructor or classmates, which of your outlines would be most promising to develop into a paragraph. Make sure that your supporting points are logical ones that actually back up your topic sentence. Ask yourself in each case, "Does this item truly support my topic sentence?"

b **Now do some prewriting.** Prepare a list of all the details you can think of that might support your point. To begin with, prepare more details than you can actually use. Here, for example, are some of the details generated by the writer of "Teensploitation Insults Teenagers" while working on the paragraph:

– characters in "ts" are unrealistic—rich, good looking, well dressed

– only set in "forever" high school or fancy locations—high school never seems to end

– teens see actors as idols, as something they can never be

– teens know real life and even high school are not like that—assumes teens are stupid

– characters in "ts" have no real pressures or ordinary problems in their lives—even parents' divorces are glamorous

– "ts" TV & movies are full of sequels & copies—nothing is original or new

– "ts" stars, shows, movies, even CDs are advertised everywhere—can't get away from it

– stuff like *Clueless, Ten Things I Hate About You* makes it seem like teens are too stupid to understand the originals—everything is candy-coated and dumbed down

– makes teens feel like this is all there is—nothing else to choose from & teens really react to peer pressure and hype

– "ts" is just insulting to teens and young people—tries to tell us what we want & what we can understand (point of view?)

c **Revise and order your supporting points and details.** Decide which details you will use to develop your paragraph. Also, number the details in the order in which you will present them. (You may also want to make an outline of your paragraph at this point.) Because emphatic order (most important reason last) is the most effective way to organize an argument paragraph, be sure to save your most powerful reason for last. Here is how the writer of "Teensploitation Insuts Teenagers" made decisions about details:

I   *Characters—(least important?)*
   1   all good looking, well off, no ordinary jobs, too much time
   2   teens idolize them or feel bad compared to them
   3   bad role models—nobody is like that

II   *High Schools and Settings—unrealistic*
   1   high school lasts forever—characters look too old, unbelievable (*Buffy, Dawson's Creek, 90210?*)
   2   so the problems and situations are stupid, don't make sense—teens are not that dumb—not like their lives
   3   shows insult teens—show lies and fairy tale lives that don't change

III   *"TS" is so dumb and so repetitive—offers no choice, no variety*
   1   it's everywhere, so not much choice—end up watching
   2   sequels & copies—don't teens want something new or different?
   3   teens feel peer pressure & media uses this
   4   dumbed-down versions of things—candy-coated (what order for details?)

d   Develop each reason with specific details. The writer found three subtopics or supporting points in her prewriting under which she could group the details she already had. She also added some new details and rephrased some of her ideas, which appear in the finished paper (page 207).

e   Think of your audience's response. As you write, imagine that your audience is a jury that will ultimately render a verdict on your argument. Have you presented a convincing case? If *you* were on the jury, would you be favourably impressed with this argument?

f   As you are working on the drafts of your paper, keep in mind the four bases: unity, support, coherence, and sentence skills.

g   Finally, edit the next-to-final draft of your paper for sentence-skills mistakes, including spelling.

■ Writing Assignment 2

Write a paragraph that uses reasons to develop a point of some kind. You may advance and defend a point of your own about which you feel strongly, or you could support any one of the following statements:

1. Junk food should be banned from school cafeterias.

2. Being young is better than being old.

3. Being old is better than being young.

4. Fall can be seen as the saddest season.

5. Classic rock music is (*or*, is not) better than a lot of today's music.

6. _____ is a sport that should be banned.

7. _____ is a subject that should be taught in every school.

8. Students in every college program should spend time working in co-op positions.

9. _____ is the one material possession that is indispensable in everyday life.

10. A college diploma is (*or* is not) essential for an ambitious person.

Use the suggestions in "How to Proceed" on pages 211–212 as a guide in writing your paragraph.

▪ Writing Assignment 3

Write a paragraph in which you take a stand on one of the controversial subjects below. As a lead-in to this writing project, your instructor might give the class a chance to "stand up for what they believe in." One side of the front of the room should be designated *strong agreement* and the other side *strong disagreement,* with the space between for varying intermediate degrees of agreement or disagreement. As the class stands in front of the room, the instructor will read one value statement at a time from the list below, and students will move to the appropriate spot, depending on their degree of agreement or disagreement. Some time will be allowed for students, first, to discuss with those near them the reasons they are standing where they are, and second, to state to those at the other end of the scale the reasons for their position.

1. Students should not be required to attend high school.

2. Prostitution should be legalized.

3. Recreational drugs should be legalized.

4. Casinos and legalized gambling benefit provincial economies.

5. Gay couples should recceive the same benefits and legal status as heterosexual couples.

6. Federal prisons should be co-ed, and prisoners should be allowed to marry.

7. Parents of girls under eighteen should be informed if their daughters receive birth-control aids.

8. The government should legalize euthanasia.

9. Canada should have one official language only, and all signs and publications should be in this language.

10. Parents should never hit their children.

Begin your paragrah by writing a sentence that expresses your attitude toward one of these value statements. For example, "I feel that prostitution should be legalized."

Outline the reason or reasons you hold the opinion that you do. Your support may be based on your own experience, the experience of someone you know, on logic, or on research. For example, an outline of a paragraph based on one student's logic proceeded as follows:

> I feel that prostitution should be legalized for the following reasons:
> 1. Prostitutes would then have to pay their fair share of income tax.
> 2. Government health centres would administer regular checkups and thus help prevent the spread of STDs.
> 3. Prostitutes would be able to work openly and independently and would not be subject to exploitation by others.
> 4. Most of all, prostitutes would no longer be so much regarded as social outcasts—an attitude that is psychologically damaging to those who may already have emotional problems.

Another outline, based on experience, proceeded as follows:

> I do not feel that prostitution should be legalized, because of a woman I know who was once a prostitute.
> 1. The attention Linda received as a prostitute prevented her from seeing and working on her personal problems.
> 2. She became embittered toward all men, whom she always suspected of wanting to exploit her.
> 3. She developed a negative self-image and felt that no one could love her.

Use your outline as the basis for writing a paragraph. Be sure to refer to the suggestions in "How to Proceed" on pages 211–212.

Writing Assignment 4

You have finally met Mr. or Ms. Right—but your parents don't approve of him or her. Specifically, they are against your doing one of the following:

> Continuing to see this person
> Going steady
> Moving in together
> Getting married at the end of the school year

Write a letter to your parents explaining in a fully detailed way why you have made your choice. Do your best to convince them that it is a good choice.

Writing Assignment 5

Writing about a Reading Selection: Read Brian Preston's selection titled "Shots on Goal" on pages 453–456. Then write an argument paper in which you agree or disagree with one of the comments about Manon Rhéaume made by her coach, another player, one of the reporters, or the author himself. Your topic sentence may be simple and direct, like one of these:

- I strongly agree with Chris McSorley's point about Manon's being a "phenomenal athlete" because of her hard work and competence.
- I disagree totally with Alexei Yashin's mother when she states that women can understand hockey as well as men, but they aren't as strong as men, so they must be smarter.

Alternatively, you could develop your own paragraph about women in violent sports like hockey and wrestling. Your topic sentence may be similar to one of the following:

- We need the presence of female skill and technical intelligence in sports where brute strength has been the only selling point.
- Women should be too intelligent to lower themselves to beating each other up in sports where brutality is essential to ticket sales.
- Men may be afraid that women will show how violent they can be if they become too successful in sports like hockey or boxing.

REVIEWING THE LEARNING OUTCOMES FOR ARGUING A POSITION

After completing any of the writing assignments in this chapter, review your paper to see how well your work responds to the following questions:

1 Does your paper open with a clear statement of your viewpoint on the topic to be argued?
2 Does your paper acknowledge and counter any opposing viewpoints close to its beginning?
3 Do you use a method of development appropriate to the type of argument you have chosen (facts and statistics for a logical argument, anecdotes or examples for an experience-based argument)?
4 Does each subtopic and detail clearly support your expressed viewpoint in a logical way?
5 Is your concluding statement justified by the evidence you have presented in the body of your paper?

Essay Development

PREVIEW

Part Three moves from the single-paragraph paper to the several-paragraph essay. The differences between a paragraph and an essay are explained and then illustrated with a paragraph that has been expanded into an essay. You are shown how to begin an essay, how to tie its supporting paragraphs together, and how to conclude it. Three student essays are presented, along with questions to increase your understanding of the essay form. Finally, directions on how to plan an essay are followed by a series of essay writing assignments.

ining a Process • Examining Cause and Effect • Comparing or Contrasting • Defining
• Dividing and Classifying • Describing a Scene or Person • Narrating an Event • Argui
tion • Explaining a Process • Examining Cause and Effect • Comparing or Contrastin
ing a Term • Dividing and Classifying • Describing a Scene or Person • Narrating an Eve
uing a Position • Explaining a Process • Examining Cause and Effect • Comparing

CHAPTER 16

Writing the Essay

LEARNING OUTCOMES

After working through the activities in this chapter and completing the stages of outlining and writing an essay in response to one of this chapter's assignments, you will have begun to achieve competence in creating an essay that

- contains an opening paragraph that attracts the reader's interest and offers a complete thesis statement and suggestion of method of development for that thesis;
- is *unified* because it opens with a clear and limited thesis in its introduction and reinforces this thesis with each of its supporting paragraphs' points and details;
- is *adequately and specifically supported* by three body paragraphs, each of which opens with a topic sentence stating its supporting point from the thesis and then offers sufficient details to explain or clarify that point;
- is *coherent* because it uses a clear method of organization appropriate to its content, and because it offers transitional phrases and sentences to link its paragraphs and to help the reader follow its pattern of ideas;
- contains a conclusion that both sums up the point that is made by its thesis and proved or explained by its supporting points and details, and also offers a parting thought to round it out; and
- communicates its ideas easily and successfully because of *effective use of sentence skills.*

WHAT IS AN ESSAY?

DIFFERENCES BETWEEN AN ESSAY AND A PARAGRAPH

An essay is simply a paper of several paragraphs, rather than one paragraph, that supports a single point. In an essay, subjects can and should be treated more fully than they would be in a single-paragraph paper.

The main idea or point developed in an essay is called the *thesis statement* or *thesis sentence* (rather than, as in a paragraph, the *topic sentence*). The thesis statement appears in the introductory paragraph, and it is then developed in the supporting paragraphs that follow. A short concluding paragraph closes the essay.

THE FORM OF AN ESSAY

The diagram below shows the form of an essay.

Introductory Paragraph

Introduction
Thesis sentence
Plan of development:
Points 1, 2, 3

The *introduction* attracts the reader's interest.
The *thesis sentence* states the main idea advanced in the paper.
The *plan of development* is a list of points that support the thesis. The points are presented in the order in which they will be developed in the paper.

First Supporting Paragraph

Topic sentence (point 1)
Specific evidence

The *topic sentence* advances the first supporting point for the thesis, and the *specific evidence* in the rest of the paragraph develops that first point.

Second Supporting Paragraph

Topic sentence (point 2)
Specific evidence

The *topic sentence* advances the second supporting point for the thesis, and the *specific evidence* in the rest of the paragraph develops that second point.

Third Supporting Paragraph

Topic sentence (point 3)
Specific evidence

The *topic sentence* advances the third supporting point for the thesis, and the *specific evidence* in the rest of the paragraph develops that third point.

Concluding Paragraph

Summary, conclusion, or both

A *summary* is a brief restatement of the thesis and its main points. A *conclusion* is a final thought or two stemming from the subject of the paper.

A MODEL ESSAY

Silvio, the writer of the paragraph on working in an apple plant (final version on page 42), later decided to develop his subject more fully. Here is the essay that resulted.

My Job in an Apple Plant

INTRODUCTORY
PARAGRAPH

[1]In the course of working my way through school, I have taken many jobs I would rather forget. [2]I have spent nine hours a day lifting heavy automobile and truck batteries off the end of an assembly belt. [3]I have risked the loss of eyes and fingers working a punch press in a textile factory. [4]I have served as an aide in a psychiatric hospital, helping care for brain-damaged men who would break into violent fits at unexpected moments. [5]But none of these jobs was as dreadful as my job in an apple plant in Prince Edward County. [6]The work was physically hard; the pay was poor; and, most of all, the working conditions were dismal.

FIRST
SUPPORTING
PARAGRAPH

[7]First of all, the job made enormous demands on my strength and energy. [8]For ten hours a night, I took cartons that rolled down a metal track and stacked them onto wooden skids in a tractor trailer. [9]Each carton contained twelve heavy cans or bottles of apple juice. [10]A carton shot down the track about every fifteen seconds. [11]I once figured out that I was lifting an average of twelve tonnes of apple juice every night. [12]When a truck was almost filled, my partner or I had to drag fourteen bulky wooden skids into the empty trailer nearby and then set up added sections of the heavy metal track so that we could start routing cartons to the back of the empty van. [13]While one of us did that, the other performed the stacking work of two people.

SECOND
SUPPORTING
PARAGRAPH

[14]I would not have minded the difficulty of the work so much if the pay had not been so poor. [15]I was paid the minimum wage at that time, $6.35 an hour, plus a quarter extra for working the night shift. [16]Because of the low salary, I felt compelled to get as much overtime pay as possible. [17]Everything over eight hours a night was time-and-a-half, so I typically worked twelve hours a night. [18]On Friday I would sometimes work straight through until Saturday at noon—eighteen hours. [19]I averaged over sixty hours a week but did not take home much more than $500.

THIRD
SUPPORTING
PARAGRAPH

[20]But even more than the low pay, what upset me about my apple plant job was the working conditions. [21]Our humourless supervisor cared only about his production record for each night and tried to keep the assembly line moving at breakneck pace. [22]During work I was limited to two ten-minute breaks and an unpaid half hour for lunch. [23]Most of my time was spent outside on the truck loading dock in near-zero-degree temperatures. [24]The steel floors of the trucks were like ice; the quickly penetrating cold made my feet feel like stone. [25]I had no shared interests with the man I loaded cartons with, and so I had to work without companionship on the job. [26]And after the production line shut down and most people left, I had to spend two hours alone scrubbing the apple vats, which were coated with a sticky residue.

CONCLUDING
PARAGRAPH

[27]I stayed on the job for five months, all the while hating the difficulty of the work, the poor money, and the conditions under which I worked. [28]By the time I quit, I was determined never to do such degrading work again.

IMPORTANT POINTS ABOUT THE ESSAY

INTRODUCTORY PARAGRAPH

An introductory paragraph has certain purposes or functions and can be constructed using various methods.

Purposes of the Introduction

An introductory paragraph should do three things:

1 Attract the reader's *interest.* Using one of the suggested methods of introduction described below can help draw the reader into your paper.

2 Present a *thesis sentence*—a clear, direct statement of the central idea that you will develop in your paper. The thesis statement, like a topic sentence, should have a keyword or words reflecting your attitude about the subject. For example, in the essay on the apple plant job, the keyword is *dreadful.*

3 Indicate a *plan of development.* This may simply be a list or *preview of the major points* that will support your thesis statement, listed *in the order in which they will be presented.* A more specific way to indicate your method of development for the body paragraphs to follow is to use *keywords identifying that method:* for example, *a description, a comparison (or contrast), the causes (or effects), the advantages (or disadvantages), a definition,* or *an analysis or examination.* In some cases, the thesis statement and plan of development may appear in the same sentence. In some cases, also, the plan of development may be omitted.

Activity

1. In "My Job in an Apple Plant," which sentences are used to attract the reader's interest?

    _____ sentences 1 to 3   _____ 1 to 4   _____ 1 to 5

2. The thesis in "My Job in an Apple Plant" is presented in

    _____ sentence 4   _____ sentence 5   _____ sentence 6

3. The thesis is followed by a plan of development.

    _____ Yes   _____ No

4. Which words in the plan of development announce the three major supporting points in the essay? Write them below.

    a. _____

    b. _____

    c. _____

Common Methods of Introduction

Here are some common methods of introduction. Use any one method, or a combination of methods, to introduce your subject in an interesting way.

1   ***Broad statement.*** Begin with a broad, general statement of your topic and narrow it down to your thesis statement. Broad, general statements ease the reader into your thesis statement by providing a background for it. In "My Job in an Apple Plant," Silvio writes generally on the topic of his worst jobs and then narrows down to a specific worst job.

2   ***Contrast.*** Start with an idea or situation that is the opposite of the one you will develop. This approach works because your readers will be surprised, and then intrigued, by the contrast between the opening idea and the thesis that follows it. Here is an example of a "contrast" introduction:

> When I was a girl, I never argued with my parents about differences between their attitudes and mine. My father would deliver his judgment on an issue, and that was usually the end of the matter. Discussion seldom changed his mind, and disagreement was not tolerated. But the situation is different with today's parents and children. My husband and I have to contend with radical differences between what our children think about a given situation and what we think about it. We have had disagreements with all three of our daughters, Stephanie, Diana, and Gisel.

3   ***"Relevance."*** Explain the importance of your topic. If you can convince your readers that the subject applies to them in some way, or is something they should know more about, they will want to continue reading. The introductory paragraph of "Consuming Canadians" (page 227) provides an example of a "relevance" introduction.

4   ***Anecdote.*** Use an incident or brief story. Stories are naturally interesting. They appeal to a reader's curiosity. In your introduction, an anecdote will grab the reader's attention right away. The story should be brief and should be related to your central idea. The incident in the story can be something that happened to you, something that you may have heard about, or something that you have read about in a newspaper or magazine. Here is an example of a paragraph that begins with a story:

> Down in the basement lived a monster. He squatted right in the centre of his dark, cement-walled cave and stretched his huge metal arms right up into the ceiling. The big metal monster was old; he had once eaten coal, we were told, and was probably mean from surviving through decades of northern Ontario winters. Now the monster was tamed and attached to the oil tank that leaned against the side of the house, so at least we knew he could not mysteriously move and come creaking after us. But he was still a monster; this we knew from his grated mouth, right in the middle of his steely face—behind those grates blazed infernal fires, day and night. This monster, the furnace, was part of a story invented by our father, and such stories are typical of "real" fairy tales, told not so much to scare children as to teach some important lessons needed for survival.

5   ***Questions.*** Ask your readers one or more questions. These questions catch the readers' interest and make them want to read on and serve as a lead-in to the thesis. Here is an example of a paragraph that begins with questions:

What would happen if we were totally honest with ourselves? Would we be able to stand the pain of giving up self-deception? Would the complete truth be too much for us to bear? Such questions will probably never be answered, for in everyday life we protect ourselves from the onslaught of too much reality. All of us cultivate defense mechanisms that prevent us from seeing, hearing, or feeling too much. Included among such defence mechanisms are rationalization, reaction formation, and substitution.

Note, however, that the thesis itself must not be a question.

6   *Quotation.* A quotation can be something you have read in a book or an article. It can also be something that you have heard: a popular saying or proverb ("Never give advice to a friend"); a current or recent advertising slogan ("Reach out and touch someone"); a favourite expression used by your friends or family ("My father always says ..."). Using a quotation in your introductory paragraph lets you add someone else's voice to your own. Here is an example of a paragraph that begins with a quotation:

"Evil," wrote Martin Buber, "is lack of direction." In my school days as a fatherless boy, with a mother too confused by her own life to really care for me, I strayed down a number of dangerous paths. Before my eighteenth birthday, I had been a car thief, a burglar, and a drug seller.

SUPPORTING PARAGRAPHS

Many college essays have three supporting points, developed in three separate paragraphs. (Some essays will have two supporting points; others, four or more.) Each of the supporting paragraphs should begin with a topic sentence that states the point to be detailed in that paragraph. Just as the thesis provides a focus or controlling idea for the entire essay, the topic sentence provides a focus for each supporting paragraph.

Activity

1.   What is the topic sentence for the first supporting paragraph of "My Job in an Apple Plant"? (*Write the sentence number here.*) _____

2.   What is the topic sentence for the second supporting paragraph? _____

3.   What is the topic sentence for the third supporting paragraph? _____

TRANSITIONAL SENTENCES

In paragraphs, transitions and other connective devices (pages 81–84) are used to help link sentences. Similarly, in an essay *transitional sentences* are used to help tie the supporting paragraphs together. Such transitional sentences usually occur near the end of one paragraph or the beginning of the next.

In "My Job in an Apple Plant," the first transitional sentence is:

I would not have minded the difficulty of the work so much if the pay had not been so poor.

In this sentence, the keyword *difficulty* reminds us of the point of the first supporting paragraph, while *pay* tells us the point to be developed in the second supporting paragraph.

Activity

Here is the other transitional sentence in "My Job in an Apple Plant":

But even more than the low pay, what upset me about my apple plant job was the working conditions.

Note: Notice that the dependent or subordinate first part of the sentence refers to the previous paragraph, and the independent (or main) part of the sentence takes the reader into the paragraph to follow.

Complete the following statement: In the sentence above, the keywords _____ _____ echo the point of the second supporting paragraph, and the keywords _____ announce the topic of the third supporting paragraph.

CONCLUDING PARAGRAPH

The concluding paragraph often summarizes the essay by briefly restating the thesis and, at times, the main supporting points of the essay. Also, the conclusion brings the paper to a natural and graceful end, sometimes leaving the reader with a final thought on the subject.

Activity

1. Which sentence in the concluding paragraph of "My Job in an Apple Plant" restates the thesis and supporting points of the essay? _____

2. Which sentence contains the concluding thought of the essay? _____

ESSAYS TO CONSIDER

Read the three student essays below and then answer the questions that follow.

Starting Over and Over Again

[1]As I walked into college this morning, I heard one student ask another, "When did *you* get here? [2]What made you start school again?" [3]"I thought it was a good plan to try again," the other student answered. [4]"Hey, it's never too late; you gotta keep trying until you get it right," was the first student's

response. [5]Today I agree with those students, but a year ago I did not feel that way. [6]Then, I thought I would never "get it right," and that nothing was worth starting all over again for. [7]I had left my country, my profession, and worked at one awful job, then failed at another. [8]So, although now I am glad "I just kept trying," and did start again for the fourth time by coming to college, I had good reasons to feel that I never wanted to start anything all over again.

[9]My first reason was that I could no longer practise the profession for which I was trained. [10]When I left the Philippines for Canada, I was starting a career as an architect. [11]Because my certification was not accepted in this country, I had trouble even getting work as a draftsman's assistant. [12]There had been a slowdown in building, and there were fewer jobs, so Canadians with drafting training were hired before I was. [13]On top of that, I was used to speaking Spanish most of the time, so my rusty English kept me from making a good impression in interviews. [14]In addition, I had no Canadian experience or references to put on my resumé. [15]Starting out again in a new country with a wife and new son, but without a profession, or much hope of work, was starting to seem like a hopeless task.

[16]Aside from not finding work related to my education, I next found another reason to dislike starting over: the type of job I had to take just so my family and I could survive. [17]I had looked into the cost of living in Canada before leaving the Philippines, and talked to friends with relatives here, but nothing prepared me for trying to get by in Vancouver, especially without steady work. [18]After registering with employment services, sending out dozens of resumés, and going to many unrewarding interviews, I finally got a full-time job—night manager of a twenty-four hour convenience store. [19]I had worked in stores and managed cash back home, so there was no challenge to the job, but the owner and never seeing my family made my life nearly unbearable. [20]The owner expected me to do all the cleaning and janitorial work for the day and night shifts as well as manage the store. [21]I would never have complained about ordinary maintenance like cleaning the glass on the counters or straightening and restocking the shelves, but trying to wash out the freezers, clean up rotting vegetables, and mop the floors while waiting on customers made work a nightly ordeal. [22]Every morning at eight, when I left the store, I hated the job and myself more. [23]And every day, all I wanted to do was sleep away my misery; I had no energy left for my wife and son, so my life felt like a treadmill to nowhere. [24]I felt starting all over again had asked for too big a sacrifice from my family, and I was no longer sure of how to change things.

[25]Because I was so desperate to change my situation, I finally experienced the main reason to dread new starts—failure. [26]A friend of my uncle's had a successful shipping company and offered me a clerical job in his front office. [27]I happily quit the convenience store and prepared to work normal hours in a suit and tie for a better wage. [28]What I had not counted on was how unprepared I was for the tasks involved in my new position. [29]Every day I was to sort out forwarding problems, speak to suppliers and customers, and write shipping reports. [30]Neither my boss nor I had considered two things: that I did not know even the basics of Canadian geography, and that my English was really not up to business standards. [31]Every day I tried to do well at my new

job, and every day, I seemed to make more and more mistakes. [32]I was embarassed when customers' parcels did not arrive at their destinations, and ashamed when my boss saw e-mails coming back full of questions about what I meant by some phrase. [33]When I was let go after two weeks, I was not surprised, but I was fed up with starting over.

[34]In summing up all these tries at starting over, I realize that I learned from each experience, even if the lessons were hard to swallow—maybe what I learned was just not to give up. [35]As I look back now, I know I learned something else—the importance of training for new beginnings, and learning that lesson led me to this new start, at college.

Consuming Canadians

[1]Almost all Canadians have become constant consumers. [2]They may grocery shop daily, or check the flyers obsessively, or shuffle coupons like decks of cards. [3]They cruise the malls, haunt the discount or "wholesale" outlets, or drive the shopping strips like starved cabbies after a fare. [4]Shopping seems like an innocent pleasure, but look at how it dominates Canadians' lives. [5]In reality, shopping, or consuming, has reached a point where it plays too large a part in daily life. [6]It is a needless substitute for other activities, has affected children's attitudes and behaviour, and now has technology as an assistant, with home shopping networks, infomercials, and online shopping.

[7]Constant food shopping in an era of refrigeration and two-career families is one of the most time-wasting and obvious signs of our consuming mania. [8]Grocery stores, once ordinary and unglamorous, now issue "Special Reports" on hot new products that informed Canadians must buy and keep up on, for reasons of health, trendiness, or just plain indulgence. [9]On a Saturday after one of these flyers appears, the aisles of supermarkets are clogged with the carts of rampaging shoppers. [10]In addition, radio and TV advertisements blanket local stations during these promotions. [11]Grocery executives are interviewed seriously about their new items, and videotapes sold, showing shoppers the VP of Foodworld turning dog food into a gourmet delight with his or her special Dijon mustard. [12]Moreover, most Saturday papers are now stuffed with as many as a dozen four-to-six-page flyers. [13]Stimulated by all this promotion, Canadians, whether motivated by the desire for a bargain or by a yen for Quadruple-Chocolate Demonic Delight, hit the stores every day, not out of need, but because of carefully managed marketing strategies.

[14]Children absorb parents' attitudes toward shopping and their views of the importance of consumer products automatically. [15]As early as age five or six, children want clothes from The Gap, Roots ballcaps, and anything worn on *Dawson's Creek*. [16]Later, in high school, the trendily clad or neatly Gapped teenager is sometimes assumed to be a better student than his or her earringed, gothic, or grunge-plaid-clad fellow student. [17]Companies like FUBU cash in on street looks and even 90s versions of grunge or "goth-wear" represent market-created consumer trends. [18]The mall as a social centre appears endlessly in teensploitation movies and TV shows: shopping, or "malling," dreaming about buying things, has replaced extra-curricular

activities, studying, or just plain hanging around. [19]Canada may be the only country where our climate has helped to create "supermalls," with amusement parks, wave-pools, and anything any child or teenager could want.

[20]Worst of all, the consuming craze now has both television and the Internet to support it. [21]In fact, no one needs to go out to shop any more. [22]Canadians have gone beyond even the very fancy catalogue for the passive in-home shopper. [23]Shopping can now be done either from the potato position on the couch or from the seat at the computer. [24]Besides the obnoxious infomercial, where some aging American celebrity lies about hair regrowth, there are more and more cable networks devoted 24/7 to offering everything from cubic zirconia to sticky pads for furniture feet. [25]And the unwary Net-surfing Canadian is lured to shop as well by online retailers and the newest temptation, online auction-houses like Ebay, who are ready to sell consumers items other consumers no longer want. [26]Whether in Moose Jaw or Come-by-Chance, all Canadian shoppers need is a credit card, a telephone, and a keyboard. [27]Canada even has its own off-the-wall home shopping star, JoJo Simard of the Psychic Network, who sells a peculiar product: the future. Canadians will buy nothing for something, apparently.

[28]Canadians really do seem to live to consume. [29]Perhaps they feel inferior and want to keep up with U.S. trends. [30]Perhaps they want their children to have more than they did. [31]Perhaps their lives really are empty. [32]Whatever the reason, Canadians are crazy to shop these days, any way they can.

An Interpretation of Lord of the Flies

[1]Modern history has shown us the evil that exists in human beings. [2]Assassinations are common, governments use torture to discourage dissent, and six million Jews were exterminated during World War II. [3]In Lord of the Flies, William Golding describes a group of schoolboys shipwrecked on an island with no authority figures to control their behaviour. [4]One of the boys soon yields to dark forces within himself, and his corruption symbolizes the evil in all of us. [5]First, Jack Merridew kills a living creature; then, he rebels against the group leader; and finally, he seizes power and sets up his own murderous society.

[6]The first stage in Jack's downfall is his killing of a living creature. [7]In Chapter 1, Jack aims at a pig but is unable to kill. [8]His upraised arm pauses "because of the enormity of the knife descending and cutting into living flesh, because of the unbearable blood," and the pig escapes. [9]Three chapters later, however, Jack leads some boys on a successful hunt. [10]He returns triumphantly with a freshly killed pig and reports excitedly to the others, "I cut the pig's throat." [11]Yet Jack twitches as he says this, and he wipes his bloody hands on his shorts as if eager to remove the stains. [12]There is still some civilization left in him.

[13]After the initial act of killing the pig, Jack's refusal to cooperate with Ralph shows us that this civilized part is rapidly disappearing. [14]With no adults around, Ralph has made some rules. [15]One is that a signal fire must be kept burning. [16]But Jack tempts the boys watching the fire to go

hunting, and the fire goes out. ¹⁷Another rule is that at a meeting, only the person holding a special seashell has the right to speak. ¹⁸In Chapter 5, another boy is speaking when Jack rudely tells him to shut up. ¹⁹Ralph accuses Jack of breaking the rules. ²⁰Jack shouts: "Bollocks to the rules! We're strong—we hunt! If there's a beast, we'll hunt it down! We'll close in and beat and beat and beat—!" ²¹He gives a "wild whoop" and leaps off the platform, throwing the meeting into chaos. ²²Jack is now much more savage than civilized.

²³The most obvious proof of Jack's corruption comes in Chapter 8, when he establishes his own murderous society. ²⁴Insisting that Ralph is not a "proper chief" because he does not hunt, Jack asks for a new election. ²⁵After he again loses, Jack announces, "I'm going off by myself. . . . Anyone who wants to hunt when I do can come too." ²⁶Eventually, nearly all the boys join Jack's "tribe." ²⁷Following his example, they paint their faces like savages, sacrifice to "the beast," brutally murder two of their schoolmates, and nearly succeed in killing Ralph as well. ²⁸Jack has now become completely savage—and so have the others.

²⁹Through Jack Merridew, then, Golding shows how easily moral laws can be forgotten. ³⁰Freed from grown-ups and their rules, Jack learns to kill living things, defy authority, and lead a tribe of murdering savages. ³¹Jack's example is a frightening reminder of humanity's potential for evil. ³²The "beast" the boys try to hunt and kill is actually within every human being.

■ Questions

1. In which essay does the thesis statement appear in the last sentence of the introductory paragraph?

   _____

2. In the essay on *Lord of the Flies,* which sentence of the introductory paragraph contains the plan of development? _____

3. Which method of introduction is used in "Starting Over and Over Again"?
   a. General to narrow   c. Incident or story
   b. Stating importance of topic   d. Questions

4. Complete the following brief outline of "Starting Over and Over Again":
   Starting over again and again was hard for three reasons:

   a. _____

   b. _____

   c. _____

5. Which *two* essays use a transitional sentence between the first and second supporting paragraphs?

   _____

   _____

6. *Complete the following statement:* Emphatic order is shown in the last supporting paragraph of "Starting Over and Over Again" with the words *most important factor;* the last supporting paragraph of "Consuming Canadians" with the words _____; in the last supporting paragraph of "An Interpretation of *Lord of the Flies*" with the words _____.

7. Which essay uses time order as well as emphatic order to organize its three supporting paragraphs? _____

8. List four major transitions used in the supporting paragraphs of "An Interpretation of *Lord of the Flies*."

   a. _____   c. _____
   b. _____   d. _____

9. Which *two* essays include a sentence in the concluding paragraph that summarizes the three supporting points?

   _____

   _____

10. Which essay includes two final thoughts in its concluding paragraph?

   _____

PLANNING THE ESSAY

OUTLINING THE ESSAY

When you write an essay, planning is crucial for success. You should plan your essay by outlining in two ways:

1 Prepare a brief outline. This should consist of a short statement of the thesis followed by the main supporting points for the thesis. Here is Silvio's outline for his essay on the apple plant:

   Working at an apple plant was my worst job.
   1. Hard work
   2. Poor pay
   3. Bad working conditions

   Do not underestimate the value of this initial outline—or the work involved in achieving it. Be prepared to do a good deal of plain hard thinking at this first and most important stage of your paper.

2 Prepare a more detailed outline. The outline form that follows will serve as a guide. Your instructor may ask you to submit a copy of this form either before you actually write an essay or along with your finished essay.

FORM FOR PLANNING AN ESSAY

To write an effective essay, use a form like the one that follows.

INTRODUCTION

Opening remarks

Thesis statement _____

_____

Plan of development

BODY

Topic sentence 1 _____

_____

Specific supporting evidence

Topic sentence 2 _____

_____

Specific supporting evidence

Topic sentence 3 _____

_____

Specific supporting evidence

CONCLUSION

Summary, closing remarks, or both

ESSAY WRITING ASSIGNMENTS

Hints: Keep the following points in mind when writing an essay on any of the topics below.

1 Your first step must be to plan your essay. Prepare both a brief outline and a more detailed outline, as explained on the preceding pages.

2 While writing your essay, use the checklist below to make sure your essay touches all four bases of effective writing.

Base 1: Unity

_____ Clearly stated thesis in the introductory paragraph of your paper

_____ All the supporting paragraphs on target in backing up your thesis

Base 2: Support

_____ Three separate supporting points for your thesis

_____ *Specific* evidence for each of the three supporting points

_____ *Plenty* of specific evidence for each supporting point

Base 3: Coherence

_____ Clear method of organization

_____ Transitions, other connecting words, or transitional sentences

_____ Effective introduction and conclusion

Base 4: Sentence Skills

_____ Clear, error-free sentences (use the checklist on the inside front cover of this book)

1 Your House or Apartment

Write an essay on the advantages *or* disadvantages (not both) of the house, apartment, or residence room where you live. In your introductory paragraph, briefly describe the place you plan to write about. End the paragraph with your thesis statement and a plan of development. Here are some suggestions for thesis statements:

The best features of my apartment are its large windows, roomy closets, and great location.

The drawbacks of my house are its unreliable oil furnace, tiny kitchen, and old-fashioned bathroom.

An inquisitive property manager, sloppy neighbours, and platoons of cockroaches came along with our rented house.

My apartment has several advantages, including friendly neighbours, lots of storage space, and a good security system.

■ 2 A Big Mistake

Write an essay about the biggest mistake you made within the past year. Describe the mistake and show how its effects have convinced you that it was the wrong thing to do. For instance, if you write about "taking on a full-time job while going to school" as your biggest mistake, show the problems it caused. (You might discuss such matters as low grades, constant exhaustion, and poor performance at work, for example.)

To get started, make a list of all the things you did last year that, with hindsight, now seem to be mistakes. Then pick out the action that has had the most serious consequences for you. Make a brief outline to guide you as you write, as in the examples below.

Thesis: Separating from my wife was the worst mistake I made last year.
1. Children have suffered
2. Financial troubles
3. Loneliness

Thesis: Buying a used car to commute to school was the worst mistake of last year.
1. Unreliable—late for class or missed class
2. Expenses for insurance, repairs
3. Led to an accident

■ 3 A Valued Possession

Write an essay about a valued material possession. Here are some suggestions:

Car	Appliance
Portable radio	Book
TV set	Photograph album
Piece of furniture	Piece of clothing
Piece of jewellery	Sound system (car or home)
Camera	Piece of hobby equipment

In your introductory paragraph, describe the possession: tell what it is, when and where you got it, and how long you have owned it. Your thesis statement should centre on the idea that there are several reasons this possession is so important to you. In each of your supporting paragraphs, provide details to back up one of the reasons.

For example, here is a brief outline of an essay written about a leather jacket:

1. It is comfortable.
2. It wears well.
3. It makes me look and feel good.

■ 4 Summarizing a Selection

Write an essay in which you summarize three of the study skills described in the selection "Power Learning" on pages 487–493. Summarizing involves condensing material by highlighting main points and key supporting details. You can eliminate minor details and most examples given in the original material. You should avoid using the exact language in the original material; put the ideas into your own words.

The introductory paragraph of the essay and suggested topic sentences for the supporting paragraphs are provided below. In addition to developing the supporting paragraphs, you should write a brief conclusion for the essay.

Introductory Paragraph

Using Study Skills

Why do some students in a college class receive As, while others get Ds and Fs? Are some people just naturally smarter? Are other students doomed to failure? Motivation—willingness to do the work—is a factor in good grades. But the main difference between successful and unsuccessful students is that the ones who do well have mastered the specific skills needed to handle college work. Fortunately, these skills can be learned by anyone. Doing well in college depends on knowing how to … *[Complete this sentence with the three study skills you decide to write about.]*

Suggested Topic Sentences for the Supporting Paragraphs (Choose Any Three)

Time control is one aid to success as a student. …
Another aid is the use of memory techniques. …
Knowing how to concentrate is another essential skill. …
Studying a textbook effectively is another key to success. …
Perhaps the most crucial step of all is effective classroom notetaking. …

5 How Study Skills Help

You may already be practising some of the study skills described in "Power Learning" (pages 487–493). If so, write an essay on how study skills are helping you to succeed in school. Your thesis might be, "Study skills are helping me to succeed in college." You could organize the essay by describing, in separate paragraphs, how three different study skills have improved your work. Your topic sentences might be similar to these:

First of all, time control has helped me to make the best use of my time.

In addition, taking good notes in class has enabled me to do well in discussions and on tests.

Finally, I can study a textbook effectively now.

Alternatively, begin applying some of the techniques and be prepared to write an essay at a later time on how the study skills helped you become a better student. Or you might want to write about three study techniques of your own that have helped you succeed in your studies.

◼ 6 Single Life

Write an essay using the third-person point of view on the advantages or drawbacks of single life. (See the model essay, "Consuming Canadians," for an example of third-person point of view, pages 227–228.) To get started, make a list of all the advantages and drawbacks you can think of. Advantages might include:

> Fewer expenses
> Fewer responsibilities
> More personal freedom
> More opportunities to move or travel

Drawbacks might include:

> Parental disapproval
> Being alone at social events
> No companion for shopping, movies, and so on
> Sadness at holiday time

After you make up two lists, select the thesis for which you feel you have more supporting material. Then organize your material into a brief outline. Be sure to include an introduction, a clear topic sentence for each supporting paragraph, and a conclusion.

Alternatively, write an essay on the advantages or drawbacks of married life. Follow the directions given above.

◼ 7 Influences on Your Writing

Are you as good a writer as you want to be? Write an essay analyzing the reasons you have become a good writer or explaining why you are not as good as you'd like to be. Begin by considering some factors that may have influenced your writing ability.

> *Your family background:* Did you see people writing at home? Did your parents respect and value the ability to write?
>
> *Your school experience:* Did you have good writing teachers? Did you have a history of failure or success with writing? Was writing fun, or was it a chore? Did your school emphasize writing?
>
> *Social influences:* How did your school friends do at writing? What were your friends' attitudes toward writing? What feelings about writing did you pick up from TV or the movies?

You might want to organize your essay by describing the three greatest influences on your writing skill (or lack of writing skill). Show how each of these has contributed to the present state of your writing.

◼ 8 A Major Decision

All of us come to various crossroads in our lives, times when we must make an important decision about which course of action to follow. Think about a major decision you had to make (or one you are planning to make). Then write an essay on the reasons for your decision. In your introduction, describe the decision you have reached. Each of the body paragraphs that follow should fully explain one of the reasons for your decision. Here are some examples of major decisions that often confront people:

Enrolling in or dropping out of college
Accepting or quitting a job
Getting married or divorced
Breaking up with a boyfriend or girlfriend
Having a baby
Moving away from home

Student papers on this topic include the essay on page 225 and the paragraphs on page 50.

9 Reviewing a TV Show or Movie

Write an essay about a television show or movie you have seen very recently. The thesis of your essay will be that the show (or movie) has both good and bad features. (If you are writing about a TV series, be sure that you evaluate only one episode. Remember also to see page 355 for correct citation of titles of movies, TV shows, and episodes.)

In your first supporting paragraph, briefly summarize the show or movie. Don't get bogged down in small details here; just give an overview, describe briefly the major characters and give the highlights of the action.

In your second supporting paragraph, explain what you feel are the best features of the show or movie. Listed below are some examples of good features you might write about:

Suspenseful, ingenious, or realistic plot
Good acting
Good scenery or special effects
Surprise ending
Good music
Believable characters

In your third supporting paragraph, explain what you feel are the worst features of the show or movie. Here are some possibilities:

Farfetched, confusing, or dull plot
Poor special effects
Bad acting
One-dimensional characters
Unrealistic dialogue

Remember to cover only a few features in each paragraph; do not try to include everything.

10 Good Qualities

We are often quick to point out a person's flaws, saying, for example, "That instructor is conceited," "My boss has no patience," or "My sister is lazy." We are usually equally hard on ourselves; we constantly analyze our own faults. We rarely, though, spend as much time thinking about another person's, or our own, good qualities. Write an essay on the good qualities of a particular person. The person might be an instructor, a job supervisor, a friend, a relative, some other person you know well, or even yourself.

11 Your High School

Imagine that you are an outside consultant called in as a neutral observer to examine the high school you attended. After your visit, you must send the school board a five-paragraph letter in which you describe the most striking features (good, bad, or a combination of both) of the school and the evidence for each of these features.

In order to write the letter, you may want to think about the following features of your high school:

Attitude of the teachers, student body, or administration
Condition of the buildings, classrooms, recreational areas, and so on
Curriculum
How classes are conducted
Extracurricular activities
Crowded or uncrowded conditions

Be sure to include an introduction, a clear topic sentence for each supporting paragraph, and a conclusion.

REVIEWING THE LEARNING OUTCOMES FOR ESSAY WRITING

When you complete any of the writing assignments in this chapter, review your paper to decide how well your essay responds to the following questions:

1 Does your essay attract the reader's interest with its opening? Is its opening well related to the essay's thesis?
2 Does your first paragraph contain a clear thesis statement and an indication of the method of organization you use?
3 Does each body paragraph open with a topic sentence dealing with one of your thesis' supporting points?
4 Does each body paragraph contain enough and specific details to explain and clarify that paragraph's point and to reinforce the point made by your thesis?
5 Are your body paragraphs linked to each other by transitional devices or transitional sentences?
6 Does your conclusion return your reader to the point of your thesis, sum up the meaning of your essay, and offer a parting thought to round off your paper?
7 Have you revised your paper carefully to avoid errors in mechanics or sentences?

PART FOUR

Sentence Skills: Grammar, Mechanics, Punctuation, Word Use, and Practice

PREVIEW

As explained in Part One, there are four steps, or bases, in effective writing. Part Four is concerned with the *fourth step: the ability to write clear, error-free sentences.* First a diagnostic test is given so that you can discover a baseline for your present understanding of important sentence skills. Then the skills themselves appear under the general headings "Grammar," "Mechanics," "Punctuation," and "Word Use," ending with a chapter on sentence variety which helps develop your sense of the various options and methods available for composing sentences. Next come mastery tests and then editing tests that reinforce many basic writing skills and give you practice in editing and proofreading. Finally, an achievement test helps you measure your improvement in important sentence skills.

S e n t e n c e - S k i l l s

D i a g n o s t i c   T e s t

PART 1

This test will help you check your knowledge of important sentence skills. Certain parts of the following word groups are underlined. Write *X* in the answer space if you think a mistake appears in the underlined part. Write *C* in the answer space if you think the underlined part is correct.

A series of headings ("Fragments," "Run-Ons," and so on) will give you clues to the mistakes to look for. However, you do not have to understand the label to find a mistake. What you are checking is your own sense of effective written English.

Fragments

1. <u>Because Tom had eaten and drunk too much.</u> He had to leave the party early. His stomach was like a volcano ready to erupt.

2. <u>After I slid my aching bones into the hot water of the tub, I realized there was no soap.</u> I didn't want to get out again.

3. I spent two hours on the phone yesterday. <u>Trying to find a garage to repair my car.</u> Eventually I had to have the car towed to a garage in another town.

4. <u>Sweating under his heavy load.</u> Brian staggered up the stairs to his apartment. He felt as though his legs were crumbling beneath him.

5. <u>I love to eat and cook Italian food, especially lasagna and ravioli.</u> I make everything from scratch.

6. One of my greatest joys in life is eating desserts. <u>Such as blueberry cheese-cake and vanilla cream puffs.</u> Almond fudge cake makes me want to dance.

Run-Ons

_____ 7. He decided to stop <u>smoking, for</u> he didn't want to die of lung cancer.

_____ 8. The window shade snapped up like a <u>gunshot her</u> cat leaped a metre off the floor.

_____ 9. Billy is the meanest little kid on his <u>block, he</u> eats only the heads of animal crackers.

_____ 10. He knew he had flunked the driver's <u>exam, he</u> ran over a stop sign.

_____ 11. My first boyfriend was five years <u>old. We</u> met every day in the playground sandbox.

_____ 12. Luisa wanted to go <u>dancing, Terrell</u> preferred going to a movie.

Irregular Verbs

_____ 13. I <u>knowed</u> her from somewhere, but I couldn't remember just where.

_____ 14. I had <u>eaten</u> so much food at the buffet dinner that I went into the bathroom just to loosen my belt.

_____ 15. When the mud slide started, the whole neighbourhood <u>began</u> going downhill.

_____ 16. Julio has <u>rode</u> the bus to school for two years while saving for a car.

Subject-Verb Agreement

_____ 17. There <u>is</u> long lines at the checkout counter.

_____ 18. The camping blanket <u>have</u> to be washed.

_____ 19. One of the crooked politicians <u>was</u> jailed for a month.

_____ 20. The bugs behind my stove <u>gets</u> high on Raid.

Consistent Verb Tense

_____ 21. I played some CDs and watched television <u>before</u> I decides to do some homework.

_____ 22. The first thing Scott does everyday is weigh himself. The scale <u>informs</u> him what kind of meals he can eat that day.

_____ 23. Sandy eats a nutritional breakfast, <u>skips</u> lunch, and then enjoys a big dinner.

_____ 24. His parents stayed together for his sake; only after he <u>graduates</u> from college were they divorced.

Pronoun Agreement, Reference, and Point of View

_____ 25. I work at a clothes shop where <u>you</u> do not get paid for all the holidays I should.

_____ 26. I enjoy movies like *The Faculty* that frighten <u>me</u>.

_____   27. A student should write <u>their</u> own papers.

_____   28. Persons camping in those woods should watch <u>their</u> step because of poison ivy.

_____   29. Angry at striking out, Mark hurled the baseball bat at the fence and broke <u>it</u>.

_____   30. I love Parmesan cheese, but <u>it</u> does not always agree with me.

Pronoun Types

_____   31. Randy and <u>me</u> would get along better if he left town.

_____   32. No one is a better cook than <u>she</u>.

Adjectives and Adverbs

_____   33. Tranh ran <u>quick</u> up the steps, taking them two at a time.

_____   34. Justin is <u>more better</u> than I am at darts.

Misplaced Modifiers

_____   35. He swatted the wasp that stung him <u>with a newspaper</u>.

_____   36. Maria returned the hamburger <u>that was spoiled</u> to the supermarket.

_____   37. My aunt once met John Candy at a benefit, <u>whom she found to be a very engaging person</u>.

_____   38. I adopted a dog from a junkyard <u>which is very close to my heart</u>.

Dangling Modifiers

_____   39. <u>Going to work</u>, Enio saw a three-car accident.

_____   40. <u>Flunking out of school</u>, my parents demanded that I get a job.

_____   41. <u>While I was waiting for the bus</u>, rain began to fall.

_____   42. <u>Braking the car suddenly</u>, the shopping bags tumbled onto the floor.

Faulty Parallelism

_____   43. Ben enjoys cross-country skiing, socializing with friends, and <u>to read comics</u>.

_____   44. Lena likes to wear soft sweaters, to eat exotic foods, and <u>to bathe in scented bath oil</u>.

_____   45. When I saw my roommate with my girlfriend, I felt worried, angry, and <u>embarrassment as well</u>.

_____   46. Francine enjoys shopping for new clothes, trying different cosmetics, and reading beauty magazines.

Capital Letters

_____   47. Warren uses <u>certs</u> mints after smoking his pipe or a cigar.

_____   48. During <u>july</u>, Frank's company works a four-day week.

_____   49. I asked my dad, <u>"When's</u> Uncle Bill getting his toupee?"

_____   50. On <u>Summer</u> days I like to sit in the backyard and sunbathe.

Apostrophe

_____   51. The <u>Wolfman's</u> bite is worse than his bark.

_____   52. <u>Alans</u> quick hands reached out to break his son's fall.

_____   53. I'll be with you shortly if <u>youll</u> just wait a minute.

_____   54. You <u>shouldn't</u> drink any more if you're hoping to get home safely.

Quotation Marks

_____   55. Someone once said, "Canadians sing about the North, but live as far south as possible."

_____   56. Say something tender to me, <u>"whispered Sean to Ina."</u>

_____   57. <u>"I hate that commercial, he muttered."</u>

_____   58. "If you don't leave soon," he warned, <u>"you'll be late for work."</u>

Comma

_____   59. Jeremy relaxes by reading <u>Donald Duck Archie and Bugs Bunny</u> comic books.

_____   60. Although I have a black belt in <u>karate</u> I decided to go easy on the demented bully who had kicked sand in my face.

_____   61. Dracula, who had a way with <u>women,</u> is his favourite movie hero.

_____   62. We could always tell when our instructor felt <u>disorganized for</u> his shirt would not be tucked into his pants.

_____   63. <u>You, my man,</u> are going to get yours.

_____   64. His father <u>shouted</u> "Why don't you go out and get a job?"

Commonly Confused Words

_____   65. Some stores will accept your credit cards but not <u>you're</u> money.

_____   66. That issue is <u>to</u> hot for any politician to handle.

_____   67. <u>They're</u> planning to trade in their old car.

_____   68. <u>Its</u> important to get this job done properly.

_____   69. You should have the brakes on your car replaced <u>write</u> away.

_____   70. <u>Who's</u> the culprit who left the paint can on the table?

Effective Word Use

_____   71. I <u>comprehended her statement</u>.

_____   72. The movie was a <u>real bomb</u>, so we left early.

_____   73. The victims of the car accident were shaken but <u>none the worse for wear</u>.

_____   74. Anne is <u>of the opinion that</u> the death penalty should be abolished.

Answers are on page 553.

PART 2 (OPTIONAL)

Do Part 2 at your instructor's request. This second part of the test will provide more detailed information about skills you need to know. On a separate piece of paper, number and correct all the items you have marked with an *X*. For example, suppose you had marked the following word groups with an *X*. (Note that these examples are not taken from the test.)

4. <u>If football games disappeared entirely from television.</u> I would not even miss them. Other people in my family would perish.

7. The kitten suddenly saw her reflection in the <u>mirror, she</u> jumped back in surprise.

15. The tree in my <u>cousins</u> front yard always sheds its leaves two weeks before others on the street.

29. When we go out to a <u>restaurant we</u> always order something we would not cook for ourselves.

Here is how you should write your corrections on a separate sheet of paper.

4. television, I

7. mirror, and

15. cousin's

29. restaurant, we

There are over forty corrections to make in all.

CHAPTER 18

Subjects and Verbs

The basic building blocks of English sentences are subjects and verbs. Understanding them is an important first step toward mastering many sentence skills.

Every sentence has a subject and a verb. Who or what the sentence speaks about is called the <u>subject</u>; what the sentence says about the subject is called the <u>verb</u>.

The <u>children</u> <u>laughed</u>.
Several <u>branches</u> <u>fell</u>.
Most <u>students</u> <u>passed</u> the test.
That <u>man</u> <u>is</u> a crook.

A SIMPLE WAY TO FIND A SUBJECT

To find a subject, ask *who* or *what* the sentence is about. As shown below, your answer is the subject.

Who is the first sentence about? <u>Children</u>
What is the second sentence about? Several <u>branches</u>
Who is the third sentence about? Most <u>students</u>
Who is the fourth sentence about? That <u>man</u>

A SIMPLE WAY TO FIND A VERB

To find a verb, ask what the sentence *says about* the subject. As shown below, your answer is the verb.

What does the first sentence *say about* the children? They <u>laughed</u>.
What does the second sentence *say about* the branches? They <u>fell</u>.
What does the third sentence *say about* the students? They <u>passed</u>.
What does the fourth sentence *say about* that man? He <u>is</u> (a crook).

A second way to find the verb is to put *I, you, we, he, she, it,* or *they* (whichever form is appropriate) in front of the word you think is a verb. If the result makes sense, you have a verb. For example, you could put *they* in front of *laughed* in the first sentence above, with the result, *they laughed,* making sense. Therefore you know that *laughed* is a verb. You could use *they* or *he,* for instance, to test the other verbs as well.

Finally, it helps to remember that most verbs show action. In the sentences already considered, the three action verbs are *laughed, fell,* and *passed.* Certain other verbs, known as *linking verbs, or verbs of appearance or perception,* do not show action. They do, however, give information about the subject. In "That man is a crook," the linking verb *is* tells us that the man is a crook. Other common linking verbs include *am, are, was, were.* Verbs indicating appearance or perception include *feel, appear, look, become,* and *seem.*

Activity

In each of the following sentences, draw one line under the subject and two lines under the verb.

1. The heavy purse cut into my shoulder.

2. Small stones pinged onto the windshield.

3. The test directions confused the students.

4. Cotton shirts feel softer than polyester ones.

5. The fog rolled into the cemetery.

6. Sparrows live in the eaves of my porch.

7. A green fly stung her on the ankle.

8. Every other night, garbage trucks rumble down my street on their way to the dump.

9. The family played badminton and volleyball, in addition to a game of softball, at the picnic.

10. With their fingers, the children drew pictures on the steamed window.

MORE ABOUT SUBJECTS AND VERBS

1   A noun is often the subject of a sentence. The words in the four examples on page 246: *children, branches, students,* and *man,* are called *nouns.* The word "noun" comes from the Latin word *nomen,* meaning "name." Nouns *name* an object, a place, a person, or another living thing. *Proper nouns* are those which are used for people's names, or for place names, such as *Mr.Khan* or *Windsor.* *Abstract nouns* identify an idea, condition, or state of being: i.e., *truth, beauty,* or *honesty.*

2 A pronoun (a word like *he, she, it, we, you,* or *they* used in place of a noun) can serve as the subject of a sentence. For example:

He seems like a lonely person.
They both like to gamble.

Without a surrounding context (so that we know who *He* or *They* refers to), such sentences may not seem clear, but they *are* complete.

3 A sentence may have more than one verb, more than one subject, or several subjects and verbs:

My heart skipped and pounded.
The radio and CD player were stolen from the car.
Minh and Elsa prepared the report together and presented it to the class.

4 The subject of a sentence never appears within a prepositional phrase. A *prepositional phrase* is simply a group of words that begins with a preposition. Note that the word "preposition" contains the word "position;" many prepositions indicate positions in time or space. Following is a list of common prepositions:

about	before	by	inside	over
above	behind	during	into	through
across	below	except	of	to
among	beneath	for	off	toward
around	beside	from	on	under
at	between	in	onto	with

Cross out prepositional phrases when looking for the subject of a sentence.

~~Under my pillow~~ I found a quarter left by the tooth fairy.
One ~~of the yellow lights at the school crossing~~ began flashing.
The funny pages ~~of the newspaper~~ disappeared.
~~In spite of my efforts,~~ Derek dropped out of school.
~~During a rainstorm,~~ I sat in my car reading magazines.

5 Many verb forms consist of more than one word. Here, for example, are some of the many forms of the verb *smile.*

smile	smiled	should smile
smiles	were smiling	will be smiling
does smile	have smiled	can smile
is smiling	had smiled	could be smiling
are smiling	had been smiling	must have smiled

Notes

a Words like *not, just, never, only,* and *always* are not part of the verb, although they may appear within the verb.

Larry <u>did</u> not <u>finish</u> the paper before class.

The road <u>was</u> just <u>completed</u> last week.

b No verb preceded by *to* (infinitive form of verb) is ever the verb of a sentence. The verb form beginning with the word *to* is called the *infinitive* form. *Infinitive* refers to the word *infinite*, or *having no limits*. The infinitive form (for example, *to do, to make*) is the beginning point for all other forms of a verb. The verb forms used as main verbs *have limits*; they are *limited* by some change to show time (tense), relation to subject (person and number), and so on. The infinitive form never changes, but is used in combination with other *finite verb forms* as in the following examples.

My car suddenly <u>began</u> to sputter on the freeway.

I <u>swerved</u> to avoid a squirrel on the road.

c No *-ing* word *by itself* is ever the verb of a sentence. (It may be part of the verb, but it must have a helping verb in front of it.)

They <u>leaving</u> early for the game. (not a sentence, because the verb is not complete)

They <u>are leaving</u> early for the game. (a sentence)

Activity

Draw a single line under the subjects and a double line under the verbs in the following sentences. Be sure to include all parts of the verb.

1. A burning odour from the wood saw filled the room.

2. At first, sticks of gum always feel powdery on your tongue.

3. Vampires and werewolves are repelled by garlic.

4. Three people in the long bank line looked impatiently at their watches.

5. The driving rain had pasted wet leaves all over the car.

6. She has decided to buy a condominium.

7. The trees in the mall were glittering with tiny white lights.

8. The puppies slipped and tumbled on the vinyl kitchen floor.

9. Tanya and Luis ate at Pizza Hut and then went to a movie.

10. We have not met our new neighbours in the apartment building.

■ Review Test

Draw a single line under subjects and a double line under verbs. Crossing out prepositional phrases may help to find the subjects.

1. A cloud of fruit flies hovered over the bananas.

2. Candle wax dripped onto the table and hardened into pools.

3. Nick and Chan are both excellent Frisbee players.

4. The leaves of my dying rubber plant resembled limp brown rags.

5. During the first week of vacation, Kevin slept until noon every day.

6. They have just decided to start working out together.

7. Psychology and digital animation are my favourite subjects.

8. The sofa in the living room has not been cleaned for over a year.

9. The water stains on her suede shoes did not disappear with brushing.

10. Kieran stayed in bed too long and, as a result, arrived late for work.

ning a Process • Examining Cause and Effect • comparing or contrasting • Definin
• Dividing and Classifying • Describing a Scene or Person • Narrating an Event • Argu
ition • Explaining a Process • Examining Cause and Effect • comparing or Contrastin
ing a Term Dividing and Classifying • Describing a Scene or Person • Narrating an Ev
uing a Position • Explaining a Process • Examining Cause and Effect • Comparing

C H A P T E R   1 9

Sentence Sense

WHAT IS SENTENCE SENSE?

As a speaker of English, you already possess the most important of all sentence skills. You have *sentence sense*—an instinctive feel for where a sentence begins, where it ends, and how it can be developed. You learned sentence sense automatically and naturally, as part of learning the English language, and you have practised it through however many years that you have been speaking English. It is as much a part of you as your ability to speak and understand English is a part of you.

Sentence sense can help you recognize and avoid fragments and run-ons, two of the most common and serious sentence-skills mistakes in written English. Sentence sense will also help you to place commas, spot awkward and unclear phrasings, and add variety to your sentences.

You may ask, "If I already have this 'sentence sense,' why do I still make mistakes in punctuating sentences?" One answer could be that your past school experiences in writing were unrewarding or unpleasant. English may have been a series of dry writing topics and heavy doses of "correct" grammar and usage, or it may have devoted no time at all to sentence skills. Or, perhaps you studied English primarily as a written language, and had little opportunity to practise speaking English every day prior to coming to Canada. For any of these reasons, or perhaps for other reasons, the instinctive sentence skills you practise while *speaking* may turn off when you start *writing*. The very acts of picking up a pen or touching a keyboard may shut down your whole natural system of language abilities and skills.

TURNING ON YOUR SENTENCE SENSE

Chances are, you don't *read a paper aloud* after you write it, or you don't do the next best thing: read it "aloud" in your head. But reading aloud is essential to turn on the natural language system within you. By reading aloud, you will be able to hear the points where your sentences begin and end. In addition, you will be able

251

to pick up any trouble spots where your thoughts are not communicated clearly and well.

The activities that follow will help you turn on and rediscover the enormous language power within you. You will be able to see how your built-in sentence sense can guide your writing just as it does your speaking.

Activity

Each item that follows lacks basic sentence punctuation. There is no period to mark the end of one sentence and no capital letter to mark the start of the next. Read each item aloud (or in your head) so that you "hear" where each sentence begins and ends. Your voice will tend to drop and pause at the point of each sentence break.

- Put a light slash mark (/) at every point where you hear a break.

Then go back and read over the item a second time. If you are now sure of each place where a split occurs, insert a period and change the first small letter after it to a capital. Minor pauses are often marked in English by commas; these are already inserted. Part of item 1 is done for you as an example.

1. I take my dog for a walk on Saturdays in the big park by the lake I do this very early in the morning before children come to the park. /that way I can let my dog run freely he jumps out the minute I open the car door and soon sees the first innocent squirrel then he is off like a shot and doesn't stop running for at least half an hour.

2. Anna hates huge tractor trailers that sometimes tailgate her Honda the enormous smoke-belching machines seem ready to swallow her small car she shakes her fist at the drivers, and she lets fly a lot of angry words recently she had a very satisfying dream she broke into a party supply store and stole fireworks she then became the first person in history to illuminate a truck

3. When I sit down to write, my mind is blank all I can think of is my name, which seems to me the most boring name in the world often I get sleepy and tell myself I should take a short nap other times I start daydreaming about things I want to buy sometimes I decide I should make a telephone call to someone I know the piece of paper in front of me is usually still blank when I leave to watch my favourite television show

4. One of the biggest regrets of my life is that I never told my father I loved him I resented the fact that he had never been able to say the words "I love you" to his children even during the long period of my father's illness, I

remained silent and unforgiving then one morning he was dead, with my words left unspoken a guilt I shall never forget tore a hole in my heart I determined not to hold in my feelings with my daughters they know they are loved, because I both show and tell them this all people, no matter who they are, want to be told that they are loved

5. Two days ago, Greg killed several flying ants in his bedroom he also sprayed a column of ants forming a colony along the kitchen baseboard yesterday, he picked the evening newspaper off the porch and two black army ants scurried onto his hand this morning, he found an ant crawling on a lollipop he had left in his shirt pocket if any more insects appear, he is going to call an exterminator he feels like the victim in a Hitchcock movie called *The Ants* he is half afraid to sleep tonight he imagines the darkness will be full of tiny squirming things waiting to crawl all over him

SUMMARY: USING SENTENCE SENSE

You probably did well in locating the end stops in these selections, proving to yourself that you *do* have sentence sense. This instinctive sense will help you deal with sentence fragments and run-ons, perhaps the two most common sentence-skills mistakes.

Remember the importance of *reading your paper aloud.* By doing so, you turn on the natural language skills that come from all your experience of speaking English. The same sentence sense that helps you communicate effectively in speaking will help you communicate effectively in writing.

CHAPTER 20

Fragments

Introductory Project

Every sentence must have a subject and a verb and must express a complete thought. A word group that lacks a subject or a verb and that does not express a complete thought is a *fragment*. Underline the statement in each numbered item that you think is *not* a complete sentence.

1. Because I could not sleep. I turned on my light and read.
2. Calling his dog's name. Todd walked up and down the street.
3. My little sister will eat anything. Except meat, vegetables, and fruit.
4. The reporter turned on her laptop computer. Then began to type quickly.

Understanding the answers: Read and complete each explanation.

1. *Because I could not sleep* is an incomplete sentence. The writer does not complete the _____ by telling us what happened because he could not sleep. Correct the fragment by joining it to the sentence that follows it:

   Because I could not sleep, I turned on my light and read.

2. *Calling his dog's name* is not a complete sentence. The word group lacks both a _____ and a verb, and it does not express a complete thought. Correct the fragment by adding it to the sentence that follows it:

   Calling his dog's name, Todd walked up and down the street.

3. *Except meat, vegetables, and fruit* is not a complete sentence. Again, the word group lacks a subject and a _____, and it does not express a complete thought. Correct the fragment by adding it to the sentence that comes before it:

   My little sister will eat anything except meat, vegetables, and fruit.

4. *Then began to type quickly* is not a complete sentence. The word group lacks a _____. One way to correct the fragment is to add the subject *she*:

   Then she began to type quickly.

Answers are on page 554.

WHAT ARE FRAGMENTS?

Every sentence must have a subject and a verb and must express a complete thought. A word group that lacks a subject or a verb and that does not express a complete thought is a *fragment*. The most common types of fragments are

1 Dependent-word fragments
2 *-ing* and *to* fragments
3 Added-detail fragments
4 Missing-subject fragments

Once you understand the specific kind or kinds of fragments that you may write, you should be able to eliminate them from your writing. The following pages explain all four types of fragments.

1 DEPENDENT-WORD FRAGMENTS

Some word groups that begin with a dependent word are fragments. Here is a list of common dependent words:

Dependent Words		
after	if, even if	when, whenever
although, though	in order that	where, wherever
as	since	whether
because	that, so that	which, whichever
before	unless	while
even though	until	who, whoever
how	what, whatever	whose

Whenever you start a sentence with one of these words, you must be careful that a fragment does not result.

The word group beginning with the dependent word *After* in the example below is a fragment.

After I learned the price of new cars. I decided to keep my old Toyota.

A *dependent statement*—one starting with a dependent word like *After*—cannot stand alone. It depends on another statement to complete the thought. "After I learned the price of new cars" is a dependent statement. It leaves us hanging. We expect in the same sentence to find out *what happened after* the writer learned the price of new cars. When a writer does not follow through and complete a thought, a fragment results.

To correct the fragment, simply follow through and complete the thought:

After I learned the price of new cars, I decided to keep my old Toyota.

Remember, then, that *dependent statements by themselves are fragments.* They *must be attached to a statement that makes sense standing alone.*

Here are two other examples of dependent-word fragments:

My daughter refused to stop smoking. <u>Unless I quit also.</u>

Bill asked for a loan. <u>Which he promised to pay back in two weeks.</u>

"Unless I quit also" is a fragment; it does not make sense standing by itself. We want to know in the same statement *what would not happen unless* the writer quit also. The writer must complete the thought. Likewise, "Which he promised to pay back in two weeks" is not in itself a complete thought. We want to know in the same statement what *which* refers to.

Correcting a Dependent-Word Fragment

In most cases you can correct a dependent-word fragment by attaching it to the sentence that comes after it or the sentence that comes before it:

After I learned the price of new cars, I decided to keep my old Toyota.
(The fragment has been attached to the sentence that comes after it.)

My daughter refused to quit smoking unless I quit also.
(The fragment has been attached to the sentence that comes before it.)

Bill asked for a loan which he promised to pay back in two weeks.
(The fragment has been attached to the sentence that comes before it.)

Another way of correcting a dependent-word fragment is simply to eliminate the dependent word by rewriting the sentence:

I learned the price of new cars and decided to keep my old Toyota.

She wanted me to quit also.

He promised to pay it back in two weeks.

Do not use this method of correction too frequently, however, for it may cut down on interest and variety in your writing style.

Notes

1 Use a comma if a dependent-word group comes at the beginning of a sentence (also see page 360):

After I learned the price of new cars, I decided to keep my old Toyota.

However, do not generally use a comma if the dependent-word group comes at the end of a sentence:

My daughter refused to stop smoking unless I quit also.

Bill asked for a loan which he promised to pay back in two weeks.

2 Sometimes the dependent words *who, that, which,* or *where* appear not at the very start, but near the start, of a word group. A fragment often results:

The city council decided to put more lights on South Street. <u>A place where several people have been harassed.</u>

"A place where several people have been harassed" is not in itself a complete thought. We want to know in the same statement *where the place was* that several people were harassed. The fragment can be corrected by attaching it to the sentence that comes before it:

The city council decided to put more lights on South Street, a place where several people have been harassed.

Activity 1

Turn each of the following dependent-word groups into a sentence by adding a complete thought. Put a comma after the dependent-word group if a dependent word starts the sentence.

Examples   Although I arrived in class late

Although I arrived in class late, I still did well on the test.

The little boy who plays with our daughter

The little boy who plays with our daughter just came down with

German measles.

1. Because the weather is bad

   _____

   _____

2. If I lend you twenty dollars

   _____

   _____

3. The car that we bought

   _____

   _____

4. Since I was tired

   _____

   _____

5. Before the instructor entered the room

   _____

   _____

Activity 2

Underline the dependent-word fragment or fragments in each item. Then correct each fragment by attaching it to the sentence that comes before or the sentence that comes after, whichever sounds more natural. Put a comma after the dependent-word group if it starts the sentence.

1. Whenever our front and back doors are open. The air current causes the
    back door to slam shut. The noise makes everyone in the house jump.

    _____

    _____

    _____

2. Mario always turns on the radio in the morning to hear the news. He wants
    to be sure that World War III has not started. Before he gets on with his day.

    _____

    _____

    _____

3. Since the line at the Department of Motor Vehicles crawls at a snail's pace.
    Eng waited two hours there. When there was only one person left in front of
    him. The office closed for the day.

    _____

    _____

    _____

4. My dog ran in joyous circles on the wide beach. Until she found a dead fish.
    Before I had a chance to drag her away. She began sniffing and nudging the
    smelly remains.

    _____

    _____

    _____

5. When the air conditioner broke down. The temperature was over thirty
    degrees. I then found an old fan. Which turned out to be broken also.

    _____

    _____

    _____

2 -*ING* AND *TO* FRAGMENTS

When an -*ing* word appears at or near the start of a word group, a fragment may
result. Such fragments often lack a subject and part of the verb. Underline the
word groups in the examples below that contain -*ing* words. Each is a fragment.

Example 1

I spent almost two hours on the phone yesterday. Trying to find a garage to
repair my car. Eventually I had to have it towed to a garage across the city.

Example 2

Anita was at first happy with the blue sports car she had bought for only five hundred dollars. Not realizing until a week later that the car averaged ten kilometres per litre of gas.

Example 3

He looked forward to the study period at school. It being the only time he could sit unbothered and dream about his future. He imagined himself as a lawyer with lots of money, a huge office, and great clothes.

People sometimes write *-ing* fragments because they think the subject in one sentence will work for the next word group as well. Thus, in the first example, the writer thinks that the subject *I* in the opening sentence will also serve as the subject for "Trying to find a garage to repair my car." But the subject must actually be *in* the sentence.

Correcting *-ing* Fragments (Participial Fragments)

1. Attach the *-ing* fragment to the sentence that comes before it or the sentence that comes after it, whichever makes sense. Example 1 could read: "I spent two hours on the phone yesterday, trying to find a garage to repair my car."
2. Add a subject and change the *-ing* verb part to the correct form of the verb. Example 2 could read: "She realized only a week later that the car averaged ten kilometres per litre of gas."
3. Change *being* to the correct form of the verb *be (am, are, is, was, were)*. Example 3 could read: "It was the only time he could sit unbothered and dream about his future."

Correcting *to* Fragments (Infinitive Fragments)

When *to* appears at or near the start of a word group, a fragment sometimes results:

I plan on working overtime. To get this job finished. Otherwise, my boss may get angry with me.

The second word group is a fragment and can be corrected by adding it to the preceding sentence:

I plan on working overtime to get this job finished.

Activity 1

Underline the *-ing* fragment in each of the items that follow. Then make it a sentence by rewriting it, using the method described in parentheses.

Example   A thunderstorm was brewing. A sudden breeze shot through the windows. <u>Driving the stuffiness out of the room.</u>
(Add the fragment to the preceding sentence.)

A sudden breeze shot through the windows, driving the stuffiness out of the room.

(In the example, a comma is used to set off "driving the stuffiness out of the room," which is extra material placed at the end of the sentence.)

1. Sweating under his heavy load. Brian staggered up the stairs to his apartment. He felt as though his legs were crumbling beneath him.
   (Add the fragment to the sentence that comes after it.)

   _____

   _____

2. He works ten hours a day. Then going to class for three hours. It is no wonder he writes sentence fragments.
   (Correct the fragment by adding the subject *he* and changing *going* to the proper form of the verb, *goes*.)

   _____

   _____

3. Kesha loved the movie *Gone with the Wind*, but Carlo hated it. His chief objection being that it lasted four hours.
   (Correct the fragment by changing *being* to the proper verb form, *was*.)

   _____

   _____

Activity 2

Underline the *-ing* or *to* fragment or fragments in each item. Then rewrite each item, correcting the fragments by using one of the three methods of correction described on page 259.

1. A mysterious package arrived on my porch yesterday. Bearing no return address. I half expected to find an heirloom inside.

   _____

   _____

2. Jeff bundled up and went outside on the bitterly cold day. To saw wood for his fireplace. He returned half frozen with only two logs.

   _____

   _____

3. Looking tired and drawn. The little girl's parents sat in the waiting room. The operation would be over in a few minutes.

   _____

   _____

4. Sighing with resignation. Teresa switched on her television. She knew that the picture would be snowy and crackling with static. Her cable being off at that time.

_____

_____

_____

_____

5. Jabbing the ice with a screwdriver. Luis attempted to speed up the defrosting process in his freezer. However, he used too much force. The result being a freezer compartment riddled with holes.

_____

_____

_____

_____

3 ADDED-DETAIL FRAGMENTS

Added-detail fragments lack a subject and a verb. They often begin with one of the following words:

also	except	including
especially	for example	such as

See if you can locate and underline the one added-detail fragment in each of the examples that follow:

Example 1

I love to cook and eat Italian food. Especially spaghetti and lasagna. I make everything from scratch.

Example 2

The class often starts late. For example, yesterday at a quarter after nine instead of at nine sharp. Today the class started at five after nine.

Example 3

He failed a number of courses before he earned his diploma. Among them, English I, Economics, and Introductory Marketing.

People often write added-detail fragments for much the same reason they write -*ing* fragments. They think the subject and verb in one sentence will serve for the next word group as well. But the subject and verb must be in *each* word group.

Correcting Added-Detail Fragments

1   Attach the fragment to the complete thought that precedes it. Example 1 could read: "I love to cook and eat Italian food, especially spaghetti and lasagna."

2   Add a subject and a verb to the fragment to make it a complete sentence. Example 2 could read: "The class often starts late. For example, yesterday it began at a quarter after nine instead of at nine sharp."

3   Change words as necessary to make the fragment part of the preceding sentence. Example 3 could read: "Among the courses he failed before he earned his diploma were English I, Economics, and Introductory Marketing."

Activity 1

Underline the fragment in each of the items below. Then make it a sentence by rewriting it, using the method described in parentheses.

Example   I am always short of pocket money. Especially for everyday items like magazines and pop. Luckily my friends often have change. (Add the fragment to the preceding sentence.)

I am always short of pocket money, especially for everyday items like

magazines and pop.

1.   Nina is trying hard for a promotion. For example, through night classes and a public speaking course. She is also working overtime for no pay.
(Correct the fragment by adding the subject and verb *she is taking.*)

_____

_____

2.   I could feel Sean's anger building. Like a land mine ready to explode. I was silent because I didn't want to be the one to set it off.
(Add the fragment to the preceding sentence.)

_____

_____

3.   We went on vacation without several essential items. Among other things, our running shoes and sweat jackets.
(Correct the fragment by adding the subject and verb *we forgot.*)

_____

_____

Activity 2

Underline the added-detail fragment in each item. Then rewrite that part of the item needed to correct the fragment. Use one of the three methods of correction described above.

1. It's always hard for me to get up for work. Especially on Mondays after a holiday weekend. However, I always wake up early on free days.

   _____

   _____

2. Tony has enormous endurance. For example, the ability to run seven kilometres in the morning and then play basketball all afternoon.

   _____

   _____

3. A counsellor gives you a chance to talk about your problems. With your family or the boss at work. You learn how to cope better with life.

   _____

   _____

4. Phil and Maria do most of their shopping through mail-order catalogues. Especially the Sears and Tilley Endurables catalogues.

   _____

   _____

5. One of my greatest joys in life is eating desserts. Such as cherry cheesecake and vanilla cream puffs. Almond fudge cake makes me want to dance.

   _____

   _____

4 MISSING-SUBJECT FRAGMENTS

In each example below, underline the word group in which the subject is missing.

Example 1

The truck skidded on the rain-slick highway. But missed a telephone pole on the side of the road.

Example 2

Michelle tried each of the appetizers on the table. And then found that, when the dinner arrived, her appetite was gone.

People write missing-subject fragments because they think the subject in one sentence will apply to the next word group as well. But the subject, as well as the verb, must be in each word group to make it a sentence.

Correcting Missing-Subject Fragments

1 Attach the fragment to the preceding sentence. Example 1 could read: "The truck skidded on the rain-slick highway but missed a telephone pole on the side of the road."

2 Add a subject (which can often be a pronoun standing for the subject in the preceding sentence). Example 2 could read: "She then found that, when the dinner arrived, her appetite was gone."

Activity

Underline the missing-subject fragment in each item. Then rewrite that part of the item needed to correct the fragment. Use one of the two methods of correction described above.

1. I tried on an old suit hanging in our basement closet. And discovered, to my surprise, that it was too tight to button.

   _____

   _____

   _____

   _____

2. When Tina had a sore throat, friends told her to gargle with salt water. Or suck on an ice cube. The worst advice she got was to avoid swallowing.

   _____

   _____

   _____

   _____

3. One of my elementary school teachers embarrassed us with her sarcasm. Also, seated us in rows from the brightest students to the dumbest. I can imagine the pain the student in the last seat must have felt.

   _____

   _____

   _____

   _____

A Review: How to Check for Fragments

1 Read your paper aloud from the *last* sentence to the *first*. You will be better able to see and hear whether each word group you read is a complete thought.

2 If you think a word group is a fragment, ask yourself: Does this contain a subject and a verb and express a complete thought?

3 More specifically, be on the lookout for the most common fragments:

- Dependent-word fragments (starting with words like *after, because, since, when,* and *before*)
- *-ing* and *to* fragments (*-ing* or *to* at or near the start of a word group)
- Added-detail fragments (starting with words like *for example, such as, also,* and *especially*)
- Missing-subject fragments (a verb is present but not the subject)

■ **Review Test 1**

Turn each of the following word groups into a complete sentence. Use the spaces provided.

Example   With sweaty palms

With sweaty palms, I walked in for the job interview.

Even when it rains

The football teams practise even when it rains.

1. When the alarm sounded

   We left the building.

2. In order to save some money

   I put it in bank.

3. Was late for the game

   so I drove there.

4. To pass the course

   I need to study harder.

5. Peter, who is very impatient

   _____

6. During the holiday season

   We go to other country.

7. The store where I worked

   It was a big one.

8. Before the movie started

   We bought some popcorn.

9. Down in the basement

   there is a big bathroom.

10. Feeling very confident

   It means you are in danger.

◼ Review Test 2

Each word group in the student paragraph below is numbered. In the space provided, write *C* if a word group is a *complete sentence;* write *F* if it is a *fragment.* You will find seven fragments in the paragraph.

A Disastrous First Date

1. C
2. C
3. F
4. C
5. F
6. C
7. C
8. F
9. C
10. F
11. C
12. C
13. F
14. C
15. F C
16. C
17. C
18. F
19. C
20. C

¹My first date with Elaine was a disaster. ²I decided to take her to a small Italian restaurant. ³That my friends told me had reasonable prices. ⁴I looked over the menu and realized I could not pronounce the names of the dishes. ⁵Such as "veal piccante," and "fettucine Alfredo." ⁶Then, I noticed a burning smell. ⁷The candle on the table was starting to blacken. ⁸And scorch the back of my menu. ⁹Trying to be casual, I quickly poured half my glass of water onto the menu. ¹⁰When the waiter returned to our table. ¹¹He asked me if I wanted to order some wine. ¹²I ordered a bottle of Baby Duck. ¹³The only wine that I had heard of and could pronounce. ¹⁴The waiter brought the wine, poured a small amount into my glass, and waited. ¹⁵I said, "You don't have to stand there. We can pour the wine ourselves." ¹⁶After the waiter put down the wine bottle and left. ¹⁷Donna told me I was supposed to taste the wine. ¹⁸Feeling like a complete fool. ¹⁹I managed to get through the dinner. ²⁰However, for weeks afterward, I felt like jumping out a tenth-storey window.

On a separate piece of paper, correct the fragments you have found. Attach each fragment to the sentence that comes before or after it, or make whatever other change is needed to turn the fragment into a sentence.

■ Review Test 3

Underline the two fragments in each item. Then rewrite the item in the space provided, making the changes needed to correct the fragments.

Example   The people at the restaurant save money. <u>By watering down the coffee. Also, using the cheapest grade of hamburger.</u> Few people go there anymore.

The people at the restaurant save money by watering down the

coffee. Also, they use the cheapest grade of hamburger.

1. Gathering speed with enormous force. The plane was suddenly in the air. Then it began to climb sharply. And several minutes later levelled off.

   _____

   _____

   _____

2. Before my neighbours went on vacation. They asked me to watch their house. I agreed to check the premises once a day. Also, to take in their mail.

   _____

   _____

   _____

3. Running untouched into the end zone. The halfback raised his arms in triumph. Then he slammed the football to the ground. And did a little victory dance.

   _____

   _____

   _____

4. It's hard to keep up with bills. Such as the telephone, gas, and electricity. After you finally mail the checques. New ones seem to arrive a day or two later.

   _____

   _____

   _____

5. While a woman ordered ten kilos of cold cuts. Customers at the deli counter waited impatiently. The woman explained that she was in charge of a school picnic. And apologized for taking up so much time.

   _____

   _____

   _____

■ Review Test 4

Write quickly for five minutes about what you like to do in your leisure time. Don't worry about spelling, punctuation, finding exact words, or organizing your thoughts. Just focus on writing as many words as you can without stopping.

After you have finished, go back and make whatever changes are needed to correct any sentence fragments in your writing.

Run-Ons

Introductory Project

A run-on occurs when two sentences are run together with no adequate sign given to mark the break between them. Shown below are four run-ons and four correctly marked sentences. See if you can complete the statement that explains how each run-on is corrected.

1. He is the meanest little kid on his block he eats only the heads of animals crackers. *Run-on*

    He is the meanest little kid on his block. He eats only the heads of animal crackers. *Correct*

    The run-on has been corrected by using a _____period_____ and a capital letter to separate the two complete thoughts.

2. Josh Evans likes to gossip about other people, he doesn't like them to gossip about him. *Run-on*

    Josh Evans likes to gossip about other people, but he doesn't like them to gossip about him. *Correct*

    The run-on has been corrected by using a joining word, _____but_____, to connect the two complete thoughts.

3. The chain on my bike likes to chew up my pants, it leaves grease marks on my ankle as well. *Run-on*

    The chain on my bike likes to chew up my pants; it leaves grease marks on my ankle as well. *Correct*

    The run-on has been corrected by using a _____;_____ to connect the two closely related thoughts.

4. The window shade snapped up like a gunshot, her cat leaped a metre off the floor. *Run-on*

    When the window shade snapped up like a gunshot, her cat leaped a metre off the floor. *Correct*

    The run-on has been corrected by using the subordinating word

    _____when._____ to connect the two closely related thoughts.

Answers are on page 554.

WHAT ARE RUN-ONS?

A *run-on* is two complete thoughts that are run together with no adequate sign given to mark the break between them.* Some run-ons have no punctuation at all to mark the break between the thoughts. Such run-ons are known as *fused sentences:* they are fused or joined together as if they were only one thought.

Fused Sentences

My grades are very good this semester my social life rates only a C.
Our father was a madman in his youth he would do anything on a dare.

In other run-ons, known as *comma splices,* a comma is used to connect or "splice" together the two complete thoughts. However, a comma alone is *not enough* to connect two complete thoughts. Some stronger connection than a comma alone is needed.

Comma Splices

My grades are very good this semester, my social life rates only a C.
Our father was a madman in his youth, he would do anything on a dare.

Comma splices are the most common kind of run-on. Students sense that some kind of connection is needed between two thoughts, and so put a comma at the dividing point. But the comma alone is not sufficient, and a stronger, clearer mark between the two thoughts is needed.

A Warning About Words That Can Lead to Run-Ons: People often write run-ons when the second complete thought begins with one of the following words:

I	we	there	now
you	they	this	then
he, she, it		that	next

Remember to be on the alert for run-ons whenever you use one of these words in a series of sentences.

*Note: Some instructors refer to each complete thought in a run-on as an *independent clause.* A *clause* is simply a group of words having a subject and a verb. A clause may be *independent* (expressing a complete thought and able to stand alone) or *dependent* (not expressing a complete thought and not able to stand alone). A run-on is two independent clauses that are run together with no adequate sign given to mark the break between them.

CORRECTING RUN-ONS

Here are four common methods of correcting a run-on.

1   Use a period and a capital letter to break the two complete thoughts into separate sentences:

My grades are very good this semester. My social life rates only a C.
Our father was a madman in his youth. He would do anything on a dare.

2   Use a comma plus a joining word (*and, but, for, or, nor, so, yet*) to connect the two complete thoughts:

My grades are very good this semester, but my social life rates only a C.
Our father was a madman in his youth, for he would do anything on a dare.

3   Use a semi-colon to connect the two complete thoughts:

My grades are very good this semester; my social life rates only a C.
Our father was a madman in his youth; he would do anything on a dare.

4   Use subordination:

Although my grades are very good this semester, my social life rates only a C.
Because my father was a madman in his youth, he would do anything on a dare.

The following pages will give you practice in all four methods of correcting a run-on. The use of subordination will be explained further on page 399, in a section of the book that deals with sentence variety.

Method 1: Period and a Capital Letter

One way of correcting a run-on is to use a period and a capital letter at the break between the two complete thoughts. Use this method especially if the thoughts are not closely related or if another method would make the sentence too long.

Activity 1

Locate the split in each of the following run-ons. Each is a *fused sentence*, that is, each consists of two sentences that are fused or joined together with no punctuation at all between them. Reading each fused sentence aloud will help you "hear" where a major break or split in the thought occurs. At such a point, your voice will probably drop and pause.

Correct the run-on by putting a period at the end of the first thought and a capital letter at the start of the next thought.

Example   Marta shuffled around the apartment in her slippers. *H*er husband couldn't stand their slapping sound on the floor.

1. The goose down jacket was not well made little feathers leaked out of the seams.

2. Liam cringed at the sound of the dentist's drill it buzzed like a twenty-kilo mosquito.

3. Last summer no one swam in the lake a little boy had dropped his pet piranhas into the water.

4. A horse's teeth never stop growing they will eventually grow outside the horse's mouth.

5. Sue's doctor told her he was an astrology nut she did not feel good about learning that.

6. Ice water is the best remedy for a burn using butter is like adding fat to a flame.

7. In the apartment the air was so dry that her skin felt parched the heat was up to thirty degrees.

8. My parents bought me an ant farm it's going to be hard to find tractors that small.

9. Lobsters are cannibalistic this is one reason they are hard to raise in captivity.

10. Julia placed an egg timer next to the phone she did not want to talk more than three minutes on her long-distance calls.

Activity 2

Locate the split in each of the following run-ons. Some of the run-ons are fused sentences, and some of them are *comma splices,* run-ons spliced or joined together with only a comma. Correct each run-on by putting a period at the end of the first thought and a capital letter at the start of the next thought.

1. A bird got into the house through the chimney we had to catch it before our cat did.

2. Some so-called health foods are not so healthy, many are made with oils that raise cholesterol levels.

3. We sat only a few metres from the magician, we still couldn't see where all the birds came from.

4. Mohammed needs only five hours of sleep each night his wife needs at least seven.

5. Our image of dentistry will soon change dentists will use lasers instead of drills.

6. Halina entered her apartment and jumped with fright someone was leaving through her bedroom window.

7. There were several unusual hair styles at the party one woman had bright green braids.

8. Jeremy saves all of his magazines, once a month, he takes them to a nearby nursing home.

9. The doctor seemed to be in a rush, I still took time to ask all the questions that were on my mind.

10. When I was little, my brother tried to feed me flies, he told me they were raisins.

Activity

Write a second sentence to go with each of the sentences that follow. Start the second sentence with the word given in italics. Your sentences can be serious or playful.

Example   She   Jackie works for the phone company.   *She climbs telephone poles in all kinds of weathers.*

It   1.   The alarm clock is unreliable. _____

_____

He   2.   My uncle has a peculiar habit. _____

_____

Then   3.   Tatiana studied for the math test for two hours. _____

_____

It   4.   I could not understand why the car would not start. _____

_____

There   5.   We saw all kinds of litter on the highway. _____

_____

Method 2: Comma and a Joining Word

A second way of correcting a run-on is to use a comma plus a joining word to connect the two complete thoughts. Joining words (also called *conjunctions*) include *and, but, for, or, nor, so,* and *yet.* Here is what the four most common joining words mean:

and   in addition to, along with

His feet hurt from the long hike, and his stomach was growling.

(*And* means "in addition": His feet hurt from the long hike; *in addition,* his stomach was growling.)

but   however, except, on the other hand, just the opposite

> I remembered to get the cocoa, but I forgot the marshmallows.

(*But* means "however": I remembered to get the cocoa; *however,* I forgot the marshmallows.)

for   because, the reason why, the cause of something

> She was afraid of not doing well in the course, for she had always struggled with English before.

(*For* means "because" or "the reason why": She was afraid of not doing well in the course; *the reason why* was that she had always struggled with English before.)

Note: If you are not comfortable using *for,* you may want to use *because* instead of *for* in the activities that follow. If you do use *because,* omit the comma before it.

so   as a result, therefore

> The windshield wiper was broken, so she was in trouble when the rain started.

(So means "as a result": The windshield wiper was broken; *as a result,* she was in trouble when the rain started.)

Activity 1

Insert the joining word (*and, but, for, so*) that logically connects the two thoughts in each sentence.

1.   The couple wanted desperately to buy the house, _____ they did not qualify for a mortgage.

2.   A lot of men today get their hair styled, _____ they use cologne and other cosmetics as well.

3.   Winston asked his wife if she had any bandages, _____ he had just sliced his finger with a paring knife.

4.   He failed the vision part of his driver's test, _____ driver's licence that day.

5.   The restaurant was beautiful, _____ the food was overpriced.

Activity 2

Add a complete and closely related thought to go with each of the following statements. Use a comma plus the italicized joining word when you write the second thought.

Example   for   Ayesha spent the day walking barefoot, *for the heel of one of*
                                                              her shoes had come off.

but   1. She wanted to go to the party _____

_____

and   2. Terry washed his car in the morning _____

_____

so   3. The day was dark and rainy _____

_____

for   4. I'm not going to eat in the school cafeteria anymore _____

_____

but   5. I asked my brother to get off the telephone _____

_____

Method 3: Semi-Colon

A third method of correcting a run-on is to use a semi-colon to mark the break between two thoughts. A *semi-colon* (;) is made up of a period above a comma and is sometimes called a *strong comma*. The semi-colon signals more of a pause than a comma alone but not quite the full pause of a period.

Semi-Colon Alone: Here are some earlier sentences that were connected with a comma plus a joining word. Notice that a semi-colon, unlike the comma alone, can be used to connect the two complete thoughts in each sentence:

A lot of men today get their hair styled; they use cologne and other cosmetics as well.

She was afraid of not doing well in the course; she had always had bad luck with English before.

The restaurant was beautiful; the food was overpriced.

The semi-colon can add to sentence variety. For some people, however, the semi-colon is a confusing mark of punctuation. Keep in mind that if you are not comfortable using it, you can and should use one of the first two methods of correcting a run-on.

Activity

Insert a semi-colon where the break occurs between the two complete thoughts in each of the following run-ons.

Example   I missed the bus by seconds; there would not be another for half an hour.

1. I spend eight hours a day in a windowless office it's a relief to get out into the open air after work.

2. The audience howled with laughter the comedian enjoyed a moment of triumph.

3. It rained all week parts of the highway were flooded.

4. Tony never goes to a certain gas station anymore he found out that the service manager overcharged him for a valve job.

5. The washer shook and banged with its unbalanced load then it began to walk across the floor.

Semi-Colon with a Transitional Word: A semi-colon is sometimes used with a transitional word and a comma to join two complete thoughts.

We were short of money; therefore, we decided not to eat out that weekend.

The roots of a geranium have to be crowded into a small pot; otherwise, the plants may not flower.

I had a paper to write; however, my brain had stopped working for the night.

Following is a list of common transitional words (also known as *adverbial conjunctions*). Brief meanings are given for the words.

Transitional Word	*Meaning*
however	but
nevertheless	but
on the other hand	but
instead	as a substitute
meanwhile	in the intervening time
otherwise	under other conditions
indeed	in fact
in addition	and
also	and
moreover	and
furthermore	and
as a result	in consequence
thus	as a result
consequently	as a result
therefore	as a result

Activity 1

Choose a logical transitional word from the list in the box and write it in the space provided. Put a semi-colon *before* the connector and a comma *after* it.

Example   Exams are over _____; *however,*_____ I still feel tense and nervous.

1. I did not understand her point _____ I asked her to repeat it.

2. With his thumbnail, Jason tried to split open the cellophane covering on the new video game _____ the cellophane refused to tear.

3. Post offices are closed for today's holiday _____ no mail will be delivered.

4. They decided not to go to the movie _____ they went to play miniature golf.

5. I had to skip lunch _____ I would have been late for class.

Activity 2

Punctuate each sentence by using a semi-colon and a comma.

Example   My brother's asthma was worsening; as a result, he quit the soccer team.

1. Manny ate an entire pizza for supper in addition he had a big chunk of pound cake for dessert.

2. The man leaned against the building in obvious pain however no one stopped to help him.

3. Our instructor was absent therefore the test was postponed.

4. I had no time to process the paper instead I printed it out neatly in black ink.

5. Benita loves the velvety texture of cherry Jell-O moreover she loves to squish it between her teeth.

Method 4: Subordination

A fourth method of joining related thoughts is to use subordination. *Subordination* is a way of showing that one thought in a sentence is not as important as, or depends on another thought.

Here are three earlier sentences that have been recast so that one idea is subordinated to (made less important than) the other idea:

When the window shade snapped up like a gunshot, her cat leaped a metre off the floor.
Because it rained all week, parts of the highway were flooded.
Although my grades are very good this year, my social life rates only a C.

Notice that when we subordinate, we use dependent words like *when, because,* and *although.* Here is a brief list of common dependent words:

> ### *Common Dependent Words*
>
> | | | |
> |---|---|---|
> | after | before | unless |
> | although | even though | until |
> | as | if | when |
> | because | since | while |

Subordination is explained further on pages 400–401.

Activity

Choose a logical dependent word from the box above and write it in the space provided.

Example _____*Because*_____ I had so much to do, I never even turned on the TV last night.

1. _____ we emerged from the darkened theatre, it took several minutes for our eyes to adjust to the light.

2. _____ "All Natural" was printed in large letters on the yogurt carton, the fine print listing the ingredients told a different story.

3. I can't study for the test this weekend _____ my boss wants me to work overtime.

4. _____ the vampire movie was over, my children were afraid to go to bed.

5. _____ you have a driver's licence and two major credit cards, that store will not accept your cheque.

A Review: How to Check for Run-Ons

1 To see if a sentence is a run-on, read it aloud and listen for a break marking two complete thoughts. Your voice will probably drop and pause at the break.

2 To check an entire paper, read it aloud from the *last* sentence to the *first*. Doing so will help you hear and see each complete thought.

3 Be on the lookout for words that can lead to run-on sentences:

I	he, she, it	they	this	next
you	we	there	that	then

4 Correct run-on sentences by using one of the following methods:
- Period and capital letter
- Comma and joining word (*and, but, for, or, nor, so, yet*)
- Semi-colon
- Subordination

Review Test 1

Some of the run-ons that follow are fused sentences, having no punctuation between the two complete thoughts; others are comma splices, having only a comma between the two complete thoughts. Correct the run-ons by using one of the following three methods:

- Period and capital letter
- Comma and joining word
- Semi-colon

Do not use the same method of correction for every sentence.

but

Example   Three people did the job, I could have done it alone.

1. The impatient driver tried to get a jump on the green light he kept edging his car into the intersection.

2. The course on the history of UFOs sounded interesting, it turned out to be very dull.

3. That clothing store is a strange place to visit you keep walking up to dummies that look like real people.

4. Everything on the menu sounded delicious they wanted to order the entire menu.

5. Chung pressed a cold washcloth against his eyes, it helped relieve his headache.

6. Marc used to be a fast-food junkie now he eats only vegetables and sunflower seeds.

7. I knew my term paper was not very good, I placed it in a shiny plastic cover to make it look better.

8. Elaine enjoys watching a talk show, Jared prefers watching a late movie.

9. My boss does not know what he is doing half the time then he tries to tell me what to do.

10. In the next minute, 100 people will die, over 240 babies will be born.

Review Test 2

Correct each run-on by using subordination. Choose from among the following dependent words:

after	before	unless
although	even though	until
as	if	when
because	since	while

Example My eyes have been watering all day, I can tell the pollen count is high.

Because my eyes have been watering all day, I can tell the pollen count is high.

1. ~~There~~ *[Even though]* There are a number of suits and jackets on sale, they all have very noticeable flaws.

_____

_____

2. *[Since]* Rust has eaten a hole in the muffler, my car sounds like a motorcycle.

_____

_____

3. *[When]* I finished my household chores, I decided to do some shopping.

_____

_____

4. The power went off for an hour during the night, all the clocks in the house must be reset.

[All the clock ... reset because the power ... right.]

_____

5. *[Although]* Electric cars eliminate exhaust pollution, the limited power of the car's battery is a serious problem.

_____

_____

■ **Review Test 3**

There are two run-ons in each passage. Correct them by using one of the following methods:

■ Period and capital letter
■ Comma and one of these joining words: *and, but,* or *so*
■ One of these dependent words: *although, because,* or *when*

1. The dog raced into the house it was happy to be among people. Its owner bent down to pet it he drew back in disgust. The dog had rolled in something with a horrible smell. *[and]*

_____

_____

_____

2. Small feet were admired in ancient China, some female infants had their feet
   tightly bound. The feet then grew into a tiny, deformed shape. The women
   could barely walk their feet were crippled for life.

[handwritten: , so some]
[handwritten: because]

_____

_____

_____

3. The four friends were losing touch with one another they decided to start a
   "chain" letter. Each woman receives the letter, she adds a page and then sends
   it on to the next friend. Each person has to write only one letter to keep the
   other three informed.

[handwritten: , so]

_____

_____

_____

4. Darryl insisted on dressing himself for nursery school. It was a cold winter
   day, he put on shorts and a tank top. He also put on cowboy boots over his
   bare feet. He liked his image in the mirror his mother made him change.

[handwritten: , but]

_____

_____

_____

■ **Review Test 4**

Write quickly for five minutes about what you did this past weekend. Don't worry
about spelling, punctuation, finding exact words, or organizing your thoughts.
Just focus on writing as many words as you can without stopping.

   After you have finished, go back and make whatever changes are needed to correct any run-ons in your writing.

Irregular Verbs

Introductory Project

You may already have a sense of which common English verbs are regular and which are not. To test yourself, fill in the past tense and past participle of the verbs below. Five are regular verbs and so take *-d* or *-ed* in the past tense and past participle. Five are irregular verbs and will probably not sound right when you try to add *-d* or *-ed*. Write *I* for *irregular* in front of these verbs. Also, see if you can write in their irregular verb forms. (The item at the top is an example.)

Present	Past	Past Participle *(used with "to have" and "to be")*
shout	shouted	shouted
1. crawl	crawled	crawled
2. bring	brought	brought
3. use	used	used
4. do	did	done
5. give	gave	given
6. laugh	laughed	laughed
7. go	went	gone
8. scare	scared	scared
9. dress	dressed	dressed
10. see	saw	seen

Answers are on page 554.

A BRIEF REVIEW OF REGULAR VERBS

Every verb has four principal parts: present, past, past participle, and present participle. These parts can be used to build all the verb tenses (the times shown by a verb).

The past and past participle of a regular verb are formed by adding *-d* or *-ed* to the present. The *past participle* is the form of the verb used with the helping verbs *have, has,* or *had* (or some form of *be* with passive verbs). The *present participle* is formed by adding *-ing* to the present. Here are the principal forms of some regular verbs:

Present	*Past*	*Past Participle*	*Present Particple*
crash	crashed	crashed	crashing
shiver	shivered	shivered	shivering
kiss	kissed	kissed	kissing
apologize	apologized	apologized	apologizing
tease	teased	teased	teasing

Most verbs in English are regular.

LIST OF IRREGULAR VERBS

Irregular verbs have irregular forms in the past tense and past participle. For example, the past tense of the irregular verb *know* is *knew;* the past participle is *known.*

Almost everyone has some degree of trouble with irregular verbs. When you are unsure about the form of a verb, you can check the following list of irregular verbs. (The present participle is not shown on this list because it is formed simply by adding *-ing* to the base form of the verb.) Or you can check a dictionary, which gives the principal parts of irregular verbs.

Present	*Past*	*Past Participle*
arise	arose	arisen
awake	awoke *or* awaked	awoke *or* awaked
be (am, are, is)	was (were)	been
become	became	become
begin	began	begun
bend	bent	bent
bite	bit	bitten
blow	blew	blown
break	broke	broken
bring	brought	brought
build	built	built

Present	*Past*	*Past Participle*
burst	burst	burst
buy	bought	bought
catch	caught	caught
choose	chose	chosen
come	came	come
cost	cost	cost
cut	cut	cut
do (does)	did	done
draw	drew	drawn
drink	drank	drunk
drive	drove	driven
eat	ate	eaten
fall	fell	fallen
feed	fed	fed
feel	felt	felt
fight	fought	fought
find	found	found
fly	flew	flown
freeze	froze	frozen
get	got	got *or* gotten
give	gave	given
go (goes)	went	gone
grow	grew	grown
have (has)	had	had
hear	heard	heard
hide	hid	hidden
hold	held	held
hurt	hurt	hurt
keep	kept	kept
know	knew	known
lay	laid	laid
lead	led	led
leave	left	left
lend	lent	lent
let	let	let
lie	lay	lain
lose	lost	lost
make	made	made
meet	met	met
pay	paid	paid
ride	rode	ridden
ring	rang	rung
run	ran	run
say	said	said
see	saw	seen

Present	Past	Past Participle
sell	sold	sold
send	sent	sent
shake	shook	shaken
shrink	shrank	shrunk
shut	shut	shut
sing	sang	sung
sit	sat	sat
sleep	slept	slept
speak	spoke	spoken
spend	spent	spent
stand	stood	stood
steal	stole	stolen
stick	stuck	stuck
sting	stung	stung
swear	swore	sworn
swim	swam	swum
take	took	taken
teach	taught	taught
tear	tore	torn
tell	told	told
think	thought	thought
wake	woke *or* waked	woken *or* waked
wear	wore	worn
win	won	won
write	wrote	written

Activity 1

Cross out the incorrect verb form in each of the following sentences. Then write the correct form of the verb in the space provided.

Example _____*drew*_____ The little boy ~~drawed~~ on the marble table with permanent ink.

_____ 1. Tomatoes were once thought to be poisonous, and they were growed only as ornamental shrubs.

_____ 2. Julio has rode the bus to school for two years while saving for a car.

_____ 3. My cats have tore little holes in all my good wool sweaters.

_____ 4. The pipes in the bathroom freezed last winter, and they burst when they thawed.

_____ 5. Every time my telephone has rang today, there has been bad news on the line.

_____ 6. Only seven people have ever knowed the formula for Coca-Cola.

_____ 7. Amy blowed up animal-shaped balloons for her son's birthday party.

_____ 8. I shaked the bottle angrily until the ketchup began to flow.

_____   9. While waiting for the doctor to arrive, I sitted in a plastic chair for over two hours.

_____   10. The pile of bones on the plate showed how much chicken the family had ate.

Activity 2

For each of the italicized verbs, fill in the three missing forms in the following order:

> **a** Present tense, which takes an *-s* ending when the subject is *he, she, it,* or any *one person* or *thing*
>
> **b** Past tense
>
> **c** Past participle—the form that goes with the helping verb *have, has,* or *had*

Example   My uncle likes to *give* away certain things. He (*a*) _____*gives*_____ old, threadbare clothes to the Salvation Army. Last year he

(*b*) _____*gave*_____ me a worthless television set in which the

picture tube was burned out. He has (*c*) _____*given*_____ away stuff that a junk dealer would reject.

1. I like to *freeze* chocolate bars. A cholcolate bar (*a*) __froze__ in

half an hour. Once I (*b*) __froze__ a bottle of cola. I put it in the freezer to chill and then forgot about it. Later I opened the freezer and

discovered it had (*c*) __frozen.__ and exploded.

2. I *know* the girl in the lavender bikini. She (*a*) __knows.__ me, too. I (*b*) __knew__ her brother before I met her. I have (*c*) __known__ him since boyhood.

3. An acquaintance of mine is a shoplifter, although he knows it's wrong to *steal.* He (*a*) __steals__ chocolate bars from supermarkets. Last month he (*b*) __stole__ a CD player and was caught by a detective. He has (*c*) __stolen__ pants and shirts by wearing several layers of clothes out of a store.

4. I *go* to parties a lot. Often Camille (*a*) __goes__ with me. She (*b*) __went__ with me just last week. I have (*c*) __gone__ to parties every Friday for the past month.

5. My brother likes to *throw* things. Sometimes he (*a*) __throws__ socks into his bureau drawer. In high school he (*b*) __threw__ footballs

while quarterbacking the team. And he has (c) ___thrown___ Frisbees in our backyard for as long as I can remember.

6. I *see* her every weekend. She (a) ___sees___ her other friends during the week. We first (b) ___saw___ each other on a cold Saturday night last winter, when we went for supper at an Indian restaurant. Since then we have (c) ___seen___ each other every weekend except when my car was broken down.

7. I often *lie* down for a few minutes after a hard day's work. Sometimes my cat (a) ___lies___ down near me. Yesterday was Saturday, so I (b) ___lay___ in bed all morning. I probably would have (c) ___lain___ in bed all afternoon, but I wanted to get some planting done in my vegetable garden.

8. I *do* not understand the assignment. It simply (a) ___does___ not make sense to me. I was surprised to learn that Shareen (b) ___did___ understand it. In fact, she had already (c) ___done___ the assignment.

9. I often find it hard to *begin* writing a paper. The assignment that I must do (a) ___begins___ to worry me while I'm watching television, but I seldom turn off the set. Once I waited until the late movie had ended before I (b) ___began___ to write. If I had (c) ___begun___ earlier, I would have gotten a decent night's sleep.

10. Alissa likes to *eat*. She (a) ___eats___ as continuously as some people smoke. Once she (b) ___ate___ a large pack of cookies in half an hour. Even if she has (c) ___eaten___ a heavy meal, she often starts munching snacks right afterward.

■ Review Test 1

Underline the correct verb in the parentheses.

1. I (shaked, shook) the bottle of medicine before I took a teaspoon of it.

2. Ahmed came into the gym and (began, begun) to practise on the parallel bars.

3. Over half the class has (taken, took) this course on a pass-fail basis.

4. Even though my father (teached, taught) me how to play baseball, I never enjoyed any part of the game.

5. Because I had (lended, lent) him the money, I had a natural concern about what he did with it.

6. The drugstore clerk (gave, gived) him the wrong change.

7. May (brang, brought) a sweatshirt with her, for she knew the mountains got cold at night.

8. My sister (was, be) at school when a stranger came asking for her at our home.

9. The mechanic (did, done) an expensive valve job on my engine without getting my permission.

10. The basketball team has (broke, broken) the school record for the most wins in one year.

11. Someone (leaved, left) his or her books in the classroom.

12. That jacket was (tore, torn) during the football game.

13. If I hadn't (threw, thrown) away the receipt, I could have gotten my money back.

14. I would have (become, became) very angry if you had not intervened.

15. As the flowerpot (fell, falled) from the windowsill, the little boy yelled, "Bombs away!"

■ Review Test 2

Write short sentences that use the form requested for the following irregular verbs.

Example Past of *grow*   *I grew ten centimetres in one year.*

1. Past of *know* _____

2. Past of *take* _____

3. Past participle of *give* _____

4. Past participle of *write* _____

5. Past of *bring* _____

6. Past participle of *speak* _____

7. Present of *begin* _____

8. Past of *go* _____

9. Past participle of *see* _____

10. Past of *drive* _____

Subject-Verb Agreement

Introductory Project

As you read each pair of sentences below, make a check mark beside the sentence that you think uses the underlined word correctly.

There <u>was</u> too many people talking at once. _____

There <u>were</u> too many people talking at once. _____

The onions in that spaghetti sauce <u>gives</u> me heartburn. _____

The onions in that spaghetti sauce <u>give</u> me heartburn. _____

The mayor and her husband <u>attends</u> our church. _____

The mayor and her husband <u>attend</u> our church. _____

Everything <u>seem</u> to slow me down when I'm in a hurry. _____

Everything <u>seems</u> to slow me down when I'm in a hurry. _____

Answers are on page 554.

A verb must agree with its subject in number. A *singular subject* (one person or thing) takes a singular verb. A *plural subject* (more than one person or thing) takes a plural verb. Mistakes in subject-verb agreement are sometimes made in the following situations (each situation is explained on the following pages):

1   When words come between the subject and the verb

2   When a verb comes before the subject

3   With compound subjects

4   With indefinite pronouns

1   WORDS BETWEEN SUBJECT AND VERB

Words that come between the subject and the verb do not change subject-verb agreement. In the sentence

The tomatoes in this salad are brown and mushy.

the subject (tomatoes) is plural, and so the verb (are) is plural. The words *in this salad* that come between the subject and the verb do not affect subject-verb agreement.

To help find the subject of certain sentences, you should cross out prepositional phrases (see page 248):

Nell, ~~with her three dogs close behind,~~ runs around the park every day.

The seams ~~in my new coat~~ have split after only two wearings.

Activity

Underline the correct verb form in the parentheses.

1. The decisions of the judge (seem, seems) questionable.

2. The flakes in this cereal (taste, tastes) like sawdust.

3. The woman in the dark sunglasses (is, are) our mayor.

4. Many people in Europe (speak, speaks) several languages.

5. A salad and small yogurt (is, are) my usual lunch.

6. That silk flower by the candles (look, looks) real.

7. One of my son's worst habits (is, are) leaving an assortment of dirty plates on the kitchen counter.

8. The rust spots on the back of Emma's car (need, needs) to be cleaned with a special polish.

9. The collection of shampoo bottles in my bathroom (overflow, overflows) the cabinet shelves.

10. A tired-looking student in my class often (sleep, sleeps) through most of the lectures.

2   VERB BEFORE SUBJECT

A verb agrees with its subject even when the verb comes *before* the subject. Words that may precede the subject include *there, here,* and, in questions, *who, which, what,* and *where.*

On Glen's doorstep were two police officers.

There are many pizza places in our town.

Here is your receipt.

Where are they going to sleep?

If you are unsure about the subject, look at the verb and ask *who* or *what*. With the first example above, you might ask, "*Who* were on the doorstep?" The answer, *police officers*, is the subject.

Activity

Write the correct form of the verb in the space provided.

is, are   1. What ____*is*____ your middle name?

was, were   2. Among the guests ____*was*____ a private detective.

do, does   3. Where ____*do*____ you go when you want to be alone?

is, are   4. There ____*are*____ many hungry people in Canadian cities.

rest, rests   5. In that grave ____*rest*____ the bones of my great-grandfather.

was, were   6. There ____*were*____ too many people in the room for me to feel comfortable.

is, are   7. Why ____*are*____ the lights turned off?

stand, stands   8. Across the street ____*stands*____ the post office.

is, are   9. Here ____*are*____ the tickets for tonight's game.

was, were   10. Stuffed into the mailbox ____*were*____ ten pieces of junk mail and three ripped magazines.

3 COMPOUND SUBJECTS

Subjects joined by *and* generally take a plural verb.

> Maple syrup and sweet butter taste delicious on pancakes.
> Fear and ignorance have a lot to do with hatred.

When subjects are joined by *either . . . or, neither . . . nor, not only . . . but also,* the verb agrees with the subject closer to the verb.

> Either the Dixie Chicks or Shania Twain deserves the award for the best country album of the year.

The nearer subject, *Shania Twain,* is singular, and so the verb is singular.

Activity

Write the correct form of the verb in the space provided.

stays, stay   1. Our cats and dog ____*stay*____ at a neighbour's house when we go on vacation.

Is, Are   2. ____*Are*____ the birthday cake and ice cream ready to be served?

holds, hold   3. Staples and Scotch tape ____*hold*____ all our old photo albums together.

was, were   4. Rent and car insurance _____were_____ my biggest expenses last month.

wants, want   5. Neither the students nor the instructor _____wants_____ to postpone the final exam till after the holidays.

is, are   6. An egg and a banana _____are_____ required for the recipe.

was, were   7. Owning a car and having money in my pocket _____were_____ the chief ambitions of my adolescence.

visits, visit   8. My aunt and uncle from Poland _____visit_____ us every other summer.

was, were   9. Before they saw a marriage therapist, Peter and Sylvia _____were_____ planning to get divorced.

acts, act   10. Not only the property owner but also her children _____act_____ unfriendly to us.

INDEFINITE PRONOUNS

The following words, known as *indefinite pronouns,* always take singular verbs:

(-**one** *words*)	(-**body** *words*)	(-**thing** *words*)	
one	nobody	nothing	each
anyone	anybody	anything	either
everyone	everybody	everything	neither
someone	somebody	something	

Note: *Both* always takes a plural verb.

Activity

Write the correct form of the verb in the space provided.

is, are   1. Everybody at my new school _____is_____ friendly.

feel, feels   2. Neither of those mattresses _____feels_____ comfortable.

knows, know   3. Nobody in my family _____knows_____ how to swim.

needs, need   4. Each of the children _____needs_____ some attention.

sounds, sound   5. Something about Robbie's story _____sounds_____ suspicious.

pitches, pitch   6. If each of us _____pitches_____ in, we can finish this job in an hour.

was, were   7. Everybody in the theatre _____was_____ getting up and leaving before the movie ended.

provides, provide   8. Neither of the restaurants _____provides_____ facilities for the physically challenged.

likes, like   9. No one in our family _____ *likes* _____ housecleaning, but we all take a turn at it.

steals, steal   10. Someone in our neighbourhood _____ *steals* _____ vegetables from people's gardens.

■ Review Test 1

Underline the correct verb in parentheses.

1. The lettuce in most of the stores in our area now (costs, cost) almost two dollars a head.

2. Nobody in the class of fifty students (understands, understand) how to solve the equation on the blackboard.

3. The packages in the shopping bag (was, were) a wonderful mystery to the children.

4. My exercise class of five students (meets, meet) every Thursday afternoon.

5. Anyone who (steals, steal) my purse won't find much inside it.

6. Business contacts and financial backing (is, are) all that I need to establish my career as a dress designer.

7. Each of those breakfast cereals (contains, contain) a high proportion of sugar.

8. The serious look in that young girl's eyes (worries, worry) me.

9. All of the cars on my block (has, have) to be moved one day a month for street cleaning.

10. The job is not for people who (stumbles, stumble) over tough decisions.

■ Review Test 2

Each of the following passages contains two mistakes in subject-verb agreement. Find these two mistakes and cross them out. Then write the correct form of each verb in the space provided.

1. Few people recalls seeing baby pigeons. The reason is simple. Baby pigeons in the nest eats a huge amount of food each day. Upon leaving the nest, they are close to the size of their parents.

   a. _____ *eat* _____

   b. _____ ~~to see~~ *recall* _____

2. Everything in the mall stores are on sale today. Customers from all over are crowding the aisles. There is terrific bargains in many departments.

   a. _____ *is* _____

   b. _____ *are* _____

3. I am disappointed in my frozen dinner. The peas looks wrinkled and dry.
    Mounds of soggy stuffing covers a tiny piece of meat.

    a. _____ look _____

    b. _____ cover. _____

4. The members of the swimming team paces nervously beside the pool.
    Finally, an official blows a whistle. Into the pool dive a swimmer with thick,
    tan arms. He paddles quickly through the water.

    a. _____ pace _____

    b. _____ dives _____

5. There are three paths through the woods. There is narrow, rocky parts on
    two of the paths. The hikers take the easiest one. Around a bend, someone
    spots a snake. It is lying in the middle of the path, sunning itself. One of the
    hikers fear snakes. He refuses to go on.

    a. _____ are _____

    b. _____ fears. _____

Consistent
Verb Tense

KEEPING TENSES CONSISTENT

Do not shift verb tenses unnecessarily. If you begin writing a paper in the present tense, don't shift suddenly to the past. If you begin in the past, don't shift without reason to the present. Notice the inconsistent verb tenses in the following example:

The shoplifter *walked* quickly toward the front of the store. When a clerk *shouts* at him, he *started* to run.

The verbs must be consistently in the present tense:

The shoplifter *walks* quickly toward the front of the store. When a clerk *shouts* at him, he *starts* to run.

Or the verbs must be consistently in the past tense:

The shoplifter *walked* quickly toward the front of the store. When a clerk *shouted* at him, he *started* to run.

Activity 1

In each item, one verb must be changed so that it agrees in tense with the other verbs. Cross out the incorrect verb and write the correct form in the space provided.

Example _____*carried*_____ Kareem wanted to be someplace else when the dentist ~~carries~~ in a long needle.

1. I played my CDs and watched television before I decide to do some home-work. _____

2. The hitchhiker stopped me as I walks from the turnpike rest station and said, "Are you on your way to Red Deer?" _____

3. Some students attend all their classes in school. They listen carefully during lectures but they don't take notes. As a result, they often failed tests.

   _____

4. His parents stayed together for his sake; only after he graduates from college were they divorced. _____

5. In the movie, artillery shells exploded on the hide of the reptile monster. It just grinned, tosses off the shells, and kept eating people. _____

6. Several months a year, monarch butterflies come to live on Point Pelee along the Lake Erie shore. Thousands and thousands of them hang from the trees and fluttered through the air in large groups. _____

7. After waking up each morning, Neil stays in bed for a while. First he stretches and yawned loudly, and then he plans his day. _____

8. The salespeople at Biggs' Department Store are very helpful. When people asked for a product the store doesn't carry or is out of, the salesperson recommends another store. _____

9. Part-time workers at the company are the first to be laid off. They are also paid less, and they received no union representation. _____

10. Smashed cars, ambulances, and police cars blocked traffic on one side of the highway. On the other side, traffic slows down as drivers looked to see what happened. _____

Activity 2

Change verbs where needed in the following passage, so that they are consistently in the past tense. Cross out each incorrect verb and write the correct form above it, as shown in the example. You will need to make nine corrections.

Late one rainy night, Mei Ling woke to the sound of steady dripping. When
she got out of bed to investigate, a drop of cold water splashed [~~splashes~~] onto her arm.
She looks up just in time to see another drop form on the ceiling, hang
suspended for a moment, and fall to the carpet. Stumbling to the kitchen,
Mei Ling reaches deep into one of the cabinets and lifts out a large roasting
pan. As she did so, pot lids and baking tins clattered out and crash onto the
counter. Mei Ling ignored them, stumbled back to the bedroom, and places
the pan on the floor under the drip. But a minute after sliding her icy feet
under the covers, Mei Ling realized she is in trouble. The sound of each drop
hitting the metal pan echoed like a cannon in the quiet room. Mei Ling feels
like crying, but she finally thought of a solution. She got out of bed and
returns a minute later with a thick bath towel. She lined the pan with the
towel and crawls back into bed.

■ Review Test

Change verbs where needed in the following passage so that they are consistently
in the past tense. Cross out each incorrect verb and then write the correct form in
the space provided. You will need to make ten corrections in all.

Balancing the green plastic bag full of garbage, Craig yanked the front
door open. As he stepped onto the front porch, he notices that a light snow
was already falling. He remembers that when he called to rent the cabin, he
was told that it was not too early to expect snow in this mountain community.
He glances up at the sky and then walks briskly to the end of the driveway.
There he deposited the overflowing bag into one of the large garbage cans.
Shivering from the cold, he turned around and starts back toward the house,
but then he pauses suddenly. At the southwest corner of the cabin, standing
on its hind legs, was an enormous black bear. For a long terrible second,
Craig was positive the bear was staring right at him. Looking for a promising
direction to run, Craig turns around and saw a small bear cub scampering
away from behind another garbage can. Before Craig had time to react, the

large bear went down on all fours, sprints past the house, and started after the cub. Craig breathed a sigh of relief, races into the cabin, and locks the door behind him.

1. _____

2. _____

3. _____

4. _____

5. _____

6. _____

7. _____

8. _____

9. _____

10. _____

CHAPTER 25

Pronoun Agreement, Reference, and Point of View

Introductory Project

Read each pair of sentences below. Then write a check mark beside the sentence that you think uses the underlined word or words correctly.

Someone in my neighbourhood lets <u>their</u> dog run loose. _____

Someone in my neighbourhood lets <u>his or her</u> dog run loose. _____

After Kieran reviewed his notes with Scott, <u>he</u> passed the exam with ease.

_____

After reviewing his notes with Scott, <u>Kieran</u> passed the exam with ease.

_____

I dislike being a server, for <u>you</u> can never count on a fair tip. _____

I dislike being a server, for <u>I</u> can never count on a fair tip. _____

Answers are on page 554.

Pronouns are words that take the place of nouns (persons, places, or things). In fact, the word *pronoun* means "for a noun." Pronouns are shortcuts that keep you from unnecessarily repeating words in writing. Here are some examples of pronouns:

Ivana had not finished *her* paper. (*Her* is a pronoun that takes the place of *Ivana's*.)

Brendan swung so heavily on the tree branch that *it* snapped. (*It* replaces *branch*.)

When the three little pigs saw the wolf, *they* pulled out cans of pepper spray. (*They* is a pronoun that takes the place of *pigs.*)

This section presents rules that will help you avoid three common mistakes people make with pronouns. The rules are as follows:

1 A pronoun must agree in number with the word or words it replaces.
2 A pronoun must refer clearly to the word it replaces.
3 Pronouns should not shift unnecessarily in point of view.

PRONOUN AGREEMENT

A pronoun must agree in number with the word or words it replaces. If the word a pronoun refers to is singular, the pronoun must be singular; if that word is plural, the pronoun must be plural. (Note that the word a pronoun refers to is also known as the *antecedent. Antecedent* means "going before" in Latin.)

Jacquie agreed to lend me her Philosopher Kings CDs.
People walking the trail must watch their step because of snakes.

In the first example, the pronoun *her* refers to the singular word *Jacquie* in the second example, the pronoun *their* refers to the plural word *People.*

Activity

Write the appropriate pronoun (*their, they, them, it*) in the blank space in each of the following sentences.

Example   I lifted the pot of hot potatoes carefully, but _____*it*_____ slipped out of my hand.

1. The value that people receive for _____ dollars these days is rapidly diminishing.

2. Rick never misses his daily workout; he believes _____ keeps him healthy.

3. Sometimes, in marriage, partners expect too much from _____ mates.

4. For some students, college is often their first experience with an undisciplined learning situation, and _____ are not always ready to accept the responsibility.

5. Our new neighbours moved in three months ago, but I have yet to meet _____.

Indefinite Pronouns

The following words, known as *indefinite pronouns,* are always singular.

(*-one* words)	(*-body* words)	
one	nobody	each
anyone	anybody	either
everyone	everybody	neither
someone	somebody	

If a pronoun in a sentence refers to one of the above singular words, the pronoun should be singular.

Each father felt that (his) child should have won the contest.

One of the women could not find (her) purse.

Everyone must be in (his) seat before the instructor takes the roll.

In each example, the circled possessive pronoun is singular because it refers to one of these special singular words.

Note: The last example is correct *if* everyone in the class is a man. If everyone in the class is a woman, the pronoun would be *her.* If the class has both women and men, the pronoun form would be *his or her:*

Everyone must be in his or her seat before the instructor takes the roll.

Some writers follow the traditional practice of using *his* to refer to both women and men. Many now use *his or her* to avoid an implied sexual bias. To avoid using *his* or the somewhat awkward *his or her,* a sentence can often be rewritten in the plural:

Students must be in their seats before the instructor takes the roll.

Activity

Underline the correct pronoun.

1. Someone has blocked the parking-lot exit with (his or her, their) car.

2. Everyone in the women's group has volunteered some of (her, their) time for the voting drive.

3. Neither of the men arrested as terrorists would reveal information about (his, their) group.

4. Not one of the women coaches will be returning to (her, their) job next year.

5. Each of the CEO's advisers offered (his or her, their) opinion about the rail strike.

PRONOUN REFERENCE

A sentence may be confusing and unclear in these circumstances:

- if a pronoun appears to refer to more than one word
- if the pronoun does not refer to any specific word.

Look at this sentence:

> Jeremy almost dropped out of high school, for he felt *they* emphasized discipline too much.

Who emphasized discipline too much? There is no specific word that *they* refers to. Be clear:

> Jeremy almost dropped out of high school, for he felt *the teachers* emphasized discipline too much.

Here are sentences with other kinds of faulty pronoun references. Read the explanations of why they are faulty and look carefully at how they are corrected.

Faulty	*Clear*
Jade told Marisa that *she* lacked self-confidence. (*Who* lacked self-confidence: Jade or Marisa? Be clear.)	Jade told Marisa, "You lack self-confidence." (Quotation marks, which can sometimes be used to correct an unclear reference, are explained on pages 352–354.)
Nazima's mother is a hairdresser, but Nazima is not interested in *it*. (There is no specific word that *it* refers to. It would not make sense to say, "Nazima is not interested in hairdresser.")	Nazima's mother is a hairdresser, but Nazima is not interested in becoming one.
Ron blamed the police officer for the ticket, *which* was foolish. (Does *which* mean that the officer's giving the ticket was foolish, or that Ron's blaming the officer was foolish? Be clear.)	Foolishly, Ron blamed the police officer for the ticket.

Activity

Rewrite each of the following sentences to make clear the vague pronoun reference. Add, change, or omit words as necessary.

Example   Our cat was friends with our hamster until he bit him.

> *Until the cat bit the hamster, the two were friends.*

1. Maria's mother let her wear her new earrings to school.

    _____

2. When I asked why I failed my driver's test, he said I drove too slowly.

    _____

3. Dad ordered my brother to paint the garage because he didn't want to do it.

    _____

4. Julian dropped his psychology courses because he thought they assigned too much reading.

    _____

5. I love Parmesan cheese on veal, but it does not always digest well.

    _____

PRONOUN POINT OF VIEW

Pronouns should not shift their point of view unnecessarily. When writing a paper, be consistent in your use of first-, second-, or third-person pronouns.

Type of Pronoun	*Singular*	*Plural*
First-person pronouns	I (my, mine, me)	we (our, us)
Second-person pronouns	you (your)	you (your)
Third-person pronouns	he (his, him)	they (their, them)
	she (her)	
	it (its)	

Note: Any person, place, or thing, as well as any indefinite pronoun like *one, anyone, someone,* and so on (page 302), is a third-person word.

For instance, if you start writing in the third person *she*, don't jump suddenly to the second person *you*. Or if you are writing in the first person *I*, don't shift unexpectedly to *one*. Look at the examples.

Inconsistent

I enjoy movies like *Bride of Chucky* that frighten *you*.
(The most common mistake people make is to let *you* slip into their writing after they start with another pronoun.)

Consistent

I enjoy movies like *Bride of Chucky* that frighten me.

As soon as a person walks into Helen's apartment, *you* can tell that Helen owns a cat.
(Again, *you* is a shift in point of view.)

As soon as a person walks into Helen's apartment, *he or she* can tell that Helen owns a cat.
(See also the note on *his or her* references on page 302.)

Activity

Cross out inconsistent pronouns in the following sentences, and write the correct form of the pronoun above each crossed-out word.

me
Example   My dreams are always the kind that haunt ~~you~~ the next day.

1. Whenever we take our children on a trip, you have to remember to bring snacks, tissues, and toys.

2. In our society, we often need a diploma before you are hired for a job.

3. A worker can take a break only after a relief person comes to take your place.

4. If a student organizes time carefully, you can accomplish a great deal of work.

5. Although I know you should watch your cholesterol intake, I can never resist an ear of corn dripping with melted butter.

■ Review Test 1

Cross out the pronoun error in each sentence and write the correction in the space provided at the left. Then circle the letter that correctly describes the type of error that was made.

Examples

___*his (or her)*___   Each player took ~~their~~ position on the court.
    Mistake in: a. pronoun reference   (b.) pronoun agreement

___*the store*___   I was angry when ~~they~~ wouldn't give me cash back when I returned the sweater I had bought.
    Mistake in: (a.) pronoun reference   b. pronoun point of view

___*I*___   I love Jello because ~~you~~ can eat about five bowls of it and still not feel full.
    Mistake in: a. pronoun agreement   (b.) pronoun point of view

_____   1. Dan asked Mr. Lalonde if he could stay an extra hour at work today.
    Mistake in: a. pronoun reference   b. pronoun agreement

_____   2. Both the front door and the back door of the abandoned house had fallen off its hinges.
    Mistake in: a. pronoun agreement   b. pronoun point of view

_____   3. I hate going to the supermarket because you always have trouble finding a parking space there.
    Mistake in: a. pronoun agreement   b. pronoun point of view

_____ 4. Neil was angry when they raised the provincial tax on cigarettes again.
Mistake in: a. pronoun agreement   b. pronoun reference

_____ 5. Every one of those musicians who played for two hours in the rain truly earned their money last night.
Mistake in: a. pronoun agreement   b. pronoun reference

_____ 6. As I entered the house, you could hear someone giggling in the hallway.
Mistake in: a. pronoun reference   b. pronoun point of view

_____ 7. Each of the beauty queens is asked a thought-provoking question and then judged on their answer.
Mistake in: a. pronoun agreement   b. pronoun reference

_____ 8. Sometimes I take the alternative route, but it takes you two hours longer.
Mistake in: a. pronoun agreement   b. pronoun point of view

_____ 9. At the dental office, I asked him if it was really necessary to take X-rays of my mouth again.
Mistake in: a. pronoun agreement   b. pronoun reference

_____ 10. My favourite subject is abnormal psychology because the case studies make you seem so normal by comparison.
Mistake in: a. pronoun agreement   b. pronoun point of view

■ Review Test 2

Underline the correct word in parentheses.

1. As we sat in class waiting for the test results, (you, we) could feel the tension.

2. Hoping to be first in line when (they, the ushers) opened the doors, we arrived two hours early for the concert.

3. If a person really wants to appreciate good coffee, (he or she, you, they) should drink it black.

4. I am hooked on science fiction stories because they allow (you, me) to escape to other worlds.

5. Tina often visits the reading centre in school, for she finds that (they, the tutors) give her helpful instruction.

6. Nobody seems to know how to add or subtract without (his or her, their) pocket calculator anymore.

7. Cindy is the kind of woman who will always do (their, her) best.

8. Each of my brothers has had (his, their) apartment broken into.

9. If someone is going to write a composition, (he or she, you, they) should prepare at least one rough draft.

10. I've been taking cold medicine, and now (it, the cold) is better.

CHAPTER 26

Pronoun Types

This chapter describes some common types of pronouns: subject and object pronouns, possessive pronouns, and demonstrative pronouns.

SUBJECT AND OBJECT PRONOUNS

Pronouns change their form depending on the purpose they serve in a sentence. In the box that follows is a list of subject and object pronouns.

Subject Pronouns	*Object Pronouns*
I	me
you	you (*no change*)
he	him
she	her
it	it (*no change*)
we	us
they	them

SUBJECT PRONOUNS

Subject pronouns are subjects of verbs.

She is wearing blue nail polish on her toes. (*She* is the subject of the verb *is wearing*.)

They ran up three flights of steps. (*They* is the subject of the verb *ran*.)

We children should have some privacy too. (*We* is the subject of the verb *should have*.)

Rules for using subject pronouns, and several kinds of mistakes people sometimes make with subject pronouns, are explained below.

1 Use a subject pronoun in spots where you have a compound (more than one) subject.

Incorrect	*Correct*
Eliza and *me* are exactly the same size.	Eliza and *I* are exactly the same size.
Her and *me* share our wardrobes with each other.	*She* and *I* share our wardrobes with each other.

Hint: If you are not sure what pronoun to use, try each pronoun by itself in the sentence. The correct pronoun will be the one that sounds right. For example, "Her shares her wardrobe" does not sound right; "She shares her wardrobe" does.

2 Use a subject pronoun after forms of the verb *to be.* Forms of *to be* include *am, are, is, was, were, has been,* and *have been.*

It was *I* who called you a minute ago and then hung up.
It may be *they* entering the coffee shop.
It was *he* who put the white tablecloth into the washing machine with a red sock.

The sentences above may sound strange and stilted to you because they are seldom used in conversation. When we speak with one another, forms such as "It was me," "It may be them," and "It is her" are widely accepted. In formal writing, however, the grammatically correct forms are still preferred.

Hint: To avoid having to use the subject pronoun form after *to be,* you can simply reword a sentence. Here is how the preceding examples could be reworded:

I was the one who called you a minute ago and then hung up.
They may be the ones entering the coffee shop.
He put the white tablecloth into the washing machine with a red sock.

3 Use subject pronouns after *than* or *as.* The subject pronoun is used because a verb is understood after the pronoun.

Mark can hold his breath longer than *I* (can). (The verb *can* is understood after *I.*)
Her thirteen-year-old daughter is as tall as *she* (is). (The verb *is* is understood after *she.*)
You drive much better than *he* (drives). (The verb *drives* is understood after *he.*)

Hint: Avoid mistakes by mentally adding the "missing" verb at the end of the sentence.

Object Pronouns

Object pronouns (*me, him, her, us, them*) are the objects of verbs or prepositions. (*Prepositions* are connecting words like *for, at, about, to, before, with,* and *of.* See also page 248.) An object, in grammatical terms, receives the action of a transitive verb or completes a prepositional phrase.

> Lee pushed *me.* (*Me* is the object of the verb *pushed.*)
> We dragged *them* all the way home. (*Them* is the object of the verb *dragged.*)
> She wrote all about *us* in her diary. (*Us* is the object of the preposition *about.*)
> Vera passed a note to *him* as she walked to the pencil sharpener. (*Him* is the object of the preposition *to.*)

People are sometimes uncertain about which pronoun to use when two objects follow the verb.

Incorrect	Correct
I argued with his sister and *he.*	I argued with his sister and *him.*
The cashier cheated Connor and *I.*	The cashier cheated Connor and *me.*

Hint: If you are not sure which pronoun to use, try each pronoun by itself in the sentence. The correct pronoun will be the one that sounds right. For example, "I argued with he" does not sound right; "I argued with him" does.

Activity

Underline the correct subject or object pronoun in each of the following sentences. Then show whether your answer is a subject or an object pronoun by circling *S* or *O* in the margin. The first one is done for you as an example.

(S) O   1. Darcy and (she, her) kept dancing even after the band stopped playing.

S O   2. The letters Mom writes to Stella and (I, me) are always printed in red.

S O   3. No one has more nerve than (he, him).

S O   4. Their relay team won because they practised more than (we, us).

S O   5. (We, Us) choir members get to perform for the governor.

S O   6. The rest of (they, them) came to the wedding by train.

S O   7. (She, Her) and Sammy got divorced and then remarried.

S O   8. My sister keeps track of all the favours she does for my brother and (I, me).

S O   9. Terrell and (he, him) look a lot alike, but they're not even related.

S O   10. Our neighbours asked Rosa and (I, me) to help with their parents' surprise party.

POSSESSIVE PRONOUNS

Possessive pronouns show ownership or possession.

Using a small branch, Siu wrote *his* initials in the wet cement.
The furniture is *mine,* but the car is hers.

Here is a list of possessive pronouns:

my, mine	our, ours
your, yours	your, yours
his	their, theirs
her, hers	
its	

Note: A possessive pronoun *never* uses an apostrophe. (Also see page 347.)

Incorrect	*Correct*
That earring is *hers'*.	That earring is *hers.*
The orange cat is *theirs'*.	The orange cat is *theirs.*

Activity

Cross out the incorrect possessive pronoun form in each of the sentences below. Write the correct form in the space at the left.

Example   _____ *hers* _____   Those gloves are ~~hers'~~.

_____ 1. A porcupine has no quills on its' belly.

_____ 2. The stereo set is theirs'.

_____ 3. You can easily tell which team is ours' by when we cheer.

_____ 4. The car with the pink car seats is hers'.

_____ 5. Grandma's silverware and dishes will be yours' when you get married.

DEMONSTRATIVE PRONOUNS

Demonstrative pronouns point to or single out a person or thing. There are four demonstrative pronouns:

this	these
that	those

Generally speaking, *this* and *these* refer to things close at hand; *that* and *those* refer to things farther away. These four pronouns are commonly used in the role of demonstrative adjectives as well.

> *This* milk has gone sour.
> My son insists on saving all *these* computer magazines.
> I almost tripped on *that* roller skate at the bottom of the steps.
> *Those* plants in the corner don't get enough light.

Note: Do not use *them, this here, that there, these here,* or *those there* to point out. Use only *this, that, these,* or *those.*

Activity

Cross out the incorrect form of the demonstrative pronoun and write the correct form in the space provided.

Example   _____Those_____   T~~hose there~~ tires look worn.

_____ 1. This here child has a high fever.

_____ 2. These here pants I'm wearing are so tight I can hardly breathe.

_____ 3. Them kids have been playing in the alley all morning.

_____ 4. That there umpire won't stand for any temper tantrums.

_____ 5. I save them old baby clothes for my daughter's dolls.

▨ Review Test

Underline the correct word in the parentheses.

1. If I left dinner up to (he, him), we'd have Shreddies every night.

2. Julia's words may have come from the script, but the smile is all (hers', hers).

3. My boyfriend offered to drive his mother and (I, me) to the mall to shop for his birthday present.

4. (Them, Those) little marks on the floor are scratches, not crumbs.

5. I took a picture of my brother and (I, me) looking into the hallway mirror.

6. When Lin and (she, her) drove back from the airport, they talked so much that they missed their exit.

7. (That there, That) orange juice box says, "Fresh," but the juice is made from concentrate.

8. Eliot swears that he dreamt about (she, her) and a speeding car the night before Irina was injured in a car accident.

9. The server brought our food to the people at the next table and gave (theirs, theirs') to us.

10. Since it was so hot out, Lee Ann and (he, him) felt they had a good excuse to study at the beach.

CHAPTER 27

Adjectives and Adverbs

ADJECTIVES

What Are Adjectives?

Adjectives describe nouns (names of persons, places, or things) or pronouns.

Emil is a *rich* man. (The adjective *rich* describes the noun *man*.)

He is also *generous*. (The adjective *generous* describes the pronoun *he*.)

Our *grey* cat sleeps a lot. (The adjective *grey* describes the noun *cat*.)

She is *old*. (The adjective *old* describes the pronoun *she*.)

Adjectives usually come before the word they describe (as in *rich man* and *grey cat*). But they also come after forms of the verb *to be* (*is, are, was, were*, and so on). They also follow verbs of appearance or perception such as *look, appear, seem, become, sound, taste*, and *smell*.

That speaker was *boring*. (The adjective *boring* describes the speaker.)

The Petersons are *homeless*. (The adjective *homeless* describes the Petersons.)

The soup looked *good*. (The adjective *good* describes the soup.)

But it tasted *salty*. (The adjective *salty* describes the pronoun *it*.)

USING ADJECTIVES TO COMPARE

For all one-syllable adjectives and some two-syllable adjectives, add *-er* when comparing two things and *-est* when comparing three or more things.

My sister's handwriting is *neater* than mine, but Mother's is the *neatest*.

Canned juice is sometimes *cheaper* than fresh juice, but frozen juice is often the *cheapest*.

For some two-syllable adjectives and all longer adjectives, add *more* when comparing two things and *most* when comparing three or more things.

> Typing something is *more efficient* than writing it by hand, but the *most efficient* way to write is on a computer.
>
> Jeans are generally *more comfortable* than slacks, but sweat pants are the *most comfortable* of all.

You can usually tell when to use *more* and *most* by the sound of a word. For example, you can probably tell by its sound that "carefuller" would be too awkward to say and that *more careful* is thus correct. In addition, there are many words for which both *-er* or *-est* and *more* or *most* are equally correct. For instance, either "a more fair rule" or "a fairer rule" is correct.

To form negative comparisons, use *less* and *least*.

> When kids called me "Dum-dum," I tried to look *less* hurt than I felt.
>
> Many people say men gossip *less* than women do, but I don't believe it.
>
> Suzanne is the most self-centred, *least* thoughtful person I know.

Points to Remember about Comparing

Point 1: Use only one form of comparison at a time. In other words, do not use both an *-er* ending and *more* or both an *-est* ending and *most*:

Incorrect	*Correct*
My Newfoundland accent is always more stronger after I visit my family in Bonavista.	My Newfoundland accent is always *stronger* after I visit my family in Bonavista.
My *most luckiest* day was the day I met my wife.	My *luckiest* day was the day I met my wife.

Point 2: Learn the irregular forms of the words shown below.

	Comparative (for Comparing Two Things)	*Superlative (for Comparing Three or More Things)*
bad	worse	worst
good, well	better	best
little (in amount)	less	least
much, many	more	most

Do not use both more and an irregular comparative or *most* and an irregular superlative.

Incorrect	*Correct*
It is *more better* to stay healthy than to have to get healthy.	It is *better* to stay healthy than to have to get healthy.

Yesterday I went on the *most best* date of my life—and all we did was go on a picnic.

Yesterday I went on the *best* date of my life—and all we did was go on a picnic.

Activity

Add to each sentence the correct form of the word in the margin.

bad

Examples   The _____*worst*_____ scare I ever had was when I thought my son was on an airplane that crashed.

wonderful

The day of my divorce was even __*more wonderful*__ than the day of my wedding.

good

1. The _____ way to diet is gradually.

popular

2. Vanilla ice cream is even _____ than chocolate ice cream.

bad

3. One of the _____ things you can do to people is ignore them.

light

4. A kilo of feathers is no _____ than a kilo of stones.

little

5. The _____ expensive way to accumulate a wardrobe is by buying used clothing whenever possible.

ADVERBS

What Are Adverbs?

Adverbs describe verbs, adjectives, or other adverbs. They usually end in *-ly*.

The referee *suddenly* stopped the fight. (The adverb *suddenly* describes the verb *stopped*.)

Her yellow rosebushes are *absolutely* beautiful. (The adverb *absolutely* describes the adjective *beautiful*.)

The auctioneer spoke so *extremely* fast that I couldn't understand him. (The adverb *extremely* describes the adverb *fast*.)

A Common Mistake with Adverbs and Adjectives

People often mistakenly use an adjective instead of an adverb after a verb.

Incorrect	*Correct*
I jog *slow*.	I jog *slowly*.
The nervous witness spoke *quiet*.	The nervous witness spoke *quietly*.
The first night I quit smoking, I wanted a cigarette *bad*.	The first night I quit smoking, I wanted a cigarette *badly*.
Reid is *real* sneaky.	Reid is *really* sneaky.

Activity

Underline the adjective or adverb needed. (Remember that adjectives describe nouns, and adverbs describe verbs or other adverbs.)

1. During a quiet moment in class, my stomach rumbled (loud, loudly).

2. I'm a (slow, slowly) reader, so I have to put aside more time to study than some of my friends.

3. Thinking no one was looking, the young man (quick, quickly) emptied his car's ashtray onto the parking lot.

4. The cottage mice wait (patient, patiently) in the shadows; at night they'll have the place to themselves.

5. I hang up the phone (immediate, immediately) whenever the speaker is a recorded message.

Well and *Good*

Two words that are often confused are *well* and *good*. *Good* is an adjective; it describes nouns. *Well* is usually an adverb; it describes verbs. *Well* (rather than *good*) is also used when referring to a person's health.

Activity

Write *well* or *good* in each of the sentences that follow.

1. I could tell by the broad grin on Delia's face that the news was _____.

2. They say he sang so _____ that even the wind stopped to listen.

3. The food at the salad bar must not have been very fresh because I didn't feel _____ after dinner.

4. When I want to do a really _____ job of washing the floor, I do it on my hands and knees.

5. The best way to get along _____ with our boss is to stay out of his way.

▓ Review Test

Underline the correct word in the parentheses.

1. In Egypt, silver was once (more valued, most valued) than gold.

2. After seeing Ben get sick, I didn't feel too (good, well) myself.

3. The (littler, less) coffee I drink, the better I feel.

4. Light walls make a room look (more large, larger) than dark walls do.

5. One of the (unfortunatest, most unfortunate) men I know is a millionaire.

6. The moths' (continuous, continuously) thumping against the screen got on my nerves.

7. Some Mennonite groups manage (good, well) without radios, telephones, or television.

8. A purple crocus had burst (silent, silently) through the snow outside our window.

9. It is (good, better) to teach people to fish than to give them fish.

10. Today a rocket can reach the moon more (quick, quickly) than it took a stagecoach to travel from one end of England to the other.

CHAPTER 28

Misplaced Modifiers

Introductory Project

Because of misplaced words, each of the sentences below has more than one possible meaning. In each case, see if you can explain the intended meaning and the unintended meaning. Also, circle the words that you think create the confusion because they are misplaced.

1. The sign in the restaurant window reads, "Wanted: Young Man—To Open Oysters with References."

   Intended meaning: _____

   Unintended meaning: _____

2. Carlo and Charlotte decided to have two children on their wedding day.

   Intended meaning: _____

   Unintended meaning: _____

3. The students no longer like the math instructor who failed the test.

   Intended meaning: _____

   Unintended meaning: _____

Answers are on page 554.

WHAT MISPLACED MODIFIERS
ARE AND HOW TO CORRECT THEM

Modifiers are descriptive words. *Misplaced modifiers* are words that, because of awkward placement, do not describe the words the writer intended them to describe. Misplaced modifiers often obscure the meaning of a sentence. To avoid them, place words as close as possible to what they describe.

Misplaced Words	*Correctly Placed Words*
Alex bought an old car from a crooked dealer *with a faulty transmission.* (The dealer had a faulty transmission?)	Alex bought an old car with a faulty transmission from a crooked dealer. (The words describing the old car are now placed next to "car.")
I *nearly* earned a hundred dollars last week. (You just missed earning a hundred dollars, but in fact earned nothing?)	I earned nearly a hundred dollars last week. (The meaning—that you earned a little under a hundred dollars—is now clear.)
Mike yelled at the howling dog *in his underwear.* (The *dog* wore underwear?)	Mike, in his underwear, yelled at the howling dog. (The words describing Mike are placed next to "Mike.")

Activity

Underline the misplaced word or words in each sentence. Then rewrite the sentence, placing related words together and thereby making the meaning clear.

Examples   The suburbs <u>nearly</u> had ten centimetres of rain.

The suburbs had nearly five centimetres.

We could see the football stadium <u>driving across the bridge</u>.

Driving across the bridge, we could see the football stadium.

1. I saw mountains of uncollected garbage walking along the city streets.

_____

2. I almost had a dozen job interviews after I sent out my résumé.

_____

3. Clark swatted the wasp that stung him with a newspaper.

_____

4. Joanne decided to live with her grandparents when she attended college to save money.

_____

5. Paula returned the hamburger to the supermarket that was spoiled.

_____

6. Roger visited the old house still weak with the flu.

_____

7. The phone almost rang fifteen times last night.

_____

8. My uncle saw a kangaroo at the window under the influence of whisky.

_____

9. We decided to send our daughter to college on the day she was born.

_____

10. Farid always opens the bills that arrive in the mailbox with a sigh.

_____

■ Review Test

Write *M* for *misplaced* or *C* for *correct* in front of each sentence.

_____ 1. Rita found it difficult to mount the horse wearing tight jeans.

_____ 2. Rita, wearing tight jeans, found it difficult to mount the horse.

_____ 3. I noticed a crack in the window walking into the delicatessen.

_____ 4. Walking into the delicatessen, I noticed a crack in the window.

_____ 5. A well-worn track shoe was found on the locker bench with holes in it.

_____ 6. A well-worn track shoe with holes in it was found on the locker bench.

_____ 7. I almost caught a hundred lightning bugs.

_____ 8. I caught almost a hundred lightning bugs.

_____ 9. In a secondhand store, Josh found a television set that had been stolen from me last month.

_____ 10. Josh found a television set in a secondhand store that had been stolen from me last month.

_____ 11. Josh found, in a secondhand store, a television set that had been stolen from me last month.

_____ 12. There were four cars parked outside the café with Alberta licence plates.

_____ 13. There were four cars with Alberta licence plates parked outside the café.

_____ 14. The Prime Minister was quoted on the *CBC News* as saying that the recession was about to end.

_____ 15. The Prime Minister was quoted as saying that the recession was about to end on the *CBC News.*

Dangling Modifiers

Introductory Project

Because of dangling words, each of the sentences below has more than one possible meaning. In each case, see if you can explain the intended meaning and the unintended meaning.

1. While smoking a pipe, my dog sat with me by the crackling fire.

   Intended meaning: _____

   Unintended meaning: _____

2. Looking at the traffic accident, his sports car went through a red light.

   Intended meaning: _____

   Unintended meaning: _____

3. After baking for several hours, Dad removed the moussaka from the oven.

   Intended meaning: _____

   Unintended meaning: _____

Answers are on pages 554–555.

WHAT DANGLING MODIFIERS ARE AND HOW TO CORRECT THEM

A modifier that opens a sentence must be *followed immediately* by the word it is meant to describe. Otherwise, the modifier is said to be *dangling*, and the sentence takes on an unintended meaning. For example, in the sentence

While smoking a pipe, my dog sat with me by the crackling fire.

the unintended meaning is that the *dog* was smoking the pipe. What the writer meant, of course, was that *he,* the writer, was smoking the pipe. The dangling modifier could be corrected by placing *I,* the word being described, directly after the opening modifier:

While smoking a pipe, *I* sat with my dog by the crackling fire.

The dangling modifier could also be corrected by placing the subject within the opening word group:

While *I* was smoking my pipe, my dog sat with me by the crackling fire.

Here are other sentences with dangling modifiers. Read the explanations of why they are dangling, and look carefully at how they are corrected.

Dangling	*Correct*
Swimming at the lake, a rock cut Samantha's foot. (*Who* was swimming at the lake? The answer is not *rock* but *Samantha.* The subject *Samantha* must be added.)	Swimming at the lake, *Samantha* cut her foot on a rock. *Or:* When *Samantha* was swimming at the lake, she cut her foot on a rock.
While eating my sandwich, five mosquitoes bit me. (*Who* is eating the sandwich? The answer is not *five mosquitoes,* as it unintentionally seems to be, but *I.* The subject *I* must be added.)	While *I* was eating my sandwich, five mosquitoes bit me. *Or:* While eating my sandwich, *I* was bitten by five mosquitoes.
Getting out of bed, the tile floor was so cold that Yoko shivered all over. (*Who* got out of bed? The answer is not *tile floor* but *Yoko.* The subject *Yoko* must be added.)	Getting out of bed, *Yoko* found the tile floor so cold that she shivered all over. *Or:* When *Yoko* got out of bed, the tile floor was so cold that she shivered all over.
To join the team, a C average or better is necessary. (*Who* is to join the team? The answer is not *C average* but *you.* The subject *you* must be added.)	To join the team, *you* must have a C average or better. *Or:* For *you* to join the team, a C average or better is necessary.

The preceding examples make clear the two ways of correcting a dangling modifier. Decide on a logical subject and do one of the following:

1 Place the subject *within* the opening word group.

When Samantha was swimming at the lake, she cut her foot on a rock.

Note: In some cases an appropriate subordinating word such as *When* must be added, and the verb may have to be changed slightly as well.

2 Place the subject right *after* the opening word group.

Swimming at the lake, Samantha cut her foot on a rock.

Activity

Ask *Who?* as you look at the opening words in each sentence. The subject that answers the question should be nearby in the sentence. If it is not, provide the logical subject by using either method of correction described above.

Example	While sleeping at the campsite, a Frisbee hit Derek on the head.
	While Derek was sleeping at the campsite, a Frisbee hit him on the head.
or	*While sleeping at the campsite, Derek was hit on the head by a Frisbee.*

1. Watching the horror movie, goose bumps covered my spine.

   _____

   _____

2. After putting on a corduroy shirt, the room didn't seem so cold.

   _____

   _____

3. Flunking out of school, my parents demanded that I get a job.

   _____

   _____

4. Covered with food stains, my brother decided to wash the tablecloth.

   _____

   _____

5. Joining several college clubs, Anton's social life became more active.

   _____

   _____

6. While visiting the African Lion Safari, a baboon scrambled onto the hood of their car.

   _____

   _____

7. Under attack by beetles, Nina sprayed her roses with insecticide.

   _____

   _____

8. Standing at the ocean's edge, the wind coated my glasses with a salty film.

   _____

   _____

9. Braking the car suddenly, my shopping bags tumbled off the seat.

   _____

   _____

10. Using binoculars, the hawk was clearly seen following its prey.

   _____

   _____

■ Review Test

Write D for *dangling* or C for *correct* in the blank next to each sentence. Remember that the opening words are a dangling modifier if they have no logical subject to modify.

_____ 1. Advertising in the paper, Ian's car was quickly sold.

_____ 2. By advertising in the paper, Ian quickly sold his car.

_____ 3. After painting the downstairs, the house needed airing to clear out the fumes.

_____ 4. After we painted the downstairs, the house needed airing to clear out the fumes.

_____ 5. Frustrated by piles of homework, Rhonda was tempted to watch television.

_____ 6. Frustrated by piles of homework, Rhonda's temptation was to watch television.

_____ 7. After I waited patiently in the bank line, the teller told me I had filled out the wrong form.

_____ 8. After waiting patiently in the bank line, the teller told me I had filled out the wrong form.

_____ 9. When dieting, desserts are especially tempting.

_____ 10. When dieting, I find desserts especially tempting.

_____ 11. Looking through the telescope, I saw a brightly lit object come into view.

_____ 12. As I was looking through the telescope, a brightly lit object came into view.

_____ 13. Looking through a telescope, a brightly lit object came into my view.

Explaining a Process · Examining Cause and Effect · Comparing or Contrasting · Defining
Term · Dividing and Classifying · Describing a Scene or Person · Narrating an Event · Arg
a Position · Explaining a Process · Examining Cause and Effect · Comparing or Contrast
Defining a Term · Dividing and Classifying · Describing a Scene or Person · Narrating an I
Arguing a Position · Explaining a Process · Examining Cause and Effect · Comparin

CHAPTER 30

Faulty Parallelism

> ### *Introductory Project*
>
> Read aloud each pair of sentences below. Make a check mark beside the sentence that reads more smoothly and clearly and sounds more natural.
>
> I made resolutions to study more, to lose weight, and watching less TV.
>
> _____
>
> I made resolutions to study more, to lose weight, and to watch less TV.
>
> _____
>
> A consumer group rates my car as noisy, expensive, and not having much safety. _____
>
> A consumer group rates my car as noisy, expensive, and unsafe. _____
>
> Pei-Ti likes wearing soft sweaters, eating exotic foods, and to bathe in scented bath oil. _____
>
> Pei-Ti likes wearing soft sweaters, eating exotic foods, and bathing in scented bath oil. _____
>
> Single life offers more freedom of choice; more security is offered by marriage. _____
>
> Single life offers more freedom of choice; marriage offers more security.
>
> _____
>
> Answers are on page 555.

PARALLELISM EXPLAINED

Words in a pair or a series should have a parallel structure. By balancing the items in a pair or a series so that they have the same kind of structure, you will make a sentence clearer and easier to read. Notice how the parallel sentences that follow read more smoothly than the nonparallel ones.

Nonparallel (Not Balanced)	*Parallel (Balanced)*
I made resolutions to lose weight, to study more, and *watching* less TV.	I made resolutions to lose weight, to study more, and to watch less TV. (A balanced series of *to* verbs: *to lose, to study, to watch*)
A consumer group rates my car as noisy, expensive, and *not having much safety.*	A consumer group rates my car as noisy, expensive, and unsafe. (A balanced series of descriptive words: *noisy, expensive, unsafe*)
Pei-Ti likes wearing soft sweaters, eating exotic foods, and *to bathe* in scented bath oil.	Pei-Ti likes wearing soft sweaters, eating exotic foods, and bathing in scented bath oil. (A balanced series of *-ing* words: *wearing, eating, bathing*)
Single life offers more freedom of choice; *more security is offered by marriage.*	Single life offers more freedom of choice; marriage offers more security. (Balanced verbs and word order: *single life offers … ; marriage offers …*)

You need not worry about balanced sentences when writing first drafts. But when you revise, you should try to put matching words and ideas into matching structures. Such parallelism will improve your writing style.

Activity

The unbalanced part of each of the following sentences is *italicized*. Rewrite the unbalanced part so that it matches the rest of the sentence. The first one is done for you as an example.

1. Mike Myers' films are clever, well-acted, and *have a lot of humour.*
   _____humorous_____

2. Filling out an income tax form is worse than wrestling a bear or *to walk* on hot coals. _____

3. The study-skills course taught me how to take more effective notes, to read a textbook chapter, and *preparing* for exams. _____

4. Nadine plans to become a model, a lawyer, or *to go into nursing*.

    _____

5. Elaine likes *to water* her garden, walking her fox terrier, and arguing with her husband. _____

6. Filled with talent and *ambitious,* Eduardo plugged away at his sales job.

    _____

7. When I saw my roommate with my girlfriend, I felt worried, angry, and *embarrassment* as well. _____

8. Cindy's cat likes sleeping in the dryer, lying in the bathtub, and *to chase* squirrels. _____

9. The bacon was fatty, *grease was on the potatoes,* and the eggs were cold.

    _____

10. People in the lobby munched popcorn, sipped pop, and *were shuffling* their feet impatiently. _____

▨ Review Test 1

On a separate piece of paper, write five sentences of your own that use parallel structure.

▨ Review Test 2

Draw a line under the unbalanced part of each sentence. Then rewrite the unbalanced part so that it matches the other item or items in the sentence. The first one is done for you as an example.

1. Our professor warned us that he would give surprise tests, <u>the assignment of term papers,</u> and allow no makeup exams.
   assign term papers _____

2. Pesky mosquitoes, humidity that is high, and sweltering heat make summer an unpleasant time for me.

   _____

3. I want a job that pays high wages, provides a complete benefits package, and offering opportunities for promotion.

   _____

4. My teenage daughter enjoys shopping for new clothes, to try different cosmetics, and reading teen magazines.

   _____

5. My car needed the brakes replaced, the front wheels aligned, and recharging of the battery.

   _____

6. I had to correct my paper for fragments, misplaced modifiers, and there were apostrophe mistakes.

   _____

7. They did not want an ordinary TV set, but a stereo set could not be afforded.

   _____

8. The neighbourhood group asked the town council to repair the potholes and that a traffic light be installed.

   _____

9. Having a headache, my stomach being upset, and a bad case of sunburn did not put me in a good mood for the evening.

   _____

10. The Grey Panthers is an organization that not only aids older citizens but also providing information for their families.

   _____

Explaining a Process • Examining Cause and Effect • Comparing or Contrasting • Defini Term • Dividing and Classifying • Describing a Scene or Person • Narrating an Event • Arg a Position • Explaining a Process • Examining Cause and Effect • Comparing or Contrast Defining a Term • Dividing and Classifying • Describing a Scene or Person • Narrating an Arguing a Position • Explaining a Process • Examining Cause and Effect • Compari

C H A P T E R   3 1

Paper Format

When you hand in a paper for any of your courses, probably the first thing you will be judged on is its format. It is important, then, that you do certain things to make your papers look attractive, neat, and easy to read.

Here are guidelines to follow in preparing a paper for an instructor:

1 Use full-sized paper (21.5×28 cm or 8½ by 11 inches).

2 Leave wide margins (2.5 cm or 1 to 1½ inches) on all four sides of each page. In particular, do not crowd the right-hand or bottom margin. The white space makes your paper more readable; also, the instructor has room for comments.

3 If you write by hand,
   a Use a blue or black pen (*not* a pencil).
   b Be careful not to overlap letters or to make decorative loops on letters. Write only on every other line.
   c Make all your letters distinct. Pay special attention to *a, e, i, o,* and *u*—five letters that people sometimes write illegibly.
   d Keep your capital letters clearly distinct from small letters. You may even want to print all the capital letters.
   e Make commas, periods, and other punctuation marks firm and clear. Leave a slight space after each period.

4 Centre the title of your paper on the first line of page 1. Do *not* put quotation marks around the title or underline the title or put a period after the title. Capitalize all the major words in a title, including the first word. Small connecting words within a title like *of, for, the, in,* and *to* are not capitalized. Skip a line between the title and the first line of your text.

5 Indent the first line of each paragraph about five spaces (1.25 cm or half an inch) from the left-hand margin.

6 When you word process, use double-spacing between lines. Also double-space after a period.

7 Whenever possible, avoid breaking (hyphenating) words at the end of lines. If you must break a word, break only between syllables. Do not break words of one syllable.

8 Write your name, the date, and the course number where your instructor asks for them.

Also keep in mind these important points about the *title* and *first sentence* of your paper:

9 The title should simply be several words that tell what the paper is about. It should usually *not* be a complete sentence. For example, if you are writing a paper about one of the most frustrating jobs you have ever had, the title could be "A Frustrating Job."

10 Do not rely on the title to help explain the first sentence of your paper. The first sentence must be independent of the title. For instance, if the title of your paper is "A Frustrating Job," the first sentence should *not* be "It was working as a babysitter." Rather, the first sentence might be "Working as a babysitter was the most frustrating job I ever had."

Activity 1

Identify the mistakes in format in the following lines from a student theme. Explain the mistakes in the spaces provided. One mistake is described for you as an example.

	"an unpleasant dining companion"
	My little brother is often an unpleasant dining companion. Last
	night was typical. For one thing, his appearance was disgusting.
	His shoes were not tied, and his shirt was unbuttoned and han-
	ging out of his pants, which he had forgotten to zip up. Traces
	of his afternoon snack of grape juice and chocolate cookies were

1. *Hyphenate only between syllables.* _____

2. _____

3. _____

4. _____

5. _____

6. _____

Activity 2

As already stated, a title should tell in several words (but *not* a complete sentence) what a paper is about. Often a title can be based on the topic sentence—the sentence that expresses the main idea of the paper. Following are five topic sentences from student papers. Write a suitable and specific title for each paper, basing the title on the topic sentence. (Note the example.)

Example   *Compromise in a Relationship*

Learning how to compromise is essential to a good relationship.

1. *Title:* _____
    Some houseplants are dangerous to children and pets.

2. *Title:* _____
    A number of fears haunted me when I was a child.

3. *Title:* _____
    To insulate a house properly, several important steps should be taken.

4. *Title:* _____
    My husband is compulsively neat.

5. *Title:* _____
    There are a number of drawbacks to having a roommate.

Activity 3

As has already been stated, you must *not* rely on the title to help explain your first sentence. In four of the five sentences that follow, the writer has, inappropriately, used the title to help explain the first sentence.

Rewrite the four sentences so that they stand independent of the title. Write *Correct* under the one sentence that is independent of the title.

Example   *Title:* My Career Plans
First sentence: They have changed in the last six months.

Rewritten: *My career plans have changed in the last six months.*

1. *Title:* Contending with Dogs
    First sentence: This is the main problem in my work as a mail carrier.

    Rewritten: _____

    _____

2. *Title:* Study Skills
    First sentence: They are necessary if a person is to do well in college.

    Rewritten: _____

    _____

3. *Title:* Summer Vacation
    First sentence: Contrary to popular belief, a summer vacation can be the most miserable experience of the year.

    Rewritten: _____

    _____

4. *Title:* My Wife and the Saturday Newspaper
    First sentence: My wife has a peculiar way of reading it.

    Rewritten: _____

    _____

5. *Title:* Overcrowded Highways
    First sentence: They are one of the chief hazards today's driver must confront.

    Rewritten: _____

    _____

◼ Review Test

In the space provided on the opposite page, rewrite the following sentences from a student paper. Correct the mistakes in format.

	"disciplining our children"
	My husband and I are becoming experts in disciplining our chil-
	dren. We have certain rules that we insist upon, and if there are
	any violations, we are swift to act. When our son simply doesn't
	do what he is told to do, he must write that particular action
	twenty times. For example, if he doesn't brush his teeth, he
	writes, "I must brush my teeth." If a child gets home after the

Capital Letters

Introductory Project

Items 1 – 13: You probably know a good deal about the uses of capital letters. Answering the questions below will help you check your knowledge.

1. Write the full name of a person you know: _____

2. In what city and province, or in what country were you born? _____

3. What is your present street address? _____

4. Name a country where you would like to travel: _____

5. Name a school that you attended: _____

6. Give the name of a store where you buy food: _____

7. Name a company where someone you know works: _____

8. What day of the week gives you the best chance to relax? _____

9. What holiday is your favourite? _____

10. What brand of toothpaste do you use? _____

11. Give the brand name of a candy or gum you like: _____

12. Name a song or a television show you enjoy: _____

13. Give the title of a magazine you read: _____

Items 14 – 16: Three capital letters are needed in the lines below. Underline the words that you think should be capitalized. Then write them, capitalized, in the spaces provided.

the caped man started his sleek black car, waved good-bye, and roared out of town. My heart thrilled when i heard someone say, "that was Batman. You don't see superheroes much, anymore."

14. _____ 15. _____ 16. _____

Answers are on page 555.

MAIN USES OF CAPITAL LETTERS

Capital letters are used with:

1 The first word in a sentence or direct quotation

2 Names of persons and the word *I*

3 Names of particular places

4 Names of days of the week, months, and holidays

5 Names of commercial products

6 Names of organizations such as religious and political groups, associations, companies, unions, and clubs

7 Titles of books, magazines, newspapers, articles, stories, poems, films, television shows, songs, papers that you write, and the like

Each use is illustrated on the pages that follow.

First Word in a Sentence or Direct Quotation

The street person touched me and asked, "Do you have any change?"

↑   ↑

(Capitalize the first word in the sentence.)   (Capitalize the first word in the direct quotation.)

"If you want a ride," said Tammy, "get ready now. Otherwise, I'm going alone."

(*If* and *Otherwise* are capitalized because they are the first words of sentences within a direct quotation. But *get* is not capitalized because it is part of the first sentence within the quotation.)

Names of Persons and the Word *I*

Last night I ran into Terry Kowalski and Liane Morrison.

Names of Particular Places

Candi graduated from St. Boniface High School in Winnipeg, Manitoba. She then moved with her parents to Red Deer, Alberta, and worked there for a time at Freda's Gift Shop. Eventually she married and moved with her husband to a Canadian Forces Base in Norfolk County, Ontario. She takes courses two nights a week at Fanshawe College. On weekends, she and her family drive to Point Pelee National Park and go birdwatching and swimming in Lake Erie. She does volunteer work at the Simcoe Hospital in connection with Holy Trinity Church. In addition, she works during the summer as a host at the Convention Centre and the Holiday Inn.

But: Use small letters if the specific name of a place is not given.

Candi sometimes remembers her unhappy days in high school and at the gift shop where she worked after graduation. She did not imagine then that she would one day be going to college and doing volunteer work for a church and a hospital in the community where she and her husband live.

Names of Days of the Week, Months, and Holidays

> I was angry at myself for forgetting that Sunday was Mother's Day.
>
> During July and August, Franco's company works a four-day week, and he has Mondays off.
>
> Aaron still has a scar on his ankle from a firecracker that exploded near him on Victoria Day and a scar on his arm where he stabbed himself with a fishhook on Labour Day weekend.

> **But:** Use small letters for the seasons—summer, fall, winter, spring.

Names of Commercial Products

> Louis uses Scope mouthwash, Certs mints, and Dentyne gum to drive away the taste of the Export cigarettes and Monte Cristo cigars that he always smokes.
>
> My sister likes to play Monopoly and Trivial Pursuit; I like chess and poker; my brother likes Scrabble, baseball, and table tennis.

> **But:** Use small letters for the *type* of product (mouthwash, mints, gum, cigarettes, and so on).

Names of Organizations Such as Religious and Political Groups, Associations, Companies, Unions, and Clubs

> Tom Wilcox attended the United Church for many years but converted to Catholicism when he married. Both he and his wife, Louise, are members of the Liberal Party. Both belong to the Canadian Automobile Association. Louise works part-time as a service representative at Eaton's. Tom is an ambulance driver and belongs to the Canadian Union of Public Employees.
>
> Enzo met Carla when he was a Boy Scout and she was a Girl Guide; she claimed he needed some guidance.

Titles of Books, Magazines, Newspapers, Articles, Stories, Poems, Films, Television Shows, Songs, Papers That You Write, and the Like

> On Sunday Anna read the first chapter of *Whale Music,* a book required for her writing course. She looked through her parents' copy of *The Globe and Mail.* She then read an article titled "Favourite Son" and a poem titled "Montreal Malaise" in *Saturday Night* magazine. At the same time, she played an old Stones' CD, *Aftermath.* In the evening, she watched *Futurama* on television and a movie, *Black Robe,* about Jesuit explorers and Native Canadians. Then, from 11 p.m. to midnight, she worked on a paper called "Trends in Mall Occupancy at the End of the Century" for her retail marketing course.

Activity

Cross out the words that need capitals in the following sentences. Then write the capitalized forms of the words in the spaces provided. The number of spaces tells you how many corrections to make in each case.

Example   I brush with crest toothpaste but get cavities all the time.   _*Crest*_

1. A spokesperson for general motors announced that the prices of all chevrolets will rise next year.

   _____   _____   _____

2. Steve graduated from Bishop Maroccco high school in june 1998.

   _____   _____   _____

3. The mild-mannered reporter named clark kent said to the Wolfman, "you'd better think twice before you mess with me, Buddy."

   _____   _____   _____

4. While watching television, Spencer drank four pepsis, ate an entire package of ritz crackers, and finished up a bag of oreo cookies.

   _____   _____   _____

5. A voyageur bus almost ran over Tony as he was riding his yamaha to a friend's home in quebec.

   _____   _____   _____

6. Before I lent my polaroid camera to Janette, I warned her, "be sure to return it by friday."

   _____   _____   _____

7. Before christmas George took his entire paycheque, went to Zellers, and bought a twenty-inch zenith television.

   _____   _____   _____

8. On their first trip to Toronto, Sam and Mattias visited the CN tower and Nathan phillips square. They also saw the Toronto bluejays at skydome.

   _____   _____   _____

9. Rob was listening to The Crash Test Dummies' recording of "Keep a Lid on Things," Erica was reading an article in *Chatelaine* titled "till Death Do Us Part," and their son was watching sharon, Lois, and Bram.

   _____   _____   _____

10. When a sign for a tim horton's rest stop appeared on the highway, anita said, "let's stop here and stretch our legs for a bit."

    _____   _____   _____

OTHER USES OF CAPITAL LETTERS

Capital letters are also used with:

1 Names that show family relationships
2 Titles of persons when used with their names

3 Specific school courses
4 Languages
5 Geographic locations
6 Historical periods and events
7 Races, nations, and nationalities
8 Opening and closing of a letter

Each use is illustrated on the pages that follow.

Names That Show Family Relationships

I got Mother to babysit for me.
I went with Grandfather to the church service.
Uncle Carlo and Aunt Rachel always enclose five dollars with birthday cards.

But: Do not capitalize words like *mother, father, grandmother, aunt,* and so on, when they are preceded by a possessive word (*my, your, his, her, our, their*).

I got my mother to babysit for me.
I went with my grandfather to the church service.
My uncle and aunt always enclose five dollars with birthday cards.

Titles of Persons When Used with Their Names

I wrote to Senator Laurent and Mayor Lastman.
Professor Snorrel sent me to Chair Ruck, who sent me to Dean Guzzi.
He drove to Dr. Jolanda Thompson's office after the cat bit him.

But: Use small letters when titles appear by themselves, without specific names.

I wrote to my senator and mayor.
The professor sent me to the chair, who sent me to the dean.
He drove to the doctor's office after the cat bit him.

Specific School Courses

I got an A in both Accounting I and Small Business Management, but I got a C in Human Behaviour.

But: Use small letters for general subject areas.

I enjoyed my business courses but not my psychology or language courses.

Languages

She knows German and Portugese, but she speaks mostly Canadian slang.

Geographic Locations

I grew up in the Maritimes. I worked in the East for a number of years and then moved to the West Coast.

But: Use small letters in directions.

A new high school is being built at the south end of town.

Because I have a compass in my car, I know that I won't be going east or west when I want to go north.

Historical Periods and Events

Mario did well answering an essay question about the Second World War, but he lost points on a question about the Great Depression.

Races, Nations, and Nationalities

The research study centred on Native Canadians and Québecois.

They have German knives and Danish glassware in the kitchen, an Indian wood carving in the bedroom, Mexican sculptures in the study, and a Persian rug in the living room.

Opening and Closing of a Letter

Dear Sir:

Dear Madam:

Sincerely yours,

Truly yours,

Note: Capitalize only the first word in a closing.

Activity

Cross out the words that need capitals in the following sentences. Then write the capitalized forms of the words in the spaces provided. The number of spaces tells you how many corrections to make in each case.

1. Although my grandfather spoke german and polish, my mother never learned either language.

    _____   _____

2. The chain letter began, "dear friend—You must mail twenty copies of this letter if you want good luck."

    _____   _____

3. Tomorrow in our culture class, dr. connalley will start lecturing on the war of 1812.

    _____   _____   _____   _____

4. aunt Catherine and uncle Hank, who are mennonites took us to their church services when we visited them on the prairies.

   _____ _____ _____ _____

5. My sister has signed up for a course titled eastern religions; she'll be studying buddhism and hinduism.

   _____ _____ _____ _____

UNNECESSARY USE OF CAPITALS

Many errors in capitalization are caused by using capitals where they are not needed.

Activity

Cross out the incorrectly capitalized words in the following sentences. Then write the correct forms of the words in the spaces provided. The number of spaces tells you how many corrections to make in each sentence.

1. Although the Commercials say that Things go better with Coke, I prefer Root Beer.

   _____ _____ _____ _____

2. The old man told the Cabdriver, "I want to go out to the Airport and don't try to cheat me."

   _____ _____

3. A front-page Newspaper story about the crash of a commercial Jet has made me nervous about my Overseas trip.

   _____ _____ _____

4. During Hurricane Hazel in the 1950s, People's Houses were flooded in Toronto.

   _____ _____ _____ _____

5. I asked the Bank Officer at Scotiabank, "How do I get an identification Card to use the automatic teller machines?"

   _____ _____ _____

■ Review Test 1

Cross out the words that need capitals in the following sentences. Then write the capitalized forms of the words in the spaces provided. The number of spaces tells you how many corrections to make in each sentence.

1. wendy and i agreed to meet on saturday before the hockey game.

   _____ _____ _____

2. Between the Gaspé peninsula and the gulf of St. Lawrence lies a long thin island called anticosti island.

   _____   _____   _____   _____

3. When I'm in the supermarket checkout line, it seems as if every magazine on display has an article called "how You Can Lose Ten kilos in two weeks."

   _____   _____   _____   _____

4. At the bookstore, each student received a free sample pack of bayer aspirin, arrid deodorant, and alberto shampoo.

   _____   _____   _____

5. "can't you be quiet?" I pleaded. "do you always have to talk while I'm watching *general hospital* on television?"

   _____   _____   _____   _____

6. On father's day, the children drove home and took their parents out to dinner at the holiday inn.

   _____   _____   _____   _____

7. I will work at the montessori Day School on mondays and fridays for the rest of september.

   _____   _____   _____   _____

8. canada trust, where my sister Amber works, is paying for her night course titled business accounting I.

   _____   _____   _____   _____

9. I subscribe to one newspaper, the *daily planet,* and two magazines, *maclean's* and *chatelaine.*

   _____   _____   _____   _____

10. On thanksgiving my brother said, "let's hurry and eat so i can go watch the game on our new sony TV."

    _____   _____   _____   _____

▓ Review Test 2

On a separate piece of paper,

1. Write seven sentences demonstrating the seven main uses of capital letters.

2. Write eight sentences demonstrating the eight additional uses of capital letters.

CHAPTER 33

Numbers and Abbreviations

NUMBERS

1 Spell out numbers that can be expressed in one or two words. Otherwise, use numerals—the numbers themselves.

> During the past five years, over five hundred lampreys have been caught in the lake.
>
> The parking fine was ten dollars.
>
> In my grandmother's attic are eighty-four pairs of old shoes.

But

> Each year about 250 baby trout are added to the lake.
>
> My costs after contesting a parking fine in court were $135.
>
> Grandmother has 110 old copies of the *Eaton's Catalogue* in her attic.

2 Be consistent when you use a series of numbers. If some numbers in a sentence or paragraph require more than two words, then use numerals throughout the selection:

> During his election campaign, Provincial Premier Lou Stanley went to 3 local fairs, 16 parades, 45 cookouts, and 112 club dinners, and delivered the same speech 176 times.

3 Use numerals for dates, times, addresses, percentages, and parts of a book.

> The letter was dated April 3, 1872.
>
> My appointment was at 6:15. (*But:* Spell out numbers before *o'clock*. For example: The doctor didn't see me until seven o'clock.)
>
> He lives at 212 West 19th Street.
>
> About 20 percent of our class has dropped out of school.
>
> Turn to page 179 in Chapter 8 and answer questions 1 – 10.

Activity

Cross out the mistakes in numbers and write the corrections in the spaces provided.

1. Roy was born on February fifteenth, nineteen seventy.

   _____

   _____

2. When the 2 children failed to return from school, over 50 people volunteered to search for them.

   _____

   _____

3. At 1 o'clock in the afternoon last Thursday, an earthquake destroyed at least 20 buildings in the town.

   _____

   _____

ABBREVIATIONS

While abbreviations are a helpful time-saver in notetaking, you should avoid most abbreviations in formal writing. Listed below are some of the few abbreviations that can acceptably be used in compositions. Note that a period is used after most abbreviations.

1 Mr., Mrs., Ms., Jr., Sr., Dr. when used with proper names:

   Mr. Tibble   Dr. Stein   Ms. O'Reilly

2 Time references:

   a.m.   p.m.   B.C. or A.D., or B.C.E. and C.E.

3 First or middle name in a signature:

   Pierre E. Trudeau   Otis T. Redding   J. Alfred Prufrock

4 Organizations and common terms known primarily by their initials:

   RCMP   UN   CBC   FM   ISP

Activity

Cross out the words that should not be abbreviated and correct them in the spaces provided.

1. On a Sat. morning I will never forget, Dec. 5, 1998, at ten min. after eight, I came downstairs and discovered that I had been robbed.

   _____   _____   _____

2. For six years I lived at First Ave. and Gordon St., right next to Mercy Memorial Hosp., in W. Edm., AB.

    _____   _____   _____   _____   _____

3. Before her biol. and Eng. exams, Linda was so nervous that her doc. gave her a tranq.

    _____   _____   _____   _____

■ **Review Test**

Cross out the mistakes in numbers and abbreviations and correct them in the spaces provided.

1. At three-fifteen p.m., an angry caller said a bomb was planted in a bus stat. locker.

    _____   _____

2. Page eighty-two is missing from my chem. book.

    _____   _____

3. Martha has over 200 copies of *People* mag.; she thinks they may be worth money someday.

    _____   _____

4. When I was eight yrs. old, I owned three cats, two dogs, and 4 rabbits.

    _____   _____

5. Approx. half the striking workers returned to work on Jan. third, nineteen ninety-seven.

    _____   _____   _____   _____

CHAPTER 34

Apostrophe

Answers are on page 555.

Introductory Project

1. Lauren's motorcycle
   my sister's boyfriend
   Grandmother's laptop
   the men's room

   What is the purpose of the *'s* in the examples above?

   _____

2. They didn't mind when their dog bit people, but now they're leashing him because he's eating all their garden vegetables.

   What is the purpose of the apostrophe in *didn't, they're,* and *he's?*

   _____

3. I used to believe that vampires lived in the old coal bin of my cellar.
   The vampire's whole body recoiled when he saw the crucifix.
   Mark ate two baked potatoes.
   One baked potato's centre was still hard.

   In each of the sentence pairs above, why is the *'s* used in the second sentence but not in the first? _____

   _____

Answers are on page 555.

The two main uses of the apostrophe are:

1 To show the omission of one or more letters in a contraction
2 To show ownership or possession

Each use is explained on the pages that follow.

APOSTROPHE IN CONTRACTIONS

A contraction is formed when two words are combined to make one word. An apostrophe is used to show where letters are omitted in forming the contraction. Here are two contractions:

have + not = haven't (*o* in *not* has been omitted)
I + will = I'll (*wi* in *will* has been omitted)

The following are some other common contractions:

I +	am = I'm		it +	is = it's
I +	have = I've		it +	has = it's
I +	had = I'd		is +	not = isn't
who +	is = who's		could +	not = couldn't
do +	not = don't		I +	would = I'd
did +	not = didn't		they +	are = they're

Note: Will + not has an unusual contraction: won't.

Activity 1

Combine the following words into contractions. One is done for you.

1.   we + are = ____*we're*____   6. you + have = _____

2.   are + not = _____   7. has + not = _____

3. you + are = _____   8. who + is = _____

4. they + have = _____   9. does + not = _____

5. would + not = _____   10. there + is = _____

Activity 2

Write the contractions for the words in parentheses. One is done for you.

1. (Are not) _____*Aren't*_____ you coming with us to the concert?

2. (I am) _____ going to take the car if (it is) _____
    all right with you.

3. (There is) _____ an extra bed upstairs if (you would)

    _____ like to stay here for the night.

4. (I will) _____ give you the name of the human resources

    director, but there (is not) _____ much chance that (he will)

    _____ speak to you.

5. Denise (should not) _____ complain about the cost of food if

    (she is) _____ not willing to grow her own by planting a back-
    yard garden.

Note: Even though contractions are common in everyday speech and in written
dialogue, usually it is best to avoid them in formal writing.

APOSTROPHE TO SHOW OWNERSHIP OR POSSESSION

To show ownership or possession, we can use such words as *belongs to, possessed
by, owned by,* or (most commonly) *of.*

> the jacket that *belongs to* Terrell
> the grades *possessed by* James
> the gas station *owned by* our cousin
> the footprints *of* the animal

But the apostrophe plus *s* (if the word is not a plural ending in *-s*) is often the
quickest and easiest way to show possession. Thus we can say:

> Terrell's jacket
> James's grades
> our cousin's gas station
> the animal's footprints

Points to Remember

1 The *'s* goes with the owner or possessor (in the examples given, *Terrell, cousin,
the animal*). What follows is the person or thing possessed (in the examples
given, *the jacket, gas station, footprints*).

2 When *'s* is handwritten, there should always be a break between the word and
the *'s.*

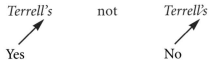

Terrell's   not   Terrell's
Yes   No

3 A singular word ending in *-s* (such as *James* in the earlier example) also shows
possession by adding an apostrophe plus *s* (*James's*).

Activity 1

Rewrite the italicized part of each of the sentences below, using the *'s* to show possession. Remember that the *'s* goes with the owner or possessor.

Example   *The toys belonging to the children* filled an entire room.

The children's toys

1. *The roller skates owned by Dawn* have been stolen.

   _____

2. *The visit of my cousin* lasted longer than I wanted it to.

   _____

3. *The fenders belonging to the car* are badly rusted.

   _____

4. *The prescription of a doctor* is needed for the pills.

   _____

5. *The jeep owned by Doris* was recalled because of an engine defect.

   _____

6. Is this *the hat of somebody?*

   _____

7. The broken saddle produced a sore on *the back of the horse.*

   _____

8. *The two dogs belonging to my neighbour* ripped open the garbage bags.

   _____

9. *The energy level possessed by the little boy* is much higher than hers.

   _____

10. *The foundation of the house* is crumbling.

    _____

Activity 2

Add *'s* to each of the following words to make them the possessors or owners of something. Then write sentences using the words. Your sentences can be serious or playful. One is done for you.

1. dog _____*dog's*_____   *That dog's bite is worse than his bark.*

2. instructor _____   _____

   _____

3. Avril _____   _____

   _____

4. store _____   _____

   _____

5. mother _____   _____

   _____

Apostrophe versus Possessive Pronouns

Do not use an apostrophe with possessive pronouns. They already show owner-ship. Possessive pronouns include *his, hers, its, yours, ours,* and *theirs.*

Incorrect	*Correct*
The bookstore lost its' lease.	The bookstore lost its lease.
The racing bikes were theirs'.	The racing bikes were theirs.
The change is yours'.	The change is yours.
His' problems are ours', too.	His problems are ours, too.
His' skin is more sunburned than hers'.	His skin is more sunburned than hers.

Apostrophe versus Simple Plurals

When you want to make a word plural, just add an *-s* at the end of the word. Do *not* add an apostrophe. For example, the plural of the word *movie* is *movies,* not *movie's* or *movies'.* Look at this sentence:

Ina admires Martin's broad shoulders, rippling muscles, and warm eyes.

The words *shoulders, muscles,* and *eyes* are simple plurals, meaning *more than one shoulder, more than one muscle, more than one eye.* The plural is shown by adding *-s* only. On the other hand, the *'s* after *Martin* shows possession—that Martin owns the shoulders, muscles, and eyes.

Activity

In the space provided under each sentence, add the one apostrophe needed and explain why the other word or words ending in *s* are simple plurals.

Example   Karens tomato plants are almost two metres tall.

Karens: *Karen's, meaning "belonging to Karen"* _____

plants: *simple plural meaning "more than one plant"* _____

1. My fathers influence on his brothers has been enormous.

   fathers: _____

   brothers: _____

2. Phils job—slaughtering pigs—was enough to make him a vegetarian.

   Phils: _____

   pigs: _____

3. As Tinas skill at studying increased, her grades improved.

   Tinas: _____

   grades: _____

4. When I walked into my doctors office, there were six people waiting who also had appointments.

   doctors: _____

   appointments: _____

5. I asked the record clerk for several blank cassette tapes and Sarah McLaughlans new CD.

   tapes: _____

   McLaughlans: _____

6. After six weeks without rain, the nearby streams started drying up, and the lakes water level fell sharply.

   weeks: _____

   streams: _____

   lakes: _____

7. Everyone wanted to enroll in Dr. Bodors class, but all the sections were closed.

   Bodors: _____

   sections: _____

8. When the brakes failed on Eriks truck, he narrowly avoided hitting several parked cars and two trees.

   Eriks: _____

   cars: _____

   trees: _____

9. My familys favourite breakfast is bacon, eggs, and home-fried potatoes.

   familys: _____

   eggs: _____

   potatoes: _____

10. We like British Columbias winters, but we prefer to spend the summers in Nova Scotia.

    British Columbias: _____

    winters: _____

    summers: _____

Apostrophe with Plural Words Ending in *-s*

Plurals that end in *-s* show possession simply by adding the apostrophe (rather than an apostrophe plus *s*):

My *parents'* van is ten years old.
The many *students'* complaints were ignored by the high school principal.
All the *Boy Scouts'* tents were damaged by the hailstorm.

Activity

In each sentence, cross out the one plural word that needs an apostrophe. Then write the word correctly, with the apostrophe, in the space provided.

Example   _____soldiers'_____   All the ~~soldiers~~ boots were polished for inspection.

1. My parents car was stolen last night.

   _____

2. The transit workers strike has just ended.

   _____

3. Two of our neighbours homes are up for sale.

   _____

4. The door to the ladies room is locked.

   _____

5. When students complaints about the cafeteria were ignored, many started to bring their own lunches.

   _____

▨ Review Test 1

In each sentence, cross out the two words that need apostrophes. Then write the words correctly in the spaces provided.

1. The contestants face fell when she learned that all she had won was a years supply of Vim cleanser.

   _____   _____

2. Weve been trying for weeks to see that movie, but theres always a long line.

   _____   _____

3. Tam's car wouldnt start until the baby-faced mechanic replaced its spark plugs and points.

   _____   _____

4. The citys budget director has trouble balancing his own familys cheque book.

   _____   _____

5. Taking Dianes elderly parents to church every week is one example of Pauls generous behaviour.

   _____   _____

6. Heres a checklist of points to follow when youre writing your class reports.

   _____   _____

7. Blair shops in the mens store for jeans and the childrens department for belts.

   _____   _____

8. The cats babies are under my chair again; I cant find a way to keep her from bringing them near me.

   _____   _____

9. Because of a family feud, Jules wasnt invited to a barbecue at her cousins house.

   _____   _____

10. Philomenas grade was the highest in the class, and Lewis grade was the lowest.

   _____   _____

■ Review Test 2

Make the following words possessive and then use at least five of them in a not-so-serious paragraph that tells a story. In addition, use at least three contractions in the paragraph.

squeegie kid	restaurant	Laurel	student
Toronto	sister	children	vampire
duck	Mike Myers	boss	Ed the Sock
customer	bartender	police car	yesterday
instructor	someone	mob	Montreal

Quotation Marks

Introductory Project

Read the following scene and underline all the words enclosed within quotation marks. Your instructor may also have you dramatize the scene, with one person reading the narration and two persons acting the two speaking parts—the young man and the old woman. The two speakers should imagine the scene as part of a stage play and try to make their words seem as real and true-to-life as possible.

An old woman in a Rolls-Royce was preparing to back into a parking space. Suddenly a small sports car appeared and pulled into the space. "That's what you can do when you're young and fast," the young man in the car yelled to the old woman. As he strolled away, laughing, he heard a terrible crunching sound. "What's that noise?" he said. Turning around, he saw the old woman backing repeatedly into and crushing his small car. "You can't do that, old lady!" he yelled.

"What do you mean, I can't?" she chuckled, as metal grated against metal. "This is what you can do when you're old and rich."

1. On the basis of the above passage, what is the purpose of quotation marks?

   _____

2. Do commas and periods that come after a quotation go inside or outside the quotation marks?

   _____

Answers are on page 555.

The two main uses of quotation marks are:

1 To set off the exact words of a speaker or a writer
2 To set off the titles of short works

Each use is explained on the pages that follow.

QUOTATION MARKS TO SET OFF EXACT WORDS OF A SPEAKER OR A WRITER

Use quotation marks when you want to show the exact words of a speaker or a writer.

> "Say something tender to me," whispered Rachel to André.
> (Quotation marks set off the exact words that Rachel spoke to André.)
> Leonard Cohen once wrote, "I want history to jump on Canada's spine with sharp skates."
> (Quotation marks set off the exact words that Leonard Cohen wrote.)
> "The only dumb question," the instructor said, "is the one you don't ask."
> (Two pairs of quotation marks are used to enclose the instructor's exact words.)
> Koji complained, "I worked so hard on this paper. I spent two days getting information in the library and two days writing it. Guess what grade I got on it."
> (Note that the end quotation marks do not come until the end of Koji's speech. Place quotation marks before the first quoted word of a speech and after the last quoted word. As long as no interruption occurs in the speech, do not use quotation marks for each new sentence.)

Punctuation Hint: In the four examples above, notice that a comma sets off the quoted part from the rest of the sentence. Also observe that commas and periods at the end of a quotation always go *inside* quotation marks.

Complete the following statements explaining how capital letters, commas, and periods are used in quotations. Refer to the four examples as guides.

1. Every quotation begins with a _____ letter.

2. When a quotation is split (as in the sentence above about dumb questions), the second part does not begin with a capital letter unless it

    is a _____ sentence.

3. _____ are used to separate the quoted part of a sentence from the rest of the sentence.

4. Commas and periods that come at the end of a quotation should go

    _____ the quotation marks.

The answers are *capital, new, Commas,* and *inside.*

Activity 1

Place quotation marks around the exact words of a speaker or writer in the sentences that follow.

1. Take some vitamin C for your cold, Anna told Dylan.

2. How are you doing in school? my uncle always asks me.

3. An epitaph on a tombstone in Nova Scotia reads, I told you I was sick!

4. Dave said, Let's walk faster. I think the game has already started.

5. Marshall McLuhan wrote, The medium is the message.

6. Cheryl said, My brother is so lazy that if opportunity knocked, he'd resent the noise.

7. It's extremely dangerous to mix alcohol and pills, Dr. Valenzuela reminded us. The combination could kill you.

8. Ice-cold drinks! shouted the vendor selling lukewarm drinks.

9. Be careful not to touch the fence, the guard warned. It's electrified.

10. Just because I'm deaf, Lin said, many people treat me as if I were stupid.

Activity 2

1. Write a sentence in which you quote a favourite expression of someone you know. Identify the relationship of the person to you.

   Example   One of my father's favourite expressions is, "Don't sweat the

                   small stuff."

   _____

   _____

   _____

2. Write a quotation that contains the words *Dylan asked Anna*. Write a second quotation that includes the words *Anna replied.*

   _____

   _____

   _____

   _____

3. Copy a sentence or two that interests you from a book or magazine. Identify the title and author of the work.

   Example   In Night Shift, *Stephen King writes, "I don't like to sleep with*

                   one leg sticking out. Because if a cool hand ever reached out

                   from under the bed and grasped my ankle, I might scream."

_____

_____

_____

_____

Indirect Quotations

An indirect quotation is a rewording of someone else's comments, rather than a word-for-word direct quotation. The word *that* often signals an indirect quotation. Quotation marks are *not* used with indirect quotations.

Direct Quotation	*Indirect Quotation*
Sean said, "The distributor cap on my car is cracked." (Sean's exact spoken words are given, so quotation marks are used.)	Sean said that the distributor cap on his car was cracked. (We learn Sean's words *in*directly, so no quotation marks are used.)
Alexandra's note to Jay read, "I'll be working late. Don't wait up for me." (The exact words that Alexandra wrote in the note are given, so quotation marks are used.)	Alexandra left a note for Jay saying she would be working late and he should not wait up for her. (We learn Alexandra's words indirectly, so no quotation marks are used.)

Activity

Rewrite the following sentences, changing words as necessary to convert the sentences into direct quotations. The first one is done for you as an example.

1. Paul asked Maria if he could turn on the hockey game.

   Paul asked Maria, "May I turn on the hockey game?"
   _____

2. Maria said that he could listen to the game on the radio.

   _____

3. Paul replied he was tired of being told what to do.

   _____

4. Maria said that as long as she paid the rent, she would make the rules.

   _____

5. Paul said that the day would come when the tables would be turned.

   _____

QUOTATION MARKS TO SET OFF TITLES OF SHORT WORKS

Titles of short works are usually set off by quotation marks, while titles of long works are underlined. Use quotation marks to set off the titles of such short works as articles in books, newspapers, or magazines; chapters in a book; short stories; poems; and songs.

On the other hand, you should underline or italicize the titles of books, newspapers, magazines, plays, movies, record albums, and television shows.

Quotation Marks	*Underlines or Italics*
the article "Yes, There are Canadian Comics"	in the book *Canuck Comics*
the article "A Day at the Beach"	in the newspaper The Vancouver Sun
the article "Biters Banquet"	in the magazine *Canadian Geographic*
the chapter "Mila, The Movie"	in the book More Than a Rose
the story "Blossom"	in the book *Sans Souci*
the poem "Suzanne"	in the book The Spice-Box of Earth
the song "Closing Time"	on the CD *The Future*
the episode "Homing Instinct"	from the TV series Traders
	the movie *The Red Violin*

Note: In printed works, titles of books, newspapers, and so on are set off by italics—slanted type that looks *like this*—instead of being underlined.

Activity

Use quotation marks or underlines as needed.

1. Spending Smart is the title of the fourth chapter of Dian Cohen's book Money.

2. No advertising is permitted in Consumer Reports, a nonprofit consumer magazine.

3. I cut out an article from MacLean's called Canadian Universities: Rankings for the Millenium to use in my sociology report.

4. Vince's favourite television show is Sliders, and his favourite movie is The Faculty.

5. Our instructor gave us a week to buy the textbook titled Personal Finance and to read the first chapter, Work and Income.

6. Every holiday season, our family watches the movie A Christmas Carol on television.

7. Allen bought Chatelaine because he wanted to read the cover article, titled Secrets Men Never Tell You.

8. Edgar Allan Poe's short story The Murders in the Rue Morgue and his poem The Raven are in a paperback titled Great Tales and Poems of Edgar Allan Poe.

9. When Victoria got her Starweek TV Magazine, she read an article titled The New Comedians and then thumbed through the listings to see when Pop-Up Video would be on that week.

10. The night before his exam, he discovered with horror that the chapter Becoming Mature was missing from Childhood and Adolescence, the psychology text that he had bought secondhand.

OTHER USES OF QUOTATION MARKS

1   Quotation marks are used to set off special words or phrases from the rest of a sentence:

Many people spell the words "a lot" as *one* word, "alot," instead of correctly spelling them as two words.
I have trouble telling the difference between "their" and "there."

Note: In printed works, *italics* are often used to set off special words or phrases. That is usually done in this book, for example.

2   Single quotation marks are used to mark off a quotation within a quotation:

The instructor said, "Know the chapter titled 'Status Symbols' in *Adolescent Development* if you expect to pass the test."
Kyra said, "One of my favourite Mae West lines is 'I used to be Snow White, but I drifted.'"

■ Review Test 1

Insert quotation marks where needed in the sentences that follow.

1. Don't you ever wash your car? Carly asked Jesse.

2. When the washer tilted and began to buzz, Zena shouted, Let's get rid of that blasted machine!

3. Take all you want, read the sign above the cafeteria salad bar, but please eat all you take.

4. After scrawling formulas all over the board with lightning speed, my math instructor was fond of asking, Any questions now?

5. Move that heap! the truck driver yelled. I'm trying to make a living here.

6. I did a summary of an article titled Adolescent Anxiety in the latest issue of Canadian Living.

7. Writer's block is something that happens to everyone at times, the instructor explained. You simply have to keep writing to break out of it.

8. A passenger in the car ahead of Kim threw food wrappers and empty cups out the window. That man, said Kim to his son, is a human pig.

9. If you are working during the day, said the counsellor, the best way to start college is with a night course or two.

10. I told the dentist that I wanted Novocaine. Don't be a sissy, he said. A little pain won't hurt. I told him that a little pain wouldn't hurt him, but it would bother me.

■ Review Test 2

Go through the comics section of a newspaper to find a comic strip that amuses you. Be sure to choose a strip where two or more characters are speaking to each other. Write a full description that will enable people who have not read the comic strip to visualize it clearly and appreciate its humour. Describe the setting and action in each panel, and enclose the words of the speakers in quotation marks.

Explaining a Process · Examining Cause and Effect · Comparing or Contrasting · Defin
Term · Dividing and Classifying · Describing a Scene or Person · Narrating an Event · Arg
a Position · Explaining a Process · Examining Cause and Effect · comparing or contrast
Defining a Term · Dividing and Classifying · Describing a Scene or Person · Narrating an
· Arguing a Position · Explaining a Process · Examining Cause and Effect · compari

C H A P T E R   3 6

Comma

Introductory Project

Commas often (though not always) signal a minor break, or pause, in a sentence. Each of the six pairs of sentences below illustrates one of the six main uses of the comma. Read each pair of sentences aloud and place a comma wherever you feel a slight pause occurs.

1. a. Ryan's interests are Lisa, television and sports.
    b. My mother put her feet up, sipped some iced tea and opened the newspaper.

2. a. Although the Lone Ranger used lots of silver bullets, he never ran out of ammunition.
    b. To open the cap of the aspirin bottle, you must first press down on it.

3. a. Kitty Katz and Serge Lamour, Canada's leading romantic stars, have made several movies together.
    b. Elsa, who is my next-door neighbour, just entered the hospital with an intestinal infection.

4. a. The wedding was scheduled for four o'clock, but the bride changed her mind at two.
    b. Franka took three coffee breaks before lunch, and then she went on a two-hour lunch break.

5. a. Delia's mother asked her, "What time do you expect to get home?"
    b. "Don't bend over to pat the dog," I warned, "or he'll kiss you."

6. a. Benjie ate seventeen hamburgers on July 29, 1998, and lived to tell about it.
    b. Benjie lives at 817 Ouellete Street, Windsor, Ontario.

Answers are on page 555.

358

SIX MAIN USES OF THE COMMA

Commas are used mainly as follows:

1 To separate items in a series
2 To set off introductory material
3 Before and after words that interrupt the flow of thought in a sentence
4 Between two complete thoughts connected by *and, but, for, or, nor, so, yet*
5 To set off a direct quotation from the rest of a sentence
6 For certain everyday material

Each use is explained on the pages that follow.

You may find it helpful to remember that the comma often marks a slight pause, or break, in a sentence. Read aloud the sentence examples given for each rule, and listen for the minor pauses, or breaks, that are signalled by commas.

Comma between Items in a Series

Use commas to separate items in a series.

> Do you drink tea with milk, lemon, or honey?
> Today the dishwasher stopped working, the garbage bag split, and the refrigerator turned into an icebox.
> The television talk shows enraged him so much he did not know whether to laugh, cry, or scream.
> Reiko awoke from a restless, nightmare-filled sleep.

Notes

a The final comma in a series is optional, but it is often used.
b A comma is used between two descriptive words in a series only if *and* inserted between the words sounds natural. You could say:

> Reiko awoke from a restless *and* nightmare-filled sleep.

But notice in the following sentence that the descriptive words do not sound natural when *and* is inserted between them. In such cases, no comma is used.

> Barbara drove a shiny blue Saturn. (A shiny *and* blue Saturn doesn't sound right, so no comma is used.)

Activity

Place commas between items in a series.

1. Godzilla lives for revenge violence and destruction.

2. My father taught me to swim by talking to me in a calm manner holding my hand firmly and throwing me into the pool.

3. Enzo added white wine mushrooms salt pepper and oregano to his spaghetti sauce.

4. Baggy threadbare jeans feel more comfortable than pyjamas to me.

5. Carmen grabbed a tiny towel bolted out of the bathroom and ran toward the ringing phone.

Comma after Introductory Material

Use a comma to set off introductory material.

> After punching the alarm clock with his fist, Bill turned over and went back to sleep.
> Looking up at the sky, I saw a man who was flying faster than a speeding bullet.
> Holding a baited trap, Jesse cautiously approached the gigantic mousehole.
> In addition, he held a broom in his hand.
> Also, he wore a football helmet in case a creature should leap out at his head.

Notes:

a If the introductory material is brief, the comma is sometimes omitted. In the activities here, you should use the comma.

b A comma is also used to set off extra material at the end of a sentence. Here are two sentences where this comma rule applies:

> A sudden breeze shot through the windows, driving the stuffiness out of the room.
> I love to cook and eat Italian food, especially penne and lasagna.

Activity

Place commas after introductory material.

1. When the president entered the room became hushed.

2. Feeling brave and silly at the same time Bernie volunteered to go on stage and help the magician.

3. While I was eating my tuna sandwich the cats circled my chair like hungry sharks.

4. Because my parents died when I was young I have learned to look after myself. Even though I am now independent I still carry a special loneliness within me.

5. At first putting extra hot pepper flakes on the pizza seemed like a good idea. However I felt otherwise when flames seemed about to shoot out of my mouth.

Comma around Words Interrupting the Flow of Thought

Use commas before and after words or phrases that interrupt the flow of thought in a sentence.

> My brother, a sports nut, owns over five-thousand hockey cards.

That game show, at long last, has been cancelled.
The children used the old Buick, rusted from disuse, as a backyard clubhouse.

Usually you can "hear" words that interrupt the flow of thought in a sentence. However, if you are not sure that certain words are interrupters, remove them from the sentence. If it still makes sense without the words, you know that the words are interrupters and the information they give is nonessential. Such nonessential information is set off with commas. In the sentence

Doris Thompson, who lives next door, won the javelin-throwing competition.

the words *who lives next door* are extra information, not needed to identify the subject of the sentence, *Doris Thompson*. Put commas around such nonessential information. On the other hand, in the sentence

The woman who lives next door won the javelin-throwing competition.

the words *who lives next door* supply essential information—information needed for us to identify the woman being spoken of. If the words were removed from the sentence, we would no longer know who won the competition. Commas are *not* used around such essential information.
Here is another example:

Wilson Hall, which the hurricane destroyed, was ninety years old.

Here the words *which the hurricane destroyed* are extra information, not needed to identify the subject of the sentence, *Wilson Hall*. Commas go around such nonessential information. On the other hand, in the sentence

The building which the hurricane destroyed was ninety years old.

the words *which the hurraine destroyed* are needed to identify the building. Commas are *not* used around such essential information.
As noted above, however, most of the time you will be able to "hear" words that interrupt the flow of thought in a sentence and will not have to think about whether the words are essential or nonessential.

Activity

Use commas to set off interrupting words.

1. On Friday my day off I went to get a haircut.

2. Dracula who had a way with women is Lyle's favourite movie hero. He feels that the Wolfman on the other hand showed no class in handling women.

3. Many people forget that Mackenzie King one of our most effective prime ministers also talked to his dead mother.

4. Mowing the grass especially when it is three centimetres high is my least favourite job.

5. A jar of chicken noodle soup which was all there was in the refrigerator did not make a very satisfying meal.

Comma between Complete Thoughts

Use a comma between two complete thoughts connected by *and, but, for, or, nor, so, yet.*

The wedding was scheduled for four o'clock, but the bride changed her mind at two.

We could always tell when our instructor felt disorganized, for his shirt would not be tucked in.

Amelia has to work some nights, so she tapes the hockey games on her VCR.

Notes

a   The comma is optional when the complete thoughts are short.

Grace's skin tans and Mark's skin freckles.

Her pop was watery but she drank it anyway.

The day was overcast so they didn't go swimming.

b   Be careful not to use a comma in sentences having *one* subject and a *double* verb. The comma is used only in sentences made up of two complete thoughts (two subjects and two verbs). In the following sentence, there is only one subject (*Kevin*) with a double verb (*will go* and *forget*). Therefore, no comma is needed:

Kevin will go partying tonight and forget all about tomorrow's exam.

Likewise, the following sentence has only one subject (*Rita*) and a double verb (*was* and *will work*); therefore, no comma is needed:

Rita was a server at the Banff Hotel last summer and probably will work there this summer.

Activity

Place a comma before a joining word that connects two complete thoughts (two subjects and two verbs). Remember, do *not* place a comma within sentences that have only one subject and a double verb.

1. The oranges in the refrigerator were covered with blue mold and the potatoes in the cupboard felt like sponges.

2. All the jeans in the shop were on sale but not a single pair was my size.

3. Phil often window shops in the malls for hours and comes home without buying anything.

4. Kurt left the dentist's office with his mouth still numb from Novocaine and he talked with a lisp for two hours.

5. I covered the walls with three coats of white paint but the purple underneath still showed through.

6. The car squealed down the entrance ramp and sped recklessly out onto the freeway.

7. The women in the dance club moved like wound-up Barbie dolls and the men in the audience sat as motionless as stones.

8. The aliens in the science fiction film visited our planet in peace but we greeted them with violence.

9. I felt like shouting at the gang of boys but didn't dare open my mouth.

10. Lenny claims he wants to succeed in college but he has missed classes all semester.

Comma with Direct Quotations

Use a comma to set off a direct quotation from the rest of a sentence.

> His father shouted, "Why don't you go out and get a job?"
> "Our modern world has lost a sense of the sacredness of life," the speaker said.
> "No," said Celia to Jerry. "I won't go to the bingo hall with you."
> "Money," wrote Marshall McLuhan, "is the poor people's credit card."

Note: Commas and periods at the end of a quotation go inside quotation marks. See also page 352.

Activity

Use commas to set off quotations from the rest of the sentence.

1. The man yelled "Call an ambulance, somebody!"

2. My partner on the dance floor said "Don't be so stiff. You look as if you'd swallowed an umbrella."

3. The question on the anatomy test read "What human organ grows faster than any other, never stops growing, and always remains the same size?"

4. The student behind me whispered "The skin."

5. "My stomach hurts" Bruce said "and I don't know whether it was the hamburger or the math test."

Comma with Everyday Material

Use a comma with certain everyday material.

Persons Spoken To

> Tina, go to bed if you're not feeling well.
> Aaron, where did you put my shoes?
> Are you coming with us, Omar?

Dates

March 4, 1998, is when Elvira buried her third husband.

Addresses

Tony's grandparents live at 183 Roxborough Avenue, Toronto, Ontario M4S 1V3.

Note: No comma is used to mark off the postal code (Canada) or zip code (U.S.).

Openings and Closings of Letters

Dear Santa,
Dear Larry,
Sincerely yours,
Truly yours,

Note: In formal letters, a colon is used after the opening: Dear Sir: *or* Dear Madam:

Numbers

The dishonest dealer turned the used car's odometer from 98,170 km to 39,170 km.

Activity

Place commas where needed.

1. I expected you to set a better example for the others Michel.

2. Janet with your help I passed the test.

3. The move stars Kitty Katz and Serge Lamour were married on September 12 1996 and lived at 3865 Marina Boulevard Vancouver British Columbia for one month.

4. They received 75000 congratulatory fan letters and were given picture contracts worth $3000000 in the first week of their marriage.

5. Kitty left Serge on October 12 1996 and ran off with their marriage counsellor.

▓ Review Test 1

Insert commas where needed. In the space provided below each sentence, summarize briefly the rule that explains the use of the comma or commas.

1. The best features of my new apartment are its large kitchen its bay windows and its low rent.

_____ seperate seyres _____

2. Because we got in line at dawn we were among the first to get tickets for the Toronto International Film Festival.

___set off introductory.___

3. "When will someone invent a telephone", Elise asked "that will only ring at convenient moments?"

___set off a direct quotation from the rest.___

4. Without opening his eyes Simon stumbled out of bed and opened the door for the whining dog.

___set off.___

5. I think Chris that you had better ask someone else for your $2500 loan.

_____

6. Hot dogs are the most common cause of choking deaths in children for a bite-size piece can easily plug up a toddler's throat.

___4.___

7. Tax forms though shortened and revised every year never seem to get any simpler.

___4.___

8. Sandra may decide to go to college full-time or she may enrol in a couple of evening courses.

___4___

9. I remember how with the terrible cruelty of children we used to make fun of the cross-eyed girl who lived on our street.

___3.   interrupt.___

10. Although that old man on the corner looks like a bum he is said to have a Swiss bank account.

___set off introductory material___

■ Review Test 2

Insert commas where needed.

1. My dog who is afraid of the dark sleeps with a night light.

2. "I wish there were some pill" said Henry "that would give you the equivalent of eight hours' sleep in four hours."

3. The hot dogs at the ball park tasted delicious but they made me sick later.

4. Janice attended class for four hours worked at the hospital for three hours and studied at home for two hours.

5. The old man as he gasped for air tried to assure the hospital clerk that he had his provincial health card somewhere.

6. Rolf and Elena sat down to watch the football game with crackers sharp cheese salty pretzels and two frosty bottles of beer.

7. Although I knew exactly what was happening the solar eclipse gave me a strong feeling of anxiety.

8. The company agreed to raise a senior bus driver's salary to $42000 by January 1 2000.

9. Even though King Kong was holding her at the very top of the Empire State Building Fay Wray kept yelling at him "Let me go!"

10. Navel oranges which Margery as a little girl called belly-button oranges are her favourite fruit.

Review Test 3

On a separate piece of paper, write six sentences, each of them demonstrating one of the six main comma rules.

CHAPTER 37

Other Punctuation Marks

Introductory Project

Each of the sentences below needs one of the following punctuation marks:

;   —   -   ( )   :

See if you can insert the correct mark in each sentence. Each mark should be used once.

1. The following holiday plants are poisonous and should be kept away from children and pets holly, mistletoe, and poinsettias.

2. The freeze dried remains of Annie's canary were in a clear bottle on her bookcase.

3. William Shakespeare 1564–1616 married a woman eight years his senior when he was eighteen.

4. Grooming in space is more difficult than on Earth no matter how much Marc Garneau combs his hair, for instance, it still tends to float loosely around his head.

5. I opened the front door, and our cat walked in proudly with a live mouse hanging from his mouth.

Answers are on page 555.

COLON (:)

Use the colon at the end of a complete statement to introduce a list, a long quotation, or an explanation.

List

The following were my worst jobs: truck loader in an apple plant, assembler in a battery factory, and attendant in a psychiatric hospital.

Explanation

There are two hockey leagues in our town: Junior A and the bantam league.

Activity

Place colons where needed.

1. Foods that are high in cholesterol include the following eggs, butter, milk, cheese, shrimp, and well-marbled meats.

2. All the signs of the flu were present hot and cold spells, heavy drainage from the sinuses, a bad cough, and an ache through the entire body.

3. In his essay, "The Role of New Media in Social Change," Marshall McLuhan wrote "One of the notable effects of the TV image on those in the primary grades seems to be the development of near-point reading. The average distance from the page of children in the first three grades has recently been measured in Toronto … The average distance is 6½ inches. The children seem to be striving to do a version of their relation to the TV image."

SEMI-COLON (;)

The main use of the semi-colon is to mark a break between two complete thoughts, as explained on page 276. Another use of the semi-colon is to mark off items in a series when the items themselves contain commas. Here are some examples:

Winning prizes at the national flower show were Roberta Collins, British Columbia, azaleas; Sally Hunt, Alberta, roses; and James Weber, Ontario, Shasta daisies.

The following books must be read for the course: *The Handmaid's Tale*, by Margaret Atwood; *The English Patient*, by Michael Ondaatje; and *Man's Search for Meaning*, by Viktor Frankl.

Activity

Place semi-colons where needed.

1. The specials at the restaurant today are eggplant Parmesan, for $5.95 black beans and rice, for $4.95 and chicken potpie, for $6.95.

2. The top of the hill in France offered an awesome view of the military cemetery thousands of headstones were arranged in perfect rows.

3. Kelley's favourite old movies are *To Catch a Thief,* starring Cary Grant and Grace Kelly *Animal Crackers,* a Marx Brothers comedy and *The Wizard of Oz,* with Judy Garland.

DASH (—)

A dash signals a pause longer than a comma but not as complete as a period. Use a dash to set off words for dramatic effect:

> I didn't go out with him a second time—once was more than enough.
> Some of you—I won't mention you by name—cheated on the test.
> It was so windy that the VW passed him on the highway—overhead.

Notes

a The dash is formed on a keyboard by striking the hyphen twice (--). In handwriting, the dash is as long as two letters would be.

b Be careful not to overuse dashes.

Activity

Place dashes where needed.

1. Riding my bike, I get plenty of exercise especially when dogs chase me.

2. I'm advising you in fact, I'm telling you not to bother me again.

3. The package finally arrived badly damaged.

HYPHEN (-)

1 Use a hyphen with two or more words that act as a single unit describing a noun.

> The fast-talking salesperson was so good that he went into politics. (*Fast* and *talking* combine to describe the salesperson.)
> I both admire and envy her well-rounded personality.
> When the dude removed his blue-tinted shades, Lonnell saw the spaced-out look in his eyes.

2 Use a hyphen to divide a word at the end of a line of writing or keyed text. When you need to divide a word at the end of a line, divide it between syllables. Use your dictionary to be sure of correct syllable divisions.

> When Tom lifted up the hood of his Toyota, he realized that one of the radiator hoses had broken.

Notes

a Do not divide words of one syllable.

b Do not divide a word if you can avoid doing so.

Activity

Place hyphens where needed.

1. High flying jets and gear grinding trucks are constant sources of noise pollution in our neighbourhood, and consequently we are going to move.

2. When Linda turned on the porch light, ten legged creatures scurried every where over the crumb filled floor.

3. Scott had ninety two dollars in his pocket when he left for the supermarket, and he had twenty two dollars when he got back.

PARENTHESES ( )

Parentheses are used to set off extra or incidental information from the rest of a sentence:

> The section of that book on the dangers of eating disorders (pages 35 to 72) is outdated.
>
> Yesterday at Hamburger House (my favourite place to eat), the guy who makes french fries asked me to go out with him.

Note: Do not use parentheses too often in your writing.

Activity

Add parentheses where needed.

1. Certain sections of the novel especially Chapter 5 made my heart race with suspense.

2. Did you hear that George Linda's first husband just got remarried?

3. Sigmund Freud 1856–1939 was the founder of psychoanalysis.

■ Review Test

At the appropriate spot, place the punctuation mark shown in the margin.

; 1. Ella's savings have dwindled to nothing she's been borrowing from me to pay her rent.

— 2. There's the idiot I'd know him anywhere who dumped garbage on our front lawn.

– 3. Today's two career couples spend more money on eating out than their parents did.

: 4. H. de Montarville Molson said "My father spoke French with a Bank of Montreal accent."

( ) 5. One-fifth of our textbook pages 401 – 498 consists of footnotes and a bibliography.

Explaining a Process · Examining Cause and Effect · Comparing or Contrasting · Defin
Term · Dividing and Classifying · Describing a Scene or Person · Narrating an Event · Arg
a Position · Explaining a Process · Examining Cause and Effect · Comparing or Contrast
Defining a Term · Dividing and Classifying · Describing a Scene or Person · Narrating an
Arguing a Position · Explaining a Process · Examining Cause and Effect · Compari

C H A P T E R   3 8

Improving Spelling

Poor spelling sometimes results from bad habits developed in early school years or sometimes is caused by a lack of familiarity or frequency with writing in English. With work, such problems can be corrected. If you can write your name without misspelling it, there is no reason why you can't do the same with almost any word in the English language. Following are seven steps you can take to improve your spelling.

STEP 1: USE THE DICTIONARY AND THE SPELL CHECKER ON YOUR PROCESSOR

Get into the habit of using the dictionary. When you write a paper, allow yourself time to look up the spelling of all those words you are unsure about. Do not overlook the value of this step just because it is such a simple one. By using the dictionary, you can probably make yourself a 95 percent better speller.

Your main asset in producing error-free documents on the word processor is your spell checker. Always spell-check your next-to-last draft of any document. Spell-checking systems allow you to identify incorrectly spelled words and to select from suggested correct spellings. Keep a dictionary open beside the keyboard as you do this, to double-check the spellings you select.

Spell-checking systems cannot differentiate between unintentional mistakes in word usage, though. "Same sound" words, homonyms like *its* and *it's* or *there, their,* and *they're,* spelled correctly but used incorrectly, cannot be corrected by a spell checker. You may want to highlight these words on your processor screen and double-check your intended meaning and spelling with the dictionary.

*Note: Your word-processing program may show the options "US Lex or Dictionary" or "UK Lex or Dictionary." "US Lex" refers to the American spelling and hyphenation patterns for words; "UK Lex," which this textbook uses, refers to the British (and predominantly Canadian) spelling and uses of hyphenation. Use one or the other set of spellings *consistently,* no matter which you use. Most Canadian colleges and universities will prefer British/Canadian spelling.

STEP 2: KEEP A PERSONAL SPELLING LIST

Keep a list of words you misspell, and study these words regularly. Use the chart on page 559 as a starter. When you accumulate additional words, write them on the back page of a frequently used notebook or on a separate sheet of paper titled "Personal Spelling List."

To master the words on your list, do the following:

1 Write down any hint that will help you remember the spelling of a word. For example, you might want to note that *occasion* is spelled with two *c*'s, or that *all right* is two words, not one word.

2 Study a word by looking at it, saying it, and spelling it. You may also want to write out the word one or more times, or "air-write" it with your finger in large, exaggerated motions.

3 When you have trouble spelling a long word, try to break the word down into syllables and see whether you can spell the syllables. For example, *inadvertent* can be spelled easily if you can hear and spell in turn its four syllables: *in ad ver tent*. Or the word *consternation* can be spelled easily if you hear and spell in turn its four syllables: *con ster na tion*. Remember, then: try to see, hear, and spell long words syllable by syllable.

4 Keep in mind that review and repeated self-testing are the keys to effective learning. When you are learning a series of words, go back after studying each new word and review all the preceding ones.

STEP 3: MASTER COMMONLY CONFUSED WORDS

Master the meanings and spellings of the commonly confused words on pages 384–390. Your instructor may assign twenty words for you to study at a time and give you a series of quizzes until you have mastered the words.

STEP 4: LEARN KEYWORDS IN MAJOR SUBJECTS

Make up and master lists of words central to the vocabulary of your major subjects. For example, a list of keywords in business might include: *economics, management, resources, scarcity, capitalism, decentralization, productivity, enterprise,* and so on; in psychology: *behaviour, investigation, experimentation, frustration, cognition, stimulus, response, organism,* and so on. Add words from your "course-specific" lists, and any words you consistently have trouble spelling to the "custom dictionary" listing in your spell checker, or set aside a specific portion of your various course notebooks to be used only for such lists.

STEP 5: UNDERSTAND BASIC SPELLING RULES

Explained briefly here are three rules that may improve your spelling. While exceptions sometimes occur, the rules hold true most of the time.

1   ***Changing*** y ***to*** i. When a word ends in a consonant plus *y*, change *y* to *i* when you add an ending.

try + ed = tried	easy + er = easier
defy + es = defies	carry + ed = carried
ready + ness = readiness	penny + less = penniless

2   ***Final silent*** e. Drop the final *e* before an ending that starts with a vowel (the vowels are *a, e, i, o,* and *u*).

create + ive = creative	believe + able = believable
nerve + ous = nervous	share + ing = sharing

Keep the final *e* before an ending that starts with a consonant.

extreme + ly = extremely	life + less = lifeless
hope + ful = hopeful	excite + ment = excitement

3   ***Doubling a final consonant.*** * Double the final consonant of a word when all three of the following are true:
  a   The word is one syllable or is accented on the last syllable.
  b   The word ends in a single consonant preceded by a single vowel.
  c   The ending you are adding starts with a vowel.

shop + er = shopper	thin + est = thinnest
equip + ed = equipped	submit + ed = submitted
swim + ing = swimming	drag + ed = dragged

Activity

Combine the following words and endings by applying the three rules above.

1. worry   + ed   = _____

2. write   + ing = _____

3. marry   + es   = _____

4. run   + ing = _____

5. terrify + ed   = _____

6. dry   + es   = _____

7. forget   + ing = _____

8. care   + ful = _____

9. control + ed   = _____

10. debate + able = _____

*In addition, Canadian spelling usually doubles the final consonant to many words ending in "l" including *cancelled*, *barrelled*, and so on. See "Canadian Spelling, Consistent Spelling, and Correctness" on page 378.

STEP 6: STUDY A BASIC WORD LIST

Study the spellings of the words in the following list. They are five hundred of the words most often used in English. Your instructor may assign twenty-five or fifty words for you to study at a time and give you a series of quizzes until you have mastered the list.

Five Hundred Basic Words

ability	around	brother	company **100**
absent	arrange	building	condition
accept	attempt	bulletin	conversation
accident	attention	bureau	copy
ache	August	business	daily
across	automobile	came	danger
address	autumn	can't	daughter
advertise	avenue	careful	daybreak
advice	awful	careless **75**	dear
after	awkward	cereal	death
again	back	certain	December
against	balance	chair	decide
agree	bargain	change	deed
all right	beautiful	charity	dentist
almost	because	cheap	deposit
a lot	become	cheat	describe
already	been **50**	cheek	did
also	before	chicken	died
although	begin	chief	different
always	being	children	dinner
amateur	believe	choose	direction
among	between	church	discover
amount	bicycle	cigarette	disease
angry	black	citizen	distance
animal **25**	blue	city	doctor
another	board	close	does **125**
answer	borrow	clothing	dollar
anxious	bottle	coffee	don't
appetite	bottom	collect	doubt
apply	brake	college	down
approach	breast	colour	dozen
approve	breathe	come	during
argue	brilliant	comfortable	each

early	grammar	knowledge	more
earth	great	labour	morning
easy	grocery **175**	laid	mother
education	grow	language	mountain
eight	guess	last	mouth
either	half	laugh	much
empty	hammer	learn	must
English	hand	led	nail
enough	handkerchief	left	near
entrance	happy	leisure	needle
evening	having	length	neighbour
everything	head	lesson	neither
examine	heard	letter **225**	never
except	heavy	life	newspaper
exercise	high	light	nickel
exit	himself	listen	niece
expect	hoarse	little	night
fact **150**	holiday	loaf	ninety
factory	home	loneliness	noise
family	hospital	long	none
far	house	lose	not
February	however	made	nothing
few	hundred	making	November **275**
fifteen	hungry	many	now
fight	husband	March	number
flower	instead	marry	ocean
forehead	intelligence	match	o'clock
foreign	interest **200**	matter	October
forty	interfere	may	offer
forward	interrupt	measure	often
found	into	medicine	old
fourteen	iron	men	omit
Friday	itself	middle	once
friend	January	might	one
from	July	million	only
gallon	June	minute	operate
garden	just	mistake	opinion
general	kindergarten	Monday **250**	opportunity
get	kitchen	money	optimist
good	knock	month	original

ought	quite	soap	thing
ounce	quiz	soldier	thirteen
overcoat	raise	something **375**	this
pain	read	sometimes	though
paper	ready	soul	thousand
part	really	soup	thread
peace	reason	south	three
pear **300**	receive	stamp	through
pencil	recognize	state	Thursday
penny	refer	still	ticket
people	religion	stockings	time
perfect	remember	straight	tired
period	repeat	street	today **425**
person	resource	strong	together
picture	restaurant	student	tomorrow
piece	ribbon	studying	tongue
pillow	ridiculous	such	tonight
place	right **350**	suffer	touch
plain	said	sugar	toward
please	same	suit	travel
pocket	sandwich	summer	trouble
policeman	Saturday	Sunday	trousers
possible	say	supper	truly
post office	school	sure	twelve
potato	scissors	sweet	uncle
power	season	take	under
prescription	see	teach	understand
president	sentence	tear **400**	United States
pretty	September	telegram	until
probably	service	telephone	upon
promise	seventeen	tenant	used
psychology	several	tenth	usual
public **325**	shoes	than	valley
pursue	should	Thanksgiving	value
put	sight	that	variety
qualify	since	theatre	vegetable
quarter	sister	them	very
quick	sixteenth	there	view **450**
quiet	sleep	therefore	villain
quit	smoke	they	visitor

voice	wear	while	world
vote	weather	white	worth
wage	Wednesday	whole	would
wagon	week	whose	writing
waist	weigh	wife	written
wait	welcome	window	wrong
wake	well	winter	year
walk	went	without	yesterday
warm	were	woman	yet
warning	what	wonder	young
watch	whether **475**	won't	your
water	which	work	you're **500**

Note: Two spelling mistakes that students often make are to write *a lot* as one word (*alot*) and to write *all right* as one word (*alright*). Do not write either *a lot* or *all right* as one word.

STEP 7: USE ELECTRONIC AIDS

Electronic spell checkers are pocket-sized devices with tiny keyboards. You key in the word the way you think it is spelled, and the checker supplies the correct spelling of related words. Some checkers even *pronounce* the word aloud for you. Canadian students will want to ask whether British/Canadian or American spelling systems are programmed into the spell checker they select, and they should find out whether or not instructors permit the use of these devices in classes and exams.

Finally, many electronic typewriters beep automatically when you misspell or mistype a word. They include built-in dictionaries that will then give you the correct spelling.

CANADIAN SPELLING, CONSISTENT SPELLING, AND CORRECTNESS

Canadian spelling is a contentious subject. You may notice that many Canadian newspapers use what we think of as "American" forms of words such as *neighbor* or *color*. These are choices made by their style guides.

Canadian spelling is neither British nor American spelling; it is a hybrid of the two, and spellings of certain words may vary from one printed source to another. Student confusion is understandable.

Check with your instructor for his or her preference, but choose *one* spelling system, and *be consistent*. Choose a Canadian dictionary, such as *The Canadian Oxford Dictionary,* which this text uses, or *Gage* or *Penguin.* If your word-processing program's spell-check system allows you to choose between British or American spelling, choose British, which is sometimes called "UK Lex."

The main differences between U.S. and Canadian spellings are in *-or/-our* endings (*honour, neighbour, labour, flavour*), *-er/-re* endings (*theatre, litre, centre, fibre*) and *-se/-ce* endings (*defence, licence, offence*).

Canadian spelling also includes more doubled *l*'s than does U.S. spelling. These double *l*'s appear in nouns such as *tranquillizer* and *counsellor*, and in present and past participle forms of verbs such as *travelling, levelled, panelled, cancelled,* and *counselled.* Whichever form your dictionary uses, remember that consistent spelling is important.

Spelling correctly has become even more important with the growth of electronic communications and with resulting changes to the workplace. The Internet and other international communications systems are integral parts of your personal and professional future. Clear and understandable communication relies on standardized spelling. Individual illiteracy, bounced off satellites and transmitted through fibre-optic cable, becomes an obstacle to information transmission and an international liability to employers and private citizens alike.

Explaining a Process • Examining Cause and Effect • Comparing or Contrasting • Defin
Term • Dividing and Classifying • Describing a Scene or Person • Narrating an Event • Arg
a Position • Explaining a Process • Examining Cause and Effect • Comparing or Contras
Defining a Term • Dividing and Classifying • Describing a Scene or Person • Narrating an
Arguing a Position • Explaining a Process • Examining Cause and Effect • Compari

CHAPTER 39

Vocabulary Development

A good vocabulary is a vital part of effective communication. A command of many words will make you a better writer, speaker, listener, and reader. Studies have shown that students with a strong vocabulary, and students who work to improve a limited vocabulary, are more successful in school. And one research study found that *a good vocabulary, more than any other factor, was common to people enjoying successful careers.* This section will describe three ways of developing your word power: (1) regular reading, (2) vocabulary wordsheets, and (3) vocabulary study books. You should keep in mind from the start, however, that none of the approaches will help unless you truly decide that vocabulary development is an important goal. Only when you have this attitude can you begin doing the sustained work needed to improve your word power.

REGULAR READING

Through reading a good deal, you will learn words by encountering them a number of times in a variety of sentences. Repeated exposure to a word in context will eventually make it a part of your working language.

You should develop the habit of reading a daily newspaper and one or more Canadian magazines like *McLean's* or *Saturday Night,* as well as magazines suited to your interests. In addition, you should try to read some books for pleasure. This may be especially difficult at times when you also have textbook reading to do. Try, however, to redirect a regular half hour to one hour of your recreational time to reading books, rather than watching television. Doing so, you may eventually reap the rewards of an improved vocabulary *and* discover that reading can be truly enjoyable. If you would like some recommendations, ask your instructor for a copy of the "List of Interesting Books" in the Instructor's Manual of *English Skills with Readings.*

VOCABULARY WORDSHEETS

Vocabulary wordsheets are another means of vocabulary development. Whenever you read, you should mark off words that you want to learn. After you have accumulated a number of words, sit down with a dictionary and look up basic information about each of them. Put this information on a wordsheet like the one shown below. Be sure also to write down a sentence in which each word appears. A word is always best learned in the context of surrounding words.

Study each word as follows. To begin with, make sure you can correctly pronounce the word and its derivations. The dictionary pronunciation key will help you pronounce each word properly. Next, study the main meanings of the word until you can say them without looking at them. Finally, spend a moment looking at the example of the word in context. Follow the same process with the second word. Then, after testing yourself on the first and the second words, go on to the third word. After you learn each new word, remember to continue to test yourself on all the words you have studied. Repeated self-testing is a key to effective learning.

Activity

In your reading, locate four words that you would like to master. Enter them in the spaces on the vocabulary wordsheet below and fill in all the needed information. Your instructor may then check your wordsheet and perhaps give you a quick oral quiz on selected words.

You may receive a standing assignment to add five words a week to a wordsheet and to study the words. Note that you can create your own wordsheets using loose-leaf paper, or your instructor may give you copies of the wordsheet that appears below.

Vocabulary Wordsheet

1. Word: ___*formidable*___ Pronunciation: ___*(fôr′ mi də bəl)*___

   Meanings: ___*1. feared or dreaded*___

   _____*2. extremely difficult*_____

   _____

   Other forms of the word: ___*formidably   formidability*___

   Use of the word in context: ___*Several formidable obstacles stand between*___

   *Matt and his goal.*_____

2. Word: _____ Pronunciation: _____

   Meanings: _____

   _____

   _____

Other forms of the word: _____

Use of the word in context: _____

_____

3. Word: _____ Pronunciation: _____

Meanings: _____

_____

_____

Other forms of the word: _____

Use of the word in context: _____

_____

4. Word: _____ Pronunciation: _____

Meanings: _____

_____

_____

Other forms of the word: _____

Use of the word in context: _____

_____

5. Word: _____ Pronunciation: _____

Meanings: _____

_____

_____

Other forms of the word: _____

Use of the word in context: _____

_____

VOCABULARY STUDY BOOKS

A third way to increase your word power is to use vocabulary study books. Many vocabulary books and programs are available. The best are those that present words in one or more contexts and then provide several reinforcement activities for each word. These books will help you increase your vocabulary if you have the determination required to work with them on a regular basis.

CHAPTER 40

Commonly Confused Words

Introductory Project

Circle the five words that are misspelled in the following passage. Then see if you can write the correct spellings in the spaces provided.

(You're) mind and body are not as separate as you might think. (Their) is a lot of evidence, for instance, that says if you believe that a placebo (a substance with no medicine) will help you, (than) it will. One man is said (too) have rapidly recovered from an advanced case of cancer after only one dose of a drug that he believed was highly effective. (Its) not clear just how placebos work, but they do show how closely the mind and body are related.

1. _____Your_____

2. _____there_____

3. _____then_____

4. _____to_____

5. _____it's_____

Answers are on page 556.

HOMONYMS

The commonly confused words on the following pages have the same sounds but different meanings and spellings; such words are known as *homonyms*. Complete the activity for each set of homonyms, and check off and study the words that give you trouble.

all ready   completely prepared
already   previously; before

> We were *all ready* to start the play, but the audience was still being seated.
> I have *already* called the police.

Fill in the blanks: I am _____All ready_____ for the economics examination

because I have _____already_____ studied the chapter three times.

brake   stop; the stopping device in a vehicle
break   come apart

> His car bumper has a sticker reading, "I *brake* for animals."
> "I am going to *break* up with Bill if he keeps seeing other women," said Rita.

Fill in the blanks: When my car's emergency _____brake_____ slipped,

the car rolled back and demolished my neighbour's rose garden, causing a

_____break_____ in our good relations with each other.

coarse   rough
course   part of a meal; a school subject; direction; certainly (as in *of course*)

> By the time the server offered the customers the second *course* of the meal, she was aware of their *coarse* eating habits.

Fill in the blanks: Theo felt that the fitness instructor's humour was too

_____coarse_____ for his taste and was glad when he finished the _____course_____.

hear   perceive with the ear
here   in this place

> "The salespeople act as though they don't see or *hear* me, even though I've been standing *here* for fifteen minutes," the woman complained.

Fill in the blanks: "Did you _____hear_____ about the distinguished visitor

who just came into town and is staying _____here_____ at this very hotel?"

hole   an empty spot
whole   entire

> "I can't believe I ate the *whole* pizza," moaned Raphael. "I think it's going to make a *hole* in my stomach lining."

Fill in the blanks: The ____*whole*____ time I was at the party I tried to conceal the ____*hole*____ I had in my trousers.

its   belonging to it
it's   shortened form of *it is* or *it has*

> The car blew *its* transmission (the transmission belonging to it, the car).
> *It's* (it has) been raining all week and *it's* (it is) raining now.

Fill in the blanks: ____*It's*____ hot and unsanitary in the restaurant kitchen I work in, and I don't think the restaurant deserves ____*its*____ good reputation.

knew   past form of *know*
new   not old

> "I had *new* wallpaper put up," said Sarah.
> "I *knew* there was some reason the place looked better," said Bill.

Fill in the blanks: Lisa ____*knew*____ that getting her hair cut would give her face a ____*new*____ look.

know   to understand
no   a negative

> "I don't *know* why my dog Fang likes to attack certain people," said Kerry. "There's *no* one thing the people have in common."

Fill in the blanks: I ____*know*____ of ____*no*____ way of telling whether the politician is honest or not.

pair   set of two
pear   fruit

> "What a great *pair* of shorts Tim bought," said Keesha to Nora. Tim didn't hear her, for he was feeling very sick after munching on a green *pear*.

Fill in the blanks: In his lunch box was a ____*pair*____ of ____*pear*____s.

passed   went by; succeeded in; handed to
past   time before the present; beyond, as in "We worked past closing time."

> Someone *passed* him a wine bottle; it was the way he chose to forget his unhappy *past*.

Fill in the blanks: I walked ____*passed* / *past*____ the instructor's office but was afraid to ask her whether or not I had ____*past* / *passed*____ the test.

peace   calm
piece   part

> Nations often risk world *peace* by fighting over a *piece* of land.

Fill in the blanks: Helen did not have any _____peace_____ until she gave her

dog a _____piece_____ of her meat loaf.

plain   simple; flat area
plane   aircraft

> The *plain,* unassuming young man on the *plane* suddenly jumped up with a
> grenade in his hand and announced, "We're all going to Tibet."

Fill in the blanks: The game-show contestant opened the small box wrapped

in _____plain_____ brown paper and found inside the keys to his own jet

_____plane_____.

principal   main; a person in charge of a school
principle   law, standard, or rule

> Pete's high school *principal* had one *principal* problem: Pete. This was
> because there were only two *principles* in Pete's life: rest and relaxation.

Fill in the blanks: The _____principal_____ reason she dropped out of school was

that she believed in the _____principle_____ of complete freedom of choice.

Note: It might help to remember that the *e* in *principle* is also in *rule*—the meaning of *principle*.

right   correct; opposite of left
write   to convey thoughts in words in print

> If you have the *right* registration form, I'll *write* your name on the class list.

Fill in the blanks: Dimitri thinks I'm weird since I _____write_____ with both

my _____right_____ and my left hand.

than   used in comparisons
then   at that time

> When we were kids, my friend Shannon had prettier clothes *than* I did. I
> really envied her then.

Fill in the blanks: Carol thought she was better _____than_____ the rest of us,

but _____then_____ she got the lowest grade on the accounting test.

Note: It might help to remember that th*e*n (with an *e*) is also a tim*e* signal.

their   belonging to them
there   at that place; neutral word used with verbs like *is, are, was, were, have,* and *had*
they're   shortened form of *they are*

> Two people own that van over *there* (at that place). *They're* (they are) going to move out of *their* apartment (the apartment belonging to them) and into the van, in order to save money.

Fill in the blanks: _____they're_____ not going to invite us to _____their_____ table because _____there_____ is no room for us to sit down.

threw   past form of *throw*
through   from one side to the other; finished

> The fans *threw* so much litter onto the field that the teams could not go *through* with the game.

Fill in the blanks: When Mr. Jefferson was _____through_____ screaming about the violence on television, he _____threw_____ the newspaper at his dog.

to   verb part, as in *to smile*; toward, as in "I'm going *to* heaven"
too   overly, as in "The pizza was *too* hot"; also, as in "The coffee was hot, *too.*"
two   number 2

> Kyle drove *to* the park *to* be alone with Cheryl. (The first *to* means "toward"; the second *to* is a verb part that goes with *be.*)
> Kyle's shirt is *too* tight; his pants are tight, *too.* (The first *too* means "overly"; the second *too* means "also.")
> You need *two* hands (2 hands) to handle a Whopper.

Fill in the blanks: _____two_____ times tonight, you have been _____too_____ ready _____to_____ make assumptions without asking questions first.

wear   to have on
where   in what place

> Tino wanted to *wear* his light pants on the hot day, but he didn't know *where* he had put them.

Fill in the blanks: Exactly _____where_____ on my leg should I _____wear_____ this elastic bandage?

weather   atmospheric conditions
whether   if it happens that; in case; if

> Some people go on vacations *whether* or not the *weather* is good.

Fill in the blanks: I always ask Bill _____whether_____ or not we're going to have a storm, for his bad knee can feel rainy _____weather_____ approaching.

whose   belonging to whom
who's   shortened form of *who is* and *who has*

> *Who's* the instructor *whose* students are complaining?

Fill in the blanks: ___who's___ the guy ___whose___ car I saw you in?

your   belonging to you
you're   shortened form of *you are*

> *You're* (meaning "you are") not going to the fair unless *your* brother (the brother belonging to you) goes with you.

Fill in the blanks: ___you're___ going to have to put aside individual differences and play together for the sake of ___your___ team.

OTHER WORDS FREQUENTLY CONFUSED

Following is a list of other words that people frequently confuse. Complete the activities for each set of words, and check off and study the words that give you trouble.

a, an   Both *a* and *an* are used before other words to mean, approximately, "one."

Generally you should use *an* before words starting with a vowel (*a, e, i, o, u*):

> an ache   an experiment   an elephant   an idiot   an ox

Generally you should use *a* before words starting with a consonant (all other letters):

> a card   a brain   a cheat   a television   a gambler

Fill in the blanks: The girls had ___an___ argument over ___a___ former boyfriend.

accept (ăk sĕpt′)   receive; agree to
except (ĕk sĕpt′)   exclude; but

> "I would *accept* your loan," said Nga to the bartender, "*except* that I'm not ready to pay 25 percent interest."

Fill in the blanks: ___Except___ for the fact that she can't ___accept___ any criticism, Lori is a good friend.

advice (ăd vīs′)   noun meaning "an opinion"
advise (ăd vīz′)   verb meaning "to counsel, to give advice"

> I *advise* you to take the *advice* of your friends and stop working so hard.

Fill in the blanks: I ___advise___ you to listen carefully to any ___advice___ you get from your boss.

affect (uh fĕkt′)   verb meaning "to influence"
effect (ĭ fĕkt′)   verb meaning "to bring about something"; noun meaning "result"

The full *effects* of marijuana and alcohol on the body are only partly known; however, both drugs clearly *affect* the brain in various ways.

Fill in the blanks: The new tax laws go into _____effect_____ next month, and they are going to _____affect_____ your income tax deductions.

among   implies three or more
between   implies only two

We had to choose from *among* 125 shades of paint but *between* only 2 fabrics.

Fill in the blanks: The layoff notices distributed _____among_____ the unhappy workers gave them a choice _____between_____ working for another month at full pay and leaving immediately with two weeks' pay.

beside   along the side of
besides   in addition to

I was lucky I wasn't standing *beside* the car when it was hit.
Besides being unattractive, these uniforms are impractical.

Fill in the blanks: _____Besides_____ the colour printer Jeff bought recently, he also has a scanner _____beside_____ his computer.

desert (dĕz′ ərt)   stretch of dry land; (di zûrt′) to abandon one's post or duty
dessert (dĭ zûrt′)   last part of a meal

Sweltering in the *desert*, I was tormented by the thought of an icy *dessert*.

Fill in the blanks: After the meal, they carried their _____dessert_____ into the living room so that they would not miss the start of the old _____desert_____ movie about Lawrence of Arabia.

fewer   used with things that can be counted
less   refers to amount, value, or degree

There were *fewer* than seven people in all my classes today.
I seem to feel *less* tired when I exercise regularly.

Fill in the blanks: With _____fewer_____ people driving large cars, we are importing _____less_____ oil than we used to.

loose (lōōs)   not fastened; not tight-fitting
lose (lōōz)   misplace; fail to win

Phil's belt is so *loose* that he always looks ready to *lose* his pants.

Fill in the blanks: At least once a week our neighbours ___lose___ their dog; it's because they let him run ___loose___.

quiet (kwī′ ĭt)   peaceful
quite (kwīt)   entirely; really; rather

After a busy day, the children are now *quiet,* and their parents are *quite* tired.

Fill in the blanks: The ___quiet___ halls of the church become ___quite___ lively during swing dance evenings.

though (thō)   despite the fact that
thought (thôt)   past form of *think*

Even *though* she worked, she *thought* she would have time to go to school.

Fill in the blanks: Yoshiko ___thought___ she would like her job, but even ___though___ the pay was good, she hated the travelling involved.

▪ Review Test 1

Underline the correct word in the parentheses. Don't try to guess. If necessary, look back at the explanations of the words.

1. Please take my (advice, advise) and (where, <u>wear</u>) something warm and practical, rather (<u>than</u>, then) something fashionable and flimsy.

2. Glen felt that if he could (loose, lose) ten kilos, the (affect, effect) on his social life might be dramatic.

3. (Their, There, <u>They're</u>) going to show seven horror films at (their, there, they're) Halloween night festival; I hope you'll be (their, there, they're).

4. (Your, <u>You're</u>) going to have to do (a, an) better job on (<u>your</u>, you're) final exam if you expect to pass the (coarse, <u>course</u>).

5. Those (to, too, <u>two</u>) issues are (to, <u>too</u>, two) hot for any politician (to, too, two) handle.

6. Even (<u>though</u>, thought) the (<u>brakes</u>, breaks) on my car were worn, I did not have (quiet, <u>quite</u>) enough money to get them replaced (<u>right</u>, write) away.

7. (<u>Accept</u>, Except) for the fact that my neighbour prowls the halls in his bathrobe in (<u>plain</u>, plane) view of all the other tenants, he is (know, <u>no</u>) stranger (<u>than</u>, then) anyone else in this rooming house.

8. Because the Randalls are so neat and fussy, (its, <u>it's</u>) hard (<u>to</u>, too, two) feel comfortable when (<u>your</u>, you're) in (<u>their</u>, there, they're) house.

9. (Whose, <u>Who's</u>) the culprit who left the paint can on the table? The paint has ruined a (knew, <u>new</u>) tablecloth, and (its, <u>it's</u>) soaked (threw, <u>through</u>) the linen and (<u>affected</u>, effected) the varnish stain on the table.

10. I would have been angry at the car that (passed, past) me at one hundred kilometres an hour on the highway, (accept, except) that I (knew, new) it would not get (passed, past) the speed trap (to, too, two) kilometres down the road.

Review Test 2

On a separate piece of paper, write short sentences using the ten words shown below.

their	principal
its	except
you're	past
too	through
then	who's

CHAPTER 41

Effective Word Choice

> ### *Introductory Project*
>
> Put a check beside the sentence in each pair that you feel makes more effective use of words.
>
> 1. I flipped out when Faith broke our date. _____
>
>   I got very angry when Faith broke our date. _____
>
> 2. Doctors as dedicated as Dr. Khan are few and far between. _____
>
>   Doctors as dedicated as Dr. Khan are rare. _____
>
> 3. Yesterday I ascertained that Elena and Wes broke up. _____
>
>   Yesterday I found out that Elena and Wes broke up. _____
>
> 4. Judging by the looks of things, it seems to me that it will probably rain very soon. _____
>
>   It looks as though it will rain soon. _____
>
> Now see if you can circle the correct number in each case:
>
> Pair (1, 2, 3, 4) contains a sentence with slang.
>
> Pair (1, 2, 3, 4) contains a sentence with a cliché.
>
> Pair (1, 2, 3, 4) contains a sentence with a pretentious word.
>
> Pair (1, 2, 3, 4) contains a wordy sentence.
>
> Answers are on page 556.

Choose your words carefully when you write. Always take the time to think about your word choices rather than simply using the first word that comes to mind. You want to develop the habit of selecting words that are appropriate and exact for your purposes. One way you can show sensitivity to language is by avoiding slang, clichés, pretentious words, and wordiness.

SLANG

We often use slang expressions when we talk because they are so vivid and colourful. However, slang is usually out of place in formal writing. Here are some examples of slang expressions:

My girlfriend *got straight* with me by saying she wanted to see other men.
Rick spent all Saturday *messing around* with his stereo.
My boss keeps *riding* me about coming to work on time.
The tires on the SUV make the car look like *something else.*
The crowd was *psyched up* when the game began.

Slang expressions have a number of drawbacks: they go out of date quickly, they become tiresome if used excessively in writing, and they may communicate clearly to some readers but not to others. Also, the use of slang can be a way of evading the specific details that are often needed to make one's meaning clear in writing. For example, in "The tires on the SUV make the car look like something else," the writer has not provided the specific details about the tires necessary for us to understand the statement clearly. In general, then, you should avoid slang in your writing. If you are in doubt about whether an expression is slang, it may help to check a recently published dictionary.

Activity

Rewrite the following sentences, replacing the italicized slang words with more formal ones.

Example   The movie was a *real bomb,* so we *cut out* early.
The movie was terrible, so we left early.

1. My boss *came down on me* for *goofing off* on the job.

   _____

   _____

2. The car was a *steal* for the money until the owner *jacked up* the price.

   _____

   _____

3. If the instructor stops *hassling* me, I am going to *get my act together* in the course.

   _____

   _____

CLICHÉS

A cliché is an expression that has been worn out through constant use. Some typical clichés are listed below:

Clichés

all work and no play	saw the light
at a loss for words	short but sweet
better late than never	sigh of relief
drop in the bucket	singing the blues
easier said than done	taking a big chance
had a hard time of it	time and time again
in the nick of time	too close for comfort
in this day and age	too little, too late
it dawned on me	took a turn for the worse
it goes without saying	under the weather
last but not least	where he (she) is
make ends meet	coming from
on top of the world	word to the wise
sad but true	work like a dog

Clichés are common in speech but make your writing seem tired and stale. Also, clichés—like slang—are often a way of evading the specific details that you must work to provide in your writing. You should, then, avoid clichés and try to express your meaning in fresh, original ways.

Activity

Underline the cliché in each of the following sentences. Then substitute specific, fresh words for the trite expression.

Example   I passed the test <u>by the skin of my teeth</u>.

I barely passed the test.

1. Anyone turning in a paper late is throwing caution to the winds.

   _____

2. Yolanda doesn't make any bones about her ambition.

   _____

3. I met with my instructor to try to iron out the problems in my paper.

   _____

PRETENTIOUS WORDS

Some people feel they can improve their writing by using fancy and elevated words rather than simple and natural words. They use artificial and stilted language that more often obscures their meaning than communicates it clearly.

Here are some unnatural-sounding sentences:

I comprehended her statement.

While partaking of our morning meal, we engaged in an animated conversation.

I am a stranger to excessive financial sums.

Law enforcement officers directed traffic when the lights malfunctioned.

The same thoughts can be expressed more clearly and effectively by using plain, natural language, as below:

I understood what she said.

While eating breakfast, we had a lively talk.

I have never had much money.

Police officers directed traffic when the lights stopped working.

Activity

Cross out the artificial words in each sentence. Then substitute clear, simple language for the artificial words.

Example   The manager ~~reproached~~ me for my ~~tardiness~~.

The manager criticized me for being late.

1. One of Irina's objectives in life is to accomplish a large family.

   _____

   _____

2. Upon entering our residence, we detected smoke in the atmosphere.

   _____

   _____

3. I am not apprehensive about the test, which encompasses five chapters of the book.

   _____

   _____

WORDINESS

Wordiness—using more words than necessary to express a meaning—is often a sign of lazy or careless writing. Your readers may resent the extra time and energy they must spend when you have not done the work needed to make your writing direct and concise.

Here are examples of wordy sentences:

Anna is of the opinion that the death penalty should be allowed.

I would like to say that my subject in this paper will be the kind of generous person that my father was.

Omitting needless words improves the sentences:

Anna supports the death penalty.

My father was a generous person.

The following box lists some wordy expressions that could be reduced to single words.

Wordy Form	*Short Form*
a large number of	many
a period of the week	a week
arrive at an agreement	agree
at an earlier point in time	before
at the present time	now
big in size	big
owing to the fact that	because
during the time that	while
five in number	five
for the reason that	because
good benefit	benefit
in every instance	always
in my own opinion	I think
in the event that	if
in the near future	soon
in this day and age	today
is able to	can
large in size	large
plan ahead for the future	plan
postponed until later	postponed
red in colour	red
return back	return

Activity

Rewrite the following sentences, omitting needless words.

1. After a lot of careful thinking, I have arrived at the conclusion that drunken drivers should receive jail terms.

    _____

    _____

2. The movie that I went to last night, which was fairly interesting, I must say, was enjoyed by me and my girlfriend.

    _____

    _____

3. Owing to inclement weather conditions of wind and rain, we have decided not to proceed with the athletic competition about to take place on the baseball diamond.

    _____

    _____

4. Without any question, there should be a law making it a requirement for parents of young children to buckle the children into car seats for safety.

    _____

    _____

5. Beyond a doubt, the only two things you can rely or depend on would be the sure facts that death comes to everyone and that the government will tax your yearly income.

    _____

    _____

■ Review Test 1

Certain words are italicized in the following sentences. In the space provided, identify the words as *slang* (S), *clichés* (C), or *pretentious words* (PW). Then rewrite the sentences, replacing the words with more effective diction.

_____ 1. We're *psyched* for tonight's Maestro concert, which is going to be *totally awesome.*

    _____

    _____

_____ 2. Getting good grades in college courses is sometimes *easier said than done.*

    _____

    _____

_____   3. I *availed myself* of the chance to *participate* in the computer course.

_____

_____

_____   4. The victims of the car accident were shaken but *none the worse for wear*.

_____

_____

_____   5. My roommate *pulled an all-nighter* and almost *conked out* during the exam.

_____

_____

▪ Review Test 2

Rewrite the following sentences, omitting needless words.

1. Workers who are on a part-time basis are attractive to a business because they do not have to be paid as much as full-time workers for a business.

2. During the time that I was sick and out of school, I missed a total of three math tests.

3. The game, which was scheduled for later today, has been cancelled by the officials because of the rainy weather.

4. At this point in time, I am quite undecided and unsure about just which classes I will take during this coming semester.

5. An inconsiderate person located in the apartment next to mine keeps her radio on too loud a good deal of the time, with the result being that it is disturbing to everyone in the neighbouring apartments.

Sentence Variety

One aspect of effective writing is to vary the kinds of sentences you write. If every sentence follows the same pattern, writing may become monotonous to read. This chapter explains four ways you can create variety and interest in your writing style. The first two ways involve coordination and subordination—important techniques for achieving different kinds of emphasis in writing.

The following are four methods you can use to make your sentences more varied and more sophisticated:

1 Add a second complete thought (coordination).
2 Add a dependent thought (subordination).
3 Begin with a special opening word or phrase.
4 Place adjectives or verbs in a series.

Each method will be discussed in turn.

ADD A SECOND COMPLETE THOUGHT

When you add a second complete thought to a simple sentence, the result is a compound (or double) sentence. The two complete statements in a compound sentence are usually connected by a comma plus a joining, or coordinating, word *(and, but, for, or, nor, so, yet)*.

A compound sentence is used when you want to give equal weight to two closely related ideas. The technique of showing that ideas have equal importance is called *coordination.*

Following are some compound sentences. Each contains two ideas that the writer regards as equal in importance.

> Barry has stopped smoking cigarettes, but he is now addicted to chewing gum.

I repeatedly failed the math quizzes, so I decided to drop the course.

Stan turned all the lights off, and then he locked the office door.

Activity

Combine the following pairs of simple sentences into compound sentences. Use a comma and a logical joining word *(and, but, for, so)* to connect each pair.

Note: If you are not sure what *and, but, for,* and *so* mean, review pages 274 and 275.

Example   • The record kept skipping.
              • There was dust on the needle.

The record kept skipping, for there was dust on the needle.

1. • The line at the deli counter was long.
    • Jake took a numbered ticket anyway.

    _____

2. • Vandals smashed the car's headlights.
    • They slashed the tires as well.

    _____

3. • I married at age seventeen.
    • I never got a chance to live on my own.

    _____

4. • Mold grew on my leather boots.
    • The closet was warm and humid.

    _____

5. • My father has a high cholesterol count.
    • He continues to eat red meat almost every day.

    _____

ADD A DEPENDENT THOUGHT

When you add a dependent thought to a simple sentence, the result is a complex sentence.* A dependent thought begins with a word or phrase like one of the following:

*The two parts of a complex sentence are sometimes called an *independent clause* and a *dependent clause*. A *clause* is simply a word group that contains a subject and a verb. An independent clause expresses a complete thought and can stand alone. A dependent clause does not express a complete thought in itself and "depends on" the independent clause to complete its meaning. Dependent clauses always begin with a dependent, or subordinating, word.

	Dependent Words	
after	if, even if	when, whenever
although, though	in order that	where, wherever
as	since	whether
because	that, so that	which, whichever
before	unless	while
even though	until	who, whoever
how	what, whatever	whose

A complex sentence is used when you want to emphasize one idea over another within a sentence. Look at the following complex sentence:

Although I lowered the thermostat, my heating bill remained high.

The idea that the writer wants to emphasize here—*my heating bill remained high*— is expressed as a complete thought. The less important idea—*Although I lowered my thermostat*—is subordinated to this complete thought. The technique of giving one idea less emphasis than another is called *subordination*.

Following are other examples of complex sentences. In each case, the part starting with the dependent word is the less emphasized part of the sentence.

Even though I was tired, I stayed up to watch the horror movie.

Before I take a bath, I check for spiders in the tub.

When Ivy feels nervous, she pulls on her earlobe.

Activity

Use logical subordinating words to combine the following pairs of simple sentences into sentences that contain a dependent thought. Place a comma after a dependent statement when it starts the sentence.

Example • Our team lost.
• We were not invited to the tournament.

Because our team lost, we were not invited to the tournament.

1. • I receive my degree in June.
   • I will begin applying for jobs.

   _____

   _____

2. • Kyra doesn't enjoy cooking.
   • She often eats at fast-food restaurants.

   _____

   _____

3. • I sent several letters of complaint.
   • The electric company never corrected my bill.

   _____

   _____

4. • Marc's car went into a skid.
   • He took his foot off the gas pedal.

   _____

   _____

5. • The final exam covered sixteen chapters.
   • The students complained.

   _____

   _____

BEGIN WITH A SPECIAL OPENING WORD OR PHRASE

Among the special openers that can be used to start sentences are (1) *-ed* words, (2) *-ing* words, (3) *-ly* words, (4) *to* word groups, and (5) prepositional phrases. Here are examples of all five kinds of openers:

-ed *word*	Tired from a long day of work, Sharon fell asleep on the sofa.
-ing *word*	Using a thick towel, Chan dried his hair quickly.
-ly *word*	Reluctantly, I agreed to rewrite the paper.
to *word group*	To get to the church on time, you must leave now.
Prepositional phrase	With Mark's help, Samantha planted the evergreen shrubs.

Activity

Combine the simple sentences into one sentence by using the opener shown in the margin and omitting repeated words. Use a comma to set off the opener from the rest of the sentence.

Example   *-ing* word: • The toaster refused to pop up.
   • It buzzed like an angry hornet.

   Buzzing like an angry hornet, the toaster refused

   to pop up.

-ed word

1. • Dimitri was annoyed by the poor TV reception.
   • He decided to get a satellite dish.

   _____

   _____

-ing word

2. • The star player glided down the court.
   • He dribbled the basketball like a pro.

_____

_____

-ly word

3. • Food will run short on our crowded planet.
   • It is inevitable.

_____

_____

to word group

4. • Andrew rented a limousine for the night.
   • He wanted to make a good impression.

_____

_____

prepositional
phrase

5. • Saysha answered the telephone.
   • She did this at 4 a.m.

_____

_____

-ed word

6. • Nathan dreaded the coming holidays.
   • He was depressed by his recent divorce.

_____

_____

-ing word

7. • The people pressed against the doors of the theatre.
   • They pushed and shoved each other.

_____

_____

-ly word

8. • I waited in the packed emergency room.
   • I was impatient.

_____

_____

to word group

9. • The little boy likes to annoy his parents.
   • He pretends he can't hear them.

_____

_____

prepositional
phrase

10. • People must wear white-soled shoes.
    • They must do this in the gym.

    _____

    _____

PLACE ADJECTIVES OR VERBS IN A SERIES

Various parts of a sentence may be placed in a series. Among these parts are adjectives (descriptive words) and verbs. Here are examples of both in a series.

Adjectives   The *black, smeary* newsprint rubbed off on my *new butcher-block* table.

Verbs   The quarterback *fumbled* the ball, *recovered* it, and *sighed* with relief.

Activity

Combine the simple sentences in each group into one sentence by using adjectives or verbs in a series and by omitting repeated words. In most cases, use a comma between the adjectives or verbs in a series.

Example   • Before Christmas, I made fruitcakes.
            • I decorated the house.
            • I wrapped dozens of toys.

            Before Christmas, I made fruitcakes, decorated the house, and

            wrapped dozens of toys.

1. • My lumpy mattress was giving me a cramp in my neck.
   • It was causing pains in my back.
   • It was making me lose sleep.

   _____

   _____

2. • Lights appeared in the fog.
   • The lights were flashing.
   • The lights were red.
   • The fog was grey.
   • The fog was soupy.

   _____

   _____

3. • Before going to bed, I locked all the doors.
   • I activated the burglar alarm.

- I slipped my wallet under my mattress.

_____

_____

4. • Joanna picked sweater hairs off her coat.
   • The hairs were fuzzy.
   • The hairs were white.
   • The coat was brown.
   • The coat was suede.

_____

_____

5. • The contact lens fell onto the floor.
   • The contact lens was thin.
   • The contact lens was slippery.
   • The floor was dirty.
   • The floor was tiled.

_____

_____

Review Test 1

On a separate piece of paper, use coordination or subordination to combine each of the following groups of simple sentences into one or more longer sentences. Omit repeated words. Since various combinations are possible, you might want to jot down several combinations in each case. Then read them aloud to find the combination that sounds best.

Keep in mind that very often the relationship among ideas in a sentence will be clearer when subordinating rather than coordinating words are used.

Example   • I don't like to ask for favours.
               • I must borrow money from my brother-in-law.
               • I know he won't turn me down.
               • I still feel guilty about it.

I don't like to ask for favours, but I must borrow money from my brother-in-law. Although I know he won't turn me down, I still feel guilty about it.

Comma Hints

a   Use a comma at the end of a word group that starts with a subordinating word (as in "Although I know he won't turn me down, …")

b   Use a comma between independent word groups connected by *and, but, for, or, nor, so, yet* (as in "I don't like to ask for favours, but …").

1. • My grandmother is eighty-six.
   • She drives to Florida alone every year.
   • She believes in being self-reliant.

2. • His name was called.
   • Luis walked into the examining room.
   • He was nervous.
   • He was determined to ask the doctor for a straight answer.

3. • They left twenty minutes early for class.
   • They were late anyway.
   • The car overheated.

4. • Jake failed the midterm exam.
   • He studied harder for the final.
   • He passed it.

5. • A volcano erupts.
   • It sends tonnes of ash into the air.
   • This creates flaming orange sunsets.

6. • Fernando got home from the shopping mall.
   • He discovered that his rented tuxedo did not fit.
   • The jacket sleeves covered his hands.
   • The pants cuffs hung over his shoes.

7. • The boys waited for the bus.
   • The wind shook the flimsy shelter.
   • They shivered with cold.
   • They were wearing thin jackets.

8. • The engine almost caught.
   • Then it died.
   • I realized no help would come.
   • I was on a lonely road.
   • It was very late.

9. • Miriam wanted white wall-to-wall carpeting.
   • She knew it was a bad buy.
   • It would look beautiful.
   • It would be very hard to clean.

10. • Gordon was leaving the store.
    • The shoplifting alarm went off.
    • He had not stolen anything.
    • The clerk had forgotten to remove the magnetic tag.
    • The tag was on a shirt Gordon had bought.

■ Review Test 2

On separate paper, write two sentences of your own that begin with (1) *-ed* words, (2) *-ing* words, (3) *-ly* words, (4) *to* word groups, and (5) prepositional phrases. Also write two sentences of your own that contain (6) a series of adjectives and (7) a series of verbs.

Explaining a Process • Examining Cause and Effect • Comparing or Contrasting • Defin
Term • Dividing and Classifying • Describing a Scene or Person • Narrating an Event • Ar
a Position • Explaining a Process • Examining Cause and Effect • Comparing or Contras
Defining a Term • Dividing and Classifying • Describing a Scene or Person • Narrating an
Arguing a Position • Explaining a Process • Examining Cause and Effect • Compari

CHAPTER 43

ESL Pointers

This section covers rules that most native speakers of English take for granted; nonetheless, the following is useful information for speakers of English as a second language (ESL).

ARTICLES WITH COUNT AND NON-COUNT NOUNS

Articles are noun markers—they signal that a noun will follow. The indefinite articles are *a* and *an*. (Use *a* before a word that begins with a consonant sound: **a** car, **a** piano, **a** uniform—the *u* in *uniform* sounds like the consonant *y* plus *u*. Use *an* before a word beginning with a vowel sound: **an** egg, **an** office, **an** honour—the *h* in *honour* is silent.) The definite article is *the*. An article may immediately precede a noun: **a** smile, **the** reason, or it may be separated from the noun by modifiers: **a** slight smile, **the** very best reason.

To know whether to use an article with a noun and which article to use, you must recognize count and non-count nouns. (A noun is a word used to name something—a person, place, thing, or idea.)

Note: There are various other noun markers, including quantity words (*some, several, a lot of*), numerals (*one, ten, 120*), demonstrative adjectives (*this, these*), possessive adjectives (*my, your, our*), and possessive nouns (*Jaime's, the school's*).

- **Count nouns** name people, places, things, or ideas that can be counted and made into plurals, such as *teacher, washroom,* and *joke* (*one teacher, two washrooms, three jokes*).
- **Non-count nouns** refer to things or ideas that cannot be counted, such as *flour, history,* and *truth.* The box below lists and illustrates common types of non-count nouns.

> ### *Common Non-Count Nouns*
>
> *Abstractions and emotions:* anger, bravery, health, pride, truth
> *Activities:* baseball, jogging, reading, teaching, travel
> *Foods:* bread, broccoli, chocolate, cheese, flour
> *Gases and vapours:* air, helium, oxygen, smoke, steam
> *Languages and areas of study:* Korean, Spanish, algebra, history, physics
> *Liquids:* blood, gasoline, lemonade, tea, water
> *Materials that come in bulk form:* aluminum, cloth, dust, sand, soap
> *Natural occurrences:* magnetism, moonlight, rain, snow, thunder
> *Other things that cannot be counted:* clothing, furniture, homework, machinery, money, news, transportation, vocabulary, work

The quantity of a non-count noun can be expressed with a word or words called a **qualifier**, such as *some, a lot of, a unit of,* and so on. (In the following two examples, the qualifiers are shown in *italic* type, and the noncount nouns are shown in **boldface** type.)

> Please have *some* **patience**.
> We need to buy *two bags of* **flour** today.

Some words can be either count or non-count nouns depending on whether they refer to one or more individual items or to something in general.

> Certain **cheeses** give some people headaches.

This sentence refers to individual cheeses; *cheese* in this case is a count noun.

> **Cheese** is made in almost every country where milk is produced.

This sentence refers to cheese in general; in this case, *cheese* is a non-count noun.

Using *a* or *an* with non-specific singular count nouns

Use *a* or *an* with singular nouns that are non-specific. A noun is non-specific when the reader doesn't know its specific identity.

> **A** left-hander faces special challenges with right-handed tools.

The sentence refers to any left-hander, not a specific one.

> Today, our cat proudly brought **a** baby bird into the house.

The reader isn't familiar with the bird. This is the first time it is mentioned.

Using *the* with specific nouns

In general, use *the* with all specific nouns—specific singular, plural, and non-count nouns.

Following are conditions that make a noun specific and therefore require the article *the*.

A noun is specific in the following cases:

- When it has already been mentioned once

  Today, our cat proudly brought a baby bird into the house. Luckily, **the** bird was still alive.

  The is used with the second mention of *bird*.

- When it is identified by a word or phrase in the sentence

  The pockets in the boy's pants are often filled with sand and dirt.

  Pockets is identified by the words *in the boy's pants.*

- When its identity is suggested by the general context

  At Willy's Diner last night, **the** service was terrible and **the** food was worse.

  The reader can conclude that the service and food being discussed were at Willy's Diner.

- When it is unique

  There will be an eclipse of **the** moon tonight.

  Earth has only one moon.

- When it is preceded by a superlative adjective (*best, biggest, wisest*)

  The best way to store broccoli is to refrigerate it in an open plastic bag.

Omitting articles

Omit articles with non-specific plurals and non-count nouns. Plurals and non-count nouns are non-specific when they refer to something in general.

Pockets didn't exist until the end of the 1700s.
Service is as important as **food** to a restaurant's success.
Iris serves her children home-made **lemonade**.

Using *the* with proper nouns

Proper nouns name particular people, places, things, or ideas and are always capitalized. Most proper nouns do not require articles; those that do, however, require *the*. Following are general guidelines about when and when not to use *the*.

Do not use *the* for most singular proper nouns, including names of the following:

- *People and animals* (Jean Chrétien, Fido)
- *Continents, provinces or state , cities, streets,* and *parks* (North America, Canada, Alberta, Lethbridge, Portage Street, Banff National Park)
- *Most countries* (France, Mexico, Russia)

- *Individual bodies of water, islands, and mountains* (Lake Erie, Prince Edward Island, Mount Everest)

Use *the* for the following types of proper nouns:

- *Plural proper nouns* (the Turners, the United States, the Great Lakes, the Rocky Mountains)
- *Names of large geographic areas, deserts, oceans, seas,* and *rivers* (the South, the Gobi Desert, the Atlantic Ocean, the Black Sea, the Mississippi River)
- *Names with the format* the _____ of _____ (the People's Republic of China, the University of Manitoba)

Activity

Underline the correct form of the noun in parentheses.

1. (A library, Library) is a valuable addition to a town.

2. This morning, the mail carrier brought me (a letter, the letter) from my cousin.

3. As I read (a letter, the letter), I began to laugh at what my cousin wrote.

4. Every night we have to do lots of (homework, homeworks).

5. We are going to visit our friends in (the British Columbia, British Columbia) next week.

6. Children should treat their parents with (the respect, respect).

7. The soldiers in battle showed a great deal of (courage, courages).

8. A famous park in Toronto is (High Park, the High Park).

9. My son would like to eat (the spaghetti, spaghetti) at every meal.

10. It is dangerous to stare directly at (the sun, sun).

SUBJECTS AND VERBS

Avoiding Repeated Subjects

In English, a particular subject can be used only once in a clause. Do not repeat a subject in the same clause by following a noun with a pronoun.

Incorrect: The *manager he* asked Dimitri to lock up tonight.
Correct: The **manager** asked Dimitri to lock up tonight.
Correct: **He** asked Dimitri to lock up tonight.

Even when the subject and verb are separated by a long word group, the subject cannot be repeated in the same clause.

Incorrect: The *girl* that danced with you *she is* my cousin.
Correct: The **girl** that danced with you **is** my cousin.

Including Pronoun Subjects and Linking Verbs

Some languages may omit a pronoun as a subject, but in English, every clause other than a command must have a subject. (In a command, the subject *you* is understood: [**You**] Hand in your papers now.)

Incorrect: The Yellowhead Highway is in central Alberta. Runs across the province.
Correct: The Yellowhead Highway is in central Alberta. **It** runs across the province.

Every English clause must also have a verb, even when the meaning of the clause is clear without the verb.

Incorrect: Angelita's piano teacher very patient.
Correct: Angelita's piano teacher is very patient.

Including *there* and *here* at the Beginning of Clauses

Some English sentences begin with *there* or *here* plus a linking verb (usually a form of *to be: is, are,* and so on). In such sentences, the verb comes before the subject.

There are masks in every culture on Earth.

The subject is the plural noun *masks,* so the plural verb *are* is used.

Here is your driver's licence.

The subject is the singular noun *licence,* so the singular verb *is* is used.
In sentences like the above, remember not to omit *there* or *here.*

Incorrect: *Are* several chickens in the Bensons' yard.
Correct: **There are** several chickens in the Bensons' yard.

Not Using the Progressive (or Continuous) Tense of Certain Verbs

The progressive (or continuous) tenses are made up of forms of *be* plus the *-ing* form of the main verb. They express actions or conditions still in progress at a particular time.

George **will be taking** classes this summer.

However, verbs for mental states, the senses, possession, and inclusion are normally not used in the progressive tense.

Incorrect: All during the movie they *were hearing* whispers behind them.
Correct: All during the movie they **heard** whispers behind them.

Incorrect: That box *is containing* a surprise for Paulo.
Correct: That box **contains** a surprise for Paulo.

Common verbs not generally used in the progressive tense are listed in the box below.

Common Verbs Not Generally Used in the Progressive Tense

Thoughts, attitudes and *desires*: agree, believe, imagine, know, like, love, prefer, think, understand, want, wish

Sense perceptions: hear, see, smell, taste

Appearances: appear, seem, look

Possession: belong, have, own, possess

Inclusion: contain, include

Using Only Transitive Verbs for the Passive Voice

Only *transitive* verbs—verbs that need direct objects to complete their meaning—can have a passive form (one in which the subject receives the action instead of performing it). Intransitive verbs cannot be used in the passive voice.

Incorrect: If you don't fix those brakes, an accident *may be happened.*

Happen is an intransitive verb—no object is needed to complete its meaning.

Correct: If you don't fix those brakes, an accident **may happen.**

If you are not sure whether a verb is transitive or intransitive, check your dictionary. Transitive verbs are indicated with an abbreviation such as *tr. v.* or *v. t.* Intransitive verbs are indicated with an abbreviation such as *intr. v.* or *v. i.*

Using Gerunds and Infinitives after Verbs (Idiomatic Verb Structures)

A gerund is the *-ing* form of a verb that is used as a noun: For Walter, **eating** is a day-long activity. An infinitive is *to* plus the basic form of the verb (the form in which the verb is listed in the dictionary): **to eat**. The infinitive can function as an adverb, an adjective, or a noun. Some verbs can be followed by only a gerund or only an infinitive; other verbs can be followed by either. Examples are given in the following lists. There are many others; watch for them in your reading.

Verb + gerund   (*admit + stealing*)
Verb + preposition + gerund   (*apologize + for + yelling*)

Some verbs can be followed by a gerund but not by an infinitive. In many cases, there is a preposition (such as *for, in,* or *of*) between the verb and the gerund. Following are some verbs and verb/preposition combinations that can be followed by gerunds but not by infinitives:

admit	deny	look forward to
apologize for	discuss	postpone
appreciate	dislike	practise
approve of	enjoy	suspect of
avoid	feel like	talk about
be used to	finish	thank for
believe in	insist on	think about

Incorrect: He must *avoid to jog* until his knee heals.
Correct: He must **avoid jogging** until his knee heals.

Incorrect: The instructor *apologized for to be* late to class.
Correct: The instructor **apologized for** being late to class.

Verb + infinitive   (*agree + to leave*)

Following are common verbs that can be followed by an infinitive but not by a gerund:

agree	decide	plan
arrange	have	refuse
claim	manage	wait

Incorrect: The children *want going* to the beach.
Correct: The children **want to go** to the beach.

Verb + noun or pronoun + infinitive   (*cause + them + to flee*)

Below are common verbs that are first followed by a noun or pronoun and then by an infinitive (not a gerund):

cause	force	remind
command	persuade	warn

Incorrect: The coach *persuaded Mario studying* harder.
Correct: The coach **persuaded Mario to study** harder.

Following are common verbs that can be followed either by an infinitive alone or by a noun or pronoun and an infinitive:

ask	need	want
expect	promise	would like

Dena **asked to have a day** off next week.

Her boss **asked her to work** on Saturday.

Verb + gerund or infinitive   (*begin + packing* or *begin + to pack*)

Following are verbs that can be followed by either a gerund or an infinitive:

begin	hate	prefer
continue	love	start

The meaning of each of the above verbs remains the same or almost the same whether a gerund or an infinitive is used.

Zoe hates **being** late.

Zoe hates **to be** late.

With the verbs below, the gerunds and the infinitives have very different meanings.

    forget   remember   stop

    Esta **stopped to call** home.

She interrupted something to call home.

    Esta **stopped calling** home.

She discontinued calling home.

Activity

Underline the correct form in parentheses.

1. The doctor (asked me, she asked me) if I smoked.
2. The coffee is very fresh. (Is, It is) strong and delicious.
3. (Are mice, There are mice) living in our kitchen.
4. The box (is containing, contains) a beautiful necklace.
5. Unless you take your foot off the brake, the car will not (be gone, go).
6. Most basketball players (very tall, are very tall).
7. Many people (enjoy to spend, enjoy spending) a day in the city.
8. The teacher (plans taking, plans to take) us on a field trip tomorrow.
9. Some old men in my neighbourhood (play cards, they play cards) every afternoon.
10. When I am happy, I feel like (to sing, singing).

ADJECTIVES

Following the Order of Adjectives in English

Adjectives modify nouns and pronouns. In English, an adjective usually comes directly before the word it describes or after a linking verb (a form of *be* or a verb of appearance or perception such as *look*, *seem* and *taste*), in which case it modifies the subject. In each of the following two sentences, the adjective is **boldfaced** and the noun it describes is *italicized*.

    That is a **false** *story*.
    The *story* is **false**.

When more than one adjective modifies the same noun, the adjectives are usually stated in a certain order, though there are often exceptions. Following is a list of the typical order of English adjectives:

Typical Order of Adjectives in a Series

1 **An article or other noun marker**: a, an, the, Lee's, this, three, your
2 **Opinion adjective**: dull, handsome, unfair, useful
3 **Size**: big, huge, little, tiny
4 **Shape**: long, short, round, square
5 **Age**: ancient, medieval, old, new, young
6 **Colour**: blue, green, scarlet, white
7 **Nationality**: Italian, Korean, Mexican, Vietnamese
8 **Religion**: Buddhist, Catholic, Jewish, Muslim
9 **Material**: cardboard, gold, marble, silk
10 **Noun used as an adjective**: house (as in *house call*), tea (as in *tea bag*), wall (as in *wall hanging*)

Here are some examples of the above order:

a long cotton scarf
the beautiful little silver cup
your new lavender evening gown
Anna's sweet Italian grandmother

In general, use no more than *two or three* adjectives after the article or other noun marker. Numerous adjectives in a series can be awkward: **the beautiful big new blue cotton** sweater.

Using the Present and Past Participles as Adjectives

The present participle ends in -*ing*. Past participles of regular verbs end in -*ed* or -*d*; a list of the past participles of many common irregular verbs begins on page 284. Both types of participles may be used as adjectives. A participle used as an adjective may precede the word it describes: It was an **exciting** *ballgame*. It may also follow a linking verb and describe the subject of the sentence: The *ballgame* was **exciting**.

While both present and past participles of a particular verb may be used as adjectives, their meanings differ. Use the present participle to describe whoever or whatever causes a feeling: an **embarrassing** *incident* (the incident is what causes the embarrassment). Use the past participle to describe whoever or whatever experiences the feeling: the **embarrassed** *parents* (the parents are the ones who are embarrassed).

The long day of holiday shopping was **tiring.**
The shoppers were **tired.**

Following are pairs of present and past participles with similar distinctions:

annoying / annoyed	exhausting / exhausted
boring / bored	fascinating / fascinated
confusing / confused	frightening / frightened
depressing / depressed	surprising / surprised
exciting / excited	

Activity

Underline the correct form in parentheses.

1. The Johnsons live in a (stone big, big stone) house.

2. Mr. Kim runs a (popular Korean, Korean popular) restaurant.

3. For her party, the little girl asked if her mother would buy her a (beautiful long velvet, beautiful velvet long) dress.

4. When their son didn't come home by bedtime, Mr. and Mrs. Singh became (worried, worrying).

5. In the centre of the city is a church with (three enormous colourful stained-glass, three stained-glass colourful enormous) windows.

PREPOSITIONS USED FOR TIME AND PLACE

The use of prepositions in English is often idiomatic, and exceptions to general rules are not rare. Therefore, correct preposition use must be learned gradually through experience. Following is a chart showing how three of the most common prepositions are used in some customary references to time and place:

The Use of On, In, and At to Refer to Time and Place

Time

On a specific day: on Monday, on January 1, on your anniversary

In a part of a day: in the morning, in the daytime (but at night)

In a month or a year: in December, in 1867

In a period of time: in an hour, in a few days, in a while

At a specific time: at 10:00 a.m., at midnight, at sunset, at dinnertime

Place

On a surface: on the desk, on the counter, on a ceiling

In a place that is enclosed: in my room, in the office, in the box

At a specific location: at the mall, at his house, at the ballpark

---

Activity

Underline the correct preposition in parentheses.

1. Can you babysit for my children (on, at) Thursday?

2. Please come to my office (on, at) 3:00 p.m.

3. You will find some computer disks (in, on) the desk drawer.

4. Miguel will begin his new job (in, at) two weeks.

5. A fight broke out between two groups of friends (on, at) the park.

Review Test

Underline the correct form in parentheses.

1. During the storm, I was startled by the loud (thunder, thunders).

2. (Is, Here is) your new textbook.

3. The ending of the movie was very (surprised, surprising).

4. Many animals that sleep all day are active (at, in) night.

5. (The people, People) in the photograph are my mother's relatives.

6. The city streets were full of (big yellow, yellow big) taxis.

7. My friend and I (are usually agreeing, usually agree) with each other.

8. In the West, New Year's Day is celebrated (in, on) January 1.

9. If the weather is nice tomorrow, let's (think about to go, think about going) to the city ourselves.

10. Most (cheese, cheeses) are made from cow's milk, but others are made from milk of sheep or goats.

Combined
Mastery Tests

SENTENCE FRAGMENTS AND RUN-ONS

■ Combined Mastery Test 1

1. _____
2. _____
3. _____
4. _____
5. _____
6. _____
7. _____
8. _____
9. _____
10. _____
11. _____
12. _____
13. _____
14. _____
15. _____
16. _____
17. _____
18. _____
19. _____
20. _____

The word groups below are numbered 1 through 20. In the space provided for each, write *C* if a word group is a complete sentence, write *F* if it is a fragment, and write *R-O* if it is a run-on. Then correct the errors.

^{1}I had a frightening dream last night, I dreamed that I was walking high up on an old railroad trestle. ^{2}It looked like the one I used to walk on recklessly. ^{3}When I was about ten years old. ^{4}At that height, my palms were sweating, just as they did when I was a boy. ^{5}I could see the ground out of the corners of my eyes, I felt a swooning, sickening sensation. ^{6}Suddenly, I realized there were rats below. ^{7}Thousands upon thousands of rats. ^{8}They knew I was up on the trestle, they were laughing. ^{9}Because they were sure they would get me. ^{10}Their teeth glinted in the moonlight, their red eyes were like thousands of small reflectors. ^{11}That almost blinded my sight. ^{12}Sensing there was something even more hideous behind me. ^{13}I kept moving forward. ^{14}Then I realized that I was coming to a gap in the trestle. ^{15}There was no way I could stop or go back I would have to cross over that empty gap. ^{16}I leaped out in despair. ^{17}Knowing I would never make it. ^{18}And felt myself falling helplessly down to the swarm of rejoicing rats. ^{19}I woke up bathed in sweat. ^{20}Half expecting to find a rat in my bed.

> **Score**   Number correct _____ × 5 = _____ percent

SENTENCE FRAGMENTS AND RUN-ONS

■ Combined Mastery Test 2

The word groups below are numbered 1 through 20. In the space provided for each, write *C* if a word group is a complete sentence, write *F* if it is a fragment, and write *R-O* if it is a run-on. Then correct the errors.

1. _____

2. _____

3. _____

4. _____

5. _____

6. _____

7. _____

8. _____

9. _____

10. _____

11. _____

12. _____

13. _____

14. _____

15. _____

16. _____

17. _____

18. _____

19. _____

20. _____

[1]My sister asked my parents and me to give up television for two weeks. [2]As an experiment for her psychology class. [3]We were too embarrassed to refuse, we reluctantly agreed. [4]The project began on a Monday morning. [5]To help us resist temptation. [6]My sister unplugged the living room set. [7]That evening the four of us sat around the dinner table much longer than usual, we found new things to talk about. [8]Later we played board games for several hours, we all went to bed pleased with ourselves. [9]Everything went well until Thursday evening of that first week. [10]My sister went out after dinner. [11]Explaining that she would be back about ten o'clock. [12]The rest of us then decided to turn on the television. [13]Just to watch the CBC news. [14]We planned to unplug the set before my sister got home. [15]And pretend nothing had happened. [16]We were settled down comfortably in our respective chairs, unfortunately, my sister walked in at that point and burst out laughing. [17]"Ah ha! I caught you," she cried. [18]She explained that part of the experiment was to see if we would stick to the agreement. [19]Especially during her absence. [20]She had predicted we would weaken, it turned out she was right.

Score Number correct _____ × 5 = _____ percent

VERBS

Combined Mastery Test 3

Each sentence contains a mistake involving (1) standard English or irregular verb forms, (2) subject-verb agreement, or (3) consistent verb tense. Circle the letter that identifies the mistake. Then cross out the incorrect verb and write the correct form in the space provided.

_____ 1. One of my apartment neighbours always keep the radio on all night.
Mistake in: a. Subject-verb agreement   b. Verb tense

_____ 2. The more the instructor explained the material and the more he wroted on the board, the more confused I got.
Mistake in: a. Irregular verb form   b. Verb tense

_____ 3. I grabbed the last carton of skim milk on the supermarket shelf, but when I checks the date on it, I realized it was not fresh.
Mistake in: a. Subject-verb agreement   b. Verb tense

_____ 4. This morning my parents argued loudly, but later they apologized to each other and embrace.
Mistake in: a. Subject-verb agreement   b. Verb tense

_____ 5. When the bell rang, Abdul takes another bite of his sandwich and then prepared for class.
Mistake in: a. Irregular verb form   b. Verb tense

_____ 6. Someone called Marlene at the office to tell her that her son had been bit by a stray dog.
Mistake in: a. Irregular verb form   b. Verb tense

_____ 7. Because I throwed away the sales slip, I couldn't return the microwave.
Mistake in: a. Irregular verb form   b. Verb tense

_____ 8. My dog and cat usually ignores each other, but once in a while they fight.
Mistake in: a. Subject-verb agreement   b. Verb tense

_____ 9. From the back of our neighbourhood bakery comes some of the best smells in the world.
Mistake in: a. Subject-verb agreement   b. Verb tense

_____ 10. The cost of new soles and heels are more than those old shoes are worth.
Mistake in: a. Subject-verb agreement   b. Verb tense

Score   Number correct _____ × 5 = _____ percent

VERBS

▪ **Combined Mastery Test 4**

Each sentence contains a mistake involving (1) standard English or irregular verb forms, (2) subject-verb agreement, or (3) consistent verb tense. Circle the letter that identifies the mistake. Then cross out the incorrect verb and write the correct form in the space provided.

_____ 1. My friend's bitter words had stinged me deeply.
Mistake in: a. Irregular verb form   b. Verb tense

_____ 2. After she poured the ammonia into the bucket, Karen reels backward because the strong fumes made her eyes tear.
Mistake in: a. Subject-verb agreement   b. Verb tense

_____ 3. Flying around in space is various pieces of debris from old space satellites.
Mistake in: a. Subject-verb agreement   b. Verb tense

_____ 4. Ella watched suspiciously as a strange car drived back and forth in front of her house.
Mistake in: a. Irregular verb form   b. Verb tense

_____ 5. Both crying and laughing helps us get rid of tension.
Mistake in: a. Subject-verb agreement   b. Verb tense

_____ 6. All my clothes were dirty, so I stayed up late and washes a load for tomorrow.
Mistake in: a. Subject-verb agreement   b. Verb tense

_____ 7. McDonald's has selled enough hamburgers to reach to the moon.
Mistake in: a. Irregular verb form   b. Verb tense

_____ 8. When Chen peeled back the bedroom wallpaper, he discovered another layer of wallpaper and uses a steamer to get that layer off.
Mistake in: a. Subject-verb agreement   b. Verb tense

_____ 9. Pina searched for the fifty-dollar bill she had hid somewhere in her dresser.
Mistake in: a. Irregular verb form   b. Verb tense

_____ 10. The realistic yellow tulips on the gravestone is made of weather-resistant fabric.
Mistake in: a. Subject-verb agreement   b. Verb tense

_____
| |
| *Score*   Number correct _____ × 5 = _____ percent |
|_____|

CAPITAL LETTERS AND PUNCTUATION

■ **Combined Mastery Test 5**

Each of the following sentences contains an error in capitalization or punctuation. Refer to the box below and write, in the space provided, the letter identifying the error. Then correct the error.

a. missing capital	c. missing quotation marks
b. missing apostrophe	d. missing comma

_____ 1. Nicole's aerobics class has been cancelled this week so she's decided to go running instead.

_____ 2. "One of the striking differences between a cat and a lie, wrote Mark Twain, "is that a cat has only nine lives."

_____ 3. My uncles cheques are printed to look like Monopoly money.

_____ 4. Did you know someone is turning the old school on ninth Street into a restaurant named Home Economics?

_____ 5. My parents always ask me where Im going and when I'll be home.

_____ 6. She doesn't talk about it much, but my aunt has been a member of alcoholics Anonymous for ten years.

_____ 7. The sweating straining horses neared the finish line.

_____ 8. Whenever he gave us the keys to the car, my father would say, Watch out for the other guy."

_____ 9. If you're going to stay up late be sure to turn down the heat before going to bed.

_____ 10. I decided to have a glass of apple juice rather than order a pepsi.

Score Number correct _____ × 10 = _____ percent	

CAPITAL LETTERS AND PUNCTUATION

■ Combined Mastery Test 6

Each of the following sentences contains an error in capitalization or punctuation. Refer to the box below and write, in the space provided, the letter identifying the error. Then correct the error.

a. missing capital	c. missing quotation marks
b. missing apostrophe	d. missing comma

_____ 1. Even though I hadn't saved the receipt I was able to return the blender to the Bay.

_____ 2. "The diners food is always reliable," said Stan. "It's consistently bad."

_____ 3. Some people are surprised to hear that manhattan is an island.

_____ 4. "To love oneself, said Oscar Wilde, "is the beginning of a lifelong romance."

_____ 5. The airplane was delayed for more than three hours and the passengers were getting impatient.

_____ 6. Lydia said to the woman behind her in the theatre, "will you stop talking, please?"

_____ 7. Walter arthritis is as good a predictor of the weather as the TV weather report.

_____ 8. "Before you can reach your goals," says my grandfather, you have to believe you can reach them."

_____ 9. There is little evidence that king Arthur, the legendary hero, really existed.

_____ 10. My cousin learned to cook when he was head chef in a b.C. logging camp.

Score Number correct _____ × 10 = _____ percent

WORD USE

■ **Combined Mastery Test 7**

Each of the following sentences contains a mistake identified in the left-hand margin. Underline the mistake and then correct it in the space provided.

Slang

1. Because Maxine has a lot of pull at work, she always has first choice of vacation time.

   _____

Wordiness

2. Truthfully, I've been wishing that the final could be postponed to a much later date sometime next week.

   _____

Cliché

3. Kate hoped her friends would be green with envy when they saw her new boyfriend.

   _____

Pretentious language

4. Bret utilizes old coffee cans to water his house plants.

   _____

Adverb error

5. The sled started slow and then picked up speed as the icy hill became steeper.

   _____

Error in comparison

6. When the weather is dry, my sinus condition feels more better.

   _____

Confused word

7. If you neglect your friends, their likely to become former friends.

   _____

Confused word

8. She's the neighbour who's dog is courting my dog.

   _____

Confused word

9. If you don't put cans, jars, and newspapers on the curb for recycling, the city won't pick up you're garbage.

   _____

Confused word

10. "Its the most economical car you can buy," the announcer said.

   _____

Score   Number correct _____ × 10 = _____ percent

WORD USE

■ Combined Mastery Test 8

Each of the following sentences contains a mistake identified in the left-hand margin. Underline the mistake and then correct it in the space provided.

Slang

1. After coming in to work late all last week, Sheila was canned.

_____

Wordiness

2. At this point in time, I'm not really sure what my major will be.

_____

Cliché

3. Jan and Alan knew they could depend on their son in their hour of need.

_____

Pretentious language

4. I plan to do a lot of comparison shopping before procuring a new dryer.

_____

Adverb error

5. The children sat very quiet as their mother read the next chapter of *Charlie and the Chocolate Factory*.

_____

Error in comparison

6. The respectfuller you treat people, the more they are likely to deserve your respect.

_____

Confused word

7. The dog has lost its' flea collar.

_____

Confused word

8. "My advise to you," said my grandmother, "is to focus on your strengths, not your fears."

_____

Confused word

9. The principle advantage of the school cafeteria is that it's three blocks from a Harvey's.

_____

Confused word

10. My parents mean well, but there goals for me aren't my goals.

_____

Score Number correct _____ × 10 = _____ percent

Editing Tests

EDITING AND PROOFREADING FOR SENTENCE-SKILLS MISTAKES

The twelve tests in this chapter will give you practice in editing and proofreading for sentence-skills mistakes. People often find it hard to proofread a paper carefully. They have put so much work into their writing, or so little, that it's almost painful for them to look at the paper one more time. You may simply have to *force* yourself to proofread and revise your writing. Remember that eliminating sentence-skills mistakes will improve an average paper and help ensure a strong grade on a good paper. Further, as you get into the habit of checking your papers, you will also get into the habit of using the sentence skills consistently. They are a basic part of clear and effective writing.

■ Editing Test 1

Identify the five mistakes in paper format in the student paper that follows. From the box below, choose the letters that describe the five mistakes and write those letters in the spaces provided.

a.	The title should not be underlined.
b.	The title should not be set off in quotation marks.
c.	There should not be a period at the end of the title.
d.	All the major words in the title should be capitalized.
e.	The title should be a phrase, not a complete sentence.
f.	The first line of the paper should stand independent of the title.
g.	A line should be skipped between the title and the first line of the paper.
h.	The first line of the paper should be indented.
i.	The right-hand margin should not be crowded.
j.	Hyphenation should occur only between syllables.

"my candy apple adventure"

	It was the best event of my day. I loved the sweetness that
	filled my mouth as I bit into the sugary coating. With my second
	bite, I munched contentedly on the apple underneath. Its
	crunchy tartness was the perfect balance to the smooth sweet-
	ness of the outside. Then the apple had a magical effect on me.
	Suddenly I remembered when I was seven years old, walking
	through the local fair grounds, holding my father's hand. We
	stopped at a refreshment stand, and he bought us each a
	candy apple. I had never had one before, and I asked him what it
	was. "This is a very special fruit," he said. "If you ever feel sad,
	all you have to do is eat a candy apple, and it will bring you
	sweetness." Now, years later, his words came back to me, and
	as I ate my candy apple, I felt the world turn sweet once more.

1. _____   2. _____   3. _____   4. _____   5. _____

■ Editing Test 2

Identify the sentence-skills mistakes at the underlined spots in the paragraph that follows. From the box below, choose the letter that describes each mistake and write it in the space provided. The same mistake may appear more than once.

a. fragment	d. apostrophe mistake
b. run-on	e. faulty parallelism
c. mistake in subject-verb agreement	

Looking Out for Yourself

It's sad but true that "If you don't look out for yourself, no one else will."

For example, some people have a false idea about the power of a college

diploma, they think that once they possesses the diploma, the world will be
     1   2

waiting on their doorstep. In fact, nobody is likely to be on their doorstep

unless, through advance planning, they has prepared themselves for a career,
                                      3

The kind in which good job opportunities exist. Even after a person has landed
                4

a job, however, a healthy amount of self-interest is needed. People who hide

in corners or with hesitation to let others know about their skills doesn't get
                 5   6

promotions or raises. Its important to take credit for a job well done, whether
               7

it involves writing a report, organized the office filing system, or calming down
                                  8

an angry customer. Also, people should feel free to ask the boss for a raise.

If they work hard and really deserve it. Those who look out for themselves get
               9

the rewards, people who depend on others to help them along get left behind.
     10

1. __b__   3. __b__   5. __e__   7. __d__   9. __a__

2. __c__   4. __a__   6. __c__   8. __e__   10. __b__

Editing Test 3

Identify the sentence-skills mistakes at the underlined spots in the paragraph that follows. From the box below, choose the letter that describes each mistake and write it in the space provided. The same mistake may appear more than once.

a. fragment	e. missing commas around an interrupter
b. run-on	
c. mistake in verb tense	f. mistake with quotation marks
d. irregular verb mistake	g. apostrophe mistake

Deceptive Appearances

Appearances can be deceptive. While looking through a library window yesterday, I saw a neatly groomed woman walk by. Her clothes were skillfully <u>tailored her</u> makeup was perfect. <u>Then thinking no one was looking she</u>

   1   2
crumpled a piece of paper in her hand. <u>And tossed it into a nearby hedge.</u>

                                                          3
Suddenly she no longer <u>looks</u> attractive to me. On another occasion, I started

                        4
talking to a person in my psychology class named Eric. Eric seemed to be a great person. He always got the class laughing with his <u>jokes, on</u> the days

                                                         5
when Eric was absent, I think even the professor missed his lively personality. Eric asked me <u>"if I wanted to get a pop in the cafeteria,"</u> and I felt happy

                  6
he had <u>chose</u> me to be a friend. <u>While we were sitting in the cafeteria.</u> Eric

        7   8
took out an envelope with several kinds of pills inside. "Want one?" he asked. "They're uppers." I didn't want <u>one, I</u> felt disappointed. <u>Erics</u> terrific

                                    9   10
personality was the product of the pills he took.

1. _____   3. _____   5. _____   7. _____   9. _____

2. _____   4. _____   6. _____   8. _____   10. _____

■ Editing Test 4

Identify the sentence-skills mistakes at the underlined spots in the paragraph that follows. From the box below, choose the letter that describes each mistake and write it in the space provided. The same mistake may appear more than once.

a.	fragment	e.	apostrophe mistake
b.	run-on	f.	dangling modifier
c.	irregular verb mistake	g.	missing quotation marks
d.	missing comma after introductory words		

A Horrifying Moment

The most horrifying moment in my life occurred in the dark hallway.

<u>Which led to my apartment house.</u> Though the hallway light was <u>out I</u>
             1   2

managed to find my apartment door. However, I could not find the keyhole

with my door key. I then pulled a book of matches from my pocket. <u>Trying to</u>
                                                 3

<u>strike a match</u>, the entire book of matches <u>bursted</u> into flames. I flicked the
     4   5

matches away but not before my coat sleeve catched fire. Within seconds, my

arm was like a torch. <u>Struggling to unsnap the buttons of my coat,</u> flames
                                    6

began to sear my skin. I was quickly going into shock. <u>And began screaming</u>
                                                 7

<u>in pain.</u> A <u>neighbours</u> door opened and a voice cried out, <u>My God!</u> I was pulled
            8   9

through an apartment and put under a bathroom shower, which extinguished

the flames. I suffered third-degree burns on my <u>arm, I</u> felt lucky to escape
                                                10

with my life.

1. _____   3. _____   5. _____   7. _____   9. _____

2. _____   4. _____   6. _____   8. _____   10. _____

■ Editing Test 5

Identify the sentence-skills mistakes at the underlined spots in the paragraph that follows. From the box below, choose the letter that describes each mistake and write it in the space provided. The same mistake may appear more than once.

a. fragment	e. faulty parallelism
b. run-on	f. apostrophe mistake
c. missing capital letter	g. missing quotation mark
d. mistake in subject-verb agreement	h. missing comma after introductory words

Why I Didn't Go to Church

I almost never attended church in my boyhood years. There was an

unwritten code that the guys on the corner <u>was</u> not to be seen in <u>churches'</u>.
                                           1   2

Although there <u>was</u> many days when I wanted to attend a church, I felt I had
                3

no choice but to stay away. If the guys had heard I had gone to church, they

would have said things like, <u>"hey,</u> angel, when are you going to <u>fly?</u> With my
                             4   5

group of friends, <u>its</u> amazing that I developed any religious feeling at all.
                   6

Another reason for not going to church was my father. When he was around

the <u>house he</u> told my mother, "Tim's not going to church. No boy of mine is a
     7

sissy." My mother and sister went to <u>church, I</u> sat with my father and read the
                                       8

Sunday paper or <u>watching television.</u> I did not start going to church until years
                 9

later. <u>When I no longer hung around with the guys on the corner or let my</u>
                                      10

<u>father have power over me.</u>

1. _____   3. _____   5. _____   7. _____   9. _____

2. _____   4. _____   6. _____   8. _____   10. _____

Editing Test 6

Identify the sentence-skills mistakes at the underlined spots in the paragraph that follows. From the box below, choose the letter that describes each mistake and write it in the space provided. The same mistake may appear more than once.

a. fragment	f. missing comma between two complete thoughts
b. run-on	
c. faulty parallelism	g. missing comma after introductory words
d. missing apostrophe	
e. missing quotation mark	h. misspelled word

Anxiety and the Telephone

Not many of us would want to do without our <u>telephones but</u> there are
1

times when the phone is a source of anxiety. For example, you might be

walking up to your front door. <u>When you hear the phone ring.</u> You struggle to
2

find your key, to unlock the door, and <u>getting</u> to the phone quickly. You know
3

the phone will stop ringing the instant you pick up the <u>receiver, then</u> you
4

wonder if you missed the call that would have made you a <u>millionare</u> or
5

introduced you to the love of your life. Another time, you may have called in

sick to work with a phony excuse. All day long, <u>youre</u> afraid to leave the house
6

in case the boss calls back. <u>And asks himself why you were feeling well</u>
7

<u>enough to go out.</u> In addition, you worry that you might unthinkingly pick up

the phone and say in a cheerful voice, <u>"Hello,</u> completely <u>forgeting</u> to use
8   9

your fake cough. In cases like <u>these having</u> a telephone is more of a curse
10

than a blessing.

1. _____   3. _____   5. _____   7. _____   9. _____

2. _____   4. _____   6. _____   8. _____   10. _____

■ Editing Test 7

See if you can locate and correct the ten sentence-skills mistakes in the following passage. The mistakes are listed in the box below. As you locate each mistake, write the number of the word group containing that mistake. Use the spaces provided. Then (on a separate piece of paper) correct the mistakes.

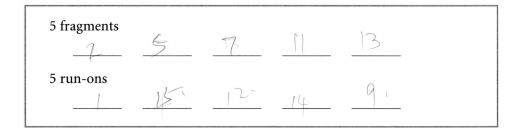

5 fragments

   2   5   7   11   13

5 run-ons

   1   15   12   14   9

Family Stories

¹When I was little, my parents invented some strange stories to explain everyday events to me, my father, for example, told me that trolls lived in our house. ²When objects such as scissors or pens were missing. ³My father would look at me and say, "The trolls took them." ⁴For years, I kept a flashlight next to my bed. ⁵Hoping to catch the trolls in the act as they carried away our possessions. ⁶Another story I still remember is my mother's explanation of pussy willows. ⁷After the fuzzy grey buds emerged in our backyard one spring. ⁸I asked Mom what they were. ⁹Pussy willows, she explained, were cats who had already lived nine lives, in this tenth life, only the tips of the cats' tails were visible to people. ¹⁰All the tails looked alike. ¹¹So that none of the cats would be jealous of the others. ¹²It was also my mother who created the legend of the birthday fairy, this fairy always knew which presents I wanted. ¹³Because my mother called up on a special invisible telephone. ¹⁴Children couldn't see these phones, every parent had a direct line to the fairy. ¹⁵My parents' stories left a great impression on me, I still feel a surge of pleasure when I think of them.

▨ Editing Test 8

See if you can locate and correct the ten sentence-skills mistakes in the following passage. The mistakes are listed in the box below. As you locate each mistake, write the number of the word group containing that mistake. Use the spaces provided. Then (on a separate piece of paper) correct the mistakes.

1 fragment _____	2 missing commas between items
1 run-on _____	in a series _____ _____
1 nonstandard verb _____	2 apostrophe mistakes _____
1 missing comma around	_____
an interrupter _____	1 capital letter mistake _____
	1 homonym mistake _____

Search for Order

¹I had an odd boss in my job as an Inventory clerk at Canadian Tire. ²Jerrys obsessions about numbers and order were irritating and interesting. ³Jerry, a thirty-year-old management trainee was a fanatic about details and order. ⁴He seemed to think that unless he had an exact, double-checked count of everything, disasters would happen. ⁵He would dig out everyones inventory sheets and sneak around the warehouse recounting as many items as he could. ⁶And look for errors in there counts and figuring. ⁷Other times, he would ask us to count how many markers and notebooks we had in our jackets and our lockers. ⁸He would make us empty our pockets and shake out our cases. ⁹Some days, I'd come upon two or three of the fellows I worked with standing at attention at their lockers, I'd know Jerry was counting markers and notebooks again. ¹⁰He were tireless in his need for perfect counts and records of everything. ¹¹It was a need he would never completely satisfy.

■ **Editing Test 9**

See if you can locate and correct the ten sentence-skills mistakes in the following passages. The mistakes are listed in the box below. As you locate each mistake, write the number of the word group containing that mistake. Use the spaces provided. Then (on a separate piece of paper) correct the mistakes.

2 fragments _____ _____   1 missing comma after

1 run-on _____   introductory words _____

1 irregular verb mistake _____   2 apostrophe mistakes _____

1 missing comma between   _____

   items in a series _____   1 faulty parallelism _____

                                 1 missing quotation mark _____

Franco's Funeral

¹Sometimes when Franco feels undervalued and depression, he likes to imagine his own funeral. ²He pictures all the people who will be there. ³He hears their hushed words sees their tears, and feels their grief. ⁴He glows with a warm sadness as the priest begins a eulogy by saying, Franco Corelli was no ordinary man. . . ." ⁵As the minister talks on Francos eyes grow moist. ⁶He laments his own passing and feels altogether appreciated and wonderful.

Feeding Time

⁷Recently I was at the cathouse in the zoo. ⁸Right before feeding time. ⁹The tigers and lions were lying about on benches and little stands. ¹⁰Basking in the late-afternoon sun. ¹¹They seemed tame and harmless. ¹²But when the meat was brung in, a remarkable change occurred. ¹³All the cats got up and moved toward the food. ¹⁴I was suddenly aware of the rippling muscles' of their bodies and their large claws and teeth. ¹⁵They seemed three times bigger, I could feel their power.

■ Editing Test 10

See if you can locate and correct the ten sentence-skills mistakes in the following passage. The mistakes are listed in the box below. As you locate each mistake, write the number of the word group containing that mistake. Use the spaces provided. Then (on a separate piece of paper) correct the mistakes.

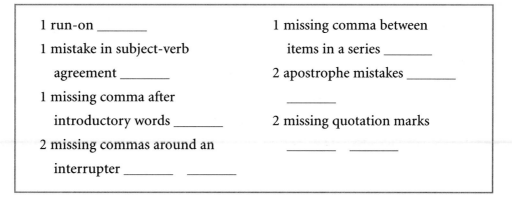

1 run-on _____	1 missing comma between
1 mistake in subject-verb	items in a series _____
agreement _____	2 apostrophe mistakes _____
1 missing comma after	_____
introductory words _____	2 missing quotation marks
2 missing commas around an	_____ _____
interrupter _____ _____	

Walking Billboards

¹Many Canadians have turned into driving, walking billboards. ²As much as we all claim to hate commercials on television we dont seem to have any qualms about turning ourselves into commercials. ³Our car bumpers for example advertise resorts brands of sunglasses, and radio stations. ⁴Also, we wear clothes marked with other peoples initials and slogans. ⁵Our fascination with the names of designers show up on the backs of our running shoes, the breast pockets of our shirts, and the right rear pockets of our blue jeans. ⁶And we wear T-shirts filled with all kinds of advertising messages. ⁷For instance, people are willing to wear shirts that read, "Dillon Construction," "Nike," or even I Got Crabs at Ed's Seafood Palace. ⁸In conclusion, we say we hate commercials, we actually pay people for the right to advertise their products.

▨ Editing Test 11

See if you can locate and correct the ten sentence-skills mistakes in the following passage. The mistakes are listed in the box below. As you locate each mistake, write the number of the word group containing that mistake. Use the spaces provided. Then (on a separate piece of paper) correct the mistakes.

3 fragments _____ _____ _____	1 mistake in pronoun point of view _____
2 run-ons _____ _____	1 dangling modifier _____
1 irregular verb mistake _____	1 missing comma between two complete thoughts _____
1 faulty parallelism _____	

Too Many Cooks

¹The problem in my college cafeteria was the succession of incompetent cooks who were put in charge. ²During the time I worked there, I watched several cooks come and go. ³The first of these was Irving. ⁴He was skinny and greasy like the undercooked bacon he served for breakfast. ⁵Irving drank, by late afternoon he begun to sway as he cooked. ⁶Once, he looked at the brightly coloured photograph on the orange juice machine. ⁷And asked why the TV was on. ⁸Having fired Irving, Marky was hired. ⁹Marky had a soft, round face that resembled a marshmallow but he had the size and temperament of a large bear. ¹⁰He'd wave one paw and growl if you entered the freezers without his permission. ¹¹He also had poor eyesight. ¹²This problem caused him to substitute flour for sugar and using pork for beef on a regular basis. ¹³After Marky was fired, Enzo arrived. ¹⁴Because he had come from Italy less than a year previously. ¹⁵He spoke little English. ¹⁶In addition, Enzo had trouble with seasoning and spices. ¹⁷His vegetables were too salty, giant bay leaves turned up in everything. ¹⁸Including the scrambled eggs. ¹⁹The cooks I worked for in the college dining hall would have made any chef go into shock.

■ Editing Test 12

See if you can locate and correct the ten sentence-skills mistakes in the following passage. The mistakes are listed in the box below. As you locate each mistake, write the number of the word group containing that mistake. Use the spaces provided. Then (on a separate piece of paper) correct the mistakes.

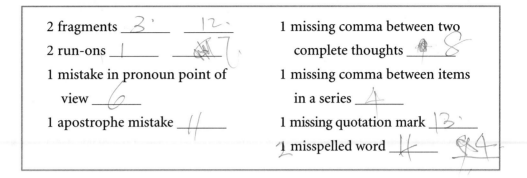

2 fragments _3_ _12_	1 missing comma between two
2 run-ons _1_ _7_	complete thoughts _8_
1 mistake in pronoun point of	1 missing comma between items
view _6_	in a series _4_
1 apostrophe mistake _11_	1 missing quotation mark _13_
	1 misspelled word _4_

My Ideal Date

¹Here are the ingredients for my ideal date, first of all, I would want to look as stunning as possible. ²I would be dressed in a black velvet dress. ³That would fit me like a layer of paint. ⁴My acessories would include a pair of black patent sandels a diamond hair clip, and a full-length black satin coat. ⁵My boyfriend, Gene, would wear a sharply tailored black tuxedo, a white silk shirt, and a bow tie. ⁶The tux would emphasize Gene's broad shoulders and narrow waist, and you would see his chest muscles under the smooth shirt fabric. ⁷Gene would pull up to my house in a long, shiny limousine, then the driver would take us to the most exclusive club in Vancouver. ⁸All eyes would be on us as we entered and photographers would rush up to take our picture for *The Sun*. ⁹As we danced on the lighted floor of the club, everyone would step aside to watch us perform our moves. ¹⁰After several bottles of champagne, Gene and I would head for an intimate restaurant on Granville Island. ¹¹As we gazed out over the lights' of the city, Gene would hand me a small velvet box containing a ten-carat ruby engagement ring. ¹²And ask me to marry him. ¹³I would thank Gene for a lovely evening and tell him gently, "Gene, I don't plan to marry until I'm thirty.

Explaining a Process · Examining Cause and Effect · Comparing or Contrasting · Defi
Term · Dividing and Classifying · Describing a Scene or Person · Narrating an Event · Ar
a Position · Explaining a Process · Examining Cause and Effect · Comparing or Contras
Defining a Term · Dividing and Classifying · Describing a Scene or Person · Narrating an
Arguing a Position · Explaining a Process · Examining Cause and Effect · Compari

CHAPTER 46

Sentence-Skills Achievement Test

PART 1

This test will help you measure your improvement in important sentence skills. Certain parts of the following word groups are underlined. Write *X* in the answer space if you think a mistake appears at the underlined part. Write *C* in the answer space if you think the underlined part is correct.

The headings ("Fragments," "Run-Ons," and so on) will give you clues to the mistakes to look for.

Fragments

_____C_____ 1. After a careless driver hit my motorcycle, I decided to buy a car. At least I would have more protection against other careless drivers.

_____X_____ 2. I was never a good student in high school. Because I spent all my time socializing with my group of friends. Good grades were not something that my group really valued.

_____X_____ 3. The elderly couple in the supermarket were not a pleasant sight. Arguing with each other. People pretended not to notice them.

_____C_____ 4. Using a magnifying glass, the little girls burned holes in the dry leaf. They then set some tissue paper on fire.

_____X_____ 5. My brother and I seldom have fights about what to watch on television. Except with baseball games. I get bored watching this sport.

_____C_____ 6. My roommate and I ate, talked, danced, and sang at a party the other night. Also, we played cards until 3 a.m. As a result, we both slept until noon the next day.

Run-Ons

_____ X   7. She decided to quit her high-pressured <u>job, she</u> didn't want to develop heart trouble.

_____ C   8. His car's wheels were not balanced <u>properly, for</u> the car began to shake when he drove over sixty kilometres an hour.

_____ X   9. I got through the interview without breaking out in a sweat <u>moustache, I</u> also managed to keep my voice under control.

_____ C   10. The craze for convenience in North America has gone too <u>far. There</u> are drive-in banks, restaurants, and even churches.

_____ X   11. My most valued possession is my stoneware <u>cooker, I</u> can make entire meals in it at a low cost.

_____ X   12. The shopping carts outside the supermarket seemed welded <u>together, Rita</u> could not separate one from another.

Irregular Verbs

_____ X   13. I learned that Dennis had <u>began</u> to see someone else while he was still going out with me.

_____ X   14. That woman has never <u>ran</u> for political office before.

_____ X   15. I <u>knowed</u> the answer to the question, but I was too nervous to think of it when the instructor called on me.

_____ X   16. They had <u>ate</u> the gallon of natural vanilla ice cream in just one night.

Subject-Verb Agreement

_____ X   17. Her watchband <u>have</u> to be fixed.

_____ X   18. There <u>is</u> two minutes left in the hockey game.

_____ X   19. He believes films that feature violence <u>is</u> a disgrace to our society.

_____ C   20. The slipcovers that she bought <u>have</u> begun to fray.

Consistent Verb Tense

_____ X   21. Kyra wanted to watch the late movie, but she was so tired she <u>falls</u> asleep before it started.

_____ C   22. When the mail carrier arrived, I <u>hoped</u> the latest issue of *Spin* magazine would be in her bag.

_____ X   23. Michelle ran down the hall without looking and <u>trips</u> over the toy truck sitting on the floor.

_____ C _____   24. Debbie enjoys riding her bike in the newly built park, which <u>features</u> a special path for bikers and runners.

Pronoun Agreement, Reference, and Point of View

_____ X _____   25. At the Saturday afternoon movie we went to, children were making so much noise that <u>you</u> could not relax.

_____ C _____   26. We did not return to the amusement park, for <u>we</u> had to pay too much for the rides and meals.

_____ C _____   27. Drivers should check the oil level in <u>their</u> cars every three months.

_____ X _____   28. At the hospital, I saw mothers with tears in their eyes wandering down the hall, hoping that <u>her</u> child's operation was a success.

_____ C _____   29. Sharon's mother was overjoyed when <u>Sharon</u> became pregnant.

_____ X _____   30. You must observe all the rules of the game, even if you do not always agree with <u>it</u>.

Pronoun Types

_____ X _____   31. Nancy and <u>her</u> often go to swing music bars.

_____ C _____   32. No one in the class is better at computers than <u>he</u>.

Adjectives and Adverbs

_____ ✓ _____   33. The little girl spoke so <u>quiet</u> I could hardly hear her.

_____ X _____   34. Kerry looks <u>more better</u> than Gina in a leather coat.

Misplaced Modifiers

_____ X _____   35. I saw sharks <u>scuba-diving</u>.

_____ C _____   36. <u>With a mile-wide grin</u>, Jessica turned in her winning lottery ticket.

_____ X _____   37. I bought a beautiful blouse in a local store <u>with long sleeves and French cuffs</u>.

_____ X _____   38. I first spotted the turtle <u>playing tag on the back lawn</u>.

Dangling Modifiers

_____ X _____   39. <u>When seven years old</u>, Jeff's father taught him to play ball.

_____ C _____   40. <u>Running across the field</u>, I caught the Frisbee.

_____ X _____   41. <u>Turning on the ignition</u>, the car backfired.

_____ X _____   42. <u>Looking at my watch</u>, a taxi nearly ran me over.

Faulty Parallelism

X 43. Much of my boyhood was devoted to getting into rock fights, crossing railway trestles, and <u>the hunt for rats in drainage tunnels</u>.

C 44. I put my books in my locker, changed into my gym clothes, and <u>hurried to the playing field</u>.

X 45. Ruth begins every day with warm-up exercises, a half-hour run, <u>and taking a hot shower</u>.

C 46. In the evening I plan to write a paper, <u>to watch a movie</u>, and to read two chapters in my biology text.

Capital Letters

X 47. When the can of <u>drano</u> didn't unclog the sink, Rob called a plumber.

X 48. I asked Bonita, "<u>what</u> time will you be leaving?"

X 49. I have to get an allergy shot once a <u>Week</u>.

C 50. Mother ordered the raincoat at the catalogue store on <u>Monday</u>, and it arrived four days later.

Apostrophe

X 51. I asked the clerk if the store had <u>Moists</u> latest CD.

C 52. <u>He's</u> failing the course because he doesn't have any confidence in his ability to do the work.

C 53. David was incensed at the dentist who charged him fifty dollars to fix his <u>son's</u> tooth.

X 54. I <u>cant</u> believe that she's not coming to the dance.

Quotation Marks

X 55. <u>"Don't forget to water the grass, my sister said</u>.

X 56. June said to Ward at bedtime, "Why is it that men's pyjamas always have such baggy <u>bottoms?" "You</u> look like a circus clown in that flannel outfit."

C 57. The red sign on the door <u>read, "Warning</u>—open only in case of an emergency."

C 58. "I can't stand that commercial," said Sue. "<u>Do you mind if I turn off the television?</u>"

Comma

C 59. Hard-luck Sam needs a <u>loan, a good-paying job, and</u> someone to show an interest in him.

_____X_____ 60. Even though I was <u>tired I</u> agreed to go shopping with my parents.

_____C_____ 61. <u>Power, not love or money, is</u> what most politicians want.

_____C_____ 62. The heel on one of Halina's shoes came <u>off, so</u> she spent the day walking barefoot.

_____X_____ 63. "Thank goodness I'm almost <u>done</u>" I said aloud with every stroke of the broom.

_____X_____ 64. I hated to ask <u>Anita who is a very stingy person to</u> lend me the money.

Commonly Confused Words

_____C_____ 65. To succeed in the job, you must learn how to control <u>your</u> temper.

_____X_____ 66. Fortunately, I was not driving very fast when my car lost <u>its'</u> brakes.

_____X_____ 67. Put your packages on the table over <u>their</u>.

_____C_____ 68. There are <u>too</u> many steps in the math formula for me to understand it.

 _C_ 69. The counselling centre can <u>advise</u> you on how to prepare for an interview.

_____X_____ 70. <u>Who's</u> white Lexus is that in front of the house?

Effective Word Use

_____X_____ 71. The teacher called to discuss Ron's <u>social maladjustment difficulties</u>.

_____X_____ 72. I thought the course would be a <u>piece of cake</u>, but a ten-page paper was required.

_____X_____ 73. When my last class ended, I felt <u>as free as a bird</u>.

_____X_____ 74. Spike gave away his television <u>owing to the fact</u> that it distracted him from studying.

PART 2 (OPTIONAL)

Do Part 2 at your instructor's request. This second part of the test will provide more detailed information about your improvement in sentence skills. On a separate piece of paper, number and correct all the items you have marked with an *X*. For example, suppose you had marked the word groups below with an *X*. (Note that these examples are not taken from the test.)

4. <u>If baseball games disappeared entirely from television</u>. I would not even miss them. Other people in my family would perish.

7. The kitten suddenly saw her reflection in the <u>mirror, she</u> jumped back in surprise.

15. The tree in my <u>cousins</u> front yard always sheds its leaves two weeks before others on the street.

29. When we go out to a <u>restaurant we</u> always order something we would not cook for ourselves.

Here is how you should write your corrections on a separate sheet of paper.

  4. television, I

  7. mirror, and

15. cousin's

29. restaurant, we

There are over forty corrections to make in all.

Fifteen Reading Selections

PREVIEW

This book assumes that writing and reading are closely connected skills, so that practising one helps the other, and neglecting one hurts the other. Part Five will enable you to work on becoming a better reader as well as a stronger writer. Following an introductory section that offers a series of tips on effective reading, there are fifteen reading selections. Each selection begins with a preview that supplies background information about the piece. After the selection are ten questions to give you practice in key reading comprehension skills. A set of discussion questions is also provided, both to deepen your understanding of the selection and to point out basic writing techniques used in the essay. Then come several writing assignments, along with guidelines to help you think about the assignments and get started working on them.

CHAPTER 47

Introduction to the Readings

The reading selections in Part Five will help you find topics for writing. Some of the selections provide helpful practical information. For example, you'll learn how to study more efficiently, how to write a test, and how to go about deciding on a career. Other selections deal with thought-provoking aspects of contemporary life. One article, for instance, deals with lying, and our attitudes toward this too-human failing; another details how one man seemed to successfully handle virtual illiteracy. Still another selection describes the experiences of Canada's only female professional goalie. Human goals and values are explored in pieces as diverse as an essay about one Native Canadian's efforts to preserve his language and culture, and another article in which a young journalist of Chinese background ponders his lack of mathematical ability. The varied subjects and tones should inspire lively class discussions as well as serious individual thought. The selections are mainly current and many are Canadian. They should also provide a continuing source of high-interest material for a wide range of writing assignments.

The selections serve another purpose as well. They will help develop reading skills with direct benefits to you as a writer. First, through close reading, you will learn how to recognize the main idea or point of a selection and how to identify and evaluate the supporting material that develops the main idea. In your writing, you will aim to achieve the same essential structure: an overall point followed by detailed and valid support for that point. Second, close reading will help you explore a selection and its possibilities thoroughly. The more you understand about what is said in a piece, the more ideas and feelings you may have about writing on an assigned topic or a related topic of your own. A third benefit of close reading is becoming more aware of authors' stylistic devices—for example, their introductions and conclusions, their ways of presenting and developing a point, their use of transitions, and their choice of language to achieve a particular tone. Recognizing these devices in other people's writing will help you enlarge your own range of writing techniques.

THE FORMAT OF EACH SELECTION

Each selection begins with a short overview that gives helpful background information. The selection is then followed by two sets of questions.

- First, there are ten reading comprehension questions to help you measure your understanding of the material. These questions involve several important reading skills: recognizing a subject or topic, determining the thesis or main idea, identifying key supporting points, making inferences, and understanding vocabulary in context. Answering the questions will enable you and your instructor to check quickly your basic understanding of a selection. More significantly, as you move from one selection to the next, you will sharpen your reading skills as well as strengthen your thinking skills—two key factors in making you a better writer.
- Following the comprehension questions are several discussion questions. In addition to dealing with issues of content, these questions focus on matters of structure, style, and tone. *Structure* refers to the ways in which the author has given shape to the work; *style* refers to word choice and the technical skills used by the writer; and *tone* is the "feeling" of a piece of work: whether it is serious, light, or comic.

Finally, several writing assignments accompany each selection. Many of the assignments provide guidelines on how to proceed, including suggestions for prewriting and appropriate methods of development. When writing your responses to the readings, you will have opportunities to apply all the methods of development presented in Part Two of this book.

HOW TO READ WELL: FOUR GENERAL STEPS

Skilful reading is an important part of becoming a skilful writer. Following are four steps that will make you a better reader—both of the selections here and in your reading at large.

1 Concentrate as You Read

To improve your concentration, follow these tips. First, read in a place where you can be quiet and alone. Don't choose a spot where a TV or stereo is on or where friends or family are talking nearby. Next, sit in an upright position when you read. If your body is in a completely relaxed position, sprawled across a bed or nestled in an easy chair, your mind is also going to be completely relaxed. The light muscular tension that comes from sitting in an upright chair promotes concentration and keeps your mind ready to work. Finally, consider using your index finger (or a pen) as a pacer while you read. Lightly underline each line of print with your index finger as you read down a page. Hold your hand slightly above the page and move your finger at a speed that is a little too fast for comfort. This pacing with your index finger, like sitting upright on a chair, creates a slight physical tension that will keep your body and mind focused and alert.

2 Skim Material before You Read It

In skimming, you spend about two minutes rapidly surveying a selection, looking for important points and skipping secondary material. Follow this sequence when skimming:

- Begin by reading the overview that precedes the selection.
- Then study the title of the selection for a few moments. A good title is the shortest possible summary of a selection; it often tells you in several words what a selection is about. For example, the title "Shots on Goal" suggests that you're going to read about a time when someone took some chances and tried for some goal.
- Next, form a basic question (or questions) out of the title. For instance, for the selection titled "Shots on Goal," you might ask, "What exactly was the goal?" "What was someone's reason for taking the shots?" "What was the result of taking the shots?" Forming questions out of the title is often a key to locating a writer's main idea—your next concern in skimming.
- Read the first two or three paragraphs and the last two or three paragraphs in the selection. Very often a writer's main idea, *if* it is directly stated, will appear in one of these paragraphs and will relate to the title. For instance, in "Why Should We Hire You?" the author states in the final paragraph that "you need to work hard in order to find the work you desire. That means knowing the reasons you should be hired and taking the steps needed to prepare a solidly based answer before you are asked The Question."
- Finally, look quickly at the rest of the selection for other clues to important points. Are there any subheadings you can relate in some way to the title? Are there any words the author has decided to emphasize by setting them off in *italic* or **boldface** type? Are there any major lists of items signalled by words such as *first*, *second*, *also*, *another*, and so on?

3 Read the Selection Straight Through with a Pen Nearby

Don't slow down or turn back; just aim to understand as much as you can the first time through. Place a check or star beside answers to basic questions you formed from the title, and beside other ideas that seem important. Number as *1, 2, 3 …* lists of important points. Circle words you don't understand. Put question marks in the margin next to passages that are unclear and that you will want to reread.

4 Work with the Material

Go back and reread passages that were not clear the first time through. Look up words that block your understanding of ideas and write their meanings in the margin. Also, reread carefully the areas you identified as most important; doing so will enlarge your understanding of the material. Now that you have a sense of the whole, prepare a short outline of the selection by answering the following questions on a sheet of paper:

- What is the main idea?
- What key points support the main idea?
- What seem to be other important points in the selection?

By working with the material in this way, you will significantly increase your understanding of a selection. *Effective reading, just like effective writing, does not happen all at once.* Rather, it is a *process.* Often you begin with a general impression of what something means, and then, by working at it, you move to a deeper level of understanding of the material.

How to Answer the Comprehension Questions: Specific Hints

Several important reading skills are involved in the ten reading comprehension questions that follow each selection. The skills are:

- Summarizing the selection by providing a title for it
- Determining the main idea
- Recognizing key supporting details
- Making inferences
- Understanding vocabulary in context

The following hints will help you apply each of these reading skills:

- **Subject or title.** Remember that the title should accurately describe the *entire* selection. It should be neither too broad nor too narrow for the material in the selection. It should answer the question "What is this about?" as specifically as possible. Note that you may at times find it easier to do the "title" question *after* the "main idea" question.
- **Main idea.** Choose the statement that you think best expresses the main idea or thesis of the entire selection. Remember that the title will often help you focus on the main idea. Then ask yourself the question, "Does most of the material in the selection support this statement?" If you can answer *Yes* to this question, you have found the thesis.
- **Key details.** If you were asked to give a two-minute summary of a selection, the major details are the ones you would include in that summary. To determine the key details, ask yourself the question, "What are the major supporting points for the thesis?"
- **Inferences.** Answer these questions by drawing on the evidence presented in the selection and on your own common sense. Ask yourself, "What reasonable judgments can I make on the basis of the information in the selection?"
- **Vocabulary in context.** To decide on the meaning of an unfamiliar word, consider its context. Ask yourself, "Are there any clues in the sentence that suggest what this word means?"

On page 560 is a chart on which you can keep track of your performance as you answer the ten questions for each selection. The chart will help you identify reading skills you may need to strengthen.

Goals and Values

SHOTS ON GOAL

Brian Preston

Hockey is Canada's gift to the world of sport, and it's a pretty violent gift at that. Fights, injuries, and flying pucks are prerequisites of a decent game, according to many fans. Well, then, what's one of the "delicate nurturing gender" doing in goal? If you're Manon Rhéaume, you're wearing a lot of kilos of equipment, enduring insults and media hype, and using all your grit and technique to take you toward the NHL. Manon plays a position which involves receiving constant physical attacks. In a traditionally male sport, she is the lone female player. The opposition she faces comes not only from the teams firing shots at her, but also from the press and even some of her teammates. Brian Preston, writing for *Saturday Night* magazine, offers readers a balanced and close-up view of the challenges and pressures Manon Rhéaume faces just trying to stay in the crease.

1 Lingering after practice, a handful of hockey players amuse themselves by seeing who can putt a puck closest to the centre face-off dot. It's called Instructor Golf, favoured pastime of summer hockey-school teachers. Two more players good-naturedly bellow at each other. Player A: "F—— you!" Player B: "F—— me!" Ad nauseam. They don't care if Manon Rhéaume hears. On this team, she's more or less one of the guys.

2 That's her handling shots from half a dozen team-mates at the far end. It's the day before Rhéaume's debut regular-season start for the Las Vegas Thunder of the International Hockey League (IHL). The only other feminine presences in this slick 13,000-seat arena are a bare-shouldered blonde pictured in a strip-club advertisement on the boards—this is Vegas, after all—and Tatania Yashin, whose super-star son, Alexei, is playing for the Thunder during the NHL lock-out. Asked what she thinks of a woman playing net, Madame Yashin, translated by her husband,

Valery, says, "Women have equal minds, they understand hockey the same as men. But it's necessary for her to be more clever, because men are more strong." Valery Yashin adds, "Our other son plays Double-A Pee Wee in Ottawa. His goalie is named Elizabeth, and she plays not bad." He watches Rhéaume take a high, hard shot off her chest. She shakes it off and sets herself to face the next shooter. "We don't know the finished results of this experiment," Yashin concludes.

Hard data will be available after tomorrow night's game, which the Thunder are hyping as potentially historic: it could be the first win ever by a woman goalie in IHL history. A reporter from Houston, whose Aeros will be Rhéaume's opponents, tells the small coterie of practice watchers that his team is licking its chops at the thought of facing her. "Not because she's a woman," he's quick to clarify. "Just because she weighs a hundred and twenty pounds." He's about to interview her for the first time, and he's having trouble remembering how to pronounce her name. "Ma-none. Ma-no. Ma-NO? Ma-NO!" It's his momentary mantra. He wonders aloud, "Is it sexist to ask if she has a boyfriend?" Yes, but he'll ask anyway. After all, she's the first pro goalie to worry about boyfriends. At least the first who can safely discuss it in public.

Chris McSorley, the Thunder's assistant coach (and brother of NHLer Marty), says Manon Rhéaume is "a phenomenal athlete, the hardest-working player we have on staff, bar none. She's where she is today because of her work ethic. She's competent enough to hold the pipes in this league, and I believe in three or four years she'll have a chance to play a regular-season game in the National Hockey League."

That eventuality would exceed even Manon Rhéaume's expectations. Still on the ice, leaning on the boards by the players' bench, she takes the Houston writer's first question: "Manon, your goal is to play in the NHL—" She interrupts to say, "I've never said that. I'm realistic. I just said I'll go as far as I can go." Another reporter, a Vegas local, butts in to ask, "Manon, will you take on Gamble?" The last time Vegas played Houston there was a huge brawl, and Thunder goalie Clint Malarchuk laid out Houston netminder Troy Gamble with a single punch. Manon laughs easily and responds, "I'll fight him if I have to." You can't help but like her. She's twenty-two, and even in a second language knows how to banter with men.

Her team-mates seem to like her too, but whether or not they take her seriously as a goalie is another matter. The Thunder collectively boast 2,500 games' worth of NHL experience: names like Bob Joyce, Jeff Sharples, Marc Habscheid, Andrew McBain, and Jim Kyte are familiar to serious hockey fans. At the first team practice these men and others took turns blasting pucks at Rhéaume's head and were surprised when she didn't flinch. "She's only added to our chemistry," Chris McSorley claims. "The players cut her no slack. She takes shots to the head, a howitzer every day. She doesn't bitch." In her autobiography *Manon: Alone in Front of the Net*, Rhéaume traces her stoicism to "a stinging remark" her father made once when she cried during a hockey game as a child: "Manon, macramé isn't painful. Choose!" She learned to "choke back my tears and return to my crease."

No-one doubts her toughness, but whether she deserves, on merit, to be signed to an IHL team is another matter. Some team-mates are sincerely enthused, like Jeff Sharples: "She's a pioneer in our sport and I think that's great." But other players have been heard to say privately that they think it's a joke, that she's in over her head in a league whose best teams are on a par with the weaker NHL squads, that she's less a legitimate player than a publicity stunt orchestrated by the team's owner, Ken Stickney. A local reporter recalls Stickney telling him gleefully, "After Gretzky, we've got the most famous hockey player in the world on our team!" The reporter replied, "Have you heard of someone named Mario Lemieux?" But Vegas hockey fans are neophytes, and a telegenic young woman probably does sell more tickets than Lemieux would.

Rhéaume is naturally offended by talk of publicity stunts. In her private dress-   8
ing room after practice, she tells me, "You know, since I started people have always said it's just for publicity. I don't face hundred-mile-an-hour shots every day and I don't have bruises everywhere on my body to have publicity. I make so many sacrifices because I love the game and I want to get better. And when people still ask and ask this question, it's hard."

The same question gets asked frequently of the Thunder's other two goalies,   9
Malarchuk and Pokey Reddick, both former NHL regulars. Reddick refuses to talk about Rhéaume. Their interaction, while not hostile, is minimal. An odd bit of theatre unfolded one morning before practice as Rhéaume, in sweats and a backward baseball cap, ever so slowly made her way towards the arena players' entrance. Reddick, thirty feet behind her and headed the same way, slowed himself to the same pace to avoid catching up to her. It looked like a turtle race. Reddick also refuses to share the net with her during practice. Rhéaume and Malarchuk split duties in the other net, essentially getting a half-share each of practice time.

At thirty-three, Clint Malarchuk has arranged to play out the twilight years of   10
his career here in Vegas; he negotiated a guaranteed four-year no-trade deal, he bought a ranch nearby and raises horses and emus. His team-mates say he's been a "first-class guy," sharing his time and a career's worth of knowledge with Rhéaume. Malarchuk speaks highly of her. "I think her skill level and her talent are quite exceptional," he says. "But she's small in stature and she's not as strong as a man." I ask if sharing a net with Rhéaume has distracted him from his own game. Last year he led the league in wins, so far this year he's been struggling, giving up close to five goals each outing. "It interrupts the flow having to share and switch," he admits. "You have to be patient. It gets a little upsetting at times because Pokey won't ever let her in his net. It's just me."

"Do you ever bug him that he should?"   11

"Oh yeah. He went along with it for like a week, but the team [management]   12
wasn't exactly honest about it either. We were told she would come out *after* practice, that we wouldn't be affected in any way. That kind of comes into it a little bit."

The next night Clint Malarchuk sits in the stands as the Thunder's third-string   13
goalie skates onto the ice ("Starting in goal, the First Lady of Hockey, Manon Rhéaume!") to the roar of 10,000-plus, the Thunder's largest weeknight crowd ever. Five guys in seats behind the net are wearing customized T-shirts, each with a giant letter on the front: M-A-N-O-N. The press box is a little more cynical. The Houston reporter predicts two periods, maximum.

Just under three minutes into the game the Aeros get a two-on-one break.   14
Rhéaume stays too far back in her net, playing the pass instead of the shooter. A 120-

pound goalie who doesn't come out and challenge leaves a lot of net to shoot at. The Aeros score on their first shot. The goal rattles her, but eventually she settles down. Her technical skills equal those of her male counterparts, but her lack of size and strength is obvious. To someone watching her, it's clear that a woman could play goal in the NHL. But that woman will be five foot eight, 160 pounds, minimum.

Watching from the stands tonight is Audrey Bakewell, pro hockey's leading power-skating instructor. She taught Clint Malarchuk when he was still a junior; with goalies she tends to concentrate on balance and agility. "A lot of my ideas are similar to Glenn Hall's in terms of stance," she says. "I taught Mike Vernon to work on figures and edges, hitting the point on the blade. With Mike Richter it was things like spinning on the spot and being able to stop a shot, taking him to the most extreme equilibrium possible and making him work at that level." Asked how it feels to be female in an overwhelmingly male preserve, she says the players have always been more accepting of her than the media, but adds the familiar refrain of any woman trying to crack a male-dominated profession: "In terms of organization and presentation, I've always had to be better than any man." **15**

Tonight Manon Rhéaume is definitely not performing better than any man. She allows three goals on twelve shots over two periods, and is replaced for the third by Reddick. After the game the Thunder's head coach, Bob Strumm, presents the media with a baseball analogy as shaky as Rhéaume's performance: she's like a starting pitcher who gives six innings of solid work, see, then she got pulled so the relief pitcher could come in and mop up. Yeah, right. Later, by the exit door where the autograph hounds wait for players to emerge, the five T-shirted guys have been reduced to three. Now they spell M-A-N. **16**

The next day Manon Rhéaume arrives at practice looking sore and dispirited. Asked if she dreamt about the game, she shakes her head. "I was so tired from the pressure," she mutters. "I was too exhausted. The pressure …" Management has decided to send her down to an easier level for a month or so, to the new Tallahassee franchise in the East Coast Hockey League, where she'll get more playing time. Last year in that league she started six games and went 5-0-1. **17**

Pokey Reddick takes his usual tack when asked for his reaction to rumours of Rhéaume's departure: "I answer no questions about Manon," he insists. "I'm just a goalie. He does all the talking for us," he says, gesturing towards Malarchuk, who's busy with another interviewer, trying to explain the decline in his play this season. He cites nagging injuries, a four-game suspension for pounding out Gamble, "plus some other things I can't comment on." The reporter says, "Those other things may be sent to the East Coast League soon," and the two of them share a smile that says they feel guilty for even thinking it, but it's true. **18**

Reading Comprehension Questions

1. Which of the following would be the best alternative title for the selection?
   a. Manon Muscles In
   b. Lightweight Fighter
   c. Choices, Sacrifices, and Bruises
   d. Girls Just Want to Play Goal

2. Which sentence best expresses the main idea of the selection?
   a. Manon Rhéaume would be back in the IHL, or in the NHL, if she'd only gain forty pounds.
   b. Manon fights hard in an all-male sport, but competing for goal time and lack of size work against her.
   c. Manon is a decent minor-league goalie, but she lacks the technique and aggressive edge to play in the NHL.
   d. Manon Rhéaume's skill is impressive, but her main selling-point is the media interest in the novelty of a female goalie.

3. What common idea do Tatania Yashin and Audrey Bakewell hold about women operating in traditionally male fields?
   a. Women can compete equally if they are physically large enough and strong enough.
   b. Women have to be able to beat men at every aspect of a given area of competition in a field.
   c. Women may eventually succeed in pro hockey and other male fields of activity, but only time will tell.
   d. Women must use and develop more intelligence, skill, and professionalism than their male counterparts in most areas of gender competition.

4. *True or false?* _____ Manon believes that she can achieve regular-season NHL status.

5. The other players on the Las Vegas Thunder team
   a. have opinions about Manon ranging from admiration to open hostility.
   b. all think Manon is tough, a great goalie, and "one of the guys."
   c. all know that she is in goal more for publicity than for any other reason.
   d. feel she causes nothing but dissension and problems for the team.

6. According to the author,
   a. Manon's abilities are motivated primarily by vengeful feelings for her father.
   b. Manon is determined and well-respected, but may never play against the top NHL teams.
   c. Manon's main problem may be the exhaustion she suffers from the number of shots she takes.
   d. team politics will prevent Manon's career from advancing much beyond very minor leagues.

7. The author implies that
   a. Thunder's management are eager to promote Manon as a player.
   b. team owners see their woman goalie as equivalent to a "supermodel."
   c. Thunder's management are less than honest about their handling of Manon.
   d. team managers prefer Clint Malarchuk and Pokey Reddick in goal.

8. *True or false?* _____ In general, hockey players are less sexist in their view of women in the sport than are the media.

9. The word *mantra* in "It's his momentary mantra" (paragraph 3) means
   a. prayer.
   b. chant.
   c. joke.
   d. phrase.

10. The word *stoicism* in "Rhéaume traces her stoicism to 'a stinging remark' her father made once when she cried during a hockey game as a child" (paragraph 6) means
   a. endurance.
   b. meanness.
   c. athletic ability.
   d. technique.

■ Discussion Questions

About Content

1. Who are the three "feminine presences[s]" in the Las Vegas arena in the opening of the article? What might each figure represent? Why?

2. Why is the reporter from Houston "licking his chops" at the idea of the Aeros playing the Thunder? Is his response an honest one? Why or why not? Where else in the selection do you find his opinion repeated?

3. Chris McSorley has his reasons for admiring Manon. What are they? Why does her response to the Las Vegas reporter in paragraph 5 get a positive response from the author?

4. According to the author's observations of Manon's performance in goal, what are her current deficiencies as a player?

About Structure

5. Preston uses which method, or combination of methods, in his opening paragraph?
   a. Broad-to-narrow
   b. Explaining the importance of the topic
   c. Anecdote
   d. Situation that is the opposite of the one to be developed

6. How many paragraphs do you read before the author allows Manon Rhéaume to speak directly? How many reported opinions have you read prior to reading her own voice in print? What is the effect of reading others' thoughts first?

7. "Shots on Goal" is written partly in chronological order—that is, in the time sequence in which the events occurred. Find, in the first sentences of paragraphs, at least three "time marker" transition phrases.

   Paragraph _____   Time marker phrase: _____

Paragraph _____   Time marker phrase: _____

Paragraph _____   Time marker phrase: _____

Where in the essay do you find these paragraphs? What is the effect of the author's use of such ordering at this point in his essay?

About Style and Tone

8. Much of Preston's article is made up of dialogue, of quotations from other sources. What does reading all these different viewpoints contribute to your perception of the possible "fairness" of Preston's look at Manon Rhéaume? Where do you find examples of Preston's own attitude toward his subject?

▓ Writing Assignments

Assignment 1: Writing a Paragraph

A writing assignment based on this selection appears on pages 214–215.

Assignment 2: Writing a Paragraph

Manon Rhéaume faces challenges and criticism from her teammates, opposing teams, the media, and undoubtedly from within herself. How do you feel about what she is trying to do?

Write a paragraph in the form of a letter in which you state your feelings about what she is doing and offer her advice or encouragement. Explain each of your points clearly, whether your details are of a personal or professional/sports-based type.

Assignment 3: Writing an Essay

Manon is a forerunner in a male-dominated field. More women enter Law Enforcement and Fire Protection programs every year, as well. There are other women, some of whom Nancy Eng mentions in her essay, such as the astronaut Sally Ride and several Canadian women politicians, who have moved into "men's work." There are also men who work at "female jobs" like nursing, and more men who enter Early Childhood Education programs at colleges.

Choose an example of a cross-over career choice for a man or a woman. What qualities would be needed by any person who entered this career? Are these qualities limited to one gender or the other? List the qualities and aptitudes before beginning to draft your essay, and break them into three categories or classifications. Review the section titled "Dividing and Classifying" in Part Two (pages 197–205) for help in this part of your prewriting.

An example of an outline for such an essay might look like this:

Thesis Statement: More men should go into Early Childhood Education, because they have three qualities which are not exclusive to women: patience, helping instincts, and stamina for dealing with young children. They would give children good male role models.

Paragraph 1: patience—no gender difference
– I helped my father raise my sisters—anyone can learn patience/e.g.
– men can be more patient as "coaches" in some skills/e.g.
– men's work often involves very painstaking, patient attention/e.g.

Paragraph 2: helping instincts—no real difference, just habit
– men already in "helping" careers: emergency-care work, etc.
– single fathers I met at school events/e.g.
– same instincts there in men, just "underdeveloped"/e.g.

Paragraph 3: stamina—men & women the same—depends on individual
– men are used to how annoying three-year-old boys are
– enduring kids is no different than enduring your teammates
– men *may* be better at certain physical demands of ECE/e.g.

Conclusion: Children need to see positive male role models, and men have many of the same qualities necessary for working with young children as women have. They just haven't realized their potential, or how useful these abilities can be.

LETTER

Judith Mackenzie

In all of our lives, there have been times when we survived some difficult situation, not because of our own efforts or toughness, but because of the kindness, grace, or generosity of others. There are also times in our lives when we are privileged to be able to help others. Both giving and receiving such generosity are our finest moments as humans: the "gift" gives to both giver and receiver endlessly. This "mystery" that is "charity" is the essence of human goodness. Sometimes highly publicized, it also occurs unnoted every day; in fact, it is often overlooked or dismissed by those too cynical to believe in it, or by those who see only the arithmetic of "give something; get something in return." In "Letter," Judith MacKenzie contemplates two intertwined personal experiences with the mysterious, and life-enriching nature of charity in action.

When I was eight years old, my father, a union organizer in the forties and fifties, was blacklisted, accused of communist activities. It meant no work—with a vengeance. My mother, then in her forties, had twin boys that spring—premature, and in premedicare times you can imagine the devastating costs for their care. I was hungry that year, hungry when I got up, hungry when I went to school, hungry when I went to sleep. In November I was asked to leave school because I only had boys' clothes to wear—hand-me-downs from a neighbour. I could come back, they said, when I dressed like a young lady.

1

The week before Christmas, the power and gas were disconnected. We ate soup **2** made from carrots, potatoes, cabbage and grain meant to feed chickens, cooked on our wood garbage burner. Even as an eight-year-old, I knew the kind of hunger we had was nothing compared to people in India and Africa. I don't think we could have died in our middle-class Vancouver suburb. But I do know that the pain of hunger is intensified and brutal when you live in the midst of plenty. As Christmas preparations increased, I felt more and more isolated, excluded, set apart. I felt a deep, abiding hunger for more than food. Christmas Eve day came, grey and full of the bleak sleety rain of a west-coast winter. Two women, strangers, struggled up our driveway, loaded down with bags. They left before my mother answered the door. The porch was full of groceries—milk, butter, bread, cheese and Christmas oranges. We never knew who they were, and after that day, pride being what it was, we never spoke of them again. But I'm forty-five years old, and I remember them well.

Since then I've crafted a life of joy and independence, if not of financial secu- **3** rity. Several years ago, living in Victoria, my son and I were walking up the street, once more in west-coast sleet and rain. It was just before Christmas and we were, as usual, counting our pennies to see if we'd have enough for all our festive treats, juggling these against the necessities. A young man stepped in front of me, very pale and carrying an old sleeping bag, and asked for spare change—not unusual in downtown Victoria. No, I said, and walked on. Something hit me like a physical blow about a block later. I left my son and walked back to find the young man. I gave him some of our Christmas luxury money—folded into a small square and tucked into his hand. It wasn't much, only ten dollars, but as I turned away, I saw the look of hopelessness turn into amazement and then joy. Well, said the rational part of my mind, Judith, you are a fool, you know he's just going up the street to the King's Hotel and spend it on drink or drugs. You've taken what belongs to your family and spent it on a frivolous romantic impulse. As I was lecturing myself on gullibility and sensible charity, I noticed the young man with the sleeping bag walking quickly up the opposite side of the street, heading straight for the King's. Well, let this be a lesson, said the rational Judith. To really rub it in, I decided to follow him. Just before the King's, he turned into a corner grocery store. I watched through the window, through the poinsettias and the stand-up Santas. I watched him buy milk, butter, bread, cheese and Christmas oranges.

Now, I have no idea how that young man arrived on the street in Victoria, nor **4** will I ever have any real grasp of the events that had led my family to a dark and hungry December. But I do know that charity cannot be treated as an RRSP. There is no best-investment way to give, no way to insure value for our dollar. Like the Magi, these three, the two older women struggling up the driveway and the young man with the sleeping bag, gave me, and continue to give me, wonderful gifts— the reminder that love and charity come most truly and abundantly from an open and unjudgemental heart.

■ **Reading Comprehension Questions**

   1. Which of the following would be the best alternative title for the selection?
     a. Christmas Gifts
     b. Giving is the Best Gift of All

      c. Charity Begins at Home
      d. Lessons in Life

2. Which sentence best expresses the main idea of the selection?
      a. Learning to give is a lifelong process.
      b. People never really know the suffering of others.
      c. Memories of generosity can make us generous.
      d. Giving freely rewards both giver and receiver.

3. The eight-year-old author felt her family's situation most acutely when
      a. she was constantly hungry and was not allowed to go to school.
      b. she realized there would be no Christmas gifts.
      c. her family was so poor they had to take handouts.
      d. she was embarrassed by the women bringing food.

4. *True or false?* _____ The author and her son were no better off than her family was during her childhood.

5. The author argues with herself about giving the young street person money because
      a. she resented people begging on the street.
      b. her past had made her prone to giving in to foolish impulses.
      c. she wanted to be logical and sensible, but remembered her own past.
      d. she was ashamed of looking stingy in front of her son.

6. The author implies that
      a. she was ashamed of wearing boys' clothes to school.
      b. schools' regulations of the time were cruel and unreasonable.
      c. wearing used "charity" clothes was painful to her.
      d. she enjoyed dressing like a "tomboy."

7. The author implies that the worst part of being hungry was
      a. the awfulness of eating food cooked on a garbage burner.
      b. her shame at starving like people in Third World countries.
      c. that the family's health was at risk because of their poor diet.
      d. feeling set apart by their deprivation in the midst of a comfortable society.

8. From the selection, we can infer that the author feels that
      a. sometimes our best actions are impulsive, rather than rational.
      b. we never understand the situations in which we find ourselves.
      c. the best gifts are those we give away.
      d. we should do without to learn the true meaning of charity.

9. The word *abiding* in "…I felt a deep, abiding hunger for more than food." (paragraph 2), means
      a. gnawing.
      b. annoying.
      c. enduring.
      d. grinding.

10. The word *gullibility* in "As I was lecturing myself on gullibility and sensible charity…" (paragraph 3) means

a. stupidity.

b. naiveté.

c. practicality.

d. generosity.

■ Discussion Questions

About Content

1. What were the reasons for the author's family's poverty during her childhood? Why was there "no work—with a vengeance" (paragraph 1) for her father?

2. Why, as Christmas approached, did the author feel a "hunger for more than food?" (paragraph 2)

3. What specific elements of the setting, characters, and their actions make the visit of the women to the family so "magical" and unexpected?

4. What are the author's reasons for saying to herself in paragraph 3, "Judith, you are a fool…", and what is she "rubbing in" as she follows the young man?

About Structure

5. "Letter" is primarily a narrative selection, and generally a brief narrative covers only a single event. However, as with "Adolescent Confusion," (pages 538–541), there are two situations narrated in "Letter", rather than one. Why might Judith MacKenzie have decided to include two events?

6. Where in the selection do you find the best statement of the author's thesis? Write the sentence(s) in the space below:

   _____

   _____

   Why has MacKenzie chosen this position for her thesis?

7. Narratives are mostly structured in *time order*. "Letter" uses transitional words and phrases to "set the stage" for each paragraph. List words and phrases that show readers when each paragraph occurs:

   (a) _____

   (b) _____

   (c) _____

   (d) _____

About Style and Tone

8. The author offers several parallel elements, as well as some elements that differ, in the two major "scenes" of her narrative. Which elements are similar in the two situations, and which are different? What is achieved by the parallels and differences?

9. "Letter" is perhaps an odd title for an essay. Why do you think MacKenzie chose this title? One element common to good personal letters and this selection is the inclusion of finely drawn details, probably aimed at evoking an emotional response. Which two of the selection's details do you find most effective, and why?

■ **Writing Assignments**

Assignment 1: Writing a Paragraph

An assignment based on this selection appears on page 204.

Assignment 2: Writing a Paragraph

Some ancient cultures believed that beggars must always be treated kindly because they might be gods in disguise. Judith MacKenzie's reaction to the street person in Victoria is probably typical of most people in today's cities: she feels torn between reason, cynicism, and sympathy. What is your reaction to being approached by one of the growing number of homeless people in Canadian cities? What would you say to someone like the young man in "Letter"?

Write a paragraph in the form of a letter, either to the person in MacKenzie's essay, or to a real person who has approached you for a handout. What would you give such a person, either as advice or as direct help, or as both? Why?

Assignment 3: Writing an Essay

Charity, or unselfish, active love for fellow humans, is held as the highest good by most of the world's cultures and religions. Indeed, in classical Judaism, the best form of charity is that where the receiver never knows the giver. Not all charity is public or even acknowledged by others. In our society, there are many types of charity, from well-publicized corporate, tax-deductible donations to the personal gift of one's time and energy to help another person.

What, to you, is the finest form of charity, and why? In an essay that explains its point with examples, discuss why one specific type of generosity is most beneficial. Think of people who exemplify human generosity or charity, or of several instances of a single person's generosity; think of situations where someone, or some group of people have acted unselfishly for another's good; such self-questioning will lead you to the specific and well-explained examples you need to argue your point of view.

WHAT GOOD FAMILIES ARE DOING RIGHT

Dolores Curran

It isn't easy to be a successful parent these days. Pressured by the conflicting demands of home and workplace, confused by changing moral standards, and drowned out by their offspring's rock music and television, today's parents seem to be facing impossible odds in their struggle to raise healthy families. Yet some parents manage to "do it all"—and even remain on speaking terms with their children. How do they do it? Dolores Curran's survey offers some significant suggestions; her article could serve as a recipe for a successful family.

I have worked with families for fifteen years, conducting hundreds of seminars, workshops, and classes on parenting, and I meet good families all the time. They're fairly easy to recognize. Good families have a kind of visible strength. They expect problems and work together to find solutions, applying common sense and trying new methods to meet new needs. And they share a common shortcoming—they can tell me in a minute what's wrong with them, but they aren't sure what's right with them. Many healthy families with whom I work, in fact, protest at being called *healthy*. They don't think they are. The professionals who work with them do.   1

To prepare the book on which this article is based, I asked respected workers in the fields of education, religion, health, family counseling,* and voluntary organizations to identify a list of possible traits of a healthy family. Together we isolated fifty-six such traits, and I sent this list to five hundred professionals who regularly work with families—teachers, doctors, principals, members of the clergy, scout directors, YMCA leaders, family counselors, social workers—asking them to pick the fifteen qualities they most commonly found in healthy families.   2

While all of these traits are important, the one most often cited as central to close family life is communication: The healthy family knows how to talk—and how to listen.   3

"Without communication you don't know one another," wrote one family counselor. "If you don't know one another, you don't care about one another, and that's what the family is all about."   4

"The most familiar complaint I hear from wives I counsel is 'He won't talk to me' and 'He doesn't listen to me,'" said a pastoral marriage counselor. "And when I share this complaint with their husbands, they don't hear *me*, either."   5

"We have kids in classes whose families are so robotized by television that they don't know one another," said a fifth-grade teacher.   6

Professional counselors are not the only ones to recognize the need. The phenomenal growth of communication groups such as Parent Effectiveness Training, Parent Awareness, Marriage Encounter, Couple Communication, and literally hundreds of others tells us that the need for effective communication—the sharing of deepest feelings—is felt by many.   7

Healthy families have also recognized this need, and they have, either instinctively or consciously, developed methods of meeting it. They know that conflicts are to be expected, that we all become angry and frustrated and discouraged. And they know how to reveal those feelings—good and bad—to each other. Honest   8

*American spellings (such as "counseling") appear in this article and others in this book which have been reprinted from U.S. sources, or from Canadian sources which use U.S. spellings.

communication isn't always easy. But when it's working well, there are certain recognizable signs or symptoms, what I call the hallmarks of the successfully communicating family.

The Family Exhibits a Strong Relationship between the Parents

According to Dr. Jerry M. Lewis—author of a significant work on families, *No Single Thread*—healthy spouses complement, rather than dominate, each other. Either husband or wife could be the leader, depending on the circumstances. In the unhealthy families he studied, the dominant spouse had to hide feelings of weakness while the submissive spouse feared being put down if he or she exposed a weakness.   9

Children in the healthy family have no question about which parent is boss. Both parents are. If children are asked who is boss, they're likely to respond, "Sometimes Mom, sometimes Dad." And, in a wonderful statement, Dr. Lewis adds, "if you ask if they're comfortable with this, they look at you as if you're crazy—as if there's no other way it ought to be."   10

My survey respondents echo Dr. Lewis. One wrote, "The healthiest families I know are ones in which the mother and father have a strong, loving relationship. This seems to flow over to the children and even beyond the home. It seems to breed security in the children and, in turn, fosters the ability to take risks, to reach out to others, to search for their own answers, become independent and develop a good self-image."   11

The Family Has Control over Television

Television has been maligned, praised, damned, cherished, and even thrown out. It has more influence on children's values than anything else except their parents. Over and over, when I'm invited to help families mend their communication ruptures, I hear "But we have no time for this." These families have literally turned their "family-together" time over to television. Even those who control the quality of programs watched and set "homework-first" regulations feel reluctant to intrude upon the individual's right to spend his or her spare time in front of the set. Many families avoid clashes over program selection by furnishing a set for each family member. One of the women who was most desperate to establish a better sense of communication in her family confided to me that they owned nine sets. Nine sets for seven people!   12

Whether the breakdown in family communication leads to excessive viewing or whether too much television breaks into family lives, we don't know. But we do know that we can become out of one another's reach when we're in front of a TV set. The term *television widow* is not humorous to thousands whose spouses are absent even when they're there. One woman remarked, "I can't get worried about whether there's life after death. I'd be satisfied with life after dinner."   13

In family-communication workshops, I ask families to make a list of phrases they most commonly hear in their home. One parent was aghast to discover that his family's most familiar comments were "What's on?" and "Move." In families like this one, communication isn't hostile—it's just missing.   14

But television doesn't have to be a villain. A 1980 Gallup Poll found that the **15** public sees great potential for television as a positive force. It can be a tremendous device for initiating discussion on subjects that may not come up elsewhere, subjects such as sexuality, corporate ethics, sportsmanship, and marital fidelity.

Even very bad programs offer material for values clarification if family mem- **16** bers view them together. My sixteen-year-old son and his father recently watched a program in which hazardous driving was part of the hero's characterization. At one point, my son turned to his dad and asked, "Is that possible to do with that kind of truck?"

"I don't know," replied my husband, "but it sure is dumb. If that load **17** shifted …" With that, they launched into a discussion on the responsibility of drivers that didn't have to originate as a parental lecture. Furthermore, as the discussion became more engrossing to them, they turned the sound down so that they could continue their conversation.

Parents frequently report similar experiences; in fact, this use of television was **18** recommended in the widely publicized 1972 Surgeon General's report as the most effective form of television gatekeeping by parents. Instead of turning off the set, parents should view programs with their children and make moral judgments and initiate discussion. Talking about the problems and attitudes of a TV family can be a lively, nonthreatening way to risk sharing real fears, hopes, and dreams.

The Family Listens and Responds

"My parents say they want me to come to them with problems, but when I do, **19** either they're busy or they only half-listen and keep on doing what they were doing—like shaving or making a grocery list. If a friend of theirs came over to talk, they'd stop, be polite, and listen," said one of the children quoted in a *Christian Science Monitor* interview by Ann McCarroll. This child put his finger on the most difficult problem of communicating in families: the inability to listen.

It is usually easier to react than to respond. When we react, we reflect our own **20** experiences and feelings; when we respond, we get into the other person's feelings. For example:

> *Tom, age seventeen:* "I don't know if I want to go to college. I don't think I'd do very well there."
> *Father:* "Nonsense. Of course you'll do well."

That's reacting. This father is cutting off communication. He's refusing either **21** to hear the boy's fears or to consider his feelings, possibly because he can't accept the idea that his son might not attend college. Here's another way of handling the same situation:

> *Tom:* "I don't know if I want to go to college. I don't think I'd do very well there."
> *Father:* "Why not?"
> *Tom:* "Because I'm not that smart."
> *Father:* "Yeah, that's scary. I worried about that, too."

Tom: "Did you ever come close to flunking out?"

Father: "No, but I worried a lot before I went because I thought college would be full of brains. Once I got there, I found out that most of the kids were just like me."

22 This father has responded rather than reacted to his son's fears. First, he searched for the reason behind his son's lack of confidence and found it was fear of academic ability (it could have been fear of leaving home, of a new environment, of peer pressure, or of any of a number of things); second, he accepted the fear as legitimate; third, he empathized by admitting to having the same fear when he was Tom's age; and, finally, he explained why his, not Tom's, fears turned out to be groundless. He did all this without denigrating or lecturing.

23 And that's tough for parents to do. Often we don't want to hear our children's fears, because those fears frighten us; or we don't want to pay attention to their dreams because their dreams aren't what we have in mind for them. Parents who deny such feelings will allow only surface conversation. It's fine as long as a child says, "School was okay today," but when she says, "I'm scared of boys," the parents are uncomfortable. They don't want her to be afraid of boys, but since they don't quite know what to say, they react with a pleasant "Oh, you'll outgrow it." She probably will, but what she needs at the moment is someone to hear and understand her pain.

24 In Ann McCarroll's interviews, she talked to one fifteen-year-old boy who said he had "*some* mother. Each morning she sits with me while I eat breakfast. We talk about anything and everything. She isn't refined or elegant or educated. She's a terrible housekeeper. But she's interested in everything I do, and she always listens to me—even if she's busy or tired."

25 That's the kind of listening found in families that experience real communication. Answers to the routine question, "How was your day?" are heard with the eyes and heart as well as the ears. Nuances are picked up and questions are asked, although problems are not necessarily solved. Members of a family who really listen to one another instinctively know that if people listen to you, they are interested in you. And that's enough for most of us.

The Family Recognizes Unspoken Messages

26 Much of our communication—especially our communication of feelings—is nonverbal. Dr. Lewis defines *empathy* as "someone responding to you in such a way that you feel deeply understood." He says, "There is probably no more important dimension in all of human relationships than the capacity for empathy. And healthy families teach empathy." Its members are allowed to be mad, glad, and sad. There's no crime in being in a bad mood, nor is there betrayal in being happy while someone else is feeling moody. The family recognizes that bad days and good days attack everyone at different times.

27 Nonverbal expressions of love, too, are the best way to show children that parents love each other. A spouse reaching for the other's hand, a wink, a squeeze on the shoulder, a "How's-your-back-this-morning?" a meaningful glance across the room—all these tell children how their parents feel about each other.

The most destructive nonverbal communication in marriage is silence. Silence **28** can mean lack of interest, hostility, denigration, boredom, or outright war. On the part of a teen or preteen, silence usually indicates pain, sometimes very deep pain. The sad irony discovered by so many family therapists is that parents who seek professional help when a teenager becomes silent have often denied the child any other way of communicating. And although they won't permit their children to become angry or to reveal doubts or to share depression, they do worry about the withdrawal that results. Rarely do they see any connection between the two.

Healthy families use signs, symbols, body language, smiles, and other gestures **29** to express caring and love. They deal with silence and withdrawal in a positive, open way. Communication doesn't mean just talking or listening; it includes all the clues to a person's feelings—his bearing, her expression, their resignation. Family members don't have to say, "I'm hurting," or, "I'm in need." A quick glance tells that. And they have developed ways of responding that indicate caring and love, whether or not there's an immediate solution to the pain.

The Family Encourages Individual Feelings and Independent Thinking

Close families encourage the emergence of individual personalities through open **30** sharing of thoughts and feelings. Unhealthy families tend to be less open, less accepting of differences among members. The family must be Republican, or Bronco supporters, or gun-control advocates, and woe to the individual who says, "Yes, but...."

Instead of finding differing opinions threatening, the healthy family finds them **31** exhilarating. It is exciting to witness such a family discussing politics, sports, or the world. Members freely say, "I don't agree with you," without risking ridicule or rebuke. They say, "I think it's wrong ..." immediately after Dad says, "I think it's right ..."; and Dad listens and responds.

Give-and-take gives children practice in articulating their thoughts at home so **32** that eventually they'll feel confident outside the home. What may seem to be verbal rambling by preteens during a family conversation is a prelude to sorting out their thinking and putting words to their thoughts.

Rigid families don't understand the dynamics of give-and-take. Some label it **33** disrespectful and argumentative; others find it confusing. Dr. John Meeks, medical director of the Psychiatric Institute of Montgomery County, Maryland, claims that argument is a way of life with normally developing adolescents. "In early adolescence they'll argue with parents about anything at all; as they grow older, the quantity of argument decreases but the quality increases." According to Dr. Meeks, arguing is something adolescents need to do. If the argument doesn't become too bitter, they have a good chance to test their own beliefs and feelings. "Incidentally," says Meeks, "parents can expect to 'lose' most of these arguments, because adolescents are not fettered by logic or even reality." Nor are they likely to be polite. Learning how to disagree respectfully is a difficult task, but good families work at it.

Encouraging individual feelings and thoughts, of course, in no way presumes **34** that parents permit their children to do whatever they want. There's a great difference between permitting a son to express an opinion on marijuana and allowing him to use it. That his opinion conflicts with his parents' opinion is OK as long as his parents make sure he knows their thinking on the subject. Whether he admits it or not, he's likely at least to consider their ideas if he respects them.

Permitting teenagers to sort out their feelings and thoughts in open discus-   35
sions at home gives them valuable experience in dealing with a bewildering array of situations they may encounter when they leave home. Cutting off discussion of behavior unacceptable to us, on the other hand, makes our young people feel guilty for even thinking about values contrary to ours and ends up making those values more attractive to them.

The Family Recognizes Turn-Off Words and Put-Down Phrases

Some families deliberately use hurtful language in their daily communication.   36
"What did you do all day around here?" can be a red flag to a woman who has spent her day on household tasks that don't show unless they're not done. "If only we had enough money" can be a rebuke to a husband who is working as hard as he can to provide for the family. "Flunk any tests today, John?" only discourages a child who may be having trouble in school.

Close families seem to recognize that a comment made in jest can be insult-   37
ing. A father in one of my groups confided that he could tease his wife about every-thing but her skiing. "I don't know why she's so sensitive about that, but I back off on it. I can say anything I want to about her cooking, her appearance, her moth-ering—whatever. But not her skiing."

One of my favorite exercises with families is to ask them to reflect upon phrases   38
they most like to hear and those they least like to hear. Recently, I invited seventy-five fourth- and fifth-graders to submit the words they most like to hear from their mothers. Here are the five big winners:

> *"I love you."*
> *"Yes."*
> *"Time to eat."*
> *"You can go."*
> *"You can stay up late."*

And on the children's list of what they least like to hear from one another are   39
the following:

> *"I'm telling."*
> *"Mom says!"*
> *"I know something you don't know."*
> *"You think you're so big."*
> *"Just see if I ever let you use my bike again."*

It can be worthwhile for a family to list the phrases members like most and   40
least to hear, and post them. Often parents aren't even aware of the reaction of their children to certain routine comments. Or keep a record of the comments heard most often over a period of a week or two. It can provide good clues to the level of

family sensitivity. If the list has a lot of "shut ups" and "stop its," that family needs to pay more attention to its relationships, especially the role that communication plays in them.

The Family Interrupts, but Equally

When Dr. Jerry M. Lewis began to study the healthy family, he and his staff video-taped families in the process of problem solving. The family was given a question, such as, "What's the main thing wrong with your family?" Answers varied, but what was most significant was what the family actually did: who took control, how individuals responded or reacted, what were the put-downs, and whether some members were entitled to speak more than others.   **41**

The researchers found that healthy families expected everyone to speak openly about feelings. Nobody was urged to hold back. In addition, these family members interrupted one another repeatedly, but no one person was interrupted more than anyone else.   **42**

Manners, particularly polite conversational techniques, are not hallmarks of the communicating family. This should make many parents feel better about their family's dinner conversation. One father reported to me that at their table people had to take a number to finish a sentence. Finishing sentences, however, doesn't seem all that important in the communicating family. Members aren't sensitive to being interrupted, either. The intensity and spontaneity of the exchange are more important than propriety in conversation.   **43**

The Family Develops a Pattern of Reconciliation

"We know how to break up," one man said, "but who ever teaches us to make up?" Survey respondents indicated that there is indeed a pattern of reconciliation in healthy families that is missing in others. "It usually isn't a kiss-and-make-up situation," explained one family therapist, "but there are certain rituals developed over a long period of time that indicate it's time to get well again. Between husband and wife, it might be a concessionary phrase to which the other is expected to respond in kind. Within a family, it might be that the person who stomps off to his or her room voluntarily reenters the family circle, where something is said to make him or her welcome."   **44**

When I asked several families how they knew a fight had ended, I got remark-ably similar answers from individuals questioned separately. "We all come out of our rooms," responded every member of one family. Three members of another family said, "Mom says, 'Anybody want a Pepsi?'" One five-year-old scratched his head and furrowed his forehead after I asked him how he knew the family fight was over. Finally, he said, "Well, Daddy gives a great big yawn and says, 'Well …'" This scene is easy to visualize, as one parent decides that the unpleasantness needs to end and it's time to end the fighting and to pull together again as a family.   **45**

Why have we neglected the important art of reconciling? "Because we have pre-tended that good families don't fight," says one therapist. "They do. It's essential to fight for good health in the family. It gets things out into the open. But we need to learn to put ourselves back together—and many families never learn this."   **46**

Close families know how to time divisive and emotional issues that may cause   47
friction. They don't bring up potentially explosive subjects right before they go out,
for example, or before bedtime. They tend to schedule discussions rather than
allow a matter to explode, and thus they keep a large measure of control over the
atmosphere in which they will fight and reconcile. Good families know that they
need enough time to discuss issues heatedly, rationally, and completely—and
enough time to reconcile. "You've got to solve it right there," said one father. "Don't
let it go on and on. It just causes more problems. Then when it's solved, let it be.
No nagging, no remembering."

The Family Fosters Table Time and Conversation

Traditionally, the dinner table has been a symbol of socialization. It's probably the   48
one time each day that parents and children are assured of uninterrupted time with
one another.

Therapists frequently call upon a patient's memory of the family table during   49
childhood in order to determine the degree of communication and interaction
there was in the patient's early life. Some patients recall nothing. Mealtime was
either so unpleasant or so unimpressive that they have blocked it out of their memories. Therapists say that there is a relationship between the love in a home and life
around the family table. It is to the table that love or discord eventually comes.

But we are spending less table time together. Fast-food dining, even within the   50
home, is becoming a way of life for too many of us. Work schedules, individual
organized activities, and television all limit the quantity and quality of mealtime
interaction. In an informal study conducted by a church group, 68 percent of the
families interviewed in three congregations saw nothing wrong with watching television while eating.

Families who do a good job of communicating tend to make the dinner meal   51
an important part of their day. A number of respondents indicated that adults in
the healthiest families refuse dinner business meetings as a matter of principle and
discourage their children from sports activities that cut into mealtime hours. "We
know which of our swimmers will or won't practice at dinnertime," said a coach,
with mixed admiration. "Some parents never allow their children to miss dinners.
Some don't care at all." These families pay close attention to the number of times
they'll be able to be together in a week, and they rearrange schedules to be sure of
spending this time together.

The family that wants to improve communication should look closely at its atti-   52
tudes toward the family table. Are family table time and conversation important? Is
table time open and friendly or warlike and sullen? Is it conducive to sharing more
than food—does it encourage the sharing of ideas, feelings, and family intimacies?

We all need to talk to one another. We need to know we're loved and appreci-   53
ated and respected. We want to share our intimacies, not just physical intimacies
but all the intimacies in our lives. Communication is the most important element
of family life because it is basic to loving relationships. It is the energy that fuels
the caring, giving, sharing, and affirming. Without genuine sharing of ourselves,
we cannot know one another's needs and fears. Good communication is what
makes all the rest of it work.

■ Reading Comprehension Questions

1. Which of the following would be the best alternative title for this selection?
   a. Successful Communication
   b. How to Solve Family Conflicts
   c. Characteristics of Families
   d. Hallmarks of the Communicating Family

2. Which sentence best expresses the article's main point?
   a. Television can and often does destroy family life.
   b. More North American families are unhappy than ever before.
   c. A number of qualities mark the healthy and communicating family.
   d. Strong families encourage independent thinking.

3. *True or false?* _____ According to the article, healthy families have no use for television.

4. Healthy families
   a. never find it hard to communicate.
   b. have no conflicts with each other.
   c. know how to reveal their feelings.
   d. permit one of the parents to make all final decisions.

5. The author has found that good families frequently make a point of being together
   a. in the mornings.
   b. after school.
   c. during dinner.
   d. before bedtime.

6. *True or false?* _____ The article implies that the most troublesome nonverbal signal is silence.

7. The article implies that
   a. verbal messages are always more accurate than nonverbal ones.
   b. in strong families, parents practise tolerance of thoughts and feelings.
   c. parents must avoid arguing with their adolescent children.
   d. parents should prevent their children from watching television.

8. From the article, we can conclude that
   a. a weak marital relationship often results in a weak family.
   b. children should not witness a disagreement between parents.
   c. children who grow up in healthy families learn not to interrupt other family members.
   d. parents always find it easier to respond to their children than to react to them.

9. The word *aghast* in "One parent was aghast to discover that his family's most familiar comments were 'What's on?' and 'Move'" (paragraph 14) means
   a. horrified.
   b. satisfied.

    c. curious.

    d. amused.

10. The word *engrossing* in "as the discussion became more engrossing to them, they turned the sound down so that they could continue their conversation" (paragraph 17) means

    a. disgusting.

    b. intellectual.

    c. foolish.

    d. interesting.

▓ Discussion Questions

About Content

1. What are the nine hallmarks of a successfully communicating family? Which of the nine do you feel are most important?

2. How do good parents control television watching? How do they make television a positive force instead of a negative one?

3. In paragraph 20, the author says, "It is usually easier to react than to respond." What is the difference between the two terms *react* and *respond*? Give an example of each word in use, based on your own experience.

4. Why, according to Curran, is a "pattern of reconciliation" (paragraph 44) crucial to good family life? Besides those patterns mentioned in the essay, can you describe a reconciliation pattern you have developed with friends or family?

About Structure

5. What is the thesis of the selection? Write here the number of the paragraph in which it is stated: _____

6. What purpose is achieved by Curran's introduction (paragraphs 1–2)? Why is a reader likely to feel her article will be reliable and worthwhile?

7. Curran frequently uses dialogue or quotations from unnamed parents or children as the basis for her examples. The conversation related in paragraphs 16–17 is one instance. Find three other dialogues used to illustrate points in the essay and write the numbers below:

Paragraphs _____ to _____

Paragraphs _____ to _____

Paragraphs _____ to _____

About Style and Tone

8. Curran enlivens the essay by using some interesting and humorous remarks from parents, children, and counsellors. One is the witty comment in

paragraph 5 from a marriage counsellor: "And when I share this complaint with their husbands, they don't hear *me*, either." Find two other places where the author keeps your interest by using humorous or enjoyable quotations, and write the numbers of the paragraphs here:

_____   _____

Writing Assignments

Assignment 1: Writing a Paragraph

A writing assignment based on this selection is on pages 195–196.

Assignment 2: Writing a Paragraph

Curran tells us five phrases that some children say they most like to hear from their parents (paragraph 38). When you were younger, what statement or action of one of your parents (or another adult) would make you especially happy—or sad? Write a paragraph that begins with a topic sentence like one of the following:

> A passing comment my grandfather once made really devastated me.
>
> When I was growing up, there were several typical ways my mother treated me that always made me sad or happy.
>
> A critical remark by my grade five teacher was the low point of my life.
>
> My mother has always had several lines that make her children feel very pleased.

You may want to write a narrative that describes in detail the particular time and place in which a statement or action occurred. Or you may want to provide three or so examples of statements or actions and their effect upon you.

To get started, make up two long lists of childhood memories involving adults—happy memories and sad memories. Then decide which memory or memories you could most vividly describe in a paragraph. Remember that your goal is to help your readers see for themselves why a particular time was sad or happy for you.

Assignment 3: Writing an Essay

In light of Curran's description of what healthy families do right, examine your own family. Which of Curran's traits of communicative families fit your family? Write an essay pointing out three things that your family is doing right in creating a communicative climate for its members. Or, if you feel your family could work harder at communicating, write the essay about three specific ways your family could improve. In either case, choose three of Curran's nine "hallmarks of the successfully communicating family" and show how they do or do not apply to your family.

In your introductory paragraph, include a thesis statement as well as a plan of development that lists the three traits you will talk about. Then present these traits in turn in three supporting paragraphs. Develop each paragraph by giving specific examples of conversations, arguments, behaviour patterns, and so on, that illustrate how your family communicates. Finally, conclude your essay with a summarizing sentence or two and a final thought about your subject.

DECOYS AND DENIAL

Frank Jones

Many students have reading and writing difficulties. A few are actually dyslexic, or have physical challenges which slow or impede their progress in communications skills. Although there is still a statistically noted incidence of various types of illiteracy in Canada today, schools are generally quicker to catch dysfunctional problems now. As you will read in the article below, such was not the case for Steve Lloyd in Ontario thirty years ago. He became a successful businessman and a collector of objects that, as author Frank Jones says, are "a bluff and an illusion." Read the story of Steve's two successes in life, and think about why "Steve's whole life has been a decoy."

Steve Lloyd is the decoy man.   1

At the Sportsmen's Show, at the Toronto Hunting and Outdoor Show, you'll   2
find Steve with some of his vast collection of wooden duck decoys talking all day—
until he generally loses his voice—about his great passion.

People wonder what his angle is. He isn't there to sell decoys or to buy them.   3
In fact, he's there at his own expense simply to convince people that Canada's old
decoys are worth preserving—and keeping here, where they belong.

That's remarkable enough. But if you think of a decoy—a wooden or plastic   4
bird used by hunters to lure ducks or geese down to the water—as a bluff and an
illusion, then Steve's whole life has been a decoy.

He's spent years pretending, hiding from a devastating truth that was only   5
revealed to *him* two years ago. And that he talked about openly for the first time
when I spoke to him last week.

First, the Steve Lloyd people know: 6

The story of how Steve, 37, fell in love with decoys sounds like something from   7
Canada's remote past. Growing up in Scarborough, he remembers, as a small boy,
being responsible for his father's basket of decoys when they went hunting in a
small boat on Frenchman's Bay.

It would be pitch dark when they'd set out. As darkness lifted, guns would pop   8
and sometimes shot would rain down from the sky.

"How careful you had to be not to break the decoys' beaks or tails! And you   9
had to count them constantly to make sure you hadn't lost any," he says.

When Steve was 12, the family moved to Belleville, and there were even more   10
opportunities for hunting with his father and his uncle.

At 21 he got married and his dad said it was time he got his own decoys.   11

"Fall was coming and I saw an ad for decoys in the paper," he says.   12

The elderly man who had placed the ad took him out to his garage. "He had   13
at least 300 to 400 on a shelf right around the garage. To him they were just working tools for hunting. He wanted $200 for them," says Steve. "I could not remem-
ber ever having $200."

He bought four of them for $2 each. Today, he estimates, the decoys would be   14
worth $1,000 each. But when Steve was later offered $10 each for his four, he
thought it was easy money.

Thus began an episode over which Steve feels a good deal of guilt. He started   15
scouting the countryside for decoys, which he sold to a Toronto dealer. He helped
create the present situation where, he says, most of Canada's priceless heritage of
decoys, including models of tiny wading birds once hunted on the Toronto Islands,
as well as huge, hollow wooden swans, are in the hands of foreigners, with many
today going to Japan.

When he really began to appreciate the art of the decoys, he started putting   16
good ones aside. A collector was born—who would one day tell thousands about
the beauty of the birds and even be featured nationwide on a CBC show.

But all his life, as he spoke in public about his great interest and rose to positions   17
of power as national sales manager for a couple of large companies, Steve had a secret.

"When will you learn to spell!" an older secretary would ask him at one of the   18
firms, trying to unravel his confused notes. It was worse than that. "I have never
read a book in my life," he admitted to me.

At school he was a dud. Spelling tests were nightmares. He simply couldn't   19
make sense of the textbooks.

"My family almost had a celebration if I had a 50 per cent mark," he says.   20

In hands-on work, he was outstanding. His high school shop teacher passed him   21
when he assembled a running engine, even though he couldn't read the manual.

As his career advanced, he developed coping mechanisms. "I hid behind the   22
phone. But if I had to write a report, I was lost."

He would even quit a job in frustration—before his shortcomings were exposed.   23

With his wife Debbie and their three daughters, he moved to Calgary for three   24
years, but returned to Brockville so the children could be close to their grandparents. For five years he worked in a factory (the only well-paying job available close
to home) before deciding, with Debbie's encouragement, that no matter how
painful it was, he must return to college to train for a better job.

It was when he was tested at St. Lawrence College that Gail Easton, a special   25
needs counsellor, discovered he had a learning disability that had prevented him
from reading and writing properly.

"I denied it at first. How could I have accomplished so much if this was true?"   26
The answer, he found: "I am always pushing myself to run with two legs when I
only have one. I didn't know anything was wrong. That's what's scary."

Now he's grateful to Gail. "She found the key that has taken away a mountain   27
of frustration. Now I sleep nights."

But knowing is different from curing. "There's no pill for this. You can't put a   28
crutch under your arm," he was told.

Ironically, the new career Steve had set his heart on was as a developmental ser-   29
vice worker: helping people with disabilities. Now he realizes he wasn't just helping "them." He was one of "them."

Working on a college placement with a small boy facing the problems he had   30
at school made him realize that maybe he had special insights, special ways of asking questions, that could bring out that bottled-up intelligence.

He knows his strong points: patience, the gift of the gab, and a love of chil-   31
dren. Today, he's bringing them all to bear at his new job at the Rideau Centre for
the developmentally handicapped at Smiths Falls. The best part: seeing if you can
make someone's day better.

He's found there is, too, a crutch for him. At work, he carries a desktop computer that, with Debbie's help, he has programmed to help him make out his reports. Most of the people he works with, he says, aren't aware of his disability.   **32**

A page of print still looks like a confusing jumble to Steve. (It will take him more than an hour to figure out what this article is about.)   **33**

But Wendy, 14, is proud of him. "My dad went back to school—and passed everything," he's heard her tell people. Alisa, 9, "reads and spells beautifully," he says. And Mallory, 6, has caught on to her dad's tricks. "Well that's very interesting," she will say when he pretends to read her a book, picking up clues from the pictures, "but it's not the story Mom read."   **34**

▓ Reading Comprehension Questions

1. Which of the following would be the best alternative title for this selection?
   a. A Collector's Passion
   b. Steve's Story
   c. Secrets, Self-Discovery, and Success
   d. Collecting a Cover Story

2. Which sentence best expresses the main idea of the selection?
   a. People develop amazing compensating skills, but facing and working on deficiencies releases us to do our best.
   b. Steve Lloyd's whole life was a sham and an amazing cover-up.
   c. Literacy problems can cripple a person's entire life.
   d. Steve Lloyd's guilt over his decoy collection nearly prevented his early success in life.

3. Steve Lloyd currently makes his living
   a. selling highly collectable duck decoys.
   b. teaching children to read.
   c. working with developmentally challenged people.
   d. as a powerful sales executive.

4. According to the author, Lloyd feels guilty because
   a. of all the decoys he bought up, which drove up prices on them.
   b. decoys became so desirable that a Canadian craft ended up as an export.
   c. he knowingly destroyed part of Canada's heritage.
   d. he kept all the finest decoys for himself.

5. Lloyd's major discovery about himself was caused by
   a. the poor pay he received at the only job he could get.
   b. the fact that he works so hard at everything he tries.
   c. his and his wife's decision that he should go back to college.
   d. the fact that he couldn't write a business report.

6. The author implies that
   a. Lloyd could make a living as a spokesperson for Canadian crafts.
   b. Lloyd liked decoys only because he enjoyed hunting so much.
   c. Lloyd collects decoys only to remind himself not to trick people any more.
   d. Lloyd's success kept him from realizing how much he was fooling himself.

7. The author implies that Steve Lloyd's compensating skills
   a. actually made him more persuasive, and more of a success in business.
   b. were strictly a result of his enthusiasm for decoys.
   c. weren't quite enough to prevent growing frustration and career problems.
   d. landed him in a dead-end job ultimately.

8. *True or false?* _____ Steve Lloyd enjoys helping others with learning disabilities because he has overcome his own.

9. The word *devastating* in "He's spent years pretending, hiding from a devastating truth that was only revealed to *him* two years ago" (paragraph 5) means
   a. horrible.
   b. hidden.
   c. shattering.
   d. obvious.

10. The words *developmentally handicapped* in "his new job at the Rideau Centre for the developmentally handicapped at Smiths Falls" (paragraph 31) mean
    a. learning skills impaired.
    b. physically challenged.
    c. motor skills impaired.
    d. mentally challenged.

Discussion Questions

About Content

1. Why does the journalist Frank Jones call Lloyd "the decoy man" in his opening sentence?

2. Read paragraphs 1–17 and find at least three qualities in Steve Lloyd which would make him someone worthy of a newspaper columnist's interest.

3. What do you find to be the most amazing fact about Steve Lloyd's school years? Why?

4. Why does Jones describe Steve Lloyd's new career choice as ironic in paragraph 29? Why might it have been an excellent choice?

About Structure

5. Jones opens his article with a simple sentence with multiple meanings, two of which are discussed in the first five paragraphs. Starting with paragraph 6, find three divisions or breaks in Lloyd's story, and indicate the paragraph numbers and "signal words" which begin those paragraphs. What is the subject of each section of the narrative? List the paragraph numbers, the signal words, and a phrase which covers the subject of each section you indicate below:

   Paragraph 6 – _____   Signal word: _____   Subject: _____

   Paragraph _____ – _____   Signal word: _____   Subject: _____

   Paragraph _____ – _____   Signal word: _____   Subject: _____

6. The author lets Steve Lloyd tell his own story in direct speech, and includes dialogue quotations from other people. How do at least three of these pieces of dialogue support the thesis of the selection?

About Style and Tone

7. The author quotes Steve Lloyd as he uses certain figures of speech called *metaphors*. A metaphor is simply the verbal substitution of one idea for another, as in "My friend is a *rock* to lean on when I'm worried." No "like" or "as" is used (such a figure of speech is a *simile*); a metaphor is a *direct* substitution of one idea for another.

    One example of a metaphor is found in paragraph 26, where Lloyd says, "I am always pushing myself to run with two legs when I only have one." What does he mean by this?

    Find two other examples of metaphors used in the dialogue quoted in the article, and explain what is meant by them.

8. Jones concludes his article with quotations from Lloyd's children. How do the first two comments confirm Lloyd's achievements? What does Mallory Lloyd's final observation about her father's story-reading talents suggest about the "decoy man"?

▪ Writing Assignments

Assignment 1: Writing a Paragraph

We have all known people who have overcome great obstacles in their lives. Sometimes, we *are* those people. Some develop coping or managing skills, so that their disability or problem is never apparent to others. Sometimes such people can be a source of inspiration, or actual help, to others.

Write a paragraph about someone you know, or about yourself, which describes three ways in which that person has dealt with a major problem or a disability. As you prepare to write, describe the problem precisely, and list the efforts or trials which the person has undergone to try to overcome, or compensate for, their obstacle. Choose the three strongest details from your list as support for your point, and conclude with a statement about the end result of this individual's efforts for him- or herself and for others.

Assignment 2: Writing a Paragraph

How successful are any of us at fooling others? Can you or I maintain a "decoy" personality which hides what we don't wish others to see? To some degree, society and manners dictate that we all must hide some of our feelings and desires to maintain ordinary levels of politeness and social function. But when, if ever, does this habit become a liability? Is the harm in maintaining "multiple personalities" only a matter of "how often" and "for how long?" Or do we sometimes end up hurting ourselves and others by hiding what we feel are vulnerable spots?

Write a paragraph about some "coping mechanisms" of your own, or those of someone you know well. Describe whatever it is that you are trying to hide or compensate for—shyness, lack of mathematical ability, feeling too short or too tall; then describe the actions and evasive manoeuvres you have used to avoid drawing attention to what you feel to be a deficiency. Have your attempts always succeeded? Or have you faced up to your perceived deficiency and dealt with it? Try to analyze where your "decoys" have taken you, and conclude with an evaluation of how you feel now about the way you coped with this aspect of yourself.

Assignment 3: Writing an Essay

How do *you* react to stories like that of Steve Lloyd and those of rich and successful people with little education? Lloyd faced his demon and put his disability to good use. The American magazine *Esquire* published a similar story, "The Man Who Couldn't Read," about a U.S. college teacher and real-estate millionaire, John Corcoran, who is now a literacy advocate. Other people, with great weaknesses in communications skills but high persuasive and mechanical abilities, have simply proceeded to sell the world their success stories while boasting that they never read a newspaper. Apparently, they can live with their "decoy" skills.

Has the advent of high-technology-based business lessened the need for communications skills? Decide how important you feel reading and writing are to your professional future in the twenty-first century. If you could barely read a memo or computer screen, much less make sense of a technical report, could you find ways around those problems?

Choose your response to this statement, made by a student:

I can live without English, and half the time I fail it anyway, but without accounting and my tech courses, I'll never make a decent salary.

Line up possible point-form responses under the headings "Agree" and "Disagree." Reread Jones' article, especially paragraphs 18–23. Consider your own career hopes or choices, and write a persuasive essay that agrees or disagrees with the student's statement above. Remember that persuading your audience depends on facts and logic, as well as on the force of your feelings. Your three supporting points should be carefully thought out and based as much on experience or your reading as possible.

A possible scratch outline for an "I disagree" essay might look like the following:

Thesis: – disagree/I'm in accounting
– numbers important, but must report to boss, etc.
– must also read tax and business reports, audits & understand
– have to write to clients after entry level & represent firm

Paragraph 1: accuracy & math skills essential to accounting, but have to read memos, write them, give presentations, talk to management

Paragraph 2: already have to read thick books on tax laws & understand annual reports & company audits—will only have to read more in future

Paragraph 3: want to be promoted, to have individual & even corporate clients to succeed/money belongs to *people*—have to write to them about what I do with it & bigger clients want formal reports/write as rep. of company

Intro 1—3 (thesis last
body 4.5.6
con clu . 7.

TRUTH OR CONSEQUENCES

Laura J. Turner

Have you ever told a lie? Answering no to that question would create an immediate contradiction for all of us. We all lie, bend the truth, give exciting excuses for things undone, and flatter people without many second thoughts. But how serious is this very human habit? When does it become a problem? When does it seem "necessary"? Laura J. Turner, formerly in public relations and now an English student at the University of Regina, has an interesting view of how we evaluate the relative "sinfulness" of this most common human habit.

When we intentionally make false statements, we lie. Lies are regarded as sins, vices, transgressions, and immoral offences. Lies are not modern phenomena: lies have been around forever. They permeate all cultures and all eras of history; lies are universal. That we should not lie is implied by one of the Ten Commandments. Nevertheless, whether we are pious or not, we generally agree that lies are socially and morally wrong. We despise lies, and more especially, we despise liars. We regard liars as social deviants, reprobates; we rank them near the bottom of the social hierarchy. Still, we all lie.   1

We are inherently prone to lying, I suppose because we are subject to original sin. To tell a lie is to be intrinsically human. Yet we regard lying as wicked depravity while, at the same time, we continue to lie. Lies come in different shapes and sizes. Though all are lies by definition, some lies are sanctioned by society, some are tolerated and others, of course, frowned upon. How are we able simultaneously to hold these conflicting viewpoints concerning lies? We classify lies as little white lies, half-truths, and barefaced lies and then impose upon them a ranking according to their degree of social acceptance or the severity of their immorality.   2

We categorize lies so that little white lies are less profane and more socially and morally acceptable than the lies of the opposite end of the scale, barefaced lies; half-truths fall in the middle range. In other words, this hierarchical system of lies we have developed enables us to justify the telling of harmless little white lies, to condone half-truths, and to disapprove of barefaced lies. *)thesis*   3

Topic sentence. We first encounter little white lies at birth; we are cooed at: "My, isn't she beautiful. She looks just like you." This is a lie, albeit a little white lie. Babies are not beautiful; they are red and wrinkly and do not resemble their parents at all. Little white lies are often told by kind, polite persons in an attempt to be socially or politically correct. When we wish to say the right thing, spare someone's feelings, pay a compliment, or make someone feel better, we make selfless statements that bend or stretch the truth, usually to benefit someone else. *white lies.*   4

Topic sentence. If we tell little white lies to be courteous, then we tell half-truths often to benefit or protect ourselves. We neglect to tell the whole truth, opting instead to omit the incriminating half of the story. Other half-truths are merely exaggerations. Many half-truths, like little white lies, are part of ordinary, daily conversation. Half-truths seem less brash and, perhaps, more socially and morally forgivable, but   5 the omitted half can haunt. Yet half-truths have become so hackneyed that many exist as clichés in our society. "I gave at the office," "the cheque is in the mail," "we'll do lunch," and "I'll call you sometime" are everyday jargon; they illustrate the social amnesty granted the telling of half-truths. *half-truths. lies.*

topic sentence (Barefaced lies are socially unacceptable). Liars of the barefaced genre are self- **6** centred and self-serving. Barefaced lies are committed in the pursuit of profit, prestige, power, vengeance, or any combination of these moral turpitudes. The barefaced liar has little or no concern for the welfare of others. A barefaced liar might be the accused in a murder trial who, without conscience, declares himself "not guilty" when, in fact, he has killed someone. A barefaced liar may be someone who emphatically declares "I *am* telling you the truth!" or "no, I definitely didn't do that!"—claiming innocence, or denying guilt, when the opposite is true. A moral felon who falls into this area of the lie labyrinth lies consciously and deliberately. Thus, the barefaced lie of the pathological liar is regarded as the most iniquitous of lies. *Barefaced lies.*

Regardless of which category one may have lied his or her way into, it is not **7** the committing of the lie, but the lie's potential to cause hurt or damage, that becomes the measure of its sinfulness. Because the majority of lies fall in the little white lie and half-truth categories, and so are less severe than barefaced lies, lying has become commonplace. One of the qualities that distinguishes humans from other creatures is our ability to justify and rationalize our behaviour, especially our deviant behaviour. Toward this end, we have ranked and classified lies so that some, such as little white lies, and half-truths, are tolerable while barefaced lies are regarded as offences. We are more able to accept white lies and half-truths because we can rationalize that the ends justify the means.

▧ Reading Comprehension Questions

1. Which of the following would be the best alternative title for this selection?
   a. The Least Deadly Sin
   b. Just Lying and Self-Justifying
   c. Little White Lies
   d. Lies Hurt Everyone

2. Which sentence best expresses the essay's main point?
   a. Lying is such a normal activity that we easily break it into categories.
   b. Compliments and conventional lies are socially acceptable.
   c. A lie's acceptability depends on how easily we can justify its harmfulness.
   d. Lying is an unavoidable part of being a sinful person.

3. *True or false?* _____ We tolerate liars simply because we all lie ourselves. *We don't tolerate all liars.*

4. The author states that white lies are less offensive than half-truths because
   a. they are told by kind, decent people.
   b. they are for the good of others, rather than for our own benefit.
   c. they are more socially acceptable than half-truths.
   d. they can't come back to haunt us.

5. Turner says that "lying has become commonplace" (paragraph 7) because
   a. it is mortal to lie, and we are all only mortal.
   b. we have given up on trying to justify our behaviour.
   c. most lies fall into the two least harmful classes of lies.
   d. we no longer see most lies as "sinful" or morally wrong.

6. The author implies that
   a. she understands exactly why people tell lies.
   b. she feels that lying can be unintentional and tolerable.
   c. our attitudes toward lying are simple and uncomplicated.
   d. she sees lying as evidence of our contradictory human nature.

7. *True or false?* _____T_____ The essay implies that we have set up an order for "lie classification" because we find our capacity for lying so hard to deal with in ethical terms.

8. From the essay, we can conclude that
   a. the purpose of a lie is often the way we reconcile guilt over having lied.
   b. humans can justify any immoral behaviour in themselves.
   c. since we understand the types of lies, they are no longer problematic.
   d. as long as we don't hurt other people, any lie is acceptable.

9. The word *permeate* in "They permeate all cultures and all eras of history; lies are universal" (paragraph 1) means
   a. dominate.
   b. destroy.
   c. spread through.
   d. distort.

10. The word *turpitudes* in "profit, prestige, power, vengeance, or any combination of these moral turpitudes" (paragraph 6) means
    a. wickednesses.
    b. goals.
    c. horrors.
    d. tendencies.

◼ Discussion Questions

About Content

1. What are the five elements of Turner's opening definition of lies? Which is the closest to an "objective dictionary definition?" Why?

2. Why do we have such problems with lying if it is such an ordinary human activity? What are the effects of our dilemna on us?

3. What are the distinctions between a half-truth and a white lie? What are the problems with half-truths?

4. Why is a barefaced lie the least acceptable form of lie? If *all* lies are intentional, why is this last type the worst?

About Structure

5. What is the effect of the short sentence at the end of the first paragraph? How does this sentence affect your understanding of the rest of the paragraph?

6. In which paragraph and in which sentence does the author reveal her categories of lies? In which paragraph does she explain her divisions?

7. How does the structure of the rest of "Truth or Consequences" follow from the transition sentence at the end of the third paragraph? What is the function of each of paragraphs 4, 5, and 6?

About Style and Tone

8. Turner uses samples of direct speech as examples of types of lies. Find and list the pieces of direct speech used.

    _____   _____

    _____   _____

    _____   _____

    _____   _____

    What is the effect on you when you read these phrases? Do they make the author's points more clearly?

Writing Assignments

Assignment 1: Writing a Paragraph

An assignment based on this selection appears on page 173.

Assignment 2: Writing a Paragraph

You have undoubtedly experienced some or all of the three types of lies Turner defines. List her three headings and, under each heading, note examples from your own life. Which did you find the most harmful or hurtful? Why? Which have you experienced the most often? Write a paragraph defining *in your own terms* the kind of lie you find the worst, and give clear examples, perhaps using direct speech, that support your definition of "the worst kind of lie."

Assignment 3: Writing an Essay

Turner writes in her final paragraph: "One of the qualities that distinguishes humans from other creatures is our ability to justify and rationalize our behaviour, especially our deviant behaviour" (paragraph 7). Consider some action or behaviour of your own of which you are not particularly proud, such as keeping extra change miscounted by a salesclerk or cheating on a girlfriend or boyfriend. How did you justify your action to yourself? How did you rationalize it? How did you finally settle things with your own conscience? How did you finally settle matters with the person or people involved? If the issue is still unsettled, what might you still do?

Write an essay about one such action in your own life. Begin with an introduction that clearly defines the nature of the "lie or wrong action" and gives a brief background for what led to your choice of action. In your prewriting, label your three body paragraphs with headings such as *my mistake*, *my reasons for doing it*, and *the consequences/how I dealt with them*. Conclude your essay with a summarizing sentence or two, and a final thought about human nature and what you may have learned.

*laining a Process · Examining Cause and Effect · Comparing or contrasting · Defini
n · Dividing and Classifying · Describing a Scene or Person · Narrating an Event · Arg
sition · Explaining a Process · Examining Cause and Effect · comparing or contrast
ning a Term · Dividing and Classifying · Describing a Scene or Person · Narrating an E
guing a Position · Explaining a Process · Examining Cause and Effect · Compari*

Education and Self-Improvement

POWER LEARNING

Sheila Akers

For many students, cramming for tests, staying up late to do assignments, and having an incomplete grasp of information are a natural part of college life. After all, there is so much to do, and almost none of it is easy. If you are one of those students who never seem able to catch up, you may find the following selection a revelation. It might convince you that even though you study hard in school, you may need to learn more about how to study better.

Jill had not been as successful in high school as she would have liked. Since college involved even more work, it was no surprise that she was not doing any better there. 1

The reason for her so-so performance was not a lack of effort. She attended most of her classes and read her textbooks. And she never missed handing in any assignment, even though it often meant staying up late the night before homework was due. Still, she just got by in her classes. Before long, she came to the conclusion that she just couldn't do any better. 2

Then one day, one of her instructors said something to make her think otherwise. "You can probably build some sort of house by banging a few boards together," he said. "But if you want a sturdy home, you'll have to use the right techniques and tools. Building carefully takes work, but it gets better results. The same can be said of your education. There are no shortcuts, but there are some proven study skills that can really help. If you don't use them, you may end up with a pretty flimsy education." 3

Prompted by this advice, Jill signed up for a course in study skills at her school.   4
She then found out a crucial fact—that learning how to learn is the key to success
in school. There are certain dependable skills that have made the difference between
disappointment and success for generations of students. These techniques won't
free you from work, but they will make your work far more productive. They include
three important areas: time control, classroom note-taking, and textbook study.

Time Control

Success in college depends on time control. Time control means that you deliberately   5
organize and plan your time, instead of letting it drift by. Planning means that you should
never be faced with a night-before-the-test "cram" session or an overdue term paper.

There are three steps involved in time control. The *first step* is to prepare a large   6
monthly calendar. Buy a calendar with a large white block around each date, or
make one yourself. At the beginning of the college semester, circle important dates
on this calendar. Circle the days on which tests are scheduled; circle the days when
papers are due. This calendar can also be used to schedule study plans. You can jot
down your plans for each day at the beginning of the week. An alternative method
would be to make plans for each day the night before. On Tuesday night, for example, you might write down "Read Chapter 5 in psychology" in the Wednesday
block. Be sure to hang this calendar in a place where you will see it every day—
your kitchen, your bedroom, even your bathroom!

The *second step* in time control is to have a weekly study schedule for the   7
semester. To prepare this schedule, make up a chart that covers all the days of the
week and all the waking hours in each day. Part of one student's schedule is shown
opposite. On your schedule, mark in all the fixed hours in each day—hours for
meals, classes, job (if any), and travel time. Next, mark in time blocks that you can
realistically use for study each day. Depending on the number of courses you are
taking and the demands of the courses, you may want to block off five, ten, or even
twenty or more hours of study time a week. Keep in mind that you should not
block off time for study that you do not truly intend to use for study. Otherwise,
your schedule will be a meaningless gimmick. Also, remember that you should
allow time for rest and relaxation in your schedule. You will be happiest, and able
to accomplish the most, when you have time for both work and play.

Time	Monday	Tuesday	Wednesday	Thursday	Friday	Saturday	Sunday
6:00 A.M.							
7:00	*B*	*B*	*B*	*B*	*B*		
8:00	*Math*	*STUDY*	*Math*	*STUDY*	*Math*		
9:00	*STUDY*	*Biology*	*STUDY*	*Biology*	*STUDY*	*Job*	
10:00	*Psychology*	↓	*Psychology*	↓	*Psychology*		
11:00	*STUDY*	*English*		*English*			
12:00 NOON	*L*		*L*	↓	*L*	↓	

The *third step* in time control is to make a daily or weekly "to do" list. This may   **8**
be the most valuable time-control method you ever use. On this list, you write
down the things you need to do for the following day or the following week. If you
choose to write a weekly list, do it on Sunday night. If you choose to write a daily
list, do it the night before. You may use a three- by five-inch notepad or a small
spiral-bound notebook for this list. Carry the list around with you during the day.
Always concentrate on doing first the most important items on your list. Mark
high-priority items with an asterisk and give them precedence over low-priority
items in order to make the best use of your time. For instance, you may find yourself wondering what to do after dinner on Thursday evening. Among the items on
your list are "Clean inside of car" and "Review chapter for math quiz." It is obviously more important for you to review your notes at this point; you can clean the
car some other time. As you complete items on your "to do" list, cross them out.
Do not worry about unfinished items. They can be rescheduled. You will still be
accomplishing a great deal and making more effective use of your time. Part of one
student's daily list is shown below.

To Do   *Tuesday*

  *1. Review biology notes before class
  *2. Proof-read English paper due today
   3. See Dick about game on Friday
  *4. Gas for car
   5. Read next chapter of psychology text

Classroom Note-Taking

One of the most important single things you can do to perform well in a college   **9**
course is to take effective class notes. The following hints should help you become
a better note-taker.

First, attend class faithfully. Your alternatives—reading the text or someone   **10**
else's notes, or both—cannot substitute for the experience of hearing ideas in person as someone presents them to you. Also, in class lectures and discussions, your
instructor typically presents and develops the main ideas and facts of the course—
the ones you will be expected to know on exams.

Another valuable hint is to make use of abbreviations while taking notes. Using   **11**
abbreviations saves time when you are trying to get down a great deal of information. Abbreviate terms that recur frequently in a lecture and put a key to your
abbreviations at the top of your notes. For example, in a sociology class, *eth* could
stand for *ethnocentrism*; in a psychology class, *STM* could stand for *short-term
memory*. (When a lecture is over, you may want to go back and write out the terms
you have abbreviated.) In addition, abbreviate words that often recur in any lecture. For instance, use *ex* for *example*, *def* for *definition*, *info* for *information*, + for
and, and so on. If you use the same abbreviations all the time, you will soon
develop a kind of personal shorthand that makes taking notes much easier.

A third hint when taking notes is to be on the lookout for signals of impor-   12
tance. Write down whatever your instructor puts on the board. If he or she takes
the time to put material on the board, it is probably important, and the chances
are good that it will come up later on exams. Always write down definitions and
enumerations. Enumerations are lists of items. They are signaled in such ways as:
"The four steps in the process are …"; "There were three reasons for …"; "The two
effects were …"; "Five characteristics of …"; and so on. Always number such enumerations in your notes (1, 2, 3, etc.). They will help you understand relationships
among ideas and organize the material of the lecture. Watch for emphasis words—
words your instructor may use to indicate that something is important. Examples
of such words are "This is an important reason …"; "A point that will keep coming up later …"; "The chief cause was …"; "The basic idea here is …"; and so on.
Always write down the important statements announced by these and other
emphasis words. Finally, if your instructor repeats a point, you can assume it is
important. You might put an R for *repeated* in the margin, so that later you will
know that your instructor has stressed it.

Next, be sure to write down the instructor's examples and mark them with an   13
X. The examples help you understand abstract points. If you do not write them
down, you are likely to forget them later when they are needed to help make sense
of an idea.

Also, be sure to write down the connections between ideas. Too many students   14
merely copy the terms the instructor puts on the board. They forget that, as time
passes, the details that serve as connecting bridges between ideas quickly fade. You
should, then, write down the relationships and connections in class. That way
you'll have them to help tie your notes together later on.

Review your notes as soon as possible after class. You must make them as clear   15
as possible while they are fresh in your mind. A day later may be too late, because
forgetting sets in very quickly. Make sure that punctuation is clear, that all words
are readable and correctly spelled, and that unfinished sentences are completed (or
at least marked off so that you can check your notes with another student's). Add
clarifying or connecting comments whenever necessary. Make sure important ideas
are clearly marked. Improve the organization if necessary, so that you can see at a
glance main points and relationships among them.

Finally, try in general to get down a written record of each class. You must do   16
this because forgetting begins almost immediately. Studies have shown that within
two weeks you are likely to have forgotten 80 percent or more of what you have
heard. And in four weeks you are lucky if 5 percent remains! This is so crucial that
it bears repeating: to guard against the relentlessness of forgetting, it is absolutely
essential to write down what you hear in class. Later on you can concentrate on
working to understand fully and to remember the ideas that have been presented
in class. And the more complete your notes are at the time of study, the more you
are likely to learn.

Textbook Study

In many college courses, success means being able to read and study a textbook   17
skillfully. For many students, unfortunately, textbooks are heavy going. After an

hour or two of study, the textbook material is as formless and as hard to understand as ever. But there is a way to attack even the most difficult textbook and make sense of it. Use a sequence in which you preview a chapter, mark it, take notes on it, and then study the notes.

Previewing. Previewing a selection is an important first step to understanding. Taking the time to preview a section or chapter can give you a bird's-eye view of the way the material is organized. You will have a sense of where you are beginning, what you will cover, and where you will end.   **18**

There are several steps in previewing a selection. First, study the title. The title   **19** is the shortest possible summary of a selection and will often tell you the limits of the material you will cover. For example, the title "FDR and the Supreme Court" tells you to expect a discussion of President Roosevelt's dealings with the Court. You know that you will probably not encounter any material dealing with FDR's foreign policies or personal life. Next, read over quickly the first and last paragraphs of the selection; these may contain important introductions to, and summaries of, the main ideas. Then examine briefly the headings and subheadings in the selection. Together, the headings and subheadings are a brief outline of what you are reading. Headings are often main ideas or important concepts in capsule form; subheadings are breakdowns of ideas within main areas. Finally, read the first sentence of some paragraphs, look for words set off in **boldface** or *italics*, and look at pictures or diagrams. After you have previewed a selection in this way, you should have a good general sense of the material to be read.

Marking. You should mark a textbook selection at the same time that you read   **20** it through carefully. Use a felt-tip highlighter to shade material that seems important, or use a regular ballpoint pen and put symbols in the margin next to the material: stars, checks, or NBs (for *nota bene*, a Latin phrase meaning "note well"). What to mark is not as mysterious as some students believe. You should try to find main ideas by looking for the following clues: definitions and examples, enumerations, and emphasis words.

1 *Definitions and examples:* Definitions are often among the most important   **21** ideas in a selection. They are particularly significant in introductory courses in almost any subject area, where much of your learning involves mastering the specialized vocabulary of that subject. In a sense, you are learning the "language" of psychology or business or whatever the subject might be.

Most definitions are abstract, and so they usually are followed by one or   **22** more examples to help clarify their meaning. Always mark off definitions and at least one example that makes a definition clear to you. In a psychology text, for example, we are told that "rationalization is an attempt to reduce anxiety by deciding that you have not really been frustrated." Several examples follow, among them: "A young man, frustrated because he was rejected when he asked for a date, convinces himself that the woman is not very attractive and is much less interesting than he had supposed."

2 *Enumerations:* Enumerations are lists of items (causes, reasons, types, and so   **23** on) that are numbered 1, 2, 3, ... or that could easily be numbered in an out-

line. They are often signaled by addition words. Many of the paragraphs in a textbook use words like *first of all, another, in addition,* and *finally* to signal items in a series. This is a very common and effective organizational method.

3   *Emphasis words:* Emphasis words tell you that an idea is important. Common   24
emphasis words include phrases such as *a major event, a key feature, the chief factor, important to note, above all,* and *most of all.* Here is an example: "The most significant contemporary use of marketing is its application to non-business areas, such as political parties."

Note-Taking.   Next, you should take notes. Go through the chapter a second   25
time, rereading the most important parts. Try to write down the main ideas in a simple outline form. For example, in taking notes on a psychology selection, you might write down the heading "Kinds of Defense Mechanisms." Below the heading you would number and describe each kind and give an example of each.

Defense Mechanisms

a.   *Definition: Unconscious attempts to reduce anxiety*
b.   *Kinds:*

(1)   *Rationalization: Attempt to reduce anxiety by deciding that you have not really been frustrated*
        Example: Man turned down for a date decides that the woman was not worth going out with anyway

(2)   *Projection: Attributing to other people motives or thoughts of one's own*
        Example: Wife who wants to have an affair accuses her husband of having one

Studying Notes.   To study your notes, use the method of repeated self-testing.   26
For example, look at the heading "Kinds of Defense Mechanisms" and say to yourself, "What are the kinds of defense mechanisms?" When you can recite them, then say to yourself, "What is rationalization?" "What is an example of rationalization?" Then ask yourself, "What is projection?" "What is an example of projection?" After you learn each section, review it, and then go on to the next section.

Do not simply read your notes; keep looking away and seeing if you can recite   27
them to yourself. This self-testing is the key to effective learning.

In summary, remember this sequence in order to deal with a textbook: previewing,   28
marking, taking notes, studying the notes. Approaching a textbook in this methodical way will give you very positive results. You will no longer feel bogged down in a swamp of words, unable to figure out what you are supposed to know. Instead, you will understand exactly what you have to do and how to go about doing it.

∎

Take a minute now to evaluate your own study habits. Do you practise many of the   29
above skills in order to control your time, take effective classroom notes, and learn

from your textbooks? If not, perhaps you should. The skills are not magic, but they are too valuable to ignore. Use them carefully and consistently, and they will make academic success possible for you. Try them, and you won't need convincing.

■ Reading Comprehension Questions

1. Which of the following would be the best alternative title for this selection?
   a. The Importance of Notetaking
   b. Good Study Skills: The Key to Success
   c. Easy Ways to Learn More
   d. How to Evaluate Your Study Habits

2. Which sentence best expresses the main idea of the selection?
   a. Good study skills can increase academic success.
   b. Notetaking is the best way to study difficult subjects.
   c. More and more schools are offering courses on study skills.
   d. Certain study techniques make college work easy for everyone.

3. Which of these is *not* a good way to organize your time?
   a. Make a monthly calendar.
   b. Keep a weekly study schedule.
   c. Prepare a "to do" list.
   d. Always use extra time for studying.

4. Which is the correct sequence of steps in studying from a textbook?
   a. Preview, self-test, take notes.
   b. Take notes, preview, mark, self-test.
   c. Take notes, mark, preview, self-test.
   d. Preview, mark, take notes, self-test.

5. When marking the textbook for main ideas, do *not*
   a. mark it while you are previewing.
   b. highlight definitions and examples.
   c. include lists of items.
   d. look for "emphasis" words.

6. *True or false?* _____ The author implies that it is better to write too much rather than too little when taking classroom notes.

7. The author implies that one value of class attendance is that you
   a. need to get the next assignment.
   b. will please the instructor, which can lead to better grades.
   c. can begin to improve your short-term memory.
   d. increase your understanding by hearing ideas in person.

8. *True or false?* _____ The author implies that studying does not require any memorization.

9. The word *abstract* in "The examples help you understand abstract points" (paragraph 13) means
   a. simple.

    b. difficult.

    c. ordinary.

    d. correct.

10. The word *capsule* in "Headings are often main ideas or important concepts in capsule form" (paragraph 19) means

    a. adjustable.

    b. larger.

    c. complicated.

    d. abbreviated.

▦ Discussion Questions

About Content

1. Evaluate Jill's college course work. What was she doing right? What was she probably doing wrong?

2. When taking notes in class, how can we tell what information is important enough to write down?

3. What are the three steps in time control? Which do you think would be most helpful to you?

4. What are some of the ways you can spot main ideas when marking a textbook chapter?

About Structure

5. Does Akers use time order or emphatic order in presenting the three study skills?

6. Write down seven different transitional words and phrases used in "Classroom Note-Taking":

    _____   _____

    _____   _____

    _____   _____

    _____

7. Akers tells us that emphasis words (paragraphs 12 and 24) are keys to important ideas. What are three emphasis words or phrases that she herself uses at different places in the article?

    _____ (paragraph _____)

    _____ (paragraph _____)

    _____ (paragraph _____)

About Style and Tone

8. Why has Akers chosen to present most of her essay in the second person—"you"? Why didn't she continue to use Jill, or another student, as an example?

■ Writing Assignments

Assignment 1: Writing a Paragraph

A writing assignment based on this selection is on page 163.

Assignment 2: Writing a Paragraph

Akers says, "A third hint on taking notes is to be on the lookout for signals of importance." Pay close attention to these signals in your classes over the next few days. Watch for use of the board, for definitions, for enumerations, and for other ways your instructors might stress information. On a special sheet of paper, keep track of these signals as they occur. Then use your notes to write a paragraph on ways that your instructors signal that certain ideas are important. Be sure to provide specific examples of what your instructors say and do. Possible topic sentences for this paragraph might be: "My psychology instructor has several ways of signalling important points in her lectures" or "My instructors use several signals in common to let students know that ideas are important."

Assignment 3: Writing an Essay

For many students, the challenge of college is not just to learn good study skills. It is also to overcome the various temptations that interfere with study time. What pulls you away from success at school? Time with friends or family? Card games? Extracurricular activities? Cable TV? Time spent daydreaming or listening to music? An unneeded part-time job?

Make a list of all the temptations that distract you from study time. Then decide on the three that interfere most with your studying time. Use these three as the basis for an essay, "Temptations in College Life."

Here is one student's outline for an essay:

Thesis statement: The local coffee shop, television, and my girlfriend often tempt me away from what I should be doing in school.

Topic sentence 1: The time I spend at the coffee shop interferes with school in three ways.
a.   Skipping classes
b.   Going right after class, instead of checking notes
c.   Long lunches with friends, instead of studying

Topic sentence 2: I also find that the time I spend watching television interferes with school.
a.   Time away from study because of sports and other shows
b.   Getting to sleep too late because of late-night TV

Topic sentence 3: Finally, I am often with my girlfriend, who is not a student and does not need to study.
a.   Time spent together on nonschool activities
b.   Studying poorly when she is around

In your final paragraph, include one or two sentences of summary and, perhaps, comment on any changes you plan to make to improve your study time.

As an alternative, you may want to write generally (rather than personally) about "Temptations Faced by College Students." In such a paper, you will use a third-person point of view rather than the first person ("I"), and you will provide examples based on your observations of others.

HOW TO WRITE A TEST

Eileen A. Brett

Writing tests never seems as trying for some students as it does for others. A few are calm, plan their attack, and finish on time. Many, however, perspire on their exam books, chew their pens, and never complete a test. If you, like the Canadian author of this text, belong to the latter group, Eileen A. Brett has some sensible down-to-earth advice about approaching and managing test-taking. Ms. Brett, a student at the University of British Columbia, writes with a light touch about a subject of serious concern. Both her recommendations and her information are concrete, specific, and, it is hoped, valuable and interesting to you.

It is the day of the final exam or perhaps it is just a unit quiz. (Of course, in today's   1
academic courses, when entire grades are sometimes comprised of quiz marks, there is no such thing as a mere quiz.) Whether quiz, test, or examination, does the very suggestion of being tested induce fear and panic? Rest assured; writing tests need not be a frightening experience. If you sit in a place without distractions, bring the right tools, relax, think positively, and organize yourself, you will survive the experience. You may even surprise yourself by doing well on the test.

As you enter the classroom the day of the test, your first priority should be to   2
choose where to sit. The important point here is not to find the most comfortable seat but to avoid windows. When a task of importance is unpleasant, eyes tend to wander toward windows and scenes of interest outside. When this happens, inevitably, concentration is relaxed. Equally distracting can be a seat at the back of the room where the back view of any number of attractive blondes or rugged athletes will be in your direct line of vision. Always choose a seat in the front row.

To be prepared you will have brought with you at least two pens and one pen-   3
cil accompanied by a bottle of correction fluid, an eraser, and a watch. Often I have forgotten this last item and suffered tremendously from judging incorrectly how much time remained. These are the essential tools of any test. The pencil may be used substantially more than the pen, for reasons that will be discussed later. One pencil is sufficient, since the walk to the pencil sharpener provides a practical excuse to exercise leg muscles. I stress, however, that this is not an opportunity to

cheat. The walk over to the pencil sharpener is not only a form of physical release, it is also a "brain break." However short this walk may be, the brain welcomes the chance to escape deep mental concentration for the non-strenuous act of sharpening a pencil.

Many students spend the remaining few minutes before the test cramming   **4** crucial bits of information into their heads. This effort is wasteful since, in my experience, last minute cramming serves to confuse and is not actually remembered anyway. Why not, instead, spend those moments in mental relaxation and deep breathing? At the same time, analyze the mood in the room. If absolutely everyone else, not having read these helpful hints, is deeply engrossed in last minute preparation, this is a fairly positive indication that the exam will be a difficult one. In this case, it is best that you breathe deeply rather than analyze. If, on the other hand, the majority is calm, cool, and collected, either the test is going to be easy or you have got the date wrong. In both cases, you have nothing to worry about.

The interval between the time the test is placed in front of you and the time   **5** you are told you may begin is the time to take the Attitude Adjustment Approach, which concerns the mindset in which you will commence writing the exam. During this time, students who want only to scrape by will decide to put minimum effort into the exam. In contrast, students who want a good, if not exceptional, grade will use this time to prepare mentally for the challenge ahead.

As the examination begins, take a moment to glance through the test. The   **6** decision as to where to start is yours. However, a word to the wise: multiple choice questions should be attacked first for two reasons. First, tidbits of information can often be gleaned from them and then reworked to fit nicely (and inconspicuously) into sentence answers or essays. Second, since the answer is right in front of you, multiple choice questions are the least painful way of easing into the task ahead.

In examinations, an organized student has the advantage over a disorganized   **7** student. An organized system for writing tests involves using a pen or pencil, depending on how confident you are with the material. Those answers of which you are fairly certain should be answered in pen. Otherwise, pencils are ideal for answering tests because answers can be changed easily. However, since numerous studies have found that, particularly with multiple choice, the first answer chosen is most often the correct one, be 110 percent sure before you change an answer. Should time permit double-checking, it will be necessary to review only those answers in pencil as answers in pen are likely to be correct. If an answer is elusive, make a mark beside the question so you will be able to quickly identify those questions to which you did not know the answers. Then move on and go back to them later.

A few techniques have been developed for writing essays. Of course, under-   **8** standing exactly what the question is asking is essential. If, for example, there is more than one essay question, ideas may flow more freely if you switch back and forth among them. When I begin to get frustrated for lack of ideas, often new thoughts will surface as I answer another question and I will quickly jot them down. Still, other people find staying with one essay until it is completed more beneficial. If all else fails, use the technique of free-writing: write on anything that is even remotely connected with the essay topic until you feel inspired. But perhaps you should take a brain break.

The technique you choose is of less importance, though, than the interest level **9** of your essays. Not many teachers enjoy perusing forty essay exams on "The Effect of Green Pesticides on Small Herbivores." If you want a good mark, you will strive to keep the professor not only awake but also excited at your discussion of genetic differences in field mice. Imagination is a wonderful asset, but if it is not one of yours, description or examples are also effective. Easy reading is also enhanced by grammatically correct writing.

Before you finish the exam, remember to finish those multiple choice questions **10** that you had found impossible to answer. If the process of elimination does not yield an answer that is satisfactory, depending on the amount of time remaining, one of two options is open: count up how many *A* answers you have, how many *B*, etc., and choose the letter that has the least number of answers; or take a reasonable guess. If all else fails, write your professor a note telling him or her of the immense satisfaction and enjoyment you derived from doing the exam, and extend holiday greetings. Then, with hope, you wait for the results and you trust that:

(a) Without your knowledge, your teacher has sent in several of your essays from the examination to Mensa, which extends the honour of membership to you.
(b) The test was for the government, which does not care anyway.
(c) The teacher appreciated your note.

Reading Comprehension Questions

1. Which of the following would be the best alternative title for the selection?
   a. Seven Steps to Success
   b. Fool-Proof Ways to Pass
   c. Tested Techniques for Taking Tests
   d. Easy Ways to Ace Exams

2. Which sentence best expresses the main idea of the selection?
   a. Mental and physical strategies and organization help you to better handle tests.
   b. Bringing the right equipment to an exam is half the battle.
   c. Writing entertaining essay answers and using a clever system for multiple-choice answers guarantee exam success.
   d. A positive mental attitude and last-minute extra studying can ensure a passing grade.

3. Which of these is *not* a good idea when you enter the exam room?
   a. Finding a chair or desk that feels comfortable
   b. Sitting away from the window
   c. Taking a seat at the front of the room
   d. Bringing enough pens

4. Brett suggests that cramming just before a test is pointless
   a. because you can't analyze the mood in the exam room.
   b. because it adds to your mental clutter and you won't remember those facts.
   c. because you can overprepare and go to the wrong location in your confusion.
   d. because you can't meditate and practise deep breathing as you cram.

5. The most important steps in approaching a test are
    a. choosing a good seat, bringing lots of equipment, and having the right attitude.
    b. arriving on time, at the right location, and handling multiple-choice questions correctly.
    c. choosing the right location and materials, being calm enough to write in an organized way, and knowing how to write a good essay answer.
    d. remembering your watch, keeping your pencils sharp, and using the information from multiple-choice questions in your essays.

6. The author implies that
    a. intense total concentration is the best mental state for dealing with a test.
    b. test results may benefit from brief pauses in concentration.
    c. large muscle exercise is necessary to do well on tests.
    d. several short strolls through the exam room are advisable.

7. *True or false?* _____ Brett implies that final marks are partly the result of decisions made by the student as he or she first looks at the exam.

8. You may conclude that
    a. a good essay answer depends on your ability to amuse the professor.
    b. a good essay answer may result from the use of correct grammar and spelling.
    c. a good essay answer results from an innovative approach, solid content, and attention to language usage.
    d. a good essay answer will result from exciting new discoveries you make in your subject area.

9. The word *gleaned* in "tidbits of information can often be gleaned from them and then reworked to fit nicely (and inconspicuously) into sentence answers or essays" (paragraph 6) means
    a. stolen.
    b. sneaked.
    c. rewritten.
    d. picked up.

10. The word *herbivores* in "The Effect of Green Pesticides on Small Herbivores" (paragraph 9) means
    a. field mice.
    b. plant-eating animals.
    c. houseflies.
    d. rodents.

Discussion Questions

About Content

1. What are Eileen A. Brett's five recommendations for writing better tests? Which of the five have you tried? Have any that you practise worked for you? Why?

2. Why should you bring only one pencil? Are you going to use the pencil more or less often than your pen? Why?

---

3. What is the "Attitude Adjustment Approach"? Why is this important?

4. What is the point of doing any multiple-choice questions first? Why bother to use two different writing implements?

About Structure

5. What method of ordering, common to all process writing, is used for this essay? In the opening paragraph, which elements recommended by this text for the first paragraphs of process writing do you find?

6. How many paragraphs does the author devote to each of the five steps she lists as parts of the process? List the stages or steps and the numbers of the paragraphs in which they are discussed.

Step 1 _____ (paragraph _____)

Step 2 _____ (paragraph _____)

Step 3 _____ (paragraph _____)

Step 4 _____ (paragraph _____)

Step 5 _____ (paragraph _____)

Which of the steps receives the most attention from the author? Why?

7. How does the writer link the stages in her process? Does she use transition words, "time marker" words and phrases, and/or repetition of important ideas? Which of these devices do you find in which paragraphs? Where are the transition devices placed?

About Style and Tone

8. The author uses some humorous phrases and a tone that is upbeat and lively. What is the effect on you as a reader of the mixture of a light tone with serious subject matter?

9. Where do you find examples of Brett's sense of humour? Some techniques to look for include (1) exaggeration, (2) unlikely combinations of ideas, and (3) unexpected ideas or turns of phrase.

List an example of each of these below:

1. _____

2. _____

3. _____

Writing Assignments

Assignment 1: Writing a Paragraph

Brett notes that the result of not knowing how to take tests is panic. She suggests that such tension may be the result of many factors, such as disorganization, last-minute cramming, mental attitude, and lack of understanding of test design and marking.

Write a paragraph about one memorable exam or test experience of your own. Decide while you are prewriting whether you have more bad or good experiences to list. Your point of view or attitude expressed will result from the list which is longer and contains clearer details or memories. Your paragraph may reflect details and suggestions from Brett's essay. A good exam experience of your own may or may not be the result of having followed some of the author's suggestions, while suffering through a particularly terrible test may bring back some very vivid details. Such strong memories may produce a good paragraph.

Your paragraph should isolate the *causes* of such a good or bad test-writing experience. The end result will be a topic sentence such as "The worst exam I ever wrote was the result of three problems: _____."

Assignment 2: Writing a Paragraph

Should such techniques as notetaking, test-writing, time-management, and study skills in general be part of your college's course offerings? Many students arrive at postsecondary education without much knowledge of such skills. Do you believe that a half-semester course covering these areas would be of use to you?

Write a paragraph that argues for or against such a course, covering *three* skills areas you believe would help you most. Be sure to choose three skills you would most like to acquire, and for each of these, list the reasons you feel these should or should not be part of college curricula. If you wish to dispute the value of such a course, you may find justification in the availability of articles such as Eileen A. Brett's, or Sheila Akers' "Power Learning," or other personal experiences which have helped your study skills.

Assignment 3: Writing an Essay

Taking tests and exams is only one of life's challenges. We all face situations and personal trials where a bit of advice, or someone else's experience and techniques, could prove useful. "How to" books are among the best-selling titles in any bookstore.

Here is a list of ordinary social situations with which you may have some experience. What these situations have in common is the often unspoken set of rules governing what to do. Select one of these topics and begin to draft an outline, listing your own set of steps for a process essay that tells someone how to handle just such an event or problem.

1. Attending the funeral of someone to whom you are not closely attached
2. Giving a speech at a wedding reception
3. Looking after someone else's child for a day
4. Saying thank you for a gift you disliked
5. Saying no to a particularly forceful salesperson
6. Refusing a date or invitation from someone you like, but are not that fond of

7. Getting out of attending a family dinner or major family celebration
8. Being best man or maid/matron of honour at a friend's wedding

You may want to refer to the chapter on process writing (pages 156–163) for a review of how to construct a process essay. In your outline, be sure to include in the opening paragraph the final result of the process, and whatever benefits you think will result from following your procedures. Indicate roughly how many steps will be involved, any anticipated difficulties, as well as any equipment or materials needed to complete the process.

Divide your list of steps or stages into three sections, and give precise details concerning how to complete each step successfully. Try not to omit any necessary steps, or leave room for mistakes caused by omitting complete instructions. Be sure to make good use of transitions to help your reader through the process.

Finish your essay with a summary of what the reader has now accomplished, and a parting thought on the value of such an achievement. You may certainly treat your subject with humour, if you are comfortable doing so.

WHY SHOULD WE HIRE YOU?

Jim Maloney

The workplace of the second millennium is a new place: perhaps a not-so-pleasant prospect for the college student, and a place of decreasing possibilities for the already-employed individual. Neither "a job for a lifetime" nor the chance of steady advancement in a field of personal expertise can be expected, much less taken for granted by anyone. A diploma, a degree, and a snappy resumé are no guarantees of a lifetime's steady employment. Instead, a sense of direction, steady and careful academic preparation, and active job research during the college years are needed to face the realities of the twenty-first-century job market. Jim Maloney, professor of English at Seneca College and long-time expert in career-based areas of writing, poses student readers "The Question"—a question he faced, and a question most companies' Human Resources personnel will ask any student reading this essay: "Why should we hire you?"

I

"Why should we hire you for this position?"   1

I remember the first time I was asked that question. I remember it the same   2
way I remember the first time a police officer asked to see my driver's licence and registration. I was no more prepared to be caught speeding than I was prepared to explain why I should be permanently employed teaching English at a community

college. In both cases, I experienced a sinking feeling in my stomach, and a quickening of my pulse: the sensations that come with being caught.

I got a speeding ticket, but I didn't get the job. 3

Looking back at the difficulty I had with that basic question, I can't believe that 4 I approached the interview so badly prepared. If I had been as prepared for the job interview as I was for doing the job, I would have felt no surprise. I had had a number of previous jobs where I was hired only for my ability to perform physical tasks, so the interviews for these jobs were far less crucial than was the simple ability to do the work. However, just as exceeding the speed limit will, when traffic police are performing properly, lead to a speeding ticket, so being interviewed for an attractive career-entry position will, when the interviewer knows what to look for, lead directly or indirectly to the question "Why should we hire you?"

The question is a significant one, not just because you will encounter it, in 5 some form, as part of a job interview, along with other "open-ended" queries designed to uncover your understanding of the position and of the suitability of your qualifications. The question is also important to consider in preparing your resume and application letter—documents crucial to creating possible interviews. Moreover, the question is relevant to you, who haven't yet finished your postsecondary career preparation and, therefore, won't be immediately facing interviews for positions in your chosen field. For you at this stage, the question "Why should we hire you?" may seem pointless, premature, or irrelevant. Try turning the question around: "Why should *I* be hired?" Now the question may have more meaning to you. Indeed, considered in this form, the question can guide you towards preparing for a career. So, thinking about how you will answer such a question will help you not only to understand the significance of the question but also to back up your answers with the right credentials, skills, and experiences.

II

Too frequently, students seem to take for granted their right, or even their access, 6 to interviews and to jobs needed to begin their careers. Such optimism can no longer be justified. Ten years ago, graduating students were warned that continued employment in one field for one company for one's entire working life was increasingly becoming a thing of the past. Students could expect three or four career shifts. Today, many college or university graduates will never have the chance even to begin careers in their chosen fields. Others may find only part-time or contract work. The last decade has produced enormous changes in the way business and industry operate in North America, and in the ways in which people are employed.

Corporate downsizing—reductions in the workforce needed by a company 7 for operating purposes—has been a fact in business life for some time now. Global competition is usually given as the reason for smaller workforce requirements, while, it is claimed, technological developments, especially computerization, have led to massive employee lay-offs with no loss to productivity. Of course, there is an alternative view of downsizing: that remaining employees are expected to be more productive—to work longer and harder—to pick up the slack. A consequence of downsizing and technological change is a reduced full-time workforce, many of whom either handle more tasks or perform more specialized technological activities. In some companies, another consequence of a smaller workforce is the replacement of permanent full-time employees who receive higher salaries and significant benefit packages with part-time or contract workers who are offered lower salaries and few, if any, benefits. Some companies have virtually nothing to offer but these limited, rather unpromising positions.

These changes are not limited to the private sector. Recently, the governments of Alberta and Ontario initiated large-scale downsizing projects in their civil services. Many job lay-offs in health care, education, and local governments have resulted from such funding cuts. For someone wishing to begin a new career, the prospects are starting to look nasty and brutish, and the immediate picture is distinctly short of jobs, hours, and rewards for new employees. Quite simply, there may not be jobs for college and university graduates who don't know how they fit into this brave new workworld. **8**

Consequently, it is now more important than ever for you to consider and act on The Question while there is still time for you to learn the needs of employers and to make yourself capable of meeting those needs. **9**

III

There are numerous reasons why students may not be seriously addressing The Question. Many students place so much trust in the educational system that they fail to look onward to life beyond graduation. Often, the very fact that students are attending college or university may be the reason they don't take advantage of their school years to prepare themselves effectively for the next step. Some students make the error of seeing an employment ad's requirement of a postsecondary diploma or degree as a guarantee of entry into that career. These students may be so impressed by their status as college or university students that they are complacent about their futures. Unfortunately, being a student is not a career and, with few exceptions, is not very profitable. Other students may find their academic work difficult and demanding enough without adding the headache of anticipating yet more demands. Still others may trust their chosen vocationally based academic program to put them on the correct job track. The problem is that they may not actually know where it is that they are going. I am amazed every semester by the number of students in specialized programs who are utterly unaware of jobs that may be available to them, of skills needed and of the actual nature of duties they may be expected to perform. Clueless in an academic fool's paradise, all of these students are caught in wishful rather than realistic thinking. **10**

But what *actual* difference will it make to familiarize yourself with job specifications and employment prospects during your education instead of when you graduate? Preparing yourself to be desirable to prospective employers can have clear advantages during your college or university years. Even if there were no other consequences, a sense of the ultimate purpose of your studies should make your efforts more significant, less abstract—less academic. Being aware of the competition you face in your chosen field could certainly make the pursuit of good grades more meaningful. If you are in a program with a variety of optional courses, your knowledge of the job market's demands will help you to make more informed **11** decisions. Should you be registered in a more rigidly structured program, knowing that the real requirements of the job you want differ from your program's offerings could indicate that you should supplement your education with additional courses beyond your curriculum. Reading job descriptions during your school years will teach you that certain types of work experience are desired, even for entry-level positions. Therefore, choosing summer or part-time work in an area related to your chosen career, even if the pay is less attractive, may ultimately be more rewarding. Most career-advice agencies now recommend volunteer work, and many students volunteer their time to organizations connected to their career paths. In the cases of both occasional and volunteer work, the contacts made and the experience gained can be very valuable. Finally, you may never need a total personality make-over, but you should think about personal characteristics of successful people in your chosen field.

IV

With all these advantages to be gained from planning ahead for employment, how do you go about finding out what employers want?   12

One place to start is within your school. Many vocationally based programs have a faculty member responsible for student employment. Some of your instructors may be actively involved in their fields; others may have informal but vital contacts with employers or former students in business and technology. You may discover that it is quite easy to gain insight into your field of interest just by sounding out your teachers. Yet another source of information is your school's student employment office. As well as placing graduating students, this facility usually offers a range of services including personality testing, career counselling, information resources on companies, and job profiles. Graduation is too late to find out what your school has to offer.   13

Don't feel limited to these paths as you try to discover a career direction. Find out requirements for actual jobs in order to become the candidate you want to be. Even though you are not applying for a permanent position now, make a habit of following not only jobs listed in your school's employment office but also those advertised in newspapers, professional journals, or occupational periodicals. Best of all, visit human resources offices of major employers in your field; check job requirements for current or future positions; meet personnel officers, and read any information available about their companies. The time spent will pay off in your career.   14

At this point, you may be ready to get in touch with someone already working in your chosen field to gain first-hand knowledge of positions you would like. You don't need to know personally someone who fits this description; one of your teachers or friends may know someone you can contact. Alternatively, speaking with or writing to an employer in your field may help you to find a person suitably placed to answer your questions about qualifications, duties, and responsibilities. You would be surprised by how easy it is to get information, even from a stranger. If you try some of these approaches, you are on your way to a personal network.   15

Today, you need to work hard to find the work you desire. That means knowing the reasons you should be hired and taking the steps needed to prepare a solidly based answer before you are asked The Question.   16

▧ Reading Comprehension Questions

1. Which of the following would be the best alternative title for this selection?
   a. Diplomas and Dim Prospects
   b. Prepare to Work to Find Work
   c. Career Confusion
   d. The Best Degree Is No Guarantee

2. Which sentence best expresses the main idea of the selection?
   a. Intelligent choices of the right courses give students fair chances of getting work on graduation.
   b. The workplace is a crowded "buyer's market," and students must work to prepare themselves to be the "right product."
   c. Today's students must expect several changes in career paths, and several different employers in their professional futures.
   d. Technological developments have eliminated many traditional job opportunities.

3. Maloney believes that
   a. students should concentrate on the employer's viewpoint as they acquire education, skills, and experience.
   b. concentrating on writing good resumés and cover letters will ensure job interviews.
   c. students can focus on career goals from the beginning of their college experience.
   d. due to changes in business and industry, finding a job in the next few years is a hopeless task.

4. Corporate downsizing has led to
   a. a need for more highly trained technological workers.
   b. a mixture of highly versatile and very specialized workers.
   c. companies consisting only of part-time workers.
   d. changes only in the private sector.

5. *True or false?* _____ Maloney believes that choice of a diploma program in a developing area of industry and careful attention to course work can maximize chances for full-time future employment.

6. The author implies that
   a. looking toward the employment market involves looking at all aspects of oneself.
   b. looking forward to job interviews is pointless and terrifying.
   c. it is never too early to start preparing a good resumé and cover letter.
   d. looking for work in the public sector is a waste of time.

7. The essay suggests that
   a. being in focused vocational training is a demanding occupation and gives students enough of an advantage in the job search.
   b. a sense of future job needs may motivate students toward better performance, better course choices, and the acquisition of suitable experience.

  c. knowing which skills will be needed and what jobs may be available will lead to success.

  d. becoming "the ideal lab technician" or "the perfect accountant" while in college is the only way to ensure job interviews.

8. *True or false?* _____ Professional contacts, college student employment offices, "go-see" interviews, and daily reading of employment ads are enough to guarantee a shot at the ideal job.

9. The word *crucial* in "documents crucial to creating possible interviews" (paragraph 5) means
  a. special.
  b. justifiable.
  c. reasonable.
  d. important.

10. The word *anticipating* in "without adding the headache of anticipating yet more demands" (paragraph 10) means
  a. awaiting.
  b. worrying about.
  c. denying.
  d. considering.

Discussion Questions

About Content

1. Why does Professor Maloney recall so vividly the first time he heard the question "Why should we hire you?"

2. The essay's proposed strategy for early focusing on future work is opposed to some traditional thinking which saw college years as a time for discovering yourself and your goals. Do you agree with Maloney's suggestions? What do you think of such "one-track" end-directed approaches to your college experience?

3. What are the early advantages the author sees for the student who is aware of future job needs and possibilities?

4. What resources are available to students within their own colleges?

About Structure

5. The thesis of many essays is found near the beginning or the end. Locate the thesis statement of "Why Should We Hire You?" and write it here.

_____

6. Which method(s) of introduction does the author use in this selection?
  a. Broad-to-narrow
  b. Explaining the importance of the topic

c. Anecdote

d. Situation opposite to the one developed

7. What methods of achieving transitions between paragraphs does Maloney use more than once in this selection?
    a. Repetition of keywords
    b. Transitional phrases
    c. Questions followed by explanations

    Find examples of at least three of these, and note them below, with the appropriate paragraph numbers.

    _____ (paragraph _____)

    _____ (paragraph _____)

    _____ (paragraph _____)

About Style and Tone

8. Maloney begins his essay with a highly personal and directly voiced confession containing a comparison between two apparently dissimilar events.

    How does the tone of the opening three paragraphs compare with that of the rest of the essay? What do you learn about the author, and how does what you discover affect your connection with him as writer? Does it make the information in the essay more or less credible? Why?

9. After the introductory paragraphs, the essay is divided into three sections. How would you subtitle each of these sections?

    1. _____

    2. _____

    3. _____

    What general method of organization do your subtitles seem to suggest?

◼ Writing Assignments

Assignment 1: Writing a Paragraph

Jim Maloney describes three types of attitudes prevalent among students. Choose the attitude that most closely resembles your own and write a paragraph that defends your position.

Assignment 2: Writing a Paragraph

Put yourself in Jim Maloney's position as he begins his essay. Imagine you have successfully graduated from your current program, have your resumé in hand, and are sitting in a job interview. Now answer "The Question" posed by the essay's title. Start with a specific job you may have in mind, or may have read about in the paper. Now, list what you think the employer may be looking for in skills, academic training, and part-time experience. Your paragraph should answer "The Question." You may want to begin with a topic sentence like "Fire Protection has been a life-long goal of mine, and I've done a lot of academic and practical preparation to get ready to enter the field." Make use of the groups of details you have listed under the headings above to build up your paragraph.

Assignment 3: Writing an Essay

You are an employer in the year 2000. *You* ask "The Question." You are a human resources officer in a company, and *you* must write the job description to be read by all those eager college graduates.

Write an essay that follows the format of a job description for a position for which your diploma is preparing you. To see examples of these, go to your Student Services office, or look at some periodicals special to your area of study for employers' advertisements. Your mission is to find and persuade that "ideal candidate" that this job is what that person is after. Be as specific in your details as possible. You can't offer "the world on a string"; you have limited salary and promotion possibilities in this uncertain economy. But you are going to be facing hundreds of applicants.

Make an outline similar to the following:

Thesis/Introduction: Omnitech Incorporated is looking for an energetic and ambitious entry-level _____. The successful candidate will have three main qualifications: _____, _____, and especially _____. (The introduction should include a brief company description and approximate salary range, as well as any special requirements, such as a willingness to travel.)

Topic Sentence 1: Your background and education will include

a. _____

b. _____

c. _____

Topic Sentence 2: The skills we are looking for are

a. _____

b. _____

c. _____

Topic Sentence 3: The types of experience we prefer are

a. _____

b. _____

c. _____

Conclude by summarizing your needs, and by emphasizing that the successful applicant will come close to or exceed all the requirements listed, and by stating that only resumés received within a certain time frame will be considered.

'THE BOY CODE' OF OUR CULTURE BREEDS BULLIES

Michele Landsberg

Is male aggressiveness an innate, hormone-driven characteristic, an inescapable left-over from the "kill or be killed" stage of our development? Anthropologists like Lionel Tiger would have us believe so, as would current writers who wish to rescue men from the grip of Political Correctness. Or, as Michele Landsberg, William Pollack, and others believe, is male aggression simply the result of relentless social conditioning to narrow or eliminate the range of available emotions in male children? Given the recurrent presence of violence in media and reality today, Landsberg questions the worldwide tendency to raise boys to be tough and emotionally limited.

1   Tenderness, optimism, empathy, imagination, responsibility, a capacity for love—are those manly qualities, or womanly? They are neither, of course, character is not colour-coded, pink or blue, from birth. It is our culture, not our genes, that insists on brutalizing boys into toughness and straitjacketing girls into the beauty myth.

2   Oh sure, our chromosomes and hormones may predispose us a certain way. But think of the energy, if not ferocity, that society invests in enforcing these gender roles. Read the birth notices: The babies are just hours old and their proud parents are already hailing them as macho new Blue Jays or beautiful princesses.

3   I've been thinking about gender conditioning again because, in the weeks since the various high school killings, one word keeps bobbing up from the swirl of anxious discussion:

4   Bullying.

5   Bullying played a malignant role in Littleton, Colorado; in Taber, Alberta, in Victoria, B.C. American psychologists estimate that 160,000 children miss school every day for fear of bullies.

6   This thuggery has long been recognized as a byproduct of what William Pollack, co-ordinator of the Centre for Men at Harvard Medical School, calls "The Boy Code." In his book *Real Boys*, Pollack argues that boys are forced, early on, to become strangers to themselves. Almost from infancy, they are shamed into denying their own emotions, donning a mask that hides any fear, doubt or neediness. Boys, writes Pollack, are wrenched away from their mothers much too soon, and mothers are disconcerted by the chorus of demands not to "baby" their boys. The trauma of a boy's premature separation from mother, at age 6 and again at adolescence, "contributes to a deep wellspring of grief and sadness" that may last a lifetime, Pollack says.

7   Extraordinarily, even after so much lip service about changing gender roles, the cruel and stupid Boy Code remains in force everywhere, even in the most enlightened households and schools, according to Pollack's research. I agree with Pollack that boys are not naturally brutish or violent—they may be energetic and active, but kindness, affection and emotional expressiveness are as instinctive to boys as to girls, until these "girlish" qualities are knocked out of them.

By prepubescence, our toys, commercials, movies, songs, TV, games, sports   8
and parental teachings have transformed most youngsters into ardent little gender
police, excluding, tormenting and mocking the "ugly" girl and the un-cool boy.

Bullying is such a fact of boyhood that you can pick up almost any man's   9
memoir at random and read about schoolyard tortures. Rudyard Kipling was bullied till he got big enough to bully back; Russell Baker, the journalist, was regularly
pummelled by a brutish "loner." Edward Ardizzone, one of Britain's most gifted
illustrators for children, was, by his own account "born to be teased and bullied,"
harassed and set upon on his nightmarish journeys from school to home. On the
most humiliating occasion, when he was 8 or 9, he was dragged behind bushes,
where a gang of boys pressed the hot ends of burnt matches to the tip of his penis.

After I wrote about Littleton and the bully factor, I received some eloquent let-   10
ters from men who will never forget what they suffered—or how close they might
have come to killing if they had had a gun. Robin Wood, an author and retired film
professor, remembers being relentlessly persecuted as an unathletic 11-year-old
English schoolboy: "I was reduced to throwing myself on the ground, blocking my
ears and screaming hysterically." No one ever came to his rescue; adults angrily
exhorted him to fight back.

I'm ashamed to remember, as a parent, making the same worse-than-useless   11
response on occasion. Now, finally, all that must change. Schools must take responsibility for the hierarchies of dominance they have helped to create, and begin to
practise inclusion instead. Peace-making programs can go some way toward coun-
teracting our overwhelmingly violent culture. In Norway, a national anti-bullying
program in the '80s reportedly cut the incidence in half. (How ironic that anti-vio-
lence and anti-racism programs have been cut by the "strong" Harris government,
even as it plans to give guns to 12-year-olds and "get tough" with street kids.)

We have to stop unnerving mothers by constant attacks on motherhood. We need   12
to overcome our deeply ingrained anxieties about masculinity, give boys as much loving nurture as we give to girls, and encourage them to be emotionally expressive.

It's not about making girls more like boys or boys more like girls; it's about   13
helping all children to become more fully human.

■ Reading Comprehension Questions

1. Which of the following would be the best alternative title for the selection?
   a. The Bully is a Fact of Life
   b. Society Stifles Boys' Emotional Growth
   c. Boys Do Not Get a Fair Chance
   d. Boys are Born Bullies

2. Which sentence best expresses the main idea of the selection?
   a. Aggressive behaviour among males is biologically determined and
      unchangeable.
   b. Boys are stuck with being little savages, whether it suits them or not.
   c. Society conditions boys to be tough and aggressive and girls to be pretty
      princesses.
   d. Boys become aggressive because they are never allowed to develop their
      other emotions.

3. *True or false?* _____ Landsberg denies any innate or genetic tendencies in males and females.

4. Boys hide many of their emotions, according to William Pollack, because
   a. they are cut off from their mothers and raised not to show "weakness."
   b. they do not know their own feelings and thus cannot express them.
   c. they are afraid to show them.
   d. they associate emotions with being "babyish" or "uncool."

5. According to Landsberg and the men whose boyhoods she examined,
   a. all boys are bullies at some point.
   b. bullying is just part of boyhood games and not very serious.
   c. boys who are tormented by bullies are usually comforted and soothed.
   d. bullying is common, but nonetheless scars those who suffer it.

6. The author implies that
   a. the absence of good parenting creates bullying.
   b. parents cooperate in forcing children into socially dictated roles.
   c. older children are often uncertain of gender roles.
   d. children may simply be naturally cruel to each other.

7. The author implies, from her choice of examples of victims of bullying, that
   a. children who are bullied are unusual cases, weaklings, or the exception to the rule.
   b. bullying is mainly a thing of the past, a product of an older system.
   c. bullying is part of the process of making boys stronger.
   d. society has tended to ignore or reinforce aggressive behaviour.

8. From the article, we can assume that Landsberg feels that:
   a. schools should get tougher with bullies and aggressive youths.
   b. boys and men should stop insulting their mothers.
   c. educators and society should de-emphasize winning and value human feelings.
   d. men should re-examine their shortcomings, imagined and real.

9. The word *predispose* in "Oh sure, our chromosomes and hormones may predispose us a certain way" (paragraph 2) means
   a. influence.
   b. force.
   c. turn.
   d. construct.

10. The word *pummelled* in "…the journalist was regularly pummelled by a brutish loner" (paragraph 9) means
   a. tormented.
   b. pounded.
   c. teased.
   d. abused.

■ **Discussion Questions**

About Content

1.　With which gender do you ordinarily associate each of the qualities Landsberg lists in her opening sentence? Why?

2.　What are the specific reasons William Pollack gives for why he believes boys "become strangers to themselves"? (paragraph 6) With which of these do you agree or disagree, and why?

3.　What emotions are "knocked out of" boys? Why? What forces and influences reinforce gender-specific emotions for boys and girls?

4.　As a parent, does Landsberg feel she had the right answer to dealing with bullying? What was her course of action?

About Structure

5.　In which paragraph do you find the author's thesis statement? Write the paragraph number and the sentence in the space provided.

_____

_____

　　In which paragraph do you find a restatement of the thesis?

6.　Paragraph 4 consists of just one word: "Bullying." What does Landsberg achieve with such a dramatically brief paragraph?

7.　Which method of introduction does the author use to begin her article?
　　a. Broad-to-narrow
　　b. Explaining the importance of the topic
　　c. Ideas opposite to those to be developed
　　d. Anecdote

About Style and Tone

8.　Many texts, including this one, advise writers to use precise and specific verbs to show their readers exactly what they mean. Landsberg uses verbs most effectively in her article; in the first paragraph, she describes culture as "brutalizing" boys and "straitjacketing" girls. Find at least two other examples of precise use of verbs and explain why these are effective.

9.　To emphasize the point and force of her thesis, Landsberg uses the basic but effective device of repetition of a keyword. Which keyword does she repeat, and where does it appear in the article, and why? What synonym for this word is used? What is the effect on you of this repetition?

■ Writing Assignments

Assignment 1: Writing a Paragraph

A writing assignment based on this selection appears on page 146.

Assignment 2: Writing a Paragraph

Why *do* all societies create images of little boys as fighters or "tigers," and of little girls as princesses or sweethearts? Is there some basically valid reason behind such stereotyping, or is it a massive error on the part of humanity? Has such gender stereotyping happened to you? If so, has it helped or hindered you in your life? How, specifically, and what have been the results?

   Using specific examples from your own experience, write a paragraph that defends or argues against this human practice.

Assignment 3: Writing an Essay

Landsberg brings up the high-school shooting tragedies in Littleton, Colorado, and in Taber, Alberta, as examples of violent behaviour ending in tragedy. She also recommends specific courses of action for society and the educational system.

   Could elementary and high schools change their curricula and values to reinforce gentler, less single-minded and "winning-oriented" behaviour? Do sports, athletic coaching, and recreational time in schools' activities promote aggression and winning at any cost, and worse, leave less assertive students on the sidelines?

   Write an "effects" essay, in which you explain the possible results of schools offering specific alternative approaches to "winning" and aggression, approaches that often result in the exclusion of quiet students. You may argue for or against such a change in educational values, but you must clearly explain why a policy or practice should or should not change, based on the possible results.

ARE WE RAISING MORALLY ILLITERATE KIDS?

Caroline Medwell

Talk of morality in youth and adult behaviour is everywhere today. Are we any more or less moral than our grandparents were? Has everyone ceased to care what is good or bad, or is the "bad apple" count the same as it ever was? People are the same mixed lot, from one generation to another, so what changes in the past twenty-five years might have affected ethics and behaviour? Well, there are at least two generations now who are predominantly products, not of "ideal" two-parent nuclear families, but of single-parent or two-working-parent families. And most people in these generations grew up with TV as a constant in their lives. Is there any single cause of "moral illiteracy?" Are children and young adults actually "morally illiterate?" Weigh your own views and experiences against those of Caroline Medwell as you read the following selection.

The two boys were about eight years old. Derek looked athletic and confident. 1 Adam seemed more fragile, his thin shoulders hunched up around his ears. On "Go!" they plunged into the water and began their race to the far end of the pool and back. The shrieks of their classmates bounced off the walls—most were cheering for the obvious favorite: "Derek! Derek!"

Adam kept his head down, concentrating on the shallow-end wall where they 2 were to turn. Derek kept a close eye on the teacher. When she turned to talk to the lifeguard, Derek, quick as a wink, spun around and started back toward the starting point, shaving about six metres off the prescribed distance. Adam turned at the shallow-end wall, as instructed, now far behind his opponent.

The crowd of boys watching from the deck fell silent for a moment, as they 3 digested the fact that Derek had cheated. Some then resumed cheering for Derek, now almost guaranteed to win. But others hesitated, then moved over to Adam's lane to lend him new-found encouragement and support.

Although Derek did reach the finish first, it was, unbelievably, a close race. The 4 teacher, sensing something amiss, declared the result to be a tie. Derek argued loudly against that verdict, insisting that he had won. Adam wrapped himself in his towel and walked slowly back to the dressing room, a contented little smile on his face.

For some reason, this small incident took on almost epic proportions in my 5 mind; a representation, I thought, of the struggle between the desire to win and the ability and willingness to play fair. That it had been enacted by two small boys was unaccountably depressing.

A short while later, I turned on the radio to hear the announcer introduce a 6 program "Is TV Turning Kids into Violent Criminals?" The psychiatrist being interviewed described "desensitized" children, who are "more likely to use violence" as a result of television viewing. He cited the example of a three-year-old Washington child who found his father's gun, picked it up, pointed it at his two-year-old playmate and shot him dead. The weekend newspaper carried an article on children who are pushed to succeed so hard by their parents that they become "problems, not prodigies."

The only item publicized that weekend indicating any kind of adult attention 7 to the needs of children highlighted the National Campaign to Save Lemon Yellow, a U.S. parent group who are fighting hard to save "eight classic crayon colors" from the Crayola 64-pack.

I couldn't help myself. I saw Nero fiddling while Rome burned. 8

To my mind, the morality of today's children looms as a more important issue than 9 discontinued crayon colors. Are our kids equipped with a solid set of values? A conscious code of ethics? A healthy respect for the people and the world around them? Or are they a generation of violent, stressed-out human beings, whose main objective is to win at any cost? Are they a generation saddled by "moral illiteracy"?

Moral illiteracy is a term coined by Burle Summers, president of the Ontario 10 Moral/Values Education Association, a volunteer group of parents, teachers and university professors. Concerned that traditional values are giving way to the fast track, the quick promotion and a "me first" attitude, members promote the teaching of qualities such as honesty, respect, courtesy, generosity, responsibility and self-discipline.

Summers cautions, however, against too literal an interpretation of the phrase 11 "morally illiterate." "I'm not saying kids are immoral," says Summers. "I am saying that they don't have the same background, the same set of rules as before." The result, he says, is five-year-olds who don't know how to share and to whom "please" and "thank you" are foreign words, 10-year-olds who laugh and chatter in the movies and put their feet up on occupied theatre seats, teens who speak rudely to store clerks and loll about on public transit seats while their elders stand precariously. The reason for such behavior, says Summers, is an "absence of certitude"— a kind of moral vacuum that creates a need to explore potential substitutes for values which were instilled in the pervious generation but seem to have gone missing in our kids.

It's true that many of us adults were raised in stable nuclear families, where 12 issues were discussed together around the family dinner table, and our parents took the time to school us in manners and good grace. Even our TV viewing revolved around such wholesome shows as *Ozzie and Harriet, Father Knows Best*, and *Leave It To Beaver*—which, if anything, erred on the side of idealism in depicting family life. Our upbringing may not have been perfect, but most of us matured with finely tuned notions of right and wrong.

Our children are not so lucky. They live in a complex world, where truth, good- 13 ness and respect are often hard to find. They spend almost as much time during the year watching TV as they do in school, and their heroes include Bart Simpson and the Teenage Mutant Ninja Turtles. Role models like Ben Johnson and Pete Rose have been barred from their respective sports for breaking the rules—and kids have noticed that this only happened after they were caught publicly. Our children live in a country which has been torn apart over the Constitution and—incredibly— embroiled in a world war.

Today's children probably have more intense life experiences every day than 14 we would have faced in a year at their age. And, at the end of these intense days, many children don't have the opportunity to discuss these experiences with their parents and, in doing so, receive guidance. One of the reasons is that many modern families are often just too busy to talk. Some families sit down to only one meal together a week, and for others, there are few social situations where children can intermingle with adults to converse, interact—and learn.

Instead, children spend a lot of time interacting with electronic gadgets. 15 Walkmans drown out the sounds of the surrounding world, running interference against two-way conversations. Video games enable children to play for hours without another human being in sight. Television, which 97 per cent of Canadian children watch for an average of 20 hours per week, offers a third form of solitary entertainment. Through that screen, children see and learn from a variety of characters. Bart Simpson, the bratty, brazen star of *The Simpsons* does say grace before dinner, but this is how it goes: "Dear God, we paid for all this stuff ourselves, so thanks for nothing." His father, Homer hears that the nuclear plant where he works is "contaminating the planet" and responds "Well, nobody's perfect."

Antonia Coffman, publicist for *The Simpsons*, points out that the characters 16 "aren't meant to be role models. The show is meant to entertain, it's not a message show." Coffman adds that both children and adults like the Simpsons because they're more realistic than the "perfect family" portrayed, for example, on *The Cosby Show*. Coffman credits kids these days with being "smarter, more savvy. They love the edge—and can see, for the most part, what's right and wrong."

Maybe so—but it may not always be the right lessons that are sinking in, espe- 17 cially if children absorb too much of this material alone or without discussion.

Marcia Williamson, a Toronto grade 2 teacher, is one of many educators who 18 is rising to the challenge of teaching values along with the regular subjects in the curriculum. Avoiding "really scary" issues like nuclear warfare, Williamson concentrates on helping her kids learn cooperation and non-violence—and how to react to everyday situations peacefully and positively. She uses films, followed by discussion, and the lessons learned are repeated around the classroom on large, colorful pieces of paper. Topics include sharing, learning from disappointment and good manners. At this level, says Williamson, you can't expect kids to perfect these skills. "All I'm doing is planting the seeds." Parent participation is crucial, so Williamson sends information home and discusses her program with the families. Without their support, she asserts, her efforts "just won't stick as well."

According to Burle Summers, "open, honest dialogue" among family members 19 is also a crucial component of values education. With respect to promoting it in the home, his advice is threefold. To start, he says, we must "sort out what's important to us—what we'd live and die for—and encourage others to reflect with us." Then, we must consider what we are doing, as a family unit or on our own, to develop respect for the individual, society, the environment, and how that respect is extended to the community around us. Thirdly, Summers asks us to "invite kids to participate in life decisions and life behavior." Do this on a daily basis, says Summers, using practical, realistic examples.

A factor Summers perceives as inhibiting the effectiveness of values education 20 is today's focus on self. "Kids are emerging from a 'me first' society," he says, "and considering the needs and rights of others can be difficult for them." It's true that children need a strong sense of themselves, and what they stand for and believe in, before they can extend or express those feelings to the world around them. Unfortunately, too many children have not been taught how to move beyond the self, and this "me first" attitude can make life difficult for those around them. Said one veteran teacher: "Teachers have a hard time these days with the lack of respect from kids—and you feel like they're getting that attitude from home." While none of the teachers I spoke with regret the freer, more open education system that we have now, most point out that it has its price.

I have three children, and I know it's not easy, and occasionally impossible, to con- 21 sistently offer them the kind of time and dialogue that the experts have described. My kids can squabble like masters, and I can be crankier sometimes than I like to imagine. But, in the interest of honesty, and inspired by my conversations with people like Burle Summers and Marcia Williamson, I decided to put into practice some of their peacemaking, thoughtful philosophies.

When my kids erupted over possession of a cereal box prize, I resisted the urge   22
to make a snap decision on who got what. Instead, I let each of them have their say, without interruption, and then asked for their solution. This turned out to be giving that particular item to the youngest ("I didn't really like it anyway," muttered one of the empty-handed two) and adding a piece of paper to the fridge door, on which we will record receipt of all such things from now on—and in doing so, know whose turn is next. And each day, I made sure I spent time with each of them, just talking about whatever was on our minds.

The results weren't always picture-perfect. I sometimes became impatient with   23
the peacemaking process and jumped ahead to a ruling on the matter. And I'll confess that when we played the one cooperative board game that we have, I found it less exciting than, say, Snakes and Ladders.

But then something happened which gave me hope. I came home yesterday   24
to find an addition to our message board. Written in a child's hand, shining out from the list of that day's activities, were the words, "Peace, Flower Power, Saving the World."

It's a start, I thought, a good start.   25

▪ Reading Comprehension questions

1. Which of the following would be the best alternative title for the selection?
   a. Media Make Children Monsters
   b. Why Morals May Be Puzzling to Kids
   c. Why Schools Can't Cope With Children Today
   d. Today's Immoral Children

2. Which sentence best expresses the main idea of the selection?
   a. Children live in a complex world full of diverse influences and little guidance, and are less morally certain than earlier generations.
   b. Media have failed to provide positive role models for children, and thus encourage violence and selfishness.
   c. Families no longer offer the consistent patterns and guidance needed to raise children with sound ethics.
   d. Ethics and morality are no longer important in today's society or its choice of role models.

3. "Moral illiteracy," according to Burle Bummers, means
   a. children do not understand what morality means.
   b. children have no role models and simply imitate society's current lack of ethics.
   c. children have not learned values and are uncertain of right and wrong.
   d. children misbehave because they prefer to challenge standards and rules.

4. Medwell believes she and her generation have a strong sense of ethics primarily because
   a. they were brought up very well.

   b. they only watched wholesome TV shows.
   c. they all grew up in two-parent nuclear families.
   d. families communicated well and taught ethical lessons.

5. *The Simpsons'* appeal, according to its publicist, lies in the fact that
   a. it reflects reality more accurately than shows with ideal families.
   b. its characters live "on the edge" of acceptable behaviour.
   c. its wisecracking characters always deliver a good message.
   d. it makes fun of everything.

6. The article implies that
   a. the media sensationalize and exaggerate child-morality issues.
   b. the media care about selling product more than about providing children with suitable role models.
   c. the media teach children violence and selfishness.
   d. the media prefer trivial items about children, rather than problematic or complex stories.

7. The article implies that
   a. electronic toys and TV create aggressive tendencies and ignorance of ethics in children.
   b. children cannot develop an ethical sense in the absence of social interaction.
   c. today's active and busy families are to blame for not teaching children moral values.
   d. children isolate themselves from reality and problems with technology and entertainment.

8. From the article, we can conclude that
   a. learning and practising ethics is best done at home.
   b. children have too little respect for others to learn from them.
   c. learning and practising ethics must be interactive and family-, community-, and school-based.
   d. children already have a sense of ethics, but cannot express it.

9. The word *prodigies* in "pushed to succeed so hard by their parents that they become "problems, not prodigies." (paragraph 6) means
   a. monsters.
   b. underachievers.
   c. geniuses.
   d. smart alecks.

10. The word *embroiled* in "…torn apart over the Constitution and—incredibly —embroiled in a world war." (paragraph 13) means
   a. attacked.
   b. overcooked.
   c. manipulated.
   d. involved.

■ Discussion Questions

About Content

1. Where in the opening anecdote, do you see examples of "the desire to win," and "the ability and willingness to play fair" (paragraph 5)? Could these events have happened in any decade, or are they typical only of today's children? Are there situations in your life in which you have taken part, or witnessed, such a struggle? How did your observations or experience affect you?

2. What examples of "moral illiteracy" among today's children and teens does Burle Summers offer? Does such behaviour confirm a judgment of today's children as "a generation of violent, stressed-out human beings, whose main objective is to win at any cost" (paragraph 9)? Why or why not? Is such behaviour prevalent, in your experience?

3. What factors, according to author Medwell, contribute to the "complex world" in which today's children live? What other factors might make their world complex as well?

4. What three recommendations does Burle Summers give for families who wish to create opportunities for dialogue about values? Are these recommendations realistic or achievable? Why or why not?

About Structure

5. What method is used to introduce and conclude the selection?
   (a) Explaining the importance of the subject
   (b) Situation opposite to the one to be developed
   (c) Anecdote related to the thesis
   (d) Asking a question

   Which standard of effective writing is achieved by the author's use of the same method for both sections?

6. Although Medwell's essay may be primarily persuasive in intention, she uses other subsidiary patterns to develop and set out her ideas. The cause-effect structure is one such pattern within the essay. Where in the selection do you find the cause-effect pattern used? Note the paragraph-groups where this pattern is used, and note in a few words the causes and effects mentioned.

7. Where in the selection do you find the following transitional devices used to link the end of one paragraph to the beginning of another? Note the words and paragraph numbers.
   (a) Repetition of a keyword or phrase
   (b) Change of direction word or phrase

About Style and Tone

8. "Are We Raising Morally Illiterate Kids?" is written from two points of view: first person (*I, we*), and the third person (*he/she*). Which paragraphs are

written in the first person? Which in the third person? In which point of view are the greater number of paragraphs written? What is the content of the paragraphs in each point of view? What is the effect of the first-person paragraphs, and what of the third-person paragraphs, in terms of the author making her point?

Writing Assignments

Assignment 1: Writing a Paragraph

An assignment based on this selection appears on page 187.

Assignment 2: Writing a Paragraph

Are you and your friends "stressed-out human beings" (paragraph 9)? What are the specific sources of stress felt by college students at the end of the twentieth century? Why is your generation's stress level different from that of your parents? Do the stresses you feel affect the ethical choices you make? How, specifically?

Write a paragraph in which you defend or argue against the following statement:

"College students today face pressures and temptations that make conventionally moral choices difficult."

Assignment 3: Writing an Essay

Everyone today lives in a media-generated environment, made of TV programming, the Internet, music videos, song lyrics, advertising, movies, and magazines. Some people feel that the media adversely inform and influence audiences, to the point of stimulating or causing violent or anti-social behaviour. Such people would inevitably cite the U.S. and Alberta high-school shooting tragedies as examples of media influencing young minds. "Are We Raising Morally Illiterate Kids?" suggests that media do offer questionable role models, such as Bart and Homer Simpson, while other people feel that viewers actually use media to help them make better moral choices.

Write an essay that looks at specific reasons why three TV shows you watch convey fair ethical standards in their characters and plot-lines. Be honest; do not use overly wholesome programs you never watch. It is entirely possible to argue that *The Simpsons*, *WWF Raw*, and *General Hospital* display reasonable ethics and moral values.

Human Groups and Society

Explaining a Process • Examining Cause and Effect • comparing or contrasting • Defin
Term • Dividing and Classifying • Describing a Scene or Person • Narrating an Event • Arc
a Position • Explaining a Process • Examining Cause and Effect • comparing or contrast
Defining a Term • Dividing and Classifying • Describing a Scene or Person • Narrating an
Arguing a Position • Explaining a Process • Examining Cause and Effect • compari

HAVE YOU SEEN MY MISSING MATH GENE?

Tony Wong

One of Canada's favourite stereotypes is that of the Asian math and computer whiz. As high school and college students, we automatically assume that the Asian student next to us will get an *A* in Accounting and can probably program our PC to do everything but cook dinner. All nations and peoples are prone to stereotyping; it's one of the ways in which our brains learn to classify and sort information. However, when we apply these categorizing principles to people, the results can range from silly social mistakes to deep-seated and harmful prejudices such as neo-Nazism and apartheid. Tony Wong, a reporter for *The Toronto Star*, takes a light-hearted look at the Canadian perception of the typical Asian: its origins in economic necessity, and its effects on him and his nontypical brother and cousin.

It seems every year I am asked to speak to Asian kids about alternate careers. 1

An alternate career for an Asian child being defined as anything but a doctor, 2
dentist, pharmacist, accountant or any vocation requiring addition.

I am uniquely qualified to give these seminars, it seems, because I must be one 3
of the few Asians, according to programs like *60 Minutes* (which once did a seg-
ment on why so many Asians are taking over the medical schools of America), who
cannot add. Or subtract or multiply.

I also stink at chess and have trouble turning on my computer. 4

To this day I have not figured out how to properly program my VCR, although   **5**
I have cleverly got rid of the flashing 12 o'clock sign by pasting electrical tape over
it. So you see, I am not bereft of resources.

If there is a math gene for Chinese folk, I have somehow missed out.   **6**

Philippe Rushton would have a field day with me, and I have not even got into   **7**
the issue of Asian versus Black versus Caucasian penis size, which has been—for
goodness sake—the topic of the good professor's latest research. I already have
enough of a complex, thank you.

But do not despair for me, for I have been living a fulfilling life despite my   **8**
handicap, although my job has been made more difficult with China's win this
summer at, what else, the International Math Olympiad, where, to top things off,
Canada's top-gun was Chinese Canadian.

This leaves folks like me in a precarious situation, burdened with trying to lead   **9**
Asian youth out of their computer and slide rule-induced stupor.

I remember one year where Metro Councillor Olivia Chow and I were dragged   **10**
out as mathematically challenged role models for a workshop on alternate career
skills for teens.

Olivia, who can actually add but faked it for my benefit, seemed doubly qual-   **11**
ified for this job as she started life as an artist before becoming a high-powered
politician.

For the occasion, I wrote a skit to demonstrate the pressures faced by Asian   **12**
kids at home. Olivia kindly agreed to play my mom, while I played a bratty kid who
wants to be an artist. I gave Olivia all the good lines.

Olivia: "Jimmy Li got into pharmacy. His mother said he got scholarship, too."   **13**

Me: "That's nice, Mom. I think I'll continue practising my Spider-Man doo-   **14**
dle. You never know when Marvel will call."

Actually my own segue into the writing life wasn't so difficult. My brother   **15**
Victor inadvertently paved the way when he decided to be an artist.

When my mother got a look at his work, which included the influences of   **16**
Matisse and Rubens with a little *Playboy* thrown in, she was not amused.

She seemed relieved when I told her I just wanted to be a starving writer.   **17**

She changed her tune, though, after a visit to the Barnes exhibition at the Art   **18**
Gallery of Ontario.

"That looks like something your brother would draw," she would exclaim see-   **19**
ing Matisse's dance of life which consists of a bunch of fat nudes frolicking. It was
then she figured that my poor brother had not been "marketed" properly, especially
after seeing that a bunch of naked people dancing in a park by a dead guy could
fetch so much money. Moreover, my brother is alive to boot.

It reminded me of the time my cousin Walter, a photographer who had shot   **20**
covers for all the top international fashion magazines, including *Vogue*, *Elle* and
Cosmopolitan, was told by his mother that he shouldn't have a studio upstairs
where no one could see him.

After all, suppose someone wanted to get a passport picture? He would lose   **21**
business. It was the ever-pragmatic Asian philosophy at work. Don't forget the walk-
by traffic. At that time, national media profiles pegged his daily fee at $50,000. But,
as my aunt would say, you never know when another $9.95 might come in handy.

So you see, there can be life after math. Diversity is the name of the game. And   22
stereotypes, like bad clichés, just won't hold any water—at least if you don't subscribe to them.

▓ Reading Comprehension Questions

1. Which of the following would be the best alternative title for this article?
   a. Adding Up Those Accurate Asians
   b. A Writer of a Different Colour
   c. Asians and the Arts
   d. Sticky Stereotypes and Tricky Truisms

2. Which sentence best expresses the main idea of the selection?
   a. Asian students are driven by their families into science-based careers.
   b. Tony Wong comes from an artistically gifted family.
   c. People of any racial group are prone to vary in their gifts and abilities.
   d. Asians are basically practical in their view of valuable life skills.

3. The stereotype of Asians as gifted only in areas of technical expertise
   a. is part of our social fabric and further exploited by media and academics.
   b. is probably true because of Chinese students' abilities in math and medicine.
   c. is a product of the Western drive for economic success.
   d. makes life almost impossible for Chinese young people gifted in other areas.

4. The author found that starting a career as a writer was less difficult because
   a. he was mathematically challenged anyway.
   b. his brother had already become an artist.
   c. his mother thought it was better than being a cartoonist.
   d. there wasn't much Asian competition in the field.

5. Wong's aunt believed that his cousin should have a street-level office
   a. because her own view of economics suggested that he might miss out on
      daily customers.
   b. because she wanted him to take passport pictures.
   c. because she didn't know what he really did for a living.
   d. because upstairs offices are bad for business.

6. The author implies that
   a. he feels threatened by Chinese abilities in technical fields.
   b. Asian students are perhaps not encouraged toward less practical careers.
   c. he is so inept that he had to become a writer to explain himself.
   d. a sense of humour is not appreciated in Asian cultures.

7. *True or false?* _____ Wong's mother's main objection to Victor
   Wong's career as an artist was that he painted mostly naked women.

8. Paragraphs 19–21 imply that Tony Wong
   a. finds the Asian culture too money-conscious.
   b. thinks his mother's values are out of touch with reality.
   c. respects the survival instinct in his culture, but sees the irony in it.
   d. envies those more successful than he is.

9. The word *precarious* in "This leaves folks like me in a precarious position, burdened with trying to lead Asian youth out of their computer and slide rule-induced stupor" (paragraph 9) means
   a. uncertain.
   b. scary.
   c. impossible.
   d. overworked.

10. The word *pragmatic* in "It was the ever-pragmatic Asian philosophy at work" (paragraph 21) means
    a. changing.
    b. working.
    c. stubborn.
    d. realistic.

■ Discussion Questions

About Content

1. What careers does Tony Wong give as those expected of Asian students? Why?

2. What reasons does the author offer for being "uniquely qualified" to give seminars on "alternate careers" for Asian students? How serious is he, do you think? Why?

3. What made Wong's mother decide that his brother's choice of career was not so stupid? What did she decide was the problem with his being an artist?

About Structure

4. Wong's article divides itself into three sections, with an introductory and a concluding paragraph. What subtitles would you give these sections? Fill in the spaces below with appropriate subtitles. *(1) intro*

   Paragraphs 2–? ___"I Am not a sterotype" 2–9___

   Paragraphs ?–14 ___"Cultural pressure" 10–14___ *body*

   Paragraphs 15–? ___"Successful Alternatives" 15–21___

   (22) conclusion.

   Why have you chosen your subtitles? What is the subject of each of these sections? How does each section advance Wong's main idea?

5. In which paragraph do you find the author's thesis? ___22___
   Why do you think he has chosen this position for his thesis?

6. What do you believe to be the keyword in the author's thesis statement? What examples in the essay support this keyword? Which examples seem to contradict the idea implied by this word?

About Style and Tone

7. Tony Wong is evidently a writer with a sense of humour. Some techniques natural to the comic writer or comedian include the following: exaggeration,

understatement or deflation, unlikely comparisons, shifts in vocabulary levels, and the use of surprising "punch lines."

Find examples of four of these comic techniques in the article, and list the phrases after the paragraph number in which you find the example required.

Exaggeration _____5, 9, 19_____ (paragraph _____)

Understatement _____2, 8, 3_____ (paragraph _____)

Shift in vocabulary level ___4–5 , 11, 19___ (paragraph _____)

Unexpected "punch line" __19, 21 , 16–17__ (paragraph _____)

8. After reading this selection, what type of publication would you expect to find it in: a weekly magazine or daily newspaper, a scholarly journal on sociology, or a text on race relations in Canada?

What do the word choices, subject matter, and tone suggest about the audience Wong is writing for?

Writing Assignments

Assignment 1: Writing a Paragraph

Tony Wong feels he is missing a math gene. Write a descriptive paragraph about some aspect of *you* that seems to be missing, or dormant, or undiscovered. Your paragraph may be humorous or straightforward in approach.

Assignment 2: Writing a Paragraph

People often surprise us because they don't always conform to our stereotypes or judgments about them based on appearances. Either their behaviour or their reasons for their actions do not follow our preconceived notions. Tony Wong's mother and his aunt are examples of apparent adherence to the Asian stereotype of practicality, but both manage to adapt to their offspring's radical career choices. Wong himself, his brother, his cousin Victor, and Toronto civic official Olivia Chow are contradictions to the stereotypical Asian.

Write a paragraph about a person whose appearance completely misled you (or someone else) at first. Describe the person's appearance and characteristics in some detail and contrast this with what you found to be the person's underlying character. Be sure to be precise in your choice of details and to contrast them with details that relate to your first impressions, so that the reader will follow your discovery of the difference between appearance and reality.

You might want to begin with a topic sentence like the following, which gives your remembered first or dominant impression of your subject, based solely on what you first observed about him or her:

Jim's three earrings, Metallica T-shirt, ripped black jeans, and shaved head had him marked as one mean punk in my mind, and the silver skull on his belt buckle did nothing to change my opinion.

Conclude your paragraph with a summary of what you learned and a statement of your current feelings about this person.

Assignment 3: Writing an Essay

Tony Wong mentions in his seventh paragraph a controversial professor from an Ontario university, Philippe Rushton. Rushton studies racial and genetic patterns in human beings. His findings, where human intelligence is concerned, have prompted criticism of his supposed racist views. When carried to an extreme, or when misapplied, judgments or findings based on race are always questionable, and have led to horrendous social problems, persecution, and such atrocities as Nazism and the recent events in Kosovo.

Although stereotyping or classifying is indeed a standard part of the learning process, wherein humans learn to distinguish one thing from another and to group similar ideas, it is very dangerous when applied to people. Most Canadian students attend colleges and universities where diversity in the classroom is the rule, not the exception. Moreover, our laws and college charters guarantee the rights of all Canadians. A fast glance at any major Canadian city's newspaper will, unfortunately, disabuse us of the notion that we have created the "perfect egalitarian society"; various racial groups continue to labour under stereotypes, and factions continue to form which support racist views.

Write an essay that tackles an experience of your own with stereotyping, whether on your part, or as applied to you by someone else. Make use of the cause and effect format for your essay. What caused you or someone else to make a premature judgment, and what were the consequences? You may choose a lighthearted approach, as Tony Wong has, or you may treat the subject seriously.

Some options for opening sentences in your thesis statement paragraphs could be as follows:

> Because I am a female student of Italian descent, people sometimes assume I must be a good cook, interested in babies, and intensely religious. Are they in for some surprises.

> When I registered in my first course in chemical engineering, and answered to the name "Littlefeather, Jim" on the attendance list, the student in the next chair raised his hand to me and said, "How." I said, "I don't know; do you?"

> Arriving from Beijing was difficult enough, but registering in a new school system, dealing with an unfamiliar language, and trying to understand the other students' behaviour all seemed just too much.

SPIRITUAL STORYTELLER

Daniel Smith

Basil Johnston is an amazing Canadian character. The author of several books, and a former teacher, he is an unpretentious and learned Native Canadian who wears his knowledge lightly and in a most charming fashion. The Canadian author of this text was fortunate enough to have had Mr. Johnston as a high-school history teacher, and can still remember his dry wit and his ability to make the dustiest patches of European politics seem interesting. Basil Johnston is a storyteller with a mission: to keep alive the language and beliefs of his Ojibway culture, and to do so by making these things relevant to our lives today.

Two precocious kids figure strongly in Basil Johnston's quest to celebrate a rich if imperiled touchstone of Canada's soul. 1

The first kid is Johnston himself, age 6. It's 60 years ago, and his entire family has just moved from the Ojibway reserve on Port Parry Island to the Cape Croker reserve on the Bruce Peninsula. 2

Johnston's mom, Mary, is determined none of the new arrivals would tumble off the Niagara Escarpment running behind his grandmother's house. So she warns them of the full assortment of perils lurking in the bush. 3

"Don't you know there are *maemaegawaehnssiwuk* (little people) out there? *Weendigoes?* (Cannibals.) And the Iroquois down there? And the white people over there?" 4

Now Basil, as is the way of the young, doesn't put much stock in these warnings until one day—after some still unrevealed misdeed involving another local kid—he hears the alien sound of a popping motorcycle engine. 5

"I thought, 'Oh, they're coming for me!'" Johnston recalls. "I ran down and hid to take my chances with the Iroquois. It turned out the motorcycle belonged to a magazine salesman. I got a damned good licking anyway. 6

"So that was my introduction to the *manitous*." 7

Johnston met a second pivotal kid some decades later in a Grade 5 classroom in North York. Johnston, now a high school teacher in Willowdale, is visiting a class that is wrapping up a five-week study of Indians. 8

Except the students hadn't pondered Indians as people, as human beings. They studied what Johnston describes as things—totem poles and lodges. Nothing about values and spiritualism and a world view so different from our own dominant Western modes of thinking. 9

"Is this all there is?" asks one downcast boy. "Of course not," replies Johnston, knowing full well he has no books, no material to direct the boy to. 10

"So that made me realize what needed to be done," Johnston concludes. 11

All his stories work out that way. They amble out, cross a bridge or two, maybe get their boots muddy, but then they always circle back to the point. "So that's how …" 12

Johnston sees story-telling as the base of all good writing and good teaching. It's the focus of his ever-broadening campaign to revive the rich folktales of the Anishinaubae—the Ojibway, Ontario's dominant Indian tribe. 13

As one of the few people around who still speaks and writes the Ojibway language, plus his experience as a teacher and later as a Royal Ontario Museum lecturer, Johnston is ideally placed to shoulder such a burden. 14

Not that he sees his calling that way. Johnston does not see himself as carrying the responsibility for the survival of a threatened culture. He's just a guy whose 15 upbringing, language, and teaching skills have come together at a time when they are needed—just as the heroes in the Anishnaubae tales arrive by seeming happenstances in the nick of time.

Not for him the endless round of political meetings and lobby efforts which bedevil the lives of so many Indian activists. He's been there, in the '60s, including a stint with the old Indian-Eskimo Association and other forerunners to today's more polished native organizations.   **16**

And he has already told the dark side of the old Indian schools, like the Spanish Indian Residential School he wrote about in *Indian School Days*,[1] before going on to become one of the first Indian post-secondary degree holders in Ontario.   **17**

Instead, from either his Richmond Hill semi or the log house he completed at Cape Croker in 1967, Johnston, at 66, avoids the political limelight to concentrate on a body of work which has brought him renown and honors across North America.   **18**

His 11th and 12th books came out this fall. *The Bear-Walker,* published by the ROM, is another collection of previously-gathered tales, some of his own and some from such story-telling pals as Sam Ozawamik and Alex McKay, who he credits for always reminding him to ask, "What does it mean?"   **19**

But the book that featured the kind of multi-city book tour few native authors have received is *The Manitous—The Spiritual World of the Ojibway.*   **20**

In *The Manitous*, Johnston finally attempts to pull together the rich pantheon of Ojibway folk heroes into a comprehensive whole, one that doubles as a one-stop peek at the Anishinaubae world view.   **21**

Many people by now have heard of Nana'b'oozoo, the half-human, half-manitou figure whose bumbling efforts to do what pops into his head so often end up doing good, despite chaos on the way. But few know of Nana'b'oozoo's brothers—Maudjee-kawiss, Pukawiss and Cheeby-aub-oozoo—and the very different gifts they brought the human beings.   **22**

The brothers and all the other manitous—from the little *maemaegawaehnssi-wuk* with their special interest in children to the more celebrated *weendigoes* and their devouring habits—aren't presented as curios from the past. Johnston argues the strengths and weaknesses of what's still known about the manitous reflect the values and lessons that form the ancient Ojibway notions of what's important for humans in the world—respect for all living things, for individual rights and responsibilities, and so on.   **23**

So the manitous aren't dead; just harder to see. Except for the weendigoes—they have become the giant lumber companies clear-cutting the vast tracts of forest, the bankers, and so on—all the agents of greed and folly which have so much impact on all our lives.   **24**

As always, Johnston has a bunch of other projects on the go. There's a children's book and another set of humor stories, in the vein of his Leacock Award-nominee *Moose Meat and Wild Rice.* And he's finishing his latest version of an Ojibway language lexicon, no small challenge for a tongue which has few of its complex grammatical niceties codified anywhere.   **25**

---

[1] *Indian School Days* is listed in the Instructor's Manual for this text. Your teacher may recommend some of Johnston's other fiction and nonfiction titles to you.

"It's all context and prefixes," explains Johnston. "The idea of the manitou cov- **26**
ers everything from the creatures themselves to manitou-like feelings or places,
depending on context.

"And the grammar! Take the word *inaendumcowin*, which means the opera- **27**
tion of the mind. It takes more than 200 different prefixes. You end up with a dictionary of some 200,000 words, and it only works if you know how it all comes
together and your ear is fine enough to distinguish those prefixes."

Johnston bristles at the oft-repeated description of his work as preserving a **28**
dying language and folklore.

"Sure, I want to draft the hardware for the teachers and for the kids who want **29**
to learn about themselves, then go on to enrich it," he says firmly. "But I'm not an
adder-to, not a historian. I want these stories to grow, not become stale. That's why
you've got to put some modern interpretations on them, to allow them to become
accessible."

Of the more than 50 aboriginal languages in full flower in Canada 500 years **30**
ago, only Ojibway—along with Cree and Inuktitut, the language of the Inuit—are
seen as having any chance of surviving another generation or two. For all the efforts
being made by Indian traditionalists, schools and cultural activists like Johnston,
the English of the television set and the bigger cities is winning the battle.

Even on the more remote Anishinaubae reserves, few people under 40 can **31**
speak their own language. Even Johnston's three adult kids, for all the childhood
grilling in those prefixes they endured from their dad, would need "a good six
months' immersion" to recover what they've lost.

"Native kids aren't flocking to night schools to recapture their language," says **32**
Johnston. "They're accepting the benefits of being native without accepting the
responsibility to live their culture."

The chapter on Nana'b'oozoo in *The Manitous*, for example, ends after his **33**
departure from the Ojibway on this discomforting note:

> Because of the present generation's indifference to its language, traditions and **34**
> heritage, the Nana'b'oozoo is unlikely to return to inspire storytellers to add to
> the national Anishinaubae legacy and the value of the bequest as it is meant to be
> enriched. And there are few who mourn the loss of the Anishinaubae nation.

Such a loss would, of course, leave Canada a poorer place as well. It's sobering **35**
to realize how few people like Basil Johnston are left, struggling against all our
modern corporate manitous to keep alive the very powers which kept the manitous of old at bay.

■ Reading Comprehension Questions

1. Which of the following would be the best alternative title for this selection?
   a. The Manitou and the Magician
   b. An Ojibway Hero
   c. Aboriginal Stories for Today's World
   d. Lost Languages and Lost Lives

2. Which sentence best expresses the main idea of the selection?
   a. Basil Johnston wants to revive Native Canadian culture through story-telling.
   b. Johnston believes profoundly in the power of Ojibway mythology.
   c. Johnston blames ecological/corporate disasters on the continuing presence of Ojibway evil spirits.
   d. Canada is at risk of losing part of its cultural identity without the work of people like Basil Johnston.

3. Six-year-old Basil Johnston believed
   a. his mother's warnings were not very important.
   b. that the motorcycle's engine was either evil spirits or the Iroquois.
   c. that he wouldn't fall off the escarpment.
   d. that the white people were the most frightening possibility.

4. The grade five students, in five weeks, had learned
   a. all about Indian living styles and culture.
   b. only Indian myths and legends.
   c. the facts about Indian homes and artifacts, but nothing about their values.
   d. the differences between Western and Native Canadian lives.

5. *True or false?* _____ Johnston wants the Ojibway language and mythology preserved as part of history.

6. The selection implies that
   a. to Johnston, the concept of manitous is valuable as a historical idea.
   b. the manitous demonstrate important universal moral and ethical values.
   c. the manitous are no longer evident in modern industrial society.
   d. manitous belong mainly in Johnston's dictionary of the Ojibway language.

7. The author implies that aboriginal languages are dying out because
   a. they are too difficult to learn, with all their complex grammar.
   b. they are not taught in schools on the reserves.
   c. English is the language of business and media, and of "the good life."
   d. they deal only with concepts and ways of living that are now in the past.

8. We can conclude from the selection that
   a. language often holds the spirit and heritage of a culture.
   b. the Ojibway won't regret the loss of their stories and language.
   c. modern and ancient myths are at war with each other.
   d. even Johnston's children are indifferent to their heritage.

9. The word *imperiled* in "Two precocious kids figure strongly in Basil Johnston's quest to celebrate a rich if imperiled touchstone of Canada's soul" (paragraph 1) means
   a. dangerous.
   b. lost.
   c. unknown.
   d. endangered.

10. The word *bequest* in "to add to the national Anishinaubae legacy and the value of the bequest as it is meant to be enriched" (paragraph 34) means
    a. history.
    b. inquiry.
    c. inherited gift.
    d. tradition.

Discussion Questions

About Content

1. What is ironic about the noise Johnston hears as he is playing near his grandmother's house? How does this little story relate to Johnston's ideas about the continuing presence of Ojibway culture?

2. Why is the student in the second anecdote described as "downcast" at the end of his five-week course in Indian culture? Why would both this child and Johnston be called "precocious" by author Smith?

3. Why does Johnston not participate in political activities for aboriginal rights, according to the selection? What does he see as his mission?

4. How many native languages have survived from the time of Canada's "discovery" by Cartier and other explorers? What does the size of this loss suggest to you?

About Structure

5. In which paragraph do you find the best expression of the author's thesis? How would you state this idea in your own words? Do you agree with Johnston?

6. What method of introduction does Daniel Smith use in this article?
    a. Explaining the importance of the topic
    b. Anecdote
    c. Broad-to-narrow
    d. Situation opposite to the one to be developed

   Why is Smith's choice of introduction particularly suitable to his subject and to the content of the article?

7. How many change-of-direction transition words do you find in this selection? List the paragraphs beginning with such words.

   _____   _____   _____   _____   _____

About Style and Tone

8. Daniel Smith uses a figure of speech in paragraph 12 to describe Basil Johnston's way of relating information. When we give a nonhuman thing human qualities, the use of this figure of speech is called *personification*.

What is personified in this paragraph? Why would such a usage be appropriate to Johnston, given what is told about him in the selection?

9. How do the Ojibway words and Johnston's explanations of the complexity of his language in the article affect you as a reader? How does it affect your perception of Native North American languages and culture?

Writing Assignments

Assignment 1: Writing a Paragraph

Each of us knows at least one person who has been a sort of "storyteller" character for us. This person might be a relative who has kept alive family stories and history, or might be a friend or acquaintance who can turn the simplest explanation into a "tall tale." Perhaps you have had a teacher, who, like Basil Johnston, used stories to teach and to entertain. Write a paragraph that is a portrait of your storyteller.

Begin by thinking of what best characterizes this person's stories and/or their storytelling style. Jot down a series of the descriptive words that come to mind under their name. Think of one or two of their best stories, and note a few phrases to remind you of the details you want to remember.

Now try to answer the question, "Why was (or is) _____ such a great (or important) storyteller to me?" Put your answer in one sentence, such as, "My best friend Lena can turn the dullest trip to the mall into an entertaining story with her funny observations about people, her bizarre chats with salespeople, and her ability to find the most disgusting washrooms in the universe." Be sure to use specific details to back up each point you make about the storyteller, their stories, or their style of telling their tales.

Assignment 2: Writing a Paragraph

Most cultures are kept alive by storytelling, what is sometimes called "the oral narrative tradition." From tiny moments in our lives, like that in Basil Johnston's grade five class when the little boy asked "Is that all there is?" come stories and memories that may become important to us. Even if we feel that our background is perhaps bland and typical of many people, there are still unique aspects to each of our lives. Your subject could be as "ordinary" as your grandmother's butter tarts, or as distinctive as the way your family celebrates a particular holiday. Write a paragraph that describes some thing or some tradition or habit which is unique to you, your family, or your cultural heritage. Explain how you came to experience this event or thing, and why it has significance to you.

Assignment 3: Writing an Essay

Is Canada the cultural mosaic it claims to be? Will the media make English the dominant language of the next century? Will our increasing dependence on technology and information media destroy the diverse cultural identities of various groups of people? In the case of Native Canadians, a loss of 47 languages seems to indicate a lack of tolerance, if not outright insensitivity, on the part of dominant cultures over the course of several centuries. As one Native rock group's lyric goes, "When Columbus came, the question was, Who discovered who?"

What about other cultural groups? English is a necessity for professional communication in most of Canada's provinces, but are we all like the young Native Canadians Johnston accuses of "accepting the benefits of being [Canadian] without accepting the responsibility to live [our] culture"? Within one generation a language can be forgotten; is a culture forgotten with it?

Write an essay that argues for or against people's retaining their own original languages in twenty-first-century Canada. You may wish to address the issue of Native Canadians, or perhaps that of another national group from which your family comes, or that of francophone Canadians. Is there a need for people to retain a knowledge of another language important to their background culture?

Here is one student's essay outline:

Thesis statement: My family is from the Ukraine, and my father tried to teach us the language, and sent us to all the cultural festivals ... but I just found them funny, and never wanted to speak Ukrainian.
– we wanted to be like our friends (all "Canadians")
– the language was too hard to learn, and we had French at school, too
– except for odd cable shows we hated, TV & radio & books were in English

Topic sentence 1: We came here to be Canadian, and no one at school, even the students whose parents came from Germany and Poland, knew more than a few words of their families' languages, so I didn't want to feel "different" or "foreign."
– our special holidays and church festivals were different enough for me
– we always felt dragged to the Ukrainian cultural events—would rather have been with our friends
– it was hard to relate to family pride in history—school didn't mention it

Topic sentence 2: Learning another language at home, on top of school work, was too difficult
– when would I use Ukrainian, outside the family?
– it's too different from English or French
– languages are not my strong point, academically

Topic sentence 3: All the TV we watch, the radio and music we listen to, and my favourite books are in English—can't imagine "Slavic Rock" ...
– only very occasional cable shows, which don't interest me at all, are in Ukrainian
– TV, music, and movies are my favourite entertainment—in English
– Stephen King and R. L. Stine write in English, and at least I enjoy reading them

WOLVERINE

By Paul Jay

Who is your idea of a Canadian superhero? A hockey player or athlete? Roberta Bondar or Marc Garneau? Bret "Hitman" Hart? Mike Myers? What do our choices of heroes and heroines say about our dreams? Or about us as a nation? What is it about our heroes and heroines that makes us choose them? How often do we choose our own idols, and how often do the media choose them for us? Paul Jay looks at his childhood superhero, and what he and his friends found to identify with in Wolverine.

1   When I was in grade five, I used to match my classmates up with corresponding superheroes. Some of these matches were natural (the too-tall David Alder became Goliath, for example), while others were more impressionistic; I can't remember who was tagged as the Incredible Hulk, only that he had a ferocious temper. The girls in my class couldn't have cared less about the game, but the boys all wanted to be one hero: Wolverine.

2   Created by New York-based Marvel Comics, Wolverine is a mutant superhero from Canada with acute animal senses, a nasty temper, and retractable, razor-sharp metal claws that he uses for gouging, slashing, and grappling with evildoers. Since his first appearance in 1974 as "Weapon X," and later as a member of the superhero team the X-Men, Wolverine has grown into one of the most popular comic-book characters around, largely because of his ornery disposition and willingness to take on any bad guy. And unlike Batman, Spider-Man, or Superman, Wolverine's been known to finish off his adversaries, when necessary.

3   Growing up in the mining town of Sudbury, Ontario—where we played superheroes in the underground tunnels of the Science North museum—my friends and I embraced Wolverine as our own. I worked with my brothers at fashioning Wolverine-style claws out of tinfoil. (The claws were, to our disappointment, more ornamental than utilitarian.) Perhaps we identified with Wolverine because he is a short-statured tough guy going toe to toe with villains twice his size; the same reason why Maple Leafs fans always save their loudest cheers for Tie Domi.

4   We also liked that Wolverine isn't overtly Canadian, like Captain Canuck, or Marvel's superhero team Alpha Flight, which personifies the American vision of Canada. Their membership includes a hero named Sasquatch, one called Snowbird, and a squat man clad all in black named, yes, Puck.

5   Wolverine represented how we wanted to see ourselves—not polite or retiring, but tough and not to be trifled with. His northern roots showed through when he was out of costume, quaffing beer or chopping wood in a plaid shift, toque, and mutton chops, like a super-powered Neil Young, with claws.

6   I noticed recently that a live-action X-Men movie is in the works, and Sudbury is being scouted as a possible location. Australian actor Russell Crowe is apparently slated for the role of Wolverine, a role that, to my mind, belongs to a Canadian. If Mr. Crowe is unavailable, I'd like to suggest Tie Domi—a man who, like Wolverine, isn't afraid to take two minutes for slashing.

■ Reading Comprehension Questions

1. Which of the following would be the best alternative title for the selection?
   a. A Cool Canadian Comic Character
   b. Sudbury Slasher Makes Good
   c. Clawing Our Way to the Top
   d. Nice Guys Want to be Tough Too

2. Which sentence best expresses the main idea of the selection?
   a. Canadians always cheer the little guy.
   b. Canadians want to be seen as tough and uncompromising.
   c. Canadians have a hidden aggressive side.
   d. Canadians never had a superhero of their own.

3. On what bases did the author and his friends assign nicknames?

4. According to the author, why has Wolverine become such a favourite with comics readers?

5. What are the three reasons why Paul Jay and his friends identified with Wolverine?

6. The author implies that
   a. Wolverine and Canadians are meaner than they seem.
   b. Canadians do not always feel like "the little guys" in any contest.
   c. Canadians, like Wolverine, have hidden personalities.
   d. Canadians are as polite as they seem.

7. *True or false?* _____ Wolverine is appealing partly because he does not represent a clichéd American view of what is Canadian.

8. The author implies that
   a. he and his friends had violent aspirations.
   b. the boys wanted to be thought of as tougher than they seemed.
   c. he shared, and still shares, the Canadian "inferiority complex."
   d. Canadians do not have enough heroes of their own.

9. The word *ornery* in "one of the most popular comic-book characters around, largely because of his ornery disposition and willingness to take on the bad guy" (paragraph 2) means
   a. aggressive.
   b. violent.
   c. cranky.
   d. nasty.

10. The words *mutton chops* in "in a plaid shift, toque, and mutton chops…" (paragraph 4) mean
    a. earflaps.
    b. large sideburns.
    c. high boots.
    d. snowshoes.

▓ Discussion Questions

About Content

1. How does Wolverine differ from other comic-book superheroes? Does this make him more or less of a superhero?

2. Which characters make up Marvel's Alpha Flight superhero team, and why would Canadian readers find them offensive?

3. Why would author Paul Jay cast Tie Domi, the Leafs player, as Wolverine?

About Structure

4. Which method of introduction does Jay use for his essay?
   a. Explaining the importance of his subject
   b. Situation opposite to the one to be developed
   c. Anecdote
   d. General-to-narrow

   Why is, or is not, this method suitable for his subject?

5. Where in the selection do you find the best statement of the author's thesis? Why, based on the content of his essay, do you believe he placed his thesis in this position?

   Write the thesis of "Wolverine" in your own words on the following lines:

   _____

   _____

6. "Wolverine" is an essay that explains with examples, but what other method of development is used by the author? Why would this other method be appropriate to the subject of the selection?

About Style and Tone

7. Humour that touches readers is often based on ordinary details of real memories or experiences. Where in "Wolverine" do you find examples of Paul Jay's use of such humour?

8. Which transitional technique is used to tie the first five paragraphs in the selection together?
   a. Transition Signal Word(s)
   b. Synonyms
   c. Repeated Word(s)

   In which sentences of these five paragraphs is this technique used? How does it function to create coherence in Jay's essay?

▩ Writing Assignments

Assignment 1: Writing a Paragraph

An assignment based on this selection appears on pages 154–155.

Assignment 2: Writing a Paragraph

"Wolverine" is an essay that tries to define why the comic-book superhero was so important to the author, and also why Wolverine has special resonance or meaning for Canadians. What, exactly, is a "superhero"? The term is used constantly in the media, but what does it mean to you?

Using the definition method of development for your paper (refer to pages 189–192), write a paragraph in which you define "superhero." Alternatively, you may write an "anti-definition," stating why you believe there is no such thing as a superhero. For either of these alternatives, you may wish to use some comparison or contrast techniques (pages 174–183) in your definition paper, as you explain what a superhero is, and is not.

Assignment 3: Writing an Essay

Who should be heroes or role models for Canadians? Should we "grow our own," or accept them ready-made from the (mainly U.S.) media? By accepting the imitating heroes from U.S. and other cultures, do Canadians further weaken their grasp on national identity?

Write a paragraph that argues *either* for *or* against the following statement:

> Because Canadians are unique, they should choose Canadians as heroes and role models.

Use specific examples to support each point in your argument. Work to provide three solidly reasoned points for each of your body paragraphs, with clear and specific details to support each point or subtopic.

ADOLESCENT CONFUSION

Maya Angelou

In this selection from her highly praised autobiographical work, *I Know Why the Caged Bird Sings*, Maya Angelou writes with honesty, humour, and sensitivity about her sexual encounter with a neighbourhood boy. Angelou captures some of the confused feelings about sex we all experience when we are growing up; she is frightened but curious, outwardly aggressive yet inwardly shy; calculating and innocent—all at the same time. Angelou's outrageous plan for finding out what it is like to be a "real woman" may seem shocking. But her candour makes us respond to her account with understanding and delight.

A classmate of mine, whose mother had rooms for herself and her daughter in a   **1**
ladies' residence, had stayed out beyond closing time. She telephoned me to ask if
she could sleep at my house. Mother gave her permission, providing my friend telephoned her mother from our house.

When she arrived, I got out of bed and we went to the upstairs kitchen to   **2**
make hot chocolate. In my room we shared mean gossip about our friends, giggled
over boys, and whined about school and the tedium of life. The unusualness of
having someone sleep in my bed (I'd never slept with anyone except my grand-
mothers) and the frivolous laughter in the middle of the night made me forget
simple courtesies. My friend had to remind me that she had nothing to sleep in.
I gave her one of my gowns, and without curiosity or interest I watched her pull
off her clothes. At none of the early stages of undressing was I in the least conscious of her body. And then suddenly, for the briefest eye span, I saw her breasts.
I was stunned.

They were shaped like light-brown falsies in the five-and-ten-cent store, but   **3**
they were real. They made all the nude paintings I had seen in museums come to
life. In a word, they were beautiful. A universe divided what she had from what I
had. She was a woman.

My gown was too snug for her and much too long, and when she wanted to   **4**
laugh at her ridiculous image I found that humor had left me without a promise
to return.

Had I been older I might have thought that I was moved by both an esthetic   **5**
sense of beauty and the pure emotion of envy. But those possibilities did not occur
to me when I needed them. All I knew was that I had been moved by looking at a
woman's breasts. So all the calm and casual words of Mother's explanation a few
weeks earlier and the clinical terms of Noah Webster did not alter the fact that in
a fundamental way there was something queer about me.

I somersaulted deeper into my snuggery of misery. After a thorough self-exam-   **6**
ination, in the light of all I had read and heard about dykes and bulldaggers, I reasoned that I had none of the obvious traits—I didn't wear trousers, or have big
shoulders or go in for sports, or walk like a man or even want to touch a woman.
I wanted to be a woman, but that seemed to me to be a world to which I was to be
eternally refused entrance.

What I needed was a boyfriend. A boyfriend would clarify my position to the   **7**
world and, even more important, to myself. A boyfriend's acceptance of me would
guide me into that strange and exotic land of frills and femininity.

Among my associates, there were no takers. Understandably the boys of my age   **8**
and social group were captivated by the yellow- or light-brown-skinned girls, with
hairy legs and smooth little lips, whose hair "hung down like horses' manes." And
even those sought-after girls were asked to "give it up or tell where it is." They were
reminded in a popular song of the times, "If you can't smile and say yes, please
don't cry and say no." If the pretties were expected to make the supreme sacrifice
in order to "belong," what could the unattractive female do? She who had been
skimming along on life's turning but never-changing periphery had to be ready to
be a "buddy" by day and maybe by night. She was called upon to be generous only
if the pretty girls were unavailable.

I believe most plain girls are virtuous because of the scarcity of opportunity   **9**
to be otherwise. They shield themselves with an aura of unavailableness (for which
after a time they begin to take credit) largely as a defense tactic.

In my particular case, I could not hide behind the curtain of voluntary good-   **10**
ness. I was being crushed by two unrelenting forces: the uneasy suspicion that I
might not be a normal female and my newly awakening sexual appetite.

I decided to take matters into my own hands. (An unfortunate but apt phrase.)   **11**

Up the hill from our house, and on the same side of the street, lived two hand-   **12**
some brothers. They were easily the most eligible young men in the neighbor-
hood. If I was going to venture into sex, I saw no reason why I shouldn't make my
experiment with the best of the lot. I didn't really expect to capture either brother
on a permanent basis, but I thought if I could hook one temporarily I might be
able to work the relationship into something more lasting.

I planned a chart for seduction with surprise as my opening ploy. One evening   **13**
as I walked up the hill suffering from youth's vague malaise (there was simply
nothing to do), the brother I had chosen came walking directly into my trap.

"Hello, Marguerite." He nearly passed me.   **14**

I put the plan into action. "Hey." I plunged, "Would you like to have a sexual   **15**
intercourse with me?" Things were going according to the chart. His mouth hung
open like a garden gate. I had the advantage and so I pressed it.

"Take me somewhere."   **16**

His response lacked dignity, but in fairness to him I admit that I had left him   **17**
little chance to be suave.

He asked, "You mean, you're going to give me some trim?"   **18**

I assured him that that was exactly what I was about to give him. Even as the   **19**
scene was being enacted, I realized the imbalance in his values. He thought I was
giving him something, and the fact of the matter was that it was my intention to
take something from him. His good looks and popularity had made him so inordinately conceited that they blinded him to that possibility.

We went to a furnished room occupied by one of his friends, who understood   **20**
the situation immediately and got his coat and left us alone. The seductee quickly
turned off the lights. I would have preferred them left on, but didn't want to appear
more aggressive than I had been already—if that was possible.

I was excited rather than nervous, and hopeful instead of frightened. I had not   **21**
considered how physical an act of seduction would be. I had anticipated long soul-
ful tongued kisses and gentle caresses. But there was no romance in the knee which
forced my legs, nor in the rub of hairy skin on my chest.

Unredeemed by shared tenderness, the time was spent in laborious gropings,   **22**
pullings, yankings, and jerkings.

Not one word was spoken.   **23**

My partner showed that our experience had reached its climax by getting up   **24**
abruptly, and my main concern was how to get home quickly. He may have sensed
that he had been used, or his lack of interest may have been an indication that I
was less than gratifying. Neither possibility bothered me.

Outside on the street we left each other with little more than "OK, see you   **25**
around."

Thanks to Mr. Freeman nine years before, I had had no pain of entry to endure, **26** and because of the absence of romantic involvement neither of us felt much had happened.

At home I reviewed the failure and tried to evaluate my new position. I had **27** had a man. I had been had. Not only didn't I enjoy it, but my normality was still a question.

What happened to the moonlight-on-the-prairie feeling? Was there something **28** so wrong with me that I couldn't share a sensation that made poets gush out rhyme after rhyme, that made Richard Arlen brave the Arctic wastes and Veronica Lake betray the entire free world?

There seemed to be no explanation for my private infirmity, but being a prod- **29** uct (is "victim" a better word?) of the Southern Negro upbringing, I decided that I "would understand it all better by and by." I went to sleep.

Three weeks later, having thought very little of the strange and strangely empty **30** night, I found myself pregnant.

▨ Reading Comprehension Questions

1. Which of the following would be the best alternative title for this selection?
   a. A Wasted Life
   b. The Story of a Teenage Pregnancy
   c. The Pain and Confusion of Growing Up
   d. A Handsome Young Man

2. Which sentence best expresses the main idea of the selection?
   a. Teenage girls feel more insecure about sex than teenage boys do.
   b. A sexual experience is the first step toward adulthood.
   c. Maya Angelou's innocence led her to a joyless experience with sex and an unplanned pregnancy.
   d. Women who are sexually aggressive often become pregnant.

3. In the days following her sexual experience, the author
   a. talked to her mother about her feelings.
   b. wrote about the incident.
   c. asked her classmates for advice.
   d. virtually ignored what had happened.

4. The author chose the boy she did to experiment with because
   a. he had shown some interest in her.
   b. she wanted to start with one of the two most eligible boys in the neighbourhood.
   c. she knew he would be kind to her.
   d. she had a crush on him.

5. The author expected that
   a. having a boyfriend would help her become a woman.
   b. she would feel guilty about her actions.
   c. she would no longer be plain.
   d. she would probably get pregnant.

6. The author implies that
   a. she would become a homosexual.
   b. she had little sense of right and wrong.
   c. she had little idea of what love, sex, or femininity really mean.
   d. none of the girls she knew had had a sexual experience.

7. *True or false?* _____ The author implies that she had discussed the facts of womanhood with her mother.

8. The author implies that
   a. she wanted the boy to marry her.
   b. she was raped as a child.
   c. the boy's lack of tenderness was expected.
   d. the movies had taught her the facts of life.

9. The word *inordinately* in "His good looks and popularity had made him so inordinately conceited" (paragraph 19) means
   a. timidly.
   b. excessively.
   c. unexpectedly.
   d. unknowingly.

10. The word *malaise* in "I walked up the hill suffering from youth's vague malaise" (paragraph 13) means
    a. patience.
    b. pleasure.
    c. ambition.
    d. uneasiness.

Discussion Questions

About Content

1. For what reasons did Angelou decide she needed a boyfriend?

2. In what ways did Angelou's actual experience differ from what she expected it to be? Find passages in the selection that describe (a) Angelou's expectations and (b) the reality of the experience.

3. What was the young man's reaction to Angelou's seduction? What does his reaction reveal about him?

About Structure

4. A narrative selection most often focuses on a single event. But this selection is developed through two narratives. What are the two narratives? Why does Angelou include both?

5. Within her narratives, Angelou uses contrast to develop her paragraphs. For example, she contrasts her body and her classmate's body, and the

"pretties" and "unattractive females." Find two other areas of contrast and write them below:

_____

_____

6. Paragraph 23 consists of just one sentence: "Not one word was spoken." What effect does Angelou achieve by making this paragraph so short?

About Style and Tone

7. Angelou enlivens her narrative with humour. Find two places where she touches on the humorous side of her experience and write the paragraph numbers here:

_____   _____

8. Find two other places where the tone is quite serious.

_____   _____

Writing Assignments

Assignment 1: Writing a Paragraph

A writing assignment based on this selection is on page 136.

Assignment 2: Writing a Paragraph

Because of her confusion and insecurity, Angelou acted without consulting anyone else about her problem. Pretend that the young Maya has come to you with her doubts and her plan to seduce a boy. What advice would you give her? In a paragraph written in the form of a letter to Maya, explain what you would say to her.

Assignment 3: Writing an Essay

Do we all need to prove ourselves on the field of romance? Why is seduction necessary? In matters of the heart, does anything ever change? Write an essay that outlines and explains an ideal first experience. Do not concentrate on graphic physical details; Angelou, and most people, suffer more from the emotional and psychological effects of unsatisfactory romantic or sexual initiations. Find the three elements that would make a good first experience for *both* partners, and define these elements clearly as you begin each of your essay's three body paragraphs.

THE IMPORTANCE OF COOKING DINNER

Nancy Eng

Do you remember the first time you tried to cook a meal? Cooking is never as easy as recipes or relatives make it seem. Food, its preparation, and the rituals of the table are important parts of our daily social and family lives. In the twenty-first century, it seems that everyone is interested in food, if not in cooking. But despite the advances of feminist advice, statistics show that most cooking is still done by women, and is regarded (other than in the elevated realm of the great chefs) as part of essential female knowledge and skills. Nancy Eng, an English student at the University of British Columbia, takes issue with the idea that the honourable womanly place in the kitchen is somehow genetically inherited.

1   This was not to be just any dinner. This meal was to be a part of my rites of passage, another step into womanhood. Like the first pair of pantyhose, the first teetering steps on high heels, and the first taste of lipstick, an entire dinner prepared on one's own has always been an initiation into the adult female ranks. Despite all the advances women have made in this male-dominated world, despite the inspiration of the Sandra Day O'Connors, the Pat Carneys, and the Sally Rides, woman continues to carry certain limiting connotations. When one thinks of women, terms like *gentle, maternal,* and *domestic* still spring even to some of the most liberal minds. No matter how capable a woman is in the work world, it is still difficult to shake the time-honoured tradition of Mom baking cookies for her family, or Grandma fixing turkey for the clan. So, as I entered the kitchen that fateful day of my fifteenth year, armed with *The Joy of Cooking* and enshrouded in a "Kiss the Cook" apron, I was ready to tackle green salad, roast chicken, and chocolate mousse. I rolled up my sleeves, took a deep breath, and went to work.

2   The salad was easy enough. For that, I didn't even need to consult the cooking bible. I managed to wash and tear up a quantity of lettuce, and I threw in a variety of appropriately coloured vegetables so that my bowl more or less resembled green salad. This accomplished, I moved on with an air of confidence to the next course.

3   The chicken sat in all its slimy glory on a roasting pan, awaiting an expert touch. Cold and slippery in my hands, it was placid and cooperative as I dangled it awkwardly from one of its slick little limbs, trying to decide which end was up. I viewed my fowl friend from several angles, puzzled as to where exactly its head had been during its previous life. The directions called for stuffing the animal, so I located my box of Stouffer's Stovetop and contemplated where it belonged. Flipping the chicken around a few more times, I finally discovered an opening. I peered into its damp darkness, feeling slightly perverse about my actions, and hoping the chicken didn't mind this kind of intrusion. I couldn't see how I was going to hold that small hole open wide enough to fill the creature up, until I spied a funnel hanging invitingly from its hook in the cupboard. Inserting the funnel's tip into the bird, I poured in the contents of the box of stuffing, not realizing the dry,

crumbly mess I was forcing in was meant to be cooked first. The chicken soon bulged slightly with uncooked stuffing and the innards, which I had not bothered to remove. Pleased with its bumpy plumpness, I went on to basting.

"Butter outer chicken generously," the book directed. I partially unwrapped a **4** cold block of margarine, hoping such a substitution wouldn't offend anyone too much, and proceeded to rub the block over the surface of the equally cold, nubbly chicken skin with as much generosity as I could muster toward raw poultry. Large clots of yellow stuck here and there on the uneven epidermis, along with some bits of gold foil from the margarine wrapper. Good enough, I thought as I flicked off some of the larger, more conspicuous pieces of foil, time for seasoning. Nothing warms the heart of an inexperienced cook more than a spice rack chock full of multicoloured substances that one can sprinkle and toss with a certain chef-like finesse. I sprinkled and tossed to my heart's content until, inspecting my master-piece, I discovered that I had liberally covered my poor chicken with cinnamon, garlic powder, and sugar. Quickly, I snapped out of my Julia Child act and reme-died my mistake by attempting to wipe off my wrongs with a paper towel. Shreds of tissue now decorated the main course, alongside the already present foil. As din-nertime was nearing, I tried to hurry myself along and ended up dusting the bird with allspice, something that sounded like a good general spice to me, but which I later discovered to be the chief flavouring for gingerbread and apple and pump-kin pies. Being behind schedule, I didn't bother with any more fancy stuff; I popped the chicken into the oven and cranked the temperature up to 500° to speed up the cooking time.

Finally, it was time to prepare the dessert. A cinch, I said: no problem. Setting **5** a large pot on the burner, I began to throw in haphazardly whatever the recipe called for: squares of semisweet chocolate, cream, butter, three separated eggs. Separated from what? I wondered; from their shells, I guess. Happy with my con-clusion, I continued, smashing the eggs along the rim of the pot, and watching the bright yellow yolks float on top of the chocolate with only a few bits of shell mix-ing in with them. I stirred the concoction vigorously, but it failed to resemble the light, fluffy delicacy from the glossy picture in the cookbook. Since the recipe said that this dessert was supposed to set awhile before serving, I left it on the stove, assuming it would magically take on the appearance of the cookbook picture by the time I spooned it out. Satisfied with my efforts, I left my dinner roasting and setting while I wandered off to watch *Donahue*.

In the middle of "Bisexual Men and Voodoo Priestesses—Compatible **6** Marriages?" a crescendo of domestic noise swelled in my ears. The smoke alarm wailed, the oven bell clanged, and the stove crackled and sputtered. Something had gone terribly wrong. Sprinting into the kitchen, I leaped up toward the smoke alarm, waving my arms frantically in an attempt to clear the smoke and shut off the ear-piercing screech. A sharp rap with a broom handle finally silenced that con-traption and allowed me to attend to what was left of dinner. The chicken was charred beyond recognition, with the bits of paper towel burning brightly and the foil glinting mockingly at me. The mousse had not transformed itself into a dessert delight that would elicit praise from my family; instead, it had melded itself to the bottom of the pot, hardening to the point where it had become an immovable part of the metal. Even my previously trouble-free salad had succumbed to the disaster surrounding it. Left sitting on the stove, the lettuce had wilted and turned an unsightly brown around its edges. As I stood in the midst of this catastrophe, in came my mother, two aunts, and my grandmother. They shook their heads sadly, and I think I actually saw tears welling up in the eyes of my grandmother. I had failed the initiation; I would never be a traditional female. No one would savour my cookies or ask for second helpings at supper. Somehow, I'd proven myself incomplete.

Suddenly, in the midst of this horrible, laughable affair, it dawned on me that   7
I didn't really mind. I didn't care. This was not the be-all and end-all; I would be a woman yet. Culinary skills or not, I would amount to something. I would be one of the new breed of women who throw aside tradition to be themselves. My heart lightened. I threw off my baking mitts, untied the apron, tossed them to my grandmother, and yelled, "Call Pizza Pizza."

■ Reading Comprehension Questions

1. Which of the following would be the best alternative title for the selection?
   a. Dinner, Denial, and Disaster
   b. Chicken à la Nancy
   c. The Importance of Poisoning Your Family
   d. Cooking Means Caring

2. Which sentence best expresses the main idea of the selection?
   a. Cooking, like caring and cleaning, is seemingly inseparable from the idea of womanhood.
   b. Cooking dinner for the family is a time-honoured coming-of-age ritual for all women.
   c. With the right cookbook, equipment, and ingredients, anyone can prepare a dinner.
   d. Failing at cooking dinner for the author meant failure in the traditional arts of womanhood.

3. The concept of womanhood, according to Nancy Eng,
   a. has changed radically because of a female astronaut and female politicians.
   b. is still narrowed by expectations of nurturing, gentleness, and domesticity.
   c. carries a double burden: workplace success and kitchen miracles.
   d. necessitates the wearing of high heels, lipstick, and an apron.

4. *True or false?* _____ The author messed up the initial preparation of every course in her meal.

5. Ms. Eng's main problem with preparing the chicken was
   a. not knowing which end to stuff.
   b. not removing the heart, liver, and gizzards prior to stuffing the bird.
   c. leaving foil and paper towel on its skin.
   d. all of the above, and more.

6. The author implies that
   a. she had at least read the recipes before trying to cook dinner.
   b. she had watched female relatives cook enough to know the basics.

   c. she had looked at the cookbook and examined her materials in advance.
   d. she mistook dressing for the event and grabbing a book for cooking.

7. Ms. Eng implies that she believed
   a. that the rules and techniques for cooking weren't that important.
   b. that all good women take time for a TV break during meal preparation.
   c. she would never be a real woman.
   d. dinner would somehow be edible, if not praiseworthy.

8. *True or false?* _____ The author implies that this has been a real life crisis, as well as a rite of passage (paragraph 1) for her.

9. The word *enshrouded* in "So, as I entered the kitchen that fateful day of my fifteenth year, armed with *The Joy of Cooking* and enshrouded in 'Kiss the Cook' apron" (paragraph 1) means
   a. dressed.
   b. disguised.
   c. wrapped up.
   d. trapped.

10. The word *crescendo* in "a crescendo of domestic noise swelled in my ears" (paragraph 6) means
   a. rumblings.
   b. build-up.
   c. shriek.
   d. cacophony.

Discussion Questions

About Content

1. What characteristics of womanhood does Eng list as persisting into the 2000s? Do you agree with her? Are these innate aspects of all women?

2. Why does the author feel "slightly perverse" (paragraph 3) about what she was doing with the stuffing mix?

3. Do you agree with Nancy Eng that "nothing warms the heart of an inexperienced cook more than a spice rack chock full of multicoloured substances" (paragraph 4)? Why do people feel this way? What's the problem with this feeling?

4. What had happened to each of the author's dishes? Why, in each case?

About Structure

5. How does the author link her title with the content of her essay in the opening paragraph? Which sentences support and expand on the meaning of the title? List the number of the sentence, note the appropriate phrase, and briefly explain how each connects to the title.

   Sentence _____   Phrase _____

Sentence _____   Phrase _____

Sentence _____   Phrase _____

6. This is a comic version of a process essay. Generally, such essays contain transitional words and phrases to direct and assist the reader in following the process. Do you think that Nancy Eng wants you to follow her process?

There are, in fact, *two* types of process essays: prescriptive ("how-to"), and descriptive (telling how by describing). Which type of process essay is "The Importance of Cooking Dinner"? Why?

7. The transitions in this essay are unusually placed. They are more like "time marker" phrases, which indicate the progress of an event or process.

Where do you find such phrases in paragraphs 2–5? What are the phrases, and what do they have in common?

About Style and Tone

8. The chicken is clearly an object for the author to contend with. Which of the rhetorical comic devices listed below does Ms. Eng use to make her description in paragraph 3 of her struggles with the bird so funny?

a. Personification (giving an object human qualities) _____

b. Alliteration (beginning closely placed words with the same letter) _____

c. Exaggeration _____

d. Puns or word-play _____

List examples of any of these comic devices which you find, and suggest why they are amusing in the context of the essay.

9. For what type of publication (and its reading audience) would such an article be likely to be written? Why?
a. a feminist magazine
b. a cookbook or cooking magazine
c. a general-interest monthly magazine
d. a sociology text

■ Writing Assignments

Assignment 1: Writing a Paragraph

There are "rites of passage" for every person: special (although sometimes quite mundane) activities, which, when first performed, have time-marking significance for all of us. These actions or events signal some change or turning-point in our lives. Some are gender-specific, such as shaving the face (as opposed to shaving the legs, which would be a female "rite of passage"), and some transcend gender boundaries, such as learning to drive.

Write a paragraph about "The Importance of…." Describe a particular "first" coming-of-age ritual which you experienced. Why was it important to you? What was its importance to that stage in your life? Consider the first time you played a game of pool, your first date, the first time you changed the oil or a tire, or some such turning point.

As Eng does, begin with some background information about yourself and the importance of the event. Then describe the stages in the process you went through in your personal "rite of passage." Be sure to use very specific details so that readers may re-experience the event along with you. Conclude with a statement of the significance, or lack thereof, which this "rite" had for you.

Assignment 2: Writing a Paragraph

We have all tried to cook something. Our first attempts may not have been as disastrous as Nancy Eng's; in fact, some of us are natural cooks, and those first scrambled eggs may have been quite edible. Write a paragraph in which you describe your first try at cooking for other people. If your first meal was suitable only for a decent burial, give the causes for the awful results; on the other hand, if you succeeded in not making your family or guests ill, make sure your paragraph tells clearly *why* you managed to cook reasonably well.

Follow the cause-and-effect format on pages 169–171 as you structure your paragraph. Begin with what you achieved, then explain the reasons for the meal that resulted, whether it was good or bad.

Assignment 3: Writing an Essay

Will you, like Nancy Eng, be among the "new breed" of men or women who have left behind the expectations and stereotypes of previous generations? Is this possible, or are certain characteristics innate within each gender? Do we want to disturb all fundamental male and female qualities as we know them?

Write a prescriptive ("how to") process essay about *your* views on "the new man" or "the new woman." Does each really exist? Do you know any examples of either? What elements would make up such creatures? Would there be changes in personality, in behaviour, in appearance? How much do we really want men and women to change, and why?

Here is your chance to play Dr. Frankenstein: Construct a new being. Tell your readers how to become "The New Man" or "The New Woman" in the traditional "three easy steps." Because this is a direct-advice process essay, address your reader directly as "you." If there are things you would rather not change about the gender in question, say so, but tell the reader how and why he or she should retain an existing quality you value.

Before beginning your outline, review the chapter on process writing (pages 156–163). Decide on your viewpoint first of all. You may take a reverse or comic view, and give instructions on how to become "a traditional gentleman" (which may, in fact, be a new creature) or "a real lady" (perhaps equally mythic). Consider what ingredients may be needed. In either case, list your steps, then group them into logical stages which become your three body paragraphs, and flesh out your instructions with careful details about becoming the "gender-perfect creature." Watch out for potential pitfalls or problems in your stages, and give lots of transitional help. Remember, you may be creating a new being.

Permissions

APPENDIX

Answers and Charts

PREVIEW

This Appendix provides answers for the Sentence-Skills Diagnostic Test on pages 241–245 and for the Introductory Projects in Part Four. It also contains four useful charts: an assignment chart and a spelling list, to be filled in by the student; an extra form for planning a paragraph; and a reading comprehension chart.

Answers to Sentence-Skills Diagnostic Test and Introductory Projects

SENTENCE-SKILLS DIAGNOSTIC TEST (PAGES 241–245)

Fragments

1. X
2. C
3. X
4. X
5. C
6. X

Run-Ons

7. C
8. X
9. X
10. X
11. C
12. X

Irregular Verbs

13. X
14. C
15. C
16. X

Subject-Verb Agreement

17. X
18. X
19. C
20. X

Consistent Verb Tense

21. X
22. C
23. C
24. X

Pronoun Agreement, Reference, and Point of View

25. X
26. C
27. X
28. C
29. X
30. C

Pronoun Types

31. X
32. C

Adjectives and Adverbs

33. X
34. X

Misplaced Modifiers

35. X
36. C

37. X
38. X

Dangling Modifiers

39. C
40. X
41. C
42. X

Faulty Parallelism

43. X
44. C
45. X
46. C

Capital Letters

47. X
48. X
49. C
50. X

Apostrophe

51. C
52. X
53. X
54. C

Quotation Marks

55. C
56. X
57. X
58. C

Comma

59. X
60. X
61. C
62. X
63. C
64. X

Commonly Confused Words

65. X
66. X
67. C
68. X
69. X
70. C

Effective Word Use

71. X
72. X
73. X
74. X

INTRODUCTORY PROJECTS

Fragments (page 254)

1. thought
2. subject
3. verb
4. subject

Run-Ons (page 270)

1. period
2. *but*
3. semi-colon
4. *When*

Irregular Verbs (page 283)

1. crawled, crawled (regular)
2. brought, brought (irregular)
3. used, used (regular)
4. did, done (irregular)
5. gave, given (irregular)
6. laughed, laughed (regular)
7. went, gone (irregular)
8. scared, scared (regular)
9. dressed, dressed (regular)
10. saw, seen (irregular)

Subject-Verb Agreement (page 290)

The second sentence in each pair is correct.

Consistent Verb Tense (page 296)

discovered . . . remembered

Pronoun Agreement, Reference, and Point of View (page 300)

The second sentence in each pair is correct.

Misplaced Modifiers (page 317)

1. Intended: A young man with references is wanted to open oysters.
   Unintended: The oysters have references.
2. Intended: On their wedding day, Carlo and Charlotte decided they would have two children.
   Unintended: Carlo and Charlotte decided to have two children who would magically appear on the day of their wedding.
3. Intended: The students who failed the test no longer like the math instructor.
   Unintended: The math instructor failed the test.

Dangling Modifiers (page 320)

1. Intended: My dog sat with me as I smoked a pipe.
   Unintended: My dog smoked a pipe.

2. Intended: He looked at a traffic accident as he drove his sports car through a red light.
   Unintended: His sports car looked at a traffic accident.
3. Intended: The moussaka baked for several hours.
   Unintended: Dad baked for several hours.

Faulty Parallelism (page 324)

The second sentence in each pair reads more smoothly and clearly.

Capital Letters (page 332)

All the answers to questions 1 to 13 should be in capital letters.
14. The   15. I   16. "That . . ."

Apostrophe (page 343)

1. The purpose of the 's is to show possession (Lauren owns the motorcycle, the boyfriend belongs to the sister, Grandmother owns the laptop, the room belongs to the men).
2. The purpose of the apostrophe is to show the omission of one or more letters in a contraction—two words shortened to form one word.
3. In each of the second sentences, the 's shows possession: the body of the vampire; the centre of the baked potato. In each of the first sentences, the s is used to form a simple plural: more than one vampire; more than one potato.

Quotation Marks (page 351)

1. The purpose of quotation marks is to set off the exact words of a speaker. (The words that the young man actually spoke aloud are set off with quotation marks, as are the words that the old woman spoke aloud.)
2. Commas and periods go inside quotation marks.

Comma (page 358)

1. a. Ryan's interests are Lisa, television, and sports.
   b. My mother put her feet up, sipped some iced tea, and opened the newspaper.
2. a. Although the Lone Ranger used lots of silver bullets, he never ran out of ammunition.
   b. To open the cap of the aspirin bottle, you must first press down on it.
3. a. Kitty Katz and Serge Lamour, Canada's leading romantic stars, have made several movies together.
   b. Elsa, who is my next-door neighbour, just entered the hospital with an intestinal infection.
4. a. The wedding was scheduled for four o'clock, but the bride changed her mind at two.
   b. Franka took three coffee breaks before lunch, and then she went on a two-hour lunch break.
5. a. Delia's mother asked her, "What time do you expect to get home?"
   b. "Don't bend over to pat the dog," I warned, "or he'll kiss you."
6. a. Benjie ate seventeen hamburgers on July 29, 1998, and lived to tell about it.
   b. Benjie lives at 817 Ouéllette Street, Windsor, Ontario.

Other Punctuation Marks (page 367)

1. pets: holly
2. freeze-dried
3. Shakespeare (1564–1616)
4. Earth; no
5. proudly—with

Commonly Confused Words (page 383)

Your mind and body. . . . *There* is a lot of evidence. . . .
then it will. . . . said *to* have. . . . *It's* not clear

Effective Word Choice (page 392)

1. "Flipped out" is slang.
2. "Few and far between" is a cliché.
3. "Ascertained" is a pretentious word.
4. The first sentence here is wordy.

C h a r t s

ASSIGNMENT CHART

Use this chart to record daily or weekly assignments in your composition class. You might want to print writing assignments and their due dates in capital letters so that they stand out clearly.

Date Given	Assignment	Date Due

Date Given	Assignment	Date Due

SPELLING LIST

Enter here the words that you misspelled in your papers (note the examples). If you add to and study this list regularly, you will not repeat the same mistakes in your writing.

Incorrect Spelling	Correct Spelling	Points to Remember
alright	all right	two words
ocasion	occasion	two "c"s

READING COMPREHENSION CHART

Write an X through the numbers of any questions you missed while answering the comprehension questions for each selection in Part Five, Fifteen Reading Selections. Then write in your comprehension score. (To calculate your score for each reading, give yourself 10 points for each item that is *not* X'd out.) The chart will make clear any skill question you get wrong repeatedly, so that you can pay special attention to that skill in the future.

Selection	Subject or Title	Thesis or Main Idea	Key Details			Inferences			Vocabulary in Context		Comprehension Score
Preston	1	2	3	4	5	6	7	8	9	10	%
MacKenzie	1	2	3	4	5	6	7	8	9	10	%
Curran	1	2	3	4	5	6	7	8	9	10	%
Jones	1	2	3	4	5	6	7	8	9	10	%
Turner	1	2	3	4	5	6	7	8	9	10	%
Akers	1	2	3	4	5	6	7	8	9	10	%
Brett	1	2	3	4	5	6	7	8	9	10	%
Maloney	1	2	3	4	5	6	7	8	9	10	%
Landsberg	1	2	3	4	5	6	7	8	9	10	%
Medwell	1	2	3	4	5	6	7	8	9	10	%
Wong	1	2	3	4	5	6	7	8	9	10	%
Smith	1	2	3	4	5	6	7	8	9	10	%
Jay	1	2	3	4	5	6	7	8	9	10	%
Angelou	1	2	3	4	5	6	7	8	9	10	%
Eng	1	2	3	4	5	6	7	8	9	10	%

Index